AF504155

PLAYFAIR FOOTBALL ANNUAL 1999–2000

52nd edition

Editor: GLENDA ROLLIN
Executive editor: JACK ROLLIN

HEADLINE

First published in 1999
by HEADLINE BOOK PUBLISHING

10 9 8 7 6 5 4 3 2 1

Cover photographs Left and back: Gareth Barry (Aston Villa) – *ASP*; right: Nicolas Anelka (Arsenal) – *Colorsport*.

ISBN 0 7472 5975 5

Typeset by Wearset, Boldon, Tyne and Wear

Printed and bound in Great Britain by
Clays Ltd, St Ives plc

HEADLINE BOOK PUBLISHING
A division of the Hodder Headline Group
338 Euston Road
London NW1 3BH

www.headline.co.uk
www.hodderheadline.com

CONTENTS

Editorial...5

The FA Premier League and the Football League
National list of Referees for season 1999–2000 6
League Review and Club Section 7
FA Premier League, Football League First, Second, Third Division
    results, tables, leading scorers 8
FA Premier and Football League Clubs 20
League positions 1973–74 to 1997–98 102
League Championship Honours 114
Relegated Clubs 121
League Title Wins 124
League Attendances 1998–99 125
Transfers 1998–99 127

English Cups
FA Cup Review 1998–99...141
AXA FA Cup 1998–99 142
Past FA Cup Finals 146
Summary of FA Cup Winners since 1871 152
Appearances in FA Cup Final...152
Worthington Cup Review 1998–99 153
Past League Cup Finals 154
Worthington Cup 1998–99 156
Auto Windscreens Shield 1998–99...160
FA Charity Shield Winners 1908–98...162

Scottish Football League
Scottish League Review 1998–99 163
Scottish League Tables 1998–99 164
Scottish League Results 1998–99...165
Scottish League Clubs 169
Scottish League Honours...184
Relegated Clubs 189
Past Scottish League Cup Finals 191
Scottish Coca-Cola Cup 1998–99...192
Tennents Scottish Cup 1998–99..193
Past Scottish Cup Finals 195

Irish and Welsh Football
Welsh League Table 1998–99 197
Northern Ireland League Table 1998–99 197
League of Wales Results 1998–99 198

European and International Football
European Review 1998–99...199
European Cup 1998–99 200
European Cup-Winners' Cup 1998–99...204
UEFA Cup 1998–99..206
Past European Cup Competition Finals..210
European Cup Draws 1999–2000 212
Euro 2000 213
Euro 2000 – Remaining Fixtures...236
Past European Championship Finals...237
Olympic Football...238
Past World Cup Finals..239
World Club Championship 242
European Super Cup 243
South American Football..244
Other British and Irish International Matches 1998–99...............245
England Under-21 Teams 1998–99 247
British Post-war International Appearances 249
British International Goalscorers since 1946..................................290
UEFA Under-21 Championship 1998–99..295

Other Football
Football Conference 1998–99 296
Dr Martens League 1998–99..298
Unibond League 1998–99...300
Ryman Football League 1998–99...302
Pontin's Central League...304
Avon Insurance Combination 305
FA Academy Under-19..305
FA Academy Under-17..306
Republic of Ireland League 307
Highland League 307
FA Umbro Trophy 1998–99..308
FA Carlsberg Vase 1998–99...308
The Times FA Youth Cup 1998–99 308

Information and Records
Useful Addresses 309
FA Premiership and Football League Fixtures 1999–2000............310
Other Fixtures 1999–2000 318

EDITORIAL

Manchester United's unique treble achievement of League, FA Cup and European Cup was the outstanding feature of the 1998–99 season. It earned for their manager a knighthood and Sir Alex Ferguson became the man of the moment, even thrust into the political arena by the Government vainly attempting to bolster its faltering campaign to back the Euro.

With HM Government also keen to secure the 2006 World Cup for England, Manchester United were pressurized into opting out of the FA Cup in 1999–2000, so that they could compete in the Club World Championship in Brazil in the winter; a prestige tournament favoured by FIFA and participation thought by the Football Association essential to keep our bid for staging the World Cup alive.

The FA also dropped hints that a reduction from 20 clubs to 18 in the Premier League would bring us in line with most of the rest of Europe. The effect of this notion would be to throw the Football League into complete confusion as they would have to accommodate 74 clubs in three divisions. Relegation of three teams to the Conference would be the only alternative, short of promoting even more clubs from outside the League and restructuring the Third Division into North and South regional divisions as of old.

The game also suffered bad publicity with both the FA and Premier League having to endure the embarrassment from officials resigning over transactions respectively concerning 'loans for votes' and 'television deals'. Whether these people had selfish motives or considered themselves to be acting in the best interests of the game is debatable, but they were clearly guilty of one thing: poor judgment.

Yes, problems in plenty exist for the game off the field, but there are just as many misgivings where the action lies on it. Experiments continue towards the use of two referees, first introduced as an alternative idea in the 1930s, with officials criticised when they have to give on the spot decisions later challenged by increasing scrutiny from television's technology.

FIFA are keen to introduce professional referees, but many will argue that paying the same officials more money will not improve their performances even if in fact it makes them more accountable. Surely it is a move which strikes at the integrity of referees who are officiating to the best of their ability.

One solution on a longer term basis could be a fast track system of encouraging former professional footballers to take up refereeing with the incentive of progressing up the ladder. In order not to discourage referees who start at grass roots level, there should be a structure in place for a quicker method for them to reach the top as well.

UEFA are anxious that all professional footballers should be trained as referees and made to officiate at matches. This is an excellent idea, but it should not be wasted. Players with this kind of ideal background would prove invaluable material to control the game which is big enough to accommodate two ways.

The other essential move must be to take timing out of the hands of referees completely. Revolutionary idea? Not a bit of it. Discussions were held 40 years ago about the same idea. Then there was no such official as the fourth official. With electronic timing, he could be the man to give spectators more value for money and stop the nonsense of holding up a board with a figure on it giving the number of minutes for time added on.

It would put an end to the farce of the statistics which claim that more goals are scored in the last minute of a match than at any other time. Not surprisingly that is, since that 60 seconds can often last several minutes.

NATIONAL LIST OF REFEREES FOR SEASON 1999–2000

#Alcock, P.E. (Halstead, Kent)
Baines, S.J. (Chesterfield)
#Barber, G.P. (Tring, Herts)
#Barry, N.S. (Scunthorpe)
Bates, A. (Stoke-on-Trent)
*Beeby, R.J. (Northampton)
#Bennett, S.G. (Orpington, Kent)
Brandwood, M.J. (Lichfield, Staffs)
Burns, W.C. (Scarborough)
Butler, A.N. (Sutton-in-Ashfield)
Cable, L.E. (Woking)
Cain, G. (Seaforth, Merseyside)
Cowburn, M.G. (Blackpool)
Crick, D.R. (Worcester Park, Surrey)
Danson, P.S. (Leicester)
Dean, M.L. (Heswall, Wirral)
Down, P. (Stoke-on-Trent)
#Dunn, S.W. (Bristol)
#Durkin, P.A. (Portland, Dorset)
#D'Urso, A.P. (Billericay, Essex)
#Elleray, D.R. (Harrow-on-the-Hill)
Fletcher, M. (Warley, West Midlands)
Foy, C.J. (St Helens, Merseyside)
Frankland, G.B. (Middlesbrough)
Furnandiz, R.D. (Doncaster)
#Gallagher, D.J. (Banbury, Oxon)
Hall, A.R. (Birmingham)
#Halsey, M.R. (Welwyn Garden City, Herts)
#Harris, R.J. (Oxford)
Heilbron, T. (Newton Aycliffe)
Hill, K.D. (Royston, Herts)
Jones, M.J. (Chester)
#Jones, P. (Loughborough)
Jones, T. (Barry-in-Furness)
Jordan, W.M. (Tring, Herts)
*Joslin, P.J. (Newark, Nottinghamshire)
*Kaye, A. (Wakefield)
Kirkby, J.A. (Sheffield)

#Knight, B. (Orpington, Kent)
Laws, D. (Whitley Bay)
Laws, G. (Whitley Bay)
Leach, K.A. (Codsall, Staffs)
Leake, A.R. (Darwen, Lancashire)
#Lodge, S.J. (Barnsley)
Lomas, E. (Manchester)
Lynch, K.M. (Kirk Hammerton, Nr York)
Mathieson, S.W. (Stockport)
Messias, M.D. (York)
Olivier, R.J. (Sutton Coldfield)
*Parkes, T.A. (Birmingham)
Pearson, R. (Peterlee, Durham)
Pike, M.S (Barrow-in-Furness)
#Poll, G. (Tring, Hertfordshire)
Pugh, D. (Bebington, Wirral)
#Reed, M.D. (Birmingham)
Rejer, P. (Tipton, West Midlands)
#Rennie, U.D. (Sheffield)
Richards, P.R. (Preston)
#Riley, M.A. (Leeds)
Robinson, J.P. (Hull)
*Ryan, M. (Preston)
Stretton, F.G. (Nottingham)
Styles, R. (Waterlooville, Hants)
Taylor, P. (Cheshunt, Hertfordshire)
*Tomlin, S.G. (Lewes, East Sussex)
Walton, P. (Long Buckby, Northants)
Warren, M.R. (Walsall)
#Wiley, A.G. (Burntwood, Staffs)
Wilkes, C.R. (Gloucester)
#Wilkie, A.B. (Chester-le-Street)
#Willard, G.S. (Worthing, West Sussex)
#Winter, J.T. (Stockton-on-Tees)
Wolstenholme, E.K. (Blackburn)
*New for season 1999–2000.
#Premier League Referee.

LEAGUE REVIEW AND CLUB SECTION

Manchester United wrested the FA Carling Premiership title back from Arsenal with a point to spare over the champions after an indifferent start. The change in United's campaign came after the 19 December 3-2 defeat at home by Middlesbrough.

From then on until the 2-1 win over Tottenham Hotspur on the last day of the season, United were unbeaten in 20 League games. Arsenal matched them for most of the second half of the season, oddly enough following a 3-2 defeat of their own at Aston Villa two weeks before United's last League reverse. Arsenal then went 19 League games of their own before losing 1-0 at Leeds. This defeat undoubtedly cost Arsenal the chance of retaining their crown, even though they had beaten United once and drawn the other game. United had gone to Elland Road previously and managed a 1-1 draw for themselves. These two results had a significant bearing on the outcome of the title race.

United called upon the services of 23 players during the League programme, none of them ever present. Goalkeeper Peter Schmeichel missed just four full games as did Gary Neville, though Roy Keane appeared in 35 matches, two of them as a substitute. His combative influence in midfield was a telling factor in United's control of play. David Beckham, excelling with crosses and dead ball situations, missed four games himself as one of his appearances was also from the substitutes bench.

The signing of Dwight Yorke from Aston Villa for £12.6 million gave an increased dimension to the United attack and his combination with Andy Cole yielded 35 goals. In defence, the arrival of Dutch centre-back Jaap Stam considerably strengthened this department.

Such were the riches at the disposal of the club that Ole Gunnar Solskjaer was unable to make more than 19 appearances, ten of them as a replacement. Yet he managed to score 12 goals including the best individual feat when he scored four goals in 13 minutes 46 seconds at Nottingham Forest on 6 February when United scored a 8-1 record away win for the Premier League.

Leeds, for their part, enjoyed a fine season of their own finishing fourth and suffering no apparent problems after the departure of manager George Graham, who took over at Tottenham. David O'Leary, previously the No. 2 at Leeds, impressively assumed the leading role at Elland Road.

Chelsea finished third and might well have done much better save for injuries to key players early in the season. West Ham United despite some inconsistency secured fifth place and also entered Europe for 1999–2000 via the Intertoto Cup. Manchester United, Arsenal and Chelsea gained places in the enlarged European Cup, while Leeds, Newcastle and Tottenham made the revamped UEFA Cup following the demise of the Cup-Winners' Cup.

Aston Villa were sixth after at one stage seeming capable of honours on their own. Liverpool, had for them a wretched season, losing both main strikers Michael Owen and Robbie Fowler through injury. Yet arguably the finest match in the Premier League had seen Liverpool win 4-2 at Villa Park in November.

At the other end of the FA Premier League, Nottingham Forest became early relegation victims, but Southampton staged a finely judged recovery to escape, leaving Charlton Athletic who headed the table early in the season and Blackburn Rovers as the other relegated teams.

In the Nationwide First Division, Sunderland romped away with the honours, collecting 105 points in the process. Bradford City gained the other automatic promotion place and Watford emerged from the play-offs to return to the top echelon. Relegated from the First Division were Bury, Oxford United and Bristol City, their positions taken by Fulham, Walsall and Manchester City, the last named making it from the play-offs.

The foursome demoted from the Second Division were York City, Northampton Town, Lincoln City and Macclesfield Town a season after winning promotion. Brentford, Cambridge United and Cardiff City took the three automatic promotion spots from the Third Division and Scunthorpe United came through from the play-offs.

There was a dramatic end to the season at the foot of the table where Carlisle United escaped the drop into the Nationwide Conference when goalkeeper Jimmy Glass on loan from Swindon Town, scored in the last second against Plymouth Argyle. Scarborough were the unfortunate losers and lost their League status after 12 years in the competition, Cheltenham Town taking their place.

FA Carling Premiership

			Home			Goals		Away			Goals			
		P	W	D	L	F	A	W	D	L	F	A	GD	Pts
1	Manchester U	38	14	4	1	45	18	8	9	2	35	19	+43	79
2	Arsenal	38	14	5	0	34	5	8	7	4	25	12	+42	78
3	Chelsea	38	12	6	1	29	13	8	9	2	28	17	+27	75
4	Leeds U	38	12	5	2	32	9	6	8	5	30	25	+28	67
5	West Ham U	38	11	3	5	32	26	5	6	8	14	27	−7	57
6	Aston Villa	38	10	3	6	33	28	5	7	7	18	18	+5	55
7	Liverpool	38	10	5	4	44	24	5	4	10	24	25	+19	54
8	Derby Co	38	8	7	4	22	19	5	6	8	18	26	−5	52
9	Middlesbrough	38	7	9	3	25	18	5	6	8	23	36	−6	51
10	Leicester C	38	7	6	6	25	25	5	7	7	15	21	−6	49
11	Tottenham H	38	7	7	5	28	26	4	7	8	19	24	−3	47
12	Sheffield W	38	7	5	7	20	15	6	2	11	21	27	−1	46
13	Newcastle U	38	7	6	6	26	25	4	7	8	22	29	−6	46
14	Everton	38	6	8	5	22	12	5	2	12	20	35	−5	43
15	Coventry C	38	8	6	5	26	21	3	3	13	13	30	−12	42
16	Wimbledon	38	7	7	5	22	21	3	5	11	18	42	−23	42
17	Southampton	38	9	4	6	29	26	2	4	13	8	38	−27	41
18	Charlton Ath	38	4	7	8	20	20	4	5	10	21	36	−15	36
19	Blackburn R	38	6	5	8	21	24	1	9	9	17	28	−14	35
20	Nottingham F	38	3	7	9	18	31	4	2	13	17	38	−34	30

LEADING GOALSCORERS 1998-99

FA CARLING PREMIERSHIP

	League	FA Cup	Worthington Cup	Other	Total
Dwight Yorke (*Manchester U*)	18	3	0	8	29
Michael Owen (*Liverpool*)	18	2	1	2	23
Jimmy Floyd Hasselbaink (*Leeds U*)	18	1	0	1	20
Andy Cole (*Manchester U*)	17	2	0	5	24
Nicolas Anelka (*Arsenal*)	17	0	0	2	19
Hamilton Ricard (*Middlesbrough*)	15	0	3	0	18
Alan Shearer (*Newcastle U*)	14	5	1	1	21
Robbie Fowler (*Liverpool*)	14	1	1	2	18
Julian Joachim (*Aston Villa*)	14	1	0	1	16
Dion Dublin (*Aston Villa*)	14	0	1	0	15
(*Including 3 League and 1 Worthington Cup goal for Coventry C*)					
Ole Gunnar Solskjaer (*Manchester U*)	13	1	3	2	19
Gianfranco Zola (*Chelsea*)	13	1	0	1	15
Dennis Bergkamp (*Arsenal*)	12	3	0	1	16
Gustavo Poyet (*Chelsea*)	11	0	2	1	14
Noel Whelan (*Coventry C*)	10	2	1	0	13
Tony Cottee (*Leicester C*)	10	1	5	0	16
Tore Andre Flo (*Chelsea*)	10	0	1	2	13
Jason Euell (*Wimbledon*)	10	0	0	0	10
Marcus Gayle (*Wimbledon*)	10	0	1	0	11

Other matches consist of European games, Auto Windscreens Shield and Football League play-offs.

Nationwide Football League Division 1

			Home				Goals	Away				Goals		
		P	W	D	L	F	A	W	D	L	F	A	GS	Pts
1	Sunderland	46	19	3	1	50	10	12	9	2	41	18	91	105
2	Bradford C	46	15	4	4	48	20	11	5	7	34	27	82	87
3	Ipswich T	46	16	1	6	37	15	10	7	6	32	17	69	86
4	Birmingham C	46	12	7	4	32	15	11	5	7	34	22	66	81
5	Watford	46	12	8	3	30	19	9	6	8	35	37	65	77
6	Bolton W	46	13	6	4	44	25	7	10	6	34	34	78	76
7	Wolverhampton W	46	11	10	2	37	19	8	6	9	27	24	64	73
8	Sheffield U	46	12	6	5	42	29	6	7	10	29	37	71	67
9	Norwich C	46	7	12	4	34	28	8	5	10	28	33	62	62
10	Huddersfield T	46	11	9	3	38	23	4	7	12	24	48	62	61
11	Grimsby T	46	11	6	6	25	18	6	4	13	15	34	40	61
12	WBA	46	12	4	7	43	33	4	7	12	26	43	69	59
13	Barnsley	46	7	9	7	35	30	7	8	8	24	26	59	59
14	Crystal Palace	46	11	10	2	43	26	3	6	14	15	45	58	58
15	Tranmere R	46	8	7	8	37	30	4	13	6	26	31	63	56
16	Stockport Co	46	7	9	7	24	21	5	8	10	25	39	49	53
17	Swindon T	46	7	8	8	40	44	6	3	14	19	37	59	50
18	Crewe Alex	46	7	6	10	27	35	5	6	12	27	43	54	48
19	Portsmouth	46	10	5	8	34	26	1	9	13	23	47	57	47
20	QPR	46	9	7	7	34	22	3	4	16	18	39	52	47
21	Port Vale	46	10	3	10	22	28	3	5	15	23	47	45	47
22	Bury	46	9	7	7	24	27	1	10	12	11	33	35	47
23	Oxford U	46	7	8	8	31	30	3	6	14	17	41	48	44
24	Bristol C	46	7	8	8	35	36	2	7	14	22	44	57	42

NATIONWIDE DIVISION 1

	League	FA Cup	Worthington Cup	Other Cups	Total
Lee Hughes *(WBA)*	31	0	1	0	32
Kevin Phillips *(Sunderland)*	23	0	2	0	25
Lee Mills *(Bradford C)*	23	1	0	0	24
Marcus Stewart *(Huddersfield T)*	22	2	2	0	26
Iffy Onuora *(Swindon T)*	20	0	0	0	20
Iwan Roberts *(Norwich C)*	19	1	3	0	23
Ade Akinbiyi *(Bristol C)*	19	0	4	0	23
Niall Quinn *(Sunderland)*	18	0	3	0	21
Brett Angell *(Stockport Co)*	17	1	0	0	18
Craig Bellamy *(Norwich C)*	17	0	2	0	19
Marcelo *(Sheffield U)*	16	3	0	0	19
Robbie Blake *(Bradford C)*	16	0	1	0	17
Dean Windass *(Oxford U)*	15	3	0	0	18
Kenny Irons *(Tranmere R)*	15	0	3	0	18
Bob Taylor *(Bolton W)*	15	0	1	0	16
Paul Groves *(Grimsby T)*	14	0	1	0	15
Dele Adebola *(Birmingham C)*	13	1	2	0	16
John Aloisi *(Portsmouth)*	13	0	3	0	16
(Also scored 5 League goals for Coventry C)					
David Johnson *(Ipswich T)*	13	0	1	0	14
James Scowcroft *(Ipswich T)*	13	0	1	0	14
Arnar Gunnlaugsson *(Bolton W)*	13	0	1	0	14
Paul Furlong *(Birmingham C)*	13	0	0	0	13

Nationwide Football League Division 2

		P	W	D	L	F	A	W	D	L	F	A	GS	Pts
				Home		**Goals**		**Away**			**Goals**			
1	Fulham	46	19	3	1	50	12	12	5	6	29	20	79	101
2	Walsall	46	13	7	3	37	23	13	2	8	26	24	63	87
3	Manchester C	46	13	6	4	38	14	9	10	4	31	19	69	82
4	Gillingham	46	15	5	3	45	17	7	9	7	30	27	75	80
5	Preston NE	46	12	6	5	46	23	10	7	6	32	27	78	79
6	Wigan Ath	46	14	5	4	44	17	8	5	10	31	31	75	76
7	Bournemouth	46	14	7	2	37	11	7	6	10	26	30	63	76
8	Stoke C	46	10	4	9	32	32	11	2	10	27	31	59	69
9	Chesterfield	46	14	5	4	34	16	3	8	12	12	28	46	64
10	Millwall	46	9	8	6	33	24	8	3	12	19	35	52	62
11	Reading	46	10	6	7	29	26	6	7	10	25	37	54	61
12	Luton T	46	10	4	9	25	26	6	6	11	26	34	51	58
13	Bristol R	46	8	9	6	35	28	5	8	10	30	28	65	56
14	Blackpool	46	7	8	8	24	24	7	6	10	20	30	44	56
15	Burnley	46	8	7	8	23	33	5	9	9	31	40	54	55
16	Notts Co	46	8	6	9	29	27	6	6	11	23	34	52	54
17	Wrexham	46	8	6	9	21	28	5	8	10	22	34	43	53
18	Colchester U	46	9	7	7	25	30	3	9	11	27	40	52	52
19	Wycombe W	46	8	5	10	31	26	5	7	11	21	32	52	51
20	Oldham Ath	46	8	4	11	26	31	6	5	12	22	35	48	51
21	York C	46	6	8	9	28	33	7	3	13	28	47	56	50
22	Northampton T	46	4	12	7	26	31	6	6	11	17	26	43	48
23	Lincoln C	46	9	4	10	27	27	4	3	16	15	47	42	46
24	Macclesfield T	46	7	4	12	24	30	4	6	13	19	33	43	43

NATIONWIDE DIVISION 2

	League	FA Cup	Worthington Cup	Other Cups	Total
Jamie Cureton *(Bristol R)*	25	2	1	1	29
Carl Asaba *(Gillingham)*	20	0	1	1	22
(Includes 1 Worthington Cup goal for Reading)					
Andy Payton *(Burnley)*	19	2	1	0	22
Stuart Barlow *(Wigan Ath)*	19	1	1	4	25
Kurt Nogan *(Preston NE)*	18	3	0	0	21
Andy Rammell *(Walsall)*	18	0	1	1	20
Shaun Goater *(Manchester C)*	17	1	2	0	20
Barry Hayles *(Fulham)*	17	1	1	0	19
(Includes 9 League and 1 Worthington Cup goal for Bristol R)					
Jason Roberts *(Bristol R)*	16	7	0	0	23
Richard Cresswell *(York C)*	16	3	0	0	19
(Also scored 1 League goal for Sheffield W)					
Robert Taylor *(Gillingham)*	16	0	0	3	19
Carlo Corazzin *(Northampton T)*	16	0	0	1	17
Geoff Horsfield *(Fulham)*	15	2	0	0	17
(Also scored 7 League and 1 Worthington Cup goal for Halifax T)					
Mark Stein *(Bournemouth)*	15	1	5	4	25
Neil Harris *(Millwall)*	15	0	0	3	18
Steve Robinson *(Bournemouth)*	13	1	1	1	16
Darren Wrack *(Walsall)*	13	0	0	1	14
Karl Connolly *(Wrexham)*	11	5	1	1	18
David Gregory *(Colchester U)*	11	0	2	1	14
Graham Kavanagh *(Stoke C)*	11	0	1	1	13
Kit Symons *(Fulham)*	11	0	0	0	11
Martin Williams *(Reading)*	11	0	0	0	11

Nationwide Football League Division 3

			Home					Away						
		P	W	D	L	F	A	W	D	L	F	A	GS	Pts
1	Brentford	46	16	5	2	45	18	10	2	11	34	38	79	85
2	Cambridge U	46	13	6	4	41	21	10	6	7	37	27	78	81
3	Cardiff C	46	13	7	3	35	17	9	7	7	25	22	60	80
4	Scunthorpe U	46	14	3	6	42	28	8	5	10	27	30	69	74
5	Rotherham U	46	11	8	4	41	26	9	5	9	38	35	79	73
6	Leyton Orient	46	12	6	5	40	30	7	9	7	28	29	68	72
7	Swansea C	46	11	9	3	33	19	8	5	10	23	29	56	71
8	Mansfield T	46	15	2	6	38	18	4	8	11	22	40	60	67
9	Peterborough U	46	11	4	8	41	29	7	8	8	31	27	72	66
10	Halifax T	46	10	8	5	33	25	7	7	9	25	31	58	66
11	Darlington	46	10	6	7	41	24	8	5	10	28	34	69	65
12	Exeter C	46	13	5	5	32	18	4	7	12	15	32	47	63
13	Plymouth Arg	46	11	6	6	32	19	6	4	13	26	35	58	61
14	Chester C	46	6	12	5	28	30	7	6	10	29	36	57	57
15	Shrewsbury T	46	11	6	6	36	29	3	8	12	16	34	52	56
16	Barnet	46	10	5	8	30	31	4	8	11	24	40	54	55
17	Brighton & HA	46	8	3	12	25	35	8	4	11	24	31	49	55
18	Southend U	46	8	6	9	24	21	6	6	11	28	37	52	54
19	Rochdale	46	9	8	6	22	21	4	7	12	20	34	42	54
20	Torquay U	46	9	9	5	29	20	3	8	12	18	38	47	53
21	Hull C	46	8	5	10	25	28	6	6	11	19	34	44	53
22	Hartlepool U	46	8	7	8	33	27	5	5	13	19	38	52	51
23	Carlisle U	46	8	8	7	25	21	3	8	12	18	32	43	49
24	Scarborough	46	8	3	12	30	39	6	3	14	20	38	50	48

Goals scored determine Nationwide Football League position where clubs are level on points. If teams still cannot be separated, the team that has conceded fewer goals is placed higher.

NATIONWIDE DIVISION 3

	League	FA Cup	Worthington Cup	Other Cups	Total
Marco Gabbiadini *(Darlington)*	23	0	0	1	24
Lloyd Owusu *(Brentford)*	22	1	2	0	25
Jamie Forrester *(Scunthorpe U)*	20	2	1	0	23
Scott Partridge *(Brentford)*	19	1	0	1	21
(Including 12 League, 1 Worthington and 1 other goal for Torquay U)					
Martin Butler *(Cambridge U)*	17	1	2	1	21
John Taylor *(Cambridge U)*	17	0	1	1	19
Lee Peacock *(Mansfield T)*	17	0	0	2	19
Steve Watkin *(Swansea C)*	17	0	0	0	17
Ken Charlery *(Barnet)*	16	0	0	0	16
Kevin Nugent *(Cardiff C)*	15	3	0	0	18
John Eyre *(Scunthorpe U)*	15	2	0	0	17
Guiliano Grazioli *(Peterborough U)*	15	0	0	0	15
Lee Steele *(Shrewsbury T)*	13	0	0	0	13
John Williams *(Cardiff C)*	12	3	1	0	16
Steve Brodie *(Scarborough)*	12	0	0	0	12
Leo Fortune-West *(Rotherham U)*	12	0	0	0	12
(Also scored 1 League goal for Lincoln C and 1 Auto-Windscreens Shield for Brentford))					
Gary Hart *(Brighton & HA)*	12	0	0	0	12
Dwight Marshall *(Plymouth Arg)*	12	0	0	0	12
John Murphy *(Chester C)*	12	0	0	0	12
Chris Tate *(Scarborough)*	12	0	0	0	12

HOME TEAM	Arsenal	Aston Villa	Blackburn R	Charlton Ath	Chelsea	Coventry C	Derby Co	Everton	Leeds U	Leicester C
Arsenal	—	1-0	1-0	0-0	1-0	2-0	1-0	1-0	3-1	5-0
Aston Villa	3-2	—	1-3	3-4	0-3	1-4	1-0	3-0	1-2	1-1
Blackburn R	1-2	2-1	—	1-0	3-4	1-2	0-0	1-2	1-0	1-0
Charlton Ath	0-1	0-1	0-0	—	0-1	1-1	1-2	1-2	1-1	0-0
Chelsea	0-0	2-1	1-1	2-1	—	2-1	2-1	3-1	1-0	2-2
Coventry C	0-1	1-2	1-1	2-1	2-1	—	1-1	3-0	2-2	1-1
Derby Co	0-0	2-1	1-0	0-2	2-2	0-0	—	2-1	2-2	2-0
Everton	0-2	0-0	0-0	4-1	0-0	2-0	0-0	—	0-0	0-0
Leeds U	1-0	0-0	1-0	4-1	0-0	2-0	4-1	1-0	—	0-1
Leicester C	1-1	2-2	1-1	1-1	2-4	1-0	1-2	2-0	1-2	—
Liverpool	0-0	0-1	2-0	3-3	1-1	2-0	1-2	3-2	1-3	0-1
Manchester U	1-1	2-1	3-2	4-1	1-1	2-0	1-0	3-1	3-2	2-2
Middlesbrough	1-6	0-0	2-1	2-0	0-0	2-0	1-1	2-2	0-0	0-0
Newcastle U	1-1	2-1	1-1	0-0	0-1	4-1	2-1	1-3	0-3	1-0
Nottingham F	0-1	2-2	2-2	0-1	1-3	1-0	2-2	0-2	1-1	1-0
Sheffield W	1-0	0-1	3-0	3-0	0-0	1-2	0-1	0-0	0-2	0-1
Southampton	0-0	1-4	3-3	3-1	0-2	2-1	0-1	2-0	3-0	2-1
Tottenham H	1-3	1-0	2-1	2-2	2-2	0-0	1-1	4-1	3-3	0-2
West Ham U	0-4	0-0	2-0	0-1	1-1	2-0	5-1	2-1	1-5	3-2
Wimbledon	1-0	0-0	1-1	2-1	1-2	2-1	2-1	1-2	1-1	0-1

Liverpool	Manchester U	Middlesbrough	Newcastle U	Nottingham F	Sheffield W	Southampton	Tottenham H	West Ham U	Wimbledon
0-0	3-0	1-1	3-0	2-1	3-0	1-1	0-0	1-0	5-1
2-4	1-1	3-1	1-0	2-0	2-1	3-0	3-2	0-0	2-0
1-3	0-0	0-0	0-0	1-2	1-4	0-2	1-1	3-0	3-1
1-0	0-1	1-1	2-2	0-0	0-1	5-0	1-4	4-2	2-0
2-1	0-0	2-0	1-1	2-1	1-1	1-0	2-0	0-1	3-0
2-1	0-1	1-2	1-5	4-0	1-0	1-0	1-1	0-0	2-1
3-2	1-1	2-1	3-4	1-0	1-0	0-0	0-1	0-2	0-0
0-0	1-4	5-0	1-0	0-1	1-2	1-0	0-1	6-0	1-1
0-0	1-1	2-0	0-1	3-1	2-1	3-0	2-0	4-0	2-2
1-0	2-6	0-1	2-0	3-1	0-2	2-0	2-1	0-0	1-1
—	2-2	3-1	4-2	5-1	2-0	7-1	3-2	2-2	3-0
2-0	—	2-3	0-0	3-0	3-0	2-1	2-1	4-1	5-1
1-3	0-1	—	2-2	1-1	4-0	3-0	0-0	1-0	3-1
1-4	1-2	1-1	—	2-0	1-1	4-0	1-1	0-3	3-1
2-2	1-8	1-2	1-2	—	2-0	1-1	0-1	0-0	0-1
1-0	3-1	3-1	1-1	3-2	—	0-0	0-0	0-1	1-2
1-2	0-3	3-3	2-1	1-2	1-0	—	1-1	1-0	3-1
2-1	2-2	0-3	2-0	2-0	0-3	3-0	—	1-2	0-0
2-1	0-0	4-0	2-0	2-1	0-4	1-0	2-1	—	3-4
1-0	1-1	2-2	1-1	1-3	2-1	0-2	3-1	0-0	—

HOME TEAM	Barnsley	Birmingham C	Bolton W	Bradford C	Bristol C	Bury	Crewe Alex	Crystal Palace	Grimsby T	Huddersfield T
Barnsley	—	0-0	2-2	0-1	2-0	1-1	2-2	4-0	0-0	7-1
Birmingham C	0-0	—	0-0	2-1	4-2	1-0	3-1	3-1	0-1	1-1
Bolton W	3-3	3-1	—	0-0	1-0	4-0	1-3	3-0	2-0	3-0
Bradford C	2-1	2-1	2-2	—	5-0	3-0	4-1	2-1	3-0	2-3
Bristol C	1-1	1-2	2-1	2-3	—	1-1	5-2	1-1	4-1	1-2
Bury	0-0	2-4	2-1	0-2	0-1	—	1-0	0-0	1-0	1-0
Crewe Alex	3-1	0-0	4-4	2-1	1-0	3-1	—	0-1	0-0	1-2
Crystal Palace	1-0	1-1	2-2	1-0	2-1	4-2	1-1	—	3-1	2-2
Grimsby T	1-2	0-3	0-1	2-0	2-1	0-0	1-1	2-0	—	1-0
Huddersfield T	0-1	1-1	3-2	2-1	2-2	2-2	0-0	4-0	2-0	—
Ipswich T	0-2	1-0	0-1	3-0	3-1	0-0	1-2	3-0	0-1	3-0
Norwich C	0-0	2-0	2-2	2-2	2-1	0-0	2-1	0-1	3-1	4-1
Oxford U	1-0	1-7	0-0	0-1	0-0	0-1	1-1	1-3	0-0	2-2
Port Vale	1-0	0-2	0-2	1-1	3-2	1-0	1-0	1-0	0-1	2-0
Portsmouth	1-3	0-1	0-2	2-4	0-1	2-1	2-0	1-1	0-1	1-0
QPR	2-1	0-1	2-0	1-3	1-1	0-0	0-1	6-0	1-2	1-1
Sheffield U	1-1	0-2	1-2	2-2	3-1	3-1	3-1	1-1	3-2	2-1
Stockport Co	0-1	1-0	0-1	1-2	2-2	0-0	1-1	1-1	2-0	1-1
Sunderland	2-3	2-1	3-1	0-0	1-1	1-0	2-0	2-0	3-1	2-0
Swindon T	1-3	0-1	3-3	1-4	3-2	1-1	1-2	2-0	2-0	3-0
Tranmere R	3-0	0-1	1-1	0-1	1-1	4-0	3-0	3-1	1-2	2-3
Watford	0-0	1-1	2-0	1-0	1-0	0-0	4-2	2-1	1-0	1-1
WBA	2-0	1-3	2-3	0-2	2-2	1-0	1-5	3-2	1-1	3-1
Wolverhampton W	1-1	3-1	1-1	2-3	3-0	1-0	3-0	0-0	2-0	2-2

DIVISION 1 1998–99 RESULTS

Ipswich T	Norwich C	Oxford U	Port Vale	Portsmouth	QPR	Sheffield U	Stockport Co	Sunderland	Swindon T	Tranmere R	Watford	WBA	Wolverhampton W
0-1	1-3	1-0	0-2	2-1	1-0	2-1	1-1	1-3	1-3	1-1	2-2	2-2	2-3
1-0	0-0	0-1	1-0	4-1	1-0	1-0	2-0	0-0	1-1	2-2	1-2	4-0	0-1
2-0	2-0	1-1	3-1	3-1	2-1	2-2	1-2	0-3	2-1	2-2	1-2	2-1	1-1
0-0	4-1	0-0	4-0	2-1	0-3	2-2	1-2	0-1	3-0	2-0	2-0	1-0	2-1
0-1	1-0	2-2	2-0	2-2	0-0	2-0	1-1	0-1	3-1	1-1	1-4	1-3	1-6
0-3	0-2	1-0	1-0	2-1	1-1	3-3	1-1	2-5	3-0	0-0	1-3	2-0	0-0
0-3	3-2	3-1	0-0	3-1	0-2	1-2	0-2	1-4	0-2	1-4	0-1	1-1	0-0
3-2	5-1	2-0	0-1	4-1	1-1	1-0	2-2	1-1	0-1	1-1	2-2	1-1	3-2
0-0	0-1	1-0	2-2	1-1	1-0	1-2	1-0	0-2	1-0	1-0	2-1	5-1	0-0
2-2	1-1	2-0	2-1	3-3	2-0	1-0	3-0	1-1	1-2	0-0	2-0	0-3	2-1
—	0-1	2-1	1-0	3-0	3-1	4-1	1-0	0-2	1-0	1-0	3-2	2-0	2-0
0-0	—	1-3	3-4	0-0	4-2	1-1	0-2	2-2	2-1	2-2	1-1	1-1	0-0
3-3	2-4	—	2-1	3-0	4-1	0-2	5-0	0-0	2-0	1-2	0-0	3-0	0-2
0-3	1-0	1-0	—	0-2	2-0	2-3	1-1	0-2	0-1	2-2	1-2	0-3	2-1
0-0	1-2	2-2	4-0	—	3-0	1-0	3-1	1-1	5-2	1-1	1-2	2-1	1-0
1-1	2-0	1-0	3-2	1-1	—	1-2	2-0	2-2	4-0	0-0	1-2	2-1	0-1
1-2	2-1	1-2	3-0	2-1	2-0	—	1-1	0-4	2-1	2-2	3-0	3-0	1-1
0-1	0-2	2-0	4-2	2-0	0-0	1-0	—	0-1	2-1	0-0	1-1	2-2	1-2
2-1	1-0	7-0	2-0	2-0	1-0	0-0	1-0	—	2-0	5-0	4-1	3-0	2-1
0-6	1-1	4-1	1-1	3-3	3-1	2-2	2-3	1-1	—	2-3	1-4	2-2	1-0
0-2	1-3	2-2	1-1	1-1	3-2	2-3	1-1	1-0	0-0	—	3-2	3-1	1-2
1-0	1-1	2-0	2-2	0-0	2-1	1-1	4-2	2-1	0-1	2-1	—	0-2	0-2
0-1	2-0	2-0	3-2	2-2	2-0	4-1	3-1	2-3	1-1	0-2	4-1	—	2-0
1-0	2-2	1-1	3-1	2-0	1-2	2-1	2-2	1-1	1-0	2-0	0-0	1-1	—

NATIONWIDE FOOTBALL LEAGUE

HOME TEAM	Blackpool	Bournemouth	Bristol R	Burnley	Chesterfield	Colchester U	Fulham	Gillingham	Lincoln C	Luton T
Blackpool	—	0-0	1-2	0-2	1-1	2-1	2-3	2-2	0-1	1-0
Bournemouth	1-1	—	1-0	5-0	0-0	2-1	1-1	3-3	2-0	1-0
Bristol R	0-2	1-0	—	3-4	0-0	1-1	2-3	0-1	3-0	1-0
Burnley	1-0	0-0	2-1	—	1-2	3-1	1-0	0-5	1-1	1-2
Chesterfield	1-2	3-1	0-0	1-0	—	3-1	1-0	1-0	3-0	3-1
Colchester U	2-2	2-1	0-3	0-4	1-0	—	0-1	1-1	1-3	2-2
Fulham	4-0	0-0	1-0	4-0	2-1	2-0	—	3-0	1-0	1-3
Gillingham	1-0	2-1	0-0	2-1	3-1	1-1	1-0	—	4-0	1-0
Lincoln C	1-2	2-1	1-0	1-1	2-0	0-0	1-2	1-2	—	2-2
Luton T	1-0	2-2	2-0	1-0	1-0	2-0	0-4	1-0	0-1	—
Macclesfield T	0-1	2-2	3-4	2-1	2-0	2-0	0-1	1-0	0-0	2-2
Manchester C	3-0	2-1	0-0	2-2	1-1	2-1	3-0	0-0	4-0	2-0
Millwall	1-0	1-2	1-1	1-2	0-0	2-0	0-1	3-3	2-0	0-1
Northampton T	0-0	2-1	3-1	2-2	1-0	3-3	1-1	0-1	0-0	1-0
Notts Co	0-1	1-2	1-1	0-0	2-0	1-3	1-0	0-1	2-3	1-2
Oldham Ath	3-0	2-3	2-1	1-1	2-0	1-0	1-1	1-4	2-0	1-1
Preston NE	1-2	0-1	2-2	4-1	2-0	2-0	0-1	1-1	5-0	2-1
Reading	1-1	3-3	0-6	1-1	1-2	1-1	0-1	0-0	2-1	3-0
Stoke C	1-3	2-0	1-4	1-4	0-0	3-3	0-1	0-0	2-0	3-1
Walsall	1-0	1-0	3-3	3-1	1-1	1-1	2-2	2-1	2-1	1-0
Wigan Ath	3-0	2-1	1-0	0-0	3-1	1-1	2-0	4-1	3-1	1-3
Wrexham	1-1	0-1	1-0	1-1	0-0	2-4	0-2	2-1	2-1	1-1
Wycombe W	2-2	0-2	1-1	2-0	1-0	2-2	1-1	0-2	4-1	0-1
York C	1-0	0-1	1-0	3-3	1-2	1-2	0-3	1-1	2-1	3-3

DIVISION 2 1998–99 RESULTS

Macclesfield T	Manchester C	Millwall	Northampton T	Notts Co	Oldham Ath	Preston NE	Reading	Stoke C	Walsall	Wigan Ath	Wrexham	Wycombe W	York C
2-1	0-0	2-3	2-1	1-0	3-0	0-0	2-0	0-1	0-2	1-1	1-1	0-0	1-2
1-0	0-0	3-0	1-1	2-0	2-0	3-1	0-1	4-0	0-1	1-0	0-0	2-0	2-1
0-0	2-2	3-0	1-1	1-1	2-2	2-2	4-1	1-0	3-4	3-2	0-0	0-2	2-0
4-3	0-6	2-1	0-2	1-1	1-0	0-1	1-1	0-2	0-0	1-1	2-1	1-1	0-1
2-0	1-1	2-1	0-0	3-0	1-3	0-1	1-0	1-1	0-1	1-1	2-1	2-0	2-1
1-1	0-1	0-0	1-0	2-1	2-2	1-0	1-1	0-1	1-0	2-1	1-3	2-1	2-1
1-0	3-0	4-1	2-0	2-1	1-0	3-0	3-1	1-0	4-1	2-0	1-1	2-0	3-3
2-2	0-2	1-1	2-3	4-0	2-1	1-1	2-1	4-0	0-1	2-0	4-0	3-0	3-1
1-0	2-1	2-0	1-0	0-1	1-3	3-4	2-2	1-2	0-1	1-0	1-0	0-1	1-2
1-2	1-1	1-2	1-0	0-1	2-0	1-1	1-1	1-2	0-1	0-4	1-2	3-1	2-1
—	0-1	0-2	0-1	0-1	1-0	3-2	2-1	1-2	1-1	0-1	0-2	1-3	1-2
2-0	—	3-0	0-0	2-1	1-2	0-1	0-1	2-1	3-1	1-0	0-0	1-2	4-0
0-0	1-1	—	2-1	1-3	1-1	2-2	1-1	2-0	1-2	3-1	3-0	2-1	3-1
0-2	2-2	1-2	—	1-1	1-1	1-1	0-1	1-3	0-1	3-3	0-2	1-1	2-2
1-1	1-1	3-1	3-1	—	0-1	2-3	1-1	1-0	2-1	0-1	1-1	1-0	4-2
1-2	0-3	0-1	0-1	1-3	—	0-1	2-0	1-0	0-2	2-3	3-2	0-0	0-2
2-2	1-1	0-1	3-0	1-1	2-1	—	4-0	3-4	1-0	2-2	3-1	2-1	3-0
1-0	1-3	2-0	0-1	1-0	1-1	2-1	—	2-1	0-1	0-1	4-0	2-1	1-0
2-0	0-1	1-0	3-1	2-3	2-0	0-1	0-4	—	2-0	2-1	1-3	2-2	2-0
2-0	1-1	3-0	0-0	3-2	3-1	1-0	0-2	1-0	—	1-2	1-0	2-2	2-3
2-0	0-1	0-1	1-0	3-0	2-0	2-2	4-1	2-3	2-0	—	1-1	0-0	5-0
2-1	0-1	0-0	1-0	1-0	1-2	0-5	3-0	0-1	2-1	0-2	—	0-2	1-1
3-0	1-0	0-1	1-2	1-1	3-0	0-1	2-3	0-1	1-2	2-1	3-0	—	1-2
0-2	2-1	2-1	1-1	1-1	0-1	0-1	1-1	2-2	1-2	1-3	1-1	3-0	—

NATIONWIDE FOOTBALL LEAGUE

HOME TEAM	Barnet	Brentford	Brighton & HA	Cambridge U	Cardiff C	Carlisle U	Chester C	Darlington	Exeter C	Halifax T
Barnet	—	0-3	0-1	3-0	1-0	1-0	0-0	3-0	0-1	2-2
Brentford	3-1	—	2-0	1-0	1-0	1-1	2-1	3-0	3-0	1-1
Brighton & HA	0-1	3-1	—	1-3	0-2	1-3	2-2	0-4	0-1	0-1
Cambridge U	3-2	0-1	2-3	—	0-0	1-0	2-1	2-1	1-1	4-0
Cardiff C	1-0	4-1	2-0	0-1	—	2-1	0-0	3-2	1-0	1-1
Carlisle U	2-1	0-1	1-0	1-1	0-1	—	1-1	3-3	1-3	0-1
Chester C	3-0	1-3	1-1	0-3	2-2	2-1	—	1-0	0-0	2-2
Darlington	0-2	2-2	1-2	0-0	3-0	1-1	1-2	—	4-0	2-2
Exeter C	1-0	0-1	1-0	0-3	0-2	2-0	0-1	0-0	—	2-1
Halifax T	1-1	1-0	1-0	3-3	1-2	1-0	3-2	0-0	1-1	—
Hartlepool U	2-2	0-1	0-0	2-2	1-1	0-0	2-0	2-3	4-3	2-0
Hull C	1-1	2-3	0-2	0-3	1-2	1-0	1-2	1-2	2-1	1-2
Leyton Orient	2-2	2-1	1-0	2-0	1-1	2-1	2-2	3-2	2-0	1-0
Mansfield T	5-0	3-1	2-0	1-3	3-0	1-1	3-0	0-1	0-1	0-1
Peterborough U	5-2	2-4	1-2	2-1	2-1	0-1	3-0	0-1	4-1	0-2
Plymouth Arg	2-0	3-0	1-2	2-2	1-1	2-0	2-0	1-2	1-0	1-0
Rochdale	0-0	2-0	2-1	0-2	1-1	1-1	3-1	0-0	1-1	1-0
Rotherham U	1-1	2-4	2-1	2-0	1-0	3-1	2-4	3-1	0-0	3-1
Scarborough	0-0	3-1	1-2	1-5	1-2	3-0	2-4	0-2	1-0	1-0
Scunthorpe U	3-1	0-0	3-1	3-2	0-2	3-1	2-1	0-1	2-0	0-4
Shrewsbury T	0-2	2-0	1-3	1-1	0-3	1-1	2-0	3-0	1-1	2-2
Southend U	2-3	1-4	3-0	0-1	0-1	0-1	0-1	2-1	0-0	0-0
Swansea C	2-1	2-1	2-2	2-0	2-1	1-1	1-1	2-0	2-0	1-2
Torquay U	1-1	3-1	1-1	0-1	0-0	2-2	0-3	2-2	1-0	4-0

DIVISION 3 1998–99 RESULTS

	Hartlepool U	Hull C	Leyton Orient	Mansfield T	Peterborough U	Plymouth Arg	Rochdale	Rotherham U	Scarborough	Scunthorpe U	Shrewsbury T	Southend U	Swansea C	Torquay U
	0-2	4-1	3-2	0-0	1-9	1-1	0-1	4-2	1-0	1-0	2-2	0-2	0-1	3-1
	3-1	0-2	0-0	3-0	3-0	3-1	2-1	0-3	1-1	2-1	0-0	4-1	4-1	3-2
	3-2	0-0	1-2	1-3	1-0	1-3	1-1	4-1	1-0	1-3	1-0	0-2	1-0	2-0
	1-2	2-0	1-0	7-2	1-1	1-0	1-1	3-2	2-3	0-0	0-0	3-0	2-1	2-0
	4-1	1-1	0-0	4-2	1-3	1-0	2-1	0-1	1-0	0-0	3-0	2-0	0-0	2-2
	2-1	0-0	1-1	0-0	1-1	2-1	0-1	0-0	1-0	0-1	2-1	3-0	1-2	3-0
	1-1	2-2	0-2	1-1	1-0	3-2	1-1	1-1	1-3	0-2	1-1	1-1	1-1	2-0
	2-0	0-1	1-1	5-1	3-0	1-2	3-0	1-2	3-0	3-1	1-0	2-1	2-2	0-2
	2-1	3-0	1-1	2-1	2-0	1-1	2-1	3-0	1-0	2-2	0-1	2-1	4-0	1-1
	2-1	0-1	1-2	2-2	2-2	2-0	0-0	2-4	1-2	1-0	2-0	3-1	2-0	1-1
	—	1-0	1-0	1-2	1-2	2-0	0-1	0-0	3-0	1-2	1-1	2-4	1-2	4-1
	4-0	—	0-1	0-0	1-0	1-0	2-1	1-0	1-1	2-3	1-1	1-1	0-2	1-0
	1-1	1-2	—	1-1	1-2	4-3	3-0	1-4	0-3	1-0	6-1	0-3	1-1	2-0
	2-0	2-0	1-2	—	1-0	2-0	3-1	0-3	3-2	2-1	1-0	0-0	1-0	2-1
	1-1	1-1	3-0	1-0	—	0-2	2-0	2-4	3-1	2-1	2-2	1-1	0-1	4-0
	0-0	0-0	2-4	3-0	0-2	—	2-1	1-0	0-0	5-0	2-0	0-3	1-2	0-0
	0-1	3-0	2-1	1-0	0-3	1-1	—	0-0	0-1	2-2	1-0	1-0	0-3	0-2
	3-0	2-1	3-1	0-0	2-2	0-2	2-2	—	4-0	0-0	0-1	2-2	1-0	2-2
	1-2	1-2	1-3	2-3	1-1	3-0	1-0	0-4	—	1-4	2-0	1-2	2-1	1-1
	1-0	3-2	2-0	3-2	1-1	0-2	0-1	4-3	5-1	—	3-0	1-1	1-2	2-0
	0-1	3-2	1-1	1-0	1-1	2-1	3-2	2-3	3-1	2-1	—	3-1	1-0	1-2
	1-1	0-1	2-2	1-2	2-0	1-0	1-1	3-0	1-0	0-1	2-1	—	2-0	0-0
	1-0	2-0	1-1	1-0	0-0	2-3	1-1	1-1	2-0	1-2	1-1	3-1	—	0-0
	3-0	2-0	1-1	0-0	0-1	1-1	2-1	2-0	0-1	1-0	0-3	2-0	1-1	—

Player	Ht	Wt	Birthplace	D.O.B.	Source
Adams Tony (D)	6 3	13 11	London	10 10 66	Apprentice
Anelka Nicolas (F)	5 11	12 03	Versailles	14 3 79	Paris St Germain
Barrett Graham (F)			Dublin	6 10 81	Trainee
Bergkamp Dennis (F)	6 0	12 05	Amsterdam	18 5 69	Internazionale
Black Tommy (M)			Chigwell	26 11 79	Trainee
Boa Morte Luis (F)	5 10	11 05	Lisbon	4 8 77	Sporting Lisbon
Bould Steve (D)	6 4	14 02	Stoke	16 11 62	Stoke C
Canoville Lee (D)			Ealing	14 3 81	Trainee
Cole Ashley (D)			Stepney	20 12 80	Trainee
Crowe Jason (D)	5 9	10 09	Sidcup	30 9 78	Trainee
Diawara Kaba (F)			Toulon	16 12 75	Bordeaux
Dixon Lee (D)	5 8	11 08	Manchester	17 3 64	Stoke C
Gray Julian (M)			Lewisham	21 9 79	Trainee
Grimandi Gilles (D)	6 0	12 07	Gap	11 11 70	Monaco
Grondin David (D)			Paris	8 5 80	St Etienne
Hughes Stephen (M)	6 0	12 05	Wokingham	18 9 76	Trainee
Kanu Nwankwo (F)	6 5	13 00	Owerri	1 8 76	Internazionale
Keown Martin (D)	6 1	12 04	Oxford	24 7 66	Everton
Lincoln Greg (M)			Cheshunt	23 3 80	Trainee
Livermore David (D)			Edmonton	20 5 80	Trainee
Ljungberg Frederik (M)			Sweden	16 4 77	Halmstad
Lukic John (G)	6 4	13 07	Chesterfield	11 12 60	Leeds U
MacDonald James (M)	6 0	12 05	Inverness	21 2 79	Trainee
Manninger Alex (G)	6 2	13 03	Salzburg	4 6 77	Graz
McGovern Brian (D)			Dublin	28 4 80	
McLeod Allan (D)			Islington	19 4 80	Trainee
Mendez Alberto (M)	5 11	11 09	Nuremberg	24 10 74	FC Feucht
Overmars Marc (F)	5 8	11 04	Emst	29 3 73	Ajax
Parlour Ray (M)	5 10	11 12	Romford	7 3 73	Trainee
Pennant Jermaine (M)			Nottingham	15 1 83	
Petit Emmanuel (M)	6 1	12 07	Dieppe	22 9 70	Monaco
Riza Omer (F)			Edmonton	8 11 79	Trainee
Seaman David (G)	6 4	14 10	Rotherham	19 9 63	QPR
Taylor Stuart (G)			Romford	28 11 80	Trainee
Upson Matthew (D)	6 1	11 05	Eye	18 4 79	Luton T
Vernazza Paulo (M)			Islington	1 11 79	Trainee
Vieira Patrick (M)	6 4	13 00	Dakar	23 6 76	AC Milan
Vivas Nelson (D)			San Nicolas	18 10 69	Lugano
Winterburn Nigel (D)	5 8	11 04	Coventry	11 12 63	Wimbledon
Wreh Christopher (F)	5 8	11 13	Liberia	14 5 75	Guincamp

League Appearances: Adams, T. 26; Anelka, N. 34(1); Bergkamp, D. 28(1); Boa Morte, L. 2(6); Bould, S. 14(5); Caballero, F. (1); Diawara, K. 2(10); Dixon, L. 36; Garde, R. 6(4); Grimandi, G. 3(5); Grondin, D. 1; Hughes, S. 4(10); Kanu, N. 5(7); Keown, M. 34; Ljungberg, F. 10(6); Manninger, A. 6; Mendez, A. (1); Overmars, M. 37; Parlour, R. 35; Petit, E. 26(1); Seaman, D. 32; Upson, M. (5); Vieira, P. 34; Vivas, N. 10(13); Winterburn, N. 30; Wreh, C. 3(9).

Goals – League (59): Anelka 17, Bergkamp 12 (2 pens), Kanu 6, Overmars 6 (2 pens), Parlour 6, Petit 4, Vieira 3, Adams 1, Hughes 1, Keown 1, Ljungberg 1, own goal 1.

Worthington Cup (2): Vivas 1, own goal 1.

FA Cup (10): Bergkamp 3, Overmars 3, Petit 2, Boa Morte 1, Kanu 1.

Ground: Arsenal Stadium, Highbury, London N5 1BU. Telephone (0171) 704 4000.

Record attendance: 73,295 v Sunderland, Div 1, 9 March 1935. **Capacity:** 38,500.

Manager: Arsène Wenger.

Secretary: K. J. Friar.
Honours – FA Premier League: Champions – 1997–98. **Football League:** Division 1 Champions – 1930–31, 1932–33, 1933–34, 1934–35, 1937–38, 1947–48, 1952–53, 1970–71, 1988–89, 1990–91. **FA Cup winners** 1929–30, 1935–36, 1949–50, 1970–71, 1978–79, 1992–93, 1997–98. **Football League Cup winners** 1986–87, 1992–93. **European Competitions: European Cup-Winners' Cup winners:** 1993–94. **Fairs Cup winners:** 1969–70.
Colours: Red shirts with white sleeves, white shorts, red and white stockings.

ASTON VILLA   FA PREMIERSHIP

Player	Ht	Wt	Birthplace	Birthdate	From
Barry Gareth (D)	5 11	12 06	Hastings	23 2 81	Trainee
Blackwood Michael (F)	5 10	11 07	Birmingham	30 9 79	Trainee
Bosnich Mark (G)	6 1	14 07	Fairfield	13 1 72	Manchester U
Byfield Darren (F)	5 11	11 11	Sutton Coldfield	29 9 76	Trainee
Calderwood Colin (D)	6 0	13 00	Glasgow	20 1 65	Tottenham H
Collymore Stan (F)	6 2	14 04	Stone	22 1 71	Liverpool
Curtolo David (M)	5 9	11 00	Stockholm	30 9 80	
Delaney Mark (M)	6 1	11 07	Haverfordwest	13 5 76	Carmarthen T
Draper Mark (F)	5 10	12 04	Long Eaton	11 11 70	Leicester C
Dublin Dion (F)	6 2	12 04	Leicester	22 4 69	Coventry C
Ehiogu Ugo (D)	6 2	14 10	Hackney	3 11 72	Trainee
Enckelman Peter (G)	6 2	12 05	Turku	10 3 77	TPS Turku
Evans Graham (F)			Wrexham	16 6 80	Caersws
Ferraresi Fabio (M)	5 9	11 02	Fano	24 5 79	Cesena
Ghent Matthew (G)	6 3	14 01	Burton	5 10 80	Trainee
Grayson Simon (D)	6 0	13 04	Ripon	16 12 69	Leicester C
Hendrie Lee (F)	5 10	11 00	Birmingham	18 5 77	Trainee
Hughes David (D)	6 4	14 02	Wrexham	1 2 78	Trainee
Jaszczun Tommy (D)	5 11	11 02	Kettering	16 9 77	Trainee
Joachim Julian (M)	5 6	12 00	Boston	20 9 74	Leicester C
Lee Alan (F)	6 2	13 09	Galway	21 8 78	Trainee
Lescott Aaron (M)	5 8	10 09	Birmingham	2 12 78	Trainee
Melaugh Gavin (M)	5 7	9 07	Derry	9 7 81	Trainee
Merson Paul (F)	6 0	13 02	Northolt	20 3 68	Middlesbrough
Mulhulland Brian (D)			Alexandria	22 8 81	Trainee
Nkubi Isaac (M)			Uganda	5 3 81	Vasteras
Oakes Michael (G)	6 2	14 07	Northwich	30 10 73	Trainee
Rachel Adam (G)	5 11	12 08	Birmingham	10 12 76	Trainee
Samuel J Lloyd (D)	5 11	11 04	Trinidad	29 3 81	Charlton Ath
Scimeca Riccardo (D)	6 0	13 11	Leamington Spa	13 6 75	Trainee
Southgate Gareth (M)	6 0	12 06	Watford	3 9 70	Crystal Palace
Standing Michael (M)	5 10	10 05	Shoreham	20 3 81	Trainee
Stone Steve (M)	5 8	12 02	Gateshead	20 8 71	Nottingham F
Tarrant Neil (M)	6 0	12 00	Darlington	24 6 79	Ross Co
Taylor Ian (M)	6 1	12 00	Birmingham	4 6 68	Sheffield W
Thompson Alan (M)	6 0	13 11	Newcastle	22 12 73	Bolton W
Vassell Darius (F)	5 7	12 00	Birmingham	13 6 80	Trainee
Walker Richard (F)	6 0	12 04	Sutton Coldfield	8 11 77	Trainee
Watson Steve (D)	6 1	12 07	North Shields	1 4 74	Newcastle U
Wright Alan (D)	5 4	9 09	Ashton-under-Lyme	28 9 71	Blackburn R

League Appearances: Barry, G. 27(5); Bosnich, M. 15; Calderwood, C. 8; Charles, G. 10(1); Collymore, S. 11(9); Delaney, M. (2); Draper, M. 13(10); Dublin, D. 24; Ehiogu, U. 23(2); Grayson, S. 4(11); Hendrie, L. 31(1); Joachim, J. 29(7); Merson, P. 21(5); Oakes, M. 23; Rachel, A. (1); Scimeca, R. 16(2); Southgate, G. 38; Stone, S. 9(1); Taylor, I. 31(2); Thompson, A. 20(5); Vassell, D. (6); Watson, S. 26(1); Wright, A. 38; Yorke, D. 1.
Goals – League (51): Joachim 14, Dublin 11 (1 pen), Merson 5, Taylor 4, Hendrie 3

(1 pen), Barry 2, Draper 2, Ehiogu 2, Scimeca 2, Thompson 2, Charles 1, Collymore 1, Southgate 1, own goal 1.
Worthington Cup (1): Draper 1.
FA Cup (3): Collymore 2, Joachim 1.
Ground: Villa Park, Trinity Rd, Birmingham B6 6HE. Telephone (0121) 327 2299.
Record attendance: 76,588 v Derby Co, FA Cup 6th rd, 2 March 1946.
Capacity: 39,217.
Manager: John Gregory.
Secretary: Steven Stride.
Honours – Football League: Division 1 Champions – 1893–94, 1895–96, 1896–97, 1898–99, 1899–1900, 1909–10, 1980–81. Division 2 Champions – 1937–38, 1959–60. Division 3 Champions – 1971–72. **FA Cup:** Winners 1887, 1895, 1897, 1905, 1913, 1920, 1957. **Football League Cup:** Winners 1961, 1975, 1977, 1994, 1996. **European Competitions: European Cup winners:** 1981–82, **European Super Cup winners:** 1982–83.
Colours: Claret and blue shirts, white shorts, sky blue stockings.

BARNET DIV. 3

Arber Mark (D)	6 1	12 11	Johannesburg	8 10 77	Tottenham H
Barnes Steve (M)	5 4	10 09	Harrow	5 1 76	Birmingham C
Basham Mike (D)	6 2	13 09	Barking	27 9 73	Peterborough U
Charlery Ken (F)	6 1	13 12	Stepney	28 11 64	Stockport Co
Currie Darren (M)	5 10	12 07	Hampstead	29 11 74	Plymouth Arg
Doolan John (M)	6 1	13 00	Liverpool	7 5 74	Mansfield T
Goodhind Warren (D)	5 11	11 02	Johannesburg	16 8 77	Trainee
Hackett Warren (D)	6 0	12 05	Plaistow	16 12 71	Mansfield T
Harrison Lee (G)	6 2	12 07	Billericay	12 9 71	Fulham
Heald Greg (D)	6 1	13 01	Enfield	26 9 71	Peterborough U
King Marlon (F)	6 1	12 03	Dulwich	26 4 80	Trainee
McGleish Scott (F)	5 10	11 07	Camden Town	10 2 74	Leyton Orient
Sawyers Robert (D)	5 10	11 03	Dudley	20 11 78	Wolverhampton W
Searle Stevie (M)	5 10	11 08	Lambeth	7 3 77	Sittingbourne
Stockley Sam (D)	6 0	12 00	Tiverton	5 9 77	Trainee
Strevens Ben (M)			Edgware	24 5 80	

League Appearances: Alsford, J. 9; Arber, M. 35; Barnes, S. 3(9); Basham, M. 32; Charlery, K. 40(2); Currie, D. 33(5); Dearden, K. 1; Devine, S. 10(10); Doolan, J. 40(2); Ford, J. 15; Gledhill, L. (1); Goodhind, W. 15; Hackett, W. 3(4); Harle, M. 11; Harrison, L. 43; Heald, G. 19; King, M. 17(5); Manuel, B. 3(9); McGleish, S. 25(11); Onwere, U. 14(5); Rust, N. 2; Sawyers, R. 21(1); Searle, S. 33(2); Simpson, P. 11(2); Stockley, S. 40(1); Wilson, P. 31.
Goals – League (54): Charlery 16, McGleish 8, King 6, Currie 4, Searle 3, Arber 2, Doolan 2, Heald 2, Onwere 2, Wilson 2 (2 pens), Alsford 1, Basham 1, Devine 1, Ford 1, Goodhind 1, Manuel 1, own goal 1.
Worthington Cup (2): Currie 1, McGleish 1.
FA Cup (1): Currie 1.
Ground: Underhill Stadium, Barnet Lane, Barnet, Herts EN5 2BE. Telephone (0181) 441 6932.
Record attendance: 11,026 v Wycombe Wanderers. FA Amateur Cup 4th Round 1951–52. **Capacity:** 4057.
Manager: John Still.
Secretary: David Stanley.
Honours – FA Amateur Cup winners 1945–46. **GM Vauxhall Conference winners** 1990–91.
Colours: Amber and black striped shirts, black shorts, black stockings.

Appleby Matty (D)	5 10	11 08	Middlesbrough	16 4 72	Darlington
Bagshaw Paul (M)	5 10	12 02	Sheffield	29 5 79	Trainee
Barker Christopher (D)	6 0	11 08	Sheffield	2 3 80	Alfreton
Barnard Darren (D)	5 9	12 03	Rinteln	30 11 71	Bristol C
Bassinder Gavin (D)	5 8	11 01	Mexborough	24 9 79	Trainee
Bullock Tony (G)	6 1	14 01	Warrington	18 2 72	Leek T
Crookes Dale (M)	5 9	12 03	Sheffield	10 3 80	Trainee
Dyer Bruce (F)	5 11	12 06	Ilford	13 4 75	Crystal Palace
Eaden Nicky (D)	5 9	12 02	Sheffield	12 12 72	Trainee
Fallon Rory (F)	6 2	11 09	Gisbourne	20 3 82	North Shore U
Fumaca Jose Antunes (M)	6 0	11 08	Belem	15 7 76	Colchester U
Gregory Andrew (M)	5 10	11 04	Barnsley	8 10 76	Trainee
Hignett Craig (F)	5 9	11 03	Whiston	12 1 70	Aberdeen
Hristov Georgi (F)	6 0	12 09	Bitola	30 1 76	Partizan Belgrade
Jones Scott (D)	5 10	12 01	Sheffield	1 5 75	Trainee
Krizan Ales (D)	5 9	12 09	Maribor	25 7 71	Branik Maribor
Marcelle Clint (M)	5 5	9 09	Port of Spain	9 11 68	Falgueiras
Markstedt Peter (D)	6 2	13 05	Vasteras	11 1 72	
McClare Sean (M)	5 11	11 08	Rotherham	12 1 78	Trainee
Morgan Chris (D)	6 1	12 08	Barnsley	9 11 77	Trainee
Moses Adrian (D)	6 0	12 07	Doncaster	4 5 75	School
O'Callaghan Brian (D)	6 1	12 12	Limerick	24 2 81	Pike Rovers
Parkin Jonathan (F)	6 4	13 07	Barnsley	30 12 81	Scholarship
Richardson Kevin (M)	5 9	11 08	Newcastle	4 12 62	Southampton
Rose Karl (F)	5 10	11 00	Barnsley	12 10 78	
Sheron Mike (F)	5 10	12 07	Liverpool	11 1 72	QPR
Siddall Richard (G)	6 1	11 06	Sheffield	24 1 82	Scholarship
Smith Andrew (M)	5 5	11 08	Blackpool	13 1 80	Trainee
Tinkler Eric (M)	6 2	12 06	Roodepoort	30 7 70	Cagliari
Turner Mike (F)	6 2	13 03	Stoke	2 4 76	Bilston T
Van der Laan Robin (M)	5 11	13 08	Schiedam	5 9 68	Derby Co
Watson David (G)	6 0	12 09	Barnsley	10 11 73	Trainee

League Appearances: Appleby, M. 33(1); Bagshaw, P. (1); Barnard, D. 26; Blackmore, C. 4(3); Bullock, M. 20(12); Bullock, T. 32; Burton, D. 3; De Zeeuw, A. 38; Dyer, B. 28; Eaden, N. 38(2); Fjortoft, J. 9(10); Goodman, D. 5(3); Hendrie, J. 6(3); Hignett, C. 24; Hristov, G. 2(1); Jones, S. 28(1); Krizan, A. 1; Leese, L. 8; Liddell, A. 3(5); Marcelle, C. 2(7); Markstedt, P. 2; McClare, S. 23(7); Moore, A. 4(1); Morgan, C. 18(1); Moses, A. 33(1); Parkin, J. (2); Pirri 2; Richardson, K. 24(2); Rose, K. 2(2); Sheridan, D. 15(10); Sheron, M. 14(1); Tinkler, E. 21(4); Turner, M. 2(11); Van der Laan, R. 13(4); Ward, A. 17; Watson, D. 6.

Goals – League (59): Ward 12 (1 pen), Hignett 9, Dyer 7, Barnard 4 (2 pens), De Zeeuw 4, Fjortoft 3, Jones 3, McClare 3, Tinkler 3, Bullock M 2, Sheron 2, Eaden 1, Hendrie 1, Sheridan 1, Turner 1, Van der Laan 1, own goals 2.

Worthington Cup (10): Fjortoft 4, Ward 3 (1 pen), Barnard 1, Eaden 1, Van der Laan 1.

FA Cup (10): Hignett 5, Bullock M 2, Dyer 1, McClare 1, Sheridan 1.

Ground: Oakwell Ground, Grove St, Barnsley S71 1ET. Telephone (01226) 211211.

Record attendance: 40,255 v Stoke C, FA Cup 5th rd, 15 February 1936. **Capacity:** 23,000.

Manager: Dave Bassett.

Secretary: Michael Spinks.

Honours – Football League: Division 3 (N) Champions – 1933–34, 1938–39, 1954–55. **FA Cup:** Winners 1912.

Colours: Red shirts, white shorts, red stockings.

BIRMINGHAM CITY   DIV. 1

Adebola Dele (F)	6 3	12 08	Lagos	23	6 75	Crewe Alex
Bass Jonathan (D)	6 0	12 02	Weston-Super-Mare	1	1 76	Trainee
Bennett Ian (G)	6 0	12 10	Worksop	10 10 71		Peterborough U
Charlton Simon (D)	5 8	11 10	Huddersfield	25 10 71		Southampton
Dyson James (D)	6 2	12 00	Wordsley	20	4 79	Trainee
Forinton Howard (F)	5 11	11 00	Boston	18	9 75	Yeovil T
Forster Nicky (F)	5 9	11 05	Caterham	8	9 73	Brentford
Furlong Paul (F)	6 0	11 00	London	1 10 68		Chelsea
Gill Jeremy (D)	5 11	11 00	Clevedon	8	9 70	Yeovil T
Grainger Martin (D)	5 10	11 07	Enfield	23	8 72	Brentford
Haarhoff James (M)			Lusaka	27	5 81	Trainee
Hey Tony (M)	5 9	11 07	Berlin	19	9 70	
Holdsworth David (D)	6 1	12 10	Walthamstow	8 11 68		Sheffield U
Holland Chris (M)	5 9	11 05	Whalley	11	9 76	Newcastle U
Hughes Bryan (M)	5 9	10 00	Liverpool	19	6 76	Wrexham
Hyde Graham (M)	5 8	12 04	Doncaster	10 11 70		Sheffield W
Johnson Andrew (F)	5 6	10 00	Bedford	10	2 81	Trainee
Johnson Michael (D)	5 11	11 00	Nottingham	4	7 73	Notts Co
Marsh Simon (D)	5 11	12 00	Ealing	29	1 77	Oxford U
McCarthy Jon (M)	5 9	11 05	Middlesbrough	18	8 70	Port Vale
McKeown, Francis (M)	5 9	11 07	Belfast	11	2 81	Sunderland
Ndlovu Peter (F)	5 8	10 02	Zimbabwe	25	2 73	Coventry C
O'Connor Martin (M)	5 8	10 08	Walsall	10 12 67		Peterborough U
Poole Kevin (G)	5 10	11 11	Bromsgrove	21	7 63	Leicester C
Purse Darren (D)	6 2	13 08	Stepney	14	2 76	Oxford U
Rea Simon (D)	6 1	13 00	Coventry	20	9 76	Trainee
Robinson Steve (M)	5 9	11 00	Nottingham	17 10 75		Trainee
Rowett Gary (D)	6 0	12 10	Bromsgrove	6	3 74	Derby Co
Wassall Darren (D)	6 0	12 07	Edgbaston	27	6 68	Derby Co

League Appearances: Ablett, G. 23(3); Adebola, D. 33(6); Bass, J. 9(2); Bennett, I. 10; Bradbury, L. 6(1); Charlton, S. 27(1); Forinton, H. (3); Forster, N. 8(25); Furlong, P. 24(5); Gill, J. 3; Grainger, M. 30(10); Holdsworth, D. 8; Holland, C. 7(7); Hughes, B. 20(8); Hyde, G. 13; Johnson, A. (4); Johnson, M. 43(2); Marsden, C. 20; Marsh, S. 6(1); McCarthy, J. 35(8); Ndlovu, P. 37(6); O'Connor, M. 35(2); Poole, K. 36; Purse, D. 11(9); Robinson, S. 20(11); Rowett, G. 42; Wassall, D. (3).
Goals – League (66): Adebola 13, Furlong 13 (3 pens), Ndlovu 10, Forster 5, Johnson M 5, Rowett 5, Grainger 4 (1 pen), O'Connor 4 (3 pens), Hughes 3, Marsden 2, Forinton 1, Holdsworth 1.
Worthington Cup (13): Marsden 3, Adebola 2, Johnson M 2, Ndlovu 2, Rowett 2, Forster 1, own goal 1.
FA Cup (2): Adebola 1, Robinson 1.
Ground: St Andrews, Birmingham B9 4NH. Telephone (0121) 772 0101.
Record attendance: 66,844 v Everton, FA Cup 5th rd,11 February 1939. **Capacity:** 30,009.
Manager: Trevor Francis.
Secretary: Alan Jones BA, MBA
Honours – Football League: Division 2 Champions – 1892–93, 1920–21, 1947–48, 1954–55, 1994–95. **Football League Cup:** Winners 1963. **Leyland Daf Cup:** Winners 1991. **Auto Windscreens Shield:** Winners 1995.
Colours: Blue shirts, blue shorts, blue/white stockings.

BLACKBURN ROVERS   DIV. 1

| Andersson Anders (M) | 5 9 | 11 09 | Tomelilla | 15 | 3 74 | Malmo |
| Baldacchino Ryan (F) | 5 9 | 12 03 | Leicester | 13 | 1 81 | Trainee |

Name	Height	Weight	Birthplace	Date of birth	Previous club
Bingham Michael (G)	6 0	12 05	Preston	21 5 81	Trainee
Blake Nathan (F)	6 0	12 08	Cardiff	27 1 72	Bolton W
Broomes Marlon (D)	6 1	12 12	Meriden	28 11 77	Trainee
Brown Keith (D)	6 0	11 00	Edinburgh	24 12 79	
Burgess Ben (F)	6 3	14 04	Buxton	9 11 81	Trainee
Carsley Lee (M)	5 9	12 00	Birmingham	28 2 74	Derby Co
Corbett James (M)	5 10	10 12	Hackney	6 7 80	Trainee
Croft Gary (D)	5 8	10 08	Stafford	17 2 74	Grimsby T
Dahlin Martin (F)	6 1	13 03	Lund	16 4 68	Roma
Dailly Christian (D)	6 0	12 05	Dundee	23 10 73	Derby Co
Davidson Callum (D)	5 10	11 00	Stirling	26 6 76	St Johnstone
Davies Kevin (F)	6 0	13 11	Sheffield	26 3 77	Southampton
Doyle Robert (M)			Dublin	15 4 82	Trainee
Duff Damien (F)	5 8	9 07	Ballyboden	2 3 79	
Dunn David (M)	5 10	12 00	Blackburn	27 12 79	Trainee
Dunning Darren (M)	5 6	11 12	Scarborough	8 1 81	Trainee
Dunning Richard (D)	5 7	11 10	Scarborough	8 1 81	Trainee
Fettis Alan (G)	6 2	13 00	Newtownards	1 2 71	Nottingham F
Filan John (G)	6 2	14 04	Sydney	8 2 70	Coventry C
Fitzpatrick Lee (M)	5 10	11 07	Manchester	31 10 78	Trainee
Flitcroft Garry (M)	6 0	11 08	Bolton	6 11 72	Manchester C
Flitcroft Steven (M)	5 10	11 01	Bolton	17 10 81	Trainee
Flowers Tim (G)	6 3	14 04	Kenilworth	3 2 67	Southampton
Forsyth Paul (F)	5 8	10 05	Dublin	11 4 81	Trainee
Foster Steve (F)	5 9	13 01	Manchester	30 12 81	Trainee
Gallacher Kevin (F)	5 8	11 03	Clydebank	23 11 66	Coventry C
Gill Wayne (M)	5 9	11 00	Chorley	28 11 75	Dundee U
Gillespie Keith (M)	5 9	11 05	Larne	18 2 75	Newcastle U
Hamilton Gary (F)			Bambridge	6 10 80	Trainee
Hawe Steven (F)			Machbrafelt	23 12 80	Trainee
Henchoz Stephane (D)	6 2	12 08	Billens	7 9 74	Hamburg
Jansen Matt (F)	5 11	11 03	Carlisle	20 10 77	Crystal Palace
Johnson Damien (M)	5 10	11 02	Lisburn	18 11 78	Trainee
Kenna Jeff (D)	5 11	12 03	Dublin	27 8 70	Southampton
Konde Oumar (M)	6 2	13 00	Basle	19 8 79	Basle
Lawless Michael (M)	5 6	10 13	Dublin	15 8 81	Trainee
McAteer Jason (M)	5 11	11 10	Birkenhead	18 6 71	Liverpool
McAvoy Andy (M)	6 0	12 00	Middlesbrough	28 8 79	Trainee
McCann Peter (D)	5 6	10 13	Dublin	18 8 81	Trainee
McKinlay Billy (M)	5 8	11 06	Glasgow	22 4 69	Dundee U
McNamee David (D)	5 11	10 07	Glasgow	10 10 80	St Mirren BC
Murphy Peter (D)	5 10	12 03	Dublin	27 10 80	Trainee
O'Brien Burton (F)	5 11	10 07	South Africa	10 6 81	S Form
Peacock Darren (D)	6 1	12 12	Bristol	3 2 68	Newcastle U
Pedersen Per (F)	5 11	13 00	Aalborg	30 3 69	Odense
Perez Sebastian (D)	5 10	12 00	Saint-Chamond	24 11 73	Bastia
Richardson Leam (D)			Leeds	19 11 79	Trainee
Scates Garth (M)			Dundonald	27 8 79	Trainee
Sutton Chris (F)	6 3	13 07	Nottingham	10 3 73	Norwich C
Taylor Martin (D)	6 4	14 00	Ashington	9 11 79	Trainee
Thomas James (F)	6 0	13 00	Swansea	16 1 79	Trainee
Ward Ashley (F)	6 1	12 02	Manchester	24 11 70	Barnsley
Wilcox Jason (F)	6 0	11 00	Bolton	15 7 71	Trainee
Williams Anthony (G)	6 1	13 08	Ogwr	20 9 77	Trainee

League Appearances: Blake, N. 9(2); Broomes, M. 8(5); Carsley, L. 7(1); Croft, G. 10(2); Dahlin, M. 2(3); Dailly, C. 14(3); Davidson, C. 34; Davies, K. 9(12); Duff, D. 18(10); Dunn, D. 10(5); Fettis, A. 2; Filan, J. 26; Flitcroft, G. 8; Flowers, T. 10(1); Gallacher, K. 13(3); Gillespie, K. 13(3); Henchoz, S. 34; Jansen, M. 10(1); Johnson, D. 14(7); Kenna, J. 22(1); Marcolin, D. 5(5); McAteer, J. 13; McKinlay, B. 14(2);

Peacock, D. 27(3); Perez, S. 4(1); Sherwood, T. 19; Sutton, C. 17; Taylor, M. 1(2); Ward, A. 17; Wilcox, J. 28(2).
Goals – League (38): Gallacher 5, Ward 5, Blake 3, Jansen 3, Sherwood 3, Sutton 3 (2 pens), Wilcox 3, Flitcroft 2, Davidson 1, Davies 1, Duff 1, Dunn 1, Gillespie 1, Johnson 1, Marcolin 1, McAteer 1, Peacock 1, Perez 1, own goal 1.
Worthington Cup (2): Sherwood 1, Sutton 1.
FA Cup (3): Davies 1, Gillespie 1, Wilcox 1.
Ground: Ewood Park, Blackburn BB2 4JF. Telephone (01254) 698888.
Record attendance: 61,783 v Bolton W, FA Cup 6th rd, 2 March, 1929. **Capacity:** 31,367.
Manager: Brian Kidd.
Secretary: Tom Finn.
Honours – FA Premier League: Champions – 1994–95. Football League: Division 1 Champions – 1911–12, 1913–14. Division 2 Champions – 1938–39. Division 3 Champions – 1974–75. **FA Cup:** Winners 1884, 1885, 1886, 1890, 1891, 1928. **Full Members' Cup:** Winners 1986–87.
Colours: Blue and white halved shirts, white shorts, white stockings, blue trim.

BLACKPOOL   DIV. 2

Aldridge Martin (F)	5 11	12 02	Northampton	4 12 74	Oxford U
Bardsley David (D)	5 10	11 07	Manchester	11 9 64	QPR
Barnes Phil (G)	6 1	11 01	Rotherham	2 3 79	Trainee
Bent Junior (F)	5 5	10 06	Huddersfield	1 3 70	Bristol C
Bryan Marvin (D)	6 0	12 02	Paddington	2 8 75	QPR
Bushell Steve (M)	5 9	11 06	Manchester	28 12 72	York C
Caig Tony (G)	6 1	12 00	Whitehaven	11 4 74	Carlisle U
Carlisle Clarke (D)	6 1	12 07	Preston	14 10 79	Trainee
Clarkson Phil (M)	5 10	12 08	Garstang	13 11 68	Scunthorpe U
Conroy Mike (F)	6 0	13 03	Glasgow	31 12 65	Fulham
Couzens Andy (M)	5 10	11 11	Shipley	4 6 75	Carlisle U
Garvey Steve (M)	5 9	11 01	Stalybridge	22 11 73	Crewe Alex
Hills John (D)	5 8	10 08	St Annes-on-Sea	21 4 78	Everton
Hughes Ian (M)	5 10	12 08	Bangor	2 8 74	Bury
Nowland Adam (F)	5 11	11 06	Preston	6 7 81	Trainee
Ormerod Brett (F)	5 11	11 04	Blackburn	18 10 76	Accrington S
Robinson Phil (D)	5 9	11 00	Manchester	28 9 80	Trainee
Shuttleworth Barry (D)	5 8	11 00	Accrington	9 7 77	Rotherham U
Thompson Phil (D)	5 11	12 00	Blackpool	1 4 81	Trainee
Worthington Nigel (D)	5 11	12 06	Ballymena	4 11 61	Stoke C

League Appearances: Aldridge, M. 19(3); Banks, S. 35; Bardsley, D. 29; Barnes, K. 2(2); Barnes, P. 1; Bent, J. 21(18); Blunt, J. 1(1); Brabin, G. 5(2); Bryan, M. 37(4); Bushell, S. 31; Butler, T. 20; Caig, T. 10; Carlisle, C. 34(5); Clarkson, P. 44; Coid, D. (1); Conroy, M. 7(1); Couzens, A. 6; Garvey, S. 6(9); Hills, J. 27(1); Hughes, I. 31(2); Jarrett, J. 2; Lawson, I. 9; Malkin, C. 24(5); Nowland, A. 13(24); Ormerod, B. 30(10); Patterson, M. 7; Robinson, P. 2(3); Rogan, A. 9(5); Shuttleworth, B. 12(2); Sturridge, S. 5; Thompson, P. 18(4); Watts, J. 9.
Goals – League (44): Clarkson 9, Ormerod 8 (1 pen), Aldridge 7 (1 pen), Bushell 3, Lawson 3, Nowland 2, Thompson 2, Bent 1, Bryan 1, Carlisle 1, Garvey 1, Hills 1, Hughes 1, Malkin 1, Shuttleworth 1, Sturridge 1, own goal 1.
Worthington Cup (5): Aldridge 2, Bent 1, Conroy 1, Malkin 1.
FA Cup (3): Aldridge 1, Blunt 1, Ormerod 1.
Ground: Bloomfield Rd Ground, Blackpool FY1 6JJ. Telephone (01253) 404331.
Record attendance: 38,098 v Wolverhampton W, Division 1, 17 September 1955.
Capacity: 11,295.
Manager: Nigel Worthington.
Secretary: Carol Banks.
Honours – Football League: Division 2 Champions – 1929–30. **FA Cup:** Winners

1953. **Anglo-Italian Cup:** Winners 1971.
Colours: All tangerine.

BOLTON WANDERERS   DIV. 1

Aljofree Hasney (D)	6 0	12 03	Manchester	11 7 78	Trainee
Banks Steve (G)	5 11	12 04	Hillingdon	9 2 72	Blackpool
Bergsson Gudni (D)	6 1	12 03	Reykjavik	21 7 65	Tottenham H
Branagan Keith (G)	6 0	13 02	Fulham	10 7 66	Millwall
Cox Neil (D)	6 0	13 02	Scunthorpe	8 10 71	Middlesbrough
Dawson Chris (D)	5 10	10 02	Coventry	22 8 79	Trainee
Elliott Robbie (D)	5 10	10 13	Gosforth	25 12 73	Newcastle U
Evans James (M)			Glasgow	27 1 82	Scholarship
Fish Mark (D)	6 4	12 11	Cape Town	14 3 74	Lazio
Frandsen Per (M)	6 1	12 06	Copenhagen	6 2 70	FC Copenhagen
Gardner Ricardo (M)	5 9	11 00	St Andrews	25 9 78	Harbour View
Glennon Matthew (G)	6 2	13 11	Stockport	8 10 78	Trainee
Gudjohnsen Eidur (F)	6 0	13 00	Reykjavik	15 9 78	KR
Hansen Bo (F)	5 10	11 00	Jutland	16 6 72	Brondby
Holden Dean (D)	6 0	11 00	Salford	15 9 79	
Holdsworth Dean (F)	5 11	11 13	Walthamstow	8 11 68	Wimbledon
Jaaskelainen Jussi (G)	6 3	12 10	Mikkeli	19 4 75	VPS
Jensen Claus (M)	5 11	12 00	Nykobing	29 4 77	Lyngby
Johansen Michael (M)	5 6	10 05	Glostrup	22 7 72	FC Copenhagen
Morrison Peter (M)	5 11	10 00	Manchester	29 6 80	Trainee
Phillips Jimmy (D)	6 0	12 07	Bolton	8 2 66	Middlesbrough
Potter Lee (F)	5 11	12 10	Salford	3 9 78	Trainee
Power Alan (M)			Dublin	18 9 80	Trainee
Smith Gordon (M)			Glasgow	18 12 80	Trainee
Snorrason Olafur (F)			Reykjavik	22 4 82	
Staton Luke (M)	5 7	10 07	Doncaster	10 3 79	Blackburn R
Strong Greg (D)	6 2	11 12	Bolton	5 9 75	Wigan Ath
Taylor Bob (F)	5 11	11 09	Easington	3 2 67	WBA
Todd Andy (D)	5 10	10 11	Derby	21 9 74	Middlesbrough
Warhurst Paul (D)	6 1	12 01	Stockport	26 9 69	Crystal Palace
Whitlow Mike (D)	6 1	11 06	Northwich	13 1 68	Leicester C

League Appearances: Aljofree, H. 1(3); Banks, S. 9; Bergsson, G. 15(2); Blake, N. 11(1); Branagan, K. 3; Cox, N. 42(2); Elliott, R. 14(8); Fish, M. 36; Frandsen, P. 44; Fullarton, J. 1; Gardner, R. 19(11); Gudjohnsen, E. 8(6); Gunnlaugsson, A. 22(5); Hansen, B. 1(7); Holdsworth, D. 22(10); Jaaskelainen, J. 34; Jensen, C. 44; Johansen, M. 40(3); Newsome, J. 6; Phillips, J. 14(1); Sellars, S. 22(3); Strong, G. 4(1); Taylor, B. 32(6); Todd, A. 18(2); Warhurst, P. 17(3); Whitlow, M. 27(1).
Goals – League (78): Taylor B 15, Gunnlaugsson 13, Holdsworth 12 (5 pens), Frandsen 8, Johansen 7, Blake 6, Gudjohnsen 5, Cox 4, Gardner 2, Jensen 2, Sellars 2, Fish 1, Strong 1.
Worthington Cup (12): Blake 3, Jensen 2, Elliott 1, Frandsen 1, Gardner 1, Gunnlaugsson 1, Johansen 1, Phillips 1, Taylor B 1.
FA Cup (1): Sellars 1.
Ground: Reebok Stadium, Burnden Way, Lostock, Bolton BL6 6JW. Telephone Bolton (01204) 673673.
Record attendance: 69,912 v Manchester C, FA Cup 5th rd, 18 February 1933.
Capacity: 25,000.
Manager: Colin Todd.
Secretary: Des McBain.
Honours – Football League: Division 1 Champions – 1996–97. Division 2 Champions – 1908–09, 1977–78. Division 3 Champions – 1972–73. **FA Cup winners** 1923, 1926, 1929, 1958. **Sherpa Van Trophy:** Winners 1989.
Colours: White shirts, navy blue shorts, blue stockings.

AFC BOURNEMOUTH DIV. 2

Name	Height	Weight	Birthplace	Date of birth	From
Bailey John (M)	5 8	10 02	London	6 5 69	Enfield
Beardsmore Russell (M)	5 8	10 04	Wigan	28 10 69	Manchester U
Boli Roger (F)	5 8	10 12	Adjame	26 9 65	Dundee U
Broadhurst Karl (D)	6 1	11 07	Portsmouth	18 3 80	Trainee
Colgan Nick (G)	6 1	13 06	Drogheda	19 9 73	Chelsea
Cox Ian (D)	6 0	12 00	Croydon	25 3 71	Crystal Palace
Day Jamie (M)	5 10	11 04	Sidcup	13 9 79	Arsenal
Dean Michael (M)	5 9	11 10	Weymouth	9 3 78	Trainee
Fletcher Carl (M)	5 10	11 07	Camberley	7 4 80	Trainee
Fletcher Steve (F)	6 2	14 09	Hartlepool	26 6 72	Hartlepool U
Griffin Anthony (D)	5 11	11 02	Bournemouth	22 3 79	Trainee
Hayter James (F)	5 9	10 13	Newport (IW)	9 4 79	Trainee
Howe Eddie (D)	5 9	11 02	Amersham	29 11 77	Trainee
Huck Willie (M)	5 10	11 09	Paris	17 3 79	Monaco
Hughes Richard (D)	5 9	9 12	Glasgow	25 6 79	Atalanta
O'Neill Jon (F)	5 11	12 00	Glasgow	2 1 74	Celtic
Ovendale Mark (G)	6 2	13 10	Leicester	22 11 73	Wisbech T
Rawlinson Mark (M)	5 10	11 04	Bolton	9 6 75	Manchester U
Robinson Steve (F)	5 9	11 02	Crumlin	10 12 74	Tottenham H
Stein Mark (F)	5 6	11 07	Capetown	29 1 66	Chelsea
Tindall Jason (M)	6 1	12 01	Stepney	15 11 77	Charlton Ath
Town David (F)	5 7	11 13	Bournemouth	9 12 76	Trainee
Warren Christer (F)	5 10	11 12	Poole	10 10 74	Southampton
Young Neil (D)	5 9	12 00	Harlow	31 8 73	Tottenham H

League Appearances: Bailey, J. 30(2); Berthe, M. 12(3); Boli, R. 5(1); Cox, I. 46; Day, J. (2); Dean, M. 1(8); Fletcher, C. (1); Fletcher, S. 38(1); Griffin, A. 1(5); Hayter, J. 16(4); Howe, E. 45; Huck, W. 6(2); Hughes, R. 43(1); Jenkins, J. (1); Lovell, S. 1(6); O'Neill, J. 18(6); Ovendale, M. 46; Rawlinson, M. 5(2); Robinson, S. 42; Rodrigues, D. (5); Stein, M. 43; Tindall, J. 6(11); Town, D. 1(9); Vincent, J. 31(1); Warren, C. 26(6); Young, N. 44.
League (63): Stein 15 (1 pen), Robinson 13 (2 pens), Fletcher S 8, Cox 5, Warren 5, O'Neill 3, Berthe 2, Hayter 2, Howe 2, Hughes 2, Vincent 2, Tindall 1 (pen), Young 1, own goals 2.
Worthington Cup (8): Stein 5, Fletcher S 1, Howe 1, Robinson 1.
FA Cup (5): Howe 2, O'Neill 1, Robinson 1, Stein 1.
Ground: Dean Court Ground, Bournemouth BH7 7AF. Telephone (01202) 395381.
Record attendance: 28,799 v Manchester U, FA Cup 6th rd, 2 March 1957.
Capacity: 10,770.
Manager: Mel Machin.
Secretary: K. R. J. MacAlister.
Honours – Football League: Division 3 Champions – 1986–87. **Associate Members' Cup:** Winners 1984.
Colours: Red shirts with black stripe, black shorts, black stockings.

BRADFORD CITY FA PREMIERSHIP

Name	Height	Weight	Birthplace	Date of birth	From
Beagrie Peter (F)	5 8	12 00	Middlesbrough	28 11 65	Manchester C
Blake Robbie (F)	5 8	11 00	Middlesbrough	4 3 76	Darlington
Bower Mark (D)	5 10	10 11	Bradford	23 1 80	Trainee
Grant Gareth (F)	5 10	10 04	Leeds	6 9 80	Trainee
Jacobs Wayne (D)	5 8	11 02	Sheffield	3 2 69	Rotherham U
Lawrence Jamie (M)	6 0	12 06	Balham	8 3 70	Leicester C

McCall Stuart (M)   5 9   11 04   Leeds   10 6 64   Rangers
Mills Lee (F)   6 2   12 09   Mexborough   10 7 70   Port Vale
Moore Darren (D)   6 3   15 08   Birmingham   22 4 74   Doncaster R
O'Brien Andrew (D)   5 10 10 06   Harrogate   29 6 79   Trainee
Patterson Andrew (F)   5 10 10 04   Kirkaldy   26 11 80   Trainee
Prudhoe Mark (G)   6 0   14 00   Washington   8 11 63   Stoke C
Rankin Isiah (F)   5 10 11 00   London   22 5 78   Arsenal
Steiner Rob (F)   6 2   13 00   Finsprong   20 6 73   Norrkoping
Todd Lee (D)   5 7   11 01   Hartlepool   7 3 72   Southampton
Walsh Gary (G)   6 3   14 11   Wigan   21 3 68   Middlesbrough
Westwood Ashley (D)   5 11 11 02   Bridgnorth   31 8 76   Crewe Alex
Whalley Gareth (M)   5 10 11 06   Manchester   19 12 73   Crewe Alex
Windass Dean (F)   5 10 12 06   Hull   1 4 69   Oxford U

League Appearances: Beagrie, P. 43; Blake, R. 35(4); Bolland, P. 2; Dreyer, J. 19(2); Edinho 1(2); Grant, G. 1(4); Jacobs, W. 42(2); Lawrence, J. 33(2); McCall, S. 43; Mills, L. 44; Moore, D. 44; O'Brien, A. 19(12); Pepper, N. 5(4); Ramage, C. (3); Rankin, I. 15(12); Sharpe, L. 6(3); Todd, L. 14(1); Walsh, G. 46; Watson, G. 5(13); Westwood, A. 17(2); Whalley, G. 45; Windass, D. 6(6); Wright, S. 21(1).
Goals – League (82): Mills 23, Blake 16, Beagrie 12 (5 pens), Rankin 4, Watson 4, Jacobs 3, McCall 3, Moore 3, Windass 3, Lawrence 2, Sharpe 2, Westwood 2, Whalley 2, Pepper 1, own goals 2.
Worthington Cup (7): Beagrie 3 (1 pen), Blake 1, Moore 1, Pepper 1, Rankin 1.
FA Cup (2): Lawrence 1, Mills 1.
Ground: Valley Parade, Bradford BD8 7DY. Telephone (01274) 773355.
Record attendance: 39,146 v Burnley, FA Cup 4th rd, 11 March 1911. **Capacity:** 18,018.
Manager: Paul Jewell.
Secretary: Jon Pollard.
Honours – Football League: Division 2 Champions – 1907–08. Division 3 Champions – 1984–85. Division 3 (N) Champions – 1928–29. **FA Cup:** Winners 1911.
Colours: Claret and amber shirts, claret shorts, amber stockings.

BRENTFORD   DIV. 2

Anderson Ijah (D)   5 8   10 06   Hackney   30 12 75   Tottenham H
Boxall Danny (D)   5 8   10 05   Croydon   24 8 77   Crystal Palace
Bryan Derek (F)   5 10 11 05   London   11 11 74   Hampton
Clark Dean (M)   5 10 12 06   Hillingdon   31 3 80   Trainee
Cullip Danny (D)   6 1   12 07   Bracknell   17 9 76   Fulham
Dearden Kevin (G)   5 11 13 12   Luton   8 3 70   Tottenham H
Evans Paul (M)   5 7   12 00   Oswestry   1 9 74   Shrewsbury T
Folan Tony (F)   6 0   11 00   Lewisham   18 9 78   Crystal Palace
Freeman Darren (F)   5 11 13 00   Brighton   22 8 73   Fulham
Hreidarsson Hermann (D)   6 0   13 01   Iceland   11 7 74   Crystal Palace
Mahon Gavin (M)   5 11 12 07   Birmingham   2 1 77   Hereford U
Oatway Charlie (M)   5 7   10 10   Hammersmith   28 11 73   Torquay U
Owusu Lloyd (F)   Slough   12 12 76   Slough T
Partridge Scott (F)   5 9   11 02   Leicester   13 10 74   Torquay U
Pearcey Jason (G)   6 1   13 12   Leamington Spa   23 7 71   Grimsby T
Powell Darren (D)   Hammersmith   10 3 76   Hampton
Quinn Robert (M)   5 11 11 02   Sidcup   8 11 76   Crystal Palace
Rowlands Martin (M)   Ealing   8 2 79   Farnborough T
Scott Andy (F)   6 1   11 05   Epsom   2 8 72   Sheffield U
Townley Leon (D)   6 2   13 06   Loughton   16 2 76   Tottenham H
Watson Paul (D)   5 8   10 10   Hastings   4 1 75   Fulham
Woodman Andy (G)   6 3   13 07   Camberwell   11 8 71   Northampton T

League Appearances: Anderson, I. 35(3); Aspinall, W. 17(2); Bates, J. 27; Boxall,

D. 37(1); Broughton, D. 1; Bryan, D. 9(11); Coyne, C. 7; Cullip, D. 2; Dearden, K. 7; Evans, P. 14; Folan, T. 19(10); Fortune-West, L. 2(9); Freeman, D. 16(6); Hebel, D. 6(9); Hreidarsson, H. 33; Jenkins, S. (1); Mahon, G. 29; Oatway, C. 7(17); Owusu, L. 42(4); Partridge, S. 12(2); Pearcey, J. 17; Powell, D. 33; Quinn, R. 34(9); Rapley, K. 3(9); Rowlands, M. 32(4); Scott, A. 31(3); Watson, P. 12; Woodman, A. 22.

Goals – League (79): Owusu 22, Partridge 7, Scott 7, Freeman 6, Bryan 4, Folan 4, Hreidarsson 4, Mahon 4, Rowlands 4, Evans 3, Rapley 3, Aspinall 2 (1 pen), Powell 2, Quinn 2, Anderson 1, Bates 1, Boxall 1, own goals 2.

Worthington Cup (8): Owusu 2, Scott 2, Bates 1, Freeman 1, Oatway 1, Rapley 1.

FA Cup (8): Folan 2, Freeman 2 (1 pen), Bates 1, Hreidarsson 1, Owusu 1, Quinn 1.

Ground: Griffin Park, Braemar Rd, Brentford, Middlesex TW8 0NT. Telephone (0208) 847 2511.

Record attendance: 39,626 v Preston NE, FA Cup 6th rd, 5 March 1938. **Capacity:** 12,763.

Manager: Ron Noades.

Secretary: Polly Kates.

Honours – Football League: Division 2 Champions – 1934–35. Division 3 Champions – 1991–92, 1998–99. Division 3 (S) Champions – 1932–33. Division 4 Champions – 1962–63.

Colours: Red and white vertical striped shirts, black shorts, black stockings.

BRIGHTON & HOVE ALBION DIV. 3

Andrews Ben (D)	6 1	12 13	Burton-on-Trent	18 11 80	Trainee
Armstrong Paul (M)	5 10	10 09	Dublin	5 10 78	Trainee
Arnott Andy (M)	6 0	12 02	Chatham	18 10 73	Fulham
Culverhouse Ian (D)	5 10	11 02	Bishop's Stortford	22 9 64	Swindon T
Hart Gary (F)	5 9	12 08	Harlow	6 11 75	Stansted
Hobson Gary (D)	6 2	13 02	North Ferriby	12 11 72	Hull C
Johnson Ross (D)	6 0	13 00	Brighton	2 1 76	Trainee
Mayo Kerry (D)	5 8	11 07	Cuckfield	21 9 77	Trainee
Ormerod Mark (G)	6 0	11 06	Bournemouth	5 2 76	Trainee
Thomas Rod (F)	5 6	11 11	London	10 10 70	Chester C
Walton Mark (G)	6 4	15 08	Merthyr	1 6 69	Fulham
Westcott John (F)	5 9	10 03	Eastbourne	31 5 79	Trainee
Wormull Simon (M)	5 10	12 03	Crawley	1 12 76	Brentford

League Appearances: Allan, D. 21(1); Andrews, B. (1); Ansah, A. 3(8); Armstrong, P. 21(7); Arnott, A. 27; Atkinson, G. 7; Barker, R. 33(10); Bennett, M. 37(1); Browne, S. 2(1); Browne, T. 13; Culverhouse, I. 35; Davies, L. 2(6); Davis, D. (1); Doherty, L. 3; Hart, G. 42(2); Hinshelwood, D. 3(1); Hobson, G. 12(1); Ifejiagwa, E. 2; Johnson, R. 30(4); King, P. 3; Mayo, K. 21(4); McArthur, D. 3; McPherson, K. 10; Mills, D. 1(1); Minton, J. 35; Moralee, J. 22(9); Nicholls, K. 4; Ormerod, M. 27; Ryan, D. 3(2); Smith, P. 8(6); Storer, S. 14(9); Sturgess, P. 28(2); Thomas, G. 2(1); Thomas, R. 11(1); Tuck, S. 2; Walton, M. 19; Westcott, J. (4).

Goals – League (49): Hart 12, Barker 10, Minton 9 (4 pens), Moralee 3, Thomas R 3, Armstrong 2 (1 pen), Arnott 2, Johnson 2, Allan 1, Ifejiagwa 1, Mayo 1, Nicholls 1, Ryan 1, own goal 1.

Worthington Cup (2): Barker 1, Storer 1.

FA Cup (2): Barker 1, Mayo 1.

Offices: Hanover House, 118 Queens Road, Brighton BN1 3XG. Telephone: (01273) 778855. **Ground:** Withdean Stadium, Tongdean Lane, Brighton. Telephone: (01634) 851854.

Record attendance: 36,747 v Fulham, Division 2, 27 December 1958.

Capacity: 10,152.

Manager: Micky Adams.

Secretary: Derek Allan.

Honours – Football League: Division 3 (S) Champions – 1957–58. Division 4 Champions – 1964–65.
Colours: Blue and white striped shirts, white shorts, blue stockings.

BRISTOL CITY   DIV. 2

Akinbiyi Ade (F)	6 1	13 09	Hackney	10 10 74	Gillingham
Andersen Braastrup (G)			Slagelse	26 3 76	Lyngby
Andersen Soren (F)	5 11	12 06	Denmark	31 1 70	Aalborg
Ashton Lee (M)			Yeovil	8 11 79	Trainee
Bell Mickey (D)	5 8	11 13	Newcastle	15 11 71	Wycombe W
Brennan Jim (D)	5 9	11 06	Toronto	8 5 77	Sora Lazio
Brown Aaron (M)	5 10	11 12	Bristol	14 3 80	Trainee
Carey Louis (D)	5 10	12 05	Bristol	20 1 77	Trainee
Cramb Colin (F)	6 0	12 09	Lanark	23 6 74	Doncaster R
Doherty Tom (M)	5 8	11 07	Bristol	17 3 79	Trainee
Dyche Sean (D)	6 0	13 05	Kettering	28 6 71	Chesterfield
Goodridge Greg (F)	5 6	11 02	Barbados	10 7 71	QPR
Hewlett Matthew (M)	6 2	12 12	Bristol	25 2 76	Trainee
Hill Matthew (D)			Bristol	26 3 81	Trainee
Hussey Stuart (M)			Southampton	4 12 80	Portsmouth
Hutchings Carl (M)	6 1	12 00	Hammersmith	24 9 74	Brentford
Jordan Andrew (D)	6 0	13 01	Manchester	14 12 79	Trainee
Langan Kevin (D)	5 11	11 02	Jersey	7 4 78	Trainee
Meechan Alex (F)			Plymouth	29 1 80	Trainee
Muntasser Jehad (M)	5 10	9 11	Tripoli	26 7 78	Prosesto
Murray Scott (M)	5 8	11 00	Aberdeen	26 5 74	Aston Villa
Phillips Steve (G)	6 1	12 07	Bath	6 5 78	Paulton R
Pinamonte Lorenzo (F)	6 3	13 04	Foggia	9 5 78	Foggia
Sebok Vilmos (D)			Hungary	13 6 73	Ujpesti
Shail Mark (D)	6 1	12 06	Sweden	15 10 66	Yeovil T
Stowell Matt (D)	5 10	11 06	Reading	1 3 77	Reading
Testimitanu Ivan (M)			Moldova	27 4 74	Zimbru Chisinau
Thorpe Tony (F)	5 8	12 06	Leicester	10 4 74	Fulham
Tinnion Brian (M)	5 11	12 13	Stanley	23 3 68	Bradford C
Torpey Steve (F)	6 3	13 06	Islington	8 12 70	Swansea C
Watts Julian (D)	6 2	13 06	Sheffield	17 3 71	Leicester C
Wilmot Ellis (M)			Bournemouth	2 11 79	Trainee
Wright Ben (M)			Munster	1 7 80	Kettering T

League Appearances: Akinbiyi, A. 44; Andersen, B. 10; Andersen, S. 26(13); Bell, M. 33; Brennan, J. 29; Brown, A. 14; Carey, L. 40(1); Cramb, C. 4(9); Doherty, T. 15(8); Dyche, S. 4(2); Edwards, C. 3; Edwards, R. 19(4); Goodridge, G. 15(15); Heaney, N. 2(1); Hewlett, M. 8(2); Hill, M. (3); Howells, D. 8; Hutchings, C. 16(5); Jordan, A. 1; Langan, K. 1; Locke, A. 26(2); Meechan, A. (1); Murray, S. 27(5); Phillips, S. 15; Pinamonte, L. 1; Sebok, V. 10(2); Shail, M. 21(3); Taylor, S. 8; Testimitanu, I. 8; Thorpe, T. 9(7); Tinnion, B. 32(3); Torpey, S. 19(2); Watts, J. 16(1); Welch, K. 21; Zwijnenberg, C. 1(2).
Goals – League (57): Akinbiyi 19, Andersen S 10, Bell 5 (4 pens), Torpey 4, Locke 3, Murray 3, Goodridge 2, Hutchings 2, Thorpe 2, Brennan 1, Doherty 1, Hewlett 1, Howells 1, Pinamonte 1, Tinnion 1, Watts 1.
Worthington Cup (8): Akinbiyi 4, Andersen S 1, Doherty 1, Hutchings 1, Thorpe 1.
FA Cup (0).
Ground: Ashton Gate, Bristol BS3 2EJ. Telephone (0117) 9630630.
Record attendance: 43,335 v Preston NE, FA Cup 5th rd, 16 February 1935.
Capacity: 21,479.
Manager: Tony Pulis.
Secretary: Michelle McDonald.

Honours – Football League: Division 2 Champions – 1905–06. Division 3 (S) Champions – 1922–23, 1926–27, 1954–55. **Welsh Cup winners** 1934. **Anglo-Scottish Cup:** Winners 1977–78. **Freight Rover Trophy winners** 1985–86.
Colours: Red shirts, red shorts, white stockings.

BRISTOL ROVERS   DIV. 2

Andreasson Marcus (D)	6 4	13 02	Liberia	13 7 78	Osters
Basford Luke (D)	5 6	9 02	Lambeth	6 1 80	Trainee
Bater Geraint (D)	5 8	10 08	Bristol	26 7 80	
Challis Trevor (D)	5 8	11 06	Paddington	23 10 75	QPR
Claridge Rob (F)	6 0	11 10	Bristol	13 3 80	Trainee
Cureton Jamie (F)	5 7	11 00	Bristol	28 8 75	Norwich C
Ellington Nathan (F)	5 10	12 10	Bradford	2 7 81	Walton & Hersham
Foster Stephen (D)	6 1	13 00	Mansfield	3 12 74	Trainee
French James (F)	6 1	12 02	Germany	24 10 79	Trainee
Hillier David (M)	5 10	12 07	Blackheath	19 12 69	Portsmouth
Holloway Ian (M)	5 7	10 10	Kingswood	12 3 63	QPR
Jones Lee (G)	6 3	15 10	Pontypridd	9 8 70	Swansea C
Kuipers Michels (G)	6 2	14 03	Amsterdam	26 6 74	
Leoni Stephane (D)	5 9	13 00	Metz	1 9 76	
Low Josh (M)	6 0	14 00	Bristol	15 2 79	Trainee
Meaker Michael (M)	5 11	12 12	Greenford	18 8 71	Reading
Pethick Robbie (D)	5 10	12 07	Tavistock	8 9 70	Portsmouth
Roberts Jason (F)	6 1	13 06	Park Royal	25 1 78	Hayes
Shore Jamie (M)	5 9	12 05	Bristol	1 9 77	Norwich C
Smith Mark (D)	6 0	13 07	Bristol	13 9 79	Trainee
Thomson Andy (D)	6 3	14 03	Swindon	28 3 74	Portsmouth
Tillson Andy (D)	6 2	13 05	Huntingdon	30 6 66	QPR
Trees Robert (M)	5 10	12 07	Manchester	18 12 77	Trainee
Trought Michael (D)	6 2	14 03	Bristol	19 10 80	Trainee
White Tom (D)	5 11	14 03	Bristol	26 1 76	Trainee
Zabek Lee (M)	6 0	13 08	Bristol	13 10 78	Trainee

League Appearances: Andreasson, M. 4(1); Andrews, B. 3; Basford, L. 6(3); Bennett, F. 1(3); Challis, T. 38; Collett, A. 3; Cureton, J. 46; Ellington, N. 1(9); Foster, S. 41(2); Hayles, B. 17; Hillier, D. 13; Holloway, I. 33(4); Ipoua, G. 15(9); Johnston, R. 1; Jones, L. 32; Kuipers, M. 1; Lee, D. 10(1); Leoni, S. 25(5); Low, J. 5(3); McKeever, M. 5(2); Meaker, M. 17(3); Penrice, G. 10(16); Pethick, R. 9; Phillips, M. 2; Pritchard, D. 11(1); Roberts, J. 32(5); Shore, J. 18(6); Smith, M. 11(3); Thomson, A. 21; Tillson, A. 18(1); Trees, R. 33(3); Trought, M. 6(3); Williams, A. 9; Zabek, L. 9(2).

Goals – League (65): Cureton 25 (6 pens), Roberts 16, Hayles 9, Ipoua 3, Meaker 2, Shore 2, Tillson 2, Bennett 1, Ellington 1, Foster 1, Lee 1, Penrice 1, Thomson 1.
Worthington Cup (2): Cureton 1, Hayles 1.
FA Cup (15): Roberts 7, Cureton 2, Shore 2, Lee 1, Leoni 1, Penrice 1, Zabek 1.
Ground: The Memorial Ground, Filton Avenue, Horfield, Bristol BS7 0AQ.
Record attendance: 9464 v Liverpool, FA Cup 4th rd, 8 February 1992 (Twerton Park). 38,472 v Preston NE, FA Cup 4th rd, 30 January 1960 (Eastville). 9274 v Leyton Orient, FA Cup 4th rd, 23 January 1999 (Memorial Ground).
Capacity: 10,861.
Manager: Ian Holloway.
Secretary: Roger Brinsford.
Honours – Football League: Division 3 (S) Champions – 1952–53. Division 3 Champions – 1989–90.
Colours: Blue and white quartered shirts, white shorts, blue stockings.

BURNLEY DIV. 2

Armstrong Gordon (D)	6 0	13 04	Newcastle	15 7 67	Bury
Branch Graham (M)	6 2	12 02	Liverpool	12 2 72	Stockport Co
Brass Chris (D)	5 9	12 06	Easington	24 7 75	Trainee
Cooke Andy (F)	5 11	12 08	Stoke	20 1 74	Newtown
Crichton Paul (G)	6 1	13 08	Pontefract	3 10 68	WBA
Davis Steve (D)	6 2	14 07	Hexham	30 10 68	Luton T
Devenney Michael (D)	5 8	10 05	Bolton	8 2 80	Trainee
Heywood Matthew (D)	6 3	14 00	Chatham	26 8 79	Trainee
Johnrose Lenny (M)	5 11	12 06	Preston	27 11 69	Bury
Little Glen (M)	6 3	13 00	Wimbledon	15 10 75	Glentoran
Mawson Craig (G)	6 2	13 04	Keighley	16 5 79	Trainee
Maylett Bradley (F)			Manchester	24 12 80	Trainee
Mellon Micky (D)	5 10	12 11	Paisley	18 3 72	Tranmere R
Payton Andy (F)	5 9	11 13	Burnley	23 10 67	Huddersfield T
Robertson Mark (M)	5 9	11 09	Sydney	6 4 77	Marconi
Scott Christopher (D)	5 11	12 05	Burnley	12 2 80	Trainee
Smith Paul (M)	6 0	13 03	Leeds	22 7 76	Trainee
Vindheim Rune (D)	5 11	12 04	Hoyancuer	18 5 72	
Weller Paul (M)	5 8	11 02	Brighton	6 3 75	Trainee

League Appearances: Armstrong, G. 40; Blatherwick, S. 3; Branch, G. 14(6); Brass, C. 33(1); Carr-Lawton, C. 2(2); Cook, P. 12; Cooke, A. 36; Cowan, T. 12; Crichton, P. 29; Davis, S. 19; Eastwood, P. 6(7); Ford, M. 11(1); Henderson, K. (7); Hewlett, M. 2; Heywood, M. 11(2); Howey, L. 3; Jepson, R. 3(12); Johnrose, L. 9(3); Little, G. 32(2); Maylett, B. (17); Mellon, M. 20; Moore, N. 10(2); Morgan, S. 17; O'Kane, J. 8; Payton, A. 39(1); Pickering, A. 21; Reid, B. 30(1); Robertson, M. 19(5); Scott, C. 9(5); Smith, C. 5(5); Smith, P. 11(1); Swan, P. 11(6); Vindheim, R. 8; Ward, G. 17; Weller, P. 1; Williams, M. 2; Williamson, J. (1); Winstanley, M. 1.

Goals – League (54): Payton 19 (1 pen), Cooke 9, Little 5, Davis 4, Reid 3, Armstrong 2, Mellon 2, Vindheim 2, Branch 1, Cook 1 (pen), Eastwood 1, Henderson 1, Jepson 1, Johnrose 1, Pickering 1, Robertson 1.

Worthington Cup (2): Cooke 1, Payton 1.

FA Cup (2): Payton 2 (1 pen).

Ground: Turf Moor, Burnley BB10 4BX. Telephone (01282) 700000.

Record attendance: 54,775 v Huddersfield T, FA Cup 3rd rd, 23 February 1924.

Capacity: 22,546.

Manager: Stan Ternent.

Secretary: Cathy Pickup.

Honours – Football League: Division 1 Champions – 1920–21, 1959–60. Division 2 Champions – 1897–98, 1972–73. Division 3 Champions – 1981–82. Division 4 Champions – 1991–92. **FA Cup winners** 1913–14. **Anglo-Scottish Cup:** Winners 1978–79.

Colours: Claret and blue shirts, blue shorts, blue stockings.

BURY DIV. 2

Avdiu Kemajl (M)	5 10	12 08	Yugoslavia	22 12 76	Esbjerg
Barnes Paul (F)	5 11	13 00	Leeds	16 11 67	Huddersfield T
Barrick Dean (D)	5 8	12 00	Hemsworth	30 9 69	Preston NE
Billy Chris (D)	5 11	12 06	Huddersfield	2 1 71	Notts Co
Borg John (M)	5 7	10 07	Salford	22 2 80	Trainee
Buggie Lee (F)			Bury	11 2 81	Trainee
Bullock Darren (M)	5 9	12 10	Worcester	12 2 69	Swindon T
D'Jaffo Laurent (F)	6 0	13 05	France	5 11 70	
Daws Nick (M)	5 11	12 13	Salford	15 3 70	Altrincham

Debenham Rob (D)	5 8	10 07	Doncaster	28 11 79	Trainee
Donnelly Mark (D)	6 1	12 07	Leeds	22 12 79	Doncaster R
Forrest Martyn (M)	5 10	12 02	Bury	2 1 79	Trainee
Hoggeth Gary (G)	6 0	11 07	South Shields	7 10 79	Trainee
James Lutel (F)	5 8	11 00	Manchester	2 6 72	
Jemson Nigel (F)	5 11	13 00	Preston	10 8 69	Oxford U
Kenny Patrick (G)	6 1	14 06	Halifax	17 5 78	Bradford PA
Kiely Dean (G)	6 0	12 13	Salford	10 10 70	York C
Linighan Brian (D)	6 4	11 04	Hartlepool	2 11 73	Sheffield W
Littlejohn Adrian (M)	5 10	11 00	Wolverhampton	26 9 71	Oldham Ath
Lucketti Chris (D)	6 2	13 06	Littleborough	28 9 71	Halifax T
Messer Gary (F)	6 1	13 00	Consett	22 9 79	Doncaster R
Preece Andy (F)	6 1	12 00	Evesham	27 3 67	Blackpool
Souter Ryan (M)	5 10	12 00	Bedford	5 2 78	Weston-Super-Mare
Swailes Chris (D)	6 2	13 07	Gateshead	19 10 70	Ipswich T
Swailes Danny (D)	6 3	12 06	Bolton	1 4 79	Trainee
Tedaldi Domenico (M)	5 11	12 00	Aberystwyth	22 10 80	Trainee
Williams Paul (M)	5 7	11 07	Leicester	11 9 69	Gillingham
Woodward Andy (D)	6 0	13 06	Stockport	23 9 73	Crewe Alex

League Appearances: Armstrong, G. (2); Avdiu, K. (6); Baldry, S. (5); Barnes, P. 6(2); Barrick, D. 16(4); Billy, C. 35(2); Bullock, D. 12; D'Jaffo, L. 35(2); Daws, N. 46; Ellis, T. 3(13); Forrest, M. (1); Foster, J. 6(1); Grobbelaar, B. 1; Hall, P. 7; James, L. 10(7); Jemson, N. 6(8); Johnrose, L. 26(1); Kiely, D. 45; Lilley, D. 5; Littlejohn, A. 11(9); Lucketti, C. 43; Matthews, R. 12(4); Patterson, M. 9(4); Preece, A. 19(20); Redmond, S. 26; Rigby, T. 1(1); Serrant, C. 15; Souter, R. (1); Swailes, C. 43; Swailes, D. ; West, D. 18(5); Williams, P. 14(1); Woodward, A. 36(1).
Goals – League (33): D'Jaffo 8 (2 pens), Preece 3, Swailes C 3, Daws 2, Ellis 2, James 2, Matthews 2, West 2, Avdiu 1, Barrick 1, Bullock 1, Johnrose 1, Lilley 1, Littlejohn 1, Lucketti 1, Williams 1, Woodward 1.
Worthington Cup (9): Matthews 3, Johnrose 2, Armstrong 1, Daws 1, D'Jaffo 1, own goal 1.
FA Cup (0).
Ground: Gigg Lane, Bury BL9 9HR. Telephone (0161) 764 4881.
Record attendance: 35,000 v Bolton W, FA Cup 3rd rd, 9 January 1960. **Capacity:** 11,841.
Manager: Neil Warnock.
Secretary: J. Neville.
Honours – Football League: Division 2 Champions – 1894–95, 1996–97. Division 3 Champions – 1960–61. **FA Cup winners** 1900, 1903. **Auto Windscreens Shield winners** 1997.
Colours: White shirts, royal blue shorts, royal blue stockings.

CAMBRIDGE UNITED　　　　　　　　　　　　DIV. 2

Armstrong Dean (M)	5 8	9 13	Chiswick	7 9 79	Trainee
Ashbee Ian (M)	6 1	13 04	Birmingham	6 9 76	Derby Co
Benjamin Trevor (F)	6 2	13 07	Kettering	8 2 79	Trainee
Butler Martin (F)	5 11	11 12	Wordsley	15 9 74	Walsall
Campbell Jamie (D)	6 1	12 07	Birmingham	21 10 72	Barnet
Chenery Ben (D)	6 1	11 11	Ipswich	28 1 77	Luton T
Duncan Andy (D)	5 11	13 04	Hexham	20 10 77	Manchester U
Ingham Andrew (M)			Leeds	21 8 81	Trainee
Joseph Marc (D)	6 1	12 12	Leicester	10 11 76	Trainee
Kyd Michael (F)	5 8	12 08	Hackney	21 5 77	Trainee
Marshall Shaun (G)	6 2	12 12	Fakenham	3 10 78	Trainee
McAvoy Larry (D)	5 8	11 00	Lambeth	7 9 79	Trainee
McNeil Martin (D)			Rutherglen	28 9 80	Trainee
Mustoe Neil (M)	5 8	12 00	Gloucester	5 11 76	Manchester U

Preece David (M)   5 6   11 01 Bridgnorth   28 5 63 Derby Co
Russell Alex (M)   5 8   11 10 Crosby   17 3 73 Rochdale
Taylor John (F)   6 2   14 00 Norwich   24 10 64 Luton T
Van Heusden Arjan (G)   6 4   14 07 Alphen   11 12 72 Port Vale
Wanless Paul (M)   6 1   13 11 Banbury   14 12 73 Lincoln C
Youngs Tom (F)   5 9   10 07 Bury St Edmunds   31 8 79 Trainee

League Appearances: Andrews, W. 1(1); Ashbee, I. 25(6); Benjamin, T. 37(5); Bruce, P. 2(2); Butler, M. 46; Campbell, J. 45; Chenery, B. 44; Duncan, A. 45; Eustace, S. 15(1); Joseph, M. 28(1); Kyd, M. 5(7); Mackenzie, N. 3(1); Marshall, S. 19; McAvoy, L. 1; McCammon, M. 1(1); McMahon, S. 1(2); McNeil, M. 4(2); Mustoe, N. 28(6); Preece, D. 5(9); Russell, A. 36(1); Taylor, J. 29(11); Van Heusden, A. 27; Walker, R. 7(14); Wanless, P. 45; Wilde, A. 1; Youngs, T. 6(4).

Goals – League (78): Butler 17 (2 pens), Taylor 17 (1 pen), Benjamin 10, Wanless 8 (1 pen), Russell 6, Ashbee 4, Campbell 4, Mustoe 3, Walker 3, Preece 2, Duncan 1, Mackenzie 1, own goals 2.

Worthington Cup (7): Benjamin 4, Butler 2 (1 pen), Taylor 1 (pen).

FA Cup (3): Benjamin 1, Butler 1, Campbell 1.

Ground: Abbey Stadium, Newmarket Rd, Cambridge CB5 8LN. Telephone (01223) 566500. **Capacity:** 9247.

Record attendance: 14,000 v Chelsea, Friendly, 1 May 1970.

Manager: Roy McFarland.

Secretary: Andrew Pincher.

Honours – Football League: Division 3 Champions – 1990–91. Division 4 Champions – 1976–77.

Colours: Amber shirts with black trim, black shorts, black stockings.

CARDIFF CITY   DIV. 2

Bonner Mark (M)   5 8   11 00 Ormskirk   7 6 74 Blackpool
Bowen Jason (M)   5 8   11 02 Merthyr   24 8 72 Reading
Cadette Nathan (M)   5 8   11 11 Cardiff   6 1 80 Trainee
Carpenter Richard (M)   6 0   13 01 Sheppey   30 9 72 Fulham
Earnshaw Robert (F)   5 6   9 09 Zambia   6 4 81 Trainee
Eckhardt Jeff (D)   6 0   12 01 Sheffield   7 10 65 Stockport Co
Ford Mike (D)   6 0   12 12 Bristol   9 2 66 Oxford U
Fowler Jason (M)   6 3   12 04 Bristol   20 8 74 Bristol C
Hallworth Jon (G)   6 3   14 08 Stockport   26 10 65 Oldham Ath
Hill Danny (M)   5 8   11 08 Edmonton   1 10 74 Oxford U
Jarman Lee (D)   6 3   14 01 Cardiff   16 12 77 Trainee
Kelly Seamus (G)   6 1   13 13 Tullamore   6 5 74 UCD
Legg Andy (M)   5 8   10 12 Swansea   28 7 66 Reading
Middleton Craig (M)   5 11 12 00 Nuneaton   10 9 70 Cambridge U
Mitchell Graham (D)   6 1   13 01 Shipley   16 2 68 Raith R
Nugent Kevin (F)   6 2   13 00 Edmonton   10 4 69 Bristol C
Phillips Lee (D)   6 0   12 10 Aberdare   18 3 79 Trainee
Roberts Chris (F)   5 10 12 03 Cardiff   22 10 79 Trainee
Thomas Dai (F)   5 11 13 07 Caerphilly   26 9 75 Watford
Williams John (F)   6 2   13 08 Birmingham   11 5 68 Exeter C
Young Scott (D)   6 1   13 02 Llywnypia   14 1 76 Trainee

League Appearances: Allen, C. 3(1); Bonner, M. 21(4); Bowen, J. 10(7); Brazier, M. 11; Carpenter, R. 41(1); Delaney, M. 28; Earnshaw, R. 1(4); Eckhardt, J. 31(4); Ford, M. 25; Fowler, J. 32(5); Hallworth, J. 41; Hill, D. 14(12); Jarman, L. 2(4); Kelly, S. 5; Legg, A. 18(6); Middleton, C. 20(15); Mitchell, G. 46; Nugent, K. 40(1); O'Sullivan, W. 38(4); Penney, D. 1; Phillips, L. 2; Roberts, C. (4); Saville, A. 2; Thomas, D. 16(8); Williams, J. 25(18); Young, S. 33.

Goals – League (60): Nugent 15 (2 pens), Williams 12, Eckhardt 5, Middleton 4, Thomas 4, Fowler 3, Bowen 2, Brazier 2, Hill 2, Legg 2, O'Sullivan 2, Bonner 1, Carpenter 1, Earnshaw 1, Jarman 1, Saville 1, Young 1, own goal 1.

Worthington Cup (2): Eckhardt 1, Williams 1.
FA Cup (13): Fowler 3, Nugent 3, Williams 3, Middleton 2, Delaney 1, Eckhardt 1.
Ground: Ninian Park, Cardiff CF1 8SX. Telephone (01222) 221001.
Record attendance: 61,566, Wales v England, 14 October 1961. **Capacity:** 15,585.
Manager: Frank Burrows.
Secretary: Ceri Whitehead.
Honours – Football League: Division 3 (S) Champions – 1946–47. **FA Cup winners** 1926–27 (only occasion the Cup has been won by a club outside England). **Welsh Cup winners** 21 times.
Colours: Blue shirts, white shorts, white stockings.

CARLISLE UNITED   DIV. 3

Anthony Graham (M)	5 7	11 02	South Shields	9 8 75	Plymouth Arg
Barr Billy (D)	5 11	11 02	Halifax	21 1 69	Crewe Alex
Brightwell David (D)	6 2	12 09	Lutterworth	7 1 71	Northampton T
Clark Peter (D)	6 1	12 04	Romford	10 12 79	Arsenal
Dobie Scott (F)	6 2	12 09	Workington	10 10 78	Trainee
Douglas Andrew (F)	5 9	10 05	Penrith	27 5 80	Trainee
Heritage Paul (G)	6 1	13 06	Sheffield	17 4 79	Barnsley
Hopper Tony (M)	5 11	12 08	Carlisle	31 5 76	Trainee
Prokas Richard (M)	5 9	11 05	Penrith	22 1 76	Trainee
Reid Paul (D)	6 2	11 08	Carlisle	18 2 82	Trainee
Searle Damon (M)	5 10	11 00	Cardiff	26 10 71	Stockport Co
Thorpe Jeff (M)	5 11	12 08	Cockermouth	17 11 72	Trainee
Thurston Mark (M)	6 2	11 08	Carlisle	10 2 80	Trainee
Tracey Richard (F)	5 11	12 04	Muirfield	9 7 79	Rotherham U
Varty Will (D)	6 0	12 00	Workington	1 10 76	Trainee
Whitehead Stuart (D)	6 0	12 02	Bromsgrove	17 7 76	Bolton W

League Appearances: Anthony, G. 21(5); Bagshaw, P. 5(4); Barr, B. 21(2); Bass, D. 8(1); Boertien, P. 8; Bowman, R. 24; Bridge-Wilkinson, M. 4(3); Brightwell, D. 41; Caig, T. 37; Clark, P. 35(1); Couzens, A. 10(5); Dobie, S. 26(7); Douglas, A. (1); Finney, S. 22(11); Glass, J. 3; Hopper, T. 17(6); Knight, R. 6; Kubicki, D. 7; McAlindon, G. 3(13); McGregor, P. 9(1); Mendes, J. 5(1); Ormerod, A. 5; Paterson, S. 18(1); Prokas, R. 33(1); Scott, R. 7; Searle, D. 43(2); Stevens, I. 31(10); Thorpe, J. 6(7); Tracey, R. 10(1); Varty, W. 5(1); Whitehead, S. 36(1).
Goals – League (43): Stevens 9, Dobie 6 (1 pen), Finney 6 (1 pen), Brightwell 4, McGregor 3, Scott 3, Tracey 3, Searle 2, Boertien 1, Bowman 1, Glass 1, Mendes 1, Paterson 1, own goals 2.
Worthington Cup (0).
FA Cup (1): Stevens 1.
Ground: Brunton Park, Carlisle CA1 1LL. Telephone (01228) 526237.
Record attendance: 27,500 v Birmingham C, FA Cup 3rd rd, 5 January 1957 and v Middlesbrough, FA Cup 5th rd, 7 February 1970. **Capacity:** 16,651.
First Team Coach: Keith Mincher.
Secretary: J. T. T. Fuller.
Honours – Football League: Division 3 Champions – 1964–65, 1994–95. **Auto Windscreens Shield winners:** 1997
Colours: Blue shirts, white shorts, white stockings.

CHARLTON ATHLETIC   DIV. 1

Allman Anthony (D)	5 9	10 07	Sidcup	14 12 80	Trainee
Barness Anthony (D)	5 11	12 01	Lewisham	25 3 73	Chelsea
Brown Steve (D)	6 1	13 10	Brighton	13 5 72	Trainee
Curbishley Alan (M)	5 10	11 07	Forest Gate	8 11 57	Brighton & HA

Fortune Jonathan (D)	6 2	11 00	Islington	23 8 80	Trainee
Hales Lee (F)	5 10	11 00	Gillingham	1 5 81	Trainee
Holmes Matty (M)	5 7	11 00	Luton	1 8 69	Blackburn R
Hunt Andy (F)	6 0	11 12	Thurrock	9 6 70	WBA
Ifejiagwa Emeka (D)	6 3	14 00	Nigeria	30 10 77	Udoji U
Ilic Sasa (G)	6 4	14 00	Melbourne	18 7 72	St Leonards Stamcroft
Izzet Kemal (M)	5 8	10 05	Whitechapel	29 9 80	Trainee
James Kevin (F)	5 9	10 07	Southwark	3 1 80	Trainee
Jones Keith (M)	5 9	10 11	Dulwich	14 10 65	Southend U
Jones Steve (F)	5 11	12 00	Cambridge	17 3 70	West Ham U
Kinsella Mark (M)	5 9	11 05	Dublin	12 8 72	Colchester U
Konchesky Paul (D)	5 10	10 05	Barking	15 5 81	Trainee
Lisbie Kevin (F)	5 9	11 00	Hackney	17 10 78	Trainee
MacDonald Charles (F)	5 9	11 00	Southwark	13 2 81	Trainee
McCammon Mark (F)	6 2	12 00	Barnet	7 8 78	Cambridge U
Mendonca Clive (F)	5 10	10 07	Islington	9 9 68	Grimsby T
Mills Danny (D)	5 11	11 09	Norwich	18 5 77	Norwich C
Newton Shaun (F)	5 8	11 00	Camberwell	20 8 75	Trainee
Nicholls Kevin (M)	5 11	11 12	Newham	2 1 79	Trainee
Parker Scott (M)	5 9	11 00	Lambeth	13 10 80	Trainee
Powell Chris (D)	5 10	11 07	Lambeth	8 9 69	Derby Co
Pringle Martin (F)	6 2	12 00	Gothenburg	18 11 70	Benfica
Redfearn Neil (M)	5 8	12 00	Dewsbury	20 6 65	Barnsley
Robinson John (F)	5 10	11 02	Bulawayo	29 8 71	Brighton & HA
Royce Simon (G)	6 2	12 10	Forest Gate	9 9 71	Southend U
Rufus Richard (D)	6 1	10 05	Lewisham	12 1 75	Trainee
Stuart Graham (M)	5 8	11 11	Tooting	24 10 70	Sheffield U
Tiler Carl (D)	6 2	13 10	Sheffield	11 2 70	Everton
Youds Eddie (D)	6 1	13 00	Liverpool	3 5 70	Bradford C

League Appearances: Barnes, J. 2(10); Barness, A. (3); Bowen, M. 2(4); Bright, M. 1(5); Brown, S. 13(5); Hunt, A. 32(2); Ilic, S. 23; Jones, K. 13(9); Jones, S. 7(18); Kinsella, M. 38; Konchesky, P. 1(1); Lisbie, K. (1); Mendonca, C. 19(6); Mills, D. 36; Mortimer, P. 10(7); Newton, S. 13(3); Parker, S. (4); Petterson, A. 7(3); Powell, C. 38; Pringle, M. 15(3); Redfearn, N. 29(1); Robinson, J. 27(3); Royce, S. 8; Rufus, R. 27; Stuart, G. 9; Tiler, C. 27; Youds, E. 21(1).

Goals – League (41): Mendonca 8 (3 pens), Hunt 7, Stuart 4 (1 pen), Pringle 3, Redfearn 3 (1 pen), Kinsella 2, Mills 2, Robinson 2, Youds 2, Bright 1, Jones K 1, Jones S 1, Mortimer 1, Rufus 1, Tiler 1, own goals 2.

Worthington Cup (4): Mortimer 1, Newton 1, Redfearn 1, Youds 1.

FA Cup (0).

Ground: The Valley, Floyd Road, Charlton, London SE7 8BL. Telephone (020) 8333 4000.

Record attendance: 75,031 v Aston Villa, FA Cup 5th rd, 12 February 1938 (at The Valley). **Capacity:** 20,043.

Manager: Alan Curbishley.

Secretary: Chris Parkes.

Honours – Football League: Division 3 (S) Champions – 1928–29, 1934–35. **FA Cup winners** 1947.

Colours: Red shirts, white shorts, red stockings.

CHELSEA

FA PREMIERSHIP

Babayaro Celestine (D)	5 9	10 12	Kaduna	29 8 78	Anderlecht
Broad Stephen (D)	6 2	12 00	Epsom	10 6 80	Trainee
Casiraghi Pierluigi (F)	5 11	12 02	Milan	4 3 69	Lazio
Clement Neil (D)	6 0	12 03	Reading	3 10 78	Trainee
Crittenden Nick (D)	5 10	11 00	Ascot	11 11 78	Trainee

Dalla Bona Samuele (D)	6 1	12 00	S. Dona di Piave	6 2 81	
De Goey Ed (G)	6 6	15 04	Gouda	20 12 66	Feyenoord
Desailly Marcel (D)	6 2	12 06	Accra	17 9 68	AC Milan
Di Matteo Roberto (M)	5 10	12 00	Schaffhausen	29 5 70	Lazio
Duberry Michael (D)	6 1	14 00	Enfield	14 10 75	Trainee
Evans Rhys (G)	6 1	12 01	Swindon	27 1 82	Trainee
Ferrer Albert (D)	5 9	11 00	Barcelona	6 6 70	Barcelona
Flo Tore Andre (F)	6 4	13 08	Strin	15 6 73	Brann
Forssell Mikael (F)	5 10	10 10	Steinfurt	15 3 81	HJK Helsinki
Goldbaek Bjarne (M)	5 10	11 06	Denmark	6 10 68	FC Copenhagen
Hampshire Steve (F)	5 10	10 10	Edinburgh	17 10 79	Trainee
Harley Jon (M)	5 10	11 10	Maidstone	26 9 79	Trainee
Hitchcock Kevin (G)	6 1	13 00	Custom House	5 10 62	Mansfield T
Hughes Paul (M)	5 11	12 06	Hammersmith	19 4 76	Trainee
Lambourde Bernard (D)	6 1	12 06	Pointe-A-Pitre	11 5 71	Bordeaux
Le Saux Graeme (D)	5 10	11 09	Jersey	17 10 68	Blackburn R
Leboeuf Franck (D)	6 0	12 00	Marseille	22 1 68	Strasbourg
Morris Jody (M)	5 5	10 11	Hammersmith	22 12 78	Trainee
Myers Andy (D)	5 10	13 11	Hounslow	3 11 73	Trainee
Nicholls Mark (F)	5 10	10 04	Hillingdon	30 5 77	Trainee
Parkin Sam (F)	6 1	12 06	Roehampton	14 3 81	School
Percassi Luca (M)	5 9	11 00	Milan	25 8 80	
Petrescu Dan (D)	5 10	11 07	Bucharest	22 12 67	Sheffield W
Poyet Gustavo (M)	6 1	13 01	Montevideo	15 11 67	Zaragoza
Richardson Jay (M)	5 9	11 00	Keston	14 11 79	Trainee
Sheerin Joe (F)	6 1	13 09	Hammersmith	1 2 79	Trainee
Slatter Danny (M)	5 8	11 01	Cardiff	15 11 80	Trainee
Terry John (D)	6 0	11 11	Barking	7 12 80	Trainee
Vialli Gianluca (F)	5 10	13 06	Cremona	9 7 64	Juventus
Wise Dennis (F)	5 6	10 11	Kensington	16 12 66	Wimbledon
Wolleaston Robert (F)	5 11	11 10	Perivale	21 12 79	Trainee
Zola Gianfranco (F)	5 6	10 10	Oliena	5 7 66	Parma

League Appearances: Babayaro, C. 26(2); Casiraghi, P. 10; De Goey, E. 35; Desailly, M. 30(1); Di Matteo, R. 26(4); Duberry, M. 18(7); Ferrer, A. 30; Flo, T. 18(12); Forssell, M. 4(6); Goldbaek, B. 13(10); Hitchcock, K. 2(1); Kharine, D. 1; Lambourde, B. 12(5); Laudrup, B. 5(2); Le Saux, G. 30(1); Leboeuf, F. 33; Morris, J. 14(4); Myers, A. 1; Newton, E. 1(6); Nicholls, M. (9); Petrescu, D. 23(9); Poyet, G. 21(7); Terry, J. (2); Vialli, G. 9; Wise, D. 21(1); Zola, G. 35(2).

Goals – League (57): Zola 13, Poyet 11, Flo 10, Goldbaek 5, Leboeuf 4 (3 pens), Petrescu 4, Babayaro 3, Di Matteo 2, Casiraghi 1, Forssell 1, Morris 1, Vialli 1, own goal 1.

Worthington Cup (10): Vialli 6, Poyet 2, Flo 1, Leboeuf 1 (pen).

FA Cup (8): Forssell 2, Vialli 2, Di Matteo 1, Leboeuf 1 (pen), Wise 1, Zola 1.

Ground: Stamford Bridge, London SW6 1HS. Telephone (0171) 385 5545.

Record attendance: 82,905 v Arsenal, Division 1, 12 October 1935.

Capacity: 35,421 (up to 41,000).

Player-Manager: Gianluca Vialli.

Secretary: Alan Shaw.

Honours – Football League: Division 1 Champions – 1954–55. **FA Cup winners** 1970, 1997. **Football League Cup winners** 1964–65, 1997–98. **Full Members' Cup winners** 1985–86. **Zenith Data Systems Cup winners** 1989–90. **European Cup-Winners' Cup winners** 1970–71, 1997–98. **Super Cup Winners:** 1999.

Colours: Royal blue with white and amber shirts and shorts, white stockings with royal blue and amber trim.

CHELTENHAM TOWN   DIV. 3

Banks Chris (D)	5 11	12 02	Stone	22 11 65	Bath C
Bloomer Bob (M)	5 10	12 07	Sheffield	21 6 66	Bristol R
Book Steve (G)	5 11	11 01	Bournemouth	7 7 69	Forest Green R

Brough John (D)   6 0   12 11 Heanor   8 1 73 Hereford U
Casey Ross (M)   5 10   10 09 Stroud   7 8 79 Trainee
Duff Michael (D)   6 1   11 08 Belfast   11 1 78 Trainee
Eaton Jason (F)   5 10   11 09 Bristol   29 1 69 Gloucester C
Freeman Mark (D)   6 2   13 08 Walsall   27 1 70 Gloucester C
Gannaway Ryan (G)   5 11   13 02 Gloucester   28 8 73 Shortwood U
Grayson Neil (F)   5 10   12 09 York   1 11 64 Northampton T
Hopkins Gareth (F)   6 2   13 08 Cheltenham   14 6 80 Trainee
Howells Lee (M)   5 11   11 12 Fremantle   14 10 68 Brisbane U
Jackson Michael (M) 5 7   10 10 Cheltenham   26 6 80 Trainee
Knight Keith (M)   5 7   11 07 Cheltenham   16 2 69 Reading
Milton Russell (M)   5 8   12 01 Folkestone   12 1 69 Dover Ath
Murphy Stephen (D)   6 0   10 11 Middlesbrough 31 8 79 Trainee
Norton David (M)   5 10   11 10 Cannock   3 3 65 Hereford U
Smith Jimmy (F)   5 9   10 04 Torquay U   22 11 69 Salisbury C
Victory Jamie (D)   5 11   12 02 London   14 11 75 Bournemouth
Walker Clive (F)   5 8   11 12 Oxford   25 6 57 Brentford
Walker Richard (D)   5 10   11 09 Derby   9 11 71 Notts Co
Watkins Dale (F)   5 8   11 12 Peterborough   4 11 71 Gloucester C
Yates Mark (M)   5 11   13 02 Birmingham   24 1 70 Kidderminster H

Conference Appearances: Bailey, D. 7(1); Banks, C. 34(1); Bloomer, B. 15(13); Brough, J. 34(6); Book, S. 42; Duff, M. 41; Eaton, J. 27(7); Freeman, M. 36(1); Grayson, N. 39(2); Howarth, N. 5(3); Howells, L. 37(1); Jackson, M. (1); Knight, K. 8(15); Milton, R. 6(11); Norton, D. 35(1); Smith, J. 2(5); Victory, J. 42; Walker, C. 17(7); Walker, R. 14(2); Watkins, D. 9(10); Yates, M. 12.
Goals – Conference (71): Grayson 17, Eaton 9, Howells 6, Watkins 6, Freeman 5, Brough 4, Victory 4, Walker C 4, Duff 3, Knight 3, Norton 3, Bailey 2, Banks 1, Smith 1, own goals 3.
FA Cup (4).Eaton 3, Howells 1.
Ground: Whaddon Road, Cheltenham, Gloucester GL52 5NA. Telephone (01242) 573558.
Record attendance: at Whaddon Road: 8326 v Reading, FA Cup 1st rd, 17 November 1956; at Cheltenham Athletic Ground: 10,389 v Blackpool, FA Cup 3rd rd, 13 January 1934.
Capacity: 6114.
Manager: Steve Cotterill.
Secretary: Reg Woodward.
Honours – Football Conference: Champions – 1998–99. **FA Trophy winners** 1997–98.
Colours: Red and white striped shirts, white shorts, red stockings.

CHESTER CITY DIV. 3

Beckett Luke (F)   5 11   11 06 Sheffield   25 11 76 Barnsley
Bennett Gary (F)   5 11   12 00 Kirby   20 9 62 Wrexham
Brown Wayne (G)   6 1   11 06 Southampton   14 1 77 Bristol C
Crosby Andy (D)   6 2   13 07 Rotherham   3 3 73 Darlington
Cutler Neil (G)   6 1   12 00 Birmingham   3 9 76 Crewe Alex
Jones Jon (F)   5 11   11 05 Wrexham   27 10 78 Trainee
Lancaster Martin (D) 6 0   12 07 Wigan   10 11 80 Trainee
Murphy John (F)   6 1   14 00 Whiston   18 10 76 Trainee
Shelton Andy (M)   5 10   12 00 Sutton Coldfield 19 6 80 Trainee
Shelton Gary (M)   5 7   11 02 Nottingham   21 3 58 Bristol C
Woods Matt (D)   6 1   12 03 Gosport   9 9 76 Trainee
Wright Darren (F)   5 6   10 00 Warrington   7 9 79 Trainee

League Appearances: Aiston, S. 11; Alsford, J. 9(1); Beckett, L. 24(4); Bennett, G. 5(2); Brown, W. 23; Carson, D. 1(1); Conroy, M. 11(4); Crosby, A. 41; Cross, J. 33(2); Cutler, N. 23; Davidson, R. 40; Fisher, N. 7(1); Flitcroft, D. 42; Jones, J. 2(6); Lancaster, M. 8(3); Moss, D. 5(2); Murphy, J. 41(1); Priest, C. 35; Reid, S. 16(6); Richardson, N. 41(2); Shelton, A. 5(17); Smeets, J. 1(2); Smith, A. 32; Thomas, R. 3(3); Woods, M. 41(2); Wright, D. 6(12).

Goals – League (57): Murphy 12, Beckett 11, Flitcroft 6 (2 pens), Crosby 4 (3 pens), Priest 4, Conroy 3, Richardson 3, Thomas 3, Smith 2 (1 pen), Alsford 1, Bennett 1, Cross 1, Davidson 1, Reid 1, Shelton 1, Woods 1, Wright 1, own goal 1.
Worthington Cup (4): Beckett 2, Smith 1, own goal 1.
FA Cup (0).
Ground: The Deva Stadium, Bumpers Lane, Chester CH1 4LT. Telephone (01244) 371376, 371809.
Record attendance: 20,500 v Chelsea, FA Cup 3rd rd (replay), 16 January, 1952 (at Sealand Road). **Capacity:** 6000.
Manager: Kevin Ratcliffe.
Secretary: Gill Dugan.
Honours – Welsh Cup winners 1908, 1933, 1947. **Debenhams Cup:** Winners 1977.
Colours: Blue and white striped shirts, white shorts, blue and white stockings.

CHESTERFIELD   DIV. 2

Beaumont Chris (M)	5 11	11 12	Sheffield	5 12 65	Stockport Co
Blatherwick Steve (D)	6 1	15 00	Nottingham	20 9 73	Burnley
Breckin Ian (D)	5 11	11 07	Rotherham	24 2 75	Rotherham U
Carss Tony (M)	5 10	11 08	Alnwick	31 3 76	Cardiff C
Curtis Tom (M)	5 8	10 08	Exeter	1 3 73	Derby Co
Ebdon Marcus (M)	5 10	11 02	Pontypool	17 10 70	Peterborough U
Holland Paul (M)	5 11	12 10	Lincoln	8 7 73	Sheffield U
Howard Jonathan (F)	5 11	11 07	Sheffield	7 10 71	Rotherham U
Lee Jason (F)	6 3	13 03	Newham	9 5 71	Watford
Lenagh Steve (D)	5 11	10 09	Durham	21 3 79	Sheffield W
Lomas Jamie (M)	5 11	10 09	Chesterfield	18 10 77	Trainee
Mercer Billy (G)	6 1	11 00	Liverpool	22 5 69	Sheffield U
Pearce Greg (M)	5 9	10 09	Bolton	26 5 80	Trainee
Reeves David (F)	6 0	12 06	Birkenhead	19 11 67	Preston NE
Simpkins Mike (D)	6 0	11 11	Sheffield	28 11 78	Trainee
Wilkinson Steve (F)	5 11	11 11	Lincoln	1 9 68	Preston NE
Willis Roger (M)	6 0	12 00	Islington	17 6 67	Peterborough U

League Appearances: Beaumont, C. 35(4); Blatherwick, S. 9(5); Breckin, I. 44; Carss, T. 2(2); Curtis, T. 24; Ebdon, M. 39(1); Hewitt, J. 40; Holland, P. 32(1); Howard, J. 34(3); Jules, M. 19(4); Leaning, A. 2; Lee, J. 14(8); Lenagh, S. 6(4); Lomas, J. 5(2); Mercer, B. 44; Morris, A. (1); Nicholson, S. 23(1); Pearce, G. (1); Perkins, C. 32(2); Reeves, D. 37(3); Simpkins, M. (1); Wilkinson, S. 18(5); Williams, M. 40; Willis, R. 7(10).
Goals – League (46): Reeves 10 (3 pens), Howard 9, Wilkinson 6, Curtis 3, Holland 3, Williams 3, Beaumont 2, Breckin 2, Hewitt 2, Blatherwick 1, Ebdon 1, Lee 1, Lenagh 1, Perkins 1, own goal 1.
Worthington Cup (4): Holland 2, Howard 1, Reeves 1.
FA Cup (0).
Ground: Recreation Ground, Chesterfield S40 4SX. Telephone (01246) 209765.
Record attendance: 30,968 v Newcastle U, Division 2, 7 April 1939. **Capacity:** 8880.
Manager: John Duncan.
Secretary: Stephanie Otter.
Honours – Football League: Division 3 (N) Champions – 1930–31, 1935–36. Division 4 Champions – 1969–70, 1984–85. **Anglo-Scottish Cup winners** 1980–81.
Colours: Blue shirts, white shorts, blue stockings.

COLCHESTER UNITED   DIV. 2

Aspinall Warren (M)	5 9	11 12	Wigan	13 9 67	Brentford
Duguid Karl (F)	5 11	11 00	Letchworth	21 3 78	Trainee
Forbes Steve (M)	6 1	13 03	Hackney	24 12 75	Millwall

Germain Steve (F)			Cannes	22 6 81	
Greene David (D)	6 3	14 03	Luton	26 10 73	Luton T
Gregory David (M)	5 10	12 03	Polstead	23 1 70	Peterborough U
Gregory Neil (F)	6 0	12 10	Ndola	7 10 72	Ipswich T
Lua-Lua Lomano (F)			Zaire	28 12 80	
Richard Fabrice (D)			Saintes	16 8 73	
Sale Mark (F)	6 5	14 09	Burton-on-Trent	27 2 72	Mansfield T
Wiles Ian (D)	6 0	11 13	Epping	28 4 80	Trainee
Wilkins Richard (M)	6 0	12 04	Streatham	25 5 65	Hereford U

League Appearances: Abrahams, P. 13(14); Adcock, T. (6); Allen, B. 4; Aspinall, W. 15; Betts, S. 22(6); Branston, G. (1); Buckle, P. 39(4); Dozzell, J. 23(6); Dublin, K. 2; Duguid, K. 23(10); Dunne, J. 32(4); Emberson, C. 37; Fernandes, T. 8; Forbes, S. 8(7); Fumaca, J. 1; Germain, S. 1(5); Greene, D. 42; Gregory, D. 43(1); Gregory, N. 29(9); Haydon, N. 7(6); Launders, B. 1; Lock, T. 14(9); Lua-Lua, L. 6(7); Okafor, S. (1); Opara, C. (1); Pounewatchy, S. 15; Rainford, D. (1); Richard, F. 10; Sale, M. 21(10); Skelton, A. 7(2); Stamps, S. 19(2); Walker, A. 1; Wiles, I. (1); Wilkins, R. 25(1); Williams, G. 38(1).

Goals – League (52): Gregory D 11 (6 pens), Greene 8, Dozzell 4, Duguid 4, Gregory N 4, Aspinall 3 (2 pens), Abrahams 2, Betts 2, Buckle 2, Forbes 2, Sale 2, Wilkins 2, Allen 1, Haydon 1, Lock 1, Lua-Lua 1, Pounewatchy 1, own goal 1.

Worthington Cup (3): Gregory D 2 (2 pens), Abrahams 1.

FA Cup (1): Adcock 1.

Ground: Layer Rd Ground, Colchester CO2 7JJ. Telephone (01206) 508800.

Record attendance: 19,072 v Reading, FA Cup 1st rd, 27 Nov, 1948. **Capacity:** 7556.

Manager: Mick Wadsworth.

Secretary: Mrs Marie Partner.

Honours – GM Vauxhall Conference winners 1991–92. **FA Trophy winners** 1991–92.

Colours: Blue and white striped shirts, navy shorts, white stockings.

COVENTRY CITY   FA PREMIERSHIP

Aloisi John (F)	6 1	12 06	Adelaide	5 2 76	Portsmouth
Barnett Christopher (M)	5 11	12 00	Derby	20 12 78	Trainee
Betts Robert (M)	5 10	11 00	Doncaster	21 12 81	School
Boateng George (M)	5 9	10 12	Nkawkaw	5 9 75	Feyenoord
Boland Willie (M)	5 9	11 02	Ennis	6 8 75	Trainee
Breen Gary (D)	6 1	11 12	London	12 12 73	Birmingham C
Brightwell Ian (M)	5 9	12 05	Lutterworth	9 4 68	Manchester C
Burrows David (D)	5 8	11 08	Dudley	25 10 68	Everton
Burrows Mark (D)	6 3	12 08	Kettering	14 8 80	Trainee
Clement Philippe (M)	6 2	13 00	Antwerp	22 3 74	Genk
Colwell Richard (D)	5 9	11 02	Wordsley	2 9 79	Trainee
Delorge Laurent (M)	5 10	11 12	Leuven	21 7 79	Gent
Doyle Daire (M)	5 10	11 06	Dublin	18 10 80	Cherry Orchard
Edworthy Marc (D)	5 11	10 03	Barnstaple	24 12 72	Crystal Palace
Eribenne Chukkie (F)	5 10	11 12	London	2 11 80	Trainee
Eustace John (M)	5 11	11 12	Solihull	3 11 79	Dundee U
Faulconbridge Craig (F)	6 1	13 00	Nuneaton	20 4 78	Dunfermline Ath
Ferguson Barry (D)	6 3	13 00	Dublin	7 9 79	Home Farm
Froggatt Steve (F)	5 11	11 00	Lincoln	9 3 73	Wolverhampton W
Gioacchini Stefano (F)			Rome	25 11 76	Venezia
Grant Martin (M)			Kirkcaldy	16 1 82	Trainee
Hall Daniel (M)			Rugby	29 12 81	Trainee
Hall Marcus (D)	6 1	12 02	Coventry	24 3 76	Trainee
Hall Paul (F)	5 8	10 02	Manchester	3 7 72	Portsmouth
Hedman Magnus (G)	6 3	14 00	Stockholm	19 3 73	AIK Stockholm

Huckerby Darren (F)	5 11	11 04	Nottingham	23 4 76	Newcastle U
Kirkland Christopher (G)	6 3	11 07	Leicester	2 5 81	Trainee
Konjic Muhamed (D)	6 3	13 00	Tulsa	14 5 70	Monaco
McAllister Gary (M)	6 1	11 11	Mothcrwcll	25 12 64	Lccds U
McPhee Gary (F)	6 0	12 00	Glasgow	18 4 80	
McPhee Stephen (M)	5 7	10 08	Glasgow	5 6 81	
Mooney Gerard (D)	5 9	11 00	Glasgow	28 8 80	Trainee
Pead Craig (M)	5 9	11 06	Bromsgrove	15 9 81	Trainee
Prenderville Barry (D)	6 0	12 08	Dublin	16 10 76	Trainee
Quinn Barry (M)	6 0	12 02	Dublin	9 5 79	Trainee
Shaw Richard (D)	5 9	12 08	Brentford	11 9 68	Crystal Palace
Shilton Sam (M)	5 11	11 06	Nottingham	21 7 78	Plymouth Arg
Soltvedt Trond Egil (M)	6 1	12 08	Voss	15 2 67	Rosenborg
Strachan Gavin (M)	5 10	11 07	Aberdeen	23 12 78	Trainee
Telfer Paul (M)	5 9	11 06	Edinburgh	21 10 71	Luton T
Whelan Noel (F)	6 2	12 03	Leeds	30 12 74	Leeds U
Williams Paul (D)	5 11	12 10	Burton	26 3 71	Derby Co

League Appearances: Aloisi, J. 7(9); Boateng, G. 29(4); Breen, G. 21(4); Burrows, D. 23; Clement, P. 6(6); Dublin, D. 10; Edworthy, M. 16(6); Froggatt, S. 23; Gioacchini, S. (3); Hall, M. 2(3); Hall, P. 2(7); Haworth, S. 1; Hedman, M. 36; Huckerby, D. 31(3); Jackson, D. (3); Konjic, M. 3(1); McAllister, G. 29; McSheffrey, G. (1); Nilsson, R. 28; Ogrizovic, S. 2; Quinn, B. 6(1); Shaw, R. 36(1); Shilton, S. 1(4); Soltvedt, T. 21(6); Telfer, P. 30(2); Wallemme, J. 4(2); Whelan, N. 31; Williams, P. 20(2).

Goals – League (39): Whelan 10, Huckerby 9, Aloisi 5, Boateng 4, Dublin 3, McAllister 3 (2 pens), Soltvedt 2, Telfer 2, Froggatt 1.

Worthington Cup (5): Boateng 1, Dublin 1, Hall P 1, Soltvedt 1, Whelan 1.

FA Cup (11): Huckerby 3, Froggatt 2, Whelan 2, Boateng 1, McAllister 1, Telfer 1, own goal 1.

Ground: Highfield Road Stadium, King Richard Street, Coventry CV2 4FW. Telephone (02476) 234000.

Record attendance: 51,455 v Wolverhampton W, Division 2, 29 April 1967.

Capacity: 23,611.

Manager: Gordon Strachan.

Secretary: Graham Hover.

Honours – Football League: Division 2 Champions – 1966–67. Division 3 Champions – 1963–64. Division 3 (S) Champions 1935–36. **FA Cup winners** 1986–87.

Colours: Sky blue and navy striped shirts with white trim, sky blue shorts and stockings with navy trim.

CREWE ALEXANDRA   DIV. 1

Bignot Marcus (D)	5 9	11 00	Birmingham	28 8 74	Kidderminster H
Charnock Phil (M)	5 10	11 03	Southport	14 2 75	Liverpool
Collins James (M)	5 8	10 00	Liverpool	28 5 78	Trainee
Critchley Neil (M)	.		Crewe	18 10 78	Trainee
Foran Mark (D)	6 3	13 04	Aldershot	30 10 73	Peterborough U
Foster Stephen (D)	5 11	11 00	Warrington	10 9 80	Trainee
Hulse Robert (M)			Crewe	25 10 79	Trainee
Jack Rodney (F)	5 7	10 07	Kingston, Jamaica	28 9 72	Torquay U
Johnson Seth (M)	5 10	11 00	Birmingham	12 3 79	Trainee
Kearton Jason (G)	6 1	12 03	Ipswich (Aus)	9 7 69	Everton
Little Colin (F)	5 10	11 00	Wythenshaw	4 11 72	Hyde U
Lunt Kenny (M)	5 10	10 00	Runcorn	20 11 79	Trainee
Macauley Steve (D)	6 1	12 03	Lytham	4 3 69	Fleetwood T
Rivers Mark (F)	5 10	11 00	Crewe	26 11 75	Trainee
Smith Peter (F)	5 10	10 00	Rhuddlan	15 9 78	Trainee

Smith Shaun (D)	5 10	11 00	Leeds	9 4 71	Halifax T
Street Kevin (M)	5 10	10 08	Crewe	25 11 77	Trainee
Unsworth Lee (D)	5 11	11 02	Eccles	25 2 73	Ashton U
Walton David (D)	6 2	14 07	Bellingham	10 4 73	Shrewsbury T
Welsby Kevin (G)	6 0	10 06	Crewe	27 8 80	Trainee
Wright David (D)	5 11	10 09	Warrington	1 5 80	Trainee
Wright Jermaine (M)	5 10	11 09	Greenwich	21 10 75	Wolverhampton W

League Appearances: Anthrobus, S. 16(5); Bignot, M. 26; Charnock, P. 40(4); Collins, J. 5(1); Foran, M. 4(2); Foster, S. (1); Jack, R. 37(2); Johnson, S. 42; Kearton, J. 46; Lightfoot, C. 19(3); Little, C. 27(10); Lunt, K. 6(12); Macauley, S. 12(8); Murphy, D. 16; Newell, M. 1(3); Rivers, M. 38(5); Smith, P. (4); Smith, S. 46; Street, K. 4(19); Unsworth, L. 15(9); Walton, D. 38; Wicks, M. 4(2); Wright, D. 20; Wright, J. 44.

Goals – League (54): Little 10, Jack 9, Rivers 7, Wright J 5, Johnson 4, Smith S 4 (3 pens), Anthrobus 3, Charnock 2, Lightfoot 2, Street 2, Collins 1, Lunt 1, Macauley 1, Murphy 1, Walton 1, Wright D 1.

Worthington Cup (7): Rivers 3, Jack 2, Little 2.

FA Cup (1): Johnson 1.

Ground: Football Ground, Gresty Rd, Crewe CW2 6EB. Telephone (01270) 213014.

Record attendance: 20,000 v Tottenham H, FA Cup 4th rd, 30 January 1960.

Capacity: 10,046.

Manager: Dario Gradi MBE.

Secretary: Mrs Gill Palin.

Honours – Welsh Cup: Winners 1936, 1937.

Colours: Red shirts, white shorts, red stockings.

CRYSTAL PALACE DIV. 1

Amsalem David (D)	6 1	12 01	Israel	4 9 71	Beitar Jerusalem
Austin Dean (D)	5 11	11 11	Hemel Hempstead	26 4 70	Tottenham H
Bradbury Lee (F)	6 2	13 10	Isle of Wight	3 7 75	Manchester C
Burton Sagi (D)	6 2	13 06	Birmingham	25 11 77	Trainee
Carlisle Wayne (M)	6 0	11 06	Lisburn	9 9 79	Trainee
Curcic Sasa (M)	5 9	11 00	Belgrade	14 2 72	Aston Villa
Del Rio Walter (D)	6 0	12 06	Buenos Aires	16 6 76	Boca Juniors
Digby Fraser (G)	6 1	12 12	Sheffield	23 4 67	Swindon T
Evans Stephen (M)	5 11	11 02	Caerphilly	25 9 80	Trainee
Foster Craig (M)	5 11	12 00	Melbourne	15 4 69	Portsmouth
Frampton Andrew (D)	5 11	10 10	Wimbledon	3 9 79	Trainee
Fullarton Jamie (M)	5 9	10 09	Bellshill	20 7 74	Bastia
Graham Gareth (M)	5 7	10 02	Belfast	6 12 78	Trainee
Gregg Matt (G)	5 11	12 00	Cheltenham	30 11 78	Torquay U
Harris Richard (D)	5 11	10 09	Croydon	23 10 80	Trainee
Hibburt James (D)	6 0	12 08	Ashford	30 10 79	Trainee
Jihai Sun (D)	5 10	10 07	Dalian	30 9 77	Dalian Wanda
Kendall Lee (G)	5 10	10 05	Newport	8 1 81	Trainee
Linighan Andy (D)	6 4	13 10	Hartlepool	18 6 62	Arsenal
Martin Andrew (F)	6 0	10 12	Cardiff	28 2 80	Trainee
McKenzie Leon (F)	5 10	10 03	Croydon	17 5 78	Trainee
Miller Kevin (G)	6 1	13 00	Falmouth	15 3 69	Watford
Morrison Clinton (F)	6 1	11 02	Tooting	14 5 79	Trainee
Mullins Hayden (M)	6 0	11 12	Reading	27 3 79	Trainee
Ormshaw Gareth (G)	6 0	12 10	Durban	8 7 79	Ramblers
Petric Gordan (D)	6 1	12 03	Belgrade	30 7 69	Rangers
Rizzo Nicky (M)	5 10	12 00	Sydney	9 6 79	Liverpool
Sharpling Christopher (F)			Bromley	21 4 81	Trainee
Smith Jamie (D)	5 8	11 02	Birmingham	17 9 74	Wolverhampton W
Svensson Mathias (F)	6 0	12 06	Boras	24 9 74	Portsmouth

Thomson Steve (M)	5 8	10 04	Glasgow	23 1 78	Trainee
Tuttle David (D)	6 2	12 10	Reading	6 2 72	Sheffield U
Woozley David (D)	6 0	12 10	Berkshire	6 12 79	Trainee
Zhiyi Fan (M)	6 0	12 01	Shanghai	22 1 70	Shanghai Shenhua

League Appearances: Amsalem, D. 6(4); Austin, D. 17(3); Bent, M. 3(9); Bradbury, L. 19(3); Burton, S. 18(5); Carlisle, W. 2(4); Crowe, J. 8; Curcic, S. 4(11); Del Rio, W. 1(1); Digby, F. 18; Dyer, B. 5(1); Edworthy, M. 1(2); Evans, S. (4); Foster, C. 30(2); Frampton, A. 4(2); Fullarton, J. 7; Graham, G. (1); Harris, R. (1); Hibburt, J. (2); Hreidarsson, H. 6(1); Jansen, M. 18; Jihai, S. 22(1); Linighan, A. 19(1); Lombardo, A. 19; Martin, A. 2(1); McKenzie, L. 10(6); Miller, K. 28; Moore, C. 23; Morrison, C. 27(10); Mullins, H. 38(2); Padovano, M. (2); Petric, G. 18; Rizzo, N. 13(6); Rodger, S. 18; Shipperley, N. 3; Smith, J. 25(1); Svensson, M. 6(2); Thomson, S. 11(5); Turner, A. (2); Tuttle, D. 17(5); Warhurst, P. 5; Woozley, D. 7; Zhiyi, F. 28(1).

Goals – League (58): Morrison 12, Jansen 7, Mullins 5, Bradbury 4 (1 pen), Curcic 4 (1 pen), Lombardo 3 (1 pen), Moore 3, Dyer 2, Foster 2, Tuttle 2, Zhiyi 2, Austin 1, Burton 1, McKenzie 1, Petric 1, Rizzo 1, Rodger 1, Shipperley 1, Svensson 1, Warhurst 1, own goals 3.

Worthington Cup (5): Lombardo 2, Hreidarsson 1, Morrison 1, Zhiyi 1.

FA Cup (1): Bradbury 1.

Ground: Selhurst Park, London SE25 6PU. Telephone (0181) 768 6000.

Record attendance: 51,482 v Burnley, Division 2, 11 May 1979. **Capacity:** 26,400.

Manager: Steve Coppell.

Club Secretary: Mike Hurst.

Honours – Football League: Division 1 – Champions 1993–94. Division 2 Champions – 1978–79. Division 3 (S) 1920–21. **Zenith Data Systems Cup winners 1991.**

Colours: Red shirts with blue trim, red shorts with blue and white trim, red stockings.

DARLINGTON   DIV. 3

Bennett Gary (D)	6 2	12 01	Manchester	4 12 61	Scarborough
Brumwell Phil (M)	5 8	11 00	Darlington	8 8 75	Trainee
Campbell Paul (M)	6 1	11 00	Middlesbrough	29 1 80	Trainee
Carruthers Martin (F)	5 11	11 07	Nottingham	7 8 72	Peterborough U
Dorner Mario (F)	5 10	13 02	Baden	21 3 70	Modling
Duffield Peter (F)	5 6	10 04	Middlesbrough	4 2 69	Raith R
Gabbiadini Marco (F)	5 10	13 04	Nottingham	21 1 68	York C
Gaughan Steve (M)	5 11	11 04	Doncaster	14 4 70	Chesterfield
Himsworth Gary (M)	5 8	11 00	York	19 12 69	York C
Hunt David (D)	5 10	12 00	Durham	5 3 80	Trainee
Leah John (M)	5 9	12 00	Shrewsbury	3 8 78	Newtown
Liddle Craig (D)	5 11	12 07	Chester-le-Street	21 10 71	Middlesbrough
Oliver Michael (M)	5 10	11 04	Middlesbrough	2 8 75	Stockport Co
Pepper Carl (D)	5 11	11 00	Darlington	26 7 80	Trainee
Preece David (G)	6 2	11 11	Sunderland	26 8 76	Sunderland
Reed Adam (D)	6 1	11 00	Bishop Auckland	18 2 75	Blackburn R
Samways Mark (G)	6 2	14 01	Doncaster	11 11 68	York C
Tutill Steve (D)	5 10	12 06	Derwent	1 10 69	York C

League Appearances: Atkinson, B. 42(1); Barnard, M. 29(4); Bennett, G. 26(3); Brumwell, P. 24(13); Campbell, P. 6(3); Carruthers, M. 11; Carter, M. 1; Costa, R. (3); Devos, J. 12; Dorner, M. 9(13); Duffield, P. 10(4); Ellison, L. 3(17); Gabbiadini, M. 40; Gaughan, S. 12(11); Heckingbottom, P. 10; Himsworth, G. 14; Hope, R. 8; Kilty, M. (2); Kubicki, D. 2(1); Leah, J. 7; Liddle, C. 44; Naylor, G. 32(10); Oliver, M. 33(3); Pepper, C. 5(1); Preece, D. 46; Reed, A. 25(4); Roberts, D. 10(14); Scott, K. 4; Shutt, C. 8(6); Tutill, S. 33(3).

Goals – League (69): Gabbiadini 23, Naylor 9, Roberts 5, Bennett 4, Dorner 3, Liddle 3, Atkinson 2, Carruthers 2, Devos 2, Duffield 2, Gaughan 2, Reed 2, Shutt 2, Barnard 1, Campbell 1, Carter 1, Costa 1, Himsworth 1, Leah 1, Oliver 1, own goal 1.
Worthington Cup (3): Devos 1, Roberts 1, own goal 1.
FA Cup (4): Atkinson 1, Barnard 1, Bennett 1, Dorner 1.
Ground: Feethams Ground, Darlington DL1 5JB. Telephone (01325) 240240.
Record attendance: 21,023 v Bolton W, League Cup 3rd rd, 14 November 1960.
Capacity: 8500.
Manager: David Hodgson.
Secretary: K. J. Lavery.
Honours – Football League: Division 3 (N) Champions – 1924–25. Division 4 Champions – 1990–91.
Colours: Black and white.

DERBY COUNTY   FA PREMIERSHIP

Name	Ht	Wt	Birthplace	Date of birth	Previous club
Baiano Francesco (F)	5 6	10 07	Naples	24 2 68	Fiorentina
Beck Mikkel (F)	6 1	13 05	Aarhus	4 5 73	Middlesbrough
Boertien Paul (D)	5 10	11 11	Carlisle	21 1 79	Carlisle U
Bohinen Lars (M)	6 1	13 00	Vadso	8 9 69	Blackburn R
Borbokis Vassilis (D)	5 9	12 02	Serres	10 2 69	Sheffield U
Bridge-Wilkinson Marc (M)	5 6	10 08	Nuneaton	16 3 79	Trainee
Burton Deon (F)	5 9	11 10	Reading	25 10 76	Portsmouth
Carbonari Horace Angel (D)	6 3	13 02	Rosario	2 5 73	Rosario Central
Christie Malcolm (F)	6 0	11 00	Peterborough	11 4 79	Nuneaton B
Delap Rory (D)	6 0	13 00	Sutton Coldfield	6 7 76	Carlisle U
Doherty Gerard (M)			Derry	24 8 81	Derry C
Dorigo Tony (D)	5 9	11 03	Adelaide	31 12 65	Torino
Elliott Steve (D)	6 1	13 12	Derby	29 10 78	Trainee
Eranio Stefano (M)	5 10	12 00	Genoa	29 12 68	AC Milan
Evatt Ian (D)			Coventry	19 11 81	Trainee
Harper Kevin (F)	5 7	12 00	Oldham	15 1 76	Hibernian
Hoult Russell (G)	6 4	14 07	Ashby	22 11 72	Leicester C
Jackson Richard (D)	5 9	9 07	Whitby	18 4 80	Scarborough
Knight Richard (G)	6 1	14 00	Burton	3 8 79	Burton Alb
Laursen Jacob (D)	5 11	12 11	Vejle	6 10 71	Silkeborg
Le Geyt Sinclair (M)			Port Elizabeth	10 7 80	
Lyons Michael (M)			Derby	24 7 81	Trainee
Murray Adam (M)	5 9	10 00	Birmingham	30 9 81	Trainee
Poom Mart (G)	6 5	13 05	Tallinn	3 2 72	Flora Tallinn
Porter Daniel (M)			Portsmouth	23 1 79	
Powell Darryl (M)	6 0	13 00	Lambeth	15 11 71	Portsmouth
Prior Spencer (D)	6 1	13 00	Rochford	22 4 71	Leicester C
Riggott Chris (D)			Derby	1 9 80	Trainee
Robinson Marvin (F)	5 11	12 09	Crewe	11 4 80	Trainee
Schnoor Stefan (D)	6 1	12 04	Neumunster	24 4 71	Hamburg
Sidhu Amrit (F)			Coventry	16 12 81	Trainee
Stimac Igor (D)	6 2	13 00	Metkovic	6 9 67	Hajduk Split
Sturridge Dean (F)	5 8	12 06	Birmingham	27 7 73	Trainee
Wanchope Paulo (F)	6 3	12 05	Heredia	31 7 76	Herediano

League Appearances: Baiano, F. 17(5); Beck, M. 6(1); Boertien, P. (1); Bohinen, L. 29(3); Borbokis, V. 3(1); Bridge-Wilkinson, M. (1); Burton, D. 14(7); Carbonari, H. 28(1); Carsley, L. 20(2); Christie, M. (2); Dailly, C. 1; Delap, R. 21(2); Dorigo, T. 17(1); Elliott, S. 7(4); Eranio, S. 18(7); Harper, K. 6(21); Hoult, R. 23; Hunt, J. (6); Kozluk, R. 3(4); Launders, B. (1); Laursen, J. 37; Murray, A. (4); Poom, M. 15(2); Powell, D. 30(3); Prior, S. 33(1); Robinson, M. (1); Schnoor, S. 20(3); Stimac, I. 14; Sturridge, D. 23(6); Wanchope, P. 33(2).

Goals – League (40): Burton 9, Wanchope 9, Carbonari 5, Sturridge 5, Baiano 4 (2 pens), Schnoor 2 (1 pen), Beck 1, Carsley 1, Dorigo 1 (pen), Harper 1, Hunt 1, Prior 1.
Worthington Cup (3): Delap 1, Sturridge 1, Wanchope 1.
FA Cup (9): Burton 3, Baiano 2, Dorigo 2 (1 pen), Eranio 1 (pen), Harper 1.
Ground: Pride Park Stadium, Derby DE24 8XL. Telephone: (01332) 202202.
Record attendance: 41,826 v Tottenham H, Division 1, 20 September 1969.
Capacity: 33,258.
Manager: Jim Smith.
Secretary: Keith Pearson ACIS.
Honours – Football League: Division 1 Champions – 1971–72, 1974–75. Division 2 Champions – 1911–12, 1914–15, 1968–69, 1986–87. Division 3 (N) 1956–57. **FA Cup winners** 1945–46.
Colours: White shirts with black trim, black shorts with white stripes, white stockings.

EVERTON FA PREMIERSHIP

Name	Ht	Wt	Birthplace	Date	Previous club
Bakayoko Ibrahima (F)			Seguela	31 12 76	Montpellier
Ball Michael (M)	6 1	11 09	Liverpool	2 10 79	Trainee
Barmby Nick (F)	5 6	11 04	Hull	11 2 74	Middlesbrough
Bilic Slaven (D)	6 3	14 03	Split	11 9 68	West Ham U
Branch Michael (F)	5 10	11 07	Liverpool	18 10 78	Trainee
Cadamarteri Danny (F)	5 8	12 11	Bradford	12 10 79	Trainee
Clarke Peter (D)	6 0	12 00	Southport	3 1 82	Trainee
Cleland Alec (D)	5 9	11 10	Glasgow	10 12 70	Rangers
Collins John (M)	5 8	10 06	Galashiels	30 1 68	Monaco
Dacourt Olivier (M)	5 9	11 00	Montreuil	25 9 74	Strasbourg
Degn Peter (M)	5 10	13 04	Denmark	6 4 77	Aarhus
Delany Dean (G)			Dublin	15 9 80	
Dempsey Gary (M)			Wexford	15 1 81	Trainee
Dunne Richard (D)	6 2	15 10	Dublin	21 9 79	Trainee
Eaton Adam (D)			Wigan	2 5 80	Trainee
Farley Adam (D)			Liverpool	12 1 80	Trainee
Farrelly Gareth (M)	6 1	13 07	Dublin	28 8 75	Aston Villa
Gemmill Scot (M)	5 11	11 06	Paisley	2 1 71	Nottingham F
Gerrard Paul (G)	6 2	14 04	Heywood	22 1 73	Oldham Ath
Grant Tony (M)	5 10	10 10	Liverpool	14 11 74	Trainee
Hibbert Anthony (M)	5 8	11 01	Liverpool	20 2 81	Trainee
Hutchison Don (M)	6 2	12 04	Gateshead	9 5 71	Sheffield U
Jeffers Francis (F)	5 10	10 02	Liverpool	25 1 81	Trainee
Jevons Phillip (M)	5 11	11 07	Liverpool	1 8 79	Trainee
Materazzi Marco (D)	6 4	14 00	Perugia	19 8 73	Perugia
McAlpine Joseph (D)			Glasgow	12 9 81	
McKay Matthew (M)	6 0	11 08	Warrington	21 1 81	Trainee
McLeod Kevin (M)	5 11	11 00	Liverpool	12 9 80	Trainee
Milligan Jamie (F)			Blackpool	3 1 80	Trainee
Myhre Thomas (G)	6 2	13 00	Sarpsborg	16 10 73	Viking
O'Kane John (D)	5 10	12 06	Nottingham	15 11 74	Manchester U
Osman Leon (M)	5 8	9 11	Billinge	17 5 81	Trainee
Oster John (F)	5 9	10 12	Boston	8 12 78	Trainee
Parkinson Joe (M)	6 0	15 05	Eccles	11 6 71	Bournemouth
Phelan Terry (D)	5 8	10 04	Manchester	16 3 67	Chelsea
Pilkington George (D)	5 11	11 00	Rugeley	7 11 81	Trainee
Regan Carl (D)			Liverpool	9 9 80	Trainee
Short Craig (D)	6 0	14 01	Bridlington	25 6 68	Derby Co
Simonsen Steve (G)	6 3	13 02	South Shields	3 4 79	Tranmere R
Unsworth Dave (D)	6 0	15 00	Chorley	16 10 73	Aston Villa

Ward Mitch (M)	5 8	11 13	Sheffield	19 6 71	Sheffield U
Watson Dave (D)	5 11	11 12	Liverpool	20 11 61	Norwich C
Weir David (D)	6 2	13 07	Falkirk	10 5 70	Hearts
Williamson Danny (M)	5 11	13 13	West Ham	5 12 73	West Ham U

League Appearances: Bakayoko, I. 17(6); Ball, M. 36(1); Barmby, N. 20(4); Bilic, S. 4; Branch, M. 1(6); Cadamarteri, D. 11(19); Campbell, K. 8; Cleland, A. 16(2); Collins, J. 19(1); Dacourt, O. 28(2); Degn, P. (4); Dunne, R. 15(1); Farley, A. (1); Farrelly, G. (1); Ferguson, D. 13; Gemmill, S. 7; Grant, T. 13(3); Hutchison, D. 29(4); Jeffers, F. 11(4); Jevons, P. (1); Madar, M. 2; Materazzi, M. 26(1); Milligan, J. (3); Myhre, T. 38; O'Kane, J. 2; Oster, J. 6(3); Short, C. 22; Spencer, J. 2(1); Thomas, T. (1); Tiler, C. 2; Unsworth, D. 33(1); Ward, M. 4(2); Watson, D. 22; Weir, D. 11(3).

Goals – League (42): Campbell 9, Jeffers 6, Bakayoko 4, Cadamarteri 4, Ferguson 4, Ball 3 (3 pens), Barmby 3, Hutchison 3, Dacourt 2, Collins 1, Gemmill 1, Materazzi 1, Unsworth 1.

Worthington Cup (7): Bakayoko 1, Collins 1, Dacourt 1, Ferguson 1, Hutchison 1, Materazzi 1, Watson 1.

FA Cup (6): Bakayoko 2, Barmby 1, Jeffers 1, Oster 1, Unsworth 1.

Ground: Goodison Park, Liverpool L4 4EL. Telephone (0151) 330 2200.

Record attendance: 78,299 v Liverpool, Division 1, 18 September 1948. **Capacity:** 40,200.

Manager: Walter Smith OBE.

Secretary: Michael J. Dunford.

Honours – Football League: Division 1 Champions – 1890–91, 1914–15, 1927–28, 1931–32, 1938–39, 1962–63, 1969–70, 1984–85, 1986–87. Division 2 Champions – 1930–31. **FA Cup:** Winners 1906, 1933, 1966, 1984, 1995. **European Competitions: European Cup-Winners' Cup winners:** 1984–85.

Colours: Royal blue shirts with white trim, white shorts, royal blue stockings.

EXETER CITY DIV. 3

Blake Noel (D)	6 2	14 02	Jamaica	12 1 62	Dundee
Breslan Geoff (M)	5 9	10 02	Torbay	4 6 80	Trainee
Curran Chris (D)	5 11	11 09	Birmingham	17 9 71	Plymouth Arg
Flack Steve (F)	6 1	11 04	Cambridge	29 5 71	Cardiff C
Gale Shaun (D)	6 1	12 02	Reading	8 10 69	Barnet
Gittens Jon (D)	5 11	12 10	Moseley	22 1 64	Torquay U
Holloway Chris (M)	5 10	11 10	Swansea	5 2 80	Trainee
McConnell Barry (F)	5 11	10 03	Exeter	1 1 77	Trainee
Potter Danny (G)	5 11	13 00	Ipswich	18 3 79	Chelsea
Power Graeme (D)	5 11	10 10	Northwick Park	7 3 77	Bristol R
Rees Jason (M)	5 5	10 00	Aberdare	22 12 69	Cambridge U
Richardson Jon (D)	6 1	12 05	Nottingham	29 8 75	Trainee
Rowbotham Darren (F)	5 10	12 13	Cardiff	22 10 66	Shrewsbury T
Wilkinson John (M)	5 8	10 12	Exeter	24 8 79	Trainee

League Appearances: Baddeley, L. 23; Bayes, A. 41; Blake, N. 4(3); Breslan, G. 24(10); Clark, B. 8(2); Crowe, G. 3(6); Curran, C. 30(4); Flack, S. 38(6); Fry, C. 27(5); Gale, S. 21(6); Gardner, J. 23(4); Gittens, J. 44; Holloway, C. 27(7); McConnell, B. 15(7); Potter, D. 5; Power, G. 40; Quailey, B. 8(4); Rees, J. 44; Richardson, J. 39(1); Rowbotham, D. 28(4); Smith, P. (1); Speakman, R. (1); Tosh, P. 8(2); Waugh, W. (7); Wilkinson, J. 6(12).

Goals – League (47): Flack 11, Rowbotham 6, McConnell 5 (1 pen), Breslan 4, Curran 4, Fry 2, Gittens 2, Quailey 2, Richardson 2, Tosh 2, Wilkinson 2, Holloway 1, Rees 1, own goals 3.

Worthington Cup (2): Richardson 2.

FA Cup (8): Flack 2, Rowbotham 2, Gardner 1, Gittens 1, Richardson 1, own goal 1.

Ground: St James Park, Exeter EX4 6PX. Telephone (01392) 254073.
Record attendance: 20,984 v Sunderland, FA Cup 6th rd (replay), 4 March 1931.
Capacity: 10,570.
Manager: Peter Fox.
Secretary: Stuart Brailey.
Honours – Football League: Division 4 Champions – 1989–90. Division 3 (S) Cup: Winners 1934.
Colours: Red and white striped shirts, black shorts, black stockings.

FULHAM   DIV. 1

Name	Ht	Wt	Birthplace	Birth date	Previous club
Arendse Andre (G)	6 4	11 05	Cape Town	27 6 67	Cape Town S
Betsy Kevin (F)	6 1	11 12	Seychelles	20 3 78	Woking
Bracewell Paul (M)	5 9	12 03	Heswall	19 7 62	Sunderland
Brazier Matthew (M)	5 8	11 08	Whipps Cross	2 7 76	QPR
Brevett Rufus (D)	5 8	11 08	Derby	24 9 69	QPR
Brooker Paul (F)	5 8	10 01	Hammersmith	25 11 76	Trainee
Coleman Chris (D)	6 2	14 04	Swansea	10 6 70	Blackburn R
Collins Wayne (M)	6 0	11 07	Manchester	4 3 69	Sheffield W
Cornwall Luke (F)	5 11	11 00	Lambeth	23 7 80	Trainee
Davis Sean (M)	5 11	12 09	Clapham	20 9 79	Trainee
Finnan Steve (M)	5 10	12 00	Limerick	20 4 76	Notts Co
Hayles Barry (F)	5 9	13 00	London	17 4 72	Bristol R
Hayward Steve (M)	5 11	12 07	Walsall	8 9 71	Carlisle U
Horsfield Geoff (F)	6 0	11 07	Barnsley	1 11 73	Halifax T
Hudson Mark (M)			Guilford	30 3 82	Trainee
Hutchinson Thomas (M)			Kingston	23 2 82	
Knight Zatyiah (M)			Solihull	2 5 80	
McAnespie Steve (D)	5 9	10 08	Kilmarnock	1 2 72	Bolton W
McGuckin Ian (D)	6 2	14 02	Middlesbrough	24 4 73	Hartlepool U
Moody Paul (F)	6 3	14 08	Portsmouth	13 6 67	Oxford U
Morgan Simon (D)	5 10	12 05	Birmingham	5 9 66	Leicester C
Neilson Alan (D)	5 11	12 08	Wegburg	26 9 72	Southampton
Peschisolido Paul (F)	5 7	11 02	Canada	25 5 71	WBA
Salako John (F)	5 9	11 10	Nigeria	11 2 69	Bolton W
Selley Ian (M)	5 9	11 05	Chertsey	14 6 74	Arsenal
Smith Neil (M)	5 8	12 02	Lambeth	30 9 71	Gillingham
Symons Kit (D)	6 1	13 07	Basingstoke	8 3 71	Manchester C
Taylor Maik (G)	6 3	13 09	Hildeshein	4 9 71	Southampton
Trollope Paul (M)	6 0	12 01	Swindon	3 6 72	Derby Co
Uhlenbeek Gus (M)	5 10	12 06	Paramaribo	20 8 70	Ipswich T

League Appearances: Albert, P. 12(1); Beardsley, P. 11(2); Betsy, K. 1(6); Bracewell, P. 25(1); Brazier, M. 1(1); Brevett, R. 45; Brooker, P. (1); Coleman, C. 45; Collins, W. 18(3); Cornwall, L. 1(3); Davis, S. 1(5); Finnan, S. 21(1); Hayles, B. 26(4); Hayward, S. 42; Horsfield, G. 26(2); Keller, F. (1); Lawrence, M. 1; Lehmann, D. 16(10); McAnespie, S. 1(2); Moody, P. 2(5); Morgan, S. 32(2); Neilson, A. 3(1); Peschisolido, P. 19(14); Salako, J. 7(3); Scott, R. 2(1); Smith, J. 9; Smith, N. 20(9); Symons, K. 45; Taylor, M. 46; Trollope, P. 17(3); Uhlenbeek, G. 11(12).
Goals – League (79): Horsfield 15, Symons 11, Hayles 8 (1 pen), Peschisolido 7 (1 pen), Morgan 5, Coleman 4, Moody 4 (1 pen), Beardsley 3, Hayward 3 (1 pen), Albert 2, Collins 2, Finnan 2, Lehmann 2, Trollope 2, Betsy 1, Bracewell 1, Brevett 1, Cornwall 1, Neilson 1, Salako 1, Smith J 1, Smith N 1, Uhlenbeek 1.
Worthington Cup (7): Lehmann 2, Beardsley 1, Coleman 1, Morgan 1, Peschisolido 1, Salako 1.
FA Cup (11): Hayward 2, Horsfield 2, Morgan 2, Peschisolido 2 (1 pen), Hayles 1, Lehmann 1, own goal 1.
Ground: Craven Cottage, Stevenage Rd, Fulham, London SW6 6HH. Telephone (0171) 893 8383.

Record attendance: 49,335 v Millwall, Division 2, 8 October 1938. Capacity: 19,250.
Manager: Paul Bracewell.
Secretary: Etain Wist.
Honours – Football League: Division 2 Champions – 1948–49, 1998–99. Division 3 (S) Champions – 1931–32.
Colours: White shirts, red and black trim, black shorts, white stockings red and black trim.

GILLINGHAM — DIV. 2

Asaba Carl (F)	6 2	13 00	London	28 1 73	Reading
Ashby Barry (D)	6 2	13 08	London	2 11 70	Brentford
Bartram Vince (G)	6 2	13 04	Birmingham	8 8 68	Arsenal
Browning Marcus (M)	6 0	12 10	Bristol	22 4 71	Huddersfield T
Bryant Matthew (D)	6 1	13 01	Bristol	21 9 70	Bristol C
Butters Guy (D)	6 3	13 12	Hillingdon	30 10 69	Portsmouth
Carr Darren (D)	6 2	13 07	Bristol	4 9 68	Chesterfield
Edge Roland (D)	5 10	11 10	Gillingham	25 11 78	Trainee
Galloway Mick (M)	5 11	12 05	Nottingham	13 10 74	Notts Co
Hessenthaler Andy (M)	5 7	11 05	Gravesend	17 6 65	Watford
Hodge John (F)	5 7	11 06	Skelmersdale	1 4 69	Walsall
Nosworthy Nayron (M)	6 1	12 07	London	11 10 80	Trainee
Patterson Mark (D)	5 9	12 04	Leeds	13 9 68	Plymouth Arg
Pennock Adrian (M)	6 1	13 05	Ipswich	27 3 71	Bournemouth
Pinnock James (F)	5 9	11 05	Dartford	1 8 78	Trainee
Saunders Mark (M)	5 11	11 12	Reading	23 7 71	Plymouth Arg
Smith Paul (M)	5 11	12 08	East Ham	18 9 71	Brentford
Statham Brian (D)	5 7	11 06	Zimbabwe	21 5 69	Brentford
Taylor Robert (F)	6 1	13 08	Norwich	30 4 71	Brentford

League Appearances: Asaba, C. 40(1); Ashby, B. 38; Bartram, V. 44; Brown, K. 2(2); Browning, M. 1(3); Bryant, M. 16(7); Butler, S. 4(3); Butters, G. 23; Carr, D. 22(8); Dobson, T. 2; Edge, R. 1(7); Elliott, S. 4(1); Galloway, M. 19(6); Hessenthaler, A. 36(3); Hodge, J. 7(27); Lisbie, K. 4(3); Nosworthy, N. (3); Patterson, M. 42; Pennock, A. 39(1); Pinnock, J. (4); Rolling, F. 1; Saunders, M. 28(6); Smith, P. 45; Southall, N. 34(8); Stannard, J. 2; Taylor, R. 43; Williams, P. 9(1).
Goals – League (75): Asaba 20, Taylor 16 (1 pen), Hessenthaler 7, Smith 6 (1 pen), Lisbie 4, Saunders 4, Southall 4, Butters 3, Galloway 3, Carr 2, Patterson 2, Ashby 1, Hodge 1, Williams 1, own goal 1.
Worthington Cup (0).
FA Cup (0).
Ground: Priestfield Stadium, Gillingham ME7 4DD. Telephone (01634) 851854, 576828.
Record attendance: 23,002 v QPR, FA Cup 3rd rd 10 January 1948. Capacity: 10,600.
Manager: Peter Taylor.
Secretary: Mrs G. E. Poynter.
Honours – Football League: Division 4 Champions – 1963–64.
Colours: Blue and black.

GRIMSBY TOWN — DIV. 1

Ashcroft Lee (F)	5 9	12 00	Preston	7 9 72	Preston NE
Black Kingsley (M)	5 10	12 00	Luton	22 6 68	Nottingham F
Bloomer Matthew (D)	6 0	12 00	Cleethorpes	3 11 78	Trainee
Buckley Adam (M)	5 9	11 00	Nottingham	2 8 79	
Burnett Wayne (M)	5 10	12 00	Lambeth	4 9 71	Huddersfield T

Butterfield Danny (D)	5 9	11 00	Boston	21 11 79	Trainee
Clare Daryl (F)	5 9	12 00	Jersey	1 8 78	Trainee
Coldicott Stacy (M)	5 8	12 00	Redditch	29 4 74	WBA
Croudson Steve (G)	6 0	12 00	Grimsby	14 9 79	Trainee
Donovan Kevin (F)	5 8	12 12	Halifax	17 12 71	WBA
Gallimore Tony (D)	5 11	13 00	Crewe	21 2 72	Carlisle U
Groves Paul (M)	5 11	13 00	Derby	28 2 66	WBA
Handyside Peter (D)	6 1	13 03	Dumfries	31 7 74	Trainee
Lester Jack (F)	5 10	11 10	Sheffield	8 10 75	Trainee
Lever Mark (D)	6 3	14 00	Beverley	29 3 70	Trainee
Livingstone Steve (F)	6 1	14 00	Middlesbrough	8 9 68	Chelsea
Love Andrew (G)	6 1	14 00	Grimsby	28 3 79	Trainee
McDermott John (D)	5 7	11 02	Middlesbrough	3 2 69	Trainee
McKenzie Mat (D)	6 0	13 00	Sheffield	3 4 79	Dunkerque
Oswin Matthew (M)			Grimsby	2 10 79	Trainee
Smith David (M)	5 8	11 04	Stonehouse	29 3 68	WBA
Smith Richard (D)	6 0	13 07	Lutterworth	3 10 70	Leicester C

League Appearances: Ashcroft, L. 21(6); Black, K. 29(13); Bloomer, M. (4); Buckley, A. (2); Burnett, W. 15(5); Butterfield, D. 9(3); Chapman, B. (1); Clare, D. 7(15); Coldicott, S. 35(2); Croudson, S. 2; Davison, A. 35; Dobbin, J. (4); Donovan, K. 27(1); Gallimore, T. 43; Groves, P. 46; Handyside, P. 30(1); Lester, J. 26(7); Lever, M. 15(9); Livingstone, S. 15(8); Love, A. 9; McDermott, J. 37; Nogan, L. 30(8); Smith, D. 30(1); Smith, R. 29(1); Widdrington, T. 16(10).

Goals – League (40): Groves 14 (4 pens), Smith D 5, Black 4, Lester 4, Ashcroft 3, Clare 3, Burnett 2, Handyside 2, Nogan 2, Widdrington 1.

Worthington Cup (4): Ashcroft 1, Clare 1, Groves 1, Nogan 1.

FA Cup (1): McDermott 1.

Ground: Blundell Park, Cleethorpes, North-East Lincolnshire DN35 7PY. Telephone (01472) 605050.

Record attendance: 31,651 v Wolverhampton W, FA Cup 5th rd, 20 February 1937.

Capacity: 10,033.

Manager: Alan Buckley.

Secretary: Ian Fleming.

Honours – Football League: Division 2 Champions – 1900–01, 1933–34. Division 3 (N) Champions – 1925–26, 1955–56. Division 3 Champions – 1979–80. Division 4 Champions – 1971-72. **League Group Cup:** Winners 1981–82. **Auto Windscreens Shield:** Winners 1997–98.

Colours: Black and white striped shirts, black shorts, black stockings.

HALIFAX TOWN DIV. 3

Butler Peter (M)	5 9	11 01	Halifax	27 8 66	WBA
Jackson Justin (F)	5 11	11 06	Nottingham	10 12 74	Notts Co
Murphy Jamie (D)	6 1	13 00	Manchester	25 2 73	Cambridge U
Murphy Stephen (M)	5 11	11 06	Dublin	5 4 78	Huddersfield T
Newton Chris (M)	6 0	11 02	Leeds	5 11 79	Huddersfield T
O'Regan Kieran (M)	5 8	10 12	Cork	9 11 63	WBA
Paterson Jamie (M)	5 3	10 02	Dumfries	26 4 73	Scunthorpe U
Power Lee (F)	6 0	11 10	Lewisham	30 6 72	Plymouth Arg
Sertori Mark (D)	6 2	14 02	Manchester	1 9 67	Scunthorpe U
Stoneman Paul (D)	6 0	12 07	Whitley Bay	26 2 73	Blackpool

League Appearances: Bradshaw, M. 41; Brown, J. 32(8); Butler, P. 33; Carter, T. 9(1); Duerden, I. 1(1); Etherington, C. 4; Grant, G. (3); Guinan, S. 12; Hanson, D. 19(12); Horsfield, G. 10; Hulme, K. 30; Jackson, J. 16; Lucas, R. 29(7); Martin, L. 37; Murphy, J. 21(2); Murphy, S. 10(2); Newton, C. 8(6); O'Regan, K. 15(4); Paterson, J. 19(5); Power, L. 14(4); Sertori, M. 39(1); Stansfield, J. 12; Stoneman, P. 40; Thackeray, A. 37(1); Williams, M. 18(6).

Goals – League (58): Paterson 10 (1 pen), Horsfield 7, Williams 6, Thackeray 5, Bradshaw 4, Hulme 4, Jackson 4, Power 4, Stoneman 4 (1 pen), Guinan 2, Hanson 2, O'Regan 2, Butler 1, Murphy J 1, Newton 1, Stansfield 1.
Worthington Cup (4): Hanson 2, Horsfield 1, Paterson 1.
FA Cup (0).
Ground: The Shay Stadium, Shaw Hill, Halifax HX1 2YS. Telephone Halifax (01422) 345543.
Record attendance: 36,885 v Tottenham H, FA Cup 5th rd, 15 February 1953.
Capacity: 9,900.
Manager: Mark Lillis.
Secretary: Hilary Molyneux Horrocks.
Honours – Football League: Division 3 (N)—Runners-up 1934–35; Division 4: Runners-up 1968–69. **Vauxhall Conference:** Champions 1997–98.
Colours: Blue shirts, white trim, blue shorts, white trim, white stockings.

HARTLEPOOL UNITED DIV. 3

Barron Michael (D)	5 11	11 06	Lumley	22 12 74	Middlesbrough
Briggs John (M)	5 11	10 10	Stockton	9 11 79	Trainee
Clark Ian (M)	5 10	11 02	Stockton	23 10 74	Doncaster R
Di Lella Gus (M)	5 9	11 09	Buenos Aires	6 10 73	
Dibble Andy (G)	6 3	16 10	Cwmbran	8 5 65	Middlesbrough
Downey Glen (D)	6 1	12 07	Newcastle	20 9 78	
Dunwell Michael (F)	5 11	12 02	Stockton	6 1 80	Trainee
Evans Nicky (M)	5 8	12 05	Carmarthen	12 5 80	Trainee
Freestone Chris (F)	5 10	12 00	Nottingham	4 9 71	Northampton T
Hollund Martin (G)	6 0	12 05	Stord	11 8 74	Brann
Hughes Danny (M)	5 10	13 00	Bangor	13 2 80	Trainee
Ingram Denny (D)	5 11	12 02	Sunderland	27 6 76	Trainee
Jones Gary (F)	6 1	13 00	Huddersfield	6 4 69	Notts Co
Knowles Darren (D)	5 6	11 01	Sheffield	8 10 70	Scarborough
Lake Craig (D)	5 11	10 02	Stockton	10 2 80	Trainee
Lee Graeme (D)	6 2	13 00	Middlesbrough	31 5 78	Trainee
McKinnon Rob (D)	5 11	11 01	Glasgow	31 7 66	Hearts
Midgley Craig (F)	5 7	11 00	Bradford	24 5 76	Bradford C
Miller Tommy (D)	6 1	12 00	Easington	8 1 79	Trainee
Smith Jeff (M)	5 10	11 01	Middlesbrough	28 6 80	Trainee
Stephenson Paul (F)	5 10	12 07	Wallsend	2 1 68	York C
Strodder Gary (D)	6 2	13 04	Mirfield	1 4 65	Notts Co
Westwood Chris (D)	5 11	12 10	Dudley	13 2 77	Wolverhampton W

League Appearances: Baker, P. 3(10); Barron, M. 38; Beardsley, P. 22; Beech, C. 16; Brightwell, S. 8(9); Clark, I. 36(3); Davies, L. 2(1); Di Lella, G. 18(5); Dunwell, M. (1); Elliott, S. 5; Evans, N. (1); Freestone, C. 9(1); Heckingbottom, P. 5; Hollund, M. 41; Howard, S. 25(3); Hughes, D. 6(2); Hutt, S. 2(2); Ingram, D. 37(1); Irvine, S. 10(8); Jones, G. 12; Knowles, D. 46; Lee, G. 23(1); McDonald, C. 5; McGuckin, I. 8; McKinnon, R. 7; Midgley, C. 26(3); Miller, T. 29(5); Miotto, S. 5; Pemberton, M. (4); Rush, D. 5(5); Smith, J. 2(1); Stephenson, P. 24(3); Stokoe, G. 15(5); Strodder, G. 13; Westwood, C. 3(1).
Goals – League (52): Beech 9, Midgley 7 (1 pen), Howard 5, Ingram 4 (4 pens), Miller 4, Freestone 3 (1 pen), Lee 3, Baker 2, Beardsley 2, Clark 2, Di Lella 2, Stephenson 2, Barron 1, Brightwell 1, Heckingbottom 1, Irvine 1, Jones 1, own goals 2.
Worthington Cup (0).
FA Cup (4): Howard 2, Midgley 1, Miller 1.
Ground: Victoria Park, Clarence Road, Hartlepool TS24 8BZ. Telephone (01429) 272584.
Record attendance: 17,426 v Manchester U, FA Cup 3rd rd, 5 January 1957.
Capacity: 7229.

Manager: Chris Turner.
Secretary: Maureen Smith.
Honours – Nil.
Colours: Royal blue and white stripes.

HUDDERSFIELD TOWN DIV. 1

Allison Wayne (F)	6 0	14 07	Huddersfield	16 10 68	Swindon T
Armstrong Craig (D)	5 11	12 10	South Shields	23 5 75	Nottingham F
Baldry Simon (M)	5 11	12 00	Huddersfield	12 2 76	Trainee
Beech Chris (M)	5 9	11 03	Blackpool	16 9 74	Hartlepool U
Beresford David (F)	5 5	11 00	Manchester	11 11 76	Oldham Ath
Brennan Damien (D)			Dublin	30 8 80	Belvedere
Collins Sam (D)	6 2	14 04	Pontefract	5 6 77	Trainee
Crossley Ryan (D)	6 0	12 00	Halifax	23 7 80	Trainee
Cuss Paul (G)	6 1	13 07	Minden	19 4 79	Trainee
Dalton Paul (F)	6 0	13 00	Middlesbrough	25 4 67	Plymouth Arg
Dyson Jon (D)	6 0	12 12	Mirfield	18 12 71	School
Edmondson Darren (D)	6 0	12 10	Ulverston	4 11 71	Carlisle U
Edwards Rob (M)	5 8	12 04	Manchester	23 2 70	Crewe Alex
Facey Delroy (F)	5 10	14 10	Huddersfield	22 4 80	Trainee
Gray Kevin (D)	5 11	14 02	Sheffield	7 1 72	Mansfield T
Heary Thomas (M)	5 10	10 06	Dublin	14 2 78	Trainee
Jenkins Steve (D)	6 0	12 08	Merthyr	16 7 72	Swansea C
Johnson Grant (M)	5 11	11 03	Dundee	24 3 72	Dundee U
Lawson Ian (F)	5 11	11 00	Huddersfield	4 11 77	Trainee
Richardson Lee J (M)	5 10	12 07	Halifax	12 3 69	Oldham Ath
Schofield Danny (F)	5 10	11 02	Doncaster	10 4 80	
Scott Paul (D)	6 0	11 11	Wakefield	5 11 79	Trainee
Stewart Marcus (F)	5 10	11 08	Bristol	7 11 72	Bristol R
Thornley Ben (F)	5 7	11 07	Bury	21 4 75	Manchester U
Vaesen Nico (G)	6 4	13 01	Hasselt	28 9 69	Aalst
Vincent Jamie (D)	5 10	11 09	London	18 6 75	Bournemouth

League Appearances: Allison, W. 44; Armstrong, C. 13; Baldry, S. 8(5); Barnes, P. 2(13); Beech, C. 13(4); Beresford, D. 13(6); Browning, M. 2(4); Collins, S. 22(1); Cowan, T. 5; Dalton, P. 7(2); Dyson, J. 10(4); Edmondson, D. 1(2); Edwards, R. 45; Facey, D. 5(15); Francis, S. 3; Gray, K. 28(6); Hamilton, D. 10; Heary, T. 3; Hessey, S. 7(3); Horne, B. 20; Jackson, M. 5; Jenkins, S. 36; Johnson, G. 36; Lawson, I. 2(4); Mattis, D. (2); Morrison, A. 12; Phillips, D. 15(8); Richardson, L. 13(2); Schofield, D. 1; Stewart, M. 43; Thornley, B. 32(3); Vaesen, N. 43; Vincent, J. 7.

Goals – League (62): Stewart 22 (4 pens), Allison 9, Johnson 4, Thornley 4, Dalton 3, Facey 3, Beech 2, Beresford 2, Edwards 2, Lawson 2, Armstrong 1, Barnes 1, Dyson 1, Gray 1, Hamilton 1, Horne 1, Jenkins 1, Phillips 1, own goal 1.

Worthington Cup (6): Allison 2, Stewart 2, Dalton 1 (pen), Johnson 1.

FA Cup (7): Allison 2, Beech 2, Stewart 2, Thornley 1.

Ground: The Alfred McAlpine Stadium, Leeds Road, Huddersfield HD1 6PX. Telephone (01484) 484100.

Record attendance: 67,037 v Arsenal, FA Cup 6th rd, 27 February 1932. **Capacity:** 24,000.

Manager: Steve Bruce.

Secretary: Ann Hough.

Honours – Football League: Division 1 Champions – 1923–24, 1924–25, 1925–26. Division 2 Champions – 1969–70. Division 4 Champions – 1969–70. **FA Cup winners** 1922.

Colours: Blue and white striped shirts, white shorts, white stockings with blue trim.

HULL CITY   DIV. 3

Alcide Colin (F)	6 2	13 11	Huddersfield	14 4 72	Lincoln C
Baker Matthew (G)	6 0	12 08	Claro	18 12 79	Trainee
Bolder Adam (M)	5 9	10 08	Hull	25 10 80	Trainee
Brabin Gary (M)	5 11	14 08	Liverpool	9 12 70	Blackpool
Brown David (F)	5 10	12 08	Bolton	2 10 78	Manchester U
D'Auria David (M)	5 8	12 00	Swansea	26 3 70	Scunthorpe U
Edwards Michael (D)	6 0	12 10	North Ferriby	25 4 80	Trainee
Ellington Lee (F)	5 10	11 07	Bradford	3 7 80	Trainee
French Jon (M)	5 10	10 10	Bristol	25 9 76	Bristol R
Greaves Mark (D)	6 1	13 00	Hull	22 1 75	Brigg Town
Hateley Mark (F)	6 2	13 00	Liverpool	7 11 61	Rangers
Hawes Steve (M)	5 8	12 04	High Wycombe	17 7 78	Sheffield U
Hocking Matthew (D)	5 11	12 00	Boston	30 1 78	Sheffield U
Joyce Warren (M)	5 9	12 01	Oldham	20 1 65	Burnley
Mann Neil (M)	5 10	12 01	Nottingham	19 11 72	Grantham T
Morley Ben (D)	5 9	10 11	Hull	22 12 80	Trainee
Oakes Andy (G)			Crewe	11 1 77	Bury
Perry Jason (D)	5 11	11 12	Caerphilly	2 4 70	Lincoln C
Swales Steve (D)	5 9	10 03	Scarborough	26 12 73	Reading
Tucker Dexter (F)	6 1	12 02	Pontefract	22 9 79	Trainee
Whitney Jon (D)	5 10	13 08	Nantwich	23 12 70	Lincoln C
Whittle Justin (D)	6 1	13 09	Derby	18 3 71	Stoke C
Whitworth Neil (D)	6 0	12 13	Ince	12 4 72	Wigan Ath
Williams Gareth (M)	6 0	12 02	Newport (IW)	12 3 67	Scarborough

League Appearances: Alcide, C. 17; Bolder, A. (1); Bonner, M. 1; Brabin, G. 21; Brown, D. 38(4); D'Auria, D. 42; Darby, D. 4(4); Dewhurst, R. 4(4); Dudley, C. 4(3); Edwards, M. 28(2); Ellington, L. 3(3); Faulconbridge, C. 4(6); French, J. 9(6); Gage, K. 2(1); Gibson, P. 4; Greaves, M. 18(7); Harrison, G. 8; Hateley, M. 8(4); Hawes, S. 18(1); Hocking, M. 24(2); Joyce, W. 28(1); Mann, N. 16(4); McGinty, B. 22(10); Morley, B. 1(11); Oakes, A. 19; Peacock, R. 13(1); Perry, J. 7(1); Rioch, G. 10(3); Saville, A. 3; Swales, S. 20(2); Whitney, J. 21; Whittle, J. 24; Whitworth, N. 18; Williams, G. 24(1); Wilson, S. 23.

Goals – League (44): Brown 11, Brabin 4, D'Auria 4 (1 pen), McGinty 4, Alcide 3, Hateley 3 (2 pens), Dudley 2, Joyce 2, Peacock 2, Whitworth 2, Bonner 1, Hocking 1, Mann 1, Whitney 1, Whittle 1, Williams 1, own goal 1.

Worthington Cup (5): Brown 3, McGinty 1, Rioch 1 (pen).

FA Cup (4): Dewhurst 1, McGinty 1, Morley 1, Rioch 1.

Ground: Boothferry Park, Hull HU4 6EU. Telephone (01482) 575263.

Record attendance: 55,019 v Manchester U, FA Cup 6th rd, 26 February 1949.

Capacity: 12,996.

Manager: Warren Joyce.

Assistant Secretary: Jackie Bell.

Honours – Football League: Division 3 (N) Champions – 1932–33, 1948–49. Division 3 Champions – 1965–66.

Colours: Black and amber striped shirts, black shorts, amber stockings with white tops.

IPSWICH TOWN   DIV. 1

Bramble Titus (D)	6 1	13 10	Ipswich	21 7 81	Trainee
Brown Wayne (D)	6 0	12 00	Barking	20 8 77	Trainee
Clapham Jamie (D)	5 9	11 08	Lincoln	7 12 75	Tottenham H
Cowell Claydon (M)			Colchester	3 9 80	Arsenal
Dyer Kieron (M)	5 8	10 01	Ipswich	29 12 78	Trainee

Friars Sean (F)	5 8	10 07	Derry	15 5 79	Liverpool
Holland Matt (M)	5 10	11 10	Bury	11 4 74	Bournemouth
Holster Marco (M)	5 6	10 11	Weesp	4 12 71	Heracles*
Inglis Kevin (M)			Glasgow	26 8 80	Trainee
Johnson David (F)	5 6	12 00	Kingston, Jam	15 8 76	Bury
Keeble Chris (M)	5 9	11 00	Colchester	17 9 78	Trainee
Kennedy John (D)	5 8	10 07	Cambridge	19 8 78	Trainee
Logan Richard (F)	6 0	12 05	Bury St Edmunds	4 1 82	Trainee
Magilton Jim (M)	6 0	14 00	Belfast	6 5 69	Sheffield W
Midgley Neil (F)	5 11	11 08	Cambridge	21 10 78	Trainee
Mowbray Tony (D)	6 1	13 07	Saltburn	22 11 63	Celtic
Naylor Richard (F)	6 0	13 07	Leeds	28 2 77	Trainee
Niven Stuart (M)	5 11	12 08	Glasgow	24 12 78	Trainee
Scowcroft James (F)	6 2	14 02	Bury St Edmunds	15 11 75	Trainee
Stockwell Mick (M)	5 7	11 07	Chelmsford	14 2 65	Apprentice
Tanner Adam (M)	6 0	13 00	Maldon	25 10 73	Trainee
Thetis Manuel (D)	6 3	14 13	France	5 11 71	Sevilla
Venus Mark (D)	6 1	12 12	Hartlepool	6 4 67	Wolverhampton W
Wilnis Fabian (D)	5 8	12 06	Paramaribo	23 8 70	De Graafschap
Wright Richard (G)	6 2	13 07	Ipswich	5 11 77	Trainee

League Appearances: Abou, S. 5; Bramble, T. 2(2); Brown, W. (1); Clapham, J. 45(1); Cundy, J. 1(3); Dyer, K. 36(1); Harewood, M. 5(1); Hodges, L. (4); Holland, M. 46; Holster, M. 1(9); Hunt, J. 2(4); Johnson, D. 41(1); Kennedy, J. 6(1); Logan, R. (2); Magilton, J. 19; Mathie, A. 2(6); Mowbray, T. 40; Naylor, R. 10(20); Petta, B. 26(6); Scowcroft, J. 29(3); Sonner, D. (4); Stockwell, M. 23(7); Tanner, A. 13(6); Taricco, M. 16; Thetis, M. 29(2); Venus, M. 44; Vernazza, P. 2; Wilnis, F. 17(1); Wright, R. 46.

Goals – League (69): Johnson 13, Scowcroft 13 (1 pen), Venus 9 (6 pens), Dyer 5, Holland 5, Naylor 5, Clapham 3, Magilton 3, Mowbray 2, Petta 2, Stockwell 2, Thetis 2, Abou 1, Harewood 1, Mathie 1, Taricco 1, Wilnis 1.

Worthington Cup (10): Holland 2, Johnson 1, Mason 1, Mathie 1, Scowcroft 1, Stockwell 1, Taricco 1, Thetis 1, own goal 1.

FA Cup (1): own goal 1.

Ground: Portman Road, Ipswich, Suffolk IP1 2DA. Telephone (01473) 400500.

Record attendance: 38,010 v Leeds U, FA Cup 6th rd, 8 March 1975. **Capacity:** 22,600.

Manager: George Burley.

Secretary: David C. Rose.

Honours – Football League: Division 1 Champions – 1961–62. Division 2 Champions – 1960–61, 1967–68, 1991–92. Division 3 (S) Champions – 1953–54, 1956–57. **FA Cup:** Winners 1977–78. **European Competitions: UEFA Cup winners:** 1980–81.

Colours: Blue shirts, white shorts, blue stockings.

LEEDS UNITED   FA PREMIERSHIP

Batty David (M)	5 8	11 10	Leeds	2 12 68	Newcastle U
Bowyer Lee (M)	5 9	10 09	London	3 1 77	Charlton Ath
Boyle Wesley (F)	5 10	11 01	Portadown	30 3 79	Trainee
Cawley Alan (M)	6 2	10 01	Sligo	3 1 82	Belvedere
Crawford Dale (F)	5 9	11 01	Sunderland	14 9 81	Trainee
Dixon Kevin (M)	5 9	12 03	Easington	27 6 80	Trainee
Evans Gareth (D)	6 0	11 11	Leeds	15 2 81	Trainee
Evans Kevin (D)	6 2	12 10	Carmarthen	16 12 80	Trainee
Feeney Warren (F)	5 10	11 00	Belfast	17 1 81	Trainee
Granville Danny (D)	6 1	12 11	Islington	19 1 75	Chelsea
Haaland Alf-Inge (M)	6 1	12 06	Stavanger	23 11 72	Nottingham F
Hackworth Tony (F)	6 1	13 07	Durham	19 5 80	Trainee
Halle Gunnar (D)	6 0	12 07	Larvik	11 8 65	Oldham Ath

Name	Ht	Wt	Birthplace	Birthdate	Signed from
Harte Ian (D)	6 0	12 04	Drogheda	31 8 77	Trainee
Hasselbaink Jimmy Floyd (F)	6 0	13 08	Paramaribo	27 3 72	Boavista
Hiden Martin (D)	6 1	12 00	Stainz	11 3 73	Rapid Vienna
Hopkin David (M)	6 1	13 13	Greenock	21 8 70	Crystal Palace
Jackson Mark (D)	6 0	12 10	Barnsley	30 9 77	Trainee
Jones Matthew (M)	5 11	11 09	Llanelli	1 9 80	Trainee
Kelly Gary (D)	5 8	11 00	Drogheda	9 7 74	Home Farm
Kennedy Alan (F)	5 8	11 00	Dublin	17 10 81	Trainee
Kewell Harry (F)	6 0	12 10	Sydney	22 9 78	NSW Academy
Knarvik Tommy (M)	5 8	11 00	Bergen	1 11 79	Skjerjard
Lagan Brian (M)	5 5	10 00	Magherafelt	3 10 80	Trainee
Lanns Jason (D)	5 8	10 07	Birmingham	2 11 81	Birmingham C
Lilley Derek (F)	5 10	12 08	Paisley	9 2 74	Morton
Loughran Anthony (D)	6 0	11 12	Liverpool	11 11 81	Trainee
Lynch Damien (D)	5 10	11 00	Dublin	31 7 79	
Martin Alan (D)	5 10	11 05	Dublin	21 11 81	Trainee
Martyn Nigel (G)	6 2	14 10	St Austell	11 8 66	Crystal Palace
Matthews Lee (F)	6 2	13 05	Middlesbrough	6 1 79	Trainee
Maybury Alan (D)	5 9	10 04	Dublin	8 8 78	Trainee
McChrystal Brian (D)	6 3	13 01	Dundalk	20 1 81	Bellurgan U
McPhail Stephen (M)	5 10	11 06	London	9 12 79	Trainee
Molenaar Robert (D)	6 2	14 09	Zaandam	27 2 69	Volendam
O'Brien Carl (M)	5 9	10 10	Dublin	6 11 81	Trainee
Porter Graeme (F)	5 6	10 00	Liverpool	24 11 81	Trainee
Radebe Lucas (D)	6 1	12 04	Johannesburg	12 4 69	Kaiser Chiefs
Ribeiro Bruno (M)	5 8	12 07	Setubal	22 10 75	Setubal
Robertson David (D)	5 11	13 01	Aberdeen	17 10 68	Rangers
Robinson Paul (G)	6 4	14 04	Beverley	15 10 79	Trainee
Santos Nuno (G)	6 1	13 00	Setubal	20 4 73	Setubal
Sharpe Lee (F)	6 0	12 10	Halesowen	27 5 71	Sampdoria
Shepherd Paul (D)	5 11	12 00	Leeds	17 11 77	Trainee
Singh Harpal (F)	5 7	10 02	Bradford	15 9 81	Trainee
Smith Alan (F)	5 9	10 13	Leeds	28 10 80	Trainee
Watson Simon (M)	5 9	10 00	Strabane	22 9 80	Trainee
Wetherall David (D)	6 4	13 05	Sheffield	14 3 71	Sheffield W
Wijnhard Clyde (F)	5 11	13 06	Paramaribo	9 11 73	Willem II
Woodgate Jonathan (D)	6 2	12 09	Middlesbrough	22 1 80	
Wright Andy (M)	5 8	9 06	Leeds	21 10 78	Trainee

League Appearances: Batty, D. 10; Bowyer, L. 35; Granville, D. 7(2); Haaland, A. 24(5); Halle, G. 14(3); Harte, I. 34(1); Hasselbaink, J. 36; Hiden, M. 14; Hopkin, D. 32(2); Jones, M. 3(5); Kewell, H. 36(2); Korsten, W. 4(3); Lilley, D. (2); Martyn, N. 34; McPhail, S. 11(6); Molenaar, R. 17; Radebe, L. 29; Ribeiro, B. 7(6); Robinson, P. 4(1); Sharpe, L. 2(2); Smith, A. 15(7); Wetherall, D. 14(7); Wijnhard, C. 11(7); Woodgate, J. 25.

Goals – League (62): Hasselbaink 18, Bowyer 9, Smith 7, Kewell 6, Harte 4 (1 pen), Hopkin 4, Wijnhard 3, Halle 2, Korsten 2, Molenaar 2, Woodgate 2, Haaland 1, Ribeiro 1, own goal 1.

Worthington Cup (2): Kewell 2.

FA Cup (9): Harte 2, Smith 2, Hasselbaink 1, Kewell 1, Riberio 1, Wetherall 1, Wijnhard 1.

Ground: Elland Road, Leeds LS11 0ES. Telephone (0113) 2266000.

Record attendance: 57,892 v Sunderland, FA Cup 5th rd (replay), 15 March 1967.

Capacity: 40,204.

Manager: David O'Leary.

Secretary: Ian Silvester.

Honours – Football League: Division 1 Champions – 1968–69, 1973–74, 1991–92. Division 2 Champions – 1923–24, 1963–64, 1989–90. **FA Cup:** Winners 1972. **Football League Cup:** Winners 1967–68. **European Competitions: European Fairs Cup winners:** 1967–68, 1970–71.
Colours: All white, yellow and blue trim.

LEICESTER CITY   FA PREMIERSHIP

Name	Ht	Wt	Birthplace	Born	Previous club
Allen Lee (F)	5 10	10 08	Islington	12 3 79	
Arphexad Pegguy (G)	6 2	13 07	Abymes	18 5 73	Lens
Boateng Daniel (M)			London	14 11 80	Arsenal
Branston Guy (D)	6 1	13 11	Leicester	9 1 79	
Brennan Karl (M)	5 6	11 00	Leicester	19 3 81	Trainee
Campbell Stuart (M)	5 10	10 08	Corby	9 12 77	Trainee
Cottee Tony (F)	5 8	11 05	West Ham	11 7 65	West Ham U
Dudfield Lawrie (F)	6 0	11 05	London	7 5 80	Kettering T
Elliott Matt (D)	6 3	14 05	Wandsworth	1 11 68	Oxford U
Emerson Paul (D)	6 1	11 06	Newtonards	29 8 78	Trainee
Fenton Graham (F)	5 10	11 09	Wallsend	22 5 74	Blackburn R
Fox Martin (D)	5 8	11 02	Sutton-in-Ashfield	21 4 79	Trainee
Goodwin Tommy (D)	6 0	12 02	Leicester	8 11 79	Trainee
Gunnlaugsson Arnar (F)	5 10	11 06	Akranes	6 3 73	Bolton W
Guppy Steve (M)	5 11	12 00	Winchester	29 3 69	Port Vale
Heskey Emile (F)	6 2	13 12	Leicester	11 1 78	Trainee
Hodges John (G)	6 0	11 05	Leicester	22 1 80	Trainee
Impey Andrew (M)	5 8	11 06	Hammersmith	13 9 71	West Ham U
Izzet Muzzy (M)	5 10	11 02	Mile End	31 10 74	Chelsea
Lennon Neil (M)	5 9	13 02	Lurgan	25 6 71	Crewe Alex
McCann Tim (M)	5 9	11 05	Belfast	22 3 80	Trainee
Oakes Stefan (M)	5 11	12 04	Leicester	6 9 78	Trainee
Savage Robbie (M)	5 11	10 07	Wrexham	18 10 74	Crewe Alex
Sinclair Frank (D)	5 10	12 07	Lambeth	3 12 71	Chelsea
Taggart Gerry (D)	6 2	14 00	Belfast	18 10 70	Bolton W
Thomas Danny (D)	5 7	10 07	Leamington Spa	1 5 81	Trainee
Ullathorne Robert (D)	5 8	10 10	Wakefield	11 10 71	Osasuna
Walsh Steve (D)	6 3	14 09	Fulwood	3 11 64	Wigan Ath
Wilson Stuart (F)	5 8	9 12	Leicester	16 9 77	Trainee
Zagorakis Theo (M)	5 9	11 08	Kavala	27 10 71	PAOK Salonika

League Appearances: Arphexad, P. 2(2); Campbell, S. 1(11); Cottee, T. 29(2); Elliott, M. 37; Fenton, G. 3(6); Gunnlaugsson, A. 5(4); Guppy, S. 38; Heskey, E. 29(1); Impey, A. 17(1); Izzet, M. 31; Kamark, P. 15(4); Keller, K. 36; Lennon, N. 37; Marshall, I. 6(4); Miller, C. 1(3); Oakes, S. 2(1); Parker, G. 2(5); Savage, R. 29(5); Sinclair, F. 30(1); Taggart, G. 9(6); Ullathorne, R. 25; Walsh, S. 17(5); Wilson, S. 1(8); Zagorakis, T. 16(3).
Goals – League (40): Cottee 10, Heskey 6, Izzet 5, Guppy 4, Elliott 3 (1 pen), Marshall 3, Walsh 3, Lennon 1, Savage 1, Sinclair 1, Zagorakis 1, own goals 2.
Worthington Cup (14): Cottee 5, Heskey 3, Fenton 1, Izzet 1, Lennon 1, Parker 1 (pen), Taggart 1, Wilson 1.
FA Cup (4): Cottee 1, Guppy 1, Sinclair 1, Ullathorne 1.
Ground: City Stadium, Filbert St, Leicester LE2 7FL. Telephone (0116) 2915000.
Record attendance: 47,298 v Tottenham H, FA Cup 5th rd, 18 February 1928.
Capacity: 22,000.
Manager: Martin O'Neill.
Football Secretary: Andrew Neville.
Honours – Football League: Division 2 Champions – 1924–25, 1936–37, 1953–54, 1956–57, 1970–71, 1979–80. **Football League Cup:** Winners 1964, 1997.
Colours: Royal blue shirts, white shorts, blue stockings.

LEYTON ORIENT

Ampadu Kwame (M)	5 10	11 10	Bradford	20 12 70	Swansea C
Baker Joe (F)	5 8	10 07	London	9 4 77	Charlton Ath
Beall Billy (M)	5 6	12 00	Enfield	4 12 77	Cambridge U
Brown Daniel (M)	6 0	12 06	Bethnal Green	12 9 80	Trainee
Canham Scott (M)	5 10	11 08	London	5 11 74	Brentford
Clark Simon (D)	6 0	12 10	Boston	12 3 67	Peterborough U
Hicks Stuart (D)	6 1	13 03	Peterborough	30 5 67	Scarborough
Inglethorpe Alex (M)	5 11	11 04	Epsom	14 11 71	Watford
Joseph Matt (D)	5 7	10 02	Bethnal Green	30 9 72	Cambridge U
Joseph Roger (D)	5 11	11 10	Paddington	24 12 65	WBA
Ling Martin (M)	5 7	10 08	West Ham	15 7 66	Swindon T
Lockwood Matt (D)	5 9	10 12	Rochford	17 10 76	Bristol R
Martin John (M)	5 5	10 00	Bethnal Green	15 7 81	
Richards Tony (F)	6 0	13 06	Newham	17 9 73	Cambridge U
Smith Dean (D)	6 0	13 00	West Bromwich	19 3 71	Hereford U
Walschaerts Wim (M)	5 11	12 00	Antwerp	5 11 72	FC Tielen
Watts Steve (F)	6 1	13 00	Lambeth	11 7 76	Fisher Ath

League Appearances: Ampadu, K. 26(3); Baker, J. (4); Barrett, S. 20; Beall, B. 21(2); Canham, S. 2(6); Clark, S. 40; Curran, D. (1); Downer, S. (1); Finney, S. 2(3); Griffiths, C. 21(3); Harris, J. 1(1); Hicks, S. 29; Inglethorpe, A. 15(8); Joseph, M. 34; Joseph, R. 13(11); Ling, M. 44; Lockwood, M. 36(1); MacKenzie, C. 26; Martin, J. 1; Maskell, C. 8(7); McCormick, S. 1(3); McDougald, J. 3(5); Morrison, D. 7(16); Omoyimni, E. 3(1); Raynor, P. 1(4); Reinelt, R. 2(5); Richards, T. 28(1); Simba, A. 19(5); Smith, D. 37; Stimson, M. 2; Walschaerts, W. 44; Warren, M. 10; Watts, S. 10(18).

Goals – League (68): Simba 10, Smith 9 (3 pens), Griffiths 8 (3 pens), Richards 7, Watts 6, Clark 4, Inglethorpe 4, Ling 4, Lockwood 3, Morrison 3, Walschaerts 3, Beall 2, Ampadu 1, Harris 1, Omoyimni 1, own goals 2.

Worthington Cup (4): Inglethorpe 1, Reinelt 1, Richards 1, Warren 1.

FA Cup (8): Richards 3, Walschaerts 2, Griffiths 1, Simba 1, Smith 1 (pen).

Ground: Leyton Stadium, Brisbane Road, Leyton, London E10 5NE. Telephone (0181) 926 1111.

Record attendance: 34,345 v West Ham U, FA Cup 4th rd, 25 January 1964.

Capacity: 13,842.

Manager: Tommy Taylor.

Secretary: Frank Woolf.

Honours – Football League: Division 3 Champions – 1969–70. Division 3 (S) Champions – 1955–56.

Colours: White shirts with red V, black shorts, red stockings.

LINCOLN CITY

DIV. 3

Barnett Jason (D)	5 9	10 10	Shrewsbury	21 4 76	Wolverhampton W
Battersby Tony (F)	6 0	12 09	Doncaster	30 8 75	Bury
Bimson Stuart (D)	5 11	11 08	Liverpool	29 9 69	Bury
Brown Grant (D)	6 0	11 12	Sunderland	19 11 69	Leicester C
Finnigan John (M)	5 8	10 11	Wakefield	29 3 76	Nottingham F
Fleming Terry (M)	5 9	10 01	Marston Green	5 1 73	Preston NE
Gain Peter (M)	6 1	11 00	Hammersmith	2 11 76	Tottenham H
Gordon Gavin (F)	6 1	12 00	Manchester	24 6 79	Hull C
Holmes Steve (D)	6 2	13 00	Middlesbrough	13 1 71	Preston NE
Miller Paul (M)	6 0	11 07	Bisley	31 1 68	Bristol R
Peacock Richard (M)	5 10	11 05	Sheffield	29 10 72	Hull C

Phillips Dave (D)	5 9	12 04	Wegberg	29 7 63	Huddersfield T
Philpott Lee (M)	5 9	11 08	Barnet	21 2 70	Blackpool
Richardson Barry (G)	6 1	12 01	Wallsend	5 8 69	Preston NE
Smith Paul (M)	5 11	11 07	Hastings	25 1 76	Nottingham F
Stones Craig (M)			Scunthorpe	31 5 80	Trainee
Thorpe Lee (F)	6 0	11 06	Wolverhampton	14 12 75	Blackpool
Vaughan John (G)	5 10	13 01	Isleworth	26 6 64	Preston NE
Walling Dean (D)	6 0	10 08	Leeds	17 4 69	Carlisle U
Wilkins Ian (D)			Lincoln	3 4 80	Trainee

League Appearances: Alcide, C. 20(3); Austin, K. 39(1); Barnett, J. 29; Battersby, T. 35(4); Bimson, S. 30(1); Brabin, G. 3(1); Brown, G. 20(1); Fenn, N. (4); Finnigan, J. 36(1); Fleming, T. 40(3); Fortune-West, L. 7(2); Gain, P. (4); Gordon, G. 21(6); Grobbelaar, B. 2; Hartfield, C. 3; Holmes, S. 37; Miller, P. 26(6); Oatway, C. 3; Peacock, R. 3(7); Perry, J. 10(2); Phillips, D. 9; Philpott, L. 15(9); Richardson, B. 13; Smith, P. 22(6); Stant, P. (3); Stones, C. (1); Thorpe, L. 35(3); Vaughan, J. 31; Walling, D. (3); Watts, J. 2; Whitney, J. 13; Wilder, C. 2(1).

Goals – League (42): Thorpe 8, Battersby 7 (1 pen), Holmes 6 (1 pen), Gordon 5, Bimson 2, Miller 2, Smith 2, Whitney 2, Alcide 1, Austin 1, Barnett 1, Brown 1, Finnigan 1, Fortune-West 1, Hartfield 1, own goal 1.

Worthington Cup (1): Battersby 1.

FA Cup (5): Alcide 1, Battersby 1, Finnigan 1, Holmes 1, Thorpe 1.

Ground: Sincil Bank, Lincoln LN5 8LD. Telephone (01522) 880011.

Record attendance: 23,196 v Derby Co, League Cup 4th rd, 15 November 1967.

Capacity: 11,729.

Manager: K. J. Reames.

Secretary: L. Jubb.

Honours – Football League: Division 3 (N) Champions – 1931–32, 1947–48, 1951–52. Division 4 Champions – 1975–76.

Colours: Red and white striped shirts, black shorts, black stockings.

LIVERPOOL   FA PREMIERSHIP

Armstrong Ian (F)			Fazackerley	16 11 81	Trainee
Babb Phil (D)	6 0	12 03	Lambeth	30 11 70	Coventry C
Berger Patrik (M)	6 1	12 06	Prague	10 11 73	Borussia Dortmund
Bjornebye Stig Inge (D)	5 10	11 09	Elverum	11 12 69	Rosenborg
Boardman John (D)			Liverpool	6 9 80	Trainee
Carragher James (M)	6 1	13 00	Liverpool	28 1 78	Trainee
Doherty Kevin (M)			Dublin	18 4 80	
Dunbavin Ian (G)			Knowsley	27 5 80	Trainee
Dundee Sean (F)	6 1	13 00	Durban	7 12 72	Karlsruhe
Ferri Jean-Michel (M)	6 0	12 00	Lyon	7 2 69	Nantes
Fowler Robbie (F)	5 11	11 10	Liverpool	9 4 75	Trainee
Friedel Brad (G)	6 3	14 00	Lakewood	18 5 71	
Gerrard Steven (M)	6 1	13 00	Whiston	30 5 80	Trainee
Gudnason Haukar (F)	5 10	12 00	Keflavik	8 9 78	Keflavik
Heggem Vegard (D)	5 11	12 00	Trondheim	13 7 75	Rosenborg
Ince Paul (M)	5 10	12 02	Ilford	21 10 67	Internazionale
James David (G)	6 5	14 02	Welwyn	1 8 70	Watford
Jones Eifion (D)	6 3	13 00	Llanrug	28 9 80	Trainee
Kippe Frode (D)			Oslo	17 1 78	Lillestrom
Kvarme Bjorn (D)	5 11	12 04	Trondheim	17 6 72	Rosenborg
Leonhardsen Oyvind (M)	5 10	11 02	Kristiansund	17 8 70	Wimbledon
Matteo Dominic (D)	6 1	11 10	Dumfries	24 4 74	Trainee
Maxwell Leyton (M)	5 8	11 00	St Asaph	3 10 79	Trainee
McManaman Steve (M)	6 0	10 06	Liverpool	11 2 72	School
Miles John (F)			Fazackerley	28 9 81	Trainee

Murphy Danny (M)	5 9	10 08	Chester	18 3 77	Crewe Alex
Murphy Neil (D)	5 9	11 00	Liverpool	19 5 80	Trainee
Navarro Alan (D)			Liverpool	31 5 81	Trainee
Newby John (F)	6 0	12 00	Warrington	28 11 78	Trainee
Nielsen Jorgen (G)	6 0	13 00	Nykobing	6 5 71	Hvidovre*
O'Brien Chris (M)			Liverpool	13 1 82	Trainee
O'Mara Paul (D)	5 9	11 00	Dublin	23 11 80	Trainee
Owen Michael (F)	5 8	11 00	Chester	14 12 79	Trainee
Partridge Richie (M)	5 8	10 10	Dublin	12 9 80	Trainee
Redknapp Jamie (M)	6 0	12 10	Barton-on-Sea	25 6 73	Bournemouth
Riedle Karlheinz (F)	5 11	12 00	Weiler	16 9 65	Borussia Dortmund
Song Rigobert (D)	6 0	13 00	Nkanglicock	1 7 76	Salernitana
Staunton Steve (D)	6 1	12 11	Drogheda	19 1 69	Aston Villa
Thompson David (M)	5 7	10 00	Birkenhead	12 9 77	Trainee
Torpey Steve (M)			Fazackerley	16 9 81	Trainee
Traore Djimi (D)	6 3	13 10	Saint Ouen	1 3 80	Laval
Warnock Stephen (M)			Ormskirk	12 12 81	Trainee
Wright Stephen (D)			Liverpool	8 2 80	Trainee

League Appearances: Babb, P. 24(1); Berger, P. 30(2); Bjornebye, S. 20(3); Carragher, J. 34; Dundee, S. (3); Ferri, J. (2); Fowler, R. 23(2); Friedel, B. 12; Gerrard, S. 4(8); Harkness, S. 4(2); Heggem, V. 27(2); Ince, P. 34; James, D. 26; Kvarme, B. 2(5); Leonhardsen, O. 7(2); Matteo, D. 16(4); McAteer, J. 6(7); McManaman, S. 25(3); Murphy, D. (1); Owen, M. 30; Redknapp, J. 33(1); Riedle, K. 16(18); Song, R. 10(3); Staunton, S. 31; Thompson, D. 4(10).

Goals – League (68): Owen 18 (1 pen), Fowler 14 (4 pens), Redknapp 8 (2 pens), Berger 7, Ince 6, Riedle 5, McManaman 4, Heggem 2, Carragher 1, Leonhardsen 1, Matteo 1, Thompson 1.

Worthington Cup (4): Fowler 1 (pen), Ince 1, Owen 1, own goal 1.

FA Cup (4): Owen 2 (1 pen), Fowler 1, Ince 1.

Ground: Anfield Road, Liverpool L4 0TH. Telephone (0151) 263 2361.

Record attendance: 61,905 v Wolverhampton W, FA Cup 4th rd, 2 February 1952.

Capacity: 45,362.

Manager: Gerard Houllier.

Secretary: Bryce Morrison.

Honours – Football League: Division 1 – Champions 1900–01, 1905–06, 1921–22, 1922–23, 1946–47, 1963–64, 1965–66, 1972–73, 1975–76, 1976–77, 1978–79, 1979–80, 1981–82, 1982–83, 1983–84, 1985–86, 1987–88, 1989–90 (Liverpool have a record number of 18 **League** Championship wins). Division 2 Champions – 1893–94, 1895–96, 1904–05, 1961–62. **FA Cup**: Winners 1965, 1974, 1986, 1989, 1992. League **Cup**: Winners 1981, 1982, 1983, 1984, 1995. Super Cup: Winners 1985–86. **European Competitions: European Cup winners:** 1976–77, 1977–78, 1980–81, 1983–84. **UEFA Cup winners:** 1972–73, 1975–76. **Super Cup winners:** 1977.

Colours: All red.

LUTON TOWN DIV. 2

Ayres James (D)	6 3	13 00	Luton	18 9 80	Trainee
Boyce Emmerson (D)	5 11	11 02	Aylesbury	24 9 79	Trainee
Davis Kelvin (G)	6 1	13 11	Bedford	29 9 76	Trainee
Doherty Gary (D)	6 1	13 00	Donegal	31 1 80	Trainee
Douglas Stuart (F)	5 8	11 05	London	9 4 78	Trainee
Fotiadis Andrew (F)	5 11	11 07	Hitchin	6 9 77	School
Fraser Stuart (D)	5 9	10 06	Edinburgh	9 1 80	Trainee
George Liam (F)	5 9	11 04	Luton	2 2 79	Trainee
Gray Phil (F)	5 9	12 07	Belfast	2 10 68	Sunderland
Johnson Marvin (D)	6 1	13 00	Wembley	29 10 68	Apprentice
Kandol Tresor (F)	6 1	11 07	Banga	30 8 81	Trainee

McGowan Gavin (D)	5 10	12 06	Blackheath	16 1 76	Arsenal
McIndoe Michael (M)	5 8	10 06	Edinburgh	2 12 79	Trainee
McLaren Paul (M)	6 1	13 00	High Wycombe	17 11 76	Trainee
Moses Jerry (M)	5 9	11 05	Kampala	22 2 81	
Scarlett Andre (M)	5 4	9 12	Brent	11 1 80	Trainee
Spring Matthew (M)	5 11	11 07	Harlow	17 11 79	Trainee
Tate Daniel (G)	5 11	11 12	Bedford	12 11 80	Trainee
Taylor Matthew (D)	5 10	11 08	Oxford	27 11 81	Trainee
Ward Scott (G)	6 2	13 00	Brent	5 10 81	Trainee
White Alan (D)	6 1	13 07	Darlington	22 3 76	Middlesbrough
Willmott Chris (D)	6 2	11 13	Bedford	30 9 77	Trainee
Zahana-Oni Landry (M)	5 9	10 09	Ivory Coast	8 8 76	Bromley

League Appearances: Abbey, N. 2; Alexander, G. 28(1); Bacque, H. 2(5); Boyce, E. 1; Cox, J. 3(5); Davies, S. 2; Davis, K. 44; Davis, S. 20; Doherty, G. 5(15); Douglas, S. 42; Dyche, S. 14; Evers, S. 27; Fotiadis, A. 8(13); Fraser, S. 5(3); George, L. 6(6); Gray, P. 32(3); Harrison, G. 14; Johnson, M. 42; Kandol, T. 2(2); Marshall, D. 3(1); McGowan, G. 27(4); McIndoe, M. 17(5); McKinnon, R. 29(1); McLaren, P. 14(9); Scarlett, A. 2(4); Showler, P. 2(1); Spring, M. 45; Thomas, M. 26(6); Thorpe, T. 7(1); White, A. 18(15); Willmott, C. 13(1); Zahana-Oni, L. 4(4).

Goals – League (51): Douglas 9, Gray 8, Davis S 6, Doherty 6, Alexander 4 (2 pens), Thorpe 4, Evers 3, Spring 3, Fotiadis 2, McKinnon 2, Dyche 1, Marshall 1, Scarlett 1, White 1.

Worthington Cup (13): Gray 3, Alexander 2 (2 pens), Davis S 2, Douglas 2, Evers 1, Fotiadis 1, Johnson 1, McLaren 1.

FA Cup (4): Davis S 2, Gray 2.

Ground: Kenilworth Road Stadium, 1 Maple Rd, Luton, Beds. LU4 8AW. Telephone (01582) 411622.

Record attendance: 30,069 v Blackpool, FA Cup 6th rd replay, 4 March 1959. **Capacity:** 9975.

Manager: Lennie Lawrence.

Secretary: Cherry Newbery.

Honours – Football League: Division 2 Champions – 1981–82. Division 4 Champions – 1967–68. Division 3 (S) Champions – 1936–37. **Football League Cup winners** 1987–88.

Colours: Orange shirts with blue side panels and blue and white knitted colar, blue shorts with orange and white stripe, blue stockings with orange stripes.

MACCLESFIELD TOWN   DIV. 3

Askey John (F)	6 0	12 02	Stoke	4 11 64	Port Vale
Brown Greg (D)	5 10	12 04	Wythenshawe	31 7 78	Chester C
Brown Steve (F)	6 0	13 10	Rochford	6 12 73	Lincoln C
Davies Simon (M)	5 11	12 04	Davenham	23 4 74	Luton T
Durkan Kieron (M)	5 10	12 09	Chester	1 12 73	Stockport Co
Griffiths Peter (M)	5 9	11 06	St Helier	13 3 80	Trainee
Hitchen Steve (D)	5 8	11 07	Salford	28 11 76	Blackburn R
Ingram Rae (D)	5 11	12 02	Manchester	6 12 74	Manchester C
Lomax Michael (D)	5 10	10 12	Whithington	7 12 79	
Mason Michael (F)	5 9	11 11	Walsall	7 8 79	
Pates Bradley (M)	5 9	11 02	Burnley	21 12 79	
Payne Steve (D)	5 11	12 05	Castleford	1 8 75	Huddersfield T
Price Ryan (G)	6 6	14 00	Wolverhampton	13 3 70	Birmingham C
Sedgemore Ben (M)	6 0	12 08	Wolverhampton	5 8 75	Mansfield T
Tinson Darren (D)	6 0	14 04	Birmingham	15 11 69	Northwich V
Tomlinson Graeme (F)	5 10	12 04	Watford	10 12 75	Manchester U
Whittaker Stuart (M)	5 7	10 06	Liverpool	2 1 75	Bolton W

League Appearances: Askey, J. 31(7); Bailey, A. 5(5); Barclay, D. 3(6); Brown, G. 5; Brown, S. 1(1); Davenport, P. (1); Davies, S. 9(3); Durkan, K. 23(3); Griffiths, P. 4; Hitchen, S. 35; Holt, M. 3(1); Howarth, N. 11(8); Ingram, R. 23(6); Landon, R. 10(4); Lomax, M. (1); Matias, P. 21(1); McDonald, M. 23; Payne, S. 32(6); Price, R. 42; Sedgemore, B. 25(10); Smith, P. 12; Sodje, E. 42; Soley, S. 5(5); Sorvel, N. 38(3); Tinson, D. 37; Tomlinson, G. 15(13); Whittaker, S. 18(9); Williams, A. 4; Wood, S. 29(13).

Goals – League (43): Askey 4, Sorvel 4, Tomlinson 4 (1 pen), Wood 4, Durkan 3, Smith 3, Sodje 3, Davies 2, Landon 2, Matias 2, McDonald 2, Payne 2, Sedgemore 2, Bailey 1, Barclay 1, Griffiths 1, Holt 1, Whittaker 1, own goal 1.

Worthington Cup (3): Askey 2, Wood 1.

FA Cup (7): Tomlinson 4, Askey 1, Sedgemore 1, Sodje 1

Ground: The Moss Rose Ground, London Road, Macclesfield, Cheshire SK11 7SP. Telephone: (01625) 264686.

Record attendance: 9008 v Winsford U, Cheshire Senior Cup 2nd rd, 4 February 1948. **Capacity:** 6028 (seated 1053, standing 4975).

Manager: Sammy McIlroy.

Secretary: Colin Garlick.

Colours: Royal blue shirts, white shorts, blue stockings.

MANCHESTER CITY   DIV. 1

Allsopp Danny (F)	6 0	12 08	Melbourne	10 8 78	Port Melbourne
Bailey Alan (F)	5 11	12 03	Macclesfield	1 11 78	Trainee
Bishop Ian (M)	5 10	12 00	Liverpool	29 5 65	West Ham U
Brown Michael R (M)	5 9	10 07	Hartlepool	25 1 77	Trainee
Cooke Terry (F)	5 8	10 03	Marston Green	5 8 76	Manchester U
Crooks Lee (D)	6 1	12 09	Wakefield	14 1 78	Trainee
Dickov Paul (F)	5 5	11 09	Glasgow	1 11 72	Arsenal
Dunfield Terry (M)	5 7	10 03	Canada	20 2 82	Trainee
Edghill Richard (D)	5 9	11 00	Oldham	23 9 74	Trainee
Fenton Nick (D)	6 1	11 08	Preston	23 11 79	Trainee
Goater Shaun (F)	6 0	12 10	Bermuda	25 2 70	Bristol C
Greenacre Chris (F)	5 11	10 06	Halifax	23 12 77	Trainee
Heaney Neil (F)	5 9	11 07	Middlesbrough	3 11 71	Southampton
Hodgson Steven (G)	5 11	11 00	Macclesfield	23 12 81	Scholarship
Holmes Shaun (D)	5 9	10 07	Derry	27 12 80	Trainee
Horlock Kevin (M)	6 0	12 00	Erith	1 11 72	Swindon T
Jobson Richard (D)	6 2	12 12	Holderness	9 5 63	Leeds U
Jordan Stephen (M)			Warrington	6 3 82	Scholarship
Killen Chris (F)	5 11	11 03	Wellington	8 10 81	Miramar R
Laycock David (M)	5 10	10 07	Hull	1 10 80	Trainee
Mason Gary (M)	5 8	10 01	Edinburgh	15 10 79	Trainee
Mike Leon (F)	6 0	12 02	Manchester	4 9 81	Scholarship
Morrison Andy (D)	5 11	12 12	Inverness	30 7 70	Huddersfield T
Pollock Jamie (M)	6 0	13 03	Stockton	16 2 74	Bolton W
Reilly Alan (M)	5 11	12 01	Dublin	22 8 80	Trainee
Russell Craig (F)	5 10	12 07	Jarrow	4 2 74	Sunderland
Shelia Murtaz (D)	6 0	13 02	Georgia	7 9 68	Alania
Taylor Gareth (F)	6 1	12 02	Weston-Super-Mare	25 2 73	Sheffield U
Tiatto Danny (D)	5 8	11 01	Melbourne	22 5 73	Baden
Tskhadadze Kakhabor (D)	6 1	12 04	Rustavi	7 9 68	Alania
Vaughan Tony (D)	6 1	12 10	Manchester	11 10 75	Ipswich T
Weaver Nick (G)	6 3	13 01	Sheffield	2 3 79	Mansfield T
Whitley Jeff (M)	5 9	10 10	Zambia	28 1 79	Trainee
Whitley Jim (M)	5 9	10 12	Zambia	14 4 75	Trainee

Wiekens Gerard (D)   6 0   12 06   Tolhuiswyk   25 2 73
Wright-Phillips Shaun (F)   5 6   10 01   London   25 10 81
Wright Tommy (G)   6 1   14 05   Belfast   29 8 63   Nottingham F

League Appearances: Allsopp, D. 3(21); Bishop, I. 21(4); Bradbury, L. 11(2); Branch, M. 4; Brown, M. 26(5); Cooke, T. 21; Crooks, L. 32(2); Dickov, P. 22(13); Edghill, R. 38; Fenton, N. 15; Goater, S. 41(2); Greenacre, C. 1; Horlock, K. 36(1); Mason, G. 18(1); Morrison, A. 21(1); Pollock, J. 24(2); Robins, M. (2); Russell, C. 5(2); Shelia, M. 3; Taylor, G. 20(6); Tiatto, D. 8(9); Tskhadadze, K. 2; Vaughan, T. 35(3); Weaver, N. 45; Whitley, Jeff 1(7); Whitley, Jim 10(8); Wiekens, G. 42; Wright, T. 1.

Goals – League (69): Goater 17, Dickov 10, Horlock 9 (1 pen), Cooke 7, Allsopp 4, Morrison 4, Taylor 4, Bradbury 3, Brown 2, Wiekens 2, Crooks 1, Pollock 1, Russell 1, Tskhadadze 1, Vaughan 1, Whitley Jeff 1, own goal 1.

Worthington Cup (10): Dickov 2, Goater 2, Allsop 1, Bradbury 1, Mason 1, Tiatto 1, Tskhadadze 1, Jim Whitley 1.

FA Cup (5): Russell 2, Brown 1, Dickov 1, Goater 1.

Ground: Maine Road, Moss Side, Manchester M14 7WN. Telephone (0161) 232 3000.

Record attendance: 84,569 v Stoke C, FA Cup 6th rd, 3 March 1934 (British record for any game outside London or Glasgow). **Capacity:** 31,458.

Manager: Joe Royle.

General Secretary: J. B. Halford.

Honours – Football League: Division 1 Champions – 1936–37, 1967–68. Division 2 Champions – 1898–99, 1902–03, 1909–10, 1927–28, 1946–47, 1965–66. **FA Cup winners** 1904, 1934, 1956, 1969. **Football League Cup winners** 1970, 1976. **European Competitions: European Cup-Winners' Cup winners:** 1969–70.

Colours: Lazer blue shirts, white shorts, navy stockings.

MANCHESTER UNITED   FA PREMIERSHIP

Beckham David (M)   6 0   11 09   Leytonstone   2 5 75   Trainee
Berg Henning (D)   6 0   12 01   Eidsvoll   1 9 69   Blackburn R
Blomqvist Jesper (F)   5 9   11 03   Tavelsjo   5 2 74   Parma
Brown Wes (D)   6 1   11 11   Manchester   13 10 79   Trainee
Butt Nicky (M)   5 10   11 05   Manchester   21 1 75   Trainee
Chadwick Luke (F)   5 11   10 09   Cambridge   18 11 80   Trainee
Clegg Michael (D)   5 8   11 10   Ashton-under-Lyne   3 7 77   Trainee
Cole Andy (F)   5 10   12 04   Nottingham   15 10 71   Newcastle U
Cosgrove Stephen (M)   5 9   10 05   Glasgow   29 12 80   Trainee
Cruyff Jordi (F)   6 1   10 12   Amsterdam   9 2 74   Barcelona
Culkin Nick (G)   6 2   13 05   York   6 7 78   York C
Curtis John (D)   5 10   11 07   Nuneaton   3 9 78   Trainee
Djordjic Bojan (M)   Belgrade   6 2 82
Evans Wayne (M)   5 9   9 12   Carmarthen   23 10 80   Trainee
Fitzpatrick Ian (F)   5 9   10 00   Manchester   22 9 80   Trainee
Ford Ryan (M)   5 9   10 04   Worksop   3 9 80   Trainee
Giggs Ryan (F)   5 11   10 10   Cardiff   29 11 73   School
Greening Jonathan (F)   6 0   11 03   Scarborough   2 1 79   York C
Healy David (F)   5 8   10 09   Downpatrick   5 8 79   Trainee
Higginbotham Danny (D)   6 1   12 03   Manchester   29 12 78   Trainee
Irwin Denis (D)   5 8   10 10   Cork   31 10 65   Oldham Ath
Johnsen Ronny (D)   6 3   13 02   Sandefjord   10 6 69   Besiktas
Keane Roy (M)   5 11   12 01   Cork   10 8 71   Nottingham F
May David (D)   6 0   13 05   Oldham   24 6 70   Blackburn R
McDermott Alan (D)   6 1   11 13   Dublin   22 1 82   Trainee
Neville Gary (D)   5 11   12 07   Bury   18 2 75   Trainee
Neville Philip (D)   5 11   11 11   Bury   21 1 77   Trainee

Nevland Erik (F)	5 10	11 12	Stavanger	10 11 77	Viking
Notman Alex (F)	5 7	10 11	Edinburgh	10 12 79	Trainee
O'Shea John (D)	6 3	11 12	Waterford	30 4 81	Waterford
Roche Lee (D)	5 10	10 11	Bolton	28 10 80	Trainee
Schmeichel Peter (G)	6 4	16 00	Gladsaxe	18 11 63	Brondby
Scholes Paul (M)	5 7	11 08	Salford	16 11 74	Trainee
Sheringham Teddy (F)	6 0	13 00	Highams Park	2 4 66	Tottenham H
Solskjaer Ole Gunnar (F)	5 10	11 06	Kristiansund	26 2 73	Molde
Stam Jaap (D)	6 3	13 09	Kampen	17 7 72	PSV Eindhoven
Stewart Michael (M)	5 11	11 06	Edinburgh	26 2 81	Trainee
Strange Gareth (M)	5 9	10 09	Bolton	3 10 81	Trainee
Teather Paul (D)	6 0	11 08	Rotherham	28 12 77	Trainee
Twiss Michael (M)	5 11	12 00	Salford	18 12 77	Trainee
Van der Gouw Raimond (G)	6 3	13 07	Oldenzaal	24 3 63	Vitesse
Wallwork Ronnie (D)	5 10	12 12	Manchester	10 9 77	Trainee
Webber Danny (F)	5 9	10 03	Manchester	28 12 81	Trainee
Wellens Richard (M)	5 9	11 05	Manchester	26 3 80	Trainee
Wheatcroft Paul (F)	5 8	9 09	Manchester	22 11 80	Trainee
Wilson Mark (M)	6 0	13 02	Scunthorpe	9 2 79	Trainee
Yorke Dwight (F)	5 10	12 04	Canaan	3 11 71	Aston Villa

League Appearances: Beckham, D. 33(1); Berg, H. 10(6); Blomqvist, J. 20(5); Brown, W. 11(3); Butt, N. 22(9); Cole, A. 26(6); Cruyff, J. (5); Curtis, J. 1(3); Giggs, R. 20(4); Greening, J. (3); Irwin, D. 26(3); Johnsen, R. 19(3); Keane, R. 33(2); May, D. 4(2); Neville, G. 34; Neville, P. 19(9); Schmeichel, P. 34; Scholes, P. 24(7); Sheringham, T. 7(10); Solskjaer, O. 9(10); Stam, J. 30; Van der Gouw, R. 4(1); Yorke, D. 32.

Goals – League (80): Yorke 18, Cole 17, Solskjaer 12, Beckham 6, Scholes 6, Giggs 3, Johnsen 3, Butt 2, Cruyff 2, Irwin 2 (2 pens), Keane 2, Sheringham 2, Blomqvist 1, Neville G 1, Stam 1, own goals 2.

Worthington Cup (5): Solskjaer 3, Nevland 1, Sheringham 1.

FA Cup (12): Yorke 3, Cole 2, Giggs 2, Beckham 1, Irwin 1 (pen), Scholes 1, Sheringham 1, Solskjaer 1.

Ground: Old Trafford, Sir Matt Busby Way, Manchester M16 0RA. Telephone (0161) 872 1661.

Record attendance: 76,962 Wolverhampton W v Grimsby T, FA Cup semi-final. 25 March 1939. **Capacity:** 56,387

Manager: Sir Alex Ferguson CBE.

Secretary: Kenneth Merrett.

Honours – FA Premier League: Champions – 1992–93, 1993–94, 1995–96, 1996–97, 1998–99. **Football League:** Division 1 Champions – 1907–8, 1910–11, 1951–52, 1955–56, 1956–57, 1964–65, 1966–67. Division 2 Champions – 1935–36, 1974–75. **FA Cup winners** 1909, 1948, 1963, 1977, 1983, 1985, 1990, 1994, 1996, 1999. **Football League Cup winners** 1991–92. **European Competitions: European Cup winners:** 1967–68, 1998–99. **European Cup-Winners' Cup winners:** 1990–91. **Super Cup winners:** 1991.

Colours: Red shirts, white shorts, black stockings.

MANSFIELD TOWN   DIV. 3

Bowling Ian (G)	6 3	13 11	Sheffield	27 7 65	Bradford C
Christie Iyseden (F)	5 10	12 02	Coventry	14 11 76	Coventry C
Clarke Darrell (M)	5 10	10 11	Mansfield	16 12 77	Trainee
Ford Tony (M)	5 9	13 00	Grimsby	14 5 59	Scunthorpe U
Hassell Bobby (D)	5 10	11 13	Derby	4 6 80	Trainee
Lormor Tony (F)	6 2	13 13	Ashington	29 10 70	Preston NE
Parkin Steve (D)	5 6	11 01	Mansfield	7 11 65	WBA
Peacock Lee (F)	6 1	13 12	Paisley	9 10 76	Carlisle U

Sisson Michael (M)   5 9   10 11   Sutton-in-Ashfield   24 11 78   Trainee
Williams Lee (D)   5 8   11 13   Edgbaston   3 2 73   Tranmere R

League Appearances: Adamson, C. 2; Allardyce, C. 6; Bowling, I. 37; Carruthers, M. (5); Cherry, S. 1; Christie, I. 18(24); Clarke, D. 24(9); Ford, T. 39(3); Hackett, W. 24(2); Harper, S. 45; Hassell, B. 1(2); Kerr, D. 30(5); L'Helgoualch, C. 3(1); Linighan, D. 10; Lormor, T. 35(6); Naylor, S. 6; Peacock, L. 42(3); Peters, M. 37; Rose, K. (1); Ryder, S. 18(4); Schofield, J. 37(5); Sedlan, J. 1(4); Sisson, M. (1); Tallon, G. 31(5); Walker, J. 18(19); Williams, L. 31(13); Willis, A. 10.

Goals – League (60): Peacock 17 (5 pens), Lormor 11, Christie 8, Harper 6, Clarke 5, Ford 2, Kerr 2, Ryder 2, Williams 2, L'Helgoualch 1, Peters 1, Tallon 1, Walker 1, own goal 1.

Worthington Cup (3): Christie 1, Clarke 1, Peters 1.

FA Cup (3): Lormor 2, Clarke 1.

Ground: Field Mill Ground, Quarry Lane, Mansfield NG18 5DA. Telephone (01623) 623567.

Record attendance: 24,467 v Nottingham F, FA Cup 3rd rd, 10 January 1953.

Capacity: 6905.

Manager: Bill Dearden.

Secretary: Christine Reynolds.

Honours – Football League: Division 3 Champions – 1976–77. Division 4 Champions – 1974–75. **Freight Rover Trophy winners** 1986–87.

Colours: Amber & royal blue shirts, royal blue shorts, royal blue stockings with amber trim.

MIDDLESBROUGH   FA PREMIERSHIP

Armstrong Alun (F)	6 0	13 08	Gateshead	22 2 75	Stockport Co
Baker Steve (D)	6 0	12 06	Pontefract	8 9 78	
Beresford Marlon (G)	6 1	13 08	Lincoln	2 6 69	Burnley
Campbell Andy (F)	6 0	11 13	Middlesbrough	18 4 79	Trainee
Canavan Michael (F)	6 1	12 02	South Shields	17 9 80	Trainee
Cooper Colin (D)	5 11	11 11	Sedgefield	28 2 67	Nottingham F
Cummins Michael (M)	6 0	12 08	Dublin	1 6 78	Trainee
Deane Brian (F)	6 3	14 00	Leeds	7 2 68	Sheffield U
Festa Gianluca (D)	5 11	13 00	Cagliari	15 3 69	Internazionale
Fleming Curtis (D)	5 10	12 05	Manchester	8 10 68	St Patrick's Ath
Gascoigne Paul (M)	5 10	12 09	Gateshead	27 5 67	Rangers
Gavin Jason (D)	6 0	11 12	Dublin	14 3 80	Trainee
Gordon Dean (D)	6 0	13 08	Thornton Heath	10 2 73	Crystal Palace
Hanson Christian (D)	6 1	11 05	Middlesbrough	3 8 81	Trainee
Harrison Craig (D)	6 0	11 08	Gateshead	10 11 77	Trainee
Jones Bradley (G)	6 3	12 01	Armadale	19 3 82	Trainee
Jones Thomas (F)	5 10	11 02	Middlesbrough	26 3 80	Trainee
Kell Richard (M)			Bishop Auckland	15 9 79	Trainee
Kelly Brian (M)			Dublin	6 2 81	Trainee
Kinder Vladimir (D)	5 9	12 03	Bratislava	9 3 69	Slovan Bratislava
Maddison Neil (M)	5 10	11 10	Darlington	2 10 69	Southampton
Moore Alan (M)	5 10	11 02	Dublin	25 11 74	Rivermount
Mustoe Robbie (M)	6 0	12 03	Oxford	28 8 68	Oxford U
O'Loughlin John (M)	5 8	10 12	Letterkenny	31 1 79	Bruncrana Hearts
O'Neill Keith (F)	6 2	12 07	Dublin	16 2 76	Norwich C
Ormerod Anthony (M)	5 11	12 00	Middlesbrough	31 3 79	Trainee
Pallister Gary (D)	6 5	15 02	Ramsgate	30 6 65	Manchester U
Prunty Sean (M)	5 9	10 11	Dublin	10 7 80	Belvedere
Ricard Hamilton (F)	6 1	13 12	Colombia	12 1 74	Deportivo Cali
Roberts Ben (G)	6 1	12 11	Bishop Auckland	2 5 75	Trainee
Schwarzer Mark (G)	6 5	15 01	Sydney	6 10 72	Bradford C
Stamp Phil (M)	5 11	14 09	Middlesbrough	12 12 75	Trainee

Name	Ht	Wt	Birthplace	Date	Previous club
Stockdale Robbie (D)	6 0	12 03	Redcar	30 11 79	Trainee
Summerbell Mark (M)	5 9	11 01	Durham	30 10 76	Trainee
Townsend Andy (M)	6 0	13 05	Maidstone	27 7 63	Aston Villa
Vickers Steve (D)	6 2	13 01	Bishop Auckland	13 10 67	Tranmere R
Walklate Steve (M)	5 11	12 00	Durham	27 9 79	Trainee
Wiltshire Luke (M)			Australia	2 10 81	

League Appearances: Armstrong, A. (6); Baker, S. 1(1); Beck, M. 13(14); Beresford, M. 4; Branca, M. (1); Campbell, A. 1(7); Cooper, C. 31(1); Cummins, M. 1; Deane, B. 24(2); Festa, G. 25; Fleming, C. 12(2); Gascoigne, P. 25(1); Gavin, J. 2; Gordon, D. 38; Harrison, C. 3(1); Kinder, V. (5); Maddison, N. 10(11); Merson, P. 3; Moore, A. 3(1); Mustoe, R. 32(1); O'Neill, K. 4(2); Pallister, G. 26; Ricard, H. 32(4); Schwarzer, M. 34; Stamp, P. 5(11); Stockdale, R. 17(2); Summerbell, M. 7(4); Townsend, A. 35; Vickers, S. 30(1).

Goals – League (48): Ricard 15 (1 pen), Deane 6, Beck 5, Mustoe 4, Gascoigne 3, Gordon 3, Festa 2, Kinder 2, Stamp 2, Armstrong 1, Cooper 1, Fleming 1, Townsend 1, Vickers 1, own goal 1.

Worthington Cup (5): Ricard 3, Festa 1, Summerbell 1.

FA Cup (1): Townsend 1.

Ground: Cellnet Riverside Stadium, Middlesbrough, Cleveland TS3 6RS. Telephone (01642) 877700

Record attendance: 53,596 v Newcastle U, Division 1, 27 December 1949.

Capacity: 35,000.

Manager: Bryan Robson.

Secretary: Karen Nelson.

Honours – Football League: Division 1 Champions 1994–95. Division 2 Champions 1926–27, 1928–29, 1973–74. **Amateur Cup winners** 1895, 1898, **Anglo-Scottish Cup:** Winners 1975–76.

Colours: Red shirts, white shorts, red stockings.

MILLWALL DIV. 2

Name	Ht	Wt	Birthplace	Date	Previous club
Barnard Richard (G)			Frimley	27 12 80	Trainee
Bircham Marc (D)	5 10	10 12	Wembley	11 5 78	Trainee
Bowry Bobby (M)	5 9	10 08	Croydon	19 5 71	Crystal Palace
Bubb Byron (M)			Harrow	17 12 81	Scholarship
Bull Ronnie (D)			Hackney	26 12 80	
Cahill Tim (M)	5 10	10 11	Sydney	6 12 79	Sydney U
Cook Andy (M)	5 9	12 00	Romsey	10 8 69	Portsmouth
Cort Leon (D)			Southwark	11 7 79	Dulwich H
Dolan Joe (D)	6 3	12 12	Harrow	27 5 80	Chelsea
Fitzgerald Scott (D)	6 0	12 12	Westminster	13 8 69	Wimbledon
Grant Kim (F)	5 10	11 05	Ghana	25 9 72	Luton T
Harris Neil (F)	5 11	12 08	Orsett	12 7 77	Cambridge C
Hicks Mark (F)			Belfast	24 7 81	
Hockton Danny (F)	6 0	11 11	Barking	7 2 79	Trainee
Ifill Paul (F)			Brighton	20 10 79	Trainee
Mead Billy (D)			London	7 1 81	
Neill Lucas (M)	6 1	12 00	Sydney	9 3 78	NSW Academy
Nethercott Stuart (D)	6 0	13 08	Ilford	21 3 73	Tottenham H
Newman Ricky (M)	5 10	12 06	Guildford	5 8 70	Crystal Palace
Odunsi Leke (M)			Walworth	5 12 80	Trainee
Reid Steven (F)	5 11	11 10	Kingston	10 3 81	Trainee
Ryan Robbie (D)	5 10	12 00	Dublin	16 5 77	Huddersfield T
Sadlier Richard (F)	6 2	12 10	Dublin	14 1 79	Belvedere
Shaw Paul (F)	5 11	12 04	Burnham	4 9 73	Arsenal
Smith Phil (G)	6 1	13 00	Harrow	14 12 79	Trainee
Stuart Jamie (D)	5 10	11 00	Southwark	15 10 76	Charlton Ath
Tyne Thomas (F)			Lambeth	2 3 81	

League Appearances: Bircham, M. 20(8); Bowry, B. 22(3); Bubb, B. 1(2); Bull, R. 1; Cahill, T. 34(2); Carter, J. 16; Cook, A. 1(1); Dolan, J. 9; Fitzgerald, S. 32; Grant, K. 4(12); Harris, N. 37(2); Hicks, M. (1); Hockton, D. 1(7); Ifill, P. 12(3); Lavin, G. 38; Law, B. 5; McDougald, J. (1); McLeary, A. 2; Neill, L. 33(2); Nethercott, S. 35(2); Newman, R. 22(2); Odunsi, L. 2(1); Reid, S. 25; Roberts, B. 11; Roberts, T. 8; Roche, S. 3; Ryan, R. 22(4); Sadlier, R. 18(13); Savage, D. (2); Shaw, P. 31(3); Smith, P. 5; Spink, N. 22; Stevens, K. 1(2); Stuart, J. 33(2).
Goals – League (52): Harris 15 (1 pen), Shaw 10, Cahill 6, Neill 6, Sadlier 5, Grant 3 (1 pen), Nethercott 2, Dolan 1, Fitzgerald 1, Hockton 1, Ifill 1, own goal 1.
Worthington Cup (1): Shaw 1.
FA Cup (0).
Ground: The Den, Zampa Road, Bermondsey SE16 3LN. Telephone (0171) 232 1222.
Record attendance: 20,093 v Arsenal, FA Cup 3rd rd, 10 January 1994. **Capacity:** 20,146.
Joint managers: Keith Stevens and Alan McLeary.
Secretary: Yvonne Haines.
Honours – Football League: Division 2 Champions – 1987–88. Division 3 (S) Champions – 1927–28, 1937–38. Division 4 Champions – 1961–62. **Football League Trophy winners** 1982–83.
Colours: White with black trim.

NEWCASTLE UNITED   FA PREMIERSHIP

Albert Philippe (D)	6 3	12 04	Bouillon	10 8 67	Anderlecht
Ameobi Foluwashola (F)	6 2	12 00	Zaria	12 10 81	Trainee
Andersson Andreas (F)	6 1	12 01	Osterhoninge	10 4 74	AC Milan
Arnison Paul (D)	5 10	10 12	Hartlepool	18 9 77	Trainee
Barton Warren (D)	5 11	12 00	Stoke Newington	19 3 69	Wimbledon
Beharall David (D)	6 0	11 07	Newcastle	8 3 79	Trainee
Boyd Mark (M)	5 9	11 02	Carlisle	22 10 81	Trainee
Brady Garry (M)	5 10	10 09	Glasgow	7 9 76	Tottenham H
Caldwell Gary (D)	5 11	11 10	Stirling	12 4 82	Trainee
Caldwell Stephen (D)	6 0	11 05	Stirling	12 9 80	Trainee
Charvet Laurent (D)	5 11	12 10	Beziers	8 5 73	Chelsea
Coppinger James (M)	5 7	10 03	Middlesbrough	10 1 81	Darlington
Dabizas Nikos (D)	6 0	11 11	Amypeo	3 8 73	Olympiakos
Dalglish Paul (F)	5 9	10 10	Glasgow	18 2 77	Liverpool
Domi Didier (D)	5 10	11 04	Sarcelles	2 5 79	Paris St Germain
Elliott Stuart (D)	5 8	11 05	London	27 8 77	Trainee
Ferguson Duncan (F)	6 4	14 06	Stirling	27 12 71	Everton
Gall Kevin (F)	5 9	11 01	Merthyr	4 2 82	Trainee
Georgiadis George (M)	5 8	10 11	Kavala	8 3 72	Panathinaikos
Given Shay (G)	6 0	11 08	Lifford	24 4 76	Blackburn R
Glass Stephen (M)	5 8	10 11	Dundee	23 5 76	Aberdeen
Griffin Andy (D)	5 8	10 10	Wigan	17 3 79	Stoke C
Hamann Dietmar (M)	6 3	12 06	Waldsasson	27 8 73	Bayern Munich
Hamilton Des (D)	5 11	12 13	Bradford	15 8 76	Bradford C
Harper Steve (G)	6 1	13 09	Easington	3 2 74	Seaham Red Star
Harris Michael (D)			Liverpool	6 12 80	Trainee
Howey Steve (D)	6 1	11 12	Sunderland	26 10 71	Trainee
Hughes Aaron (D)	6 0	11 02	Magherafelt	8 11 79	Trainee
Kerr Brian (M)	5 8	11 00	Motherwell	12 10 81	Trainee
Ketsbaia Temuri (F)	5 8	10 12	Gale	18 3 68	AEK Athens
Knight Paul (F)	5 7	10 07	Dublin	16 10 80	Trainee
Lee Robert (M)	5 10	11 03	Hornchurch	1 2 66	Charlton Ath
Maric Silvio (M)	5 10	11 02	Zagreb	20 3 75	Croatia Zagreb

McClen Jamie (M)	5 8	10 07	Newcastle	13 5 79	Trainee
McMahon David (F)	6 1	11 05	Dublin	17 1 81	Trainee
Pearce Stuart (D)	5 10	12 06	Shepherd's Bush	24 4 62	Nottingham F
Perez Lionel (G)	5 11	13 04	Bagnols Coze	24 4 67	Sunderland
Pistone Alessandro (D)	5 11	11 05	Milan	27 7 75	Internazionale
Robinson Paul (F)	5 10	10 12	Sunderland	20 11 78	Darlington
Saha Louis (F)	5 11	11 06	Paris	8 8 78	Metz
Serrant Carl (D)	5 11	11 02	Bradford	12 9 75	Oldham Ath
Shearer Alan (F)	5 11	12 06	Newcastle	13 8 70	Blackburn R
Solano Norberto (M)	5 9	11 06	Callao	12 12 74	Boca Juniors
Speed Gary (M)	5 10	10 12	Mancot	8 9 69	Everton
Talbot Paul (D)	5 10	10 09	Gateshead	11 8 79	Trainee
Walker Andrew (M)			Salford	2 1 81	Trainee

League Appearances: Albert, P. 3(3); Andersson, A. 11(4); Barnes, J. (1); Barton, W. 17(7); Batty, D. 6(2); Beharall, D. 4; Brady, G. 3(6); Charvet, L. 30(1); Dabizas, N. 25(5); Dalglish, P. 6(5); Domi, D. 14; Ferguson, D. 7; Georgiadis, G. 7(3); Gillespie, K. 5(2); Given, S. 31; Glass, S. 18(4); Griffin, A. 14; Guivarc'h, S. 2(2); Hamann, D. 22(1); Harper, S. 7(1); Howey, S. 14; Hughes, A. 12(2); Ketsbaia, T. 14(12); Lee, R. 20(6); Maric, S. 9(1); McClen, J. 1; Pearce, S. 12; Pistone, A. 2(1); Saha, L. 5(6); Serrant, C. 3(1); Shearer, A. 29(1); Solano, N. 24(5); Speed, G. 34(4); Watson, S. 7.
Goals – League (48): Shearer 14 (6 pens), Solano 6, Ketsbaia 5, Hamann 4, Speed 4, Dabizas 3, Glass 3, Andersson 2, Ferguson 2, Charvet 1, Dalglish 1, Guivarc'h 1, Saha 1, own goal 1.
Worthington Cup (2): Dalglish 1, Shearer 1.
FA Cup (12): Shearer 5, Ketsbaia 3, Georgiadis 1, Hamann 1, Saha 1, Speed 1.
Ground: St James' Park, Newcastle-upon-Tyne NE1 4ST. Telephone (0191) 201 8400.
Record attendance: 68,386 v Chelsea, Division 1, 3 Sept 1930. **Capacity:** 36,834.
Manager: Ruud Gullit.
Assistant secretary: Tony Toward.
Honours – Football League: Division 1 – Champions 1904–05, 1906–07, 1908–09, 1926–27, 1992–93. Division 2 Champions – 1964–65. **FA Cup winners** 1910, 1924, 1932, 1951, 1952, 1955. **Texaco Cup winners** 1973–74, 1974–75. **European Competitions: European Fairs Cup winners:** 1968–69. **Anglo-Italian Cup winners:** 1973.
Colours: Black and white striped shirts, black shorts, black stockings.

NORTHAMPTON TOWN DIV. 3

Corazzin Carlo (F)	5 10	12 07	Canada	25 12 71	Plymouth Arg
Dobson Tony (D)	6 1	12 06	Coventry	5 2 69	WBA
Frain John (D)	5 9	11 09	Birmingham	8 10 68	Birmingham C
Gibb Ali (F)	5 9	11 07	Salisbury	17 2 76	Norwich C
Hendon Ian (D)	6 0	12 10	Ilford	5 12 71	Notts Co
Hodgson Dougie (D)	6 2	13 10	Frankston	27 2 69	Oldham Ath
Hope Richard (D)	6 2	12 06	Stockton	22 6 78	Darlington
Howard Steve (F)	6 2	14 06	Durham	10 5 76	Hartlepool U
Howey Lee (D)	6 2	13 09	Sunderland	1 1 69	Burnley
Hughes Garry (D)	6 1	11 09	Birmingham	19 11 79	Trainee
Hunt James (M)	5 8	10 03	Derby	17 12 76	Notts Co
Hunter Roy (M)	5 10	12 08	Saltburn	29 10 73	WBA
Lee Christian (F)	6 2	11 07	Aylesbury	8 10 76	Doncaster R
Matthew Damian (M)	5 11	10 10	Islington	23 9 70	Burnley
Morrow Andrew (F)	5 8	9 07	Bangor	5 10 80	Trainee
Parrish Sean (M)	5 10	11 08	Wrexham	14 3 72	Doncaster R
Sampson Ian (D)	6 2	13 03	Wakefield	14 11 68	Sunderland
Savage Dave (M)	6 1	12 07	Dublin	30 7 73	Millwall

Spedding Duncan (D)	6 1	11 01	Frimley	7 9 77	Southampton
Turley Billy (G)	6 4	14 10	Wolverhampton	15 7 73	Evesham U
Wilkinson Paul (F)	6 1	12 04	Louth	30 10 64	Millwall

League Appearances: Bishop, C. 4; Clarke, A. 2(2); Clarkson, I. 3(2); Corazzin, C. 36(3); Dobson, T. 8(3); Frain, J. 40(1); Francis, S. 3; Freestone, C. 17(15); Gibb, A. 30(11); Heggs, C. 8(5); Hendon, I. 7; Hill, C. 22(5); Hodgson, D. 7(1); Hope, R. 17(2); Howard, S. 12; Howey, L. 25; Hunt, J. 24(11); Hunter, R. 15(3); Lee, C. 9(10); Matthew, D. 1; Parrish, S. 33; Peer, D. 21(5); Sampson, I. 42; Savage, D. 18(9); Seal, D. 5(1); Spedding, D. 15(9); Turley, B. 25; Warburton, R. 12; Warner, M. 5(4); Wilder, C. 1; Wilkinson, P. 12(3); Wilson, K. 8; Witter, T. 1(3); Woodman, A. 18.

Goals – League (43): Corazzin 16 (6 pens), Howey 6, Savage 5, Freestone 2, Hunt 2, Heggs 1, Hodgson 1, Hunter 1, Lee 1, Parrish 1, Peer 1, Sampson 1, Spedding 1, Warburton 1, Wilkinson 1, Wilson 1, own goal 1.

Worthington Cup (6): Freestone 3, Heggs 2, Parrish 1.

FA Cup (2): Sampson 1, own goal 1.

Ground: Sixfields Stadium, Upton Way, Northampton NN5 5QA. Telephone (01604) 757773.

Record attendance: 24,523 v Fulham, Division 1, 23 April 1966. **Capacity:** 7653.

Manager: Ian Atkins.

Secretary: Norman Howells.

Honours – Football League: Division 3 Champions – 1962–63. Division 4 Champions – 1986–87.

Colours: Claret with white shirts, white shorts, white stockings.

NORWICH CITY   DIV. 1

Anselin Cedric (M)	5 7	11 00	Lens	24 7 77	Bordeaux
Bellamy Craig (F)	5 8	10 05	Cardiff	13 1 79	Trainee
Carey Shaun (M)	5 10	11 03	Kettering	13 5 76	Trainee
Coote Adrian (F)	6 1	12 00	Gt Yarmouth	30 9 78	Trainee
Eadie Darren (F)	5 9	11 03	Chippenham	10 6 75	Trainee
Fleming Craig (D)	5 11	13 00	Halifax	6 10 71	Oldham Ath
Forbes Adrian (F)	5 7	11 02	Greenford	23 1 79	Trainee
Fuglestad Erik (D)	5 9	11 02	Randaberg	13 8 74	Viking
Grant Peter (M)	5 10	11 08	Bellshill	30 8 65	Celtic
Green Robert (G)	6 3	12 12	Chertsey	18 1 80	Trainee
Jackson Matt (D)	6 0	13 00	Leeds	19 10 71	Everton
Kenton Darren (D)	5 11	11 10	Wandsworth	13 9 78	Trainee
Llewellyn Chris (F)	6 0	11 07	Merthyr	28 8 79	Trainee
MacKay Malcolm (D)	6 3	13 06	Bellshill	19 2 72	Celtic
Marshall Andy (G)	6 2	14 00	Bury	14 4 75	Trainee
Marshall Lee (M)	6 2	12 06	Islington	21 1 79	Enfield
Milligan Mike (M)	5 10	11 06	Manchester	20 2 67	Oldham Ath
Mulryne Philip (M)	5 8	11 02	Belfast	1 1 78	Manchester U
Roberts Iwan (F)	6 3	13 06	Bangor	26 6 68	Wolverhampton W
Russell Darel (M)	6 0	12 00	Mile End	22 10 80	Trainee
Scott Kevin (D)	6 3	14 03	Easington	17 12 66	Tottenham H
Sutch Daryl (D)	5 11	12 09	Lowestoft	11 9 71	Trainee
Way Darren (M)	5 6	10 09	Plymouth	21 11 79	Trainee
Wilson Che (D)	5 11	11 04	Ely	17 1 79	Trainee

League Appearances: Adams, N. 15(3); Anselin, C. 7; Bellamy, C. 38(2); Brannan, G. 10(1); Carey, S. 7(3); Coote, A. 2(4); Dalglish, P. 3(2); Eadie, D. 21(1); Fleming, C. 35(2); Forbes, A. 7(8); Fuglestad, E. 22(2); Grant, P. 31(2); Green, R. 2; Hughes, P. 2(2); Jackson, M. 36(1); Kenton, D. 22; Llewellyn, C. 21(10); MacKay, M. 24(3); Marshall, A. 37; Marshall, L. 38(6); Milligan, M. 1(1); Mulryne, P. 6(1); O'Neill, K. 14(4); Roberts, I. 40(5); Russell, D. 8(5); Segura, V. 2(2); Sutch, D. 34(2); Watt, M.

7(1); Wilson, C. 14(3).
Goals – League (62): Roberts 19, Bellamy 17 (2 pens), Adams 3 (2 pens), Eadie 3, Fleming 3, Marshall L 3, Llewellyn 2, Mulryne 2, Anselin 1, Brannan 1, Hughes 1, Jackson 1, Kenton 1, MacKay 1, O'Neill 1, Russell 1, own goals 2.
Worthington Cup (7): Roberts 3, Bellamy 2, O'Neill 1, own goal 1.
FA Cup (1): Roberts 1.
Ground: Carrow Road, Norwich NR1 1JE. Telephone (01603) 760760.
Record attendance: 43,984 v Leicester C, FA Cup 6th rd, 30 March 1963. **Capacity:** 21,414.
Manager: Bruce Rioch.
Secretary: Kevin Platt.
Honours – Football League: Division 2 Champions – 1971–72, 1985–86. Division 3 (S) Champions – 1933–34. **Football League Cup:** Winners 1962, 1985.
Colours: All yellow.

NOTTINGHAM FOREST   DIV. 1

Name	Ht	Wt	Birthplace	Birthdate	Previous club
Allou Bernard (M)	5 8	11 00	Cocody	19 6 75	Paris St Germain
Bart-Williams Chris (M)	5 11	12 07	Freetown	16 6 74	Sheffield W
Bonalair Thierry (D)	5 9	10 08	Paris	14 6 66	Neuchatel Xamax
Burns John (M)	5 10	11 02	Dublin	4 12 77	Belvedere
Carter Nicky (F)	5 11	11 07	Stoke	29 11 81	Trainee
Chettle Steve (D)	6 1	13 04	Nottingham	27 9 68	Apprentice
Cooper Richard (D)	5 9	10 07	Nottingham	27 9 79	Trainee
Crossley Mark (G)	6 0	15 09	Barnsley	16 6 69	Trainee
Dawson Kevin (D)	6 0	10 07	Northallerton	18 6 81	Trainee
Doig Chris (D)	6 2	12 06	Dumfries	13 2 81	Trainee
Edds Gareth (M)	5 11	10 12	Sydney	3 2 81	Trainee
Edwards Christian (D)	6 2	12 03	Caerphilly	23 11 75	Swansea C
Foy Keith (M)	5 11	12 03	Crumlin	30 12 81	Trainee
Freedman Dougie (F)	5 9	12 05	Glasgow	21 1 74	Wolverhampton W
Freeman David (F)	5 10	11 07	Dublin	25 11 79	Cherry Orchard
Goodlad Mark (G)	6 0	13 02	Barnsley	9 9 80	Trainee
Gray Andy (M)	6 0	13 00	Harrogate	15 11 77	Leeds U
Guinan Stephen (F)	6 1	13 06	Birmingham	24 12 75	Trainee
Harewood Marlon (F)	6 1	13 03	Hampstead	25 8 79	Trainee
Hjelde Jon Olav (D)	6 2	13 05	Levanger	30 7 72	Rosenborg
Hodgson Richard (F)	5 10	11 06	Sunderland	1 10 79	Trainee
Hudson Niall (M)	5 10	10 02	Ilkeston	7 1 82	Trainee
Johnson Andy (M)	6 1	13 03	Bristol	2 5 74	Norwich C
Louis-Jean Mathieu (D)	5 9	10 08	Mont-St-Aignan	22 2 76	Le Havre
Mattsson Jesper (D)	6 1	13 01	Visby	18 4 68	Halmstad
McNamara Niall (F)	5 11	11 09	Eire	26 1 82	Trainee
Melton Steve (M)	5 11	12 03	Lincoln	3 10 78	Trainee
Palmer Carlton (M)	6 2	13 00	Oldbury	5 12 65	Southampton
Pascolo Marco (G)	6 2	14 04	Sion	2 5 66	Cagliari
Prutton David (D)	6 1	11 06	Hull	12 9 81	Trainee
Quashie Nigel (M)	5 9	12 08	Nunhead	20 7 78	QPR
Rogers Alan (D)	5 10	12 08	Liverpool	3 1 77	Tranmere R
Shipperley Neil (F)	6 1	14 01	Chatham	30 10 74	Crystal Palace
Turner Matthew (F)	5 9	10 00	Nottingham	29 12 81	Trainee
Van Hooijdonk Pierre (F)	6 4	13 07	Steenbergen	29 11 69	Celtic
Williams Gareth (M)	5 11	11 08	Glasgow	16 12 81	Trainee
Woan Ian (F)	5 10	12 07	Wirral	14 12 67	Runcorn

League Appearances: Allou, B. (2); Armstrong, C. 20(2); Bart-Williams, C. 20(4); Beasant, D. 26; Bonalair, T. 24(4); Chettle, S. 32(2); Crossley, M. 12; Darcheville,

J. 14(2); Doig, C. 1(1); Edwards, C. 7(5); Freedman, D. 20(11); Gemmill, S. 18(2); Gough, R. 7; Gray, A. 3(5); Harewood, M. 11(12); Harkes, J. 3; Hjelde, J. 16(1); Hodges, G. 3(2); Johnson, A. 25(3); Louis-Jean, M. 15(1); Lyttle, D. 5(5); Mattsson, J. 5(1); Melton, S. 1; Palmer, C. 13; Porfirio, H. 3(6); Quashie, N. 12(4); Rogers, A. 34; Shipperley, N. 12(8); Stensaas, S. 6(1); Stone, S. 26; Thomas, G. 5; Van Hooijdonk, P. 19(2); Woan, I. (2).

Goals – League (35): Freedman 9, Van Hooijdonk 6, Rogers 4, Bart-Williams 3, Stone 3, Chettle 2 (2 pens), Darcheville 2, Bonalair 1, Harewood 1, Hjelde 1, Porfirio 1, Shipperley 1, Thomas 1.

Worthington Cup (9): Freedman 3, Harewood 2, Stone 2, Armstrong 1, Johnson 1. **FA Cup** (0).

Ground: City Ground, Nottingham NG2 5FJ. Telephone (0115) 9824444.

Record attendance: 49,945 v Manchester U, Division 1, 28 October 1967. **Capacity:** 30,602.

Manager: David Platt.

Secretary: Paul White.

Honours – Football League: Division 1 – Champions 1977–78, 1997–98. Division 2 Champions – 1906–07, 1921–22. Division 3 (S) Champions – 1950–51. **FA Cup:** Winners 1898, 1959. **Football League Cup:** Winners 1977–78, 1978–79, 1988–89, 1989–90. **Anglo-Scottish Cup:** Winners 1976–77. **Simod Cup:** Winners 1989. **Zenith Data Systems Cup:** Winners 1991–92. **European Competitions: European Cup winners:** 1978–79, 1979–80. **Super Cup winners:** 1979–80.

Colours: Red shirts, black shoulders, white shorts, red stockings.

NOTTS COUNTY DIV. 2

Beadle Peter (F)	6 1	13 07	Lambeth	13 5 72	Port Vale
Bolland Paul (M)	5 10	10 12	Bradford	23 12 79	Bradford C
Darby Duane (F)	5 11	12 06	Birmingham	17 10 73	Hull C
Dyer Alex (M)	5 11	12 00	Forest Gate	14 11 65	Huddersfield T
Fairclough Chris (D)	5 11	11 07	Nottingham	12 4 64	Bolton W
Farrell Sean (F)	6 1	13 07	Watford	28 2 69	Peterborough U
Gibson Paul (G)	6 2	13 06	Sheffield	1 11 76	Manchester U
Holmes Richard (D)			Grantham	7 11 80	Trainee
Hughes Andy (M)	6 0	11 00	Manchester	2 1 78	Oldham Ath
Liburd Richard (D)	5 9	11 01	Nottingham	26 9 73	Carlisle U
Murray Shaun (M)	5 8	11 02	Newcastle	7 12 70	Bradford C
Owers Gary (M)	5 11	12 07	Newcastle	3 10 68	Bristol C
Pearce Dennis (D)	5 9	11 00	Wolverhampton	10 9 74	Wolverhampton W
Rapley Kevin (F)	5 9	10 08	Reading	21 9 77	Brentford
Redmile Matthew (D)	6 4	14 10	Nottingham	12 11 76	Trainee
Richardson Ian (M)	5 11	11 01	Barking	22 10 70	Dagenham & Redbridge
Robson Mark (F)	5 7	10 02	Newham	22 5 69	Charlton Ath
Stallard Mark (F)	6 0	12 10	Derby	24 10 74	Wycombe W
Tierney Fran (M)	5 10	11 00	Liverpool	9 10 75	Crewe Alex
Ward Darren (G)	5 11	12 09	Worksop	11 5 74	Mansfield T
Warren Mark (D)	6 0	12 02	Clapton	12 11 74	Leyton Orient
Webster Adam (M)			Leicester	3 7 80	

League Appearances: Beadle, P. 13(1); Billy, C. 3(3); Bolland, P. 12(1); Creaney, G. 13(3); Devlin, P. 5; Dudley, C. (4); Dyer, A. 19(10); Fairclough, C. 16; Farrell, S. 7(4); Finnan, S. 12(1); Foley, D. 2; Garcia, T. 10(9); Gibson, P. 1; Goram, A. 1; Grant, K. 6; Hendon, I. 32; Holmes, R. 3(5); Hughes, A. 21(9); Jackson, J. 3(7); Jones, G. 23(5); Liburd, R. 27(8); Matthews, L. 4(1); Murray, S. 32(3); Owers, G. 36(3); Parkin, B. 1; Pearce, D. 31(2); Quayle, M. 2(3); Rapley, K. 10(6); Redmile, M. 39(2); Richardson, I. 23; Robson, M. (2); Stallard, M. 13(1); Strodder, G. 8(3); Tierney, F. 13(7); Torpey, S. 4(2); Ward, D. 43; Warren, M. 18.

Goals – League (52): Richardson 7, Hendon 6 (5 pens), Stallard 4, Beadle 3, Creaney 3 (1 pen), Farrell 3, Hughes 3, Murray 3, Owers 3, Tierney 3, Garcia 2, Jones 2, Rapley 2, Fairclough 1, Grant 1, Liburd 1, Pearce 1, Redmile 1, Strodder 1, Torpey 1, own goal 1.
Worthington Cup (1): Torpey 1.
FA Cup (8): Jones 6, Murray 1, Owers 1.:
Ground: County Ground, Meadow Lane, Nottingham NG2 3HJ. Telephone (0115) 952 9000.
Record attendance: 47,310 v York C, FA Cup 6th rd, 12 March 1955. **Capacity:** 20,300.
Manager: Sam Allardyce.
Secretary: Ian Moat.
Honours – Football League: Division 2 Champions – 1896–97, 1913–14, 1922–23. Division 3 Champions – 1997–98. Division 3 (S) Champions – 1930–31, 1949–50. Division 4 Champions – 1970–71. **FA Cup:** Winners 1893–94. **Anglo-Italian Cup:** Winners 1995.
Colours: Black and white striped shirts, black shorts, black stockings.

OLDHAM ATHLETIC DIV. 2

Name			Birthplace	D.O.B.	Previous club
Allott Mark (F)	5 11	10 12	Middleton	16 3 78	Trainee
Boshell Daniel (M)			Bradford	30 5 81	Trainee
Campbell Jamie (M)			Glasgow	2 12 80	Trainee
Clitheroe Lee (F)	5 10	10 07	Chorley	18 11 78	Trainee
Dudley Craig (F)	5 11	11 02	Ollerton	12 9 79	Notts Co
Duxbury Lee (M)	5 10	10 07	Keighley	7 10 69	Bradford C
Garnett Shaun (D)	6 2	13 01	Wallasey	22 11 69	Swansea C
Graham Richard (D)	6 2	12 09	Dewsbury	28 11 74	Trainee
Holt Andy (D)	6 1	11 02	Manchester	21 5 78	Trainee
Hotte Mark (M)	5 11	11 00	Bradford	27 9 78	Trainee
Innes Mark (D)	5 10	12 04	Bellshill	27 9 78	Trainee
Kelly Gary (G)	5 11	12 08	Fulwood	3 8 66	Bury
McGinlay John (F)	5 10	12 02	Inverness	8 4 64	Bradford C
McLean Ian (D)	5 10	11 04	Leeds	13 9 78	Trainee
McNiven David (F)	5 10	12 00	Leeds	27 5 78	Trainee
McNiven Scott (D)	5 10	10 08	Leeds	27 5 78	Trainee
Miskelly David (G)	6 0	12 02	Ards	3 9 79	Trainee
Philliskirk Tony (F)	6 2	12 12	Sunderland	10 2 65	Cardiff C
Rickers Paul (M)	5 10	10 07	Dewsbury	9 5 75	Trainee
Salt Philip (M)	5 10	11 02	Huddersfield	2 3 79	Trainee
Sheridan John (M)	5 10	12 01	Stretford	1 10 64	Bolton W
Sugden Ryan (M)			Bradford	26 12 80	Trainee
Swan Iain (D)	6 2	11 03	Glasgow	4 7 80	Trainee
Thom Stuart (D)	6 2	11 10	Dewsbury	27 12 76	Nottingham F
Tipton Matthew (F)	5 10	11 02	Bridgend	29 6 80	Trainee
Walsh Danny (D)	5 9	12 03	Manchester	16 9 78	Trainee
Wardle Darren (M)			Bury	2 1 81	
Whitehall Steve (F)	5 11	11 07	Bromborough	8 12 66	Mansfield T

League Appearances: Allott, M. 32(9); Beavers, P. 7; Clitheroe, L. 1(1); Duxbury, L. 41; Garnett, S. 36(1); Graham, R. 11; Gray, A. 4; Hodgson, D. (1); Holt, A. 39(4); Hotte, M. (1); Innes, M. 8(5); Kelly, G. 45; Littlejohn, A. 11(5); Mardon, P. 12; McGinlay, J. 4(3); McLean, I. 5; McNiven, D. 1(5); McNiven, S. 33(4); Miskelly, D. 1; Orlygsson, T. 19(3); Reid, P. 40; Rickers, P. 44(1); Ritchie, A. (1); Salt, P. 3(6); Sheridan, J. 30; Sinnott, L. 14(4); Spooner, N. 2; Sugden, R. (2); Swan, I. 1; Thom, S. 19(6); Tipton, M. 15(13); Walsh, D. (1); Whitehall, S. 28(8).
Goals – League (48): Allott 7, Duxbury 6, Holt 5, Rickers 4, Whitehall 4, Graham 3, Mardon 3, Beavers 2, Garnett 2, Littlejohn 2, Sheridan 2, Tipton 2, Innes 1, McGinlay 1, McNiven S 1, Reid 1 (pen), Thom 1, own goal 1.

Worthington Cup (3): Allott 1, Littlejohn 1, Reid 1 (pen).
FA Cup (5): McGinlay 2 (1 pen), Duxbury 1, McNiven S 1, Salt 1.
Ground: Boundary Park, Oldham OL1 2PA. Telephone (0161) 624 4972.
Record attendance: 47,671 v Sheffield W, FA Cup 4th rd. 25 January 1930.
Capacity: 13,559.
Manager: Andy Ritchie.
Secretary: Alan Hardy.
Honours – Football League: Division 2 Champions – 1990–91, Division 3 (N) Champions – 1952–53. Division 3 Champions – 1973–74.
Colours: All blue.

OXFORD UNITED DIV. 2

Beauchamp Joey (M)	5 10	12 07	Oxford	13 3 71	Swindon T
Cook Jamie (F)	5 10	10 10	Oxford	2 8 79	Trainee
Davis Steve (D)	6 1	13 05	Birmingham	26 7 65	Barnsley
Folland Robbie (F)	5 9	10 07	Swansea	16 9 79	Trainee
Francis Kevin (F)	6 7	16 12	Moseley	6 12 67	Birmingham C
Gilchrist Phil (D)	6 0	13 04	Stockton	25 8 73	Hartlepool U
Gray Martin (M)	5 9	11 04	Stockton	17 8 71	Sunderland
Lundin Paul (G)	6 4	14 00	Osby	21 11 64	Osters
Powell Paul (M)	5 8	11 01	Wallingford	30 6 78	Trainee
Robinson Les (D)	5 9	12 02	Shirebrook	1 3 67	Doncaster R
Tait Paul (M)	5 11	11 10	Sutton Coldfield	31 7 71	Birmingham C
Thomson Andy (F)	5 10	11 05	Motherwell	1 4 71	Southend U
Watson Mark (D)	6 0	12 04	Vancouver	8 9 70	Osters
Weatherstone Simon (F)	5 10	12 04	Reading	26 1 80	Trainee
Whelan Phil (D)	6 3	13 05	Stockport	7 3 72	Middlesbrough

League Appearances: Banger, N. 22(10); Beauchamp, J. 31(6); Cook, J. 9(10); Davis, S. 3; Francis, K. 12(6); Gerrard, P. 16; Gilchrist, P. 39; Gray, M. 40; Hill, D. 1(8); Jackson, E. 1; Lundin, P. 7; Marsh, S. 20(1); Murphy, M. 33(10); Powell, P. 40(4); Remy, C. 10(2); Robinson, L. 44; Rose, A. 1(3); Salmon, M. 1; Smith, D. 19(3); Tait, P. 17; Thomson, A. 25(13); Warren, M. 4; Watson, M. 23; Weatherstone, S. 4(8); Whelan, P. 14(1); Whitehead, P. 21; Williams, M. (2); Wilsterman, B. 12(5); Windass, D. 33; Wright, T. 4(2).
Goals – League (48): Windass 15 (3 pens), Thomson 7, Banger 5, Beauchamp 4, Murphy 4, Powell 3, Gilchrist 2, Marsh 2, Wilsterman 2, Cook 1, Francis 1, Remy 1, Weatherstone 1.
Worthington Cup (4): Murphy 2, Weatherstone 1, Whelan 1.
FA Cup (6): Windass 3 (1 pen), Murphy 2, Gilchrist 1.
Ground: Manor Ground, Headington, Oxford OX3 7RS. Telephone (01865) 761503.
Record attendance: 22,750 v Preston NE, FA Cup 6th rd, 29 February 1964.
Capacity: 9572.
Manager: Malcolm Shotton.
Secretary: Mick Brown.
Honours – Football League: Division 2 Champions – 1984–85. Division 3 Champions – 1967–68, 1983–84. **Football League Cup:** Winners 1985–86.
Colours: Yellow shirts with navy trim, navy shorts and stockings.

PETERBOROUGH UNITED DIV. 3

Broughton Drewe (F)	6 3	12 01	Hitchin	25 10 78	Brentford
Butler Steve (F)	6 1	12 02	Birmingham	21 1 62	Gillingham
Campbell James (D)	6 2	11 12	Kent	16 11 79	Trainee

Castle Steve (M)	5 11	11 07	Ilford	17 5 66	Birmingham C
Chapple Phil (D)	6 2	13 01	Norwich	21 11 66	Charlton Ath
Clarke Andy (F)	5 10	11 07	Islington	22 7 67	Wimbledon
Cleaver Chris (F)	5 10	11 07	Hitchin	24 3 79	Trainee
Connor Dan (G)	6 2	12 09	Dublin	31 1 81	Trainee
Danielsson Helgi (M)	5 11	10 10	Reykjavik	13 7 81	Fylkir
Davies Simon (M)	5 10	12 03	Haverfordwest	23 10 79	Trainee
Drury Adam (D)	5 10	11 06	Cottenham	29 8 78	Trainee
Edwards Andy (D)	6 2	12 00	Epping	17 9 71	Birmingham C
Etherington Matthew (F)	5 10	10 07	Truro	14 8 81	School
Farrell Dave (F)	5 9	11 07	Birmingham	11 11 71	Wycombe W
French Daniel (M)	5 11	11 01	Peterborough	25 11 79	Trainee
Gill Matthew (M)	5 11	11 10	Cambridge	8 11 80	Trainee
Green Francis (F)	5 9	11 04	Derby	23 4 80	Ilkeston T
Griemink Bart (G)	6 3	15 04	Holland	29 3 72	Birmingham C
Haley Grant (D)	5 8	10 02	Bristol	20 9 79	Trainee
Hanlon Ritchie (M)	5 10	11 12	Kenton	25 5 78	Southend U
Hann Matthew (M)	5 9	10 04	Saffron Walden	6 9 80	Trainee
Hooper Dean (D)	5 10	12 12	Harefield	13 4 71	Swindon T
Inman Niall (M)	5 9	11 06	Wakefield	6 2 78	Trainee
Jelleyman Gareth (D)	5 10	10 02	Holywell	14 11 80	Trainee
Kenna Warren (D)	6 1	13 06	Southampton	18 5 80	Trainee
Koogi Anders (M)	5 10	10 11	Roskilde	8 9 79	Trainee
Lewis Neil (D)	5 8	10 05	Wolverhampton	28 6 74	Leicester C
Lyttle Gerard (D)	5 7	11 01	Belfast	27 11 77	Star of the Stea
Martin Jae (M)	5 11	11 00	London	5 2 76	Lincoln C
Rowe Zeke (F)	5 10	11 08	Stoke Newington	30 10 73	Chelsea
Scott Richard (M)	5 9	10 10	Dudley	29 9 74	Shrewsbury T
Shields Tony (M)	5 8	10 01	Derry	4 6 80	Trainee
Tyler Mark (G)	5 11	12 00	Norwich	2 4 77	Trainee
Wicks Matthew (D)	6 2	13 05	Reading	8 9 78	Crewe Alex

League Appearances: Allardyce, C. 4; Andrews, W. 8(2); Bodley, M. 24; Broughton, D. 14(11); Butler, S. 13(1); Carruthers, M. 13(1); Castle, S. 26; Chapple, P. 1; Cleaver, C. (2); Connor, D. 2; Davies, S. 43; De Souza, M. 3; Drury, A. 39(1); Edwards, A. 41; Etherington, M. 21(8); Farrell, D. 28(9); Forbes, S. 1(2); Gill, M. 22(4); Grazioli, G. 21(13); Green, F. 3(4); Griemink, B. 17; Hanlon, R. (4); Hann, M. (4); Hooper, D. 36(2); Houghton, S. 7(1); Inman, N. 1(2); Koogi, A. (1); Legg, A. 5; Linton, D. 8; Martin, J. (4); McKenzie, L. 14; McMenamin, C. 4(1); Payne, D. 8(1); Quinn, J. 7; Rennie, D. 9; Rowe, Z. (7); Scott, R. 19(8); Shields, T. 6(3); Tyler, M. 27; Wicks, M. 11.

Goals – League (72): Grazioli 15, McKenzie 8, Broughton 7 (2 pens), Andrews 5, Quinn 5, Castle 4, Davies 4, Farrell 4 (1 pen), Scott 4, Etherington 3, Butler 2 (1 pen), Carruthers 2, Edwards 2, Hooper 2, Green 1, Hanlon 1, Houghton 1, Inman 1, own goal 1.

Worthington Cup (1): Carruthers 1.

FA Cup (0).

Ground: London Road Ground, Peterborough PE2 8AL. Telephone (01733) 563947.

Record attendance: 30,096 v Swansea T, FA Cup 5th rd, 20 February 1965.

Capacity: 15,314.

Manager: Barry Fry.

Secretary: Caroline Hand.

Honours – Football League: Division 4 Champions – 1960–61, 1973–74.

Colours: Royal blue shirts, white shorts, blue stockings with white tops.

PLYMOUTH ARGYLE

DIV. 3

| Ashton Jon (D) | 6 0 | 13 00 | Plymouth | 4 8 79 | Trainee |
| Barlow Martin (M) | 5 7 | 10 03 | Barnstable | 25 6 71 | Trainee |

Bastow Darren (M)   Torquay   22 12 81   Trainee
Beswetherick John (D)   5 11   11 04   Liverpool   15 1 78   Trainee
Ford Liam (F)   5 7   10 03   Bradford   8 9 79   Trainee
Gibbs Paul (D)   5 10   11 09   Gorleston   26 10 72   Torquay U
Hargreaves Chris (M)   5 11   12 02   Cleethorpes   12 5 72   Hereford U
Heathcote Mike (D)   6 2   12 08   Durham   10 9 65   Cambridge U
McCall Steve (M)   5 11   12 10   Carlisle   15 10 60   Torquay U
McCarthy Sean (F)   6 1   12 05   Bridgend   12 9 67   Oldham Ath
McGovern Brendan (M)   5 10   12 07   Camborne   9 2 80   Trainee
Phillips Lee (F)   5 10   12 00   Penzance   16 9 80   School
Rowbotham Jason (D)   5 9   11 09   Cardiff   3 1 69   Wycombe W
Sheffield Jon (G)   5 11   11 06   Bedworth   1 2 69   Peterborough U
Wotton Paul (M)   5 11   11 08   Plymouth   17 8 77   Trainee

League Appearances: Ashton, J. 22(4); Barlow, M. 45; Barrett, A. (1); Bastow, D. 21(8); Beswetherick, J. 18(4); Branston, G. 7; Collins, S. 40; Crittenden, N. 1(1); Crowe, G. 3(8); Dungey, J. 7; Edmondson, D. 4; Flash, R. 4(1); Ford, L. (1); Forinton, H. 8(1); Gibbs, P. 27; Gritton, M. (2); Guinan, S. 11; Hargreaves, C. 30(2); Heathcote, M. 43; Jean, E. 21(8); Marker, N. 4; Marshall, D. 25(3); Mauge, R. 31(1); McCall, S. 14(3); McCarthy, S. 14(2); McGovern, B. (2); Phillips, L. 8(7); Power, L. 7(9); Sale, M. 8; Sheffield, J. 39; Sweeney, T. 6(7); Taylor, C. 6; Wills, K. (2); Wotton, P. 32(4).

Goals – League (58): Marshall 12, Guinan 7, Barlow 5 (1 pen), Forinton 3, Gibbs 3 (2 pens), Heathcote 3, Jean 3, Mauge 3, McCarthy 3, Bastow 2, Collins 2, Hargreaves 2, Branston 1, Crowe 1, Phillips 1, Sale 1, Sweeney 1, Taylor 1, Wotton 1 (pen), own goals 3.

Worthington Cup (3): McCarthy 2, Jean 1.

FA Cup (4): Heathcote 1, Sweeney 1, Wotton 1 (pen), own goal 1

Ground: Home Park, Plymouth, Devon PL2 3DQ. Telephone (01752) 562561.

Record attendance: 43,596 v Aston Villa, Division 2, 10 October 1936.

Capacity: 19,630.

Manager: Kevin Hodges.

Secretary: Roger Matthews.

Honours – Football League: Division 3 (S) Champions – 1929–30, 1951–52. Division 3 Champions – 1958–59.

Colours: Green and white shirts, white shorts, green, black and white stockings.

PORTSMOUTH   DIV. 1

Awford Andy (D)   5 9   11 02   Worcester   14 7 72   Worcester C
Claridge Steve (F)   5 9   13 00   Portsmouth   10 4 66   Wolverhampton W
Durnin John (M)   5 10   11 10   Liverpool   18 8 65   Oxford U
Flahavan Aaron (G)   6 1   11 12   Southampton   15 12 75   Trainee
Holbrook Adam (M)   5 9   11 04   Newport (IW)   17 10 80   Trainee
Igoe Sammy (M)   5 6   9 07   Spelthorne   30 9 75   Trainee
McLoughlin Alan (M)   5 8   10 10   Manchester   20 4 67   Southampton
McNab Joe (M)   5 4   9 00   Brighton   29 10 80   Manchester C
McNab Neil (M)   5 6   10 03   Brighton   29 10 80   Manchester C
Miglioranzi Stefani (M) 6 0   11 12   Pacos de Caldas   20 9 77   St Johns Univ
Nightingale Luke (F)   5 10   12 05   Portsmouth   22 12 80   Trainee
Peron Jean-Francois (M) 5 8   10 04   St Omer   11 10 65   Walsall
Perrett Russell (D)   6 2   13 00   Barton-on-Sea   18 6 73   AFC Lymington
Pettefer Carl (M)   5 6   10 11   Taplow   22 3 81   Trainee
Phillips Martin (M)   5 9   10 03   Exeter   13 3 76   Manchester C
Robinson Matthew (D)   5 11   11 04   Exeter   23 12 74   Southampton
Simpson Fitzroy (M)   5 8   12 00   Trowbridge   26 2 70   Manchester C
Simpson Robbie (F)   5 10   11 06   Luton   3 3 76   Tottenham H

Soley Steve (M)	5 11	12 08	Widnes	22 4 71	Leek T
Tardif Chris (G)	6 0	12 05	Guernsey	19 9 79	Trainee
Thogersen Thomas (D)	6 1	13 00	Copenhagen	2 4 68	Brondby
Vlachos Michalis (D)	5 11	12 08	Athens	20 9 67	AEK Athens
Waterman David (D)	5 10	13 02	Guernsey	16 5 77	Trainee
Whitbread Adrian (D)	6 1	13 00	Epping	22 10 71	West Ham U

League Appearances: Aloisi, J. 22; Andreasson, S. (2); Awford, A. 35; Claridge, S. 39; Durnin, J. 16(10); Flahavan, A. 13; Hillier, D. 11(5); Igoe, S. 39(1); Knight, A. 20; Kyzeridis, N. 2(2); McLoughlin, A. 41; Miglioranzi, S. 4(3); Nightingale, L. 6(13); Peron, J. 37(1); Perrett, R. 12(3); Pethick, R. 4(6); Petterson, A. 13; Phillips, M. 2(15); Robinson, M. 27(2); Simpson, F. 38(3); Soley, S. 1(7); Thogersen, T. 29(5); Thomson, A. 14; Vlachos, M. 29(1); Waterman, D. 10; Whitbread, A. 33; Whittingham, G. 9.

Goals – League (57): Aloisi 13, Claridge 9 (1 pen), Durnin 7, McLoughlin 7 (4 pens), Whittingham 7, Igoe 5, Nightingale 3, Awford 1, Peron 1, Phillips 1, Robinson 1, Simpson 1, own goal 1.

Worthington Cup (9): Aloisi 3, McLoughlin 3 (2 pens), Hillier 1, Vlachos 1, Whitbread 1.

FA Cup (2): Claridge 1, Nightingale 1.

Ground: Fratton Park, Frogmore Rd, Portsmouth PO4 8RA. Telephone (01705) 731204.

Record attendance: 51,385 v Derby Co, FA Cup 6th rd, 26 February 1949.

Capacity: 19, 179.

Manager: Alan Ball.

Secretary: Paul Weld.

Honours – Football League: Division 1 Champions – 1948–49, 1949–50. Division 3 (S) Champions – 1923–24. Division 3 Champions – 1961–62, 1982–83. **FA Cup:** Winners 1939.

Colours: Blue shirts, white shorts, red stockings.

PORT VALE   DIV. 1

Barnett Dave (D)	6 1	12 08	Birmingham	16 4 67	Dunfermline Ath
Bent Marcus (F)	6 2	12 04	Hammersmith	19 5 78	Crystal Palace
Bogie Ian (M)	5 7	11 10	Newcastle	6 12 67	Leyton Orient
Brammer Dave (M)	5 10	12 00	Bromborough	28 2 75	Wrexham
Brisco Neil (M)	6 0	11 05	Billinge	26 1 78	Manchester C
Burns Liam (D)	6 0	13 03	Belfast	30 10 78	Trainee
Butler Tony (D)	6 2	12 03	Stockport	28 9 72	Blackpool
Carragher Matthew (D)	5 9	11 06	Liverpool	14 1 76	Wigan Ath
Corden Wayne (M)	5 10	11 05	Leek	1 11 75	Trainee
Eyre Richard (M)	5 8	11 08	Poynton	15 9 76	Trainee
Gardner Anthony (D)	6 5	13 00	Staffordshire	19 9 80	Trainee
Griffiths Carl (F)	5 10	11 05	Oswestry	15 7 71	Leyton Orient
Musselwhite Paul (G)	6 2	14 04	Portsmouth	22 12 68	Scunthorpe U
Naylor Tony (F)	5 7	10 07	Manchester	29 3 68	Crewe Alex
O'Callaghan George (M)	6 1	10 05	Cork	5 9 79	Trainee
Pilkington Kevin (G)	6 1	13 00	Hitchin	8 3 74	Manchester U
Rougier Tony (F)	5 10	14 07	Trinidad	17 7 71	Hibernian
Smith Alex (M)	5 9	9 09	Liverpool	15 2 76	Chester C
Snijders Mark (D)	6 2	14 04	Alkmaar	12 3 72	
Talbot Stuart (M)	5 11	13 07	Birmingham	14 6 73	Moor Green
Tankard Allen (D)	5 10	13 04	Fleet	21 5 69	Wigan Ath
Walsh Michael (D)	6 0	12 08	Rotherham	5 8 77	Scunthorpe U

League Appearances: Ainsworth, G. 15; Allen, C. 2(3); Aspin, N. 28(2); Barker, S. 23(4); Barnett, D. 26(1); Beadle, P. 18(5); Beesley, P. 33(2); Bent, M. 10(5);

Berntsen, R. 1; Bogie, I. 31(4); Brammer, D. 9; Brisco, N. 1; Burns, L. 2(2); Butler, T. 4; Carragher, M. 8(2); Clarke, A. 2(4); Corden, W. 4(12); Eyre, R. 8(3); Foyle, M. 32(3); Gardner, A. 14(1); Griffiths, C. 3; Horlaville, C. 1(1); Jansson, J. 5(2); Koordes, R. 13(2); Lee, A. 7(4); Lyttle, D. 7; McGill, D. (3); McGlinchey, B. 10(5); McQuade, J. (3); Mean, S. 1; Musselwhite, P. 38; Naylor, T. 14(8); O'Callaghan, G. 4; Pilkington, K. 8; Pounewatchy, S. 2; Rougier, T. 8(5); Russell, C. 8; Smith, A. 7(1); Snijders, M. 6(4); Talbot, S. 29(4); Tankard, A. 37; Walsh, M. 18(1); Widdrington, T. 9.

Goals – League (45): Foyle 9, Beadle 6, Ainsworth 5, Naylor 4, Tankard 4, Beesley 3, Barker 2 (1 pen), Bogie 2, Lee 2, Allen 1, Gardner 1, Griffiths 1, McGlinchey 1, Russell 1, Walsh 1, Widdrington 1 (pen), own goal 1.

Worthington Cup (3): Naylor 2, Ainsworth 1.

FA Cup (0).

Ground: Vale Park, Burslem, Stoke-on-Trent ST6 1AW. Telephone (01782) 814134.

Record attendance: 50,000 v Aston Villa, FA Cup 5th rd, 20 February 1960.

Capacity: 22,356

Manager: Brian Horton.

Secretary: F. W. Lodey.

Honours – Football League: Division 3 (N) Champions – 1929–30, 1953–54. Division 4 Champions – 1958–59.

Colours: White shirts, black shorts, black and white stockings.

PRESTON NORTH END   DIV. 2

Alexander Graham (D)	5 10	12 02	Coventry	10 10 71	Luton T
Appleton Michael (M)	5 8	11 00	Salford	4 12 75	Manchester U
Cartwright Lee (F)	5 8	10 06	Rossendale	19 9 72	Trainee
Eyres David (F)	5 11	11 05	Liverpool	26 2 64	Burnley
Gregan Sean (M)	6 2	12 03	Stockton	29 3 74	Darlington
Harris Jason (F)	6 1	11 10	Sutton	24 11 76	Leyton Orient
Jackson Michael (D)	5 11	11 09	Chester	4 12 73	Bury
Kidd Ryan (D)	5 11	10 08	Radcliffe	16 10 71	Port Vale
King Stuart (M)			Derry	20 3 81	Trainee
Lucas David (G)	6 1	11 06	Preston	23 11 77	
Ludden Dominic (D)	5 7	10 09	Basildon	30 3 74	Watford
Macken Jonathan (F)	5 10	12 00	Manchester	7 9 77	Trainee
McKenna Paul (M)	5 8	11 11	Chorley	20 10 77	Trainee
Moilanen Teuvo (G)	6 5	12 06	Oulu	12 12 73	Jaro
Morgan Paul (D)	6 0	11 03	Belfast	23 10 78	Trainee
Murdock Colin (D)	6 1	12 00	Ballymena	2 7 75	Manchester U
Nogan Kurt (F)	5 10	11 01	Cardiff	9 9 70	Burnley
Parkinson Gary (D)	5 10	11 08	Middlesbrough	10 1 68	Burnley
Rankine Mark (M)	5 9	11 06	Doncaster	30 9 69	Wolverhampton W
Wright Mark (F)	5 10	11 04	Chorley	4 9 81	Schoolboy

League Appearances: Alexander, G. 10; Appleton, M. 13(12); Basham, S. 15(2); Byfield, D. 3(2); Cartwright, L. 14(13); Clement, N. 4; Darby, J. 12(8); Eyres, D. 33(1); Gray, A. 5; Gregan, S. 40(1); Harris, J. 9(25); Harrison, C. 6; Holt, M. (3); Jackson, M. 44; Kidd, R. 27(1); Lucas, D. 31; Ludden, D. 26(6); Macken, J. 30(12); McGregor, P. 1(3); McKenna, P. 31(5); Moilanen, T. 15; Murdock, C. 28(5); Nogan, K. 39(3); Parkinson, G. 27; Rankine, M. 42; Wright, M. 1.

Goals – League (78): Nogan 18, Basham 10, Eyres 8, Jackson 8, Macken 8, Harris 6, Cartwright 4, Gregan 3, Kidd 3, Rankine 3, Appleton 2, Byfield 1, Darby 1, Murdock 1, Parkinson 1 (pen), own goal 1.

Worthington Cup (0).

FA Cup (7): Nogan 3, Darby 1, Harris 1, McKenna 1, Rankine 1

Ground: Deepdale, Preston PR1 6RU. Telephone (01772) 902020.
Record attendance: 42,684 v Arsenal, Division 1, 23 April 1938. **Capacity:** 21,412.
Manager: David Moyes.
Secretary: M. Wearmouth.
Honours – Football League: Division 1 Champions – 1888–89 (first champions), 1889–90. Division 2 Champions – 1903–04, 1912–13, 1950–51. Division 3 Champions – 1970–71, 1995–96. **FA Cup winners** 1889, 1938.
Colours: White shirts, navy shorts, white stockings.

QUEENS PARK RANGERS — DIV. 1

Name	Height	Weight	Birthplace	Birthdate	Previous club
Bankole Ademola (G)	6 3	12 08	Lagos	9 9 69	Crewe Alex
Baraclough Ian (D)	6 1	12 02	Leicester	4 12 70	Notts Co
Breacker Tim (D)	5 11	13 00	Bicester	2 7 65	West Ham U
Brown Carlos (M)	5 11	10 06	Edmonton	22 4 81	Trainee
Bruce Paul (F)	5 10	12 01	London	18 2 78	Trainee
Bubb Alvin (M)	5 5	10 00	Paddington	11 10 80	Trainee
Cass Matthew (D)	5 7	10 05	Liverpool	16 12 79	Trainee
Currie Michael (F)	5 10	11 00	Westminster	19 10 79	Trainee
Darlington Jermaine (D)	5 10	12 05	London	11 4 74	Aylesbury U
Dowie Iain (F)	6 1	13 07	Hatfield	9 1 65	West Ham U
Gallen Kevin (F)	5 11	12 10	Hammersmith	21 9 75	Trainee
Graham Richard (M)	5 8	10 06	Newry	5 8 79	Trainee
Harper Lee (G)	6 1	13 11	Chelsea	30 10 71	Arsenal
Heinola Antti (D)	5 7	10 05	Helsinki	20 3 73	Heracles
Jeanne Leon (M)	5 6	10 00	Cardiff	17 11 80	Trainee
Jones Vinnie (M)	6 0	11 12	Watford	5 1 65	Wimbledon
Kulcsar George (M)	6 1	13 08	Budapest	12 8 67	Bradford C
Langley Richard (M)	5 10	11 04	London	27 12 79	Trainee
Lopez Rik (F)	5 10	11 04	Northwick Park	25 12 79	Arsenal
Lusardi Mario (F)	5 9	10 02	Islington	27 9 79	Trainee
Mahoney-Johnson Michael (F)	5 10	12 10	Paddington	6 11 76	Trainee
McFlynn Terry (M)	5 9	10 05	Magherafelt	27 3 81	Trainee
Miklosko Ludek (G)	6 5	14 00	Protesov	9 12 61	West Ham U
Morrow Steve (D)	6 0	11 03	Bangor	2 7 70	Arsenal
Murray Paul (M)	5 8	10 05	Carlisle	31 8 76	Carlisle U
Ord Richard (D)	6 2	12 08	Murton	3 3 70	Sunderland
Owen Karl (D)	5 10	10 06	Coventry	12 10 79	Trainee
Peacock Gavin (M)	5 8	11 08	Eltham	18 11 67	Chelsea
Perry Mark (M)	5 11	12 09	Perivale	19 10 78	Trainee
Plummer Chris (D)	6 2	12 12	Isleworth	12 10 76	Trainee
Purser Wayne (F)	5 9	11 04	Basildon	13 4 80	Trainee
Ready Karl (D)	6 1	12 10	Neath	14 8 72	Trainee
Rose Matthew (D)	5 11	11 01	Dartford	24 9 75	Arsenal
Rowland Keith (D)	5 10	10 00	Portadown	1 9 71	West Ham U
Scully Tony (F)	5 7	11 05	Dublin	12 6 76	Manchester C
Slade Steve (F)	6 0	10 13	Hackney	6 10 75	Tottenham H
Weare Ross (F)	6 2	13 05	Perivale	19 3 77	East Ham U
Whittle David (M)	5 10	12 07	Waterford	2 12 78	Trainee
Wright Daniel (F)	5 8	10 06	London	24 9 81	Trainee

League Appearances: Baraclough, I. 41(2); Breacker, T. 18; Darlington, J. 4; Dowie, I. 7(12); Gallen, K. 41(3); Graham, R. (2); Harper, L. 15; Heinola, A. 23; Jeanne, L. 7(3); Jones, V. 1(1); Kiwomya, C. 12(4); Kulcsar, G. 17; Langley, R. 7(1); Linighan, A. 4(3); Maddix, D. 37; Miklosko, L. 31; Morrow, S. 24; Murray, P. 32(7); Peacock, G. 41(1); Perry, M. 1; Plummer, C. 8(2); Ready, K. 40(1); Rose, M.

27(2); Rowland, K. 16(14); Scully, T. 10(13); Sheron, M. 21(2); Slade, S. 10(10); Steiner, R. 5(7); Yates, S. 6.
Goals – League (52): Gallen 8, Peacock 8 (2 pens), Sheron 8, Kiwomya 6, Maddix 4, Rowland 3 (1 pen), Steiner 3, Ready 2, Scully 2, Baraclough 1, Breacker 1, Dowie 1, Kulcsar 1, Langley 1, Murray 1, Slade 1, own goal 1.
Worthington Cup (3): Maddix 1, Sheron 1, Slade 1.
FA Cup (0).
Ground: South Africa Road, W12 7PA. Telephone (0181) 743 0262.
Record attendance: 35,353 v Leeds U, Division 1, 27 April 1974. **Capacity:** 19,148.
Manager: Gerry Francis.
Secretary: Sheila Marson.
Honours – Football League: Division 2 Champions – 1982–83. Division 3 (S) Champions – 1947–48. Division 3 Champions – 1966–67. **Football League Cup winners** 1966–67.
Colours: Blue and white hooped shirts, blue shorts, blue stockings.

READING DIV. 2

Barras Tony (D)	6 0	13 00	Stockton	29 3 71	York C
Bernal Andy (D)	5 10	12 05	Canberra	16 7 66	Ipswich T
Brayson Paul (F)	5 6	10 10	Newcastle	16 9 77	Newcastle U
Brebner Grant (M)	5 10	11 11	Edinburgh	6 12 77	Manchester U
Caskey Darren (M)	5 8	11 09	Basildon	21 8 74	Tottenham H
Casper Chris (D)	6 0	12 02	Burnley	28 4 75	Manchester U
Crawford Jimmy (M)	5 11	11 06	Chicago	1 5 74	Newcastle U
Evers Sean (M)	5 9	9 11	Hitchin	10 10 77	Luton T
Glasgow Byron (M)	5 6	10 11	Tooting	18 2 79	Trainee
Gray Stuart (D)	5 11	11 02	Harrogate	18 12 73	Celtic
Gurney Andy (D)	5 11	12 02	Bristol	25 1 74	Torquay U
Hammond Nicky (G)	6 0	11 13	Hornchurch	7 9 67	Plymouth Arg
Hodges Lee (F)	6 0	12 00	Epping	4 9 73	Barnet
Howie Scott (G)	6 3	13 07	Motherwell	4 1 72	Motherwell
Kromheer Elroy (D)	6 4	12 07	Amsterdam	15 1 70	Zwolle
Lockwood Adam (D)	5 11	11 08	Wakefield	26 10 81	Trainee
McIntyre Jim (F)	5 11	12 00	Alexandria	24 5 72	Kilmarnock
McLaren Andy (M)	5 10	10 06	Glasgow	5 6 73	Dundee U
Murty Graeme (M)	5 10	11 10	Saltburn	13 11 74	York C
Parkinson Phil (M)	6 0	12 09	Chorley	1 12 67	Bury
Polston John (D)	5 11	11 12	Walthamstow	10 6 68	Norwich C
Primus Linvoy (D)	6 0	13 07	Forest Gate	14 9 73	Barnet
Sarr Mass (F)	5 8	11 13	Monrovia	6 2 73	Hajduk Split
Scott Keith (F)	6 2	14 07	Westminster	9 6 67	Wycombe W
Van der Kwaak Peter (G)	6 4	13 12	Haarlem	12 10 68	Dordrecht
Williams Martin (F)	5 9	11 12	Luton	12 7 73	Luton T

League Appearances: Asaba, C. (1); Barras, T. 4(2); Bernal, A. 18(4); Booty, M. 7(1); Bowen, J. 1; Brayson, P. 13(15); Brebner, G. 36(3); Caskey, D. 42; Casper, C. 32; Clement, N. 11; Crawford, J. 9(2); Davies, G. 1; Evers, S. (1); Fleck, R. 2(2); Glasgow, B. 28(4); Gray, S. 25(2); Gurney, A. 5(3); Hammond, N. 1; Hodges, L. (1); Houghton, R. 13(5); Howie, S. 42; Hunter, B. 2(1); Kromheer, E. 11; Lambert, J. 1; Legg, A. 2; Maybury, A. 8; McIntyre, J. 22(10); McKeever, M. 6(1); McLaren, A. 7; McPherson, K. 13(2); Murty, G. 8(1); Parkinson, P. 42; Polston, J. 4; Primus, L. 31; Reilly, M. 4(2); Roach, N. 3(2); Sarr, M. 18(10); Scott, K. 5(4); Stamp, N. (1); Thorpe, T. 6; Van der Kwaak, P. 3; Williams, M. 20(6); Wright, A. (2).
Goals – League (54): Williams 11 (3 pens), Brebner 9, Caskey 7, McIntyre 6, Parkinson 5, Sarr 3, Gray 2, McKeever 2, Scott 2, Barras 1, Clement 1, Fleck 1, Glasgow 1, McLaren 1, Thorpe 1 (pen), own goal 1.
Worthington Cup (4): Caskey 2 (2 pens), Asaba 1, Brebner 1.

FA Cup (0).
Ground: Madejski Stadium, Junction 11, M4, Reading, Berks RG2 0FL.
Telephone (0118) 968 1100.
Record attendance: 33,042 v Brentford, FA Cup 5th rd, 19 February 1927.
Capacity: 15,000.
Manager: Tommy Burns.
Secretary: Ms Andrea Barker.
Honours – Football League: Division 2 Champions – 1993–94. Division 3
Champions – 1985–86. Division 3 (S) Champions – 1925–26. Division 4 Champions
– 1978–79. **Simod Cup winners** 1987–88.
Colours: Royal blue and white hooped shirts, blue shorts, white and blue stockings.

ROCHDALE DIV. 3

Bayliss Dave (D)	5 11	12 00	Liverpool	8 6 76	Trainee
Carden Paul (M)	5 9	11 10	Liverpool	29 3 79	Blackpool
Edwards Neil (G)	5 8	11 02	Aberdare	5 12 70	Stockport Co
Hicks Graham (D)			Oldham	17 2 81	Trainee
Holt Michael (F)	5 10	11 03	Barnoldswick	28 7 77	Preston NE
Jones Gary (M)	5 11	11 07	Birkenhead	3 6 77	Caernarfon Town
Lancashire Graham (F)	5 9	12 04	Blackpool	19 10 72	Wigan Ath
Morris Andy (F)	6 4	14 07	Sheffield	17 11 67	Chesterfield
Peake Jason (M)	5 11	12 13	Leicester	29 9 71	Bury
Priestley Phil (G)			Wigan	30 3 76	Atherton LR
Stoker Gareth (M)	5 9	11 04	Bishop Auckland	22 2 73	Cardiff C
Stokes Dean (D)	5 8	11 02	Birmingham	23 5 70	Port Vale

League Appearances: Bailey, M. 12(7); Barlow, A. 25(4); Bayliss, D. 22(3);
Bryson, I. 31(8); Carden, P. 24(1); De Souza, M. 5; Diaz, I. 12(2); Edwards, N. 45;
Farrell, A. 36(2); Gray, D. (3); Hicks, G. 1; Hill, K. 33; Holt, M. 17(7); Johnson, A.
13(3); Jones, G. 11(9); Lancashire, G. 7(4); Leonard, M. 2(6); Lydiate, J. 14; Monington, M. 37; Morris, A. 25; Painter, R. 35(5); Peake, J. 36(2); Priestley, P. 1; Spar-
row, P. 21(4); Stoker, G. 11(1); Stokes, D. 10(1); Stuart, M. 9(10); Williams, M.
11(3).
Goals – League (42): Holt 7, Morris 7, Painter 6 (1 pen), Peake 5, Lancashire 3 (1
pen), Monington 3, Diaz 2, Sparrow 2, Bailey 1, Barlow A 1, Bayliss 1, Hill 1, Lydi-
ate 1, Stoker 1, Williams 1.
Worthington Cup (0).
FA Cup (3): Bryson 2, Monington 1.
Ground: Spotland, Sandy Lane, Rochdale OL11 5DS. Telephone (01706) 644648.
Record attendance: 24,231 v Notts Co, FA Cup 2nd rd, 10 December 1949.
Capacity: 9,223.
Manager: Steve Parkin.
Secretary: Mrs Karen Jagger.
Honours – Nil.
Colours: Blue shirts with white trim, blue shorts, blue stockings with white hoop.

ROTHERHAM UNITED DIV. 3

Beech Chris (D)	5 9	12 09	Congleton	5 11 75	Cardiff C
Berry Trevor (M)	5 6	11 00	Haslemere	1 8 74	Aston Villa
Dillon Paul (D)	5 9	10 11	Limerick	22 10 78	Trainee
Fortune-West Leo (F)	6 4	13 01	Stratford	9 4 71	Brentford
Garner Darren (M)	5 9	12 07	Plymouth	10 12 71	Plymouth Arg
Glover Lee (F)	5 11	11 09	Kettering	24 4 70	Port Vale
Hudson Danny (M)	5 8	10 03	Mexborough	25 6 79	Trainee

Hurst Paul (D)	5 4	90	Sheffield	25 9 74	Trainee
Ingledow Jamie (M)	5 7	11 01	Barnsley	23 8 80	Trainee
Martindale Gary (F)	6 1	11 13	Liverpool	24 6 71	Notts Co
Monkhouse Andy (F)	6 0	13 09	Leeds	23 10 80	Trainee
Pettinger Paul (G)	6 0	13 00	Sheffield	1 10 75	Carlisle U
Pollitt Mike (G)	6 3	14 12	Farnworth	29 2 72	Sunderland
Scott Rob (F)	6 1	12 04	Epsom	15 8 73	Fulham
Sedgwick Chris (F)	5 11	10 10	Sheffield	28 4 80	Trainee
Warne Paul (F)	5 8	11 01	Norwich	8 5 73	Wigan Ath
Warner Vance (D)	6 0	13 04	Leeds	3 9 74	Nottingham F
White Jason (F)	6 1	12 12	Meriden	19 10 71	Northampton T
Williams Mark (D)	6 0	11 02	Liverpool	10 11 78	Trainee

League Appearances: Beech, C. 24; Berry, T. 11(7); Bos, G. 1(1); Clark, M. 1; Dillon, P. 25(1); Fortune-West, L. 20; Garner, D. 40; Glover, L. 18(1); Hudson, D. 19(7); Hurst, P. 31(1); Ingledow, J. 15(6); Jackson, J. 2; Knill, A. 35(1); Martindale, G. 6(4); Monkhouse, A. (5); Pollitt, M. 46; Raven, P. 11; Richardson, N. 4(1); Roscoe, A. 27(11); Scott, G. 13; Scott, R. 5(1); Sedgwick, C. 24(9); Strodder, G. 3; Thompson, S. 28(5); Tracey, R. (3); Varty, W. 14; Warne, P. 19; Warner, V. 23; Whelan, P. 13; White, J. 18(8); Williams, M. 10(1).

Goals – League (79): Fortune-West 12, Glover 10 (2 pens), Warne 8, Roscoe 5, Thompson 5 (3 pens), White 5, Garner 4, Hudson 4, Sedgwick 4 (1 pen), Whelan 4, Knill 3, Berry 2, Hurst 2, Ingledow 2, Martindale 2, Raven 2, Dillon 1, Jackson 1, Monkhouse 1, Scott R 1, Warner 1.

Worthington Cup (0).

FA Cup (8): Garner 2, Glover 2, Berry 1, Hudson 1, Hurst 1, Scott R 1.

Ground: Millmoor Ground, Rotherham S60 1HR. Telephone (01709) 512434.

Record attendance: 25,000 v Sheffield U, Division 2, 13 December 1952 and v Sheffield W, Division 2, 26 January 1952. **Capacity:** 11,514

Manager: Ronnie Moore.

Honours – Football League: Division 3 Champions – 1980–81. Division 3 (N) Champions – 1950–51. Division 4 Champions – 1988–89. **Auto Windscreens Shield:** Winners 1996

Colours: Red shirts, white shorts, red stockings.

SCARBOROUGH   NATIONWIDE CONFERENCE

Brodie Steve (F)	5 7	10 08	Sunderland	14 1 73	Sunderland
Carr Graeme (M)	5 10	11 00	Chester-le-Street	28 10 78	Trainee
Hoyland Jamie (M)	6 0	14 07	Sheffield	23 1 66	Burnley
Martin Kevin (G)	6 1	12 05	Bromsgrove	22 6 76	Trainee
McNaughton Michael (D)	6 2	14 00	Blackpool	29 1 80	Trainee
Milbourne Ian (F)	5 9	11 02	Hexham	21 1 79	Trainee
Rennison Shaun ()			Northallerton	23 11 80	Trainee
Roberts Darren (F)	6 0	12 04	Birmingham	12 10 69	Darlington
Russell Matthew (M)	6 0	11 05	Leeds	17 1 78	Trainee
Tate Chris (F)	6 0	12 00	York	27 12 77	York C
Worrall Ben (M)	5 5	10 00	Swindon	7 12 75	Swindon T

League Appearances: Atkinson, G. 15; Atkinson, P. 23(4); Brodie, S. 43; Bullimore, W. 33(2); Campbell, N. 3(8); Carr, G. 5(5); Dabelsteen, T. 5; Elliott, T. 20; Goodlad, M. 3; Greenacre, C. 10(2); Hodges, G. 1; Hoyland, J. 44; Jackson, R. 19(1); Jones, N. 8(1); Kay, J. 23(1); Lydiate, J. 26(1); Marinkov, A. 22; McAuley, S. 6(1); McNaughton, M. 22(9); Milbourne, I. 2(14); Mountfield, D. 5(1); Naisbett, P. 2; Parks, T. 15; Porter, G. 11(2); Radigan, N. 4(5); Rainford, D. (2); Rennison, S. 15; Renshaw, I. (1); Roberts, D. 18; Robinson, L. 17(12); Russell, M. 20(17); Saville, A. (9); Tate, C. 18(7); Todd, A. (1); Weaver, L. 6; Williams, G. 17; Worrall, B. 25(6).

Goals – League (50): Brodie 12, Tate 12, Marinkov 4 (2 pens), Hoyland 3, Roberts 3, Robinson 3, Russell 3, Greenacre 2, Williams 2, Atkinson G 1, Bullimore 1, Dabelsteen 1, Lydiate 1, McNaughton 1, Rennison 1.
Worthington Cup (0).
FA Cup (1): Williams 1.
Ground: The McCain Stadium, Seamer Road, Scarborough YO12 4HF. Telephone (01723) 735094.
Record attendance: 11,130 v Luton T, FA Cup 3rd rd, 8 January 1938.
Capacity: 6899.
Manager: Colin Addison.
Secretary: Mrs Gillian Russell.
Honours – FA Trophy: Winners 1973, 1976, 1977. **GM Vauxhall Conference:** Winners 1987.
Colours: White shirts and shorts with red and green trim, red and white stockings.

SCUNTHORPE UNITED · DIV. 2

Calvo-Garcia Alexander (M)	5 11	11 10	Ordizia	1	1 72	Eibar
Clarke Tim (G)	6 3	15 12	Stourbridge	19	9 68	York C
Dawson Andrew (D)	5 10	11 02	Northallerton	20	10 78	Nottingham F
Evans Tom (G)	6 1	13 02	Doncaster	31	12 76	Crystal Palace
Gayle John (F)	6 3	15 00	Bromsgrove	30	7 64	Northampton T
Graves Wayne (M)	5 8	10 07	Scunthorpe	18	9 80	Trainee
Harsley Paul (M)	5 10	11 03	Scunthorpe	29	5 78	Trainee
Hope Chris (D)	6 1	12 08	Sheffield	14	11 73	Nottingham F
Housham Steven (M)	5 10	12 03	Gainsborough T	24	2 76	Trainee
Logan Richard (M)	6 0	13 03	Barnsley	24	5 69	Plymouth Arg
Marshall Lee (M)	5 10	10 08	Nottingham	1	8 75	Stockport Co
McAuley Sean (D)	5 11	12 02	Sheffield	23	6 72	Hartlepool U
Sheldon Gareth (F)	5 11	11 10	Birmingham	31	1 80	Trainee
Stamp Darryn (F)	6 1	11 10	Beverley	21	9 78	
Stanton Nathan (D)	5 11	12 00	Nottingham	6	5 81	Trainee
Wilcox Russ (D)	6 0	12 13	Hemsworth	25	3 64	Preston NE

League Appearances: Atkinson, G. (1); Bull, G. 4(20); Calvo-Garcia, A. 42(1); Clarke, T. 22; Dawson, A. 24; Evans, T. 24; Eyre, J. 41; Fickling, A. 28(1); Forrester, J. 46; Gayle, J. 36(1); Harsley, P. 32(2); Hope, C. 46; Housham, S. 11(5); Logan, R. 38(3); Marshall, L. 5(14); McAuley, S. 16(1); Sheldon, G. 5(6); Stamp, D. 5(20); Stanton, N. 3(1); Walker, J. 40(1); Wilcox, R. 24(4); Witter, T. 14.
Goals – League (69): Forrester 20, Eyre 15 (4 pens), Calvo-Garcia 9, Logan 6, Hope 5, Gayle 4, Stamp 4, Marshall 1, Sheldon 1, Walker 1, Wilcox 1, own goals 2.
Worthington Cup (1): Forrester 1.
FA Cup (6): Eyre 2 (1 pen), Forrester 2, Harsley 1, Housham 1.
Ground: Glanford Park, Scunthorpe, South Humberside DN15 8TD. Telephone (01724) 848077.
Record attendance: Old Showground: 23,935 v Portsmouth, FA Cup 4th rd, 30 January 1954. Glanford Park: 8775 v Rotherham U, Division 4, 1 May 1989.
Capacity: 9183.
Manager: Brian Laws.
Secretary: A. D. Rowing.
Honours – Division 3 (N) Champions – 1957–58.
Colours: Sky blue with claret shirts, white shorts, white stockings with claret trim.

SHEFFIELD UNITED · DIV. 1

Cullen Jon (M)	6 0	11 10	Durham	10	1 73	Hartlepool U
Davies Kevin (M)	6 0	12 00	Sheffield	15	11 78	Trainee
Dellas Traianos (D)	6 4	15 00	Salonika	31	1 76	Aris Salonika

Derry Shaun (M)	5 10	10 13	Nottingham	6 12 77	Notts Co
Devlin Paul (F)	5 8	11 05	Birmingham	14 4 72	Birmingham C
Doane Ben (D)	5 10	12 00	Sheffield	22 12 79	Trainee
Ford Bobby (M)	5 8	11 00	Bristol	22 9 74	Oxford U
Hamilton Ian (M)	5 10	12 03	Stevenage	14 12 67	WBA
Hunt Jonathan (M)	5 10	11 13	London	2 11 71	Derby Co
Kelly Alan (G)	6 3	14 02	Preston	11 8 68	Preston NE
Kozluk Robert (D)	5 8	10 12	Sutton-in-Ashfield	5 8 77	Derby Co
Macari Paul (F)	5 8	11 06	Manchester	23 8 76	Stoke C
Marcelo (F)	6 0	13 08	Niteroi	11 10 69	Alaves
Marker Nicky (D)	6 0	13 00	Exeter	3 5 65	Blackburn R
Morris Lee (F)	5 10	10 06	Driffield	30 4 80	Trainee
O'Connor Jon (D)	6 0	11 00	Darlington	29 10 76	Everton
Quinn Wayne (M)	5 10	11 11	Truro	19 11 76	
Tebily Oliver (D)	6 0	13 00	Abidjan	19 12 75	Chateauroux
Tracey Simon (G)	6 0	13 12	Woolwich	9 12 67	Wimbledon
Woodhouse Curtis (M)	5 8	11 00	Driffield	17 4 80	Trainee

League Appearances: Borbokis, V. 19; Bruce, S. 10; Campbell, A. 11; Cullen, J. (2); Dellas, T. 9(8); Derry, S. 23(3); Devlin, P. 23(10); Donis, G. 5(2); Ford, B. 27(3); Goram, A. 7; Hamilton, D. 6; Hamilton, I. 27(3); Henry, N. 3(3); Holdsworth, D. 16; Hunt, J. 12(1); Jacobsen, A. 8(4); Katchuro, P. 8(8); Kelly, A. 22; Kozluk, R. 10; Marcelo 26(9); Marker, N. 17(1); Morris, L. 14(6); Nilsen, R. 14(3); O'Connor, J. 2; Quinn, W. 41(3); Sandford, L. 34(1); Saunders, D. 19; Stuart, G. 25; Taylor, G. 7(5); Tebily, O. 7(1); Tracey, S. 17(1); Twiss, M. 2(10); Wilder, C. 4; Woodhouse, C. 31(2).

Goals – League (71): Marcelo 16 (1 pen), Saunders 7, Katchuro 6, Morris 6, Stuart 6, Devlin 5, Campbell 3, Dellas 3, Marker 3, Woodhouse 3, Borbokis 2, Hamilton I 2, Hunt 2, Donis 1, Holdsworth 1, Quinn 1, Taylor 1, Twiss 1, own goals 2.

Worthington Cup (7): Saunders 3, Borbokis 1, Ford 1, Hamilton I 1, Taylor 1.

FA Cup (10): Marcelo 3, Holdsworth 2, Morris 2, Borbokis 1, Devlin 1, Stuart 1.

Ground: Bramall Lane Ground, Sheffield S2 4SU. Telephone (0114) 2215757

Record attendance: 68,287 v Leeds U, FA Cup 5th rd, 15 February 1936.

Capacity: 30,370.

Manager: Adrian Heath.

Secretary: D. Capper AFA.

Honours – Football League: Division 1 Champions – 1897–98. Division 2 Champions – 1952–53. Division 4 Champions – 1981–82. **FA Cup:** Winners 1899, 1902, 1915, 1925.

Colours: Red and white striped shirts with black trim, black shorts and black stockings with red trim.

SHEFFIELD WEDNESDAY   FA PREMIERSHIP

Agogo Manuel (M)	5 9	11 07	Accra	1 8 79	Willesden
Alexandersson Niclas (M)	6 2	11 07	Halmstad	29 12 71	IFK Gothenburg
Atherton Peter (D)	5 11	13 13	Wigan	6 4 70	Coventry C
Bennett Neil (G)	6 1	11 13	Dewsbury	29 10 80	Trainee
Bettney Scott (D)	5 9	12 06	Hull	12 3 80	Trainee
Billington David (D)	5 7	10 07	Oxford	15 10 80	Trainee
Booth Andy (F)	6 1	13 00	Huddersfield	6 12 73	Huddersfield T
Brennan Dean (M)	5 9	11 04	Dublin	17 6 80	
Briscoe Lee (F)	5 11	11 13	Pontefract	30 9 75	Trainee
Bromby Leigh (D)	6 0	11 05	Dewsbury	2 6 80	
Carbone Benito (F)	5 6	10 09	Begnara	14 8 71	Internazionale
Clarke Matthew (G)	6 4	13 10	Sheffield	3 11 73	Rotherham U
Coubrough James (M)			Bradford	4 10 80	Trainee
Cresswell Richard (F)	6 1	11 07	Bridlington	20 9 77	York C

Douglas Andrew (F)	5 7	10 09	Edmonton	7 2 80	Arsenal
Emerson (D)	6 1	14 07	Porto Alegre	30 3 72	Benfica
Geary Derek (D)	5 6	10 08	Dublin	19 6 80	
Hamshaw Matthew (M)			Rotherham	1 1 82	Trainee
Haslam Nathan (M)			Middlesbrough	13 1 81	Trainee
Haslam Steven (M)	5 11	11 00	Sheffield	6 9 79	Trainee
Hibbins John (M)	6 2	12 09	Sheffield	17 11 79	Trainee
Higgins Alex (M)	5 9	10 12	Sheffield	22 7 81	Trainee
Hinchcliffe Andy (D)	5 10	12 10	Manchester	5 2 69	Everton
Holmes Peter (M)	5 11	10 05	Bishop Auckland	18 11 80	Trainee
Humphreys Richie (F)	5 11	14 07	Sheffield	30 11 77	Trainee
Hutton John (F)	5 10	11 12	Easington	23 9 80	Trainee
Jones Stuart (G)	6 1	13 11	Bristol	24 10 77	Weston-Super-Mare
Jonk Wim (M)	6 1	12 02	Volendam	12 10 66	PSV Eindhoven
McKeever Mark (M)	5 9	11 08	Derry	16 11 78	Trainee
Morrison Owen (F)			Derry	8 12 81	Trainee
Newsome Jon (D)	6 3	13 10	Sheffield	6 9 70	Norwich C
Nicholson Kevin (D)	5 8	11 05	Derby	2 10 80	Trainee
Nolan Ian (D)	5 11	12 02	Liverpool	9 7 70	Tranmere R
Oakes Scott (M)	5 11	11 12	Leicester	5 8 72	Luton T
Pressman Kevin (G)	6 1	15 05	Fareham	6 11 67	Apprentice
Quinn Alan (F)	5 9	10 05	Dublin	13 6 79	
Rudi Petter (D)	6 3	12 11	Kristiansund	17 9 73	Molde
Sanetti Francesco (F)	5 11	12 07	Rome	11 1 79	Genoa
Scott Philip (M)	5 9	11 01	Perth	14 11 74	St Johnstone
Sonner Danny (M)	6 0	12 08	Wigan	9 1 72	Ipswich T
Srnicek Pavel (G)	6 2	14 07	Bohumin	10 3 68	Newcastle U
Staniforth Thomas (M)			Carlisle	15 12 80	Trainee
Walker Des (D)	5 11	11 12	Hackney	26 11 65	Sampdoria

League Appearances: Agogo, M. (1); Alexandersson, N. 31(1); Atherton, P. 38; Barrett, E. (5); Booth, A. 34; Briscoe, L. 5(11); Carbone, B. 31; Cobian, J. 7(2); Cresswell, R. 1(6); Di Canio, P. 5(1); Emerson 38; Haslam, S. 2; Hinchcliffe, A. 32; Humphreys, R. 10(9); Hyde, G. (1); Jonk, W. 38; Magilton, J. 1(5); McKeever, M. 1(2); Morrison, O. (1); Newsome, J. 2(3); Oakes, S. (1); Pressman, K. 14(1); Quinn, A. 1; Rudi, P. 33(1); Sanetti, F. (3); Scott, P. (4); Sonner, D. 24(2); Srnicek, P. 24; Stefanovic, D. 8(3); Walker, D. 37; Whittingham, G. 1(1).
Goals – League (41): Carbone 8 (1 pen), Booth 6, Rudi 6, Alexandersson 3, Di Canio 3, Hinchcliffe 3, Sonner 3, Atherton 2, Jonk 2, Briscoe 1, Cresswell 1, Emerson 1, Humphreys 1, Scott 1.
Worthington Cup (1): own goal 1.
FA Cup (6): Humphreys 2, Carbone 1, Emerson 1, Rudi 1, Stefanovic 1.
Ground: Hillsborough, Sheffield, S6 1SW. Telephone (0114) 2212121
Record attendance: 72,841 v Manchester C, FA Cup 5th rd, 17 February 1934.
Capacity: 39,859
Manager: Danny Wilson.
Secretary: Alan D. Sykes.
Honours – Football League: Division 1 Champions – 1902–03, 1903–04, 1928–29, 1929–30. Division 2 Champions – 1899–1900, 1925–26, 1951–52, 1955–56, 1958–59. **FA Cup winners** 1896, 1907, 1935. **Football League Cup winners** 1990–91.
Colours: Blue and white striped shirts, black shorts, black stockings.

SHREWSBURY TOWN   DIV. 3

Berkley Austin (M)	5 9	10 10	Gravesend	28 1 73	Swindon T
Cooksey Scott (G)	6 3	13 10	Birmingham	24 6 72	Peterborough U
Craven Dean (M)	5 6	10 10	Shrewsbury	17 2 79	WBA

Edwards Paul (G)	6 0	11 05	Liverpool	22 2 65	Crewe Alex
Hanmer Gary (D)	5 6	10 02	Shrewsbury	12 10 73	Newtown
Herbert Craig (D)	5 10	11 00	Coventry	9 11 75	WBA
Jagielka Steve (F)	5 8	11 03	Manchester	10 3 78	Trainee
Jobling Kevin (M)	5 8	12 00	Sunderland	1 1 68	Grimsby T
Kerrigan Steve (F)	6 1	12 04	Bailleston	9 10 72	Ayr U
Preece Roger (M)	5 8	10 13	Much Wenlock	9 6 69	Chester C
Steele Lee (F)	5 8	12 05	Liverpool	7 12 73	Northwich V
Thompson Glyn (G)	6 3	11 03	Shrewsbury	24 2 81	Trainee
Tretton Andrew (D)	6 0	12 08	Derby	9 10 76	Chesterfield
Whelan Spencer (D)	6 2	13 00	Liverpool	17 9 71	Chester C
Wilding Peter (D)	6 1	12 09	Shrewsbury	28 11 68	Telford U

League Appearances: Beavers, P. 2; Berkley, A. 41; Brown, M. 15(19); Cooksey, S. 2; Craven, D. 6(4); Drysdale, L. 2; Edwards, P. 43; Evans, P. 32; Gayle, B. 43; Hanmer, G. 46; Hayfield, M. 1(1); Herbert, C. 6(2); Jagielka, S. 13(18); Jobling, K. 41; Jones, M. (1); Kerrigan, S. 32(5); Preece, R. 16(4); Rutherford, M. (3); Seabury, K. 44; Steele, L. 33(5); Thompson, G. 1; Tretton, A. 22(1); Whelan, S. 8(1); White, D. 7(4); Wilding, P. 42; Winstanley, M. 8.

Goals – League (52): Steele 13, Kerrigan 10, Berkley 8, Evans 6 (2 pens), Seabury 5, Brown 2, Preece 2, Gayle 1, Jagielka 1, Jobling 1, own goals 3.

Worthington Cup (4): Evans 3 (2 pens), Jobling 1.

FA Cup (0).

Ground: Gay Meadow, Shrewsbury SY2 6AB. Telephone (01743) 360111.

Record attendance: 18,917 v Walsall, Division 3, 26 April 1961. **Capacity:** 8000.

Manager: Jake King.

Secretary: M. J. Starkey.

Honours – Football League: Division 3 Champions – 1978–79, 1993–94. **Welsh Cup winners** 1891, 1938, 1977, 1979, 1984, 1985.

Colours: Blue shirts, white trim, blue shorts, blue stockings, white trim.

SOUTHAMPTON   FA PREMIERSHIP

Basham Steve (F)	5 11	12 04	Southampton	2 12 77	Trainee
Beattie James (F)	6 0	13 03	Lancaster	27 2 78	Blackburn R
Benali Francis (M)	5 9	11 03	Southampton	30 12 68	Apprentice
Beresford John (M)	5 7	12 00	Sheffield	4 9 66	Newcastle U
Bevan Scott (G)	6 6	15 03	Southampton	16 9 79	Trainee
Bradley Shayne (F)	6 0	13 06	Gloucester	8 12 79	Trainee
Bridge Wayne (F)	5 10	12 04	Southampton	5 8 80	Trainee
Colleter Patrick (D)	5 8	11 04	Brest	6 11 65	Marseille
Collins Chris (D)	6 0	13 01	Chatham	26 9 79	Trainee
Dodd Jason (D)	5 9	12 08	Bath	2 11 70	Bath C
Dryden Richard (D)	6 0	14 09	Stroud	14 6 69	Bristol C
Gibbens Kevin (M)	5 10	13 02	Southampton	4 11 79	Trainee
Hiley Scott (D)	5 9	11 12	Plymouth	27 9 68	Manchester C
Hirst David (F)	5 11	14 10	Cudworth	7 12 67	Sheffield W
Howells David (M)	6 0	12 03	Guildford	15 12 67	Tottenham H
Hughes David (M)	5 11	11 07	St Albans	30 12 72	Trainee
Hughes Mark (F)	5 9	13 04	Wrexham	1 11 63	Chelsea
Jones Paul (G)	6 2	15 03	Chirk	18 4 67	Stockport Co
Kachloul Hassan (M)	6 1	12 09	Agadir	19 2 73	St Etienne
Le Tissier Matthew (F)	6 0	14 01	Guernsey	14 10 68	Trainee
Lundekvam Claus (D)	6 3	13 03	Austevoll	22 2 73	Brann
Marsden Chris (M)	6 0	12 07	Sheffield	3 10 69	Birmingham C
Marshall Scott (D)	6 1	12 13	Edinburgh	1 5 73	Celtic
Monk Gary (D)	6 1	13 05	Bedford	6 3 79	Trainee
Monkou Ken (D)	6 3	14 11	Surinam	29 11 64	Chelsea

Moss Neil (G)   6 2   13 07   New Milton   10 5 75   Bournemouth
Oakley Matthew (M)   5 10 12 06   Peterborough   17 8 77   Trainee
Ostenstad Egil (F)   5 11 13 00   Haugesund   2 1 72   Viking
Pakhar (Pahars) Marian (F) 5 8   10 09   Latvia   5 8 76   Skonto Riga
Paul Mark (F)   5 6   10 10   Peterborough   3 1 79   Kings Lynn
Ripley Stuart (F)   5 11 13 05   Middlesbrough   20 11 67   Blackburn R
Rodrigues Danny (F)   5 10 11 07   Madeira   3 3 80   Farense
Stensgaard Michael (G)   6 2   13 11   Denmark   1 9 74   FC Copenhagen
Warner Phil (D)   5 10 11 09   Southampton   2 2 79   Trainee
Williams Andy (F)   5 9   10 12   Bristol   8 10 77   Trainee

League Appearances: Basham, S. (4); Beattie, J. 22(13); Benali, F. 19(4); Beresford, J. 1(3); Bradley, S. (3); Bridge, W. 15(8); Colleter, P. 16; Dodd, J. 27(1); Dryden, R. 4; Gibbens, K. 2(2); Hiley, S. 27(2); Hirst, D. (2); Howells, D. 8(1); Hughes, D. 6(3); Hughes, M. 32; Jones, P. 31; Kachloul, H. 18(4); Le Tissier, M. 20(10); Lundekvam, C. 30(3); Marsden, C. 14; Marshall, S. 2; Monk, G. 4; Monkou, K. 22; Moss, N. 7; Oakley, M. 21(1); Ostenstad, E. 27(7); Pakhar (Pahars), M. 4(2); Palmer, C. 18(1); Ripley, S. 16(6); Warner, P. 5; Williams, A. (1).

Goals – League (37): Le Tissier 7 (1 pen), Ostenstad 7, Beattie 5, Kachloul 5, Pakhar (Pahars) 3, Marsden 2, Oakley 2, Basham 1, Colleter 1, Dodd 1 (pen), Howells 1, Hughes M 1, Monkou 1.

Worthington Cup (1): Beattie 1.

FA Cup (1): Ostenstad 1.

Ground: The Dell, Milton Road, Southampton SO15 2XH. Telephone (01703) 220505.

Record attendance: 31,044 v Manchester U, Division 1, 8 October 1969. **Capacity:** 15,000.

Manager: Dave Jones.

Secretary: Brian Truscott.

Honours – Football League: Division 3 (S) Champions – 1921–22. Division 3 Champions – 1959–60. **FA Cup:** Winners 1975–76.

Colours: Red and white striped shirts, black shorts, black stockings with red trim.

SOUTHEND UNITED   DIV. 3

Beard Mark (M)   5 10 10 12   Roehampton   8 10 74   Sheffield U
Booty Martyn (D)   5 9   12 06   Kirby Muxloe   30 5 71   Reading
Burns Alex (F)   5 9   12 09   Bellshill   4 8 73   Motherwell
Byrne Paul (M)   5 11 13 00   Dublin   30 6 72   Celtic
Campbell Neil (F)   6 2   13 10   Middlesbrough   26 1 77   Scarborough
Coleman Simon (D)   6 0   12 03   Worksop   13 6 68   Bolton W
Conlon Barry (F)   6 2   13 07   Drogheda   1 10 78   Manchester C
Fitzpatrick Trevor (F)   6 1   12 10   Surrey   19 2 80   Trainee
Hails Julian (M)   5 10 11 02   Lincoln   20 11 67   Fulham
Houghton Scott (M)   5 7   12 03   Hitchin   22 10 71   Peterborough U
Jones Nathan (D)   5 7   10 12   Rhondda   28 5 73   Merthyr T
Livett Simon (M)   5 10 12 07   Plaistow   8 1 69   Cambridge U
Maher Kevin (M)   5 11 12 08   Ilford   17 10 76   Tottenham H
Margetson Martyn (G)   6 0   14 00   West Neath   8 9 71   Manchester C
Morley David (D)   6 2   13 02   St Helens   25 9 77   Manchester C
Morrish Adam (M)   Greenwich   28 6 80   Trainee
Newman Rob (D)   6 1   13 10   Bradford-on-Avon   13 12 63   Norwich C
Perkins Chris (D)   5 11 12 11   Stepney   1 3 80   Trainee
Roach Neville (F)   5 10 11 12   Reading   29 9 78   Reading
Roget Leo (D)   6 1   12 02   Ilford   1 8 77   Trainee
Whyte David (F)   5 8   12 00   Greenwich   20 4 71   Bristol R

League Appearances: Beard, M. 36(1); Booty, M. 18(2); Burns, A. 26(5); Campbell, N. 9(3); Capleton, M. 14; Clarke, A. 14(10); Coleman, S. 41(1); Conlon, B.

28(6); Coyne, C. (1); De Souza, M. 2; Dublin, K. 6(3); Fitzpatrick, T. 7(16); Gooding, M. 19(4); Hails, J. 11; Harris, A. 1; Hodges, L. 10; Houghton, S. 26(1); Hunter, B. 5; Iorfa, D. (2); Jones, N. 5(12); Livett, S. 19(4); Maher, K. 34; Margetson, M. 32; McGavin, S. 4(7); Morley, D. 26(1); Newman, R. 36; Patterson, M. 5; Rapley, K. 9; Roach, N. 7(1); Roget, L. 11(3); Stimson, M. 17; Unger, L. 14; Whyte, D. 14(4).
Goals – League (52): Conlon 7, Newman 7, Burns 5, Fitzpatrick 5, Coleman 4, Maher 4, Rapley 4, Clarke 3, Houghton 3, Campbell 2, Hunter 2, Whyte 2, Hails 1, Hodges 1, Livett 1, Roach 1.
Worthington Cup (2): Clarke 1, Newman 1.
FA Cup (0).
Ground: Roots Hall Football Ground, Victoria Avenue, Southend-on-Sea SS2 6NQ. Telephone (01702) 304050
Record attendance: 31,090 v Liverpool FA Cup 3rd rd, 10 January 1979. **Capacity:** 12,306
Manager: Alan Little.
Secretary: Miss H. Giles.
Honours – Football League: Division 4 Champions – 1980–81.
Colours: Royal blue and white.

STOCKPORT COUNTY   DIV. 1

Angell Brett (F)	6 2	13 10	Marlborough	20 8 68	Sunderland
Bennett Tom (M)	5 11	11 08	Falkirk	12 12 69	Wolverhampton W
Byrne Chris (M)	5 9	10 02	Hulme	9 2 75	Macclesfield T
Connelly Sean (D)	5 10	11 10	Sheffield	26 6 70	Hallam
Cook Paul (M)	5 11	11 00	Liverpool	22 6 67	Tranmere R
Cooper Kevin (F)	5 8	10 07	Derby	8 2 75	Derby Co
Dinning Tony (D)	6 0	12 00	Wallsend	12 4 75	Trainee
Ellis Tony (F)	5 11	11 00	Salford	20 10 64	Bury
Flynn Mike (D)	6 0	11 02	Oldham	23 2 69	Preston NE
Gannon Jim (D)	6 2	13 00	Southwark	7 9 68	Sheffield U
Gray Ian (G)	6 2	13 00	Manchester	25 2 75	Rochdale
Mannion Sean (M)	5 8	11 05	Dublin	3 3 80	Stella Maris
Matthews Rob (F)	6 0	12 05	Slough	14 10 70	Bury
McIntosh Martin (D)	6 3	12 05	East Kilbride	19 3 71	Hamilton A
Moore Ian (F)	5 11	12 02	Birkenhead	26 8 76	Nottingham F
Nash Carlo (G)	6 5	14 01	Bolton	13 9 73	Crystal Palace
Phillips Wayne (M)	5 11	11 00	Bangor	15 12 70	Wrexham
Smith David (M)	5 10	12 11	Liverpool	26 12 70	Oxford U
Travis Simon (D)	5 7	10 00	Preston	22 3 77	Torquay U
Wilbraham Aaron (F)	6 3	12 04	Knutsford	21 10 79	Trainee
Woodthorpe Colin (D)	6 0	11 08	Ellesmere Pt	13 1 69	Aberdeen

League Appearances: Alsaker, P. 1; Angell, B. 42; Bennett, T. 3(4); Branch, G. 10(4); Byrne, C. 11; Byrne, D. 2; Connelly, S. 33(2); Cook, P. 23(1); Cooper, K. 27(11); Dinning, T. 35(6); Ellis, T. 16; Flynn, M. 46; Gannon, J. 28(10); Grant, S. 1(12); Gray, I. 3; Hughes, P. 7; Mannion, S. (1); Matthews, R. 19(4); McInnes, D. 13; McIntosh, M. 41; Moore, I. 32(6); Nash, C. 43; Phillips, W. 7(2); Smith, D. 17; Travis, S. 1(8); Wilbraham, A. 8(18); Woodthorpe, C. 37.
Goals – League (49): Angell 17, Ellis 6 (1 pen), Dinning 5 (5 pens), Branch 3, McIntosh 3, Moore 3, Byrne C 2, Matthews 2, Woodthorpe 2, Connelly 1, Cooper 1, Flynn 1, Grant 1, Smith 1, own goal 1.
Worthington Cup (2): Byrne 1, Moore 1.
FA Cup (3): Angell 1, Woodthorpe 1, own goal 1.
Ground: Edgeley Park, Hardcastle Road, Stockport, Cheshire SK3 9DD. Telephone (0161) 286 8888.
Record attendance: 27,833 v Liverpool, FA Cup 5th rd, 11 February 1950.

Capacity: 11,540.
Manager: Andy Kilner.
Secretary: Gary Glendenning BA (HONS) FCCA.
Honours – Football League: Division 3 (N) Champions – 1921–22, 1936–37. Division 4 Champions – 1966–67.
Colours: Blue shirts with white chest band, blue shorts, blue stockings with white trim.

STOKE CITY DIV. 2

Bullock Matthew (M)	5 8	11 00	Stoke	1 11 80	Trainee
Cartwright Jamie (M)	5 7	9 06	Lichfield	11 10 79	Trainee
Clarke Clive (D)	6 1	12 05	Dublin	14 1 80	Trainee
Collins Lee (D)	6 2	13 05	Bellshill	10 9 77	Aston Villa
Crowe Dean (F)	5 5	11 02	Stockport	6 6 79	Trainee
Dixon Calvin (M)			Walsall	20 10 80	Trainee
Fraser Stuart (G)	6 0	12 00	Cheltenham	1 8 78	
Godbold Jamie (M)	5 4	9 0	Great Yarmouth	10 1 80	Trainee
Goodfellow Marc (M)			Burton	20 9 81	
Heath Robert (M)	5 9	10 07	Newcastle-Under-Lyme	31 8 78	
Kavanagh Graham (M)	5 10	12 06	Dublin	2 12 73	Middlesbrough
Kavanagh Jason (D)	5 8	12 09	Meriden	23 11 71	Wycombe W
Lightbourne Kyle (F)	6 2	12 00	Bermuda	29 9 68	Coventry C
MacKenzie Neil (M)	6 2	12 05	Birmingham	15 4 76	
McGeough David (M)			Drogheda	10 11 80	
Mohan Nicky (D)	6 0	13 07	Middlesbrough	6 10 70	Wycombe W
Muggleton Carl (G)	6 2	13 03	Leicester	13 9 68	Celtic
Neal Lewis (M)			Leicester	14 7 81	
O'Connor James (M)	5 8	11 00	Dublin	1 9 79	Trainee
Oldfield David (M)	6 1	13 04	Perth (Aus)	30 5 68	Luton T
Petty Ben (D)	6 1	13 03	Solihull	22 3 77	Aston Villa
Robinson Phil (M)	5 10	11 06	Stafford	6 1 67	Notts Co
Scheuber Stuart (M)			Rhuddlan	3 4 81	Trainee
Short Chris (D)	5 10	12 03	Munster	9 5 70	Sheffield U
Sigurdsson Kris (D)	5 11	11 11	Akureyri	7 10 80	
Sigurdsson Larus (D)	6 0	13 11	Akureyri	4 6 73	Thor
Small Bryan (D)	5 9	11 09	Birmingham	15 11 71	Bury
Taaffe Steven (F)	5 5	9 08	Stoke	10 9 79	Trainee
Thorne Peter (F)	6 0	13 07	Manchester	21 6 73	Swindon T
Ward Gavin (G)	6 2	13 06	Sutton Coldfield	30 6 70	Bolton W
Wooliscroft Ashley (D)	5 10	11 02	Stoke	28 12 79	Trainee

League Appearances: Clarke, C. 2; Collins, L. 4; Connor, P. 2(1); Crowe, D. 19(19); Forsyth, R. 13(5); Fraser, S. (1); Heath, R. 7(3); Kavanagh, G. 36; Kavanagh, J. 8; Keen, K. 43(1); Lightbourne, K. 28(8); Mackenzie, N. 3(3); Mohan, N. 15; Muggleton, C. 40; O'Connor, J. 4; Oldfield, D. 43(3); Petty, B. 9(2); Pickering, A. (1); Robinson, P. 39(1); Short, C. 19(2); Sigurdsson, L. 38; Small, B. 35(2); Strong, G. 5; Sturridge, S. 1(2); Taaffe, S. 1(2); Thorne, P. 33(1); Tweed, S. (1); Wallace, R. 11(20); Ward, G. 6; Whittle, J. 9(5); Woods, S. 33; Wooliscroft, A. (1).
Goals – League (59): Kavanagh G 11 (4 pens), Thorne 9, Crowe 8 (1 pen), Lightbourne 7, Oldfield 6, Sigurdsson L 4, Wallace 3, Connor 2, Forsyth 2, Keen 2, Robinson 1, Strong 1, Whittle 1, own goals 2.
Worthington Cup (2): Kavanagh G 1, Thorne 1.
FA Cup (1): Lightbourne 1.
Ground: Britannia Stadium, Stoke-on-Trent ST4 4EG. Telephone: (01782) 592222.
Record attendance: 51,380 v Arsenal, Division 1, 29 March 1937. **Capacity:** 24,054.
Manager: Gary Megson.

Honours – Football League: Division 2 Champions – 1932–33, 1962–63, 1992–93. Division 3 (N) Champions – 1926–27. **Football League Cup:** Winners 1971–72. **Autoglass Trophy winners** 1992.
Colours: Red and white striped shirts, white shorts, red and white stockings.

SUNDERLAND   FA PREMIERSHIP

Name					
Aiston Sam (F)	6 0	12 01	Newcastle	21 11 76	Newcastle U
Ball Kevin (M)	5 9	11 06	Hastings	12 11 64	Portsmouth
Beavers Paul (F)	6 0	12 05	Blackpool	2 10 78	Trainee
Bridges Michael (F)	6 1	11 00	North Shields	5 8 78	Trainee
Butler Paul (D)	6 0	13 05	Manchester	2 11 72	Bury
Butler Thomas (M)	5 8	10 07	Ballymun	25 4 81	Trainee
Clark Lee (M)	5 8	11 07	Wallsend	27 10 72	Newcastle U
Convery Mark (F)	5 6	10 05	Newcastle	29 5 81	Trainee
Craddock Jody (D)	6 0	11 01	Bromsgrove	25 7 75	Cambridge U
Dichio Daniele (F)	6 3	12 08	Hammersmith	19 10 74	Lecce
Dickman Jonjo (D)	5 8	10 05	Hexham	22 9 81	
Duke David (M)	5 10	11 00	Inverness	7 11 78	Redby CA
Gray Michael (D)	5 7	10 08	Sunderland	3 8 74	Trainee
Harrison Gerry (D)	5 8	12 05	Lambeth	15 4 72	Burnley
Holloway Darren (D)	6 0	12 04	Bishop Auckland	3 10 77	Trainee
Johnston Allan (F)	5 7	9 07	Glasgow	14 12 73	Rennes
Kyle Kevin (F)	5 8	12 00	Stranraer	7 6 81	
Lumsdon Chris (M)	5 11	10 03	Newcastle	15 12 79	Trainee
Lynch Finbar (F)	5 8	10 01	Dublin	24 1 82	Belvedere
Makin Chris (D)	5 10	12 10	Manchester	8 5 73	Marseille
Maley Mark (D)	5 8	12 00	Newcastle	26 1 81	Trainee
Marriott Andy (G)	6 2	10 10	Sutton-in-Ashfield	11 10 70	Wrexham
McCann Gavin (M)	5 11	11 00	Blackpool	10 1 78	Everton
McCartney George (D)	6 0	12 06	Belfast	29 4 81	Trainee
McGill Brendan (M)	5 9	10 05	Dublin	22 3 81	
Phillips Kevin (F)	5 7	11 00	Hitchin	25 7 73	Watford
Porter Christopher (M)			Sunderland	10 11 79	Trainee
Proctor Michael (F)	5 11	12 00	Sunderland	3 10 80	Trainee
Quinn Niall (F)	6 4	12 04	Dublin	6 10 66	Manchester C
Rae Alex (M)	5 8	11 08	Glasgow	30 9 69	Millwall
Shannon Greg (G)	6 0	11 00	Maghreafelt	15 2 81	Trainee
Sorensen Thomas (G)	6 3	12 05	Fredericia	12 6 76	Odense
Summerbee Nicky (F)	5 8	11 08	Altrincham	26 8 71	Manchester C
Thirlwell Paul (M)	5 11	11 04	Newcastle	13 2 79	Trainee
Wainwright Neil (F)	5 10	10 02	Warrington	4 11 77	Wrexham
Weaver Luke (G)	6 2	13 02	Woolwich	26 6 79	Leyton Orient
Williams Darren (D)	5 9	11 00	Middlesbrough	28 4 77	York C

League Appearances: Aiston, S. (1); Ball, K. 42; Bridges, M. 13(17); Butler, P. 44; Clark, L. 26(1); Craddock, J. 3(3); Dichio, D. 16(20); Gray, M. 36(1); Holloway, D. 1(5); Johnston, A. 40; Makin, C. 37(1); Marriott, A. 1; McCann, G. 5(6); Melville, A. 44; Mullin, J. 8(1); Phillips, K. 26; Quinn, N. 36(3); Rae, A. 12(3); Scott, M. 14(2); Smith, M. 4(4); Sorensen, T. 45; Summerbee, N. 36; Thirlwell, P. 1(1); Wainwright, N. (2); Williams, D. 16(9).
Goals – League (91): Phillips 23 (3 pens), Quinn 18, Dichio 10 (1 pen), Bridges 8, Johnston 7, Clark 3, Smith 3, Summerbee 3, Ball 2, Butler 2, Gray 2, Melville 2, Mullin 2, Rae 2, Scott 2 (2 pens), own goals 2.
Worthington Cup (16): Bridges 4, Quinn 3, Dichio 2, Phillips 2, Johnston 1, McCann 1, Scott 1, Smith 1, own goal 1.
FA Cup (1): McCann 1.
Ground: Sunderland Stadium of Light, Sunderland, Tyne and Wear SR5 1SU. Telephone: (0191) 5515000.

Record attendance: 75,118 v Derby Co, FA Cup 6th rd replay, 8 March 1933 (at Roker Park). **Capacity:** 42,000.
Manager: Peter Reid.
Secretary: Mark Blackbourne.
Honours – Football League: Division 1 Champions – 1891–92, 1892–93, 1894–95, 1901–02, 1912–13, 1935–36, 1995–96, 1998–99. Division 2 Champions – 1975–76. Division 3 Champions – 1987–88. **FA Cup:** Winners 1937, 1973.
Colours: Red and white striped shirts, black shorts, black stockings, red turnover.

SWANSEA CITY   DIV. 3

Alsop Julian (F)	6 5	14 08	Nuneaton	28 5 73	Bristol R
Appleby Ritchie (M)	5 9	11 03	Stockton	18 9 75	Ipswich T
Bird Tony (F)	5 11	12 10	Cardiff	1 9 74	Cardiff C
Bound Matthew (D)	6 2	14 00	Bradford-on-Avon	9 11 72	Stockport Co
Casey Ryan (M)	6 0	10 12	Coventry	3 1 79	Trainee
Coates Jonathan (M)	5 8	10 04	Swansea	27 5 75	Trainee
Cusack Nick (M)	6 0	12 05	Rotherham	24 12 65	Fulham
Davies Jamie (F)	6 0	11 09	Swansea	12 2 80	Trainee
Freestone Roger (G)	6 3	14 06	Newport	19 8 68	Chelsea
Hartfield Charlie (M)	6 0	13 08	London	4 9 71	Sheffield U
Howard Mike (D)	5 9	11 13	Birkenhead	2 12 78	Tranmere R
Jenkins Lee (M)	5 9	10 00	Pontypool	28 6 79	Trainee
Jones Jason (G)	6 2	12 10	Wrexham	10 5 79	Liverpool
Jones Steve (D)	5 10	12 02	Bristol	25 12 70	Cheltenham T
Lacey Damien (D)	5 9	11 03	Bridgend	3 8 77	Trainee
O'Leary Kristian (D)	6 0	13 04	Port Talbot	30 8 77	Trainee
Phillips Gareth (M)	5 7	11 02	Church Village	19 8 79	Trainee
Price Jason (D)	6 0	11 05	Aberdare	12 4 77	Aberaman Ath
Roberts Stuart (M)	5 6	9 8	Carmarthen	22 7 80	Trainee
Smith Jason (D)	6 1	13 06	Bromsgrove	6 9 74	Coventry C
Thomas Martin (M)	5 8	11 06	Lyndhurst	12 9 73	Fulham
Walker Keith (D)	6 0	12 08	Edinburgh	17 4 66	St Mirren
Watkin Steve (F)	5 10	11 10	Wrexham	16 6 71	Wrexham

League Appearances: Alsop, J. 37(4); Appleby, R. 36(3); Bird, T. 8(21); Bound, M. 45; Casey, R. 5(5); Clode, M. 2; Coates, J. 30(3); Cusack, N. 42(1); Davies, J. (1); Freestone, R. 38; Gregg, M. 5; Howard, M. 38(1); Jenkins, L. 6(6); Jones, J. 3; Jones, S. 31(1); Lacey, D. 7(5); Newhouse, A. 5(1); O'Gorman, D. 2(3); O'Leary, K. 17(2); Phillips, G. (1); Price, J. 25(3); Roberts, S. 15(17); Smith, J. 42; Thomas, M. 26(4); Walker, K. 1; Watkin, S. 40(3).
Goals – League (56): Watkin 17 (2 pens), Alsop 10, Price 4, Smith 4, Appleby 3, Bird 3, Roberts 3, Thomas 3, Bound 2, Jones S 2, O'Leary 2, Casey 1, Cusack 1, Howard 1.
Worthington Cup (1): Cusack 1.
FA Cup (6): Thomas 2, Alsop 1, Appleby 1, Price 1, Smith 1.
Ground: Vetch Field, Swansea SA1 3SU. Telephone (01792) 474114.
Record attendance: 32,796 v Arsenal, FA Cup 4th rd, 17 February 1968. **Capacity:** 10,402.
Team Manager: John Hollins MBE.
Secretary: Vicki Townsend.
Honours – Football League: Division 3 (S) Champions – 1924–25, 1948–49.
Autoglass Trophy: Winners 1994. **Welsh Cup:** Winners 9 times.
Colours: White shirts with maroon and black trim, white shorts, white stockings.

SWINDON TOWN   DIV. 1

Collins Lee (M)	5 9	11 02	Bellshill	3	2 74	Albion R
Cowe Steve (F)	5 7	10 02	Gloucester	29	9 74	Aston Villa
Cuervo Philippe (M)	5 11	11 03	Ris-oranges	13	8 69	
Davies Gareth (D)	6 1	11 03	Hereford	11	12 73	Reading
Davis Sol (D)	5 7	11 00	Cheltenham	4	9 79	Trainee
Glass Jimmy (G)	6 1	13 04	Swindon	1	8 73	Bournemouth
Gooden Ty (M)	5 8	12 06	Canvey Island	23	10 72	Wycombe W
Griffin Charlie (F)			Bath	25	6 79	Bristol R
Hall Gareth (D)	5 8	12 00	Croydon	12	3 69	Sunderland
Hay Chris (F)	6 0	12 05	Glasgow	28	8 74	Celtic
Howe Bobby (M)	5 7	10 06	Annitsford	6	11 73	Nottingham F
Hulbert Robin (M)			Plymouth	14	3 80	Trainee
Leitch Scott (M)	5 10	12 00	Motherwell	6	10 69	Hearts
Mildenhall Steve (G)	6 4	14 01	Swindon	13	5 78	Trainee
Ndah George (F)	6 1	11 04	Dulwich	23	12 74	Crystal Palace
Onuora Iffy (F)	6 0	13 01	Glasgow	28	7 67	Gillingham
Reeves Alan (D)	6 0	12 00	Birkenhead	19	11 67	Wimbledon
Robinson Mark (D)	5 9	12 04	Rochdale	21	11 68	Newcastle U
Talia Frank (G)	6 1	13 06	Melbourne	20	7 72	Blackburn R
Taylor Craig (D)	6 1	12 03	Plymouth	24	1 74	Dorchester T
Walters Mark (M)	5 9	11 05	Birmingham	2	6 64	Southampton
Willis Adam (D)	6 1	13 02	Nuneaton	21	9 76	Coventry C

League Appearances: Borrows, B. 40; Bradley, S. 6(1); Bullock, D. 17(5); Campagna, S. (2); Collins, L. 2(2); Cowe, S. 2(3); Cuervo, P. 2(4); Davies, G. 6; Davis, S. 21(4); Fenn, N. 4; Glass, J. 3; Gooden, T. 36(2); Griffin, C. 1(4); Hall, G. 39(2); Hay, C. 16(11); Howe, B. 20(3); Hulbert, R. 7(9); Kerslake, D. 12(2); Leitch, S. 23(1); Linton, D. 7(1); McAreavey, P. (1); McHugh, F. 1; Ndah, G. 40(1); Onuora, I. 40(3); Reeves, A. 23(1); Robinson, M. 25(4); Talia, F. 43; Taylor, C. 18(3); Walters, M. 31(7); Watson, K. 9(9); Williams, J. 1(2); Willis, A. 11.

Goals – League (59): Onuora 20 (1 pen), Ndah 11, Walters 10 (3 pens), Hay 6, Howe 3, Reeves 2, Bullock 1, Gooden 1, Griffin 1, Hall 1, own goals 3.

Worthington Cup (2): Ndah 1, Reeves 1.

FA Cup (1): Walters 1.

Ground: County Ground, Swindon, Wiltshire SN1 2ED. Telephone (01793) 333 700.

Record attendance: 32,000 v Arsenal, FA Cup 3rd rd, 15 January 1972. **Capacity:** 15,728.

Manager: Jimmy Quinn.

Secretary: David Norris.

Honours – Football League: Division 2 Champions – 1995–96. Division 4 Champions – 1985–86. **Football League Cup:** Winners 1968–69. **Anglo-Italian Cup:** Winners 1970.

Colours: Red shirts, white shorts, red stockings.

TORQUAY UNITED   DIV. 3

Aggrey Jimmy (D)	6 3	13 06	London	26	10 78	Chelsea
Bedeau Anthony (F)	5 10	11 00	Hammersmith	24	3 79	Trainee
Donaldson O'Neill (F)	6 0	12 04	Birmingham	24	11 69	Stoke C
Hapgood Leon (F)	5 6	10 00	Torbay	7	8 79	Trainee
Healy Brian (M)	6 1	13 02	Glasgow	27	12 68	Morecambe
Herrera Robbie (D)	5 7	10 06	Torbay	12	6 70	Fulham

Hill Kevin (M)	5 8	10 03	Exeter	6 3 76	Torrington
Neil Gary (F)	6 0	12 10	Glasgow	16 8 78	Leicester C
Platts Mark (F)	5 8	11 12	Sheffield	23 5 79	Sheffield W
Simb Jean-Pierre (F)	6 1	11 05	Paris	4 9 74	FC Paris
Thomas Wayne (D)	5 11	11 02	Gloucester	17 5 79	Trainee
Tully Stephen (M)	5 7	10 04	Paignton	10 2 80	Trainee
Watson Alex (D)	6 1	12 00	Liverpool	5 4 68	Bournemouth
Williams Eifion (F)	5 11	11 00	Bangor	15 11 75	Barry T

League Appearances: Aggrey, J. 22(3); Bedeau, A. 28(8); Clayton, G. 15; Donaldson, O. 7(5); Forrester, M. 1(4); Gregg, M. 11; Gurney, A. 20; Hadley, S. (2); Hapgood, L. 11(6); Harries, P. 5; Healy, B. 16(3); Herrera, R. 39(1); Hill, K. 22(13); Jermyn, M. (1); Leadbitter, C. 37; Lee, A. 6(1); McFarlane, A. 5(10); McGorry, B. 31(3); Monk, G. 6; Neil, G. 6(1); Nichols, J. 5(1); Partridge, S. 29; Platts, M. 7(1); Robinson, J. 29; Russell, L. 9; Simb, J. 3(6); Southall, N. 25; Thomas, W. 44; Tully, S. 31(6); Veysey, K. 10; Waddle, C. 7; Watson, A. 8; Williams, E. 7; Witter, T. 4; Worthington, M. (1).

Goals – League (47): Partridge 12, Bedeau 9, Hill 5, Williams 5, McFarlane 3, Healy 2 (1 pen), Lee 2, Tully 2, Donaldson 1, Gurney 1, Leadbitter 1, McGorry 1, Robinson 1, Simb 1, Thomas 1.

Worthington Cup (2): Bedeau 1, Thomas 1.

FA Cup (1): Partridge 1.

Ground: Plainmoor Ground, Torquay, Devon TQ1 3PS. Telephone (01803) 328666.

Record attendance: 21,908 v Huddersfield T, FA Cup 4th rd, 29 January 1955.

Capacity: 6003.

Manager: Wes Saunders.

Secretary: Miss H. Kindeleit.

Honours – Nil

Colours: Yellow and navy striped shirts, navy shorts, yellow stockings.

TOTTENHAM HOTSPUR   FA PREMIERSHIP

Allen Rory (F)	5 11	11 02	Beckenham	17 10 77	Trainee
Anderton Darren (F)	6 1	12 05	Southampton	3 3 72	Portsmouth
Armstrong Chris (F)	6 0	12 10	Newcastle	19 6 71	Crystal Palace
Baardsen Espen (G)	6 5	13 03	San Rafael	7 12 77	San Francisco AB
Campbell Sol (D)	6 21	14 04	Newham	18 9 74	Trainee
Carr Stephen (D)	5 9	12 04	Dublin	29 8 76	Trainee
Clemence Stephen (M)	5 11	11 07	Liverpool	31 3 78	Trainee
Crouch Peter (F)	6 2	11 12	Macclesfield	30 1 81	Trainee
Darcy Ross (D)	6 0	12 02	Balbriggan	21 3 78	Trainee
Dominguez Jose (F)	5 3	10 00	Lisbon	16 2 74	Sporting Lisbon
Edinburgh Justin (D)	5 10	12 01	Basildon	18 12 69	Southend U
Fenn Neale (F)	5 10	12 08	Edmonton	18 1 77	Trainee
Ferdinand Les (F)	5 11	13 05	Acton	18 12 66	Newcastle U
Fox Ruel (F)	5 6	10 05	Ipswich	14 1 68	Newcastle U
Freund Steffen (M)	5 11	12 06	Brandenburg	19 1 70	Borussia Dortmund
Ginola David (F)	5 11	11 10	Gassin	25 1 67	Newcastle U
Gower Mark (M)			Edmonton	5 10 78	Motherwell
Hillier Ian (D)	5 11	11 05	Neath	26 12 79	Trainee
Iversen Steffen (F)	6 1	11 08	Oslo	10 11 76	
King Ledley (D)	6 2	13 08	London	12 10 80	Trainee
Lee David (M)	5 11	11 08	Basildon	28 3 80	Trainee
McVeigh Paul (F)	5 6	10 05	Belfast	6 12 77	Trainee
Nielsen Allan (M)	5 8	11 02	Esbjerg	13 3 71	Brondby

Piercy John (M)   5 11   11 12   Forest Gate   18 9 79   Trainee
Saib Moussa (M)   5 9   11 08   Theniet-El-Had   5 3 69   Valencia
Scales John (D)   6 2   13 05   Harrogate   4 7 66   Liverpool
Sherwood Tim (M)   6 1   12 09   St Albans   2 2 69   Blackburn R
Taricco Mauricio (D)   5 8   11 05   Buenos Aires   10 3 73   Ipswich T
Thelwell Alton (D)   London   5 9 80   Trainee
Tramezzani Paolo (D)   6 1   13 06   Reggio-Emilia   30 7 70   Piacenza
Vaughan Wayne (M)   Barking   18 2 80   Trainee
Vega Ramon (D)   6 3   13 00   Olten   14 6 71   Cagliari
Walker Ian (G)   6 2   13 01   Watford   31 10 71   Trainee
Webb Simon (M)   5 11   12 03   Castle Bar   19 1 78   Trainee
Young Luke (M)   Harlow   19 7 79   Trainee

League Appearances: Allen, R. (5); Anderton, D. 31(1); Armstrong, C. 24(10); Baardsen, E. 12; Berti, N. 4; Calderwood, C. 11(1); Campbell, S. 37; Carr, S. 37; Clemence, S. 9(9); Dominguez, J. 2(11); Edinburgh, J. 14(2); Ferdinand, L. 22(2); Fox, R. 17(3); Freund, S. 17; Ginola, D. 30; Iversen, S. 22(5); King, L. (1); Nielsen, A. 24(4); Nilsen, R. 3; Saib, M. (4); Scales, J. 7; Segers, H. 1; Sherwood, T. 12(2); Sinton, A. 12(10); Taricco, M. 12(1); Tramezzani, P. 6; Vega, R. 13(3); Walker, I. 25; Young, L. 14(1).

Goals – League (47): Iversen 9, Armstrong 7, Campbell 6, Ferdinand 5, Anderton 3 (2 pens), Fox 3, Ginola 3, Nielsen 3, Dominguez 2, Sherwood 2, Vega 2, own goals 2.

Worthington Cup (17): Armstrong 5, Nielsen 3, Campbell 2, Iversen 2, Carr 1, Dominguez 1, Ginola 1, Scales 1, Vega 1.

FA Cup (13): Ginola 3, Nielsen 3, Anderton 2 (1 pen), Iversen 2, Fox 1, Sherwood 1, Sinton 1.

Ground: 748 High Rd, Tottenham, London N17 0AP. Telephone (0181) 365 5000.

Record attendance: 75,038 v Sunderland, FA Cup 6th rd, 5 March 1938.

Capacity: 36,236.

Manager: George Graham.

Secretary: Peter Barnes.

Honours – Football League: Division 1 Champions – 1950–51, 1960–61. Division 2 Champions – 1919–20, 1949–50. **FA Cup:** Winners 1901 (as non-**League** club), 1921, 1961, 1962, 1967, 1981, 1982, 1991. **Football League Cup:** Winners 1970–71, 1972–73, 1998–99. **European Competitions: European Cup-Winners' Cup winners:** 1962–63. **UEFA Cup winners:** 1971–72, 1983–84.

Colours: White shirts, navy blue shorts, navy blue stockings.

TRANMERE ROVERS   DIV. 1

Achterberg John (G)   6 1   13 00   Utrecht   8 7 71   Eindhoven
Allen Graham (D)   6 0   12 00   Bolton   8 4 77   Everton
Challinor Dave (D)   6 1   12 00   Chester   2 10 75   Brombrough Pool
Frail Stephen (D)   5 11   12 03   Glasgow   10 8 69   Hearts
Gibson Neil (M)   5 11   11 08   St Asaph   10 10 79   Trainee
Hill Clint (D)   6 0   11 06   Liverpool   19 10 78   Trainee
Hinds Richard (D)   6 2   12 00   Sheffield   22 8 80   Schoolboy
Holmes Tommy (D)   6 0   12 06   Bevington   1 9 79   Trainee
Irons Kenny (M)   5 10   11 02   Liverpool   4 11 70   Trainee
Jones Gary (F)   6 3   13 05   Chester   10 5 75   Trainee
Jones Lee (F)   5 8   10 06   Wrexham   29 5 73   Liverpool
Joy Ian (M)   5 10   11 00   San Diego   14 7 81   Trainee
Kelly David (F)   5 11   11 10   Birmingham   25 11 65   Sunderland
Koumas Jason (M)   5 10   11 06   Wrexham   25 9 79   Trainee
Mahon Alan (M)   5 9   11 05   Dublin   4 4 78   Crumplin U
McGreal John (D)   6 1   11 06   Birkenhead   2 6 72   Trainee

Moran Andy (F)	5 11	11 02	Wigan	7 10 79	Trainee
Morgan Alan (D)	5 9	11 00	Aberystwyth	2 11 73	Trainee
Parkinson Andy (F)	5 8	10 12	Liverpool	27 5 79	Liverpool
Santos Georges (D)	6 3	14 08	Marseille	15 8 70	Toulon
Taylor Perry (M)	5 11	12 02	Birkenhead	29 1 81	Trainee
Taylor Scott (F)	5 10	11 06	Chertsey	5 5 76	Bolton W
Thompson Andy (D)	5 5	10 06	Cannock	9 11 67	Wolverhampton W
Williams Ryan (F)	5 4	11 02	Chesterfield	31 8 78	Mansfield T

League Appearances: Achterberg, J. 24; Allen, G. 41; Challinor, D. 29(5); Coyne, D. 17; Frail, S. 5; Gibson, N. (1); Hill, C. 33; Hinds, R. 1(1); Irons, K. 43; Jones, G. 15(11); Jones, L. 18(12); Kelly, D. 16(11); Koumas, J. 11(12); Mahon, A. 34(5); McGreal, J. 36; Mellon, M. 21(3); Morgan, A. 4(2); Morrissey, J. 5(19); O'Brien, L. 18(5); Parkinson, A. 20(9); Russell, C. 3(1); Santos, G. 37; Sharps, I. (1); Shepherd, P. (1); Simonsen, S. 5; Taylor, S. 31(5); Thompson, A. 37; Williams, R. 2(3).

Goals – League (63): Irons 15 (6 pens), Taylor 9, Mahon 6 (1 pen), Allen 5, Jones G 5, Hill 4, Kelly 4, Koumas 3, Challinor 2, Jones L 2, O'Brien 2, Parkinson 2, Mellon 1, Santos 1, Thompson 1, own goal 1.

Worthington Cup (8): Irons 3 (2 pens), Kelly 2, Jones L 1, Koumas 1, Parkinson 1.

FA Cup (0).

Ground: Prenton Park, Prenton Road West, Birkenhead L42 9PN. Telephone (0151) 608 4194.

Record attendance: 24,424 v Stoke C, FA Cup 4th rd, 5 February 1972.

Capacity: 16,789.

Manager: John Aldridge.

Secretary: Mick Horton.

Honours – Football League Division 3 (N) Champions – 1937–38. **Welsh Cup:** Winners 1935. **Leyland Daf Cup:** Winners 1990.

Colours: White shirts, blue shorts.

WALSALL DIV. 1

Birch Gary (M)			Birmingham	8 10 81	Trainee
Brissett Jason (F)	5 10	12 05	Redbridge	7 9 74	Bournemouth
Carter Alfonso (M)			Birmingham	23 8 80	Trainee
Eyjolfsson Siggi (F)	6 2	12 09	Reykjavik	1 12 73	From IA Akranes
Gadsby Matthew (D)	6 1	11 12	Sutton Coldfield	6 9 79	Trainee
Green Richard (D)	6 1	14 00	Wolverhampton	22 11 67	Gillingham
Keates Dean (M)	5 5	10 07	Walsall	30 6 78	Trainee
Larusson Bjarni (M)			Iceland	11 3 76	Hibernian
Marsh Chris (D)	5 10	13 04	Dudley	14 1 70	Trainee
Mavrak Darko (M)			Mostar	19 1 69	Norrkoping
Platt Clive (F)	6 3	13 04	Wolverhampton	27 10 77	Trainee
Rammell Andy (F)	6 1	14 00	Nuneaton	10 2 67	Southend U
Ricketts Michael (F)	6 1	12 05	Birmingham	4 12 78	Trainee
Roper Ian (D)	6 3	13 09	Nuneaton	20 6 77	Trainee
Thomas Wayne (M)	5 8	12 02	Walsall	28 8 78	Trainee
Viveash Adrian (D)	6 1	13 05	Swindon	30 9 69	Swindon T
Walker James (G)	5 10	13 01	Sutton-in-Ashfield	9 7 73	Notts Co
Wrack Darren (M)	5 10	12 02	Cleethorpes	5 5 76	Grimsby T

League Appearances: Brissett, J. 27(8); Carter, A. (1); Cramb, C. 4; Davis, N. (1); Dyer, W. (1); Evans, W. 6(5); Eyjolfsson, S. (10); Gadsby, M. 3(3); Green, R. 22(8); Henry, N. 8; Keates, D. 38(5); Keister, J. 2; Lambert, J. 4(2); Larusson, B. 33(3); Marsh, C. 43; Mavrak, D. 12(1); Otta, W. 6(2); Platt, C. 6(1); Pointon, N. 43; Porter, G. 14(1); Rammell, A. 39; Ricketts, M. 2(6); Roper, I. 29(3); Simpson, P. 10; Steiner, R. 10; Thomas, W. 1(11); Viveash, A. 40; Walker, J. 46; Watson, A. 12(9); Wrack, D. 46.

Goals – League (63): Rammell 18, Wrack 13 (2 pens), Cramb 4 (2 pens), Larusson 3, Otta 3, Steiner 3, Watson 3, Brissett 2, Keates 2, Marsh 2, Mavrak 2, Eyjolfsson 1, Green 1, Platt 1, Roper 1, Simpson 1, own goals 3.
Worthington Cup (1): Rammell 1.
FA Cup (1): Roper 1.
Ground: Bescot Stadium, Bescot Cresent, Walsall WS1 4SA. Telephone (01922) 622791.
Record attendance: 10,628 B International, England v Switzerland, 20 May 1991.
Capacity: 9000.
Manager: Ray Graydon.
Secretary/Commercial Manager: Roy Whalley.
Honours – Football League: Division 4 Champions – 1959–60.
Colours: Red shirts with black trim, black shorts with white trim, red stockings with white band.

WATFORD FA PREMIERSHIP

Name	Ht	Wt	Birthplace	Birthdate	Previous club
Bakalli Adrian (M)			Brussels	22 11 76	Molenbeek
Chamberlain Alec (G)	6 2	13 10	March	20 6 64	Sunderland
Day Chris (G)	6 3	13 06	Walthamstow	28 7 75	Crystal Palace
Easton Clint (M)	5 11	10 04	Barking	1 10 77	Trainee
Gibbs Nigel (D)	5 7	11 06	St Albans	20 11 65	Apprentice
Gudmundsson Johann (M)	6 0	12 00	Reykjavik	5 12 77	Keflavik
Hazan Alon (M)	6 1	13 08	Ashdod	14 9 67	Ironi Ashdod
Hyde Micah (M)	5 10	11 12	Newham	10 11 74	Cambridge U
Iroha Ben (M)	5 8	11 06	Calabar	29 11 69	San Jose Clash
Johnson Lee (M)			Newmarket	7 6 81	Trainee
Johnson Richard (M)	5 10	12 07	Kurri Kurri	27 4 74	Trainee
Kennedy Peter (D)	5 10	11 05	Lisburn	10 9 73	Portadown
Langston Matthew (M)			Brighton	2 4 81	Trainee
Millen Keith (D)	6 2	13 00	Croydon	26 9 66	Brentford
Mooney Tommy (D)	5 11	13 10	Teesside North	11 8 71	Southend U
Ngonge Michel (F)	6 0	12 08	Huy	10 1 67	Samsunspor
Noel-Williams Gifton (F)	6 1	13 09	Islington	21 1 80	Trainee
Page Robert (D)	6 0	12 13	Llwynipia	3 9 74	Trainee
Palmer Steve (M)	6 1	13 05	Brighton	31 3 68	Ipswich T
Panayi James (D)	6 1	13 12	Hammersmith	24 1 80	Trainee
Perpetuini David (M)	5 9	10 07	Hitchin	26 9 79	Trainee
Pluck Colin (D)	6 0	12 05	London	6 9 78	Trainee
Robinson Paul (D)	5 9	11 10	Watford	14 12 78	Trainee
Rosenthal Ronny (F)	5 11	13 04	Haifa	4 10 63	Tottenham H
Smart Allan (F)	6 2	12 11	Perth	8 7 74	Carlisle U
Smith Tommy (F)	5 9	10 11	Hemel Hempstead	22 5 80	Trainee
Ward Darran (D)	6 0	14 02	Kenton	13 9 78	Trainee
Wright Nick (F)	5 9	11 13	Derby	15 10 75	Carlisle U
Yates Dean (D)	6 2	12 06	Leicester	26 10 67	Derby Co

League Appearances: Bazeley, D. 36(4); Bonnot, A. 1(3); Chamberlain, A. 46; Daley, T. 6(6); Easton, C. 7; Gibbs, N. 9(1); Gudmundsson, J. 6(7); Hazan, A. 8(15); Hyde, M. 43(1); Iroha, B. 8(2); Johnson, R. 40; Kennedy, P. 46; Lee, J. 1; Millen, K. 10(1); Mooney, T. 20(16); Ngonge, M. 13(9); Noel-Williams, G. 19(7); Page, R. 37(2); Palmer, S. 40(1); Perpetuini, D. 1; Robinson, P. 26(3); Rosenthal, R. 1(4); Smart, A. 34(1); Smith, T. 3(5); Ward, D. 1; Whittingham, G. 4(1); Wright, N. 31(2); Yates, D. 9.
Goals – League (65): Noel-Williams 10, Mooney 9, Smart 7, Kennedy 6 (2 pens), Wright 6, Johnson 4, Ngonge 4, Bazeley 2, Gudmundsson 2, Hazan 2, Hyde 2, Palmer 2, Smith 2, Daley 1, Lee 1, Millen 1, Yates 1, own goals 3.
Worthington Cup (1): Ngonge 1.

FA Cup (2): Johnson 1, Kennedy 1.
Ground: Vicarage Road Stadium, Watford WD1 8ER. Telephone (01923) 496000.
Record attendance: 34,099 v Manchester U, FA Cup 4th rd (replay), 3 February 1969. **Capacity:** 22,000.
General Manager: Graham Taylor.
Secretary: John Alexander.
Honours – Football League: Division 3 Champions – 1968–69. Division 2 Champions – 1997–98. Division 4 Champions – 1977–78.
Colours: Yellow shirts with red and black trim, red shorts, red stockings with black trim.

WEST BROMWICH ALBION   DIV. 1

Name	Height	Weight	Birthplace	Birthdate	Previous club
Adamson Christopher (G)	5 11	11 00	Ashington	4 11 78	Trainee
Angel Mark (M)	5 8	11 02	Newcastle	23 8 75	Oxford U
Burgess Daryl (D)	5 11	11 04	Birmingham	24 1 71	Trainee
Carbon Matt (D)	6 2	12 05	Nottingham	8 6 75	Derby Co
Chambers Adam (D)	5 10	11 08	Sandwell	20 11 80	Trainee
Chambers James (D)	5 10	11 08	Sandwell	20 11 80	Trainee
De Freitas Fabian (F)	6 0	12 00	Paramaribo	28 7 72	Osasuna
Evans Micky (F)	6 0	12 03	Plymouth	1 1 73	Southampton
Flynn Sean (M)	5 8	11 09	Birmingham	13 3 68	Derby Co
Gabbidon Daniel (D)	5 10	11 02	Cwmbran	8 8 79	Trainee
Holmes Paul (D)	5 10	11 00	Stocksbridge	18 2 68	Everton
Hughes Lee (F)	5 10	11 06	Birmingham	22 5 76	Kidderminster H
Kilbane Kevin (F)	6 0	12 07	Preston	1 2 77	Preston NE
Mardon Paul (D)	6 0	11 10	Bristol	14 9 69	Birmingham C
Maresca Enzo (M)	5 11	12 00	Salerno	10 2 80	
McDermott Andy (D)	5 9	11 03	Sydney	24 3 77	QPR
Miller Alan (G)	6 3	14 06	Epping	29 3 70	Middlesbrough
Oliver Adam (M)	5 9	11 02	Sandwell	25 10 80	Trainee
Potter Graham (D)	6 1	11 12	Solihull	20 5 75	Southampton
Quailey Brian (F)	6 1	13 11	Leicester	21 3 78	Nuneaton B
Quinn James (F)	6 1	12 10	Coventry	15 12 74	Blackpool
Raven Paul (D)	6 1	12 11	Salisbury	28 7 70	Doncaster R
Richards Justin (F)	6 0	11 10	Sandwell	16 10 80	Trainee
Sneekes Richard (M)	5 11	12 03	Amsterdam	30 10 68	Bolton W
Whitehead Phil (G)	6 3	15 04	Halifax	17 12 69	Oxford U

League Appearances: Angel, M. 4(18); Bortolazzi, M. 25(10); Burgess, D. 15(5); Carbon, M. 38(1); De Freitas, F. 22(15); Evans, M. 17(3); Flynn, S. 33(5); Gabbidon, D. 2; Holmes, P. 17; Hughes, L. 42; Kilbane, K. 44; Mardon, P. 12(6); Maresca, E. 9(13); McDermott, A. 20; Miller, A. 20; Murphy, S. 30(7); Oliver, A. (1); Potter, G. 19(3); Quailey, B. 1(1); Quinn, J. 39(4); Raven, P. 6(1); Richards, J. (1); Sneekes, R. 35(5); Van Blerk, J. 30; Whitehead, P. 26.
Goals – League (69): Hughes 31 (5 pens), De Freitas 7, Kilbane 6, Quinn 6, Murphy 4, Sneekes 4, Bortolazzi 2, Carbon 2, Evans 2, Flynn 2, Maresca 2, Angel 1.
Worthington Cup (2): Evans 1, Hughes 1.
FA Cup (0).
Ground: The Hawthorns, West Bromwich B71 4LF. Telephone (0121) 525 8888.
Record attendance: 64,815 v Arsenal, FA Cup 6th rd, 6 March 1937. **Capacity:** 25,396.
Manager: Denis Smith.
Secretary: Dr. John J. Evans BA, PHD. (Wales).
Honours – Football League: Division 1 Champions – 1919–20. Division 2 Champions – 1901–02, 1910–11. **FA Cup:** Winners 1888, 1892, 1931, 1954, 1968.
Football League Cup: Winners 1965–66.
Colours: Navy blue and white striped shirts, white shorts, blue and white stockings.

	Ht	Wt		Birthdate	
Abou Samassi (F)	6 1	12 08	Gagnoa	4 4 73	Cannes
Alexander Gary (F)			South London	15 8 79	Trainee
Berkovic Eyal (M)	5 7	10 02	Haifa	2 4 72	Southampton
Bullard Jimmy (M)	5 10	11 07	Newham	23 10 78	Gravesend & N
Bywater Steve (G)			Manchester	7 6 81	Trainee
Carrick Michael (F)			Wallsend	28 7 81	Trainee
Cole Joe (M)	5 9	11 00	North London	8 11 81	Trainee
Coyne Chris (D)	6 1	13 10	Brisbane	20 12 78	Perth SC
Di Canio Paolo (F)	5 9	11 07	Rome	9 7 68	Sheffield W
Dicks Julian (D)	5 10	13 00	Bristol	8 8 68	Liverpool
Etherington Craig (M)			Basildon	16 9 79	Trainee
Ferdinand Rio (D)	6 2	12 00	Peckham	8 11 78	Trainee
Ferrante Michael (M)			Melbourne	28 4 81	Australia IOS
Foe Marc Vivien (M)	6 2	13 06	Yaounde	1 5 75	Lens
Forrest Craig (G)	6 4	14 04	Vancouver	20 9 67	Ipswich T
Garcia Richard (F)			Perth	4 9 81	Trainee
Hislop Shaka (G)	6 4	14 04	Hackney	22 2 69	Newcastle U
Hodges Lee (M)	5 5	10 02	Newham	2 3 78	Trainee
Holligan Gavin (F)	6 0	13 00	Lambeth	13 6 80	Kingstonian
Keller Marc (M)	5 9	12 03	Colmar	14 1 68	Karlsruhe
Kitson Paul (F)	5 11	10 12	Murton	9 1 71	Newcastle U
Lampard Frank (M)	6 0	11 12	Romford	20 6 78	Trainee
Lazaridis Stan (D)	5 9	12 00	Perth	16 8 72	West Adelaide
Lomas Steve (M)	6 0	12 08	Hanover	18 1 74	Manchester C
Margas Javier (D)			Chile	10 5 69	Univ Catolica
McCann Grant (M)			Belfast	14 4 80	Trainee
Minto Scott (D)	5 10	12 04	Cheshire	6 8 71	Benfica
Moncur John (M)	5 7	9 10	Mile End	22 9 66	Swindon T
O'Reilly Alex (G)			Epping	15 9 79	Trainee
Omoyimni Emmanuel (F)	5 6	10 07	Nigeria	28 12 77	Trainee
Pearce Ian (D)	6 3	14 04	Bury St Edmunds	7 5 74	Blackburn R
Potts Steve (D)	5 7	10 11	Hartford (USA)	7 5 67	Apprentice
Purces Stephen (M)			Essex	14 1 80	Trainee
Ruddock Neil (D)	6 2	12 12	South London	9 5 68	Liverpool
Sinclair Trevor (F)	5 10	12 05	Dulwich	2 3 72	QPR
Wright Ian (F)	5 10	11 08	Woolwich	3 11 63	Arsenal

League Appearances: Abou, S. 2(1); Berkovic, E. 28(2); Breacker, T. 2(1); Cole, J. 2(6); Coyne, C. (1); Di Canio, P. 12(1); Dicks, J. 9; Ferdinand, R. 31; Foe, M. 13; Forrest, C. 1(1); Hartson, J. 16(1); Hislop, S. 37; Hodges, L. (1); Holligan, G. (1); Impey, A. 6(2); Keller, M. 17(4); Kitson, P. 13(4); Lampard, F. 38; Lazaridis, S. 11(4); Lomas, S. 30; Margas, J. 3; Minto, S. 14(1); Moncur, J. 6(8); Omoyimni, E. (3); Pearce, I. 33; Potts, S. 11(8); Ruddock, N. 27; Sinclair, T. 36; Wright, I. 20(2).

Goals – League (46): Wright 9, Sinclair 7, Keller 5, Lampard 5 (1 pen), Di Canio 4, Hartson 4, Berkovic 3, Kitson 3, Pearce 2, Ruddock 2, Lomas 1, own goal 1.

Worthington Cup (1): Lampard 1.

FA Cup (1): Dicks 1.

Ground: Boleyn Ground, Green Street, Upton Park, London E13 9AZ. Telephone (0181) 548 2748.

Record attendance: 42,322 v Tottenham H, Division 1, 17 October 1970. **Capacity:** 26,012.

Manager: Harry Redknapp.

Secretary: Graham Mackrell FCCA.

Honours – Football League: Division 2 Champions – 1957–58, 1980–81. **FA Cup:** Winners 1964, 1975, 1980. **European Competitions: European Cup-Winners' Cup winners:** 1964–65.

Colours: Claret shirts with blue sleeves, white shorts, light blue with claret hooped stockings.

WIGAN ATHLETIC   DIV. 2

Balmer Stuart (D)	6 0	12 11	Falkirk	20 9 69	Charlton Ath
Barlow Stuart (F)	5 10	11 01	Liverpool	16 7 68	Oldham Ath
Bradshaw Carl (D)	5 10	11 08	Sheffield	2 10 68	Norwich C
Carroll Roy (G)	6 2	13 05	Enniskillen	30 9 77	Hull C
Fitzhenry Neil (D)	6 0	12 02	Billinge	24 9 78	Trainee
Green Scott (D)	5 10	13 04	Walsall	15 1 70	Bolton W
Griffiths Gareth (D)	6 4	14 01	Winsford	10 4 70	Port Vale
Haworth Simon (F)	6 1	13 01	Cardiff	30 3 77	Coventry C
Jones Graeme (F)	6 0	14 04	Gateshead	13 3 70	Doncaster R
Kilford Ian (M)	5 10	11 03	Bristol	6 10 73	Nottingham F
Lee David (F)	5 7	11 01	Whitefield	5 11 67	Bolton W
Liddell Andy (F)	5 6	11 06	Leeds	28 6 73	Barnsley
Martinez Roberto (M)	5 11	12 03	Balaguer	13 7 73	Balaguer
McGibbon Pat (D)	6 2	14 01	Lurgan	6 9 73	Manchester U
Nixon Eric (G)	6 4	14 00	Manchester	4 10 62	Stockport C
O'Connell Brendan (M)	5 9	12 01	London	12 11 66	Charlton Ath
O'Neill Michael (M)	5 11	10 10	Portadown	5 7 69	Coventry C
Porter Andy (M)	5 9	12 03	Holmes Chapel	17 9 68	Port Vale
Smeets Jorg (F)	5 6	10 04	Bussum	5 11 70	

League Appearances: Balmer, S. 36; Barlow, S. 39(2); Bradshaw, C. 39; Carroll, R. 43; Fitzhenry, N. 1; Green, S. 32(5); Greenall, C. 40; Griffiths, G. 20; Haworth, S. 19(1); Jenkinson, L. 3(4); Jones, G. 8(12); Kilford, I. 16(7); Lee, D. 20(16); Liddell, A. 28; Lowe, D. 5(11); Martinez, R. 3(7); McGibbon, P. 35(1); Nixon, E. 3; O'Neill, M. 35(1); Porter, A. 6(10); Rogers, P. 42; Sharp, K. 25(6); Smeets, J. (1); Warne, P. 8(3).
Goals – League (75): Barlow 19 (2 pens), Haworth 10, Liddell 10, Bradshaw 6 (5 pens), Greenall 6, Lee 6, McGibbon 5, Jones 3, Rogers 2, Sharp 2, Balmer 1, Lowe 1, Porter 1, Warne 1, own goals 2.
Worthington Cup (4): Barlow 1, Griffiths 1, Lee 1, own goal 1.
FA Cup (5): Lowe 2, Barlow 1, Greenall 1, Haworth 1.
Ground: J. J. B. Stadium, Robin Park, Wigan WN6 7BA. Telephone (01942) 244433.
Record attendance: 27,500 v Hereford U, FA Cup 2nd rd, 12 December 1953.
Capacity: 25,000
Manager: John Benson.
Secretary: Mrs Brenda Spencer.
Honours – Football League: Division 3 Champions – 1996–97. **Freight Rover Trophy:** Winners 1984–85. **Auto Windscreens Shield:** Winners 1998–99.
Colours: Blue shirts with white side panel, blue shorts and stockings.

WIMBLEDON   FA PREMIERSHIP

Agyemang Patrick (F)	6 1	12 00	London	29 9 80	Trainee
Ainsworth Gareth (M)	5 8	13 02	Blackburn	10 5 73	Port Vale
Ardley Neal (M)	5 11	11 09	Epsom	1 9 72	Trainee
Blackwell Dean (D)	6 1	12 10	Camden	5 12 69	Trainee
Castledine Stewart (M)	6 1	12 00	Wandsworth	22 1 73	Trainee
Cort Carl (F)	6 4	12 07	Southwark	1 11 77	
Cunningham Kenny (D)	5 11	11 02	Dublin	28 6 71	Millwall
Earle Robbie (M)	5 9	10 10	Newcastle-Under-Lyme	27 1 65	Port Vale
Ekoku Efan (F)	6 2	12 00	Manchester	8 6 67	Norwich C
Euell Jason (F)	5 11	11 02	Lambeth	6 2 77	Trainee
Favata Sebastian (D)	5 10	11 07	Carshalton	18 10 80	Trainee
Francis Damien (M)	6 0	10 10	Wandsworth	27 2 79	Trainee

Gayle Marcus (F)	6 1	12 09	Hammersmith	27 9 70	Brentford
Gier Robert (M)	5 9	11 07	Bracknell	6 1 81	Trainee
Goodman Jon (F)	6 0	12 03	Walthamstow	2 6 71	Millwall
Gray Wayne (F)	5 10	12 07	London	7 11 80	Trainee
Halliwell Bryn (G)	5 11	12 00	Epsom	1 10 80	Trainee
Hartson John (F)	6 0	13 00	Swansea	5 4 75	West Ham U
Hawkins Peter (D)	6 0	11 04	Maidstone	19 9 78	Trainee
Heald Paul (G)	6 2	12 05	Wath-on-Dearne	20 9 68	Leyton Orient
Hinds Leigh (F)	5 8	10 10	Beckenham	17 8 78	Trainee
Hughes Ceri (M)	5 10	12 07	Pontypridd	26 2 71	Luton T
Hughes Michael (M)	5 6	10 08	Larne	2 8 71	West Ham U
Jupp Duncan (D)	6 0	12 11	Guildford	25 1 75	Fulham
Kennedy Mark (F)	5 11	11 00	Dublin	15 5 76	Liverpool
Kimble Alan (D)	5 10	12 04	Poole	6 8 66	Cambridge U
Leaburn Carl (F)	6 3	13 00	Lewisham	30 3 69	Charlton Ath
McAllister Brian (D)	5 11	12 05	Glasgow	30 11 70	Trainee
Owusu Ansah (M)	5 11	11 02	Hackney	22 11 79	Trainee
Perry Chris (D)	5 8	10 08	Carshalton	26 4 73	Trainee
Roberts Andy (M)	5 10	13 00	Dartford	20 3 74	Crystal Palace
Sullivan Neil (G)	6 0	12 01	Sutton	24 2 70	Trainee
Thatcher Ben (D)	5 11	12 07	Swindon	30 11 75	Millwall
Thurgood Sean (D)	6 2	12 09	Hayling Island	11 2 80	Alton T
Williamson Russell (D)	5 4	8 10	Epping	17 3 80	Trainee
Willy Mark (M)	5 11	12 00	Sidcup	5 8 80	Trainee

League Appearances: Ainsworth, G. 5(3); Ardley, N. 16(7); Blackwell, D. 27(1); Castledine, S. 1; Cort, C. 6(10); Cunningham, K. 35; Earle, R. 35; Ekoku, E. 11(11); Euell, J. 31(2); Fear, P. (2); Gayle, M. 31(4); Goodman, J. (1); Hartson, J. 12(2); Hughes, C. 8(6); Hughes, M. 28(2); Jupp, D. 3(3); Kennedy, M. 7(10); Kimble, A. 22(4); Leaburn, C. 14(8); Perry, C. 34; Roberts, A. 23(5); Sullivan, N. 38; Thatcher, B. 31.

Goals – League (40): Euell 10, Gayle 10, Ekoku 6, Earle 5, Cort 3, Hartson 2, Hughes M 2, Roberts 2.

Worthington Cup (11): Ardley 3, Ekoku 3, Earle 1, Gayle 1, Hughes M 1 (pen), Kennedy 1, Leaburn 1.

FA Cup (2): Earle 1, Cort 1

Ground: Selhurst Park, South Norwood, London SE25 6PY. Telephone (0181) 771 2233.

Record attendance: 30,115 v Manchester U, FA Premier **League**, 9 May 1993.

Capacity: 26,297.

Manager: Egil Olsen.

Secretary: Steve Rooke.

Honours – Football League: Division 4 Champions – 1982–83. **FA Cup:** Winners 1987–88.

Colours: All navy blue with yellow trim.

WOLVERHAMPTON WANDERERS DIV. 1

Andrews Keith (M)	5 11	11 05	Dublin	13 9 80	Trainee
Bull Steve (F)	5 11	11 04	Tipton	28 3 65	WBA
Corica Steve (M)	5 8	10 10	Cairns	24 3 73	Marconi
Crowe Seamie (M)	5 7	11 07	Galway	18 11 80	Trainee
Emblen Neil (M)	6 1	13 03	Bromley	19 6 71	Crystal Palace
Flo Havard (F)	6 2	13 08	Volda	4 4 70	Werder Bremen
Green Ryan (D)	5 8	10 10	Cardiff	20 10 80	Danes Court
Hackett Stephen (D)			Dublin	17 9 80	Trainee
Jones Mark (F)	5 9	12 06	Walsall	7 9 79	Trainee
Keane Robbie (F)	5 9	11 07	Dublin	8 7 80	Trainee
Larkin Colin (M)			Dundalk	27 4 82	Trainee

Loughlin Paul (M)			Dublin	5 10 81	Stella Maris
Middleton Darren (F)	6 1	11 13	Lichfield	28 12 78	Aston Villa
Murray Matthew (G)	6 4	13 11	Solihull	2 5 81	Trainee
Muscat Kevin (D)	5 11	11 07	Crawley	7 8 73	Crystal Palace
Naylor Lee (D)	5 8	11 08	Bloxwich	19 3 80	Trainee
Niestroj Robert (M)	5 10	11 03	Oppeln	2 12 74	Fortuna Dusseldorf
Osborn Simon (M)	5 8	11 04	New Addington	9 1 72	QPR
Robinson Carl (M)	5 10	11 10	Llandrindod Wells	13 10 76	Trainee
Sedgley Steve (D)	6 1	13 13	Enfield	26 5 68	Ipswich T
Simms Gordon (D)	6 1	12 06	Larne	23 3 81	Trainee
Stowell Mike (G)	6 2	13 10	Portsmouth	19 4 65	Everton
Williams Adrian (D)	6 2	12 06	Reading	16 8 71	Reading

League Appearances: Atkins, M. 15; Bull, S. 11(4); Connolly, D. 18(14); Corica, S. 20(11); Curle, K. 44; Emblen, N. 30(3); Ferguson, D. 2(2); Fernando 17(2); Flo, H. 18(1); Foley, D. 2(3); Froggatt, S. 8; Gilkes, M. 25(5); Green, R. 1; Jones, M. (2); Keane, R. 30(3); Muscat, K. 37; Naylor, L. 17(6); Niestroj, R. 2(3); Osborn, S. 36(1); Richards, D. 40(1); Robinson, C. 29(5); Sedgley, S. 41(3); Simpson, P. 8(3); Stowell, M. 46; Whittingham, G. 9(1).

Goals – League (64): Keane 11, Robinson 8, Connolly 6, Flo 5, Curle 4 (4 pens), Muscat 4 (2 pens), Bull 3, Richards 3, Sedgley 3, Corica 2, Emblen 2, Fernando 2, Foley 2, Osborn 2, Simpson 2, Naylor 1, Whittingham 1, own goals 3.

Worthington Cup (8): Bull 3, Keane 3, Ferguson 1, Osborn 1.

FA Cup (3): Keane 2, Flo 1.

Ground: Molineux Grounds, Wolverhampton WV1 4QR. Telephone (01902) 655000.

Record attendance: 61,315 v Liverpool, FA Cup 5th rd, 11 February 1939.

Capacity: 28,525.

Manager: Colin Lee.

Secretary: Richard Skirrow.

Honours – Football League: Division 1 Champions – 1953–54, 1957–58, 1958–59. Division 2 Champions – 1931–32, 1976–77. Division 3 (N) Champions – 1923–24. Division 3 Champions – 1988–89. Division 4 Champions – 1987–88. **FA Cup:** Winners 1893, 1908, 1949, 1960. **Football League Cup:** Winners 1973–74, 1979–80. **Sherpa Van Trophy winners** 1988.

Colours: Gold shirts, black shorts, gold stockings.

WREXHAM DIV. 2

Barrett Paul (M)	5 9	11 04	Newcastle	13 4 78	Newcastle U
Brace Deryn (D)	5 7	10 12	Haverfordwest	15 3 75	Trainee
Carey Brian (D)	6 3	13 02	Cork	31 5 68	Leicester C
Cartwright Mark (G)	6 2	13 06	Chester	13 1 73	York C
Chalk Martyn (F)	5 6	11 03	Swindon	30 8 69	Stockport Co
Connolly Karl (F)	5 10	11 01	Prescot	9 2 70	Napoli (Liverpool)
Cooper Steve (D)	5 9	11 03	Pontypridd	10 12 79	
Edwards Jake (F)	6 1	12 08	Manchester	11 5 76	USA College
Gibson Robin (F)	5 7	10 07	Crewe	15 11 79	Trainee
Hardy Phil (D)	5 7	11 08	Chester	9 4 73	Trainee
Humes Tony (D)	6 0	12 00	Blyth	19 3 66	Ipswich T
McGregor Mark (D)	5 10	11 05	Chester	16 2 77	Trainee
Morrell Andy (F)	5 11	11 06	Doncaster	28 9 74	
Owen Gareth (M)	5 8	12 00	Chester	21 10 71	Trainee
Ridler Dave (D)	6 0	12 02	Liverpool	12 3 76	Prescot T
Roberts Neil (F)	5 10	11 02	Wrexham	7 4 78	Trainee
Roberts Steve (D)	6 2	11 06	Wrexham	24 2 80	Trainee
Russell Kevin (M)	5 9	10 12	Portsmouth	6 12 66	Notts Co
Spink Dean (D)	6 1	12 12	Halesowen	22 1 67	Shrewsbury T

Thomas Steve (M)   5 10   11 07   Hartlepool   23 6 79   Trainee
Walsh Dave (G)   6 1   12 05   Wrexham   29 4 79   Trainee
Williams Danny (M)   6 1   13 00   Wrexham   12 7 79   Liverpool

League Appearances: Barrett, P. 8(2); Brace, D. 15(2); Brammer, D. 31(3); Carey, B. 36; Cartwright, M. 30; Chalk, M. 19(9); Connolly, K. 43(1); Cooke, T. 10; Edwards, J. 4(5); Elliott, S. 8(1); Gibson, R. 3(4); Griffiths, C. 4; Hardy, P. 31(2); Humes, T. 10(2); McGregor, M. 43; Morrell, A. 4(3); Owen, G. 35; Ridler, D. 35(1); Rishworth, S. (4); Roberts, N. 11(11); Rush, I. 12(5); Russell, K. 25(6); Skinner, C. 12; Spink, D. 26(8); Thomas, A. (1); Thomas, S. 1(3); Ward, P. 25; Whitley, J. 9; Wright, T. 16.

Goals – League (43): Connolly 11 (3 pens), Griffiths 3, Owen 3, Roberts 3, Spink 3, Brammer 2, Carey 2, Russell 2, Skinner 2, Ward 2, Whitley 2, Edwards 1, Gibson 1, McGregor 1, Ridler 1, own goals 4.

Worthington Cup (2): Connolly 1 (pen), Roberts 1.

FA Cup (9): Connolly 5, Brammer 1, Roberts 1 (pen), Russell 1, own goal 1.

Ground: Racecourse Ground, Mold Road, Wrexham LL11 2AH. Telephone (01978) 262129.

Record attendance: 34,445 v Manchester U, FA Cup 4th rd, 26 January 1957.

Capacity: 15,500.

Manager: Brian Flynn.

Secretary: D. L. Rhodes.

Honours – Football League: Division 3 Champions – 1977–78. **Welsh Cup:** Winners 22 times.

Colours: Red shirts, white shorts, red stockings.

WYCOMBE WANDERERS   DIV. 2

Baird Andy (D)   5 8   11 13   East Kilbride   18 1 79   Trainee
Bates Jamie (D)   5 11   14 06   Croydon   24 2 68   Brentford
Beeton Alan (D)   5 11   11 13   Watford   4 10 78   Trainee
Brown Steve (M)   5 11   11 12   Northampton   6 7 66   Northampton T
Bulman Dannie (M)   5 9   11 12   Ashford   24 1 79   Ashford T
Carroll Dave (M)   6 0   11 12   Paisley   20 9 66   Ruislip Manor
Cousins Jason (D)   5 10   12 07   Hayes   4 10 70   Brentford
Devine Sean (F)   5 11   13 00   Lewisham   6 9 72   Barnet
Emblen Paul (F)   5 11   12 12   Bromley   3 4 76   Charlton Ath
Harkin Maurice (F)   5 9   11 05   Derry   16 8 79   Trainee
Holsgrove Lee (D)   6 1   12 06   Wendover   13 12 79   Millwall
Lawrence Matthew (D)   6 1   12 12   Northampton   19 6 74   Fulham
Lee Martyn (M)   5 7   9 00   Guilford   10 9 80   Trainee
McCarthy Paul (D)   5 10   13 10   Cork   4 8 71   Brighton & HA
McSporran Jermaine (F)   5 7   10 12   Manchester   1 1 77
Osborn Mark (M)   Bletchley   18 6 81   Trainee
Rogers Mark (D)   6 1   12 12   Geulph   3 11 75
Ryan Keith (M)   5 11   12 06   Northampton   25 6 70   Berkhamsted T
Senda Daniel (F)   5 9   10 02   Harrow   17 4 81   Southampton
Simpson Michael (M)   5 6   11 07   Nottingham   28 2 74   Notts Co
Taylor Martin (G)   5 11   13 11   Tamworth   9 12 66   Derby Co
Thompson Richard (F)   5 7   12 02   Lambeth   2 5 74   Crawley T
Vinnicombe Chris (D)   5 8   10 12   Exeter   20 10 70   Burnley
Westhead Mark (G)   6 2   14 05   Blackpool   19 7 75   Bolton W
Wraight Gary (D)   5 9   11 13   Epping   5 3 79   Trainee

League Appearances: Baird, A. 25(3); Bates, J. 9; Beeton, A. 11(5); Brown, S. 34(4); Bulman, D. 5(6); Carroll, D. 27(5); Cornforth, J. 9(4); Cousins, J. 34; Devine, S. 11(1); Emblen, P. 28(7); Forsyth, M. 4; Harkin, M. 1(1); Holsgrove, L. (1); Kavanagh, J. 14(4); Lawrence, M. 34; Lee, M. 2(1); McCarthy, P. 26(3); McGavin, S. 1(4); McSporran, J. 11(15); Mohan, N. 25; Read, P. 11(5); Robson, M. 1(3);

Ryan, K. 26(2); Scott, K. 23(2); Senda, D. (6); Simpson, M. 31(2); Stallard, M. 12(3); Taylor, M. 44; Vinnicombe, C. 39(2); Westhead, M. 2; Wraight, G. 6.
Goals – League (52): Devine 8, Baird 6, Carroll 6 (1 pen), Scott 6, McSporran 4, Simpson 4 (1 pen), Brown 3, Cousins 2, Emblen 2, Lawrence 2, Mohan 2, Stallard 2, Bulman 1, Cornforth 1 (pen), McCarthy 1, Read 1, Ryan 1.
Worthington Cup (4): Brown 2, Read 1, Stallard 1.
FA Cup (4): Baird 1, Carroll 1 (pen), Reid 1, Scott 1
Ground: Adams Park, Hillbottom Road, Sands, High Wycombe HP12 4HJ. Telephone (01494) 472100.
Record attendance: 9002 v West Ham U, FA Cup 3rd rd, 7 January 1995. **Capacity:** 10,000.
Manager: Lawrie Sanchez.
Secretary: Ian Moat.
Honours – GM Vauxhall Conference winners: 1993. **FA Trophy winners:** 1991, 1993.
Colours: Light & dark blue quartered shirts, light blue shorts, light blue stockings.

YORK CITY   DIV. 3

Name			Birthplace		Signed
Agnew Steve (M)	5 10	10 06	Shipley	9 11 65	Sunderland
Connelly Gordon (M)	6 0	11 07	Glasgow	1 11 76	
Dawson Andrew (D)	6 0	12 00	York	8 12 79	Trainee
Garratt Martin (M)	5 10	11 00	York	22 2 80	
Hall Wayne (D)	5 9	10 06	Rotherham	25 10 68	Darlington
Jones Barry (D)	5 10	11 07	Prescot	20 6 70	Wrexham
Jordan Scott (M)	5 9	11 02	Newcastle	19 7 75	Trainee
McMillan Andy (D)	5 11	11 09	Bloemfontein	22 6 68	
Mimms Bobby (G)	6 2	14 01	York	12 10 63	Rotherham U
Pouton Alan (M)	6 0	12 02	Newcastle	1 2 77	Newcastle U
Reed Martin (D)	5 11	11 07	Scarborough	10 1 78	Trainee
Rennison Graham (D)	6 1	12 00	Northallerton	2 10 78	Trainee
Rowe Rodney (F)	5 8	12 08	Plymouth	30 7 75	Huddersfield T
Skinner Craig (M)	5 8	11 00	Bury	21 10 70	Wrexham
Tinkler Mark (M)	5 11	11 04	Bishop Auckland	21 10 74	Leeds U
Thompson Neil (D)	6 0	13 08	Beverely	2 10 63	Barnsley
Williams Marc (F)	5 9	11 07	Bangor	8 2 73	Halifax T
Woods Neil (F)	6 0	12 11	York	30 7 66	Grimsby T

League Appearances: Agnew, S. 19(1); Barras, T. 24; Carruthers, M. 3(3); Connelly, G. 28; Cresswell, R. 36; Dawson, A. 7(4); Fairclough, C. 11; Garratt, M. 33(5); Hall, W. 26(1); Himsworth, G. 12(1); Hocking, M. 4(2); Jones, B. 44(1); Jordan, S. 27(5); McMillan, A. 33; Mimms, B. 35; Pouton, A. 24(3); Prendergast, R. 1(2); Reed, M. 8(4); Rowe, R. 24(15); Skinner, C. 3(2); Thompson, N. 24; Tinkler, M. 36(1); Tolson, N. 17(11); Warrington, A. 11; Williams, M. 11; Woods, N. 5(3).
Goals – League (56): Cresswell 16 (3 pens), Rowe 7, Thompson 6 (3 pens), Jordan 5, Connelly 4, Williams 4, Tolson 3, Agnew 2, Jones 2, Tinkler 2, Dawson 1, Garratt 1, Hall 1, Pouton 1, own goal 1.
Worthington Cup (1): Thompson 1.
FA Cup (5): Cresswell 3, Jordan 2.
Ground: Bootham Crescent, York YO3 7AQ. Telephone (01904) 624447.
Record attendance: 28,123 v Huddersfield T, FA Cup 6th rd, 5 March 1938.
Capacity: 9534.
Manager: Neil Thompson.
Secretary: Keith Usher.
Honours – Football League: Division 4 Champions – 1983–84.
Colours: Red shirts, navy shorts, red stockings.

LEAGUE POSITIONS: FA PREMIER from 1992–93 and DIVISION 1 1973–74 to 1991–92

	1997–98	1996–97	1995–96	1994–95	1993–94	1992–93	1991–92	1990–91	1989–90	1988–89	1987–88	1986–87	1985–86
Arsenal	1	3	5	12	4	10	4	1	4	1	6	4	7
Aston Villa	7	5	4	18	10	2	7	17	2	17	–	22	16
Barnsley	19	–	–	–	–	–	–	–	–	–	–	–	–
Birmingham C	–	–	–	–	–	–	–	–	–	–	–	–	21
Blackburn R	6	13	7	1	2	4	–	–	–	–	–	–	–
Bolton W	18	–	20	–	–	–	–	–	–	–	–	–	–
Brighton & HA	–	–	–	–	–	–	–	–	–	–	–	–	–
Bristol C	–	–	–	–	–	–	–	–	–	–	–	–	–
Burnley	–	–	–	–	–	–	–	–	–	–	–	–	–
Carlisle U	–	–	–	–	–	–	–	–	–	–	–	–	–
Charlton Ath	–	–	–	–	–	–	–	–	19	14	17	19	–
Chelsea	4	6	11	11	14	11	14	11	5	–	18	14	6
Coventry C	11	17	16	16	11	15	19	16	12	7	10	10	17
Crystal Palace	20	–	–	19	–	20	10	3	15	–	–	–	–
Derby Co	9	12	–	–	–	–	–	20	16	5	15	–	–
Everton	17	15	6	15	17	13	12	9	6	8	4	1	2
Ipswich T	–	–	–	22	19	16	–	–	–	–	–	–	20
Leeds U	5	11	13	5	5	17	1	4	–	–	–	–	–
Leicester C	10	9	–	21	–	–	–	–	–	–	–	20	19
Liverpool	3	4	3	4	8	6	6	2	1	2	1	2	1
Luton T	–	–	–	–	–	–	20	18	17	16	9	7	9
Manchester C	–	–	18	17	16	9	5	5	14	–	–	21	15
Manchester U	2	1	1	2	1	1	2	6	13	11	2	11	4
Middlesbrough	–	19	12	–	–	21	–	–	–	18	–	–	–
Millwall	–	–	–	–	–	–	–	–	20	10	–	–	–
Newcastle U	13	2	2	6	3	–	–	–	–	20	8	17	11
Norwich C	–	–	–	20	12	3	18	15	10	4	14	5	–
Nottingham F	–	20	9	3	–	22	8	8	9	3	3	8	8
Notts Co	–	–	–	–	–	–	21	–	–	–	–	–	–
Oldham Ath	–	–	–	–	21	19	17	–	–	–	–	–	–
Oxford U	–	–	–	–	–	–	–	–	–	–	21	18	18
Portsmouth	–	–	–	–	–	–	–	–	–	–	19	–	–
QPR	–	–	19	8	9	5	11	12	11	9	5	16	13
Sheffield U	–	–	–	–	20	14	9	13	–	–	–	–	–
Sheffield W	16	7	15	13	7	7	3	–	18	15	11	13	5
Southampton	12	16	17	10	18	18	16	14	7	13	12	12	14
Stoke C	–	–	–	–	–	–	–	–	–	–	–	–	–
Sunderland	–	18	–	–	–	–	–	19	–	–	–	–	–
Swansea C	–	–	–	–	–	–	–	–	–	–	–	–	–
Swindon T	–	–	–	–	22	–	–	–	–	–	–	–	–
Tottenham H	14	10	8	7	15	8	15	10	3	6	13	3	10
Watford	–	–	–	–	–	–	–	–	–	–	20	9	12
WBA	–	–	–	–	–	–	–	–	–	–	–	–	22
West Ham U	8	14	10	14	13	–	22	–	–	19	16	15	3
Wimbledon	15	8	14	9	6	12	13	7	8	12	7	6	–
Wolv'hampton W	–	–	–	–	–	–	–	–	–	–	–	–	–

1984–85	1983–84	1982–83	1981–82	1980–81	1979–80	1978–79	1977–78	1976–77	1975–76	1974–75	1973–74	
7	6	10	5	3	4	7	5	8	17	16	10	Arsenal
10	10	6	11	1	7	8	8	4	16	–	–	Aston Villa
–	–	–	–	–	–	–	–	–	–	–	–	Barnsley
–	20	17	16	13	–	21	11	13	19	17	19	Birmingham C
–	–	–	–	–	–	–	–	–	–	–	–	Blackburn R
–	–	–	–	22	17	–	–	–	–	–	–	Bolton W
–	–	22	13	19	16	–	–	–	–	–	–	Brighton & HA
–	–	–	–	–	20	13	17	18	–	–	–	Bristol C
–	–	–	–	–	–	–	–	–	21	10	6	Burnley
–	–	–	–	–	–	–	–	–	–	22	–	Carlisle U
–	–	–	–	–	–	–	–	–	–	–	–	Charlton Ath
6	–	–	–	–	22	16	–	–	21	17		Chelsea
18	19	19	14	16	15	10	7	19	14	14	16	Coventry C
–	–	–	–	22	13	–	–	–	–	–	–	Crystal Palace
–	–	–	–	21	19	12	15	4	1	3		Derby Co
1	7	7	8	15	19	4	3	9	11	4	7	Everton
17	12	9	2	2	3	6	18	3	6	3	4	Ipswich T
–	–	–	20	9	11	5	9	10	5	9	1	Leeds U
15	15	–	–	21	–	–	22	11	7	18	9	Leicester C
2	1	1	1	5	1	1	2	1	1	2	2	Liverpool
13	16	18	–	–	–	–	–	–	–	20	–	Luton T
–	–	20	10	12	17	15	4	2	8	8	14	Manchester C
4	4	3	3	8	2	9	10	6	3	–	21	Manchester U
–	–	–	22	14	9	12	14	12	13	7	–	Middlesbrough
–	–	–	–	–	–	–	–	–	–	–	–	Millwall
14	–	–	–	–	–	–	21	5	15	15	15	Newcastle U
20	14	14	–	20	12	16	13	16	10	–	22	Norwich C
9	3	5	12	7	5	2	1	–	–	–	–	Nottingham F
–	21	15	15	–	–	–	–	–	–	–	–	Notts Co
–	–	–	–	–	–	–	–	–	–	–	–	Oldham Ath
–	–	–	–	–	–	–	–	–	–	–	–	Oxford U
–	–	–	–	–	–	–	–	–	–	–	–	Portsmouth
19	5	–	–	–	–	20	19	14	2	11	8	QPR
–	–	–	–	–	–	–	–	–	22	6	13	Sheffield U
8	–	–	–	–	–	–	–	–	–	–	–	Sheffield W
5	2	12	7	6	8	14	–	–	–	–	20	Southampton
22	18	13	18	11	18	–	–	21	12	5	5	Stoke C
21	13	16	19	17	–	–	–	20	–	–	–	Sunderland
–	–	21	6	–	–	–	–	–	–	–	–	Swansea C
–	–	–	–	–	–	–	–	–	–	–	–	Swindon T
3	8	4	4	10	14	11	–	22	9	19	11	Tottenham H
11	11	2	–	–	–	–	–	–	–	–	–	Watford
12	17	11	17	4	10	3	6	7	–	–	–	WBA
16	9	8	9	–	–	–	20	17	18	13	18	West Ham U
–	–	–	–	–	–	–	–	–	–	–	–	Wimbledon
–	22	–	21	18	6	18	15	–	20	12	12	Wolv'hampton W

LEAGUE POSITIONS: DIVISION 1 from 1992–93 and DIVISION 2 1973–74 to 1991–92

	1997-98	1996-97	1995-96	1994-95	1993-94	1992-93	1991-92	1990-91	1989-90	1988-89	1987-88	1986-87	1985-86
Aston Villa	–	–	–	–	–	–	–	–	–	–	2	–	–
Barnsley	–	2	10	6	18	13	16	8	19	7	14	11	12
Birmingham C	7	10	15	–	22	19	–	–	–	23	19	19	–
Blackburn R	–	–	–	–	–	–	6	19	5	5	5	12	19
Blackpool	–	–	–	–	–	–	–	–	–	–	–	–	–
Bolton W	–	1	–	3	14	–	–	–	–	–	–	–	–
Bournemouth	–	–	–	–	–	–	–	–	22	12	17	–	–
Bradford C	13	21	–	–	–	–	–	–	23	14	4	10	13
Brentford	–	–	–	–	–	22	–	–	–	–	–	–	–
Brighton & HA	–	–	–	–	–	–	23	6	18	19	–	22	11
Bristol C	–	–	–	23	13	15	17	9	–	–	–	–	–
Bristol R	–	–	–	–	–	24	13	13	–	–	–	–	–
Burnley	–	–	–	22	–	–	–	–	–	–	–	–	–
Bury	17	–	–	–	–	–	–	–	–	–	–	–	–
Cambridge U	–	–	–	–	–	23	5	–	–	–	–	–	–
Cardiff C	–	–	–	–	–	–	–	–	–	–	–	–	–
Carlisle U	–	–	–	–	–	–	–	–	–	–	–	–	20
Charlton Ath	4	15	6	15	11	12	7	16	–	–	–	–	2
Chelsea	–	–	–	–	–	–	–	–	–	1	–	–	–
Crewe Alex	11	–	–	–	–	–	–	–	–	–	–	–	–
Crystal Palace	–	6	3	–	1	–	–	–	–	3	6	6	5
Derby Co	–	–	2	9	6	8	3	–	–	–	–	1	–
Fulham	–	–	–	–	–	–	–	–	–	–	–	–	22
Grimsby T	–	22	17	10	16	9	19	–	–	–	–	21	15
Hereford U	–	–	–	–	–	–	–	–	–	–	–	–	–
Huddersfield T	16	20	8	–	–	–	–	–	–	–	23	17	16
Hull C	–	–	–	–	–	–	–	24	14	21	15	14	6
Ipswich T	5	4	7	–	–	–	1	14	9	8	8	5	–
Leeds U	–	–	–	–	–	–	–	–	1	10	7	4	14
Leicester C	–	–	5	–	4	6	4	22	13	15	13	–	–
Leyton Orient	–	–	–	–	–	–	–	–	–	–	–	–	–
Luton T	–	–	24	16	20	20	–	–	–	–	–	–	–
Manchester C	22	14	–	–	–	–	–	–	–	2	9	–	–
Manchester U	–	–	–	–	–	–	–	–	–	–	–	–	–
Mansfield T	–	–	–	–	–	–	–	–	–	–	–	–	–
Middlesbrough	2	–	–	1	9	–	2	7	21	–	3	–	21
Millwall	–	–	22	12	3	7	15	5	–	–	1	16	9
Newcastle U	–	–	–	–	–	1	20	11	3	–	–	–	–
Norwich C	15	13	16	–	–	–	–	–	–	–	–	–	1
Nottingham F	1	–	–	–	2	–	–	–	–	–	–	–	–
Notts Co	–	–	–	24	7	17	–	4	–	–	–	–	–
Oldham Ath	–	23	18	14	–	–	–	1	8	16	10	3	8
Oxford U	12	17	–	–	23	14	21	10	17	17	–	–	–
Peterborough U	–	–	–	–	24	10	–	–	–	–	–	–	–
Plymouth Arg	–	–	–	–	–	–	22	18	16	18	16	7	–
Port Vale	19	8	12	17	–	–	24	15	11	–	–	–	–
Portsmouth	20	7	21	18	17	3	9	17	12	20	–	2	4
Preston NE	–	–	–	–	–	–	–	–	–	–	–	–	–
QPR	21	9	–	–	–	–	–	–	–	–	–	–	–

1984–85	1983–84	1982–83	1981–82	1980–81	1979–80	1978–79	1977–78	1976–77	1975–76	1974–75	1973–74	
–	–	–	–	–	–	–	–	–	–	2	14	Aston Villa
11	14	10	6	–	–	–	–	–	–	–	–	Barnsley
2	–	–	–	–	3	–	–	–	–	–	–	Birmingham C
5	6	11	10	4	–	22	5	12	15	–	–	Blackburn R
–	–	–	–	–	–	–	20	5	10	7	5	Blackpool
–	–	22	19	18	–	–	1	4	4	10	11	Bolton W
–	–	–	–	–	–	–	–	–	–	–	–	Bournemouth
–	–	–	–	–	–	–	–	–	–	–	–	Bradford C
–	–	–	–	–	–	–	–	–	–	–	–	Brentford
6	9	–	–	–	–	2	4	–	–	–	–	Brighton & HA
–	–	–	–	21	–	–	–	–	2	5	16	Bristol C
–	–	–	–	22	19	16	18	15	18	19	–	Bristol R
–	–	21	–	–	21	13	11	16	–	–	–	Burnley
–	–	–	–	–	–	–	–	–	–	–	–	Bury
–	22	12	14	13	8	12	–	–	–	–	–	Cambridge U
21	15	–	20	19	15	9	19	18	–	21	17	Cardiff C
16	7	14	–	–	–	–	–	20	19	–	3	Carlisle U
17	13	17	13	–	22	19	17	7	9	–	–	Charlton Ath
–	1	18	12	12	4	–	–	2	11	–	–	Chelsea
–	–	–	–	–	–	–	–	–	–	–	–	Crewe Alex
15	18	15	15	–	–	1	9	–	–	–	20	Crystal Palace
–	20	13	16	6	–	–	–	–	–	–	–	Derby Co
9	11	4	–	–	20	10	10	17	12	9	13	Fulham
10	5	19	17	7	–	–	–	–	–	–	–	Grimsby T
–	–	–	–	–	–	–	–	22	–	–	–	Hereford U
13	12	–	–	–	–	–	–	–	–	–	–	Huddersfield T
–	–	–	–	–	–	–	22	14	14	8	9	Hull C
–	–	–	–	–	–	–	–	–	–	–	–	Ipswich T
7	10	8	–	–	–	–	–	–	–	–	–	Leeds U
–	–	3	8	–	1	17	–	–	–	–	–	Leicester C
–	–	–	22	17	14	11	14	19	13	12	4	Leyton Orient
–	–	–	1	5	6	18	13	6	7	–	2	Luton T
3	4	–	–	–	–	–	–	–	–	–	–	Manchester C
–	–	–	–	–	–	–	–	–	–	1	–	Manchester U
–	–	–	–	–	–	–	21	–	–	–	–	Mansfield T
19	17	16	–	–	–	–	–	–	–	–	1	Middlesbrough
–	–	–	–	–	21	16	10	–	–	20	12	Millwall
–	3	5	9	11	9	8	–	–	–	–	–	Newcastle U
–	–	–	3	–	–	–	–	–	–	3	–	Norwich C
–	–	–	–	–	–	–	–	3	8	16	7	Nottingham F
20	–	–	–	2	17	6	15	8	5	14	10	Notts Co
14	19	7	11	15	11	14	8	13	17	18	–	Oldham Ath
1	–	–	–	–	–	–	–	–	20	11	18	Oxford U
–	–	–	–	–	–	–	–	–	–	–	–	Peterborough U
–	–	–	–	–	–	–	–	21	16	–	–	Plymouth Arg
–	–	–	–	–	–	–	–	–	–	–	–	Port Vale
4	16	–	–	–	–	–	–	–	22	17	15	Portsmouth
–	–	–	20	10	7	–	–	–	–	–	21	Preston NE
–	–	1	5	8	5	–	–	–	–	–	–	QPR

LEAGUE POSITIONS: DIVISION 1 from 1992–93 and DIVISION 2 1973–74 to 1991–92 (cont.)

	1997–98	1996–97	1995–96	1994–95	1993–94	1992–93	1991–92	1990–91	1989–90	1988–89	1987–88	1986–87	1985–86
Reading	24	18	19	2	–	–	–	–	–	–	22	13	–
Rotherham U	–	–	–	–	–	–	–	–	–	–	–	–	–
Sheffield U	6	5	9	8	–	–	–	–	2	–	21	9	7
Sheffield W	–	–	–	–	–	–	–	3	–	–	–	–	–
Shrewsbury T	–	–	–	–	–	–	–	–	–	22	18	18	17
Southampton	–	–	–	–	–	–	–	–	–	–	–	–	–
Southend U	–	24	14	13	15	18	12	–	–	–	–	–	–
Stockport Co	8	–	–	–	–	–	–	–	–	–	–	–	–
Stoke C	23	12	4	11	10	–	–	–	24	13	11	8	10
Sunderland	3	–	1	20	12	21	18	–	6	11	–	20	18
Swansea C	–	–	–	–	–	–	–	–	–	–	–	–	–
Swindon T	18	19	–	21	–	5	8	21	4	6	12	–	–
Tottenham H	–	–	–	–	–	–	–	–	–	–	–	–	–
Tranmere R	14	11	13	5	5	4	14	–	–	–	–	–	–
Walsall	–	–	–	–	–	–	–	–	–	24	–	–	–
Watford	–	–	23	7	19	16	10	20	15	4	–	–	–
WBA	10	16	11	19	21	–	–	23	20	9	20	15	–
West Ham U	–	–	–	–	–	2	–	2	7	–	–	–	–
Wimbledon	–	–	–	–	–	–	–	–	–	–	–	–	3
Wolv'hampton W	9	3	20	4	8	11	11	12	10	–	–	–	–
Wrexham	–	–	–	–	–	–	–	–	–	–	–	–	–
York C	–	–	–	–	–	–	–	–	–	–	–	–	–

LEAGUE POSITIONS: DIVISION 2 from 1992–93 and DIVISION 3 1973–74 to 1991–92

	1997–98	1996–97	1995–96	1994–95	1993–94	1992–93	1991–92	1990–91	1989–90	1988–89	1987–88	1986–87	1985–86
Aldershot	–	–	–	–	–	–	–	–	–	24	20	–	–
Barnet	–	–	–	–	24	–	–	–	–	–	–	–	–
Barnsley	–	–	–	–	–	–	–	–	–	–	–	–	–
Birmingham C	–	–	–	1	–	–	2	12	7	–	–	–	–
Blackburn R	–	–	–	–	–	–	–	–	–	–	–	–	–
Blackpool	12	7	3	12	20	18	–	–	23	19	10	9	12
Bolton W	–	–	–	–	–	2	13	4	6	10	–	21	18
Bournemouth	9	16	14	19	17	17	8	9	–	–	–	1	15
Bradford C	–	–	6	14	7	10	16	8	–	–	–	–	–
Brentford	21	4	15	2	16	–	1	6	13	7	12	11	10
Brighton & HA	–	–	23	16	14	9	–	–	–	–	2	–	–
Bristol C	2	5	13	–	–	–	–	–	2	11	5	6	9
Bristol R	5	17	10	4	8	–	–	–	1	5	8	19	16

	1984–85	1983–84	1982–83	1981–82	1980–81	1979–80	1978–79	1977–78	1976–77	1975–76	1974–75	1973–74
Reading	–	–	–	–	–	–	–	–	–	–	–	–
Rotherham U	–	–	20	7	–	–	–	–	–	–	–	–
Sheffield U	18	–	–	–	–	–	20	12	11	–	–	–
Sheffield W	–	2	6	4	10	–	–	–	–	–	22	19
Shrewsbury T	8	8	9	18	14	13	–	–	–	–	–	–
Southampton	–	–	–	–	–	–	–	2	9	6	13	–
Southend U	–	–	–	–	–	–	–	–	–	–	–	–
Stockport Co	–	–	–	–	–	–	–	–	–	–	–	–
Stoke C	–	–	–	–	–	–	3	7	–	–	–	–
Sunderland	–	–	–	–	–	2	4	6	–	1	4	6
Swansea C	–	21	–	–	3	12	–	–	–	–	–	–
Swindon T	–	–	–	–	–	–	–	–	–	–	–	22
Tottenham H	–	–	–	–	–	–	–	3	–	–	–	–
Tranmere R	–	–	–	–	–	–	–	–	–	–	–	–
Walsall	–	–	–	–	–	–	–	–	–	–	–	–
Watford	–	–	–	2	9	18	–	–	–	–	–	–
WBA	–	–	–	–	–	–	–	–	–	3	6	8
West Ham U	–	–	–	–	1	7	5	–	–	–	–	–
Wimbledon	12	–	–	–	–	–	–	–	–	–	–	–
Wolv'hampton W	22	–	2	–	–	–	–	–	1	–	–	–
Wrexham	–	–	–	21	16	16	15	–	–	–	–	–
York C	–	–	–	–	–	–	–	–	–	21	15	–

	1984–85	1983–84	1982–83	1981–82	1980–81	1979–80	1978–79	1977–78	1976–77	1975–76	1974–75	1973–74
Aldershot	–	–	–	–	–	–	–	–	–	21	20	8
Barnet	–	–	–	–	–	–	–	–	–	–	–	–
Barnsley	–	–	–	–	2	11	–	–	–	–	–	–
Birmingham C	–	–	–	–	–	–	–	–	–	–	–	–
Blackburn R	–	–	–	–	–	2	–	–	–	–	1	13
Blackpool	–	–	–	23	18	12	–	–	–	–	–	–
Bolton W	17	10	–	–	–	–	–	–	–	–	–	–
Bournemouth	10	17	14	–	–	–	–	–	–	–	21	11
Bradford C	1	7	12	–	–	–	–	22	–	–	–	–
Brentford	13	20	9	8	9	19	10	–	–	–	–	–
Brighton & HA	–	–	–	–	–	–	–	–	2	4	19	19
Bristol C	5	–	–	23	–	–	–	–	–	–	–	–
Bristol R	6	5	7	15	–	–	–	–	–	–	–	2

LEAGUE POSITIONS: DIVISION 2 from 1992–93 and DIVISION 3 1973–74 to 1991–92 (cont.)

	1997–98	1996–97	1995–96	1994–95	1993–94	1992–93	1991–92	1990–91	1989–90	1988–89	1987–88	1986–87	1985–86
Burnley	20	9	17	–	6	13	–	–	–	–	–	–	–
Bury	–	1	–	–	–	–	21	7	5	13	14	16	20
Cambridge U	–	–	–	20	10	–	–	1	–	–	–	–	–
Cardiff C	–	–	–	22	19	–	–	–	21	16	–	–	22
Carlisle U	23	–	21	–	–	–	–	–	–	–	–	22	–
Charlton Ath	–	–	–	–	–	–	–	–	–	–	–	–	–
Chester C	–	–	–	23	–	24	18	19	16	8	15	15	–
Chesterfield	10	10	7	–	–	–	–	–	–	22	18	17	17
Colchester U	–	–	–	–	–	–	–	–	–	–	–	–	–
Crewe Alex	–	6	5	3	–	–	–	22	12	–	–	–	–
Crystal Palace	–	–	–	–	–	–	–	–	–	–	–	–	–
Darlington	–	–	–	–	–	–	24	–	–	–	–	22	13
Derby Co	–	–	–	–	–	–	–	–	–	–	–	–	3
Doncaster R	–	–	–	–	–	–	–	–	–	–	24	13	11
Exeter C	–	–	–	–	22	19	20	16	–	–	–	–	–
Fulham	6	–	–	–	21	12	9	21	20	4	9	18	–
Gillingham	8	11	–	–	–	–	–	–	–	23	13	5	5
Grimsby T	3	–	–	–	–	–	3	–	–	22	–	–	–
Halifax T	–	–	–	–	–	–	–	–	–	–	–	–	–
Hartlepool U	–	–	–	–	23	16	11	–	–	–	–	–	–
Hereford U	–	–	–	–	–	–	–	–	–	–	–	–	–
Huddersfield T	–	–	–	5	11	15	3	11	8	14	–	–	–
Hull C	–	–	24	8	9	20	14	–	–	–	–	–	–
Leyton Orient	–	–	–	24	18	7	10	13	14	–	–	–	–
Lincoln C	–	–	–	–	–	–	–	–	–	–	–	21	19
Luton T	17	3	–	–	–	–	–	–	–	–	–	–	–
Mansfield T	–	–	–	–	–	22	–	24	15	15	19	10	–
Middlesbrough	–	–	–	–	–	–	–	–	–	–	–	2	–
Millwall	18	14	–	–	–	–	–	–	–	–	–	–	–
Newport Co	–	–	–	–	–	–	–	–	–	–	–	23	19
Northampton T	4	–	–	–	–	–	–	–	22	20	6	–	–
Notts Co	–	24	4	–	–	–	–	–	3	9	4	7	8
Oldham Ath	13	–	–	–	–	–	–	–	–	–	–	–	–
Oxford U	–	–	2	7	–	–	–	–	–	–	–	–	–
Peterborough U	–	21	19	15	–	–	6	–	–	–	–	–	–
Plymouth Arg	22	19	–	21	3	14	–	–	–	–	–	–	2
Portsmouth	–	–	–	–	–	–	–	–	–	–	–	–	–
Port Vale	–	–	–	–	2	3	–	–	–	3	11	12	–
Preston NE	15	15	–	–	–	21	17	17	19	6	16	–	–
Reading	–	–	–	–	1	8	12	15	10	18	–	–	1
Rochdale	–	–	–	–	–	–	–	–	–	–	–	–	–
Rotherham U	–	23	16	17	15	11	–	23	9	–	21	14	14
Scunthorpe U	–	–	–	–	–	–	–	–	–	–	–	–	–
Sheffield U	–	–	–	–	–	–	–	–	–	2	–	–	–
Sheffield W	–	–	–	–	–	–	–	–	–	–	–	–	–
Shrewsbury T	–	22	18	18	–	–	22	18	11	–	–	–	–
Southend U	24	–	–	–	–	–	–	2	–	21	17	–	–
Southport	–	–	–	–	–	–	–	–	–	–	–	–	–

1984–85	1983–84	1982–83	1981–82	1980–81	1979–80	1978–79	1977–78	1976–77	1975–76	1974–75	1973–74	
21	12	–	1	8	–	–	–	–	–	–	–	Burnley
–	–	–	–	–	21	19	15	7	13	14	–	Bury
24	–	–	–	–	–	–	2	–	–	–	21	Cambridge U
–	–	2	–	–	–	–	–	–	2	–	–	Cardiff C
–	–	–	2	19	6	6	13	–	–	–	–	Carlisle U
–	–	–	–	3	–	–	–	–	–	3	14	Charlton Ath
–	–	–	24	18	9	16	5	13	17	–	–	Chester C
–	–	24	11	5	4	20	9	18	15	15	5	Chesterfield
–	–	–	–	22	5	7	8	–	22	11	–	Colchester U
–	–	–	–	–	–	–	–	–	–	–	–	Crewe Alex
–	–	–	–	–	–	–	–	3	5	5	–	Crystal Palace
–	–	–	–	–	–	–	–	–	–	–	–	Darlington
7	–	–	–	–	–	–	–	–	–	–	–	Derby C
14	–	23	19	–	–	–	–	–	–	–	–	Doncaster R
–	24	19	18	11	8	9	17	–	–	–	–	Exeter C
–	–	–	3	13	–	–	–	–	–	–	–	Fulham
4	8	13	6	15	16	4	7	12	14	10	–	Gillingham
–	–	–	–	–	1	–	–	23	18	16	6	Grimsby T
–	–	–	–	–	–	–	–	–	24	17	9	Halifax T
–	–	–	–	–	–	–	–	–	–	–	–	Hartlepool U
–	–	–	–	–	–	23	–	1	12	18		Hereford U
–	–	3	17	4	–	–	–	–	–	24	10	Huddersfield T
3	4	–	–	24	20	8	–	–	–	–	–	Hull C
22	11	20	–	–	–	–	–	–	–	–	–	Leyton Orient
14	6	4	–	–	–	24	16	9	–	–	–	Lincoln C
–	–	–	–	–	–	–	–	–	–	–	–	Luton T
–	–	–	–	–	23	18	–	1	11	–	–	Mansfield T
–	–	–	–	–	–	–	–	–	–	–	–	Middlesbrough
2	9	17	9	16	14	–	–	–	3	–	–	Millwall
18	13	4	16	12	–	–	–	–	–	–	–	Newport Co
–	–	–	–	–	–	–	22	–	–	–	–	Northampton T
–	–	–	–	–	–	–	–	–	–	–	–	Notts Co
–	–	–	–	–	–	–	–	–	–	–	1	Oldham Ath
–	1	5	5	14	17	11	18	17	–	–	–	Oxford U
–	–	–	–	–	21	4	16	10	7	–		Peterborough U
15	19	8	10	7	15	15	19	–	–	2	17	Plymouth Arg
–	–	1	13	6	–	–	24	20	–	–	–	Portsmouth
–	23	–	–	–	–	–	21	19	12	6	20	Port Vale
23	16	16	14	–	–	–	3	6	8	9	–	Preston NE
9	–	21	12	10	7	–	–	21	–	–	–	Reading
–	–	–	–	–	–	–	–	–	–	–	24	Rochdale
12	18	–	–	1	13	17	20	4	16	–	–	Rotherham U
–	21	–	–	–	–	–	–	–	–	–	–	Scunthorpe U
–	3	11	–	21	12	–	–	–	–	–	–	Sheffield U
–	–	–	–	–	3	14	14	8	20	–	–	Sheffield W
–	–	–	–	–	–	1	11	10	9	–	22	Shrewsbury T
–	22	15	7	–	22	13	–	–	23	18	12	Southend U
–	–	–	–	–	–	–	–	–	–	–	23	Southport

LEAGUE POSITIONS: DIVISION 2 from 1992–93 and DIVISION 3 1973–74 to 1991–92 (cont.)

	1997–98	1996–97	1995–96	1994–95	1993–94	1992–93	1991–92	1990–91	1989–90	1988–89	1987–88	1986–87	1985–86
Stockport Co	–	2	9	11	4	6	5	–	–	–	–	–	–
Stoke C	–	–	–	–	–	1	4	14	–	–	–	–	–
Sunderland	–	–	–	–	–	–	–	–	–	–	1	–	–
Swansea C	–	–	22	10	13	5	19	20	17	12	–	–	24
Swindon T	–	–	1	–	–	–	–	–	–	–	–	3	–
Torquay U	–	–	–	–	–	–	23	–	–	–	–	–	–
Tranmere R	–	–	–	–	–	–	–	5	4	–	–	–	–
Walsall	19	12	11	–	–	5	–	–	24	–	3	8	6
Watford	1	13	–	–	–	–	–	–	–	–	–	–	–
WBA	–	–	–	–	–	4	7	–	–	–	–	–	–
Wigan Ath	11	–	–	–	–	23	15	10	18	17	7	4	4
Wimbledon	–	–	–	–	–	–	–	–	–	–	–	–	–
Wolv'hampton W	–	–	–	–	–	–	–	–	–	1	–	–	23
Wrexham	7	8	8	13	12	–	–	–	–	–	–	–	–
Wycombe W	14	18	12	6	–	–	–	–	–	–	–	–	–
York C	16	20	20	9	5	–	–	–	–	–	23	20	7

LEAGUE POSITIONS: DIVISION 3 from 1992–93 and DIVISION 4 1973–74 to 1991–92

	1997–98	1996–97	1995–96	1994–95	1993–94	1992–93	1991–92	1990–91	1989–90	1988–89	1987–88	1986–87	1985–86
Aldershot	–	–	–	–	–	–	*	23	22	–	–	6	16
Barnet	7	15	9	11	–	3	7	–	–	–	–	–	–
Barnsley	–	–	–	–	–	–	–	–	–	–	–	–	–
Blackpool	–	–	–	–	–	–	4	5	–	–	–	–	–
Bolton W	–	–	–	–	–	–	–	–	–	–	3	–	–
Bournemouth	–	–	–	–	–	–	–	–	–	–	–	–	–
Bradford C	–	–	–	–	–	–	–	–	–	–	–	–	–
Brentford	–	–	–	–	–	–	–	–	–	–	–	–	–
Brighton & HA	23	23	–	–	–	–	–	–	–	–	–	–	–
Bristol C	–	–	–	–	–	–	–	–	–	–	–	–	–
Burnley	–	–	–	–	–	–	1	6	16	16	10	22	14
Bury	–	–	3	4	13	7	–	–	–	–	–	–	–
Cambridge U	16	10	16	–	–	–	–	–	6	8	15	11	22
Cardiff C	21	7	22	–	–	1	9	13	–	–	2	13	–
Carlisle U	–	3	–	1	7	18	22	20	8	12	23	–	–
Chester C	14	6	8	–	2	–	–	–	–	–	–	–	2
Chesterfield	–	–	–	3	8	12	13	18	7	–	–	–	–

*Record expunged

1984-85	1983-84	1982-83	1981-82	1980-81	1979-80	1978-79	1977-78	1976-77	1975-76	1974-75	1973-74	
–	–	–	–	–	–	–	–	–	–	–	–	Stockport Co
–	–	–	–	–	–	–	–	–	–	–	–	Stoke C
–	–	–	–	–	–	–	–	–	–	–	–	Sunderland
20	–	–	–	–	3	–	–	–	–	–	–	Swansea C
–	–	–	22	17	10	5	10	11	19	4	–	Swindon T
–	–	–	–	–	–	–	–	–	–	–	–	Torquay U
–	–	–	–	–	–	23	12	14	–	22	16	Tranmere R
11	6	10	20	20	–	22	6	15	7	8	15	Walsall
–	–	–	–	–	–	2	–	–	–	23	7	Watford
–	–	–	–	–	–	–	–	–	–	–	–	WBA
16	15	18	–	–	–	–	–	–	–	–	–	Wigan Ath
–	2	–	21	–	24	–	–	–	–	–	–	Wimbledon
–	–	–	–	–	–	–	–	–	–	–	–	Wolv'hampton W
–	–	22	–	–	–	–	1	5	6	13	4	Wrexham
–	–	–	–	–	–	–	–	–	–	–	–	Wycombe W
8	–	–	–	–	–	–	–	24	–	–	3	York C

1984-85	1983-84	1982-83	1981-82	1980-81	1979-80	1978-79	1977-78	1976-77	1975-76	1974-75	1973-74	
13	5	18	16	6	10	5	5	17	–	–	–	Aldershot
–	–	–	–	–	–	–	–	–	–	–	–	Barnet
–	–	–	–	–	–	4	7	6	12	15	13	Barnsley
2	6	21	12	–	–	–	–	–	–	–	–	Blackpool
–	–	–	–	–	–	–	–	–	–	–	–	Bolton W
–	–	–	4	13	11	18	17	13	6	–	–	Bournemouth
–	–	–	2	14	5	15	–	4	17	10	8	Bradford C
–	–	–	–	–	–	–	4	15	18	8	19	Brentford
–	–	–	–	–	–	–	–	–	–	–	–	Brighton & HA
–	4	14	–	–	–	–	–	–	–	–	–	Bristol C
–	–	–	–	–	–	–	–	–	–	–	–	Burnley
4	15	5	9	12	–	–	–	–	–	–	4	Bury
–	–	–	–	–	–	–	–	1	13	6	–	Cambridge U
–	–	–	–	–	–	–	–	–	–	–	–	Cardiff C
–	–	–	–	–	–	–	–	–	–	–	–	Carlisle U
16	24	13	9	–	–	–	–	–	–	4	7	Chester C
1	13	–	–	–	–	–	–	–	–	–	–	Chesterfield

LEAGUE POSITIONS: DIVISION 3 from 1992–93 and DIVISION 4 1973–74 to 1991–92 (cont.)

	1997-98	1996-97	1995-96	1994-95	1993-94	1992-93	1991-92	1990-91	1989-90	1988-89	1987-88	1986-87	1985-86
Colchester U	4	8	7	10	17	10	–	–	24	22	9	5	6
Crewe Alex	–	–	–	–	3	6	6	–	–	3	17	17	12
Darlington	19	18	5	20	21	15	–	1	–	24	13	–	–
Doncaster R	24	19	13	9	15	16	21	11	20	23	–	–	–
Exeter C	15	22	14	22	–	–	–	–	1	13	22	14	21
Fulham	–	2	17	8	–	–	–	–	–	–	–	–	–
Gillingham	–	–	2	19	16	21	11	15	14	–	–	–	–
Grimsby T	–	–	–	–	–	–	–	–	2	9	–	–	–
Halifax T	–	–	–	–	–	22	20	22	23	21	18	15	20
Hartlepool U	17	20	20	18	–	–	–	3	19	19	16	18	7
Hereford U	–	24	6	16	20	17	17	17	17	15	19	16	10
Huddersfield T	–	–	–	–	–	–	–	–	–	–	–	–	–
Hull C	22	17	–	–	–	–	–	–	–	–	–	–	–
Leyton Orient	11	16	21	–	–	–	–	–	–	6	8	7	5
Lincoln C	3	9	18	12	18	8	10	14	10	10	–	24	–
Macclesfield T	2	–	–	–	–	–	–	–	–	–	–	–	–
Maidstone U	–	–	–	–	–	–	18	19	5	–	–	–	–
Mansfield T	12	11	19	6	12	–	3	–	–	–	–	–	3
Newport Co	–	–	–	–	–	–	–	–	–	–	24	–	–
Northampton T	–	4	11	17	22	20	16	10	–	–	–	1	8
Notts Co	1	–	–	–	–	–	–	–	–	–	–	–	–
Peterborough U	10	–	–	–	–	–	–	4	9	17	7	10	17
Plymouth Arg	–	–	4	–	–	–	–	–	–	–	–	–	–
Portsmouth	–	–	–	–	–	–	–	–	–	–	–	–	–
Port Vale	–	–	–	–	–	–	–	–	–	–	–	–	4
Preston NE	–	–	1	5	5	–	–	–	–	–	–	2	23
Reading	–	–	–	–	–	–	–	–	–	–	–	–	–
Rochdale	18	14	15	15	9	11	8	12	12	18	21	21	18
Rotherham U	9	–	–	–	–	2	–	–	1	–	–	–	–
Scarborough	6	12	23	21	14	13	12	9	18	5	12	–	–
Scunthorpe U	8	13	12	7	11	14	5	8	11	4	4	8	15
Sheffield U	–	–	–	–	–	–	–	–	–	–	–	–	–
Shrewsbury T	13	–	–	–	1	9	–	–	–	–	–	–	–
Southend U	–	–	–	–	–	–	–	–	3	–	–	3	9
Southport	–	–	–	–	–	–	–	–	–	–	–	–	–
Stockport Co	–	–	–	–	–	–	–	2	4	20	20	19	11
Swansea C	20	5	–	–	–	–	–	–	–	–	6	12	–
Swindon T	–	–	–	–	–	–	–	–	–	–	–	–	1
Torquay U	5	21	24	13	6	19	–	7	15	14	5	23	24
Tranmere R	–	–	–	–	–	–	–	–	–	2	14	20	19
Walsall	–	–	–	2	10	5	15	16	–	–	–	–	–
Watford	–	–	–	–	–	–	–	–	–	–	–	–	–
Wigan Ath	–	1	10	14	19	–	–	–	–	–	–	–	–
Wimbledon	–	–	–	–	–	–	–	–	–	–	–	–	–
Wolv'hampton W	–	–	–	–	–	–	–	–	–	–	1	4	–
Workington	–	–	–	–	–	–	–	–	–	–	–	–	–
Wrexham	–	–	–	–	–	2	14	24	21	7	11	9	13
Wycombe W	–	–	–	–	4	–	–	–	–	–	–	–	–
York C	–	–	–	–	–	4	19	21	13	11	–	–	–

1984–85	1983–84	1982–83	1981–82	1980–81	1979–80	1978–79	1977–78	1976–77	1975–76	1974–75	1973–74	
7	8	6	6	–	–	–	–	3	–	–	3	Colchester U
10	16	23	24	18	23	24	15	12	16	18	21	Crewe Alex
3	14	17	3	8	22	21	19	11	20	21	20	Darlington
–	2	–	–	3	12	22	12	8	10	17	22	Doncaster R
18	–	–	–				–	2	7	9	10	Exeter C
–	–	–	–	–	–	–	–	–	–	–	–	Fulham
–	–	–	–	–	–	–	–	–	–	–	2	Gillingham
–	–	–	–	–	–	2	6	–	–	–	–	Grimsby T
21	21	11	19	23	18	23	20	21	–	–	–	Halifax T
19	23	22	14	9	19	13	21	22	14	13	11	Hartlepool U
5	11	24	10	22	21	14	–	–	–	–	–	Hereford U
–	–	–	–	–	1	9	11	9	5	–	–	Huddersfield T
–	–	2	8	–	–	–	–	–	–	–	–	Hull C
–	–	–	–	–	–	–	–	–	–	–	–	Leyton Orient
–	–	–	–	2	7	–	–	–	1	5	12	Lincoln C
–	–	–	–	–	–	–	–	–	–	–	–	Macclesfield T
–	–	–	–	–	–	–	–	–	–	–	–	Maidstone U
14	19	10	20	7	–	–	–	–	–	1	17	Mansfield T
–	–	–	–	–	3	8	16	19	22	12	9	Newport C
23	18	15	22	10	13	19	10	–	2	16	5	Northampton T
–	–	–	–	–	–	–	–	–	–	–	–	Notts Co
11	7	9	5	5	8	–	–	–	–	–	1	Peterborough U
–	–	–	–	–	–	–	–	–	–	–	–	Plymouth Arg
–	–	–	–	–	4	7	–	–	–	–	–	Portsmouth
12	–	3	7	19	20	16	–	–	–	–	–	Port Vale
–	–	–	–	–	–	–	–	–	–	–	–	Preston NE
–	3	–	–	–	–	1	8	–	3	7	6	Reading
17	22	20	21	15	24	20	24	18	15	19	–	Rochdale
–	–	–	–	–	–	–	–	–	–	3	15	Rotherham U
–	–	–	–	–	–	–	–	–	–	–	–	Scarborough
9	–	4	23	16	14	12	14	20	19	24	18	Scunthorpe U
–	–	–	1	–	–	–	–	–	–	–	–	Sheffield U
–	–	–	–	–	–	–	–	–	–	2	–	Shrewsbury T
20	–	–	–	1	–	–	2	10	–	–	–	Southend U
–	–	–	–	–	–	–	23	23	23	11	–	Southport
22	12	16	18	20	16	17	18	14	21	20	24	Stockport Co
–	–	–	–	–	–	–	3	5	11	22	14	Swansea C
8	17	8	–	–	–	–	–	–	–	–	–	Swindon T
24	9	12	15	17	9	11	9	16	9	14	16	Torquay U
6	10	19	11	21	15	–	–	–	4	–	–	Tranmere R
–	–	–	–	2	–	–	–	–	–	–	–	Walsall
–	–	–	–	–	–	1	7	8	–	–	–	Watford
–	–	–	3	11	6	6	–	–	–	–	–	Wigan Ath
–	–	1	–	4	–	3	13	–	–	–	–	Wimbledon
–	–	–	–	–	–	–	–	–	–	–	–	Wolv'hampton W
–	–	–	–	–	–	–	–	24	24	23	23	Workington
15	20	–	–	–	–	–	–	–	–	–	–	Wrexham
–	–	–	–	–	–	–	–	–	–	–	–	Wycombe W
–	1	7	17	24	17	10	22	–	–	–	–	York C

LEAGUE CHAMPIONSHIP HONOURS

FA PREMIER LEAGUE

Maximum points: 126

	First	Pts	Second	Pts	Third	Pts
1992–93	Manchester U	84	Aston Villa	74	Norwich C	72
1993–94	Manchester U	92	Blackburn R	84	Newcastle U	77
1994–95	Blackburn R	89	Manchester U	88	Nottingham F	77

Maximum points: 114

	First	Pts	Second	Pts	Third	Pts
1995–96	Manchester U	82	Newcastle U	78	Liverpool	71
1996–97	Manchester U	75	Newcastle U*	68	Arsenal*	68
1997–98	Arsenal	78	Manchester U	77	Liverpool	65
1998–99	Manchester U	79	Arsenal	78	Chelsea	75

DIVISION 1

Maximum points: 138

	First	Pts	Second	Pts	Third	Pts
1992–93	Newcastle U	96	West Ham U*	88	Portsmouth††	88
1993–94	Crystal Palace	90	Nottingham F	83	Millwall††	74
1994–95	Middlesbrough	82	Reading††	79	Bolton W	77
1995–96	Sunderland	83	Derby Co	79	Crystal Palace††	75
1996–97	Bolton W	98	Barnsley	80	Wolverhampton W††	76
1997–98	Nottingham F	94	Middlesbrough	91	Sunderland††	90
1998–99	Sunderland	105	Bradford C	87	Ipswich T††	86

DIVISION 2

Maximum points: 138

	First	Pts	Second	Pts	Third	Pts
1992–93	Stoke C	93	Bolton W	90	Port Vale††	89
1993–94	Reading	89	Port Vale	88	Plymouth Arg††	85
1994–95	Birmingham C	89	Brentford††	85	Crewe Alex††	83
1995–96	Swindon T	92	Oxford U	83	Blackpool††	82
1996–97	Bury	84	Stockport Co	82	Luton T††	78
1997–98	Watford	88	Bristol C	85	Grimsby T	72
1998–99	Fulham	101	Walsall	87	Manchester C	82

DIVISION 3

Maximum points: 126

	First	Pts	Second	Pts	Third	Pts
1992–93	Cardiff C	83	Wrexham	80	Barnet	79
1993–94	Shrewsbury T	79	Chester C	74	Crewe Alex	73
1994–95	Carlisle U	91	Walsall	83	Chesterfield	81

Maximum points: 138

	First	Pts	Second	Pts	Third	Pts
1995–96	Preston NE	86	Gillingham	83	Bury	79
1996–97	Wigan Ath*	87	Fulham	87	Carlisle U	84
1997–98	Notts Co	99	Macclesfield T	82	Lincoln C	75
1998–99	Brentford	85	Cambridge U	81	Cardiff C	80

†† *Not promoted after play-offs.*

FOOTBALL LEAGUE

Maximum points: a 44; *b* 60

	First	Pts	Second	Pts	Third	Pts
1888–89*a*	Preston NE	40	Aston Villa	29	Wolverhampton W	28
1889–90*a*	Preston NE	33	Everton	31	Blackburn R	27
1890–91*a*	Everton	29	Preston NE	27	Notts Co	26
1891–92*b*	Sunderland	42	Preston NE	37	Bolton W	36

DIVISION 1 to 1991–92

Maximum points: a 44; *b* 52; *c* 60; *d* 68; *e* 76; *f* 84; *g* 126; *h* 120; *k* 114.

	First	Pts	Second	Pts	Third	Pts
1892–93*c*	Sunderland	48	Preston NE	37	Everton	36
1893–94*c*	Aston Villa	44	Sunderland	38	Derby Co	36

	First	Pts	Second	Pts	Third	Pts
1894–95*c*	Sunderland	47	Everton	42	Aston Villa	39
1895–96*c*	Aston Villa	45	Derby Co	41	Everton	39
1896–97*c*	Aston Villa	47	Sheffield U*	36	Derby Co	36
1897–98*c*	Sheffield U	42	Sunderland	37	Wolverhampton W*	35
1898–99*d*	Aston Villa	45	Liverpool	43	Burnley	39
1899–1900*d*	Aston Villa	50	Sheffield U	48	Sunderland	41
1900–01*d*	Liverpool	45	Sunderland	43	Notts Co	40
1901–02*d*	Sunderland	44	Everton	41	Newcastle U	37
1902–03*d*	The Wednesday	42	Aston Villa*	41	Sunderland	41
1903–04*d*	The Wednesday	47	Manchester C	44	Everton	43
1904–05*d*	Newcastle U	48	Everton	47	Manchester C	46
1905–06*e*	Liverpool	51	Preston NE	47	The Wednesday	44
1906–07*e*	Newcastle U	51	Bristol C	48	Everton*	45
1907–08*e*	Manchester U	52	Aston Villa*	43	Manchester C	43
1908–09*e*	Newcastle U	53	Everton	46	Sunderland	44
1909–10*e*	Aston Villa	53	Liverpool	48	Blackburn R*	45
1910–11*e*	Manchester U	52	Aston Villa	51	Sunderland*	45
1911–12*e*	Blackburn R	49	Everton	46	Newcastle U	44
1912–13*e*	Sunderland	54	Aston Villa	50	Sheffield W	49
1913–14*e*	Blackburn R	51	Aston Villa	44	Middlesbrough*	43
1914–15*e*	Everton	46	Oldham Ath	45	Blackburn R*	43
1919–20*f*	WBA	60	Burnley	51	Chelsea	49
1920–21*f*	Burnley	59	Manchester C	54	Bolton W	52
1921–22*f*	Liverpool	57	Tottenham H	51	Burnley	49
1922–23*f*	Liverpool	60	Sunderland	54	Huddersfield T	53
1923–24*f*	Huddersfield T*	57	Cardiff C	57	Sunderland	53
1924–25*f*	Huddersfield T	58	WBA	56	Bolton W	55
1925–26*f*	Huddersfield T	57	Arsenal	52	Sunderland	48
1926–27*f*	Newcastle U	56	Huddersfield T	51	Sunderland	49
1927–28*f*	Everton	53	Huddersfield T	51	Leicester C	48
1928–29*f*	Sheffield W	52	Leicester C	51	Aston Villa	50
1929–30*f*	Sheffield W	60	Derby Co	50	Manchester C*	47
1930–31*f*	Arsenal	66	Aston Villa	59	Sheffield W	52
1931–32*f*	Everton	56	Arsenal	54	Sheffield W	50
1932–33*f*	Arsenal	58	Aston Villa	54	Sheffield W	51
1933–34*f*	Arsenal	59	Huddersfield T	56	Tottenham H	49
1934–35*f*	Arsenal	58	Sunderland	54	Sheffield W	49
1935–36*f*	Sunderland	56	Derby Co*	48	Huddersfield T	48
1936–37*f*	Manchester C	57	Charlton Ath	54	Arsenal	52
1937–38*f*	Arsenal	52	Wolverhampton W	51	Preston NE	49
1938–39*f*	Everton	59	Wolverhampton W	55	Charlton Ath	50
1946–47*f*	Liverpool	57	Manchester U*	56	Wolverhampton W	56
1947–48*f*	Arsenal	59	Manchester U*	52	Burnley	52
1948–49*f*	Portsmouth	58	Manchester U*	53	Derby Co	53
1949–50*f*	Portsmouth*	53	Wolverhampton W	53	Sunderland	52
1950–51*f*	Tottenham H	60	Manchester U	56	Blackpool	50
1951–52*f*	Manchester U	57	Tottenham H*	53	Arsenal	53
1952–53*f*	Arsenal*	54	Preston NE	54	Wolverhampton W	51
1953–54*f*	Wolverhampton W	57	WBA	53	Huddersfield T	51
1954–55*f*	Chelsea	52	Wolverhampton W*	48	Portsmouth*	48
1955–56*f*	Manchester U	60	Blackpool*	49	Wolverhampton W	49
1956–57*f*	Manchester U	64	Tottenham H*	56	Preston NE	56
1957–58*f*	Wolverhampton W	64	Preston NE	59	Tottenham H	51
1958–59*f*	Wolverhampton W	61	Manchester U	55	Arsenal*	50
1959–60*f*	Burnley	55	Wolverhampton W	54	Tottenham H	53
1960–61*f*	Tottenham H	66	Sheffield W	58	Wolverhampton W	57

	First	Pts	Second	Pts	Third	Pts
1961–62f	Ipswich T	56	Burnley	53	Tottenham H	52
1962–63f	Everton	61	Tottenham H	55	Burnley	54
1963–64f	Liverpool	57	Manchester U	53	Everton	52
1964–65f	Manchester U*	61	Leeds U	61	Chelsea	56
1965–66f	Liverpool	61	Leeds U*	55	Burnley	55
1966–67f	Manchester U	60	Nottingham F*	56	Tottenham H	56
1967–68f	Manchester C	58	Manchester U	56	Liverpool	55
1968–69f	Leeds U	67	Liverpool	61	Everton	57
1969–70f	Everton	66	Leeds U	57	Chelsea	55
1970–71f	Arsenal	65	Leeds U	64	Tottenham H*	52
1971–72f	Derby Co	58	Leeds U*	57	Liverpool*	57
1972–73f	Liverpool	60	Arsenal	57	Leeds U	53
1973–74f	Leeds U	62	Liverpool	57	Derby Co	48
1974–75f	Derby Co	53	Liverpool*	51	Ipswich T	51
1975–76f	Liverpool	60	QPR	59	Manchester U	56
1976–77f	Liverpool	57	Manchester C	56	Ipswich T	52
1977–78f	Nottingham F	64	Liverpool	57	Everton	55
1978–79f	Liverpool	68	Nottingham F	60	WBA	59
1979–80f	Liverpool	60	Manchester U	58	Ipswich T	53
1980–81f	Aston Villa	60	Ipswich T	56	Arsenal	53
1981–82g	Liverpool	87	Ipswich T	83	Manchester U	78
1982–83g	Liverpool	82	Watford	71	Manchester U	70
1983–84g	Liverpool	80	Southampton	77	Nottingham F*	74
1984–85g	Everton	90	Liverpool*	77	Tottenham H	77
1985–86g	Liverpool	88	Everton	86	West Ham U	84
1986–87g	Everton	86	Liverpool	77	Tottenham H	71
1987–88h	Liverpool	90	Manchester U	81	Nottingham F	73
1988–89k	Arsenal*	76	Liverpool	76	Nottingham F	64
1989–90k	Liverpool	79	Aston Villa	70	Tottenham H	63
1990–91k	Arsenal†	83	Liverpool	76	Crystal Palace	69
1991–92g	Leeds U	82	Manchester U	78	Sheffield W	75

No official competition during 1915–19 and 1939–46; Regional Leagues operating.
* *Won or placed on goal average (ratio)/goal difference.*
† *2 pts deducted*

DIVISION 2 to 1991–92

Maximum points: a 44; b 56; c 60; d 68; e 76; f 84; g 126; h 132; k 138.

	First	Pts	Second	Pts	Third	Pts
1892–93a	Small Heath	36	Sheffield U	35	Darwen	30
1893–94b	Liverpool	50	Small Heath	42	Notts Co	39
1894–95c	Bury	48	Notts Co	39	Newton Heath*	38
1895–96c	Liverpool*	46	Manchester C	46	Grimsby T*	42
1896–97c	Notts Co	42	Newton Heath	39	Grimsby T	38
1897–98c	Burnley	48	Newcastle U	45	Manchester C	39
1898–99d	Manchester C	52	Glossop NE	46	Leicester Fosse	45
1899–1900d	The Wednesday	54	Bolton W	52	Small Heath	46
1900–01d	Grimsby T	49	Small Heath	48	Burnley	44
1901–02d	WBA	55	Middlesbrough	51	Preston NE*	42
1902–03d	Manchester C	54	Small Heath	51	Woolwich A	48
1903–04d	Preston NE	50	Woolwich A	49	Manchester U	48
1904–05d	Liverpool	58	Bolton W	56	Manchester U	53
1905–06e	Bristol C	66	Manchester U	62	Chelsea	53
1906–07e	Nottingham F	60	Chelsea	57	Leicester Fosse	48
1907–08e	Bradford C	54	Leicester Fosse	52	Oldham Ath	50
1908–09e	Bolton W	52	Tottenham H*	51	WBA	51
1909–10e	Manchester C	54	Oldham Ath*	53	Hull C*	53
1910–11e	WBA	53	Bolton W	51	Chelsea	49

	First	Pts	Second	Pts	Third	Pts
1911–12e	Derby Co*	54	Chelsea	54	Burnley	52
1912–13e	Preston NE	53	Burnley	50	Birmingham	46
1913–14e	Notts Co	53	Bradford PA*	49	Woolwich A	49
1914–15e	Derby Co	53	Preston NE	50	Barnsley	47
1919–20f	Tottenham H	70	Huddersfield T	64	Birmingham	56
1920–21f	Birmingham*	58	Cardiff C	58	Bristol C	51
1921–22f	Nottingham F	56	Stoke C*	52	Barnsley	52
1922–23f	Notts Co	53	West Ham U*	51	Leicester C	51
1923–24f	Leeds U	54	Bury*	51	Derby Co	51
1924–25f	Leicester C	59	Manchester U	57	Derby Co	55
1925–26f	Sheffield W	60	Derby Co	57	Chelsea	52
1926–27f	Middlesbrough	62	Portsmouth*	54	Manchester C	54
1927–28f	Manchester C	59	Leeds U	57	Chelsea	54
1928–29f	Middlesbrough	55	Grimsby T	53	Bradford PA*	48
1929–30f	Blackpool	58	Chelsea	55	Oldham Ath	53
1930–31f	Everton	61	WBA	54	Tottenham H	51
1931–32f	Wolverhampton W	56	Leeds U	54	Stoke C	52
1932–33f	Stoke C	56	Tottenham H	55	Fulham	50
1933–34f	Grimsby T	59	Preston NE	52	Bolton W*	51
1934–35f	Brentford	61	Bolton W*	56	West Ham U	56
1935–36f	Manchester U	56	Charlton Ath	55	Sheffield U*	52
1936–37f	Leicester C	56	Blackpool	55	Bury	52
1937–38f	Aston Villa	57	Manchester U*	53	Sheffield U	53
1938–39f	Blackburn R	55	Sheffield U	54	Sheffield W	53
1946–47f	Manchester C	62	Burnley	58	Birmingham C	55
1947–48f	Birmingham C	59	Newcastle U	56	Southampton	52
1948–49f	Fulham	57	WBA	56	Southampton	55
1949–50f	Tottenham H	61	Sheffield W*	52	Sheffield U*	52
1950–51f	Preston NE	57	Manchester C	52	Cardiff C	50
1951–52f	Sheffield W	53	Cardiff C*	51	Birmingham C	51
1952–53f	Sheffield U	60	Huddersfield T	58	Luton T	52
1953–54f	Leicester C*	56	Everton	56	Blackburn R	55
1954–55f	Birmingham C*	54	Luton T*	54	Rotherham U	54
1955–56f	Sheffield W	55	Leeds U	52	Liverpool*	48
1956–57f	Leicester C	61	Nottingham F	54	Liverpool	53
1957–58f	West Ham U	57	Blackburn R	56	Charlton Ath	55
1958–59f	Sheffield W	62	Fulham	60	Sheffield U*	53
1959–60f	Aston Villa	59	Cardiff C	58	Liverpool*	50
1960–61f	Ipswich T	59	Sheffield U	58	Liverpool	52
1961–62f	Liverpool	62	Leyton Orient	54	Sunderland	53
1962–63f	Stoke C	53	Chelsea*	52	Sunderland	52
1963–64f	Leeds U	63	Sunderland	61	Preston NE	56
1964–65f	Newcastle U	57	Northampton T	56	Bolton W	50
1965–66f	Manchester C	59	Southampton	54	Coventry C	53
1966–67f	Coventry C	59	Wolverhampton W	58	Carlisle U	52
1967–68f	Ipswich T	59	QPR*	58	Blackpool	58
1968–69f	Derby Co	63	Crystal Palace	56	Charlton Ath	50
1969–70f	Huddersfield T	60	Blackpool	53	Leicester C	51
1970–71f	Leicester C	59	Sheffield U	56	Cardiff C*	53
1971–72f	Norwich C	57	Birmingham C	56	Millwall	55
1972–73f	Burnley	62	QPR	61	Aston Villa	50
1973–74f	Middlesbrough	65	Luton T	50	Carlisle U	49
1974–75f	Manchester U	61	Aston Villa	58	Norwich C	53
1975–76f	Sunderland	56	Bristol C*	53	WBA	53
1976–77f	Wolverhampton W	57	Chelsea	55	Nottingham F	52
1977–78f	Bolton W	58	Southampton	57	Tottenham H*	56
1978–79f	Crystal Palace	57	Brighton & HA*	56	Stoke C	56

	First	Pts	Second	Pts	Third	Pts
1979–80f	Leicester C	55	Sunderland	54	Birmingham C*	53
1980–81f	West Ham U	66	Notts Co	53	Swansea C*	50
1981–82g	Luton T	88	Watford	80	Norwich C	71
1982–83g	QPR	85	Wolverhampton W	75	Leicester C	70
1983–84g	Chelsea*	88	Sheffield W	88	Newcastle U	80
1984–85g	Oxford U	84	Birmingham C	82	Manchester C	74
1985–86g	Norwich C	84	Charlton Ath	77	Wimbledon	76
1986–87g	Derby Co	84	Portsmouth	78	Oldham Ath††	75
1987–88h	Millwall	82	Aston Villa*	78	Middlesbrough	78
1988–89k	Chelsea	99	Manchester C	82	Crystal Palace	81
1989–90k	Leeds U*	85	Sheffield U	85	Newcastle U††	80
1990–91k	Oldham Ath	88	West Ham U	87	Sheffield W	82
1991–92k	Ipswich T	84	Middlesbrough	80	Derby Co	78

No official competition during 1915–19 and 1939–46; Regional Leagues operating.
** Won or placed on goal average (ratio)/goal difference.*
†† Not promoted after play-offs.

DIVISION 3 to 1991–92

Maximum points: 92; 138 from 1981–82.

	First	Pts	Second	Pts	Third	Pts
1958–59	Plymouth Arg	62	Hull C	61	Brentford*	57
1959–60	Southampton	61	Norwich C	59	Shrewsbury T*	52
1960–61	Bury	68	Walsall	62	QPR	60
1961–62	Portsmouth	65	Grimsby T	62	Bournemouth*	59
1962–63	Northampton T	62	Swindon T	58	Port Vale	54
1963–64	Coventry C*	60	Crystal Palace	60	Watford	58
1964–65	Carlisle U	60	Bristol C*	59	Mansfield T	59
1965–66	Hull C	69	Millwall	65	QPR	57
1966–67	QPR	67	Middlesbrough	55	Watford	54
1967–68	Oxford U	57	Bury	56	Shrewsbury T	55
1968–69	Watford*	64	Swindon T	64	Luton T	61
1969–70	Orient	62	Luton T	60	Bristol R	56
1970–71	Preston NE	61	Fulham	60	Halifax T	56
1971–72	Aston Villa	70	Brighton & HA	65	Bournemouth*	62
1972–73	Bolton W	61	Notts Co	57	Blackburn R	55
1973–74	Oldham Ath	62	Bristol R*	61	York C	61
1974–75	Blackburn R	60	Plymouth Arg	59	Charlton Ath	55
1975–76	Hereford U	63	Cardiff C	57	Millwall	56
1976–77	Mansfield T	64	Brighton & HA	61	Crystal Palace*	59
1977–78	Wrexham	61	Cambridge U	58	Preston NE*	56
1978–79	Shrewsbury T	61	Watford*	60	Swansea C	60
1979–80	Grimsby T	62	Blackburn R	59	Sheffield W	58
1980–81	Rotherham U	61	Barnsley*	59	Charlton Ath	59
1981–82	Burnley*	80	Carlisle U	80	Fulham	78
1982–83	Portsmouth	91	Cardiff C	86	Huddersfield T	82
1983–84	Oxford U	95	Wimbledon	87	Sheffield U*	83
1984–85	Bradford C	94	Millwall	90	Hull C	87
1985–86	Reading	94	Plymouth Arg	87	Derby Co	84
1986–87	Bournemouth	97	Middlesbrough	94	Swindon T	87
1987–88	Sunderland	93	Brighton & HA	84	Walsall	82
1988–89	Wolverhampton W	92	Sheffield U*	84	Port Vale	84
1989–90	Bristol R	93	Bristol C	91	Notts Co	87
1990–91	Cambridge U	86	Southend U	85	Grimsby T*	83
1991–92	Brentford	82	Birmingham C	81	Huddersfield T	78

** Won or placed on goal average (ratio)/goal difference.*

DIVISION 4 (1958–1992)

Maximum points: 92; 138 from 1981–82.

	First	Pts	Second	Pts	Third	Pts
1958–59	Port Vale	64	Coventry C*	60	York C	60
1959–60	Walsall	65	Notts Co*	60	Torquay U	60
1960–61	Peterborough U	66	Crystal Palace	64	Northampton T*	60
1961–62†	Millwall	56	Colchester U	55	Wrexham	53
1962–63	Brentford	62	Oldham Ath*	59	Crewe Alex	59
1963–64	Gillingham*	60	Carlisle U	60	Workington	59
1964–65	Brighton & HA	63	Millwall*	62	York C	62
1965–66	Doncaster R*	59	Darlington	59	Torquay U	58
1966–67	Stockport Co	64	Southport*	59	Barrow	59
1967–68	Luton T	66	Barnsley	61	Hartlepools U	60
1968–69	Doncaster R	59	Halifax T	57	Rochdale*	56
1969–70	Chesterfield	64	Wrexham	61	Swansea C	60
1970–71	Notts Co	69	Bournemouth	60	Oldham Ath	59
1971–72	Grimsby T	63	Southend U	60	Brentford	59
1972–73	Southport	62	Hereford U	58	Cambridge U	57
1973–74	Peterborough U	65	Gillingham	62	Colchester U	60
1974–75	Mansfield T	68	Shrewsbury T	62	Rotherham U	59
1975–76	Lincoln C	74	Northampton T	68	Reading	60
1976–77	Cambridge U	65	Exeter C	62	Colchester U*	59
1977–78	Watford	71	Southend U	60	Swansea C*	56
1978–79	Reading	65	Grimsby T*	61	Wimbledon*	61
1979–80	Huddersfield T	66	Walsall	64	Newport Co	61
1980–81	Southend U	67	Lincoln C	65	Doncaster R	56
1981–82	Sheffield U	96	Bradford C*	91	Wigan Ath	91
1982–83	Wimbledon	98	Hull C	90	Port Vale	88
1983–84	York C	101	Doncaster R	85	Reading*	82
1984–85	Chesterfield	91	Blackpool	86	Darlington	85
1985–86	Swindon T	102	Chester C	84	Mansfield T	81
1986–87	Northampton T	99	Preston NE	90	Southend U	80
1987–88	Wolverhampton W	90	Cardiff C	85	Bolton W	78
1988–89	Rotherham U	82	Tranmere R	80	Crewe Alex	78
1989–90	Exeter C	89	Grimsby T	79	Southend U	75
1990–91	Darlington	83	Stockport Co*	82	Hartlepool U	82
1991–92††*Burnley		83	Rotherham U*	77	Mansfield T	77

†*Maximum points:* 88 owing to Accrington Stanley's resignation. ††*Not promoted after play-offs.*
†**Maximum points:* 126 owing to Aldershot being expelled.

DIVISION 3—SOUTH (1920–1958)

1920–21 Season as Division 3.
Maximum points: a 84; *b* 92.

	First	Pts	Second	Pts	Third	Pts
1920–21*a*	Crystal Palace	59	Southampton	54	QPR	53
1921–22*a*	Southampton*	61	Plymouth Arg	61	Portsmouth	53
1922–23*a*	Bristol C	59	Plymouth Arg*	53	Swansea T	53
1923–24*a*	Portsmouth	59	Plymouth Arg	55	Millwall	54
1924–25*a*	Swansea T	57	Plymouth Arg	56	Bristol C	53
1925–26*a*	Reading	57	Plymouth Arg	56	Millwall	53
1926–27*a*	Bristol C	62	Plymouth Arg	60	Millwall	56
1927–28*a*	Millwall	65	Northampton T	55	Plymouth Arg	53
1928–29*a*	Charlton Ath*	54	Crystal Palace	54	Northampton T*	52
1929–30*a*	Plymouth Arg	68	Brentford	61	QPR	51
1930–31*a*	Notts Co	59	Crystal Palace	51	Brentford	50
1931–32*a*	Fulham	57	Reading	55	Southend U	53
1932–33*a*	Brentford	62	Exeter C	58	Norwich C	57

	First	Pts	Second	Pts	Third	Pts
1933–34a	Norwich C	61	Coventry C*	54	Reading*	54
1934–35a	Charlton Ath	61	Reading	53	Coventry C	51
1935–36a	Coventry C	57	Luton T	56	Reading	54
1936–37a	Luton T	58	Notts Co	56	Brighton & HA	53
1937–38a	Millwall	56	Bristol C	55	QPR*	53
1938–39a	Newport Co	55	Crystal Palace	52	Brighton & HA	49
1939–46	Competition cancelled owing to war.					
1946–47a	Cardiff C	66	QPR	57	Bristol C	51
1947–48a	QPR	61	Bournemouth	57	Walsall	51
1948–49a	Swansea T	62	Reading	55	Bournemouth	52
1949–50a	Notts Co	58	Northampton T*	51	Southend U	51
1950–51b	Nottingham F	70	Norwich C	64	Reading*	57
1951–52b	Plymouth Arg	66	Reading*	61	Norwich C	61
1952–53b	Bristol R	64	Millwall*	62	Northampton T	62
1953–54b	Ipswich T	64	Brighton & HA	61	Bristol C	56
1954–55b	Bristol C	70	Leyton Orient	61	Southampton	59
1955–56b	Leyton Orient	66	Brighton & HA	65	Ipswich T	64
1956–57b	Ipswich T*	59	Torquay U	59	Colchester U	58
1957–58b	Brighton & HA	60	Brentford*	58	Plymouth Arg	58

** Won or placed on goal average (ratio).*

DIVISION 3—NORTH (1921–1958)
Maximum points: a 76; b 84; c 80; d 92.

	First	Pts	Second	Pts	Third	Pts
1921–22a	Stockport Co	56	Darlington*	50	Grimsby T	50
1922–23a	Nelson	51	Bradford PA	47	Walsall	46
1923–24b	Wolverhampton W	63	Rochdale	62	Chesterfield	54
1924–25b	Darlington	58	Nelson*	53	New Brighton	53
1925–26b	Grimsby T	61	Bradford PA	60	Rochdale	59
1926–27b	Stoke C	63	Rochdale	58	Bradford PA	55
1927–28b	Bradford PA	63	Lincoln C	55	Stockport Co	54
1928–29g	Bradford C	63	Stockport Co	62	Wrexham	52
1929–30b	Port Vale	67	Stockport Co	63	Darlington*	50
1930–31b	Chesterfield	58	Lincoln C	57	Wrexham*	54
1931–32c	Lincoln C*	57	Gateshead	57	Chester	50
1932–33b	Hull C	59	Wrexham	57	Stockport Co	54
1933–34b	Barnsley	62	Chesterfield	61	Stockport Co	59
1934–35b	Doncaster R	57	Halifax T	55	Chester	54
1935–36b	Chesterfield	60	Chester*	55	Tranmere R	55
1936–37b	Stockport Co	60	Lincoln C	57	Chester	53
1937–38b	Tranmere R	56	Doncaster R	54	Hull C	53
1938–39b	Barnsley	67	Doncaster R	56	Bradford C	52
1939–46	Competition cancelled owing to war.					
1946–47b	Doncaster R	72	Rotherham U	60	Chester	56
1947–48b	Lincoln C	60	Rotherham U	59	Wrexham	50
1948–49b	Hull C	65	Rotherham U	62	Doncaster R	50
1949–50b	Doncaster R	55	Gateshead	53	Rochdale*	51
1950–51d	Rotherham U	71	Mansfield T	64	Carlisle U	62
1951–52d	Lincoln C	69	Grimsby T	66	Stockport Co	59
1952–53d	Oldham Ath	59	Port Vale	58	Wrexham	56
1953–54d	Port Vale	69	Barnsley	58	Scunthorpe U	57
1954–55d	Barnsley	65	Accrington S	61	Scunthorpe U*	58
1955–56d	Grimsby T	68	Derby Co	63	Accrington S	59
1956–57d	Derby Co	63	Hartlepools U	59	Accrington S*	58
1957–58d	Scunthorpe U	66	Accrington S	59	Bradford C	57

** Won or placed on goal average (ratio).*

(Not accounted for in previous section)
1986–87   Aldershot to Division 3.
1987–88   Swansea C to Divison 3.
1988–89   Leyton Orient to Division 3.
1989–90   Cambridge U to Division 3; Notts Co to Division 2; Sunderland to Division 1.
1990–91   Notts Co to Division 1; Tranmere R to Division 2; Torquay U to Division 3.
1991–92   Blackburn R to Premier League; Peterborough U to Division 1.
1992–93   Swindon T to Premier League; WBA to Division 1; York C to Division 2.
1993–94   Leicester C to Premier League; Burnley to Division 1; Wycombe W to Division 2.
1994–95   Huddersfield T to Division 1.
1995–96   Leicester C to Premier League; Bradford C to Division 1; Plymouth Arg to Division 2.
1996–97   Crystal Palace to Premier League; Crewe Alex to Division 1; Northampton T to Division 2.
1997–98   Charlton Ath to Premier League; Colchester U to Division 2.
1998–99   Watford to Premier League; Scunthorpe to Division 2.

RELEGATED CLUBS

FA PREMIER LEAGUE TO DIVISION 1

1992–93 Crystal Palace, Middlesbrough, Nottingham F
1993–94 Sheffield U, Oldham Ath, Swindon T
1994–95 Crystal Palace, Norwich C, Leicester C, Ipswich T
1995–96 Manchester C, QPR, Bolton W
1996–97 Sunderland, Middlesbrough, Nottingham F
1997–98 Bolton W, Barnsley, Crystal Palace
1998–99 Charlton Ath, Blackburn R, Nottingham F

DIVISION 1 TO DIVISION 2

1898–99 Bolton W and Sheffield W
1899–1900 Burnley and Glossop
1900–01 Preston NE and WBA
1901–02 Small Heath and Manchester C
1902–03 Grimsby T and Bolton W
1903–04 Liverpool and WBA
1904–05 League extended. Bury and Notts Co, two bottom clubs in First Division, re-elected.
1905–06 Nottingham F and Wolverhampton W
1906–07 Derby Co and Stoke C
1907–08 Bolton W and Birmingham C
1908–09 Manchester C and Leicester Fosse
1909–10 Bolton W and Chelsea
1910–11 Bristol C and Nottingham F
1911–12 Preston NE and Bury
1912–13 Notts Co and Woolwich Arsenal
1913–14 Preston NE and Derby Co
1914–15 Tottenham H and Chelsea*
1919–20 Notts Co and Sheffield W
1920–21 Derby Co and Bradford PA
1921–22 Bradford C and Manchester U
1922–23 Stoke C and Oldham Ath
1923–24 Chelsea and Middlesbrough
1924–25 Preston NE and Nottingham F
1925–26 Manchester C and Notts Co

1926–27 Leeds U and WBA
1927–28 Tottenham H and Middlesbrough
1928–29 Bury and Cardiff C
1929–30 Burnley and Everton
1930–31 Leeds U and Manchester U
1931–32 Grimsby T and West Ham U
1932–33 Bolton W and Blackpool
1933–34 Newcastle U and Sheffield U
1934–35 Leicester C and Tottenham H
1935–36 Aston Villa and Blackburn R
1936–37 Manchester U and Sheffield W
1937–38 Manchester C and WBA
1938–39 Birmingham C and Leicester C
1946–47 Brentford and Leeds U
1947–48 Blackburn R and Grimsby T
1948–49 Preston NE and Sheffield U
1949–50 Manchester C and Birmingham C
1950–51 Sheffield W and Everton
1951–52 Huddersfield T and Fulham
1952–53 Stoke C and Derby Co
1953–54 Middlesbrough and Liverpool
1954–55 Leicester C and Sheffield W
1955–56 Huddersfield T and Sheffield U
1956–57 Charlton Ath and Cardiff C
1957–58 Sheffield W and Sunderland
1958–59 Portsmouth and Aston Villa

1959–60 Luton T and Leeds U
1960–61 Preston NE and Newcastle U
1961–62 Chelsea and Cardiff C
1962–63 Manchester C and Leyton Orient
1963–64 Bolton W and Ipswich T
1964–65 Wolverhampton W and
        Birmingham C
1965–66 Northampton T and
        Blackburn R
1966–67 Aston Villa and Blackpool
1967–68 Fulham and Sheffield U
1968–69 Leicester C and QPR
1969–70 Sunderland and Sheffield W
1970–71 Burnley and Blackpool
1971–72 Huddersfield T and Nottingham F
1972–73 Crystal Palace and WBA
1973–74 Southampton, Manchester U,
        Norwich C
1974–75 Luton T, Chelsea, Carlisle U
1975–76 Wolverhampton W, Burnley,
        Sheffield U
1976–77 Sunderland, Stoke C,
        Tottenham H
1977–78 West Ham U, Newcastle U,
        Leicester C
1978–79 QPR, Birmingham C, Chelsea
1979–80 Bristol C, Derby Co, Bolton W
1980–81 Norwich C, Leicester C, Crystal
        Palace

1981–82 Leeds U, Wolverhampton W,
        Middlesbrough
1982–83 Manchester C, Swansea C,
        Brighton & HA
1983–84 Birmingham C, Notts Co,
        Wolverhampton W
1984–85 Norwich C, Sunderland, Stoke C
1985–86 Ipswich T, Birmingham C, WBA
1986–87 Leicester C, Manchester C,
        Aston Villa
1987–88 Chelsea**, Portsmouth,
        Watford, Oxford U
1988–89 Middlesbrough, West Ham U,
        Newcastle U
1989–90 Sheffield W, Charlton Ath,
        Millwall
1990–91 Sunderland and Derby Co
1991–92 Luton T, Notts Co, West Ham U
1992–93 Brentford, Cambridge U,
        Bristol R
1993–94 Birmingham C, Oxford U,
        Peterborough U
1994–95 Swindon T, Burnley, Bristol C,
        Notts Co
1995–96 Millwall, Watford, Luton T
1996–97 Grimsby T, Oldham Ath,
        Southend U
1997–98 Manchester C, Stoke C, Reading
1998–99 Bury, Oxford U, Bristol C

**Relegated after play-offs.*
Subsequently re-elected to Division 1 when League was extended after the War.

DIVISION 2 TO DIVISION 3

1920–21 Stockport Co
1921–22 Bradford PA and Bristol C
1922–23 Rotherham Co and
        Wolverhampton W
1923–24 Nelson and Bristol C
1924–25 Crystal Palace and Coventry C
1925–26 Stoke C and Stockport Co
1926–27 Darlington and Bradford C
1927–28 Fulham and South Shields
1928–29 Port Vale and Clapton Orient
1929–30 Hull C and Notts Co
1930–31 Reading and Cardiff C
1931–32 Barnsley and Bristol C
1932–33 Chesterfield and Charlton Ath
1933–34 Millwall and Lincoln C
1934–35 Oldham Ath and Notts Co
1935–36 Port Vale and Hull C
1936–37 Doncaster R and Bradford C
1937–38 Barnsley and Stockport Co
1938–39 Norwich C and Tranmere R
1946–47 Swansea T and Newport Co
1947–48 Doncaster R and Millwall
1948–49 Nottingham F and Lincoln C
1949–50 Plymouth Arg and Bradford PA
1950–51 Grimsby T and Chesterfield
1951–52 Coventry C and QPR

1952–53 Southampton and Barnsley
1953–54 Brentford and Oldham Ath
1954–55 Ipswich T and Derby Co
1955–56 Plymouth Arg and Hull C
1956–57 Port Vale and Bury
1957–58 Doncaster R and Notts Co
1958–59 Barnsley and Grimsby T
1959–60 Bristol C and Hull C
1960–61 Lincoln C and Portsmouth
1961–62 Brighton & HA and Bristol R
1962–63 Walsall and Luton T
1963–64 Grimsby T and Scunthorpe U
1964–65 Swindon T and Swansea T
1965–66 Middlesbrough and Leyton Orient
1966–67 Northampton T and Bury
1967–68 Plymouth Arg and
        Rotherham U
1968–69 Fulham and Bury
1969–70 Preston NE and Aston Villa
1970–71 Blackburn R and Bolton W
1971–72 Charlton Ath and Watford
1972–73 Huddersfield T and Brighton &
        HA
1973–74 Crystal Palace, Preston NE,
        Swindon T
1974–75 Millwall, Cardiff C, Sheffield W

1975–76 Oxford U, York C, Portsmouth
1976–77 Carlisle U, Plymouth Arg,
Hereford U
1977–78 Blackpool, Mansfield T, Hull C
1978–79 Sheffield U, Millwall,
Blackburn R
1979–80 Fulham, Burnley,
Charlton Ath
1980–81 Preston NE, Bristol C,
Bristol R
1981–82 Cardiff C, Wrexham, Orient
1982–83 Rotherham U, Burnley,
Bolton W
1983–84 Derby Co, Swansea C,
Cambridge U
1984–85 Notts Co, Cardiff C,
Wolverhampton W
1985–86 Carlisle U, Middlesbrough,
Fulham
1986–87 Sunderland**, Grimsby T,
Brighton & HA
1987–88 Huddersfield T, Reading,
Sheffield U**

1988–89 Shrewsbury T, Birmingham C,
Walsall
1989–90 Bournemouth, Bradford C,
Stoke C
1990–91 WBA and Hull C
1991–92 Plymouth Arg, Brighton & HA,
Port Vale
1992–93 Preston NE, Mansfield T, Wigan
Ath, Chester C
1993–94 Fulham, Exeter C,
Hartlepool U, Barnet
1994–95 Cambridge U, Plymouth Arg,
Cardiff C, Chester C, Leyton
Orient
1995–96 Carlisle U, Swansea C, Brighton
& HA, Hull C
1996–97 Peterborough U, Shrewsbury T,
Rotherham U, Notts Co
1997–98 Brentford, Plymouth Arg,
Carlisle U, Southend U
1998–99 York C, Northampton T,
Lincoln C, Macclesfield T

DIVISION 3 TO DIVISION 4

1958–59 Rochdale, Notts Co,
Doncaster R, Stockport Co
1959–60 Accrington S, Wrexham,
Mansfield T, York C
1960–61 Chesterfield, Colchester U,
Bradford C, Tranmere R
1961–62 Newport Co, Brentford, Lincoln
C, Torquay U
1962–63 Bradford PA, Brighton & HA,
Carlisle U, Halifax T
1963–64 Millwall, Crewe Alex, Wrexham,
Notts Co
1964–65 Luton T, Port Vale,
Colchester U, Barnsley
1965–66 Southend U, Exeter C,
Brentford, York C
1966–67 Doncaster R, Workington,
Darlington, Swansea T
1967–68 Scunthorpe U, Colchester U,
Grimsby T,
Peterborough U (demoted)
1968–69 Oldham Ath, Crewe Alex,
Hartlepool, Northampton T
1969–70 Bournemouth, Southport,
Barrow, Stockport Co
1970–71 Reading, Bury, Doncaster R,
Gillingham
1971–72 Mansfield T, Barnsley, Torquay
U, Bradford C
1972–73 Rotherham U, Brentford,
Swansea C, Scunthorpe U
1973–74 Cambridge U, Shrewsbury T,
Southport, Rochdale
1974–75 Bournemouth, Tranmere R,
Watford, Huddersfield T

1975–76 Aldershot, Colchester U,
Southend U, Halifax T
1976–77 Reading, Northampton T,
Grimsby T, York C
1977–78 Port Vale, Bradford C,
Hereford U, Portsmouth
1978–79 Peterborough U, Walsall,
Tranmere R, Lincoln C
1979–80 Bury, Southend U, Mansfield T,
Wimbledon
1980–81 Sheffield U, Colchester U,
Blackpool, Hull C
1981–82 Wimbledon, Swindon T,
Bristol C, Chester
1982–83 Reading, Wrexham,
Doncaster R, Chesterfield
1983–84 Scunthorpe U, Southend U,
Port Vale, Exeter C
1984–85 Burnley, Orient, Preston NE,
Cambridge U
1985–86 Lincoln C, Cardiff C,
Wolverhampton W, Swansea C
1986–87 Bolton W**, Carlisle U,
Darlington, Newport Co
1987–88 Doncaster R, York C, Grimsby
T, Rotherham U**
1988–89 Southend U, Chesterfield,
Gillingham, Aldershot
1989–90 Cardiff C, Northampton T,
Blackpool, Walsall
1990–91 Crewe Alex, Rotherham U,
Mansfield T
1991–92 Bury, Shrewsbury T, Torquay U,
Darlington

***Relegated after play-offs.*

LEAGUE TITLE WINS

FA PREMIER LEAGUE – Manchester U 5, Arsenal 1, Blackburn R 1.

LEAGUE DIVISION 1 – Liverpool 18, Arsenal 10, Everton 9, Sunderland 8, Manchester U 7, Aston Villa 7, Newcastle U 5, Sheffield W 4, Huddersfield T 3, Leeds U 3, Wolverhampton W 3, Blackburn R 2, Nottingham F 2, Portsmouth 2, Preston NE 2, Burnley 2, Manchester C 2, Tottenham H 2, Derby Co 2, Bolton W 1, Chelsea 1, Sheffield U 1, WBA 1, Ipswich T 1, Crystal Palace 1, Middlesbrough 1.

LEAGUE DIVISION 2 – Leicester C 6, Manchester C 6, Sheffield W 5, Birmingham C (one as Small Heath) 5, Derby Co 4, Liverpool 4, Ipswich T 3, Leeds U 3, Notts Co 3, Preston NE 3, Middlesbrough 3, Stoke C 3, Bury 2, Grimsby T 2, Norwich C 2, Nottingham F 2, Tottenham H 2, WBA 2, Aston Villa 2, Burnley 2, Chelsea 2, Manchester U 2, West Ham U 2, Wolverhampton W 2, Bolton W 2, Fulham 2, Swindon T, Huddersfield T, Bristol C, Brentford, Bradford C, Everton, Sheffield U, Newcastle U, Coventry C, Blackpool, Blackburn R, Sunderland, Crystal Palace, Luton T, QPR, Oxford U, Millwall, Oldham Ath, Reading, Watford 1 each.

LEAGUE DIVISION 3 – Portsmouth 2, Oxford U 2, Carlisle U 2, Preston NE 2, Shrewsbury T 2, Brentford 2, Plymouth Arg, Southampton, Bury, Northampton T, Coventry C, Hull C, QPR, Watford, Leyton Orient, Aston Villa, Bolton W, Oldham Ath, Blackburn R, Hereford U, Mansfield T, Wrexham, Grimsby T, Rotherham U, Burnley, Bradford C, Bournemouth, Reading, Sunderland, Wolverhampton W, Bristol R, Cambridge U, Cardiff C, Wigan Ath, Notts Co 1 each.

LEAGUE DIVISION 4 – Chesterfield 2, Doncaster R 2, Peterborough U 2, Port Vale, Walsall, Millwall, Brentford, Gillingham, Brighton, Stockport Co, Luton T, Notts Co, Grimsby T, Southport, Mansfield T, Lincoln C, Cambridge U, Watford, Reading, Huddersfield T, Southend U, Sheffield U, Wimbledon, York C, Swindon T, Northampton T, Wolverhampton W, Rotherham U, Exeter C, Darlington, Burnley 1 each.

To 1957–58

DIVISION 3 (South) – Bristol C 3; Charlton Ath, Ipswich T, Millwall, Notts Co, Plymouth Arg, Swansea T 2 each; Brentford, Bristol R, Cardiff C, Crystal Palace, Coventry C, Fulham, Leyton Orient, Luton T, Newport Co, Nottingham F, Norwich C, Portsmouth, QPR, Reading, Southampton, Brighton & HA 1 each.

DIVISION 3 (North) – Barnsley, Doncaster R, Lincoln C 3 each; Chesterfield, Grimsby T, Hull C, Port Vale, Stockport Co 2 each; Bradford PA, Bradford C, Darlington, Derby Co, Nelson, Oldham Ath, Rotherham U, Stoke C, Tranmere R, Wolverhampton W, Scunthorpe U 1 each.

LEAGUE ATTENDANCES 1998–99

FA CARLING PREMIERSHIP ATTENDANCES

	Average Gate			Season 1998/99	
	1997/98	1998/99	+/−%	Highest	Lowest
Arsenal	38,053	38,024	−0.08	38,308	37,323
Aston Villa	36,137	36,937	+2.21	39,241	29,559
Blackburn Rovers	25,253	25,773	+2.06	30,436	21,754
Charlton Athletic	13,275	19,816	+49.27	20,048	16,488
Chelsea	32,901	34,754	+5.63	35,017	34,000
Coventry City	19,718	20,773	+5.35	23,091	16,003
Derby County	29,105	29,193	+0.30	32,913	25,710
Everton	35,376	36,202	+2.34	40,185	30,357
Leeds United	34,725	35,773	+3.02	40,255	30,012
Leicester City	20,615	20,469	−0.71	22,091	17,725
Liverpool	40,628	43,321	+6.63	44,852	36,019
Manchester United	55,168	55,188	+0.04	55,316	55,052
Middlesbrough	29,994	34,386	+14.64	34,687	33,387
Newcastle United	36,680	36,690	+0.03	36,784	36,352
Nottingham Forest	20,584	24,415	+18.61	30,025	20,480
Sheffield Wednesday	28,709	26,745	−6.84	39,475	19,321
Southampton	15,159	15,140	−0.13	15,255	14,354
Tottenham Hotspur	29,143	34,149	+17.18	36,125	28,338
West Ham United	24,967	25,639	+2.69	26,044	23,153
Wimbledon	16,675	18,207	+9.19	26,121	11,717

NATIONWIDE FOOTBALL LEAGUE: DIVISION ONE ATTENDANCES

	Average Gate			Season 1998/99	
	1997/98	1998/99	+/−%	Highest	Lowest
Barnsley	18,449	16,269	−11.8	18,114	14,733
Birmingham City	18,708	20,794	+11.2	29,060	15,935
Bolton Wanderers	24,352	18,240	−25.1	24,625	13,324
Bradford City	15,564	14,298	−8.1	15,887	12,595
Bristol City	11,846	12,860	+8.6	16,257	9,810
Bury	6,177	5,476	−11.3	8,669	3,436
Crewe Alexandra	5,243	5,269	+0.5	5,759	4,489
Crystal Palace	21,983	17,123	−22.1	22,096	12,919
Grimsby Town	5,601	6,681	+19.3	9,528	4,789
Huddersfield Town	12,145	12,976	+6.8	20,741	9,717
Ipswich Town	14,973	16,920	+13.0	22,162	11,596
Norwich City	14,444	15,761	+9.1	19,511	11,137
Oxford United	7,512	7,040	−6.3	9,434	5,587
Port Vale	8,432	6,991	−17.1	10,465	4,980
Portsmouth	11,149	11,973	+7.4	17,022	8,180
Queens Park Rangers	13,083	11,793	−9.9	18,498	8,070
Sheffield United	17,942	16,243	−9.5	25,612	12,293
Stockport County	8,322	7,900	−5.1	10,548	6,048
Sunderland	33,492	38,745	+15.7	41,634	33,870
Swindon Town	10,298	8,651	−16.0	11,718	5,765
Tranmere Rovers	7,999	6,930	−13.4	14,248	4,937
Watford	11,532	11,822	+2.5	20,303	8,682
West Bromwich Albion	16,662	14,585	−12.5	22,682	9,601
Wolverhampton Wanderers	23,281	22,620	−2.8	27,589	18,480

NATIONWIDE FOOTBALL LEAGUE: DIVISION TWO ATTENDANCES

	Average Gate			Season 1998/99	
	1997/98	1998/99	+/−%	Highest	Lowest
AFC Bournemouth	4,732	7,117	+50.4	10,964	4,863
Blackpool	5,220	5,116	−2.0	10,868	2,990
Bristol Rovers	6,413	6,263	−2.3	8,033	4,833
Burnley	10,481	10,605	+1.2	17,251	8,526
Chesterfield	4,756	4,564	−4.0	8,245	2,621
Colchester United	3,137	4,479	+44.2	6,554	3,228
Fulham	9,018	11,387	+26.3	17,176	7,447
Gillingham	6,450	6,339	−1.7	10,400	4,575
Lincoln City	3,968	4,654	+17.3	8,145	2,518
Luton Town	6,501	5,527	−15.0	9,070	4,021
Macclesfield Town	2,913	3,311	+13.7	6,381	1,868
Manchester City	28,196	28,261	+0.2	32,471	24,291
Millwall	7,023	6,958	−0.9	12,726	4,249
Northampton Town	6,389	6,073	−4.9	7,557	4,710
Notts County	5,711	5,617	−1.6	10,316	3,294
Oldham Athletic	5,586	5,628	+0.8	12,976	3,913
Preston North End	9,460	11,926	+26.1	20,857	8,656
Reading	9,676	11,265	+16.4	20,055	7,914
Stoke City	15,025	12,732	−15.3	23,272	6,569
Walsall	4,062	5,457	+34.3	9,517	3,098
Wigan Athletic	3,968	4,250	+7.1	6,700	2,784
Wrexham	4,090	3,948	−3.5	9,048	1,871
Wycombe Wanderers	5,415	5,121	−5.4	8,129	3,361
York City	3,853	3,646	−5.4	7,527	2,075

NATIONWIDE FOOTBALL LEAGUE: DIVISION THREE ATTENDANCES

	Average Gate			Season 1998/99	
	1997/98	1998/99	+/−%	Highest	Lowest
Barnet	2,254	2,107	−6.5	3,129	1,314
Brentford	5,029	5,444	+8.3	9,535	3,674
Brighton & Hove Albion	2,329	3,253	+39.7	4,838	1,793
Cambridge United	2,898	4,583	+58.1	8,936	2,385
Cardiff City	3,610	7,131	+97.5	12,455	3,742
Carlisle United	5,381	3,319	−38.3	7,599	2,273
Chester City	2,255	2,562	+13.6	3,926	1,729
Darlington	2,314	3,181	+37.5	5,899	2,085
Exeter City	3,988	3,154	−20.9	6,746	1,929
Halifax Town	3,002	2,541	+18.1	4,455	1,906
Hartlepool United	2,258	2,690	+19.1	5,098	1,593
Hull City	4,684	6,051	+29.2	13,949	3,433
Leyton Orient	4,374	4,672	+6.8	6,537	3,186
Mansfield Town	2,720	2,963	+8.9	4,095	2,292
Peterborough United	6,192	5,306	−14.3	10,168	3,785
Plymouth Argyle	5,323	5,323	n/c	11,936	3,589
Rochdale	1,847	2,125	+15.1	5,374	1,344
Rotherham United	3,648	3,988	+9.3	5,943	2,696
Scarborough	2,489	2,211	−11.2	4,769	1,056
Scunthorpe United	3,006	3,741	+24.5	5,633	2,421
Shrewsbury Town	2,403	2,575	+7.2	3,247	1,620
Southend United	4,148	4,317	+4.1	6,700	3,250
Swansea City	3,443	5,225	+51.8	9,226	3,360
Torquay United	2,679	2,600	−2.9	5,719	1,715

TRANSFERS 1998–99

May 1998	*From*	*To*
22 Corbett, James J.	Gillingham	Blackburn Rovers

June 1998
11 Beckett, Luke J.	Barnsley	Chester
10 Bradley, Russell	Hartlepool United	Hednesford Town
16 Brebner, Grant I.	Manchester United	Reading
2 Davies, Kevin C.	Southampton	Blackburn Rovers
12 Finnigan, John F.	Nottingham Forest	Lincoln City
24 Glass, James R.	AFC Bournemouth	Swindon Town
23 Reeves, Alan	Wimbledon	Swindon Town
18 Stowell, Matthew D.	Slough Town	Bristol City
12 Thompson, Alan	Bolton Wanderers	Aston Villa
23 Thorpe, Anthony	Fulham	Bristol City
15 Wicks, Matthew	Arsenal	Crewe Alexandra

July 1998
4 Angel, Mark	Oxford United	West Bromwich Albion
15 Barclay, Dominic A.	Bristol City	Macclesfield Town
17 Beattie, James S.	Blackburn Rovers	Southampton
8 Bennett, Gary E.	Scarborough	Darlington
10 Berthe, Mohamed	West Ham United	AFC Bournemouth
9 Boxall, Daniel J.	Crystal Palace	Brentford
15 Brady, Garry	Tottenham Hotspur	Newcastle United
22 Bruce, Stephen R.	Birmingham City	Sheffield United
27 Butler, Paul J.	Bury	Sunderland
29 Carpenter, Richard	Fulham	Cardiff City
15 Challis, Trevor	Queens Park Rangers	Bristol Rovers
17 Gordon, Dean D.	Crystal Palace	Middlesbrough
8 Granville, Daniel P.	Chelsea	Leeds United
31 Holsgrove, Paul	Brighton & Hove Albion	Hibernian
15 Hughes, Leslie M.	Chelsea	Southampton
15 Liddle, Craig	Middlesbrough	Darlington
16 Lormor, Anthony	Preston North End	Mansfield Town
31 Moore, Ian R.	Nottingham Forest	Stockport County
18 Murty, Graeme S.	York City	Reading
9 Mustoe, Neil J.	Wigan Athletic	Cambridge United
24 Ord, Richard J.	Sunderland	Queens Park Rangers
30 Owers, Gary	Bristol City	Notts County
28 Owusu, Lloyd	Slough Town	Brentford
24 Pallister, Gary A.	Manchester United	Middlesbrough
1 Powell, Christopher G.	Derby County	Charlton Athletic
9 Quinn, Robert J.	Crystal Palace	Brentford
1 Redfearn, Neil D.	Barnsley	Charlton Athletic
17 Richardson, Kevin	Southampton	Barnsley
10 Ripley, Stuart E.	Blackburn Rovers	Southampton
31 Ruddock, Neil	Liverpool	West Ham United
20 Scott, Richard P.	Shrewsbury Town	Peterborough United
9 Serrant, Carl	Oldham Athletic	Newcastle United
3 Smart, Alan A.C.	Carlisle United	Watford
17 Spedding, Duncan	Southampton	Northampton Town
3 Thornley, Benjamin L.	Manchester United	Huddersfield Town
28 Unsworth, David G.	West Ham United	Aston Villa
17 Van der Laan, Robertus P.	Derby County	Barnsley
9 Wainwright, Neil	Wrexham	Sunderland
30 Walsh, Michael S.	Scunthorpe United	Port Vale
15 Walton, Mark A.	Fulham	Brighton & Hove Albion
24 Whalley, Gareth	Crewe Alexandra	Bradford City
10 Whitehall, Steven C.	Mansfield Town	Oldham Athletic
30 Wright, Darren J.	Cheltenham Town	Stafford Rangers
27 Wright, Ian E.	Arsenal	West Ham United
7 Wright, Nicholas J.	Carlisle United	Watford

August 1998
27 Armstrong, Gordon I.	Bury	Burnley
12 Ashcroft, Lee	Preston North End	Grimsby Town
14 Battersby, Anthony	Bury	Lincoln City

6 Beadle, Peter C.	Bristol Rovers	Port Vale
28 Beesley, Paul	Manchester City	Port Vale
6 Butler, Peter J.F.	West Bromwich Albion	Halifax Town
7 Carr, Darren J.	Chesterfield	Gillingham
10 Claridge, Stephen E.	Wolverhampton Wanderers	Portsmouth
6 Coldicott, Stacy	West Bromwich Albion	Grimsby Town
22 Cooper, Colin T.	Nottingham Forest	Middlesbrough
22 Dailly, Christian	Derby County	Blackburn Rovers
28 Edworthy, Marc	Crystal Palace	Coventry City
12 Freedman, Douglas A.	Wolverhampton Wanderers	Nottingham Forest
10 Hall, Paul A.	Portsmouth	Coventry City
4 Herrera, Roberto	Fulham	Torquay United
24 Hiley, Scott P.	Manchester City	Southampton
6 Hooper, Dean R.	Kingstonian	Peterborough United
12 Hughes, Richard D.	Arsenal	AFC Bournemouth
14 Jack, Rodney A.	Torquay United	Crewe Alexandra
28 Lee, Jason B.	Watford	Chesterfield
20 Lowndes, Nathan P.	Watford	St Johnstone
20 McCarthy, Sean C.	Oldham Athletic	Plymouth Argyle
7 Mills, Lee	Port Vale	Bradford City
28 Morley, David T.	Manchester City	Southend United
27 Phillips, Martin J.	Manchester City	Portsmouth
22 Prior, Spencer	Leicester City	Derby County
25 Quashie, Nigel F.	Queens Park Rangers	Nottingham Forest
14 Rankin, Isaiah	Arsenal	Bradford City
12 Rizzo, Nicholas A.	Liverpool	Crystal Palace
7 Roberts, Jason A.D.	Wolverhampton Wanderers	Bristol Rovers
17 Rowett, Gary	Derby County	Birmingham City
20 Savage, Robert	Crewe Alexandra	Leicester City
14 Sinclair, Frank M.	Chelsea	Leicester City
28 Swan, Peter H.	Bury	Burnley
6 Taylor, Robert A.	Brentford	Gillingham
20 Thomas, David J.	Watford	Cardiff City
6 Todd, Lee	Southampton	Bradford City
22 Unsworth, David G.	Aston Villa	Everton
20 Vickers, Ashley J.	Peterborough United	St Albans City
11 Whalley, Gareth	Crewe Alexandra	Bradford City
6 Windass, Dean	Aberdeen	Oxford United
6 Wrack, Darren	Grimsby Town	Walsall
22 Yorke, Dwight	Aston Villa	Manchester United

Temporary transfers

28 Allen, Graham	Everton	Tranmere Rovers
17 Arnott, Andrew J.	Fulham	Rushden & Diamonds
28 Asaba, Carl E.	Reading	Gillingham
18 Barrett, Scott	Cambridge United	Kingstonian
10 Battersby, Anthony	Bury	Lincoln City
7 Beardsley, Peter A.	Bolton Wanderers	Fulham
21 Brannan, Gerard D.	Manchester City	Norwich City
7 Branston, Guy P.B.	Leicester City	Colchester United
28 Brazier, Matthew R.	Fulham	Cardiff City
13 Brooker, Paul	Fulham	Stevenage Borough
4 Brown, Simon J.	Tottenham Hotspur	Fulham
28 Clarke, Andrew W.	Wimbledon	Port Vale
21 Coyne, Christopher	West Ham United	Brentford
7 Crichton, Paul A.	West Bromwich Albion	Burnley
6 Crowe, Glen M.	Wolverhampton Wanderers	Exeter City
11 De Souza, Juan M.I.	Peterborough United	Southend United
28 Emblen, Paul D.	Charlton Athletic	Wycombe Wanderers
10 Green, Richard E.	Gillingham	Walsall
28 Harris, Jason A.S.	Leyton Orient	Preston North End
4 Hiley, Scott	Manchester City	Southampton
5 Hughes, Richard	Arsenal	AFC Bournemouth
20 Hunt, Jonathan R.	Derby County	Sheffield United
28 Kenny, Patrick	Bradford Park Avenue	Bury
7 McCarthy, Sean C.	Oldham Athletic	Plymouth Argyle
14 McIntyre, Kevin	Tranmere Rovers	Doncaster Rovers
13 McKenzie, Leon M.	Crystal Palace	Peterborough United
17 Marriott, Andrew	Wrexham	Sunderland
21 Mean, Scott	West Ham United	Port Vale

14 Mimms, Robert A.   Rotherham United   York City
30 Naylor, Martin P.   Shrewsbury Town   Telford United
28 Nixon, Eric W.   Stockport County   Wigan Athletic
 7 Russell, Craig S.   Manchester City   Tranmere Rovers
18 Scott, Robert   Fulham   Carlisle United
26 Simpson, Colin R.   Leyton Orient   Hendon
 7 Torpey, Stephen D.J.   Bristol City   Notts County
 7 Twiss, Michael J.   Manchester United   Sheffield United
14 Ward, Gavin J.   Bolton Wanderers   Burnley

September 1998

23 Allen, Graham   Everton   Tranmere Rovers
 2 Asaba, Carl E.   Reading   Gillingham
18 Balmer, Stuart M.   Charlton Athletic   Wigan Athletic
16 Betsy, Kevin   Woking   Fulham
11 Dobson, Anthony J.   West Bromwich Albion   Northampton Town
18 Emblen, Paul D.   Charlton Athletic   Wycombe Wanderers
22 Folan, Anthony S.   Crystal Palace   Brentford
 2 Gray, Andrew D.   Leeds United   Nottingham Forest
11 Green, Richard E.   Gillingham   Walsall
24 Harris, Jason A.S.   Leyton Orient   Preston North End
24 Hreidarsson, Hermann   Crystal Palace   Brentford
 3 Kenny, Patrick J.   Bradford Park Avenue   Bury
21 Mackay, Malcolm   Celtic   Norwich City
10 Merson, Paul C.   Middlesbrough   Aston Villa
 9 Mustafa, Tarkan   Barnet   Kingstonian
18 O'Neill, Michael A.   Coventry City   Wigan Athletic
 3 Peron, Jean F.   Walsall   Portsmouth
23 Priestley, Philip A.   Atherton LR   Rochdale
 8 Samuels, Dean   Barnet   Stevenage Borough
22 Shipperley, Neil J.   Crystal Palace   Nottingham Forest
23 Simonsen, Steven P.A.   Tranmere Rovers   Everton
30 Tiler, Carl   Everton   Charlton Athletic

Temporary transfers

 7 Adams, Kieran C.   Barnet   Dover Athletic
17 Alsford, Julian   Dundee United   Barnet
18 Arber, Mark A.   Tottenham Hotspur   Barnet
 8 Baldry, Simon   Huddersfield Town   Bury
 7 Beardsley, Peter A.   Bolton Wanderers   Fulham
18 Blatherwick, Steven S.   Burnley   Chesterfield
 7 Brady, Matthew J.   Barnet   Dover Athletic
21 Brannan, Gerard D.   Manchester City   Norwich City
18 Brown, Simon J.   Tottenham Hotspur   Kingstonian
25 Campbell, Neil A.   Scarborough   Telford United
16 Casper, Christopher M.   Manchester United   Reading
 7 Conlon, Barry J.   Manchester City   Southend United
11 Crowe, Glen   Wolverhampton Wanderers   Exeter City
11 Davies, Lawrence   Bradford City   Hartlepool United
 4 Dobson, Anthony J.   West Bromwich Albion   Gillingham
11 Edmondson, Darren S.   Huddersfield Town   Plymouth Argyle
18 Hale, Matthew J.   Bristol City   Dorchester Town
17 Hartfield, Charles J.   Swansea City   Lincoln City
25 Hathaway, Ian A.   Colchester United   Aldershot Town
25 Hecklingbottom, Paul   Sunderland   Hartlepool United
25 Holt, Michael A.   Preston North End   Macclesfield Town
25 Larusson, Bjarnolfur   Hibernian   Walsall
18 Mackay, Malcolm   Celtic   Norwich City
24 Matthews, Lee J.   Leeds United   Notts County
 8 McCormick, Steven   Dundee   Leyton Orient
25 McGregor, Paul A.   Nottingham Forest   Carlisle United
14 McIntyre, Kevin   Tranmere Rovers   Doncaster Rovers
13 Mimms, Robert A.   Rotherham United   York City
25 Monk, Garry A.   Southampton   Torquay United
17 Parks, Anthony   Burnley   Barrow
 4 Reeve, Daniel J.   Colchester United   Heybridge Swifts
18 Saville, Andrew V.   Cardiff City   Hull City
17 Simpson, Paul D.   Wolverhampton Wanderers   Walsall
25 Smith, Peter L.   Crewe Alexandra   Macclesfield Town
15 Statham, Brian   Gillingham   Woking

15 Sturgess, Paul C. | Millwall | Brighton & Hove Albion
15 Ward, Gavin J. | Bolton Wanderers | Burnley
17 Winstanley, Mark A. | Burnley | Shrewsbury Town

October 1998
23 Arnott, Andrew J. | Fulham | Brighton & Hove Albion
23 Barnes, Steven L. | Birmingham City | Barnet
26 Beall, Matthew J. | Cambridge United | Leyton Orient
30 Blake, Nathan A. | Bolton Wanderers | Blackburn Rovers
21 Boli, Roger Z. | Dundee United | AFC Bournemouth
28 Brannan, Gerald D. | Manchester City | Motherwell
30 Broughton, Drewe O. | Norwich City | Brentford
29 Butler, Stephen | Gillingham | Peterborough United
 2 Caffel, Jason R. | Oxford City | Whitney Town
 9 Conlon, Barry J. | Manchester City | Southend United
23 Dyer, Bruce A. | Crystal Palace | Barnsley
 1 Froggatt, Stephen J. | Wolverhampton Wanderers | Coventry City
24 Gregg, Matthew S. | Torquay United | Crystal Palace
 2 Haworth, Simon O. | Coventry City | Wigan Athletic
23 Heggs, Carl S. | Northampton Town | Rushden & Diamonds
12 Hodgson, Douglas J. | Oldham Athletic | Northampton Town
12 Horsfield, Geoffrey M. | Halifax Town | Fulham
 9 Jones, David J. | Blackpool | Doncaster Rovers
 2 Lawrence, Matthew J. | Fulham | Wycombe Wanderers
15 Liddell, Andrew M. | Barnsley | Wigan Athletic
 5 Marriott, Andrew | Wrexham | Sunderland
16 Mathie, Alexander | Ipswich Town | Dundee United
16 Mimms, Robert A. | Rotherham United | York City
23 Morgan, Philip J. | Macclesfield Town | Hednesford Town
 7 Savage, David T. | Millwall | Northampton Town
15 Sonner, Daniel J. | Ipswich Town | Sheffield Wednesday
 9 Taylor, Scott J. | Bolton Wanderers | Tranmere Rovers
 8 Thomas, Roderick C. | Chester City | Brighton & Hove Albion
23 Warburton, Raymond | Northampton Town | Rushden & Diamonds
15 Watson, Stephen C. | Newcastle United | Aston Villa
14 Watts, Stephen | Fisher Athletic | Leyton Orient

Temporary transfers
22 Allen, Christopher A. | Nottingham Forest | Cardiff City
 2 Andrews, Wayne M.H. | Watford | Cambridge United
20 Arber, Mark A. | Tottenham Hotspur | Barnet
11 Beardsley, Peter A. | Bolton Wanderers | Fulham
29 Bradbury, Lee M. | Manchester City | Crystal Palace
29 Branch, Paul M. | Everton | Manchester City
 2 Breacker, Timothy S. | West Ham United | Queens Park Rangers
18 Casper, Christopher M. | Manchester United | Reading
30 Cooke, Terence J. | Manchester United | Wrexham
19 Crittenden, Nicholas J. | Chelsea | Plymouth Argyle
23 Dennis, Kevin J. | Brentford | Chesham United
29 Desouza, Juan M.I. | Peterborough United | Rochdale
23 Devlin, Paul J. | Sheffield United | Notts County
16 Earnshaw, Mark W. | Oldham Athletic | Blyth Spartans
23 Elliott, Stuart T. | Newcastle United | Gillingham
 8 Fortune-West, Leo O. | Lincoln City | Rotherham United
16 Guinan, Stephen | Nottingham Forest | Halifax Town
19 Hale, Matthew | Bristol City | Dorchester Town
16 Hamilton, Derick V. | Newcastle United | Sheffield United
 9 Hodgson, Douglas J.H. | Oldham Athletic | Northampton Town
20 Hunt, Jonathan R. | Derby County | Ipswich Town
23 Ifejiagwa, Emeka | Charlton Athletic | Brighton & Hove Albion
29 Jackson, Mark G. | Leeds United | Huddersfield Town
16 Lambert, Christopher J.P. | Reading | Walsall
23 Landon, Richard J. | Macclesfield Town | Nuneaton Borough
15 Legg, Andrew | Reading | Peterborough United
16 Lough, Lee A. | Luton Town | Ashford Town
29 McKenzie, Leon M. | Crystal Palace | Peterborough United
 2 Miklosko, Ludek | West Ham United | Queens Park Rangers
30 Moore, Alan | Middlesbrough | Barnsley
30 Morrish, Adam | Southend United | Dartford
29 Morrison, Andrew C. | Huddersfield Town | Manchester City

8 Nixon, Eric W.   Stockport County   Wigan Athletic
21 Oatway, Anthony   Brentford   Lincoln City
31 O'Kane, John A.   Everton   Burnley
31 Ormshaw, Gareth D.   Crystal Palace   Maidenhead United
30 Perkins, Christopher P.   Southend United   Purfleet
27 Plummer, Dwane J.   Bristol City   Stevenage Borough
29 Raven, Paul D.   West Bromwich Albion   Rotherham United
17 Robson, Mark A.   Notts County   Wycombe Wanderers
 6 Simpson, Colin R.   Leyton Orient   Boreham Wood
26 Smith, Peter L.   Crewe Alexandra   Macclesfield Town
30 Smith, Philip A.   Millwall   Bromley
30 Spooner, Nicholas M.   Bolton Wanderers   Oldham Athletic
18 Sturgess, Paul C.   Millwall   Brighton & Hove Albion
16 Taylor, Craig   Swindon Town   Plymouth Argyle
21 Thom, Stuart P.   Nottingham Forest   Oldham Athletic
 2 Vernazza, Paolo A.   Arsenal   Ipswich Town
16 Whittaker, David A.   Crewe Alexandra   Belper Town
16 Williams, Anthony S.   Blackburn Rovers   Macclesfield Town
 9 Wilson, Paul R.   Barnet   Aldershot Town
18 Winstanley, Mark A.   Burnley   Shrewsbury Town

November 1998
 3 Ainsworth, Gareth   Port Vale   Wimbledon
19 Arber, Mark A.   Tottenham Hotspur   Barnet
 4 Bradbury, Lee M.   Manchester City   Crystal Palace
17 Broughton, Drewe O.   Brentford   Peterborough United
 4 Casper, Christopher M.   Manchester United   Reading
19 Crichton, Paul A.   West Bromwich Albion   Burnley
25 Ferguson, Duncan   Everton   Newcastle United
13 Finnan, Stephen J.   Notts County   Fulham
17 Fortune-West, Leopold O.   Lincoln City   Brentford
17 Hayles, Barrington E.   Bristol Rovers   Fulham
25 Impey, Andrew R.   West Ham United   Leicester City
13 Littlejohn, Adrian S.   Oldham Athletic   Bury
12 Matthews, Robert D.   Bury   Stockport County
27 McCann, Gavin P.   Everton   Sunderland
 5 McSporran, Jermaine   Oxford City   Wycombe Wanderers
 6 Morrison, Andrew C.   Huddersfield Town   Manchester City
26 Pepper, Colin N.   Bradford City   Aberdeen
11 Petric, Gordon   Rangers   Crystal Palace
18 Plummer, Dwayne   Bristol City   Stevenage Borough
 5 Reilly, Mark   Reading   Kilmarnock
20 Scott, Robert   Fulham   Rotherham United
 6 Sturgess, Paul C.   Millwall   Brighton & Hove Albion
26 Taylor, Gareth K.   Sheffield United   Manchester City
 6 Thom, Stuart P.   Nottingham Forest   Oldham Athletic
 6 Whelan, Spencer R.   Chester City   Shrewsbury Town
27 Whittle, Justin P.   Stoke City   Hull City
27 Williams, Gareth J.   Scarborough   Hull City

Temporary transfers
 7 Adams, Kieran C.   Barnet   Chesham United
27 Aiston, Sam J.   Sunderland   Chester City
12 Amaral, Neto (Edinho)   Bradford City   Dunfermline Athletic
27 Beech, Christopher S.   Hartlepool United   Huddersfield Town
20 Branston, Guy P.B.   Leicester City   Plymouth Argyle
27 Brookes, Darren P.   Doncaster Rovers   Worksop Town
26 Brown, Simon J.   Tottenham Hotspur   Gravesend & Northfleet
20 Browning, Marcus T.   Huddersfield Town   Gillingham
26 Bunn, James T.   Tottenham Hotspur   Gravesend & Northfleet
 6 Byfield, Darren   Aston Villa   Preston North End
19 Clement, Neil   Chelsea   Reading
10 Crowe, Jason W.R.   Arsenal   Crystal Palace
29 Devlin, Paul J.   Sheffield United   Notts County
13 Dobie, Robert S.   Carlisle United   Clydebank
 9 Dublin, Keith B.L.   Southend United   Colchester United
10 Dudley, Craig B.   Notts County   Hull City
19 Earnshaw, Mark W.   Oldham Athletic   Blyth Spartans
20 Elliott, Stuart T.   Newcastle United   Gillingham
13 Fenn, Neale M.C.   Tottenham Hotspur   Swindon Town

21 Follett, Richard J. | Nottingham Forest | King's Lynn
26 Gibson, Paul R. | Manchester United | Hull City
16 Guinan, Stephen | Nottingham Forest | Halifax Town
27 Hewlett, Paul M. | Bristol City | Burnley
20 Hodges, Lee L. | West Ham United | Ipswich Town
26 Holsgrove, Lee | Wycombe Wanderers | Aldershot Town
16 Holt, Michael A. | Preston North End | Rochdale
20 Houghton, Scott A. | Peterborough United | Southend United
 6 Howey, Lee M. | Burnley | Northampton Town
 6 Jackson, Justin J. | Notts County | Morecambe
12 Jones, Stuart C. | Sheffield Wednesday | Crewe Alexandra
 6 Lawson, Ian J. | Huddersfield Town | Blackpool
27 Lee, Alan D. | Aston Villa | Torquay United
25 Linighan, Brian | Bury | Cambridge City
30 Lovelock, Andrew J. | Crewe Alexandra | Witton Albion
27 Low, Joshua D. | Bristol Rovers | Farnborough Town
20 Lyttle, Desmond | Nottingham Forest | Port Vale
20 McGregor, Paul A. | Nottingham Forest | Carlisle United
 5 McInnes, Derek | Rangers | Stockport County
27 McIntyre, Kevin | Tranmere Rovers | Barrow
30 McKenzie, Leon M. | Crystal Palace | Peterborough United
18 Mendes, Junior | St Mirren | Carlisle United
24 Miklosko, Ludek | West Ham United | Queens Park Rangers
30 Morrish, Adam | Southend United | Dartford
18 Newsome, Jon | Sheffield Wednesday | Bolton Wanderers
26 O'Kane, John A. | Everton | Burnley
29 Ormshaw, Gareth D. | Crystal Palace | Maidenhead United
13 Petterson, Andrew K. | Charlton Athletic | Portsmouth
20 Rapley, Kevin J. | Brentford | Southend United
30 Raven, Paul D. | West Bromwich Albion | Rotherham United
27 Simpson, Colin R. | Leyton Orient | Sutton United
24 Smith, Peter L. | Crewe Alexandra | Macclesfield Town
 6 Steiner, Robert H. | Bradford City | Queens Park Rangers
12 Theobald, David J. | Ipswich Town | Braintree Town
25 Warhurst, Paul | Crystal Palace | Bolton Wanderers
 5 Warne, Paul | Wigan Athletic | Kettering Town
 3 Whittingham, Guy | Sheffield Wednesday | Wolverhampton Wanderers
 6 Wilder, Christopher J. | Sheffield United | Northampton Town
 3 Wilkins, Ian J. | Lincoln City | Grantham Town
 5 Williams, Paul R.C. | Gillingham | Bury

December 1998

18 Aloisi, John | Portsmouth | Coventry City
 9 Batty, David | Newcastle United | Leeds United
 1 Blatherwick, Steven S. | Burnley | Chesterfield
31 Branch, Graham | Stockport County | Burnley
17 Davies, Simon I. | Luton Town | Macclesfield Town
31 Davis, Stephen M. | Luton Town | Burnley
 9 De Souza, Juan M. | Peterborough United | Rushden & Diamonds
18 Gillespie, Keith R. | Newcastle United | Blackburn Rovers
 9 Hanlon, Ritchie K. | Rushden & Diamonds | Peterborough United
16 Healy, Brian | Morecambe | Torquay United
24 Hope, Richard P. | Darlington | Northampton Town
23 Houghton, Scott A. | Peterborough United | Southend United
30 Jenkinson, Leigh | Wigan Athletic | Heart of Midlothian
18 Kelly, Raymond | Manchester City | Bohemians
10 Marsh, Simon T. | Oxford United | Birmingham City
30 Miklosko, Ludek | West Ham United | Queens Park Rangers
16 Oakes, Andrew M. | Winsford United | Hull City
18 Perry, Jason | Lincoln City | Hull City
17 Pickering, Albert G. | Stoke City | Burnley
 4 Taricco, Mauricio R. | Ipswich Town | Tottenham Hotspur
18 Tweed, Steven | Stoke City | Dundee
31 Ward, Ashley S. | Barnsley | Blackburn Rovers
 1 Whitehead, Philip M. | Oxford United | West Bromwich Albion
18 Whitney, John D. | Lincoln City | Hull City
10 Williams, Paul R.C. | Gillingham | Bury

Temporary transfers

 3 Abou, Samassi | West Ham United | Ipswich Town

11 Adams, Kieran C.	Barnet	Chesham United
27 Aiston, Sam J.	Sunderland	Chester City
23 Allen, Lee S.	Leicester City	King's Lynn
7 Beavers, Paul M.	Sunderland	Shrewsbury Town
17 Boylan, Lee M.	West Ham United	Kingstonian
11 Brabin, Gary	Blackpool	Lincoln City
22 Branston, Guy	Leicester City	Plymouth Argyle
27 Brookes, Darren P.	Doncaster Rovers	Worksop Town
4 Burton, Deon J.	Derby County	Barnsley
4 Byfield, Darren	Aston Villa	Preston North End
10 Campbell, Andrew P.	Middlesbrough	Sheffield United
12 Conroy, Michael K.	Blackpool	Chester City
18 Dawson, Andrew	Nottingham Forest	Scunthorpe United
18 Dobbin, James	Grimsby Town	Southport
10 Dudley, Craig B.	Notts County	Hull City
18 Earnshaw, Mark W.	Oldham Athletic	Blyth Spartans
11 Edwards, Christian N.H.	Nottingham Forest	Bristol City
27 Emsden, Nigel G.	Basingstoke Town	Oxford City
18 Faulconbridge, Craig M.	Coventry City	Hull City
31 Fenn, Neale M.C.	Tottenham Hotspur	Lincoln City
8 Foley, Dominic J.	Wolverhampton Wanderers	Notts County
23 Follett, Richard J.	Nottingham Forest	King's Lynn
18 Forinton, Howard L.	Birmingham City	Plymouth Argyle
24 French, James R.	Bristol Rovers	Newport AFC
31 Gain, Peter	Tottenham Hotspur	Lincoln City
18 Gerrard, Paul W.	Everton	Oxford United
1 Graham, Gareth L.	Crystal Palace	Merthyr Tydfil
24 Grant, Kim T.	Millwall	Notts County
22 Gray, David	Rochdale	Chorley
11 Greenacre, Christopher M.	Manchester City	Scarborough
15 Guinan, Stephen	Nottingham Forest	Halifax Town
24 Harrison, Gerald R.	Sunderland	Luton Town
18 Hayter, James E.	AFC Bournemouth	Salisbury City
29 Holsgrove, Lee	Wycombe Wanderers	Aldershot Town
16 Holt, Michael A.	Preston North End	Rochdale
18 Hope, Richard P.	Darlington	Northampton Town
6 Howey, Lee M.	Burnley	Northampton Town
17 Hughes, John P.	Chelsea	Stockport County
17 Jelleyman, Gareth A.	Peterborough United	Boston United
12 Jones, Stuart C.	Sheffield Wednesday	Crewe Alexandra
18 Key, Lance W.	Rochdale	Northwich Victoria
7 Landon, Richard J.	Macclesfield Town	Atherstone United
27 Lee, Alan D.	Aston Villa	Torquay United
23 Linighan, Brian	Bury	Cambridge City
23 Lyttle, Desmond	Nottingham Forest	Port Vale
4 Mason, Philip	Aylesbury United	Oxford City
24 McConnell, Barry	Exeter City	Weston-Super-Mare
18 McGuckin, Thomas I.	Fulham	Hartlepool United
31 McIntyre, Kevin	Tranmere Rovers	Doncaster Rovers
11 McKeever, Mark	Sheffield Wednesday	Bristol Rovers
1 Martin, Andrew P.	Crystal Palace	Merthyr Tyfil
4 Morrisey, Terence	Oxford City	Abingdon Town
11 Naylor, Stuart W.	Bristol City	Mansfield Town
8 Oakes, Andrew M.	Winsford United	Hull City
11 Patterson, Mark A.	Bury	Blackpool
11 Perkins, Christopher P.	Southend United	Dartford
14 Petterson, Andrew K.	Charlton Athletic	Portsmouth
11 Power, Lee M.	Plymouth Argyle	Halifax Town
23 Quailey, Brian S.	West Bromwich Albion	Exeter City
31 Rainford, David J.	Colchester United	Scarborough
22 Rapley, Kevin J.	Brentford	Southend United
11 Salmon, Michael B.	Charlton Athletic	Oxford United
28 Simpson, Colin	Leyton Orient	Sutton United
11 Simpson, Paul D.	Wolverhampton Wanderers	Walsall
4 Steiner, Robert	Bradford City	Queens Park Rangers
30 Walker, Richard M.	Aston Villa	Cambridge United
24 Warren, Mark W.	Leyton Orient	Oxford United
18 Watts, Julian	Bristol City	Lincoln City
11 Weaver, Luke D.S.	Sunderland	Scarborough
31 Webster, Colin J.L.	Crewe Alexandra	Congleton Town

  2 Whittingham, Guy   Sheffield Wednesday   Wolverhampton Wanderers
 24 Winstanley, Mark A.   Burnley   Scunthorpe United
  8 Wright, Andrew J.   Leeds United   Reading

January 1999
 27 Beech, Christopher S.   Hartlepool United   Huddersfield Town
 15 Bent, Marcus N.   Crystal Palace   Port Vale
  8 Brabin, Gary   Blackpool   Hull City
 22 Campbell, Neil A.   Scarborough   Southend United
 28 Di Canio, Paolo   Sheffield Wednesday   West Ham United
 28 Francis, Stephen S.   Huddersfield Town   Northampton Town
 29 Griffin, Charles   Chippenham Town   Swindon Town
 15 Gurney, Andrew R.   Torquay United   Reading
 15 Hartson, John   West Ham United   Wimbledon
 16 Holt, Michael A.   Preston North End   Rochdale
 19 Jansen, Matthew B.   Crystal Palace   Blackburn Rovers
 28 McAteer, Jason W.   Liverpool   Blackburn Rovers
 19 McIntyre, Kevin   Tranmere Rovers   Doncaster Rovers
  8 Mellon, Michael J.   Tranmere Rovers   Burnley
 21 Palmer, Carlton L.   Southampton   Nottingham Forest
 21 Peacock, Richard J.   Hull City   Lincoln City
 14 Pennant, Jermaine   Notts County   Arsenal
 14 Power, Lee M.   Plymouth Argyle   Halifax Town
  4 Rougier, Anthony L.   Hibernian   Port Vale
 27 Sheron, Michael N.   Queens Park Rangers   Barnsley
  8 Souter, Ryan J.   Weston-Super-Mare   Bury
  4 Staton, Luke R.   Blackburn Rovers   Bolton Wanderers
 15 Tait, Paul   Birmingham City   Oxford United
 15 Thomson, Andrew J.   Portsmouth   Bristol Rovers
  7 Warhurst, Paul   Crystal Palace   Bolton Wanderers
 15 Warne, Paul   Wigan Athletic   Rotherham United
 28 Warren, Mark W.   Leyton Orient   Notts County
 28 Woodman, Andrew J.   Northampton Town   Brentford
  4 Zahana-Oni, Landry   Bromley   Luton Town

Temporary transfers
 14 Adams, Kieran C.   Barnet   Billericay Town
 25 Albert, Philippe   Newcastle United   Fulham
 29 Allen, Lee S.   Leicester City   King's Lynn
 29 Bailey, Alan   Manchester City   Macclesfield Town
 29 Beckett, Duane L.   Doncaster Rovers   Spennymoor United
 14 Bolland, Paul G.   Bradford City   Notts County
  8 Bonner, Mark   Cardiff City   Hull City
  7 Booty, Martyn J.   Reading   Southend United
 20 Branston, Guy   Leicester City   Plymouth Argyle
 28 Brookes, Darren P.   Doncaster Rovers   Worksop Town
  4 Brown, Greg J.   Macclesfield Town   Chorley
 13 Campbell, Andrew P.   Middlesbrough   Sheffield United
 13 Campbell, James R.   Peterborough United   Wisbech Town
  9 Canoville, Dean   Millwall   Walton & Hersham
 29 Carruthers, Martin G.   Peterborough United   York City
 29 Claridge, Robert R.   Bristol Rovers   Weston-Super-Mare
 15 Clarke, Andrew W.   Wimbledon   Northampton Town
 29 Cleaver, Christopher W.   Peterborough United   Grantham Town
 18 Clement, Neil   Chelsea   Reading
 11 Conroy, Michael K.   Blackpool   Chester City
 15 Cooke, Terence J.   Manchester United   Manchester City
 17 Dawson, Andrew   Nottingham Forest   Scunthorpe United
 15 Duffield, Peter   Falkirk   Darlington
  4 Dyche, Sean M.   Bristol City   Luton Town
 29 Elliott, Stuart T.   Newcastle United   Hartlepool United
 19 Forinton, Howard L.   Birmingham City   Plymouth Argyle
 29 Gerrard, Paul W.   Everton   Oxford United
 24 Grant, Kim T.   Millwall   Notts County
 20 Gray, David   Rochdale   Chorley
 12 Greenacre, Christopher   Manchester City   Scarborough
 13 Griffiths, Carl B.   Leyton Orient   Wrexham
 28 Harewood, Marlon A.   Nottingham Forest   Ipswich Town
 15 Harrison, Craig   Middlesbrough   Preston North End
 24 Harrison, Gerald R.   Sunderland   Luton Town

18 Hayter, James E.   AFC Bournemouth   Salisbury City
 7 Howey, Lee M.   Burnley   Northampton Town
12 Hughes, John P.   Chelsea   Stockport County
 8 Jackson, John   Middlesbrough   Bishop Auckland
21 Jackson, Justin J.   Notts County   Rotherham United
 8 Lawson, Ian J.   Huddersfield Town   Blackpool
22 Longworth, Steven P.   Blackpool   Lancaster City
 9 Lovelock, Andrew J.   Crewe Alexandra   Witton Albion
15 Magilton, James   Sheffield Wednesday   Ipswich Town
 8 Mardon, Paul J.   West Bromwich Albion   Oldham Athletic
15 McGuckin, Thomas I.   Fulham   Hartlepool United
11 McKeever, Mark   Sheffield Wednesday   Bristol Rovers
 1 Morrish, Adam   Southend United   Dartford
15 Naylor, Stuart W.   Bristol City   Mansfield Town
19 Ormerod, Anthony   Middlesbrough   Carlisle United
 1 Ormshaw, Gareth D.   Crystal Palace   Maidenhead United
11 Patterson, Mark A.   Bury   Blackpool
15 Perkins, Christopher P. Southend United   Dartford
14 Petterson, Andrew K.   Charlton Athletic   Portsmouth
27 Quailey, Brian S.   West Bromwich Albion   Exeter City
27 Rapley, Kevin J.   Brentford   Southend United
19 Rimmer, Stephen A.   Manchester City   Doncaster Rovers
29 Russell, Craig S.   Manchester City   Port Vale
29 Scott, Kevin W.   Norwich City   Darlington
29 Simpson, Philip M.   Barnet   Farnborough Town
29 Strodder, Gary J.   Notts County   Rotherham United
18 Swailes, Daniel   Bury   Gainsborough Trinity
12 Weaver, Luke D.S.   Sunderland   Scarborough
14 Whitley, Jeffrey   Manchester City   Wrexham
28 Whittingham, Guy   Sheffield Wednesday   Portsmouth
 7 Williams, Anthony S.   Blackburn Rovers   Macclesfield Town
15 Williamson, Michael P.   Crewe Alexandra   Congleton Town
22 Woodman, Andrew J.   Northampton Town   Brentford

February 1999
26 Armstrong, Steven C.   Nottingham Forest   Huddersfield Town
18 Beadle, Peter C.   Port Vale   Notts County
10 Breacker, Timothy S.   West Ham United   Queens Park Rangers
15 Bullock, Darren J.   Swindon Town   Bury
19 Collins, Lee D.   Aston Villa   Stoke City
 4 Crowe, Glen M.   Wolverhampton Wanderers   Plymouth Argyle
18 Ellington, Nathan   Walton & Hersham   Bristol Rovers
 3 Ellis, Anthony J.   Bury   Stockport County
26 Fortune-West, Leo O.   Brentford   Rotherham United
 5 Gunnlaugsson, Arnar B.   Bolton Wanderers   Leicester City
24 Hillier, David   Portsmouth   Bristol Rovers
24 Howard, Steven J.   Hartlepool United   Northampton Town
19 Howey, Lee M.   Burnley   Northampton Town
 5 Hyde, Graham   Sheffield Wednesday   Birmingham City
11 Jackson, Justin J.   Notts County   Halifax Town
12 Johnrose, Leonard   Bury   Burnley
17 Marinkov, Alexandre   Scarborough   Hibernian
 2 Marsden, Christopher   Birmingham City   Southampton
19 McNamee, David   St Mirren   Blackburn Rovers
19 O'Brien, Burton   St Mirren   Blackburn Rovers
19 Partridge, Scott M.   Torquay United   Brentford
19 Pethick, Robert J.   Portsmouth   Bristol Rovers
25 Rapley, Kevin J.   Brentford   Notts County
 5 Roberts, Darren A.   Darlington   Scarborough
 5 Sherwood, Tim A.   Blackburn Rovers   Tottenham Hotspur
19 Simpson, Philip M.   Barnet   Yeovil Town
25 Strodder, Gary J.   Notts County   Hartlepool United
25 Ward, Gavin J.   Bolton Wanderers   Stoke City

Temporary transfers
15 Adams, Kieran C.   Barnet   Billericay Town
13 Aiston, Sam J.   Sunderland   Chester City
22 Albert, Phillipe   Newcastle United   Fulham
 4 Alcide, Colin J.   Lincoln City   Hull City
24 Allen, Bradley J.   Charlton Athletic   Colchester United

26 Allen, Lee S.	Leicester City	King's Lynn
5 Andrews, Wayne M.H.	Watford	Peterborough United
10 Aspinall, Warren	Brentford	Colchester United
27 Bankole, Ademola	Queens Park Rangers	Grimsby Town
19 Barrick, Dean	Bury	Ayr United
5 Basham, Steven	Southampton	Preston North End
14 Bolland, Paul G.	Bradford City	Notts County
19 Brown, Simon J.	Tottenham Hotspur	Aylesbury United
19 Brown, Stephen R.	Macclesfield Town	Dover Athletic
12 Campbell, James R.	Peterborough United	Cambridge City
15 Canoville, Dean	Millwall	Walton & Hersham
15 Cowe, Steven M.	Swindon Town	Hereford United
27 Cramb, Colin	Bristol City	Walsall
26 Critchley, Neil	Crewe Alexandra	Winsford United
17 Dawson, Andrew	Nottingham Forest	Scunthorpe United
5 Dearden, Kevin C.	Brentford	Barnet
5 Dennis, Kevin J.	Brentford	Welling United
26 Denys, Ryan H.	Brentford	Carshalton Athletic
7 Dyche, Sean M.	Bristol City	Luton Town
15 Earnshaw, Robert	Cardiff City	Middlesbrough
10 Eastwood, Philip J.	Burnley	Kettering Town
4 Etherington, Craig	West Ham United	Halifax Town
5 Goodlad, Mark	Nottingham Forest	Scarborough
12 Grant, Gareth M.	Bradford City	Halifax Town
23 Gray, Andrew D.	Nottingham Forest	Preston North End
12 Gregg, Matthew S.	Crystal Palace	Swansea City
12 Greenacre, Christopher	Manchester City	Scarborough
18 Hall, Paul A.	Coventry City	Bury
15 Hamilton, Derick V.	Newcastle United	Huddersfield Town
26 Harries, Paul G.	Crystal Palace	Torquay United
23 Howard, Steven J.	Hartlepool United	Northampton Town
12 Hunter, Barry V.	Reading	Southend United
25 Jones, Mark C.	Aylesbury United	Oxford City
26 Longworth, Steven P.	Blackpool	Accrington Stanley
12 Lydiate, Jason L.	Scarborough	Rochdale
11 McKinnon, Robert	Heart of Midlothian	Hartlepool United
18 Magilton, James	Sheffield Wednesday	Ipswich Town
13 Mahoney-Johnson, Michael A.	Queens Park Rangers	Aylesbury United
7 Mardon, Paul	West Bromwich Albion	Oldham Athletic
26 Marker, Nicholas R.T.	Sheffield United	Plymouth Argyle
18 Mason, Michael	Macclesfield Town	Burton Albion
19 Morrish, Adam	Southend United	Witham Town
12 Murphy, Daniel B.	Liverpool	Crewe Alexandra
26 Nicholls, Kevin J.R.	Charlton Athletic	Brighton & Hove Albion
12 Perkins, Christopher P.	Southend United	Dartford
24 Phillips, Martin J.	Portsmouth	Bristol Rovers
19 Quayle, Mark L.	Notts County	Grantham Town
23 Rapley, Kevin J.	Brentford	Notts County
26 Roach, Neville	Reading	Southend United
12 Roberts, Ben J.	Middlesbrough	Millwall
18 Serrant, Carl	Newcastle United	Bury
23 Shepherd, Paul	Leeds United	Tranmere Rovers
11 Simpson, Colin R.	Leyton Orient	Farnborough Town
12 Statham, Brian	Gillingham	Stevenage Borough
16 Stoker, Gareth	Cardiff City	Rochdale
2 Strevens, Benjamin J.	Barnet	Wingate & Finchley
17 Swailes, Daniel	Bury	Gainsborough Trinity
5 Thorpe, Anthony L.	Bristol City	Reading
26 Tosh, Paul J.	Hibernian	Exeter City
5 Vaughan, Wayne S.	Tottenham Hotspur	Witham Town
1 Webster, Colin J.	Crewe Alexandra	Congleton Town
26 Whittaker, David A.	Crewe Alexandra	Winsford United
26 Wright, Thomas J.	Manchester City	Wrexham

March 1999

31 Adams, Kieran C.	Barnet	Billericay Town
10 Alcide, Colin J.	Lincoln City	Hull City
25 Alexander, Graham	Luton Town	Preston North End
19 Andrews, Bradley J.	Norwich City	Bristol Rovers

25 Banks, Steven | Blackpool | Bolton Wanderers
15 Barnes, Paul L. | Huddersfield Town | Bury
25 Barras, Anthony | York City | Reading
26 Beck, Mikkel | Middlesbrough | Derby County
19 Berthe, Mohamed | AFC Bournemouth | Heart of Midlothian
25 Boertien, Paul | Carlisle United | Derby County
12 Borbokis, Vassilis | Sheffield United | Derby County
24 Brammer, David | Wrexham | Port Vale
25 Browning, Marcus T. | Huddersfield Town | Gillingham
25 Butler, Philip A. | Blackpool | Port Vale
25 Caig, Antony | Carlisle United | Blackpool
24 Calderwood, Colin | Tottenham Hotspur | Aston Villa
25 Carruthers, Martin G. | Peterborough United | Darlington
23 Carsley, Lee K. | Derby County | Blackburn Rovers
24 Couzens, Andrew J. | Carlisle United | Blackpool
17 Cowan, Thomas | Huddersfield Town | Burnley
26 Cresswell, Richard P.W. | York City | Sheffield Wednesday
25 Darlington, Jermaine C. | Aylesbury United | Queens Park Rangers
19 Dawson, Andrew | Nottingham Forest | Scunthorpe United
 3 Day, James R. | Arsenal | AFC Bournemouth
10 Delaney, Mark A. | Cardiff City | Aston Villa
25 Dudley, Craig B. | Notts County | Oldham Athletic
 3 Evans, Paul D. | Shrewsbury Town | Brentford
25 Evers, Sean A. | Luton Town | Reading
25 Finney, Stephen K. | Carlisle United | Leyton Orient
26 Freestone, Christopher M. | Northampton Town | Hartlepool United
26 Gain, Peter | Tottenham Hotspur | Lincoln City
25 Gemmill, Scot | Nottingham Forest | Everton
25 Gibson, Paul R. | Manchester United | Notts County
25 Griffiths, Carl B. | Leyton Orient | Port Vale
26 Hendon, Ian M. | Notts County | Northampton Town
 5 Himsworth, Gary P. | York City | Darlington
23 Holdsworth, David G. | Sheffield United | Birmingham City
26 Huck, William R.F. | Arsenal | AFC Bournemouth
 2 Hughes, Daniel P. | Wolverhampton Wanderers | Hartlepool United
12 Hunt, Jonathan R. | Derby County | Sheffield United
25 Jackson, Richard | Scarborough | Derby County
10 Jones, Gary | Notts County | Hartlepool United
 8 Kavanagh, Jason C. | Wycombe Wanderers | Stoke City
12 Kozluk, Robert | Derby County | Sheffield United
23 Magilton, James | Sheffield Wednesday | Ipswich Town
24 McGregor, Paul A. | Nottingham Forest | Preston North End
25 McLaren, Andrew | Dundee United | Reading
 3 Mohan, Nicholas | Wycombe Wanderers | Stoke City
31 Moore, Craig A. | Crystal Palace | Rangers
26 Mulryne, Philip P. | Manchester United | Norwich City
19 O'Neill, Keith P. | Norwich City | Middlesbrough
25 Phillips, David O. | Huddersfield Town | Lincoln City
 1 Roach, Neville | Reading | Southend United
24 Scott, Keith | Wycombe Wanderers | Reading
26 Scott, Philip C. | St Johnstone | Sheffield Wednesday
25 Smith, Alexander P. | Chester City | Port Vale
 3 Stallard, Mark | Wycombe Wanderers | Notts County
 6 Stoker, Gareth | Cardiff City | Rochdale
12 Stone, Steven B. | Nottingham Forest | Aston Villa
24 Stuart, Graham C. | Sheffield United | Charlton Athletic
25 Tracey, Richard S. | Rotherham United | Carlisle United
25 Vincent, Jamie R. | AFC Bournemouth | Huddersfield Town
12 Watson, Andrew | Garforth Town | Doncaster Rovers
25 Weare, Ross | East Ham United | Queens Park Rangers
 3 Wicks, Matthew J. | Crewe Alexandra | Peterborough United
22 Williams, Daniel I.L. | Liverpool | Wrexham
19 Williams, Marc L. | Halifax Town | York City
 5 Windass, Dean | Oxford United | Bradford City
10 Wright, Benjamin | Kettering Town | Bristol City

Temporary transfers
18 Adams, Kieran C. | Barnet | Billericay Town
26 Adcock, Anthony C. | Colchester United | Heybridge Swifts
25 Albert, Philippe | Newcastle United | Fulham

9 Alcide, Colin J.	Lincoln City	Hull City
11 Aspinall, Warren	Brentford	Colchester United
30 Avdiu, Kemasl	Bury	Partick Thistle
25 Bagshaw, Paul J.	Barnsley	Carlisle United
30 Bailey, Alan	Manchester City	Macclesfield Town
19 Berkeley, Dominic A.	Macclesfield Town	Kettering Town
19 Barras, Anthony	York City	Reading
31 Bartley, Daniel R.	West Ham United	Dorchester Town
7 Basham, Steven	Southampton	Preston North End
25 Beavers, Paul M.	Sunderland	Oldham Athletic
3 Berthe, Mohamed	AFC Bournemouth	Brentford
17 Bolland, Paul G.	Bradford City	Notts County
25 Bradbury, Lee M.	Crystal Palace	Birmingham City
25 Bradley, Shayne	Southampton	Swindon Town
18 Branston, Guy	Leicester City	Rushden & Diamonds
5 Bridge-Wilkinson, Marc	Derby County	Carlisle United
31 Briscoe, Anthony M.	Shrewsbury Town	Tamworth
5 Brown, Greg J.	Macclesfield Town	Morecambe
22 Brown, Simon J.	Tottenham Hotspur	Aylesbury United
25 Bruce, Paul M.	Queens Park Rangers	Cambridge United
19 Butler, Stephen	Peterborough United	Stevenage Borough
25 Cadette, Nathan D.	Cardiff City	Merthyr Tydfil
25 Campbell, Andrew P.	Middlesbrough	Sheffield United
1 Carruthers, Martin G.	Peterborough United	York City
2 Claridge, Robert R.	Bristol Rovers	Weston-Super-Mare
1 Cleaver, Christopher W.	Peterborough United	Grantham Town
25 Clement, Neil	Chelsea	Preston North End
2 Collett, Andrew A.	Bristol Rovers	Rushden & Diamonds
25 Connor, Paul	Middlesbrough	Stoke City
25 Conroy, Michael K.	Blackpool	Chester City
12 Cook, Paul A.	Stockport County	Burnley
25 Cornwall, Lucas C.	Fulham	Queens Park Rangers
5 Couzens, Andrew J.	Carlisle United	Blackpool
12 Cowan, Thomas	Huddersfield Town	Burnley
14 Cowe, Steven M.	Swindon Town	Hereford United
25 Coyne, Christopher	West Ham United	Southend United
28 Critchley, Neil	Crewe Alexandra	Winsford United
25 Dalglish, Paul	Newcastle United	Norwich City
25 Darby, Duane A.	Notts County	Hull City
11 Dearden, Kevin C.	Brentford	Huddersfield Town
8 Dennis, Kevin J.	Brentford	Welling United
26 Denys, Ryan H.	Brentford	Carshalton Athletic
18 Devine, Sean T.	Barnet	Wycombe Wanderers
31 Douglas, Andrew R.	Sheffield Wednesday	Slough Town
3 Dublin, Keith B.L.	Southend United	Canvey Island
17 Dudley, Craig B.	Notts County	Telford United
25 Dyche, Sean M.	Bristol City	Luton Town
22 Elliott, Stuart T.	Newcastle United	Wrexham
17 Fairclough, Courtney H.	Notts County	York City
25 Follett, Richard J.	Nottingham Forest	Scunthorpe United
3 Forbes, Steven D.	Colchester United	Peterborough United
25 French, James R.	Bristol Rovers	Merthyr Tydfil
25 Fullarton, Jamie	Crystal Palace	Bolton Wanderers
2 Gerrard, Paul W.	Everton	Oxford United
25 Gray, Andrew D.	Nottingham Forest	Oldham Athletic
25 Greenacre, Christopher M.	Manchester City	Northampton Town
24 Guinan, Stephen	Nottingham Forest	Plymouth Argyle
24 Hamilton, Derick	Newcastle United	Huddersfield Town
25 Hanlon, Ritchie K.	Peterborough United	Welling United
2 Harrison, Gerald R.	Sunderland	Luton Town
25 Harrison, Gerald R.	Sunderland	Hull City
5 Haydon, Nicholas	Colchester United	Kettering Town
12 Heaney, Neil	Manchester City	Bristol City
31 Henshaw, Terrence R.	Notts County	Burton Albion
26 Hocking, Matthew J.	Hull City	York City
25 Hodges, Lee L.	West Ham United	Southend United
25 Howells, David	Southampton	Bristol City
24 Hughes, John P.	Chelsea	Norwich City
25 Hurst, Richard A.	Queens Park Rangers	Aylesbury United

5 Hutt, Stephen	Hartlepool United	Bishop Auckland
19 Jackson, Elliott	Oxford United	Stevenage Borough
25 Jenkins, Stephen M.	Southampton	Brentford
26 Jones, Mark C.	Aylesbury United	Oxford City
26 Jones, Nathan J.	Southend United	Scarborough
25 Kenny, Patrick J.	Bury	Whitby Town
26 Knight, Richard	Derby County	Carlisle United
25 Launders, Brian T.	Derby County	Colchester United
2 Lee, Alan D.	Aston Villa	Port Vale
25 Lilley, Derek	Leeds United	Bury
25 Linighan, Andrew	Crystal Palace	Queens Park Rangers
19 Linton, Desmond M.	Peterborough United	Swindon Town
5 Lisbie, Kevin A.	Charlton Athletic	Gillingham
31 Lovelock, Andrew J.	Crewe Alexandra	Altrincham
12 Lydidate, Jason L.	Scarborough	Rochdale
5 Mackenzie, Christopher N.	Leyton Orient	Nuneaton Borough
24 Mackenzie, Neil D.	Stoke City	Cambridge United
25 McAuley, Sean	Scunthorpe United	Scarborough
8 McKeever, Mark A.	Sheffield Wednesday	Reading
19 Magilton, James	Sheffield Wednesday	Ipswich Town
8 Mardon, Paul	West Bromwich Albion	Oldham Athletic
8 Martin, Jae A.	Peterborough United	Grantham Town
25 Maybury, Alan	Leeds United	Reading
26 Miller, Charles	Rangers	Leicester City
2 Mohan, Nicholas	Wycombe Wanderers	Stoke City
29 Morrish, Adam	Southend United	Witham Town
16 Murphy, Daniel B.	Liverpool	Crewe Alexandra
25 Neil, Gary D.C.	Leicester City	Torquay United
25 Nielsen, Jorgen T.	Liverpool	Wolverhampton Wanderers
19 Omoyimni, Emmanuel	West Ham United	Leyton Orient
9 Platts, Mark A.	Sheffield Wednesday	Torquay United
1 Quailey, Brian S.	West Bromwich Albion	Exeter City
19 Quayle, Mark	Notts County	Grantham Town
31 Rigby, Anthony A.	Bury	Altrincham
12 Roberts, Ben J.	Middlesbrough	Millwall
25 Roberts, Christian J.	Cardiff City	Hereford United
26 Rose, Karl B.	Barnsley	Mansfield Town
12 Rowe, Ezekiel B.	Peterborough United	Welling United
1 Russell, Craig S.	Manchester City	Port Vale
25 Russell, Lee	Portsmouth	Torquay United
25 Sale, Mark D.	Colchester United	Plymouth Argyle
23 Serrant, Carl	Newcastle United	Bury
26 Sharpe, Lee S.	Leeds United	Bradford City
30 Simpson, Colin R.	Leyton Orient	Bromley
25 Smeets, Jorg	Wigan Athletic	Chester City
25 Smith, James J.A.	Crystal Palace	Fulham
25 Smith, Paul D.	Charlton Athletic	Barnet
19 Soley, Stephen	Portsmouth	Macclesfield Town
31 Spiller, Richard B.	Bristol City	Weymouth
2 Steiner, Robert H.	Bradford City	Queens Park Rangers
25 Steiner, Robert H.	Bradford City	Walsall
4 Strevens, Benjamin J.	Barnet	Wingate & Finchley
25 Strong, Greg	Bolton Wanderers	Stoke City
25 Stuart, Mark R.	Rochdale	Southport
9 Sturridge, Simon A.	Stoke City	Blackpool
30 Thompson, Scott R.	Chester City	Witton Albion
25 Thorpe, Anthony L.	Bristol City	Luton Town
12 Tracey, Richard S.	Rotherham United	Carlisle United
2 Tucker, Dexter C.	Hull City	Gainsborough Trinity
26 Tuttle, David P.	Crystal Palace	Charlton Athletic
12 Varty, John W.	Carlisle United	Rotherham United
10 Vaughan, Wayne S.	Tottenham Hotspur	Witham Town
25 Watts, Julian	Bristol City	Blackpool
12 Whelan, Philip J.	Oxford United	Rotherham United
5 White, Thomas M.	Bristol Rovers	Kingstonian
25 Whittaker, David A.	Crewe Alexandra	Winsford United
1 Whittingham, Guy	Sheffield Wednesday	Portsmouth
18 Whittingham, Guy	Sheffield Wednesday	Watford
24 Widdrington, Thomas	Grimsby Town	Port Vale

25 Wilder, Christopher J.   Sheffield United   Lincoln City
 5 Williams, Anthony S.   Blackburn Rovers   Huddersfield Town
24 Williams, Anthony S.   Blackburn Rovers   Bristol Rovers
15 Williams, Jamie L.   Coventry City   Hinckley United
31 Williamson, Michael P.   Crewe Alexandra   Nantwich Town
25 Willis, Adam P.   Swindon Town   Mansfield Town

April 1999
16 Bolland, Paul G.   Bradford City   Notts County
27 Buggie, Lee D.   Bolton Wanderers   Bury
22 Cooke, Terence J.   Manchester United   Manchester City
16 Devine, Sean T.   Barnet   Wycombe Wanderers
 9 Duffield, Peter   Falkirk   Darlington

Temporary transfers
30 Adamson, Christopher   West Bromwich Albion   Mansfield Town
 7 Basham, Steven   Southampton   Preston North End
28 Connor, Paul   Middlesbrough   Stoke City
13 Cook, Paul A.   Stockport County   Burnley
30 Cowe, Steven M.   Swindon Town   Hereford United
 4 Dublin, Keith B.L.   Southend United   Canvey Island
22 Glass, James R.   Swindon Town   Carlisle United
 1 Hamlet, Gareth   Halifax Town   Farsley Celtic
 7 Hanlon, Ritchie K.   Peterborough United   Welling United
29 Hodges, Lee L.   West Ham United   Southend United
 2 Hutt, Stephen   Hartlepool United   Bishop Auckland
 6 Lee, Alan D.   Aston Villa   Port Vale
 3 Lisbie, Kevin   Charlton Athletic   Gillingham
 7 Nielsen, Jorgen T.   Liverpool   Wolverhampton Wanderers
16 Russell, Lee E.   Portsmouth   Torquay United
13 Smith, James A.   Crystal Palace   Fulham
19 Soley, Steven   Portsmouth   Macclesfield Town
 6 Strevens, Benjamin J.   Barnet   Wingate & Finchley
22 Stuart, Mark R.   Rochdale   Southport
 1 Thompson, Scott R.   Chester City   Witton Albion
 1 Tucker, Dexter C.   Hull City   Gainsborough Trinity
14 Varty, John W.   Carlisle United   Rotherham United
15 Williams, Jamie L.   Coventry City   Hinckley United

May 1999
25 Brown, Daniel   Leyton Orient   Barnet
28 Burton, Sagi   Crystal Palace   Colchester United
26 Hocking, Matthew J.   Hull City   York City
21 Johnson, Seth A.M.   Crewe Alexandra   Derby County
27 Kiely, Dean L.   Bury   Charlton Athletic
27 Low, Joshua D.   Bristol Rovers   Leyton Orient
29 Walling, Dean A.   Lincoln City   Doncaster Rovers

Temporary transfers
 8 Varty, John W.   Carlisle United   Rotherham United
 8 Whelan, Philip J.   Oxford United   Rotherham United

June 1999
11 Dalglish, Paul   Newcastle United   Norwich City
29 Eaton, Adam P.   Everton   Preston North End
25 Forster, Nicholas   Birmingham City   Reading
 4 Gray, Martin   Oxford United   Darlington
11 Halle, Gunnar   Leeds United   Bradford City
17 Irons, Kenneth   Tranmere Rovers   Huddersfield Town
23 James, David B.   Liverpool   Aston Villa
14 Lucketti, Christopher   Bury   Huddersfield Town
21 Nicholls, Kevin J.   Charlton Athletic   Wigan Athletic
 7 Oakes, Andrew M.   Hull City   Derby County
 5 Town, David   AFC Bournemouth   Rushden & Diamonds
15 Turley, William L.   Northampton Town   Rushden & Diamonds

FA CUP REVIEW 1998–99

Although there was little doubt that Manchester United deserved their 2-0 FA Cup final success, both goals came to effectively stifle Newcastle's best periods in the game.

Yet the match itself had started badly enough for United when Roy Keane was soon limping after a challenge from Gary Speed. The Republic of Ireland international was replaced by Teddy Sheringham as early as the ninth minute. The newcomer's impact was such that within two minutes he had flattened Newcastle's promising start by opening the scoring. A carpeted move had cut a path through Newcastle's defence following an exploratory exchange of passes.

Newcastle manager Ruud Gullit decided to go for broke on the restart with Duncan Ferguson on for Dietmar Hamann. Again Newcastle had the better of the possession, but in the 53rd minute the excercise became academic when Scholes made it 2-0 for United with a low shot from 20 yards. Temuri Ketsbaia did hit a post and Silvio Maric should have done better than shoot wide with a clear-cut opportunity, but the feeling was that United would only have stepped up a gear had Newcastle reduced the arrears.

Long before either club had thought about the Third Round, let alone the final, the non-league hopefuls had trod the Road to Wembley in the early autumn. None did better in this respect than Ford United of the Ryman League, Division Three, who played eight games before reaching the First Round proper to face Preston North End and found no disgrace in defeat at the club who had achieved the very first League and Cup double in 1889.

Northern League Bedlington Terriers were comfortable winners over Second Division Colchester United at this stage.

The Second Round saw those perennial giant-killers Yeovil Town record their 18th Football League scalp when they beat Northampton Town 2-0. Non-league moneybags Rushden & Diamonds reached the Third Round and forced Leeds to a replay, but Yeovil lost after a second attempt to Cardiff.

Meanwhile Manchester United had taken revenge for their Premiership defeat by Middlesbrough, by beating the Riverside Stadium team 3-1 at Old Trafford. Newcastle had edged out Crystal Palace 2-1.

Newcastle had a reasonably comfortable 3-0 win over Bradford City in the Fourth Round, but United were more severely tested before they overcame Liverpool 2-1 with goals in the last two minutes. Fulham were the surprise packets of the round, winning 2-0 at Aston Villa, but Chelsea needed a replay to defeat struggling Oxford after a controversial late penalty had earned them a second chance.

The Fifth Round was dominated by the strange affair of Arsenal v Sheffield United. A Nwankwo Kanu goal resulting from a sporting throw-in which went horribly wrong left Arsenal 2-1 winners but with a bad taste in everyone's mouth. Arsenal generously responded by offering a replay which was accepted. This ended with exactly the same scoreline.

Even so, Manchester United disposed of Fulham, the conquerors of Villa 1-0 and Newcastle needed a second attempt to remove Blackburn Rovers from the competition.

Newcastle did even better in the quarter-finals, beating Everton 4-1, but United needed a second attempt before eliminating Chelsea.

If the goal of this round had been David Ginola's solo effort to defeat Barnsley, the goal of the competition came in the semi-finals when Manchester United won their replay with Arsenal, who had quietly but efficiently moved towards the last stages of defending their crown.

Ryan Giggs' run from inside his own half took him through the Arsenal defence in the 109th minute of extra time in the replay and ended with a memorable goal. United had had Keane sent off in the 74th minute. Dennis Bergkamp, scorer of Arsenal's goal also missed a penalty.

By an odd twist of coincidence, Alan Shearer had scored a 109th minute penalty for Newcastle in their 2-0 win over Tottenham.

AXA FA CUP 1998–99

FIRST ROUND

Manchester C	(2) 3	Halifax T	(0) 0
Swansea C	(2) 3	Millwall	(0) 0
Basingstoke T	(0) 1	Bournemouth	(1) 2
Bedlington T	(2) 4	Colchester U	(0) 1
Brentford	(2) 5	Camberley T	(0) 0
Bristol R	(0) 3	Welling U	(0) 0
Cardiff C	(3) 6	Chester C	(0) 0
Cheltenham T	(0) 0	Lincoln C	(0) 1
Dulwich H	(0) 0	Southport	(0) 1
Enfield	(0) 2	York C	(2) 2
Hartlepool U	(1) 2	Carlisle U	(0) 1
Hednesford T	(0) 3	Barnet	(0) 1
Kingstonian	(0) 1	Burton A	(0) 0
Leyton Orient	(1) 4	Brighton & HA	(1) 2
Macclesfield T	(0) 2	Slough T	(2) 2
Mansfield T	(1) 2	Hayes	(0) 1
Northampton T	(0) 2	Lancaster C	(1) 1
Oldham Ath	(2) 2	Gillingham	(0) 0
Plymouth Arg	(0) 0	Kidderminster H	(0) 0
Preston NE	(1) 3	Ford U	(0) 0
Reading	(0) 0	Stoke C	(1) 1
Runcorn	(0) 1	Stevenage B	(0) 1
Rushden & D	(1) 1	Shrewsbury T	(0) 0
Salisbury C	(0) 0	Hull C	(0) 2
Scarborough	(0) 1	Rochdale	(0) 1
Southend U	(0) 0	Doncaster R	(1) 1
Tamworth	(1) 2	Exeter C	(1) 2
Telford U	(0) 0	Cambridge U	(1) 2
Walsall	(0) 1	Gresley R	(0) 0
Wigan Ath	(2) 4	Blackpool	(1) 3
Woking	(0) 0	Scunthorpe U	(1) 1
Worcester C	(0) 0	Torquay U	(0) 1
Wrexham	(0) 1	Peterborough U	(0) 0
Wycombe W	(0) 1	Chesterfield	(0) 0
Yeovil T	(1) 2	West Auckland T	(2) 2
Boreham Wood	(0) 2	Luton T	(1) 3
Emley	(1) 1	Rotherham U	(0) 1
Fulham	(1) 1	Leigh RMI	(1) 1
Hendon	(0) 0	Notts Co	(0) 0
Darlington	(0) 3	Burnley	(1) 2

(at Middlesbrough.)

FIRST ROUND REPLAYS

Stevenage B	(0) 2	Runcorn	(0) 0
Exeter C	(3) 4	Tamworth	(0) 1
Kidderminster H	0	Plymouth Arg	0

(Abandoned at half-time; fog.)

Leigh RMI	(0) 0	Fulham	(2) 2
Rochdale	(1) 2	Scarborough	(0) 0
Rotherham U	(1) 3	Emley	(1) 1
Slough T	(1) 1	Macclesfield T	(1) 1

(aet; Macclesfield T won 9-8 on penalties.)

| West Auckland T | (0) 1 | Yeovil T | (0) 1 |

(aet; Yeovil T won 5-3 on penalties.)

| York C | (2) 2 | Enfield | (1) 1 |
| Kidderminster H | (0) 0 | Plymouth Arg | (0) 0 |

(aet; Plymouth Arg won 5-4 on penalties.)

| Notts Co | (0) 3 | Hendon | (0) 0 |

SECOND ROUND

Darlington	(1) 1	Manchester C	(0) 1
Cardiff C	(1) 3	Hednesford T	(0) 1
Doncaster R	(0) 0	Rushden & D	(0) 0
Exeter C	(1) 2	Bristol R	(1) 2
Fulham	(1) 4	Hartlepool U	(1) 2
Lincoln C	(1) 4	Stevenage B	(0) 1
Luton T	(1) 1	Hull C	(1) 2
Macclesfield T	(1) 4	Cambridge U	(0) 1
Mansfield T	(0) 1	Southport	(1) 2
Notts Co	(1) 1	Wigan Ath	(0) 1
Oldham Ath	(0) 1	Brentford	(1) 1
Preston NE	(0) 2	Walsall	(0) 0
Rochdale	(0) 0	Rotherham U	(0) 0
Scunthorpe U	(0) 2	Bedlington T	(0) 0
Swansea C	(1) 1	Stoke C	(0) 0
Torquay U	(0) 0	Bournemouth	(1) 1
Wrexham	(1) 2	York C	(1) 1
Wycombe W	(1) 1	Plymouth Arg	(0) 1
Yeovil T	(1) 2	Northampton T	(0) 0
Kingstonian	(0) 0	Leyton Orient	(0) 0

SECOND ROUND REPLAYS

| Brentford | (1) 2 | Oldham Ath | (1) 2 |

(aet; Oldham Ath won 4-2 on penalties.)

Bristol R	(1) 5	Exeter C	(0) 0
Leyton Orient	(1) 2	Kingstonian	(0) 1
Manchester C	(0) 1	Darlington	(0) 0

(aet).

Plymouth Arg	(2) 3	Wycombe W	(0) 2
Rotherham U	(1) 4	Rochdale	(0) 0
Rushden & D	(1) 4	Doncaster R	(1) 2
Wigan Ath	(0) 0	Notts Co	(0) 0

(aet; Notts Co won 4-2 on penalties.)

THIRD ROUND

Aston Villa	(1) 3	Hull C	(0) 0
Blackburn R	(1) 2	Charlton Ath	(0) 0
Bolton W	(0) 1	Wolverhampton W	(1) 2
Bournemouth	(1) 1	WBA	(0) 0
Bradford C	(1) 2	Grimsby T	(0) 1
Bristol C	(0) 0	Everton	(0) 2
Bury	(0) 0	Stockport Co	(3) 3
Cardiff C	(0) 1	Yeovil T	(0) 1
Coventry C	(3) 7	Macclesfield T	(0) 0
Crewe Alex	(0) 1	Oxford U	(2) 3
Leicester C	(2) 4	Birmingham C	(1) 2
Lincoln C	(0) 0	Sunderland	(1) 1
Newcastle U	(0) 2	Crystal Palace	(1) 1
Nottingham F	(0) 0	Portsmouth	(1) 1

Oldham Ath	(0) 0	Chelsea	(0) 2
Plymouth Arg	(0) 0	Derby Co	(2) 3
QPR	(0) 0	Huddersfield T	(1) 1
Rotherham U	(0) 0	Bristol R	(1) 1
Rushden & D	(0) 0	Leeds U	(0) 0
Sheffield U	(1) 1	Notts Co	(0) 1
Southampton	(0) 1	Fulham	(1) 1
Southport	(0) 0	Leyton Orient	(0) 2
Swindon T	(0) 0	Barnsley	(0) 0
Tottenham H	(4) 5	Watford	(2) 2
Tranmere R	(0) 0	Ipswich T	(0) 1
West Ham U	(0) 1	Swansea C	(0) 1
Wimbledon	(0) 1	Manchester C	(0) 0
Wrexham	(1) 4	Scunthorpe U	(0) 3
Manchester U	(0) 3	Middlesbrough	(0) 1
Port Vale	(0) 0	Liverpool	(2) 3
Sheffield W	(3) 4	Norwich C	(1) 1
Preston NE	(2) 2	Arsenal	(1) 4

THIRD ROUND REPLAYS

Yeovil T	(0) 1	Cardiff C	(1) 2
(aet).			
Fulham	(0) 1	Southampton	(0) 0
Leeds U	(1) 3	Rushden & D	(1) 1
Swansea C	(1) 1	West Ham U	(0) 0
Barnsley	(0) 3	Swindon T	(0) 1
Notts Co	(1) 3	Sheffield U	(1) 4
(aet).			

FOURTH ROUND

Aston Villa	(0) 0	Fulham	(2) 2
Barnsley	(1) 3	Bournemouth	(0) 1
Blackburn R	(0) 1	Sunderland	(0) 0
Bristol R	(0) 3	Leyton Orient	(0) 0
Everton	(1) 1	Ipswich T	(0) 0
Leicester C	(0) 0	Coventry C	(1) 3
Newcastle U	(1) 3	Bradford C	(0) 0
Portsmouth	(1) 1	Leeds U	(2) 5
Sheffield W	(1) 2	Stockport Co	(0) 0
Swansea C	(0) 0	Derby Co	(0) 1
Wimbledon	(0) 1	Tottenham H	(0) 1
Wrexham	(1) 1	Huddersfield T	(1) 1
Manchester U	(0) 2	Liverpool	(1) 1
Wolverhampton W	(1) 1	Arsenal	(1) 2
Oxford U	(0) 1	Chelsea	(0) 1
Sheffield U	(1) 4	Cardiff C	(1) 1

FOURTH ROUND REPLAYS

Tottenham H	(1) 3	Wimbledon	(0) 0
Chelsea	(2) 4	Oxford U	(1) 2
Huddersfield T	(2) 2	Wrexham	(1) 1

FIFTH ROUND

Arsenal	(1) 2	Sheffield U	(0) 1
(Match void after Arsenal's plea for replay was accepted by F.A.)			
Barnsley	(2) 4	Bristol R	(0) 1

Everton	(1) 2	Coventry C	(0) 1
Huddersfield T	(1) 2	Derby Co	(0) 2
Leeds U	(0) 1	Tottenham H	(0) 1
Sheffield W	(0) 0	Chelsea	(0) 1
Manchester U	(1) 1	Fulham	(0) 0
Newcastle U	(0) 0	Blackburn R	(0) 0
Arsenal	(2) 2	Sheffield U	(0) 1

FIFTH ROUND REPLAYS

Blackburn R	(0) 0	Newcastle U	(1) 1
Derby Co	(1) 3	Huddersfield T	(1) 1
Tottenham H	(0) 2	Leeds U	(0) 0

SIXTH ROUND

Arsenal	(0) 1	Derby Co	(0) 0
Manchester U	(0) 0	Chelsea	(0) 0
Newcastle U	(1) 4	Everton	(0) 1
Barnsley	(0) 0	Tottenham H	(0) 1

SIXTH ROUND REPLAY

| Chelsea | (0) 0 | Manchester U | (1) 2 |

SEMI-FINALS

Newcastle U	(0) 2	Tottenham H	(0) 0
(aet.)			
Manchester U	(0) 0	Arsenal	(0) 0
(aet.)			

SEMI-FINAL REPLAY

| Manchester U | (1) 2 | Arsenal | (0) 1 |
| *(aet.)* | | | |

FINAL (at Wembley)

22 MAY

Manchester U (1) 2 *(Sheringham 11, Scholes 53)*
Newcastle U (0) 0   79,101

Manchester U: Schmeichel; Neville G, Neville P, May, Keane (Sheringham), Johnsen, Beckham, Scholes (Stam), Cole (Yorke), Solskjaer, Giggs.
Newcastle U: Harper; Griffin, Domi, Dabizas, Charvet, Solano (Maric), Lee, Hamann (Ferguson), Shearer, Ketsbaia (Glass), Speed.
Referee: P. Jones (Loughborough).

PAST FA CUP FINALS

Details of one goalscorer is not available in 1878.

1872	The Wanderers ....1 *Betts*	Royal Engineers 0
1873	The Wanderers ....2 *Kinnaird, Wollaston*	Oxford University 0
1874	Oxford University...................2 *Mackarness, Patton*	Royal Engineers 0
1875	Royal Engineers ....1 *Renny-Tailyour*	Old Etonians ....1* *Bonsor*
Replay	Royal Engineers ....2 *Renny-Tailyour, Stafford*	Old Etonians 0
1876	The Wanderers ....1 *Edwards*	Old Etonians ....1* *Bonsor*
Replay	The Wanderers ....3 *Wollaston, Hughes 2*	Old Etonians 0
1877	The Wanderers ....2 *Lindsay, Kenrick*	Oxford University ....1* *Kinnaird (og)*
1878	The Wanderers ....3 *Kenrick 2, Kinnaird*	Royal Engineers ....1 *Unknown*
1879	Old Etonians ....1 *Clerke*	Clapham Rovers 0
1880	Clapham Rovers ....1 *Lloyd-Jones*	Oxford University 0
1881	Old Carthusians ....3 *Wyngard, Parry, Todd*	Old Etonians 0
1882	Old Etonians ....1 *Anderson*	Blackburn Rovers................................0
1883	Blackburn Olympic ....2 *Costley, Matthews*	Old Etonians ....1* *Goodhart*
1884	Blackburn Rovers...................2 *Sowerbutts, Forrest*	Queen's Park, Glasgow ....1 *Christie*
1885	Blackburn Rovers...................2 *Forrest, Brown*	Queen's Park, Glasgow 0
1886	Blackburn Rovers...................0	West Bromwich Albion 0
Replay	Blackburn Rovers...................2 *Brown, Sowerbutts*	West Bromwich Albion 0
1887	Aston Villa ....2 *Hunter, Hodgetts*	West Bromwich Albion 0
1888	West Bromwich Albion ....2 *Woodhall, Bayliss*	Preston NE ....1 *Dewhurst*
1889	Preston NE ....3 *Dewhurst, J. Ross, Thompson*	Wolverhampton W 0
1890	Blackburn Rovers...................6 *Walton, John Southworth,* *Lofthouse, Townley 3*	Sheffield W ....1 *Bennett*

Year	Winners	Score	Runners-up	Score
1891	Blackburn Rovers	3	Notts Co	1
	Dewar, John Southworth, Townley		*Oswald*	
1892	West Browmwich Albion	3	Aston Villa	0
	Geddes, Nicholls, Reynolds			
1893	Wolverhampton W	1	Everton	0
	Allen			
1894	Notts Co	4	Bolton W	1
	Watson, Logan 3		*Cassidy*	
1895	Aston Villa	1	West Bromwich Albion	0
	J. Devey			
1896	Sheffield W	2	Wolverhampton W	1
	Spiksley 2		*Black*	
1897	Aston Villa	3	Everton	2
	Campbell, Wheldon, Crabtree		*Boyle, Bell*	
1898	Nottingham F	3	Derby Co	1
	Cape 2, McPherson		*Bloomer*	
1899	Sheffield U	4	Derby Co	1
	Bennett, Beers, Almond, Priest		*Boag*	
1900	Bury	4	Southampton	0
	McLuckie 2, Wood, Plant			
1901	Tottenham H	2	Sheffield U	2
	Brown 2		*Bennett, Priest*	
Replay	Tottenham H	3	Sheffield U	1
	Cameron, Smith, Brown		*Priest*	
1902	Sheffield U	1	Southampton	1
	Common		*Wood*	
Replay	Sheffield U	2	Southampton	1
	Hedley, Barnes		*Brown*	
1903	Bury	6	Derby Co	0
	Ross, Sagar, Leeming 2, Wood, Plant			
1904	Manchester C	1	Bolton W	0
	Meredith			
1905	Aston Villa	2	Newcastle U	0
	Hampton 2			
1906	Everton	1	Newcastle U	0
	Young			
1907	Sheffield W	2	Everton	1
	Stewart, Simpson		*Sharp*	
1908	Wolverhampton W	3	Newcastle U	1
	Hunt, Hedley, Harrison		*Howey*	
1909	Manchester U	1	Bristol C	0
	A. Turnbull			
1910	Newcastle U	1	Barnsley	1
	Rutherford		*Tufnell*	
Replay	Newcastle U	2	Barnsley	0
	Shepherd 2 (1 pen)			

1911	Bradford C.....................0	Newcastle U 0
Replay	Bradford C.....................1	Newcastle U 0
	Speirs	
1912	Barnsley 0	West Bromwich Albion 0
Replay	Barnsley 1	West Bromwich Albion 0*
	Tufnell	
1913	Aston Villa 1	Sunderland 0
	Barber	
1914	Burnley 1	Liverpool 0
	Freeman	
1915	Sheffield U.....................3	Chelsea 0
	Simmons, Masterman, Kitchen	
1920	Aston Villa 1	Huddersfield T.......................0*
	Kirton	
1921	Tottenham H....................1	Wolverhampton W...................0
	Dimmock	
1922	Huddersfield T 1	Preston NE...........................0
	Smith (pen)	
1923	Bolton W 2	West Ham U 0
	Jack, J.R. Smith	
1924	Newcastle U 2	Aston Villa 0
	Harris, Seymour	
1925	Sheffield U.....................1	Cardiff C..............................0
	Tunstall	
1926	Bolton W 1	Manchester C.........................0
	Jack	
1927	Cardiff C........................1	Arsenal 0
	Ferguson	
1928	Blackburn Rovers...............3	Huddersfield T.......................1
	Roscamp 2, McLean	*A. Jackson*
1929	Bolton W 2	Portsmouth...........................0
	Butler, Blackmore	
1930	Arsenal.........................2	Huddersfield T.......................0
	James, Lambert	
1931	West Bromwich Albion 2	Birmingham 1
	W.G. Richardson 2	*Bradford*
1932	Newcastle U 2	Arsenal 1
	Allen 2	*John*
1933	Everton 3	Manchester C.........................0
	Stein, Dean, Dunn	
1934	Manchester C 2	Portsmouth...........................1
	Tilson 2	*Rutherford*
1935	Sheffield W 4	West Bromwich Albion 2
	Rimmer 2, Palethorpe, Hooper	*Boyes, Sandford*
1936	Arsenal.........................1	Sheffield U...........................0
	Drake	
1937	Sunderland 3	Preston NE...........................1
	Gurney, Carter, Burbanks	*F. O'Donnell*

1938	Preston NE ....1 *Mutch (pen)*	Huddersfield T 0*
1939	Portsmouth ....4 *Parker 2, Barlow,* *Anderson*	Wolverhampton W ....1 *Dorsett*
1946	Derby Co ....4 *H. Turner (og), Doherty,* *Stamps 2*	Charlton Ath ....1* *H. Turner*
1947	Charlton Ath ....1 *Duffy*	Burnley 0*
1948	Manchester U ....4 *Rowley 2, Pearson,* *Anderson*	Blackpool ....2 *Shimwell (pen), Mortensen*
1949	Wolverhampton W ....3 *Pye 2, Smyth,*	Leicester C ....1 *Griffiths*
1950	Arsenal ....2 *Lewis 2*	Liverpool 0
1951	Newcastle U ....2 *Milburn 2*	Blackpool 0
1952	Newcastle U ....1 *G. Robledo*	Arsenal 0
1953	Blackpool ....4 *Mortensen 3, Perry*	Bolton W ....3 *Lofthouse, Moir, Bell*
1954	West Bromwich Albion ....3 *Allen 2 (1 pen), Griffin*	Preston NE ....2 *Morrison, Wayman*
1955	Newcastle U ....3 *Milburn, Mitchell,* *Hannah*	Manchester C ....1 *Johnstone*
1956	Manchester C ....3 *Hayes, Dyson, Johnstone*	Birmingham C ....1 *Kinsey*
1957	Aston Villa ....2 *McParland 2*	Manchester U ....1 *T. Taylor*
1958	Bolton W ....2 *Lofthouse 2*	Manchester U 0
1959	Nottingham F ....2 *Dwight, Wilson*	Luton T ....1 *Pacey*
1960	Wolverhampton W ....3 *McGrath (og), Deeley 2*	Blackburn Rovers 0
1961	Tottenham H ....2 *Smith, Dyson*	Leicester C 0
1962	Tottenham H ....3 *Greaves, Smith,* *Blanchflower (pen)*	Burnley ....1 *Robson*
1963	Manchester U ....3 *Herd 2, Law*	Leicester C ....1 *Keyworth*
1964	West Ham U ....3 *Sissons, Hurst, Boyce*	Preston NE ....2 *Holden, Dawson*
1965	Liverpool ....2 *Hunt, St John*	Leeds U ....1* *Bremner*

1966	Everton 3	Sheffield W 2
	Trebilcock 2, Temple	*McCalliog, Ford*
1967	Tottenham H 2	Chelsea 1
	Robertson, Saul	*Tambling*
1968	West Browmwich Albion 1	Everton 0*
	Astle	
1969	Manchester C 1	Leicester C 0
	Young	
1970	Chelsea 2	Leeds U 2*
	Houseman, Hutchinson	*Charlton, Jones*
Replay	Chelsea 2	Leeds U 1*
	Osgood, Webb	*Jones*
1971	Arsenal 2	Liverpool 1*
	Kelly, George	*Heighway*
1972	Leeds U 1	Arsenal 0
	Clarke	
1973	Sunderland 1	Leeds U 0
	Porterfield	
1974	Liverpool 3	Newcastle 0
	Keegan 2, Heighway	
1975	West Ham U 2	Fulham 0
	A. Taylor 2	
1976	Southampton 1	Manchester U 0
	Stokes	
1977	Manchester U 2	Liverpool 1
	Pearson, J. Greenhoff	*Case*
1978	Ipswich T 1	Arsenal 0
	Osborne	
1979	Arsenal 3	Manchester U 2
	Talbot, Stapleton,	*McQueen, McIlroy*
	Sunderland	
1980	West Ham U 1	Arsenal 0
	Brooking	
1981	Tottenham H 1	Manchester C 1*
	Hutchison (og)	*Hutchison*
Replay	Totteham H 3	Manchester C 2
	Villa 2, Crooks	*MacKenzie, Reeves (pen)*
1982	Tottenham H 1	QPR 1*
	Hoddle	*Fenwick*
Replay	Tottenham H 1	QPR 0
	Hoddle (pen)	
1983	Manchester U 2	Brighton & HA 2*
	Stapleton, Wilkins	*Smith, Stevens*
Replay	Manchester U 4	Brighton & HA 0
	Robson 2, Whiteside, Muhren (pen)	
1984	Everton 2	Watford 0
	Sharp, Gray	
1985	Manchester U 1	Everton 0*
	Whiteside	

1986	Liverpool	3	Everton	1
	Rush 2, Johnston		*Lineker*	
1987	Coventry C	3	Tottenham H	2*
	Bennett, Houchen,		*C. Allen, Kilcline (og)*	
	Mabbutt (og)			
1988	Wimbledon	1	Liverpool	0
	Sanchez			
1989	Liverpool	3	Everton	2*
	Aldridge, Rush 2		*McCall 2*	
1990	Manchester U	3	Crystal Palace	3*
	Robson, Hughes 2		*O'Reilly, Wright 2*	
Replay	Manchester U	1	Crystal Palace	0
	Martin			
1991	Tottenham H	2	Nottingham F	1*
	Stewart, Walker (og)		*Pearce*	
1992	Liverpool	2	Sunderland	0
	Thomas, Rush			
1993	Arsenal	1	Sheffield W	1*
	Wright		*Hirst*	
Replay	Arsenal	2	Sheffield W	1*
	Wright, Linighan		*Waddle*	
1994	Manchester U	4	Chelsea	0
	Cantona 2 (2 pens),			
	Hughes, McClair			
1995	Everton	1	Manchester U	0
	Rideout			
1996	Manchester U	1	Liverpool	0
	Cantona			
1997	Chelsea	2	Middlesbrough	0
	Di Matteo, Newton			
1998	Arsenal	2	Newcastle U	0
	Overmars, Anelka			

After extra time

SUMMARY OF FA CUP WINNERS SINCE 1871

Manchester United..........................10
Tottenham Hotspur...........................8
Arsenal..7
Aston Villa 7
Blackburn Rovers.............................6
Newcastle United.............................6
Everton 5
Liverpool...5
The Wanderers 5
West Bromwich Albion 5
Bolton Wanderers 4
Manchester City...............................4
Sheffield United...............................4
Wolverhampton Wanderers..............4
Sheffield Wednesday........................3
West Ham United..............................3
Bury...2
Chelsea..2
Nottingham Forest............................2
Old Etonians 2
Preston North End 2

Sunderland 2
Barnsley...1
Blackburn Olympic 1
Blackpool...1
Bradford City 1
Burnley 1
Cardiff City......................................1
Charlton Athletic..............................1
Clapham Rovers 1
Coventry City 1
Derby County 1
Huddersfield Town...........................1
Ipswich Town 1
Leeds United 1
Notts County 1
Old Carthusians 1
Oxford University 1
Portsmouth 1
Royal Engineers 1
Southampton 1
Wimbledon.......................................1

APPEARANCES IN FA CUP FINAL

Manchester United..........................15
Arsenal..13
Newcastle United 13
Everton 12
Liverpool...11
West Bromwich Albion 10
Aston Villa 9
Tottenham Hotspur...........................9
Blackburn Rovers.............................8
Manchester City...............................8
Wolverhampton Wanderers..............8
Bolton Wanderers 7
Preston North End 7
Old Etonians 6
Sheffield United...............................6
Sheffield Wednesday........................6
Chelsea..5
Huddersfield Town...........................5
The Wanderers 5
Derby County 4
Leeds United....................................4
Leicester City 4
Oxford University 4
Royal Engineers 4
Sunderland 4
West Ham United..............................4
Blackpool...3

Burnley 3
Nottingham Forest 3
Portsmouth.......................................3
Southampton....................................3
Barnsley...2
Birmingham City 2
Bury...2
Cardiff City......................................2
Charlton Athletic..............................2
Clapham Rovers 2
Notts County 2
Queen's Park (Glasgow) 2
Blackburn Olympic 1
Bradford City 1
Brighton & Hove Albion....................1
Bristol City 1
Coventry City...................................1
Crystal Palace..................................1
Fulham 1
Ipswich Town 1
Luton Town.......................................1
Middlesbrough.................................1
Old Carthusians 1
Queen's Park Rangers 1
Watford..1
Wimbledon.......................................1

WORTHINGTON CUP REVIEW 1998–99

Despite new sponsors the League Cup continued its formula from the previous season. Again the eight clubs involved in European action were exempted to the third round. Significantly perhaps only two of these Chelsea and Manchester United survived until the quarter-finals and both finalists had to play from the second round onwards.

The competition had started quietly enough with newly promoted Macclesfield Town beating Stoke 3-1 and holding on a 3-2 aggregate win. This was in sharp contrast to their miserable League form. Returning newcomers Halifax had a curious time with Wrexham. Halifax won 2-0 at Wrexham despite playing for over an hour with ten players, then lost the second leg by the same score again finishing a man short. Halifax won 4-2 on penalties. Top scorers were Manchester City 2-0 winners at Notts County and 7-1 at Maine Road. Wolverhampton Wanderers' Steve Bull notched a hat-trick in the 5-0 second leg win over Barnet and Paul Evans' treble for Shrewsbury included two penalties.

Macclesfield's run ended abruptly as Birmingham City beat them 3-0 away and 6-0 at home. Halifax lost 5-2 on aggregate to their Yorkshire neighbours Bradford City.

Leicester began their campaign with a 6-1 aggregate success over Chesterfield, while Tottenham beat Brentford 3-2 home and away.

The final itself watched by a crowd of 77,892 was a disappointing affair, Tottenham Hotspur scoring in injury time through Allan Nielsen to defeat Leicester City 1-0. Spurs had had Justin Edinburgh sent off for retaliation against Rob Savage in the 63rd minute. For Spurs it was their third success having won the League Cup in 1971 and 1973. Leicester had had two previous wins of their own in 1964 and 1997.

Spurs other honour was to see their former French international David Ginola voted Footballer of the Year by the Football Writers and also by his fellow professionals.

Premier League casualties were evident from the second round. Southampton lost 1-0 to Fulham at The Dell after a 1-1 draw at Craven Cottage and Sheffield Wednesday were beaten at Hillsborough by Cambridge United with a single goal and were similarly held in the second leg.

The third victims of such giant-killing were West Ham United, 2-0 losers at Northampton Town and only managing to pull one goal back in injury time at Upton Park.

In the third round Northampton began promisingly against another London club Tottenham and took the lead before losing 3-1. Luton Town accounted for Coventry City 2-0 and Cambridge gave Nottingham Forest a shock, just losing 4-3 on penalties after a 3-3 draw. Leicester won 2-1 at Charlton.

Embarrassingly, Manchester United were taken to extra time by First Division Bury at Old Trafford in front of a crowd of 52,495 before scoring twice to put some respectability on the scoreline. Chelsea's player-manager Gianluca Vialli was a hat-trickster in the 4-1 win over Aston Villa.

In the fourth round it was Everton's turn to bow out. Sunderland held them 1-1 at Goodison Park and then edged home 5-4 on penalties. Chelsea won 5-0 at an under-strengthed Arsenal and though Manchester United have rarely taken the competition seriously, they reached the quarter-finals by beating Forest 2-1.

However, Tottenham indicated their intention with a fine 3-1 victory at Liverpool and a late penalty enabled Leicester to progress 2-1 at the expense of Leeds.

In the quarter-finals, Football League interest was guaranteed when Sunderland were paired with Luton. The north-east promotion candidates were 3-0 winners via an own goal and two scored in the last minute. Wimbledon beat Chelsea 2-1 and one goal was sufficient for Leicester to oust Blackburn Rovers. Tottenham's credentials were enhanced following a 3-1 win of their own against Manchester United.

The first leg of the semi-finals saw Sunderland lose home advantage when they were beaten 2-1 by Leicester. Wimbledon came back from White Hart Lane with a goalless draw against Spurs. In the return games, Sunderland managed a 1-1 draw at Leicester but it was insufficient and Tottenham won 1-0 at Selhurst Park.

PAST LEAGUE CUP FINALS

Played as two legs up to 1966

1961	Rotherham U 2	Aston Villa 0
	Webster, Kirkman	
	Aston Villa 3	Rotherham U 0*
	O'Neill, Burrows, McParland	
1962	Rochdale 0	Norwich C....................................3
		Lythgoe 2, Punton
	Norwich C.....................................1	Rochdale.......................................0
	Hill	
1963	Birmingham C................................3	Aston Villa 1
	Leek 2, Bloomfield	*Thomson*
	Aston Villa 0	Birmingham C..............................0
1964	Stoke C...1	Leicester C....................................1
	Bebbington	*Gibson*
	Leicester C....................................3	Stoke C..2
	Stringfellow, Gibson, Riley	*Viollet, Kinnell*
1965	Chelsea...3	Leicester C....................................2
	Tambling, Venables (pen), McCreadie	*Appleton, Goodfellow*
	Leicester C....................................0	Chelsea..0
1966	West Ham U 2	WBA 1
	Moore, Byrne	*Astle*
	WBA 4	West Ham U 1
	Kaye, Brown, Clark, Williams	*Peters*
1967	QPR..3	WBA 2
	Morgan R, Marsh, Lazarus	*Clark C 2*
1968	Leeds U 1	Arsenal...0
	Cooper	
1969	Swindon T.....................................3	Arsenal...1*
	Smart, Rogers 2	*Gould*
1970	Manchester C 2	WBA 1*
	Doyle, Pardoe	*Astle*
1971	Tottenham H..................................2	Aston Villa 0
	Chivers 2	
1972	Chelsea...1	Stoke C..2
	Osgood	*Conroy, Eastham*
1973	Tottenham H..................................1	Norwich C.....................................0
	Coates	
1974	Wolverhampton W 2	Manchester C 1
	Hibbitt, Richards	*Bell*
1975	Aston Villa 1	Norwich C.....................................0
	Graydon	
1976	Manchester C 2	Newcastle U 1
	Barnes, Tueart	*Gowling*
1977	Aston Villa 0	Everton 0
Replay	Aston Villa 1	Everton 1*
	Kenyon (og)	*Latchford*

Replay	Aston Villa 3	Everton 2*
	Little 2, Nicholl	*Latchford, Lyons*
1978	Nottingham F 0	Liverpool 0*
Replay	Nottingham F 1	Liverpool 0
	Robertson (pen)	
1979	Nottingham F 3	Southampton 2
	Birtles 2, Woodcock	*Peach, Holmes*
1980	Wolverhampton W 1	Nottingham F 0
	Gray	
1981	Liverpool 1	West Ham U.............................1*
	Kennedy A	*Stewart (pen)*
Replay	Liverpool 2	West Ham U.............................1
	Dalglish, Hansen	*Goddard*
1982	Liverpool 3	Tottenham H............................1*
	Whelan 2, Rush	*Archibald*
1983	Liverpool 2	Manchester U...........................1*
	Kennedy A, Whelan	*Whiteside*
1984	Liverpool 0	Everton 0*
Replay	Liverpool 1	Everton 0
	Souness	
1985	Norwich C.................................1	Sunderland 0
	Chisholm (og)	
1986	Oxford U...................................3	QPR...0
	Hebberd, Houghton, Charles	
1987	Arsenal......................................2	Liverpool 1
	Nicholas 2	*Rush*
1988	Luton T 3	Arsenal......................................2
	Stein B 2, Wilson	*Hayes, Smith*
1989	Nottingham F 3	Luton T 1
	Clough 2, Webb	*Harford*
1990	Nottingham F 1	Oldham Ath 0
	Jemson	
1991	Sheffield W 1	Manchester U............................0
	Sheridan	
1992	Manchester U............................1	Nottingham F 0
	McClair	
1993	Arsenal......................................2	Sheffield W 1
	Merson, Morrow	*Harkes*
1994	Aston Villa 3	Manchester U............................1
	Atkinson, Saunders 2 (1 pen)	*Hughes*
1995	Liverpool 2	Bolton W 1
	McManaman 2	*Thompson*
1996	Aston Villa 3	Leeds U......................................0
	Milosevic, Taylor, Yorke	
1997	Leicester C.................................1	Middlesbrough 1*
	Heskey	*Ravanelli*
Replay	Leicester C.................................1	Middlesbrough 0*
	Claridge	
1998	Chelsea......................................2	Middlesbrough 0*
	Sinclair, Di Matteo	

After extra time

WORTHINGTON CUP 1998–99

FIRST ROUND, FIRST LEG

Barnet	(0) 2	Wolverhampton W	(0) 1
Birmingham C	(0) 2	Millwall	(0) 0
Blackpool	(1) 1	Scunthorpe U	(0) 0
Bolton W	(0) 1	Hartlepool U	(0) 0
Bournemouth	(1) 2	Colchester U	(0) 0
Bradford C	(0) 1	Lincoln C	(0) 1
Bristol C	(3) 4	Shrewsbury T	(0) 0
Bury	(1) 1	Burnley	(1) 1
Cambridge U	(1) 1	Watford	(0) 0
Exeter C	(0) 1	Ipswich T	(1) 1
Fulham	(1) 2	Cardiff C	(1) 1
Huddersfield T	(1) 3	Mansfield T	(2) 2
Leyton Orient	(1) 1	Bristol R	(0) 1
Luton T	(0) 2	Oxford U	(2) 3
Macclesfield T	(1) 3	Stoke C	(1) 1
Northampton T	(1) 2	Brighton & HA	(0) 1
Notts Co	(0) 0	Manchester C	(0) 2
Oldham Ath	(3) 3	Crewe Alex	(1) 2
Peterborough U	(0) 1	Reading	(0) 1
Plymouth Arg	(1) 1	Portsmouth	(3) 3
Port Vale	(0) 1	Chester C	(2) 2
Rotherham U	(0) 0	Chesterfield	(1) 1
Sheffield U	(1) 3	Darlington	(0) 1
Southend U	(0) 1	Gillingham	(0) 0
Stockport Co	(1) 2	Hull C	(2) 2
Swansea C	(0) 1	Norwich C	(0) 1
Torquay U	(1) 1	Crystal Palace	(1) 1
Tranmere R	(1) 3	Carlisle U	(0) 0
Walsall	(0) 0	QPR	(0) 0
WBA	(2) 2	Brentford	(0) 1
Wigan Ath	(0) 1	Rochdale	(0) 0
Wrexham	(0) 0	Halifax T	(1) 2
York C	(0) 0	Sunderland	(2) 2
Grimsby T	(0) 0	Preston NE	(0) 0
Scarborough	(0) 0	Barnsley	(1) 1
Swindon T	(1) 2	Wycombe W	(0) 1

FIRST ROUND, SECOND LEG

Barnsley	(2) 3	Scarborough	(0) 0
Brentford	(0) 3	WBA	(0) 0
Bristol R	(1) 1	Leyton Orient	(1) 2
Burnley	(1) 1	Bury	(1) 4
Cardiff C	(0) 1	Fulham	(2) 2
Carlisle U	(0) 0	Tranmere R	(0) 1
Chester C	(0) 2	Port Vale	(1) 2
Chesterfield	(0) 2	Rotherham U	(0) 0
Colchester U	(1) 3	Bournemouth	(2) 2
Crewe Alex	(1) 2	Oldham Ath	(0) 0
Darlington	(0) 2	Sheffield U	(0) 2
Gillingham	(0) 0	Southend U	(0) 1
Halifax T	(0) 0	Wrexham	(1) 2

(aet; Halifax T won 4-2 on penalties.)

| Hull C | (0) 0 | Stockport Co | (0) 0 |

(aet; Hull C won on away goals.)

Ipswich T	(3) 5	Exeter C	(1) 1
Lincoln C	(0) 0	Bradford C	(0) 1
Mansfield T	(0) 1	Huddersfield T	(1) 1
Norwich C	(0) 1	Swansea C	(0) 0
Oxford U	(1) 1	Luton T	(1) 3
Portsmouth	(2) 3	Plymouth Arg	(1) 2
Preston NE	(0) 0	Grimsby T	(0) 0

(aet; Grimsby T won 7-6 on penalties.)

Rochdale	(0) 0	Wigan Ath	(0) 1
Scunthorpe U	(1) 1	Blackpool	(1) 1
Shrewsbury T	(2) 4	Bristol C	(2) 3
Sunderland	(0) 2	York C	(0) 1
Watford	(0) 1	Cambridge U	(0) 1
Wolverhampton W	(3) 5	Barnet	(0) 0
Wycombe W	(1) 2	Swindon T	(0) 0
Brighton & HA	(0) 1	Northampton T	(0) 1
Manchester C	(4) 7	Notts Co	(0) 1
Millwall	(1) 1	Birmingham C	(1) 1
Stoke C	(0) 1	Macclesfield T	(0) 0
Crystal Palace	(1) 2	Torquay U	(0) 1
Hartlepool U	(0) 0	Bolton W	(0) 3
QPR	(0) 3	Walsall	(0) 1
Reading	(1) 2	Peterborough U	(0) 0

SECOND ROUND, FIRST LEG

Barnsley	(1) 3	Reading	(0) 0
Blackpool	(1) 2	Tranmere R	(1) 1
Bolton W	(1) 3	Hull C	(0) 1
Bournemouth	(1) 1	Wolverhampton W	(0) 1
Brentford	(1) 2	Tottenham H	(1) 3
Bury	(2) 3	Crystal Palace	(0) 0
Fulham	(0) 1	Southampton	(0) 1
Halifax T	(0) 1	Bradford C	(1) 2
Huddersfield T	(1) 1	Everton	(1) 1
Ipswich T	(0) 2	Luton T	(0) 1
Leyton Orient	(0) 1	Nottingham F	(4) 5
Macclesfield T	(0) 0	Birmingham C	(0) 3
Northampton T	(0) 2	West Ham U	(0) 0
Portsmouth	(2) 2	Wimbledon	(1) 1
Sheffield U	(1) 2	Grimsby T	(0) 1
Sunderland	(2) 3	Chester C	(0) 0
Bristol C	(1) 1	Crewe Alex	(1) 1
Coventry C	(0) 1	Southend U	(0) 0
Derby Co	(1) 1	Manchester C	(1) 1
Leicester C	(1) 3	Chesterfield	(0) 0
Middlesbrough	(1) 2	Wycombe W	(0) 0
Norwich C	(1) 1	Wigan Ath	(0) 0
QPR	(0) 0	Charlton Ath	(2) 2
Sheffield W	(0) 0	Cambridge U	(1) 1

SECOND ROUND, SECOND LEG

| Birmingham C | (3) 6 | Macclesfield T | (0) 0 |
| Bradford C | (0) 3 | Halifax T | (0) 1 |

Cambridge U	(0) 1	Sheffield W	(0) 1
Charlton Ath	(1) 1	QPR	(0) 0
Chester C	(0) 0	Sunderland	(1) 1
Chesterfield	(1) 1	Leicester C	(0) 3
Crewe Alex	(0) 2	Bristol C	(0) 0
Grimsby T	(0) 2	Sheffield U	(0) 0
Hull C	(1) 2	Bolton W	(1) 3
Luton T	(0) 4	Ipswich T	(1) 2
Nottingham F	(0) 0	Leyton Orient	(0) 0
Southend U	(0) 0	Coventry C	(3) 4
Tranmere R	(1) 3	Blackpool	(1) 1
West Ham U	(0) 1	Northampton T	(0) 0
Wigan Ath	(0) 2	Norwich C	(2) 3
Wimbledon	(1) 4	Portsmouth	(1) 1
Wolverhampton W	(0) 1	Bournemouth	(1) 2
Wycombe W	(1) 1	Middlesbrough	(0) 1
Crystal Palace	(1) 2	Bury	(1) 1
Everton	(2) 2	Huddersfield T	(1) 1
Manchester C	(0) 0	Derby Co	(1) 1
Reading	(0) 1	Barnsley	(0) 1
Southampton	(0) 0	Fulham	(1) 1
Tottenham H	(1) 3	Brentford	(1) 2

THIRD ROUND

Barnsley	(1) 2	Bournemouth	(0) 1
Charlton Ath	(0) 1	Leicester C	(0) 2
Liverpool	(0) 3	Fulham	(0) 1
Luton T	(0) 2	Coventry C	(0) 0
Northampton T	(1) 1	Tottenham H	(1) 3
Norwich C	(0) 1	Bolton W	(0) 1

(aet; Bolton W won 3-1 on penalties.)

| Nottingham F | (2) 3 | Cambridge U | (0) 3 |

(aet; Nottingham F won 4-3 on penalties.)

Sunderland	(0) 2	Grimsby T	(1) 1
Tranmere R	(0) 0	Newcastle U	(1) 1
Birmingham C	(1) 1	Wimbledon	(1) 2
Chelsea	(1) 4	Aston Villa	(1) 1
Crewe Alex	(0) 0	Blackburn R	(0) 1
Derby Co	(0) 1	Arsenal	(1) 2
Leeds U	(1) 1	Bradford C	(0) 0
Manchester U	(0) 2	Bury	(0) 0
Middlesbrough	(0) 2	Everton	(0) 3

FOURTH ROUND

Bolton W	(0) 1	Wimbledon	(1) 2
Liverpool	(0) 1	Tottenham H	(2) 3
Luton T	(0) 1	Barnsley	(0) 0
Arsenal	(0) 0	Chelsea	(1) 5
Everton	(0) 1	Sunderland	(1) 1

(aet; Sunderland won 5-4 on penalties.)

Leicester C	(0) 2	Leeds U	(1) 1
Manchester U	(0) 2	Nottingham F	(0) 1
Newcastle U	(1) 1	Blackburn R	(1) 1

(aet; Blackburn R won 4-2 on penalties.)

FIFTH ROUND

| Sunderland | (1) 3 | Luton T | (0) 0 |

Wimbledon	(1) 2	Chelsea	(0) 1
Leicester C	(0) 1	Blackburn R	(0) 0
Tottenham H	(0) 3	Manchester U	(0) 1

SEMI-FINALS, FIRST LEG

| Sunderland | (0) 1 | Leicester C | (1) 2 |
| Tottenham H | (0) 0 | Wimbledon | (0) 0 |

SEMI-FINALS, SECOND LEG

| Wimbledon | (0) 0 | Tottenham H | (1) 1 |
| Leicester C | (0) 1 | Sunderland | (1) 1 |

FINAL (at Wembley)

21 MAR

Leicester C (0) 0
Tottenham H (0) 1 *(Nielsen 90)*   77,892

Leicester C: Keller; Ullathorne, Guppy, Elliott, Walsh, Taggart, Lennon, Izzet, Cottee, Savage (Zagorakis), Heskey (Marshall).
Tottenham H: Walker; Carr, Edinburgh, Freund, Vega, Campbell, Anderton, Nielsen, Iversen, Ferdinand, Ginola (Sinton).
Referee: T. Heilbron (Newton Aycliffe).

AUTO WINDSCREENS SHIELD 1998–99

FIRST ROUND

Colchester U	(1) 1	Gillingham	(4) 5
Blackpool	(0) 0	Stoke C	(1) 2
Burnley	(0) 0	Preston NE	(0) 1
Chester C	(1) 1	Hartlepool U	(0) 2

(aet; Hartlepool U won in sudden death.)

Macclesfield T	(0) 0	Wrexham	(0) 1
Manchester C	(0) 1	Mansfield T	(0) 2
Oldham Ath	(0) 0	Darlington	(0) 1

(aet; Darlington won in sudden death.)

Rotherham U	(0) 0	Wigan Ath	(1) 3
Bournemouth	(1) 2	Reading	(0) 0
Brentford	(1) 2	Plymouth Arg	(0) 0
Peterborough U	(3) 3	Leyton Orient	(0) 0
Shrewsbury T	(0) 0	Wycombe W	(0) 1

(aet; Wycombe W won in sudden death.)

Swansea C	(2) 4	Barnet	(0) 1
Walsall	(0) 2	Bristol R	(0) 2

(aet; Walsall won 5-4 on penalties.)

Millwall	(2) 2	Cardiff C	(0) 0
Notts Co	(0) 0	Hull C	(1) 1

SECOND ROUND

Halifax T	(1) 4	York C	(1) 2
Hull C	(0) 1	Wrexham	(1) 2
Lincoln C	(1) 1	Mansfield T	(0) 0
Bournemouth	(3) 5	Peterborough U	(1) 1
Brighton & HA	(1) 1	Millwall	(2) 5
Cambridge U	(1) 3	Northampton T	(1) 2
Exeter C	(1) 3	Southend U	(0) 1
Luton T	(0) 0	Walsall	(1) 3
Swansea C	(0) 0	Gillingham	(0) 1
Torquay U	(0) 2	Fulham	(0) 1

(aet; Torquay U won on sudden death.)

Wycombe W	(0) 1	Brentford	(2) 4
Darlington	(0) 0	Chesterfield	(0) 2

NORTHERN QUARTER-FINALS

Wrexham	(1) 3	Chesterfield	(0) 2

SECOND ROUND

Hartlepool U	(0) 2	Preston NE	(0) 2

(aet; Hartlepool U won 4-3 on penalties.)

Scunthorpe U	(1) 1	Carlisle U	(0) 1

(aet; Carlisle U won 4-3 on penalties.)

Wigan Ath	(1) 3	Scarborough	(0) 0

SOUTHERN QUARTER-FINALS

Brentford	(0) 0	Walsall	(0) 0

(aet; Walsall won 4-3 on penalties.)

Cambridge U	(1) 1	Exeter C	(0) 1

(aet; Cambridge U won 5-3 on penalties.)

Torquay U	(0) 0	Gillingham	(1) 1

NORTHERN QUARTER-FINALS

Carlisle U	(0) 0	Wigan Ath	(1) 3
Hartlepool U	(0) 0	Lincoln C	(0) 3

SECOND ROUND

Rochdale	(2) 2	Stoke C	(0) 1

(at Stoke.)

SOUTHERN QUARTER-FINALS

Bournemouth	(1) 1	Millwall	(1) 1

(aet; Millwall won 4-3 on penalties.)

NORTHERN SEMI-FINALS

Lincoln C	(0) 1	Wrexham	(1) 2

(aet; Wrexham won on sudden death.)

SOUTHERN SEMI-FINALS

Millwall	(0) 1	Gillingham	(0) 0

(aet; Millwall won on sudden death.)

Walsall	(1) 1	Cambridge U	(0) 1

(aet; Walsall won 4-3 on penalites.)

NORTHERN QUARTER-FINALS

Rochdale	(0) 2	Halifax T	(0) 1

(aet; Rochdale won on sudden death.)

NORTHERN SEMI-FINALS

Rochdale	(0) 0	Wigan Ath	(1) 2

SOUTHERN FINAL, FIRST LEG

Millwall	(1) 1	Walsall	(0) 0

NORTHERN FINAL, FIRST LEG

Wigan Ath	(0) 2	Wrexham	(0) 0

SOUTHERN FINAL, SECOND LEG

Walsall	(0) 1	Millwall	(1) 1

NORTHERN FINAL, SECOND LEG

Wrexham	(1) 2	Wigan Ath	(1) 3

FINAL (at Wembley)

18 APR

Millwall (0) 0
Wigan Ath (0) 1 *(Rogers 90)*   55,349

Millwall: Roberts B; Lavin, Stuart, Cahill, Nethercott, Dolan, Newman, Ifill, Harris, Sadlier, Reid.
Wigan Ath: Carroll; Bradshaw, Sharp, McGibbon, Balmer, Rogers, Liddell, Greenall, Haworth, O'Neill, Barlow (Lee).
Referee: C. Wilkes (Gloucester).

FA CHARITY SHIELD WINNERS 1908–98

1908	Manchester U v QPR	
	4-0 after 1-1 draw	
1909	Newcastle U v Northampton T	2-0
1910	Brighton v Aston Villa	1-0
1911	Manchester U v Swindon T	8-4
1912	Blackburn R v QPR	2-1
1913	Professionals v Amateurs	7-2
1920	Tottenham H v Burnley	2-0
1921	Huddersfield T v Liverpool	1-0
1922	Not played	
1923	Professionals v Amateurs	2-0
1924	Professionals v Amateurs	3-1
1925	Amateurs v Professionals	6-1
1926	Amateurs v Professionals	6-3
1927	Cardiff C v Corinthians	2-1
1928	Everton v Blackburn R	2-1
1929	Professionals v Amateurs	3-0
1930	Arsenal v Sheffield W	2-1
1931	Arsenal v WBA	1-0
1932	Everton v Newcastle U	5-3
1933	Arsenal v Everton	3-0
1934	Arsenal v Manchester C	4-0
1935	Sheffield W v Arsenal	1-0
1936	Sunderland v Arsenal	2-1
1937	Manchester C v Sunderland	2-0
1938	Arsenal v Preston NE	2-1
1948	Arsenal v Manchester U	4-3
1949	Portsmouth v Wolverhampton W	1-1*
1950	World Cup Team v	4-2
	Canadian Touring Team	
1951	Tottenham H v Newcastle U	2-1
1952	Manchester U v Newcastle U	4-2
1953	Arsenal v Blackpool	3-1
1954	Wolverhampton W v WBA	4-4*
1955	Chelsea v Newcastle U	3-0
1956	Manchester U v Manchester C	1-0
1957	Manchester U v Aston Villa	4-0
1958	Bolton W v Wolverhampton W	4-1
1959	Wolverhampton W v	3-1
	Nottingham F	
1960	Burnley v Wolverhampton W	2-2*
1961	Tottenham H v FA XI	3-2
1962	Tottenham H v Ipswich T	5-1
1963	Everton v Manchester U	4-0
1964	Liverpool v West Ham U	2-2*
1965	Manchester U v Liverpool	2-2*
1966	Liverpool v Everton	1-0
1967	Manchester U v Tottenham H	3-3*
1968	Manchester C v WBA	6-1
1969	Leeds U v Manchester C	2-1
1970	Everton v Chelsea	2-1
1971	Leicester C v Liverpool	1-0
1972	Manchester C v Aston Villa	1-0
1973	Burnley v Manchester C	1-0
1974	Liverpool† v Leeds U	1-1
1975	Derby Co v West Ham U	2-0
1976	Liverpool v Southampton	1-0
1977	Liverpool v Manchester U	0-0*
1978	Nottingham F v Ipswich T	5-0
1979	Liverpool v Arsenal	3-1
1980	Liverpool v West Ham U	1-0
1981	Aston Villa v Tottenham H	2-2*
1982	Liverpool v Tottenham H	1-0
1983	Manchester U v Liverpool	2-0
1984	Everton v Liverpool	1-0
1985	Everton v Manchester U	2-0
1986	Everton v Liverpool	1-1*
1987	Everton v Coventry C	1-0
1988	Liverpool v Wimbledon	2-1
1989	Liverpool v Arsenal	1-0
1990	Liverpool v Manchester U	1-1*
1991	Arsenal v Tottenham H	0-0*
1992	Leeds U v Liverpool	4-3
1993	Manchester U† v Arsenal	1-1
1994	Manchester U v Blackburn R	2-0
1995	Everton v Blackburn R	1-0
1996	Manchester U v Newcastle U	4-0
1997	Manchester U† v Chelsea	1-1

*Each club retained shield for six months. †Won on penalties.

AXA FA CHARITY SHIELD 1998

Arsenal (1) 3, Manchester U (0) 0

At Wembley, 9 August 1998, attendance 67,342

Arsenal: Seaman; Dixon, Winterburn, Vieira (Grimandi), Keown, Adams (Bould), Parlour, Anelka, Petit (Boa Morte), Bergkamp (Wreh), Overmars (Hughes).
Scorers: Overmars 33, Wreh 56, Anelka 71.

Manchester U: Schmeichel; Neville G, Irwin, Johnsen, Keane (Berg), Stam, Beckham, Butt (Solskjaer), Cole (Sheringham), Scholes (Neville P), Giggs (Cruyff).

Referee: G. Poll (Tring).

SCOTTISH LEAGUE REVIEW 1998–99

Rangers won the inaugural Scottish Premier League, clinching the title against their eternal rivals Celtic on 2 May in a bruising encounter which unhappily saw several unsavoury incidents on and off the pitch. Three players were dismissed and referee Hugh Dallas was struck by a coin. Fans invaded the pitch three times.

Neil McCann opened the scoring for Rangers in the 12th minute and Celtic were further distressed when Stephane Mahe was sent off just after half an hour's play for a second bookable offence.

Celtic went two down a minute before the interval when Jorg Albertz converted a penalty for Rangers. McCann made it 3-0 in the 76th minute to end the affair as a contest. Ten minutes later Rod Wallace, the Rangers striker was sent off for a foul and a minute before the final whistle Victor Riseth received his second booking and thus a red card leaving Celtic with nine men. It was a bitter disappointment for Celtic on their own ground before a crowd of 59,918.

However, Henrik Larsson, the Swedish international won both the Scottish Football Writers Award as Player of the Year and a similar accolade as the Scottish Professional Footballers choice.

The season had opened with the champions-to-be losing 2-1 at Hearts. Celtic lost their second match 3-2 at Aberdeen, who then led the table. But after four games it was Rangers leading Celtic.

Kilmarnock held on surprisingly well to Rangers heels in the following weeks to keep Celtic in third place. Amazingly there was no change in the order of such things until well into February. Moreover it only altered when Kilmarnock's match with Dunfermline Athletic was postponed. Ironically it proved a turning point for Killie because in their next game they were beaten 5-0 at home by Rangers. At the other end of the League, Dundee, the promoted team were everyone's favourites to return whence they came. There were problems with the Dens Park ground and it seemed the ideal solution for the Tayside Blues to be the fall guys. But Dundee had other ideas.

In fact Hearts, the momentary leaders slumped so dramatically that by mid-March only goal difference kept them above cellar dwellers Dunfermline. Worse followed the next week when Dunfermline had a rare 1-0 success against St Johnstone and Dundee beat Hearts 2-0 to put the Tynecastle team on the bottom. Only then did they begin to show some form to escape leaving the unfortunate Dunfermline to become the relegated team.

In the Scottish League, Falkirk, Inverness Caley and Ross County were clear leaders in their respective division after only four games. Towards the end of October, Hibernian were looking good, Falkirk fading, Livingston moving above Caley and Stenhousemuir edging out Ross County.

Ayr United then put in a challenging burst to go above Hibs before subsiding as Falkirk recovered. All three top teams increased their lead with the New Year. Caley caught Livingston in March but surrendered the lead to their rivals again the following month as the two teams see-sawed before Livingston prevailed. Falkirk and Stenhousemuir earned promotion for steady performances over the second half of the season. Luckless Stranraer, the first to be relegated in the League, won only one game away, their first at Hibernian.

In the League Cup Rangers lifted the trophy with a 2-1 win over St Johnstone, who had a consistent season overall, finishing a highly respectable third in the Scottish Premier League and earning a place in the UEFA Cup for 1999–2000 in the process. With Rangers in the European Cup, St Johnstone joined Celtic and Kilmarnock in the remaining competition. The Tennant's Scottish Cup Final gave Rangers the treble; a goal by Rod Wallace in the 49th minute overcoming Celtic.

Finally a word of praise for Stenhousemuir's 42 year old Graeme Armstrong who finished the season with a record 879 League appearances in a career spanning 24 seasons.

SCOTTISH LEAGUE TABLES 1998–99

Premier Division

	P	W	D	L	F	A	W	D	L	F	A	Pts	GD
Rangers	36	12	5	1	32	11	11	3	4	46	20	77	+47
Celtic	36	14	2	2	49	12	7	6	5	35	23	71	+49
St Johnstone	36	8	7	3	24	18	7	5	6	15	20	57	+1
Kilmarnock	36	8	7	3	24	15	6	7	5	23	14	56	+18
Dundee	36	7	4	7	18	23	6	3	9	18	33	46	−20
Hearts	36	8	2	8	27	26	3	7	8	17	24	42	−6
Motherwell	36	6	5	7	20	31	4	6	8	15	23	41	−19
Aberdeen	36	6	4	8	24	35	4	3	11	19	36	37	−28
Dundee U	36	2	8	8	13	22	6	2	10	24	26	34	−11
Dunfermline Ath	36	4	7	7	18	29	0	9	9	10	30	28	−31

The header groups: Home / Goals, Away / Goals.

First Division

	P	W	D	L	F	A	W	D	L	F	A	Pts	GD
Hibernian	36	16	1	1	45	13	12	4	2	39	20	89	+51
Falkirk	36	9	5	4	28	18	11	1	6	32	20	66	+22
Ayr U	36	8	4	6	38	23	11	1	6	28	19	62	+24
Airdrieonians	36	6	2	10	17	29	12	3	3	25	14	59	−1
St Mirren	36	10	2	6	26	25	4	8	6	16	18	52	−1
Greenock Morton	36	5	5	8	20	24	9	2	7	25	17	49	+4
Clydebank	36	5	6	7	17	18	6	7	5	19	20	46	−2
Raith R	36	5	5	8	19	27	3	6	9	18	30	35	−20
Hamilton A	36	3	5	10	13	26	3	5	10	17	36	28	−32
Stranraer	36	2	2	14	14	31	3	0	15	15	43	17	−45

Second Division

	P	W	D	L	F	A	W	D	L	F	A	Pts	GD
Livingston	36	13	4	1	32	12	9	7	2	34	23	77	+31
Inverness CT	36	14	4	0	44	20	7	5	6	36	28	72	+32
Clyde	36	10	4	4	28	16	5	4	9	18	26	53	+4
Queen of the S	36	7	8	3	26	17	6	1	11	24	28	48	+5
Alloa Ath	36	8	3	7	41	30	5	4	9	24	26	46	+9
Stirling A	36	7	3	8	27	28	5	5	8	23	35	44	−13
Arbroath	36	7	4	7	19	25	5	4	9	18	27	44	−15
Partick T	36	7	4	7	18	19	5	3	10	18	26	43	−9
East Fife	36	7	3	8	22	31	5	3	10	20	33	42	−22
Forfar Ath	36	6	3	9	31	34	2	4	12	17	36	31	−22

Third Division

	P	W	D	L	F	A	W	D	L	F	A	Pts	GD
Ross Co	36	12	1	5	39	16	12	4	2	48	26	77	+45
Stenhousemuir	36	9	2	7	34	26	10	5	3	28	16	64	+20
Brechin C	36	7	6	5	21	19	10	2	6	26	24	59	+4
Dumbarton	36	6	5	7	25	21	10	4	4	28	19	57	+13
Berwick R	36	7	3	8	28	27	5	11	2	25	22	50	+4
Queen's Park	36	6	7	5	22	21	5	4	9	19	25	44	−5
Albion R	36	5	4	9	22	36	7	4	7	21	27	44	−20
East Stirlingshire	36	4	10	4	27	22	5	3	10	23	26	40	+2
Cowdenbeath	36	5	2	11	19	30	3	5	10	15	35	31	−31
Montrose	36	5	4	9	26	31	3	2	13	16	43	30	−32

BELL'S SCOTTISH LEAGUE—PREMIER DIVISION RESULTS 1998–99

	Aberdeen	Celtic	Dundee	Dundee U	Dunfermline Ath	Hearts	Kilmarnock	Motherwell	Rangers	St Johnstone
Aberdeen	—	3-2	2-2	0-3	2-1	2-0	0-1	1-1	1-1	0-1
	—	1-5	1-2	0-4	3-1	2-5	2-1	1-1	2-4	1-0
Celtic	2-0	—	6-1	2-1	5-0	1-1	1-1	2-0	5-1	0-1
	3-2	—	5-0	2-1	5-0	3-0	1-0	1-0	0-3	5-0
Dundee	0-2	1-1	—	2-2	1-0	1-0	1-1	1-0	0-4	0-1
	1-2	0-3	—	1-3	3-1	2-0	2-1	1-0	1-1	0-1
Dundee U	1-0	1-1	0-1	—	1-1	0-0	0-2	2-2	0-0	1-1
	3-0	1-2	0-2	—	1-1	1-3	0-0	0-3	1-2	0-1
Dunfermline Ath	1-1	2-2	2-0	2-1	—	1-1	0-3	1-1	0-2	1-1
	1-2	1-2	2-0	2-2	—	0-0	0-6	1-2	0-3	1-0
Hearts	2-0	2-1	0-2	0-1	2-1	—	2-1	3-0	2-1	1-1
	0-2	2-4	1-2	4-1	2-0	—	2-2	0-2	2-3	0-2
Kilmarnock	4-0	2-0	2-1	2-0	0-0	3-0	—	0-0	1-3	2-2
	4-2	0-0	0-0	2-0	0-0	1-0	—	0-1	0-5	1-1
Motherwell	2-2	1-2	2-1	1-0	0-0	3-2	0-0	—	1-0	1-0
	1-1	1-7	1-2	2-0	1-1	0-4	1-2	—	1-5	1-2
Rangers	2-1	0-0	1-0	2-1	1-1	3-0	1-0	2-1	—	4-0
	3-1	2-2	6-1	0-1	1-0	0-0	1-1	2-1	—	1-0
St Johnstone	2-0	2-1	1-1	1-3	1-1	1-1	0-0	5-0	0-7	—
	4-1	1-0	1-0	1-0	1-1	0-0	0-1	0-0	3-1	—

BELL'S SCOTTISH LEAGUE—DIVISION ONE RESULTS 1998–99

	Airdrieonians	Ayr U	Clydebank	Falkirk	Hamilton A	Hibernian	Morton	Raith R	St Mirren	Stranraer
Airdrieonians	—	0-2	0-0	0-3	3-2	1-3	0-1	0-1	1-0	3-2
	—	0-2	2-0	1-2	1-0	1-4	0-2	2-2	0-3	2-0
Ayr U	1-2	—	4-1	4-2	2-3	3-3	1-0	0-2	1-1	7-1
	0-1	—	0-0	1-2	5-0	1-3	1-0	1-0	2-2	4-0
Clydebank	0-1	0-1	—	0-1	0-0	2-2	2-1	1-1	1-0	2-1
	0-1	2-1	—	1-2	0-0	2-0	1-2	0-0	2-2	1-2
Falkirk	0-1	1-0	2-2	—	2-1	1-1	2-1	1-1	1-1	1-0
	1-1	3-0	0-2	—	6-1	1-2	1-2	1-0	1-0	3-2
Hamilton A	1-1	1-3	1-2	2-1	—	2-2	0-0	3-2	0-0	1-2
	0-2	0-2	0-1	0-2	—	0-2	0-2	1-2	0-0	1-0
Hibernian	1-0	4-2	2-1	2-1	0-0	—	2-1	3-1	4-1	1-2
	3-0	3-0	3-0	2-1	4-0	—	2-1	5-1	2-1	2-0
Morton	0-0	1-2	2-2	0-3	1-2	0-1	—	2-0	0-1	3-0
	0-2	1-4	1-1	3-2	3-0	1-3	—	1-1	0-0	1-0
Raith R	1-3	0-0	0-1	1-1	0-2	1-3	0-0	—	1-0	2-0
	0-1	2-4	2-1	2-1	1-1	1-3	1-3	—	1-1	3-2
St Mirren	1-5	0-2	0-0	0-2	3-2	2-0	1-0	2-1	—	1-0
	3-0	1-0	1-1	0-3	1-0	1-2	1-5	3-1	—	5-1
Stranraer	1-2	0-1	0-2	1-2	2-1	0-1	2-3	2-2	0-1	—
	1-2	0-2	0-2	0-1	2-2	0-4	0-1	2-0	1-2	—

BELL'S SCOTTISH LEAGUE—DIVISION TWO RESULTS 1998–99

	Alloa Ath	Arbroath	Clyde	East Fife	Forfar Ath	Inverness CT	Livingston	Partick Th	Queen of the S	Stirling Alb
Alloa Ath	—	1-1	3-0	5-1	1-2	1-1	3-4	3-1	2-1	7-0
	—	1-2	1-0	3-1	3-1	1-4	1-3	0-1	3-5	2-2
Arbroath	0-2	—	0-0	0-2	2-1	0-1	2-2	1-0	2-1	0-3
	1-2	—	0-3	2-1	2-2	3-1	1-1	2-1	0-2	1-0
Clyde	2-1	3-0	—	0-0	3-1	4-1	1-1	1-2	2-0	2-1
	0-1	1-1	—	1-0	1-0	1-1	0-3	0-1	2-1	4-1
East Fife	2-2	0-3	0-0	—	1-0	1-5	2-3	1-3	2-0	2-3
	0-4	1-2	2-1	—	2-1	3-2	1-1	1-0	0-1	1-0
Forfar Ath	1-2	1-3	2-2	1-2	—	2-2	1-2	0-1	1-0	1-2
	3-1	5-2	3-1	2-4	—	0-3	1-2	2-1	2-1	3-3
Inverness CT	3-2	2-1	1-1	4-2	2-2	—	2-1	3-2	3-2	3-1
	1-1	2-0	3-0	4-0	2-0	—	3-1	3-2	1-0	2-2
Livingston	2-1	2-1	2-0	3-1	1-1	2-1	—	1-0	2-0	1-1
	1-0	1-0	2-0	1-0	5-0	4-3	—	1-1	1-2	0-0
Partick Th	1-0	2-0	0-2	0-1	2-0	0-1	1-3	—	2-2	1-0
	2-1	0-0	0-1	2-2	1-0	2-1	1-1	—	1-3	0-1
Queen of the S	2-1	0-0	2-1	0-0	3-0	2-2	0-1	0-0	—	2-3
	0-0	3-0	2-1	2-0	0-3	1-1	2-2	2-2	—	3-0
Stirling Alb	4-2	0-1	1-2	3-2	3-1	0-1	1-3	2-0	1-0	—
	1-1	2-1	2-3	0-1	2-2	1-5	0-0	3-0	1-3	—

BELL'S SCOTTISH LEAGUE—DIVISION THREE RESULTS 1998–99

	Albion R	Berwick R	Brechin C	Cowdenbeath	Dumbarton	East Stirling	Montrose	Queen's P	Ross Co	Stenhousemuir
Albion R	—	1-1	1-4	0-1	0-2	3-1	4-1	2-1	0-8	1-3
	—	0-3	4-1	1-1	0-2	0-2	0-0	1-0	3-3	1-2
Berwick R	2-1	—	3-0	3-1	3-1	1-2	1-1	0-3	0-2	1-2
	1-1	—	2-3	2-1	0-1	1-2	4-1	0-2	2-2	2-1
Brechin C	1-0	1-1	—	2-1	0-0	0-0	3-0	2-2	0-1	1-0
	3-1	0-3	—.	1-1	3-3	1-0	2-3	1-0	0-1	0-2
Cowdenbeath	2-3	1-1	0-1	—	0-2	2-1	4-1	0-3	1-2	0-2
	0-2	1-2	0-2	—	2-1	3-2	1-0	0-0	2-3	0-2
Dumbarton	2-0	0-0	1-2	5-0	—	2-2	0-2	1-0	1-2	0-2
	1-1	1-1	2-0	6-1	—	0-2	2-1	0-1	0-0	1-4
East Stirling	0-1	0-0	1-1	1-1	1-2	—	3-1	1-1	2-2	1-1
	4-1	3-3	4-1	0-0	1-2	—	2-1	1-1	1-2	1-1
Montrose	1-2	1-1	1-2	1-1	1-1	2-0	—	1-0	3-6	0-0
	2-3	0-3	1-3	1-2	4-2	1-0	—	3-0	2-3	1-2
Queen's P	0-0	1-1	1-1	2-0	0-1	0-4	3-0	—	4-2	0-0
	0-0	1-1	0-2	2-1	1-1	2-1	1-2	—	0-3	4-1
Ross Co	1-2	3-1	0-1	2-0	2-0	1-0	3-1	5-1	—	0-1
	2-0	6-0	2-1	1-0	1-2	4-2	3-0	1-2	—	2-2
Stenhousemuir	4-1	1-2	0-1	1-2	0-3	1-0	4-0	2-1	2-4	—
	1-2	1-1	1-0	4-1	0-2	2-2	3-1	4-1	3-2	—

ABERDEEN   PREMIER LEAGUE

Ground: Pittodrie Stadium, Aberdeen AB24 5QH (01224) 650400
Ground capacity: 22,199. **Colours:** All red with white trim.
Manager: Ebbe Skovdahl.
League Appearances: Anderson R 13(3); Bernard P 8(1); Bett B 1; Buchan J 19(4); Dodds W 6; Dow A 22(3); Gillies R 4(7); Good I (1); Hamilton J 6(1); Hart M 5(9); Hignett C 13; Inglis J 16(1); Jess E 36; Kiriakov I 17(5); Leighton J 22; Mayer A 13; Newell M 14(9); Notman A (2); Pepper N 7(3); Perry M 32; Rowson D 18(4); Smith G 30; Stillie D 8; Warner A 6; Whyte D 35; Winters R 28; Wyness D 6(8); Young Darr 11; Young Dere (4).
Goals – League (43): Jess 14, Winters 12, Perry 4, Buchan 2, Hignett 2, Mayer 2, Newell 2, Bernard 1, Hamilton 1, Inglis 1, Wyness 1, own goal 1.
Scottish Cup (0).
League Cup (3): Dodds 3.

AIRDRIEONIANS   DIV. 1

Ground: Shyberry Excelsior Stadium, Airdrie ML679
8QZ (01236) 622000
Ground capacity: 6300. **Colours:** White shirts with red diamond, white shorts.
Manager: Gary Mackay.
League Appearances: Black K 30(1); Brady D (1); Cooper S 25(2); Easton S 3(4); Evans G 21(5); Farrell D 20(4); Farrell G 6(12); Greacen S (1); Jack P 21(1); Johnston F 26(5); Mackay G 4(6); Martin J 28; McCann A 27(4); McCloy B 2(2); McCormick S 4(8); McGrillen P 20(3); McGuire D 2(2); McKeown S 2(11); Moore A 21(7); Sandison J 33(1); Sissoko H (1); Smith A 23(2); Stewart A 31(1); Taylor S 8(4); Thomson S 8; Wilson M 31.
Goals – League (42): Cooper 8, Black 7 (4 pens), Evans 6, McCann 4, Moore 4, McCormick 2, Taylor 2 (1 pen), Wilson 2, Farrell D 1, Farrell G 1, Johnston 1, McGrillen 1, McKeown 1, Sissoko 1, own goal 1.
Scottish Cup (1): Cooper 1.
League Cup (4): Moore 2, Wilson 2.

ALBION ROVERS   DIV. 3

Ground: Cliftonhill Stadium, Main Street, Coatbridge ML5 3RB (01236) 606334
Ground capacity: 2496. **Colours:** Yellow shirts with black trim, black shorts.
Manager: Mark Shanks.
League Appearances: Blair P 12; Bottiglieri E 10; Bruce D 6(1); Diack I 14(5); Docherty R 6; Donaldson E 35(1); Duncan G 26; Goldie G (1); Greenock R 15(7); Hamilton J 23; Harty M 8(13); Limond W 3(2); Lorimer D 31(5); McBride K 1(3); McBride M (1); McColm R 1; McGowan C (2); McGowan N 33; McIlhatton L (2); McLean M 35; McLees J 29(2); McQuade K (2); McStay J 32; Melvin M 33(1); Mitchell C 1; Murphy J 11(3); Ross A 5; Shaw M 9(12); Silvestro C 4(1); Sinclair C 2(2); Smith J 1; Sturrock G 10(12).

Goals – League (43): Lorimer 10 (2 pens), McLees 6, Donaldson 5, Melvin 5, Diack 4, McStay 3, Blair 2, Murphy 2, Bottiglieri 1, Bruce 1, Hamilton 1, Ross 1, Shaw 1, own goal 1.
Scottish Cup (7): Lorimer 2, Murphy 2, Diack 1, Hamilton 1, Melvin 1.
League Cup (1): Donaldson 1.

ALLOA ATHLETIC   DIV. 2

Ground: Recreation Park, Alloa FK10 1RR (01259) 722695
Ground capacity: 3142. **Colours:** Gold shirts with black trim, black shorts.
Manager: Terry Christie.
League Appearances: Allan G 2(1); Armstrong G 1(1); Beaton D 6; Cairns M 36; Cameron M 21(7); Clark D 9(5); Cowan M 18; Donaghy M 10(1); Duthie M 5(3); Gilmour J (1); Haddow L 12(1); Irvine W 33; Mackay S 6(13); McAneny P 33(1); McCulloch K 6; McKechnie G 20(5); McLeod K (2); Nelson M 19(7); Pew D 21(8); Ramsay S 15(4); Sharp R 15(2); Simpson P 25(8); Valentine C 34; Wilson M 22(3); Wilson S 27(1)
Goals – League (65): Cameron 15, Irvine 15 (4 pens), Simpson 10, McKechnie 9, Cowan 3, Clark 2, Duthie 2, McAneny 2, Mackay 2, Beaton 1, Pew 1, Ramsay 1, Wilson M 1, Wilson S 1.
Scottish Cup (1): Cameron 1.
League Cup (5): Mckechnie 2, Cameron 1, Simpson 1, Wilson M 1.

ARBROATH   DIV. 2

Ground: Gayfield Park, Arbroath DD11 1QB (01241) 872157
Ground capacity: 6488. **Colours:** Maroon shirts with sky blue trim, white shorts.
Manager: David Baikie.
League Appearances: Arbuckle D 23(5); Burns K (1); Cooper C 13(4); Crawford J 35; Devine C 5(1); Donnachie B 2(1); Elliott J 8(3); Florence S 24; Gallagher J 31(1); Grant B 2(6); Hinchcliffe C 25; Jones K 22(1); McAulay J 34(1); McGlashan C 27; McGlashan J 14; McWalter M 3(2); Mercer J 22(7); Mitchell B 2; O'Driscoll J 3(1); Peters S 10(2); Scott S 1(2); Scott W 15(5); Sellars B 22(8); Spence W 5(6); Thomson N 14(9); Tindal K 23(8); Wight C 11.
Goals – League (37): McGlashan C 12 (1 pen), Sellars 5, Arbuckle 4, Gallagher 4 (2 pens), Tindal 3, Crawford 2, McGlashan J 2, Cooper 1 (pen), Devine 1, Mercer 1, Peters 1, own goal 1.
Scottish Cup (1): Gallagher 1 (pen).
League Cup (0).

AYR UNITED   DIV. 1

Ground: Somerset Park, Ayr KA8 9NB (01292) 263435
Ground capacity: 12,178. **Colours:** White shirts with black sleeves, black shorts.
Manager: Gordon Dalziel.
League Appearances: Agnew P 1(2); Armstrong G (2); Barrick D 11; Bowman G (4); Bradford J 2(3); Burns G 4(6); Campbell M 9; Castilla D 21; Craig D 22; Crilly M (3); Davies J 27(2); Dick J 1(3); Duthie M (5); Ferguson I 9(13); Findlay W

15(7); Hamilton B 2(1); Horace A (4); Hurst G 34; Kelly R 7(11); Lyons A 31(1); Millen A 34; Miller C 4(2); Nelson C 15; Nolan V (1); Reynolds M 11(7); Robertson J 21; Scally N 2; Stewart D (1); Teale G 23; Traynor J 22(7); Walker A 31(2); Welsh C 25(1); Winnie D 12.
Goals – League (66): Hurst 18, Walker 15 (3 pens), Ferguson 8 (2 pens), Lyons 8, Teale 4 (1 pen), Davies 3, Craig 2, Findlay 2 (1 pen), Bradford 1, Burns 1, Kelly 1, Millen 1, Reynolds 1, Robertson 1.
Scottish Cup (5): Walker 3 (2 pens), Lyons 1, Teale 1.
League Cup (8): Hurst 2, Armstrong 1, Davies 1, Lyons 1, Walker 1, Welsh 1, own goal 1.

BERWICK RANGERS DIV. 3

Ground: Shielfield Park, Berwick-on-Tweed TD15 2EF (01289) 307424
Ground capacity: 4131. **Colours:** Black with two inch gold stripe, black shorts.
Manager: Paul Smith.
League Appearances: Baigrie J 1(7); Beaton D 28; Buglass K (1); Burgess M 1; Campbell C 25(1); Clark J 2; Cunningham T 1; Dixon A (4); Forrester P 28(2); Fraser G 26(3); Haddow L 3; Hunter M 12(3); Irvine N 2; Laidlaw S 2(2); Leask M 24(6); McCole D (1); McLeod J 7(1); McNicoll G 34; Neil M 19(1); Neill A 35; O'Connor G 35; Quinn B (11); Rafferty K 24(8); Ramage I 20(9); Reilly D 1(1); Ritchie I 9; Seaton S 4(5); Shaw G 14(7); Sinclair C 2; Smith D 9(6); Smith S (3); Watt D 28(2).
Goals – League (53): Leask 12, Forrester 9, Smith D 7, Watt 7, Rafferty 5, Shaw 4, Hunter 2, Neil M 2, Ramage 2, Baigrie 1, McNicoll 1, Neill A 1.
Scottish Cup (0).
League Cup (2): Forrester 1, Laidlaw 1.

BRECHIN CITY DIV. 3

Ground: Glebe Park, Brechin DD9 6BJ (01356) 622856
Ground capacity: 3980. **Colours:** Red with white trim.
Manager: John Young.
League Appearances: Bain K 31; Black R 32(1); Boylan P 6; Boyle S 8; Brown R 13(3); Buick G 15(7); Butter J 3; Cairney H 34; Campbell S 27(1); Christie G 11(5); Dailly M 10(6); Dickson J 34(2); Garden S 33; Hutcheon A 6(15); Kerrigan S 14(12); Laing K 5; MacLeod I (3); McKellar J 22(7); Riley P 12; Smart C 11(1); Smith G 26; Sorbie S 31; Williamson K 12(1).
Goals – League (47): Dickson 15 (3 pens), Sorbie 12, Bain 5, Kerrigan 4, Black 2, Campbell 2, McKellar 2, Christie 1, Dailly 1, Hutcheon 1, Smart 1, Smith 1.
Scottish Cup (5): Dickson 2, Sorbie 2, Kerrigan 1.
League Cup (2): Hutcheon 2.

CELTIC PREMIER LEAGUE

Ground: Celtic Park, Glasgow G40 3RE (0141) 556 2611
Ground capacity: 60,506. **Colours:** Green and white hooped shirts, white shorts.
Head Coach: John Barnes.
League Appearances: Annoni E 9(5); Blinker R 13(2); Boyd T 31; Brattbakk H 16(8); Burchill M 5(16); Burley C 20(1); Corr B (1); Donnelly S 20(3); Gould J 28;

Hannah D 5(4); Healy C 2(1); Jackson D 4(2); Johnson T 3; Kerr S 4; Lambert P 33; Larsson H 35; Mackay M 1; Mahe S 24; Marshall S 1(1); McBride J (1); McCondichie A 1; McKinlay T 11(7); McNamara J 15(1); Mjallby J 17; Moravcik L 14; O'Donnell P 13(2); Rieper M 7; Riseth V 26(1); Stubbs A 22(1); Viduka M 8(1); Warner A 3; Wieghorst M 5(2).
Goals – League (84): Larsson 29 (7 pens), Burchill 9, Burley 9, Moravcik 6, Brattbakk 5, Donnelly 5, Viduka 5, Blinker 4, Johnson 3, Riseth 3, O'Donnell 2, Lambert 1, Mackay 1, Mjallby 1, Stubbs 1.
Scottish Cup (12): Larsson 5, Viduka 3, Blinker 1, Brattbakk 1, O'Donnell 1, own goal 1.
League Cup (0).

CLYDE

DIV. 2

Ground: Broadwood Stadium, Cumbernauld G68 9NE (01236) 451511
Ground capacity: 8200. **Colours:** White shirts with red and black trim, black shorts.
Manager: Allan Maitland.
League Appearances: Balfour R 3; Barratt J 13(7); Brownlie P (1); Campbell P (4); Carrigan B 19(12); Convery S 30; Cranmer C 23(5); Dillon J (2); Grant A 28(6); Hay P 6(5); Keogh P 34(2); McCusker R 35; McDonald I 14(4); McGhee G (1); McGraw M 5; McHarg S 7(9); McIntyre G 2; McLay A 29; McMillan A 9; McPhee G 2(2); Mitchell J 2(4); Murray D 25(4); O'Brien A 1(15); Peters S 1(1); Rice B 8(10); Sexton D 1; Smith B 35; Spittal I 35; Wylie D 29(1).
Goals – League (46): Convery 12 (2 pens), McCusker 10 (2 pens), Keogh 6, Barratt 3, Carrigan 3, O'Brien 3, Grant 2, McGraw 2, McHarg 2, Cranmer 1, McLay 1, Spittal 1.
Scottish Cup (11): McCusker 3 (1 pen), Carrigan 2, Convery 2, McHarg 2, Grant 1, McLay 1.
League Cup (1): McPhee 1.

CLYDEBANK

DIV. 1

Ground: Cappielow Park, Greenock. (Office) (0141) 9559048. (Match days only) (01475) 723571
Ground capacity: 14,891. **Colours:** Red and white stripes, black shorts.
Player/Manager: Ian McCall.
League Appearances: Anthony M 9(4); Brannigan K 31; Brown A 1(14); Callaghan S 5; Dobie S 6; Docherty S 17(11); Elliot B 4; Gardner L 24(11); Inglis N 1; Love G 7; Lovering P 12; McDonald C 22(8); McKelvie D (9); McKinstrey J 7(2); McLaughlin J 32; McMillan A 1(1); McWilliams D 5(4); Miller S 28(4); Morrison S 2(1); Murdoch S 13(3); Naker R 1; Newlands R 1; Nicholls D 34; Ritchie I 11(2); Robertson A 7(4); Ross S 3; Scott C 28; Smith T 20(1); Taggart C 25(10); Teale G 7(1); Wishart F 32.
Goals – League (36): McDonald 9, McLaughlin 3, Miller 3, Smith 3, Brannigan 2, Docherty 2 (1 pen), Elliot 2, Gardner 2, Taggart 2, Teale 2, Anthony 1 (pen), Brown 1, Love 1, McWilliams 1, Nicholls 1, Robertson 1.
Scottish Cup (6): Nicholls 3, Gardner 1, McMillan 1, Ritchie 1.
League Cup (1): McDonald 1.

COWDENBEATH   DIV. 3

Ground: Central Park, Cowdenbeath KY4 9EY (01383) 610166
Ground capacity: 5268. **Colours:** Royal blue stripes with red trim, white shorts.
Manager: Craig Levein.
League Appearances: Bannatyne P (2); Blair D 2(1); Bowsher C 7(1); Bradley M 19; Brown G 23(12); Bruno P 1; Burns J 23(4); Carnie G 8; Cuthbert L 15(2); Dair L 3; Dinse R 2; Findlay G 5; Godfrey R 9; Graham C 11(4); Hamilton A 22(4); Horn R 8; Humphreys M 10(3); Hunter G 2; Hutchison S 27; Lakie J 1; Lynch J 1; Malcolm S 4; Martin A (1); McKenzie J 5; McMillan A 1; McMillan C 7(6); Melvin A (6); Millar P 1(2); Milne K 23; Mitchell W 13(2); Murray D 7(1); Paterson G 1; Pryde D 2(3); Ritchie A 4(3); Robertson M 13(4); Smith P (1); Snedden S 29(1); Stewart W 26(3); Thomson R 21(1); Urquhart M 11(2); Ward M (3); Welsh B 4(8); Winter C 25.
Goals – League (34): Stewart 7, Milne 6, Brown 5, Bradley 2, Hamilton 2, Snedden 2, Thomson 2, Winter 2, Bowsher 1, Dair 1, Graham 1, Hunter 1, Robertson 1, Welsh 1.
Scottish Cup (2): Burns 1, Snedden 1.
League Cup (0).

DUMBARTON   DIV. 3

Ground: Boghead Park, Dumbarton G82 2JA (01389) 762569
Ground capacity: 5503. **Colours:** White with yelllow trim, white shorts.
Manager: Jimmy Brown.
League Appearances: Barnes D 1; Bradford J 4; Brittain C 22(1); Brown A 2(5); Bruce J 17; Dennison P 2; Finnegan P 1(2); Flannery P 33; Glancy M 5(5); Gow S 6(3); Grace A 18(2); Harvey P 7(2); Jack S 35; King T 29; McKinnon C 27; Meechan K 33; Melvin M 2(9); Melvin W 24(6); Miller K 2(7); Mooney M 28(4); Reid D 9(1); Robertson J 21(5); Sharp L 17; Smith C 3(6); Stewart D 9(1); Wilkinson B 4(2); Wilson W 35.
Goals – League (53): Flannery 17, Robertson 8 (4 pens), Mooney 4 (1 pen), King 3, McKinnon 3, Melvin W 3, Smith 3, Bradford 2, Sharp 2 (1 pen), Brittain 1, Bruce 1, Glancy 1, Gow 1, Grace 1, Jack 1, Stewart 1, Wilson 1.
Scottish Cup (1): Flannery 1.
League Cup (0).

DUNDEE   PREMIER LEAGUE

Ground: Dens Park, Dundee DD3 7JY (01382) 889966
Ground capacity: 10,531. **Colours:** Dark blue shirts with red and white trim, white shorts.
Manager: John Scott.
League Appearances: Adamczuk D 24(2); Anderson I 17(11); Annand E 19(10); Bayne G (2); Boyack S 8; Coyne T 8(8); Douglas R 35; Falconer W 31(2); Fleming D 1; Garcin E 2(1); Grady J 20(6); Grant B (4); Hunter G 3; Irvine B 33; Langfield J 1(1); Maddison L 21; Magee D 1(1); McCormick S (1); McInally J 14(1); McSkimming S 25(4); Miller W 26; O'Driscoll J (1); Pounewatchy S 2(1); Rae G 23(7); Raeside R 19(2); Robertson H 9(1); Rogers D 7(4); Sharp L 4(2); Smith B 29(4); Strachan G 4(2); Tweed S 10.

Goals – League (36): Annand 9, Adamczuk 6, Falconer 4, Anderson 3, Grady 3, Irvine 3, Boyack 2, McSkimming 2, Rae 1, Sharp 1, Tweed 1, own goal 1.
Scottish Cup (1): Annand 1.
League Cup (0).

DUNDEE UNITED

PREMIER LEAGUE

Ground: Tannadice Park, Dundee DD3 7JW (01382) 833166
Ground capacity: 14,209. **Colours:** Tangerine shirts with black trim, black shorts.
Manager: Paul Sturrock.
League Appearances: Boli R 3; Combe A 10; De Vos J 23(2); Dijkstra S 26(1); Dodds W 29(1); Dolan J 4(1); Duffy C 12(3); Easton C 28(2); Eustace J 8(3); Hannah D 13; Jenkins I 5(1); Jonsson S 12(2); Malpas M 31; Mathie A 13(9); McConalogue S (1); McCulloch S 9; McLaren A 3(5); McLaughlin B 1(2); McNally M 4(1); McSwegan G 5; Miller J 14(10); Mols T 11; Murray N 2(1); Olofsson K 32(2); Partridge D (1); Pascual B 16; Paterson J 8(7); Patterson D 17(2); Pedersen E 6; Skoldmark M 22(3); Thompson S 5(10); Valeriani J (1); Winters R 1(2); Worrall D 3(1); Zetterlund L 20(1).
Goals – League (37): Dodds 17 (3 pens), Olofsson 7, McSwegan 3, Miller 2, Easton 1, Eustace 1, Hannah 1, Jonsson 1, Mathie 1, Thompson 1, Winters 1, Zetterlund 1.
Scottish Cup (8): Olofsson 3, Dodds 1, Duffy 1, Murray 1, Patterson D 1, Skoldmark 1.
League Cup (2): Boli 1, McSwegan 1.

DUNFERMLINE ATHLETIC

DIV. 1

Ground: East End Park, Dunfermline KY12 7RB (01383) 724295
Ground capacity: 12,500. **Colours:** Black and white striped shirts, black shorts.
Manager: Dick Campbell.
League Appearances: Boyle S 1; Britton G 13(8); Butler L 35; Coyle O 11; Dair J 9(1); Den Bieman I (2); Dolan J 10; Edinho 5(4); Faulconbridge C 1(5); Ferguson D 18(3); Fraser J 2(4); French H 15(6); Graham D 14(7); Huxford R 22(3); Ireland C 21(2); Johnson G 18; Linighan D 1; MacDonald W (1); Martin C 2(1); McCulloch S 19; McGroarty C 3(1); Millar M 13(8); Nish C (2); Petrie S 19(11); Shaw G 10(8); Shields G 36; Smith A 29(6); Squires J 19(2); Templeman C 5(7); Thomson S 20(1); Tod A 24(1); Westwater I 1.
Goals – League (28): Smith 8 (2 pens), Britton 2, French 2, Graham 2, Petrie 2, Shaw 2, Squires 2, Thomson 2, Boyle 1, Coyle 1, Edinho 1, McCulloch 1, Millar 1 (pen), Tod 1.
Scottish Cup (2): Smith 2.
League Cup (0).

EAST FIFE

DIV. 3

Ground: Bayview Park, Methil, Fife KY8 3RW (01333) 426323
Ground capacity: 2000 (all seated). **Colours:** Amber shirts with black trim, black shorts.
Manager: Steve Kirk.

League Appearances: Abercromby M 7(3); Allan G 21(2); Archibald E (2); Brown G 13(4); Butter J 2; Coyle R 25(1); Cusick J 32; Dair L 13(3); Dixon A 1; Dyer M 4(2); Findlay M 1; Fisher D (3); Gartshore P 1(5); Gibb R 28(3); Harrison T 17; Honeyman B 2(1); Johnston G 17; Kirk S 17(10); Lawrie A 13; MacFarlane C (1); Martin J 11(9); McCulloch W 34; McNeil J 4(7); McPherson G 3(6); Moffat B 35; Mooney R 3(2); Munro K 36; Peters S 5(2); Ramsay S 7; Robertson G 7; Skeldon K 18(4); Strathdee J 7(4); Venables R 12(1).
Goals – League (42): Moffat 13, Dair 5, Kirk 5, Allan 3, Brown 3, Martin 3, Honeyman 2, Cusick 1, Dyer 1, Gartshore 1, Gibb 1, Lawrie 1, Ramsay 1, Robertson 1, own goal 1.
Scottish Cup (2): Coyle 1, Moffat 1.
League Cup (3): Coyle 1, Cusick 1, Kirk 1.

EAST STIRLINGSHIRE   DIV. 3

Ground: Firs Park, Falkirk FK2 7AY (01324) 623583
Ground capacity: 1880. **Colours:** Black and white stripes, black shorts.
Manager: Hugh McCann.
League Appearances: Abdulraham K (1); Barr A 23(3); Brown M 21(6); Bruce G 4; Ferguson B 16(2); Hardie M 20(3); Hoxley P 1(2); Hunter S (4); Kennedy K 7(11); Laidlaw S 14; Lepper N 1(1); McBeth P (3); McDougall G 13; McGoldrick K 19(1); McNeill W 22(6); Millar D 1; Muirhead D 34; Patterson P 36; Ross B 32; Russell G 13(1); Scott A (4); Sime A (5); Smith J 28; Storrar A 21(8); Thompson B 19; Walker S 25; Ward H 26(5).
Goals – League (50): McNeill 8, Laidlaw 6, Muirhead 6, Patterson 5, Ward 5, Walker 4, Barr 3, Hardie 3, Kennedy 3, Smith 3, McGoldrick 2, own goals 2.
Scottish Cup (2): Walker 2.
League Cup (0).

FALKIRK   DIV. 1

Ground: Brockville Park, Falkirk FK1 5AX (01324) 624121
Ground capacity: 9706. **Colours:** Navy blue shirts, white shorts.
Manager: Alex Totten.
League Appearances: Corrigan M 21(3); Crabbe S 36; Den Bieman I 24; Duffield P 10(7); Hagen D 9(3); Hamilton B 12(4); Henry J 11(1); Hogarth M 5; Hutchison G 24(9); James K 11(2); Keith M 27(2); Kerr M 1(1); Mathers P 31; McAllister K 35; McCart C 12(2); McKee C 2(2); McKenzie S 33(2); McQuilken J 21(1); McStay G 4(6); Morrison S (1); Moss D 16(1); O'Hara G 2; Oliver N 7(1); Rennie S 3; Seaton A 16(8); Sinclair D 23.
Goals – League (60): Keith 17, Crabbe 10 (4 pens), Hutchison 6, McAllister 6, Henry 5, Moss 5, Corrigan 3, Duffield 3, Hamilton 2, McCart 1, McKenzie 1, McStay 1.
Scottish Cup (6): Moss 3, Crabbe 1 (pen), McAllister 1, own goal 1.
League Cup (5): McKee 2, Crabbe 1, Keith 1, Oliver 1.

FORFAR ATHLETIC   DIV. 3

Ground: Station Park, Forfar, Angus (01307) 463576
Ground capacity: 8732. **Colours:** Sky blue and navy shirts, navy shorts.

Manager: Ian McPhee.
League Appearances: Allison J 19(8); Bowes M (1); Brand R 24(10); Cargill A 30(3); Christie S 1(3); Craig D 26(2); Ferguson G 19; Gibson A 8(1); Gillies K 17(4); Glennie S (1); Gray A (2); Hamilton J 5; Honeyman B 17(6); Johnston G 4(2); Mann R 18; McCheyne G 27(1); McIlravey P 6(3); McLauchlan M 24(9); McLean B 12(8); Moffat J 11; Nairn J 22(1); Rattray A 20; Raynes S 27(5); Robertson D 25; Sharp R 9; Tully C 6; Watson G 19.
Goals – League (48): Brand 10, Cargill 7, Honeyman 6, McLauchlan 6 (1 pen), McLean 6, McCheyne 2, McIlravey 2, Mann 2 (2 pens), Nairn 2, Rattray 2, Craig 1, Gibson 1, Tully 1.
Scottish Cup (3): Brand 2, Craig 1.
League Cup (0).

GREENOCK MORTON   DIV. 1

Ground: Cappielow Park, Greenock (01475) 723571
Ground capacity: 14,891. **Colours:** Royal blue and white shirts, white shorts.
Manager: Billy Stark.
League Appearances: Aitken S 19(3); Anderson D 16; Anderson J 33; Archdeacon O 33; Blaikie A 3(9); Blair P (2); Collins D 18; Curran H 34; Duffield P 2(1); Fenwick P 30; Foster M 14(5); George M 1(2); Hawke W 27(4); Juttla J 4(5); Matheson R 17(14); Maxwell A 30; McCormick S 3(2); McDonald S (1); McPherson C 20(13); Morrow J 4(1); Murie D 6(1); Slavin B 11(4); Thomas K 22; Twaddle K 31; Tweedie G 2(2); Whalen S (1); Wright K 10(6); Wylie D 6.
Goals – League (45): Thomas 9 (1 pen), Anderson J 6, Wright 6, Curran 5, Fenwick 5, Twaddle 5, Hawke 3, Anderson D 1, Blaikie 1, McCormick 1, McPherson 1, Matheson 1, own goal 1.
Scottish Cup (8): Archdeacon 2, Thomas 2, Twaddle 2, Matheson 1, own goal 1.
League Cup (0).

HAMILTON ACADEMICAL   DIV. 2

Ground: Firhill Stadium, Glasgow G20 7AL. (Match days only): (0141) 5791971(Weekdays): (01698) 286103
Ground capacity: 14,538. **Colours:** Red and white hooped shirts, white shorts.
Manager: Colin Miller.
League Appearances: Berry N 14(1); Bonnar M (1); Clark G 14(11); Cunnington E 33; Davidson W 3(1); Geraghty M 18(5); Henderson D 25; Henderson N 24(4); Hillcoat C 25; Hillcoat J 9; Kelly R (1); Kerr A 1(1); Krivokapic M (1); Lynn G 1; MacFarlane I 15; MacLaren R 12(3); Martin M 2(1); McAulay I 21(3); McCormick S 12(9); McFarlane D 5(10); McGill D 3; McKenzie P 13(5); Miller C 7(1); Moore M 3(9); Muir D (1); Oliver N 6; Rajamaki M 4(3); Reid C 6; Renicks S 32; Robertson S 6; Tait T 21(1); Thomson S 33(1); Wales G 28(2).
Goals – League (30): Wales 11 (2 pens), Geraghty 5, McCormick 4, Henderson D 3, Berry 1, Cunnington 1, McFarlane D 1, Moore 1, Renicks 1, Tait 1, Thomson 1.
Scottish Cup (2): Clark 1, Wales 1.
League Cup (3): Geraghty 1, McFarlane D 1, Renicks 1.

HEART OF MIDLOTHIAN   PREMIER LEAGUE

Ground: Tynecastle Park, Gorgie Road, Edinburgh EH11 2NL (0131) 200 7200
Ground capacity: 18,000. **Colours:** Maroon shirts, white shorts.
Manager: Jim Jefferies.
League Appearances: Adam S 28(1); Berthe M 1; Callaghan S 2; Cameron C 10(1); Carricondo J 1(10); Flîgel T 18(2); Fulton S 27; Guerin V 9(10); Hamilton J 20(5); Holmes D 1(5); Jackson D 9; James K 1(3); Jenkinson L 3(2); Kirk A (5); Lilley D 3(1); Locke G 22(3); Makel L 6(8); McCann N 8; McKenzie R 10; McKinnon R 14(2); McPherson D 17(1); McSwegan G 17(4); Murie D (4); Murray G 18(3); Naysmith G 23(3); O'Neill K (3); Pressley S 29(1); Quitongo J 5(7); Ritchie P 29; Rousset G 26; Salvatori S 11(1); Severin S 5(2); Weir D 23.
Goals – League (44): Adam 10, McSwegan 7, Cameron 6, Hamilton 6 (1 pen), McCann 3, Flögel 2, Fulton 2, Guerin 1, Jackson 1, Lilley 1, Locke 1, Makel 1, Pressley 1, Ritchie 1, Weir 1.
Scottish Cup (1): Hamilton 1.
League Cup (5): Adam 1, Fulton 1, Hamilton 1, Holmes 1, McKinnon 1.

HIBERNIAN   PREMIER LEAGUE

Ground: Easter Road Stadium, Edinburgh EH7 5QG (0131) 661 2159
Ground capacity: 16,032. **Colours:** Green shirts with white sleeves and collar, white shorts.
Manager: Alex McLeish.
League Appearances: Anderson D 6; Bannerman S 2(10); Bottiglieri E (1); Collins D 16; Crawford S 28(7); Dempsie M 5(3); Dennis S 29(2); Dietrich C 1; Elliot D 8; Gottskalksson O 36; Guggi P 7(1); Harper K (2); Hartley P 6(6); Holsgrove P 9(8); Hughes J 22(1); Latapy R 23; Lavety B 9(17); Lovell S 26(5); Lovering P 17; Marinkov A 10; McGinlay P 29(1); McManus T (1); Miller K 5(2); Paatelainen M 25(1); Paton E 1(3); Prenderville B 13; Reid A (1); Renwick M 15(1); Rougier A 10(5); Sauzee F 9; Shannon R 1; Skinner J 24; Smith T 3(2); Tosh P 1.
Goals – League (84): Crawford 14 (4 pens), McGinlay 12, Paatelainen 12, Lovell 11, Latapy 6, Hartley 5 (4 pens), Dennis 3, Hughes 3, Guggi 2, Lavety 2, Prenderville 2, Sauzee 2, Skinner 2, Harper 1, Holsgrove 1, Lovering 1, Marenko 1, Miller 1, Rougier 1, own goals 2.
Scottish Cup (2): Latapy 1, Lovering 1.
League Cup (3): Crawford 1 (pen), Lovell 1, Skinner 1.

INVERNESS CALEDONIAN THISTLE   DIV. 1

Ground: Caledonian Stadium, East Longman, Inverness IV1 1FF (01463) 222880
Ground capacity: 5600. **Colours:** Blue shirts with white trim, blue shorts.
Manager: Steven W.Paterson.
League Appearances: Addicoat W 5(4); Allan A 9(4); Bavidge M 1(7); Calder J 22; Cherry P 24(3); Christie C 33(1); Craig D (1); Farquhar G 9(3); Fridge L 14; Glancy M 9(4); Hastings R 23; MacArthur I 1(3); Mann R 13; McCulloch M 32(1); McLean S 34(1); Nicol G 1(3); Robertson H 12; Robson B 4(11); Shearer D 21(9); Sheerin P 34(2); Stewart I 1(5); Teasdale M 36; Tokely R 23(1); Wilson B 35(1).

Goals – League (80): McLean 20, Wilson 14 (1 pen), Shearer 12, Sheerin 10 (5 pens), Christie 4, McCulloch 4, Teasdale 4, Cherry 3, Glancy 3, Stewart 2, Bavidge 1, Robertson 1, Tokely 1, own goal 1.
Scottish Cup (1): own goal 1.
League Cup (4): Cherry 1, McLean 1, Shearer 1, Sheerin 1.

KILMARNOCK   PREMIER LEAGUE

Ground: Rugby Park, Kilmarnock KA1 2DP (01563) 525184
Ground capacity: 18,128. **Colours:** Blue and white striped shirts, blue shorts.
Manager: Bobby Williamson.
League Appearances: Bagan D 1(4); Baker M 23; Burke A 2(17); Durrant I 36; Hamilton S 5; Henry J 7(4); Holt G 33; Innes C 4; Kerr D 16; Lauchlan J 14; MacPherson A 31; Mahood A 16(12); Marshall G 36; McCoist A 16(10); McCutcheon G 2(11); McGowne K 32; Mitchell A 27(5); Montgomerie R 22; Nevin P 2(1); Reilly M 17(1); Roberts M 9(13); Vareille J 20(3); Wright P 25(8).
Goals – League (47): McCoist 7, Wright 6 (2 pens), Varcille 5, Durrant 4 (1 pen), McGowne 4, Mitchell 4, Henry 3, Holt 3, Roberts 3, McCutcheon 2, Mahood 2, Innes 1, MacPherson 1, Nevin 1, own goal 1.
Scottish Cup (0).
League Cup (3): Wright 2 (1 pen), McCoist 1.

LIVINGSTON   DIV. 1

Ground: Almondvale Stadium, Livingston EH54 7DN (01506) 417 000
Ground capacity: 6100. **Colours:** Black with yellow trim, black shorts.
Manager: Jim Leishman.
League Appearances: Alexander N 21; Bennett N 13(7); Bingham D 29; Boyle J 34; Conway F 10(2); Coughlan G 6; Courts T (1); Deas P 35; Ferguson I 3(1); Feroz C 1(10); Fleming D 14(1); Forrest G 2(3); Harvey P 1(3); King C 29; Little I 7(7); Macdonald W 5; Magee K 2(1); McCaldon I 15; McCormick J 10(22); McManus A 31; McMartin G (4); McPhee B 9(19); Millar J 30; Rajamaki M 3(2); Robertson J 30(6); Sherry J 20(2); Sweeney S 10; Watson G 26(1).
Goals – League (66): Robertson 12, Bingham 11 (3 pens), King 9, McPhee 9, Deas 5, McCormick 4, Millar 4, Sherry 4, Fleming 3, Boyle 1, Feroz 1, Little 1, McManus 1, Watson 1.
Scottish Cup (8): Bingham 2 (1 pen), Robertson 2, Fleming 1, McCormick 1, Millar 1, own goal 1.
League Cup (4): Bingham 2 (1 pen), Millar 1, Robertson 1.

MONTROSE   DIV. 3

Ground: Links Park, Montrose DD10 8QD (01674) 673200
Ground capacity: 4338. **Colours:** Royal blue with white sleeves, white shorts.
Manager: Kevin Drinkell.
League Appearances: Andrew B 13(11); Coulston D 19; Craib M 31; Craig M 15; Duffy K 21; Farnan C 30(1); Fitzpatrick F 21(1); Henry J 3(5); Higgins G 7; Hutton D 3(3); Irvine B (1); Loney J 14(2); Lyon M 6(3); Magee K 13; Mailer C 32;

McGlashan C 8; McWilliam R 4(13); Meldrum G 35; Murray M 15; Niddrie K 21(1); O'Driscoll J 9; Paterson G 14; Shand M 9(4); Stevenson C 1(4); Taylor S 30(2); Watt J 13(5); Winiarski S 5(2); Wylie R 4(1).
Goals – League (42): Taylor 7 (1 pen), Craig 5 (1 pen), Magee 5, Paterson 4, Andrew 3, Coulston 3, Farnan 3, Higgins 2, Lyon 2, Duffy 1, Hutton 1, Loney 1, McGlashan 1 (pen), McWilliam 1, Mailer 1, Niddrie 1, Shand 1.
Scottish Cup (1): Taylor 1.
League Cup (1): Andrew 1.

MOTHERWELL   PREMIER LEAGUE

Ground: Fir Park, Motherwell ML1 2QN (01698) 333333
Ground capacity: 13,742. **Colours:** Amber shirts with claret trim, white shorts.
Manager: Billy Davies.
League Appearances: Adams D 11(15); Bacque H (1); Brannan G 25; Christie K 4(1); Coyle O 26; Craigan S 6(4); Denham G (1); Doesburg M 29(1); Goodman D 8; Goram A 13; Gower M 8(1); Halliday S 2(2); Kaven M 16; Matthaei R 14(3); May E 10(2); McClair B 8(3); McCulloch L 14(12); McGowan J 32; McMillan S 30; Michels J 7(3); Miller G 1(3); Nevin P 14(16); Nicholas S 1(6); Nyyssonen K 3; Ramsay D (4); Ross I 8(4); Shivute E (1); Spencer J 21; Stirling J 4(1); Teale S 29; Thomas A 10; Valakari S 35; Woods S 7.
Goals – League (35): Coyle 7, Spencer 7, Brannan 5 (1 pen), Adams 3, McCulloch 3, McMillan 2, Goodman 1, Gower 1, McGowan 1, Nicholas 1, Nyyssonen 1, Ramsay 1, Stirling 1, Teale 1 (pen).
Scottish Cup (5): Brannan 1, Coyle 1, McCulloch 1, Thomas 1, own goal 1.
League Cup (1): Halliday 1.

PARTICK THISTLE   DIV. 2

Ground: Firhill Park, Glasgow G20 7AL (0141) 579 1971
Ground capacity: 14,538. **Colours:** Red and yellow hooped shirts, black shorts.
Manager: John Lambie.
League Appearances: Archibald A 33; Arthur K 28; Avdiu K 6; Bonar S 7(7); Bryce T 18(1); Burns G 6; Callaghan T 14(11); Callaghan W 7(6); Connell G 32(1); Dair L 1; Donaghy M 1; Dunn R 26(8); Flannigan C 8(8); Frame A 4(3); Gaughan K 22(4); Hood G 6; Houston S (2); Howie W (1); Jamieson W 25; Johnston S 4(11); Kennedy D 24; Lauchlan M 22(5); Martin A (1); McArthur S 8(1); McCann K 1; McDonald P 29(2); McHarg S 1(1); McKenzie J 3(4); McKeown D 30; Morgan A 12(1); Ross S 8; Tosh P 10.
Goals – League (36): Dunn 10, Morgan 6 (3 pens), Lauchlan 5 (1 pen), Bryce 3, McDonald 3 (1 pen), Jamieson 2, Archibald 1, Ardiu 1, Connell 1, Flannigan 1, Houston 1, Tosh 1, own goal 1.
Scottish Cup (8): Dunn 4 (1 pen), Tosh 4.
League Cup (2): Lauchlan 1, Morgan 1.

QUEEN OF THE SOUTH   DIV. 2

Ground: Palmerston Park, Dumfries DG2 9BA (01387) 254853
Ground capacity: 8352. **Colours:** Royal blue shirts, white shorts.
League Appearances: Adams C 18(9); Aitken A 27(2); Armstrong G 4(3); Bailey

L 16(10); Boyle D 6(5); Bryce T 1(5); Caldwell B 2(13); Cleeland M 26(2); Doig K 9; Eadie K 15(5); Leslie S 21(1); Lilley D 27; Love G 9; MacLeod J 4; Mallan S 24(7); Mathieson D 36; McAllister J 25(2); McCaig J 1(1); McGuffie R 1; McKee C 2; Milligan R 1; Moffat A 2; Nesovic A 20(3); Potts C 5; Rowe G 28(2); Russell G 5(1); Thomson J 18; Townsley D 21(6); Turner T 5; Weir M 17(2).
Goals – League (50): Mallan 15 (1 pen), Townsley 10, Rowe 7, Eadie 5 (1 pen), Adams 4, Nesovic 3, Armstrong 1, Bailey 1, Caldwell 1, Cleeland 1, Leslie 1, Potts 1.
Scottish Cup (1): Nesovic 1.
League Cup (1): Eadie 1.

QUEEN'S PARK   DIV. 3

Ground: Hampden Park, Glasgow G42 9BA (0141) 632 1275
Ground capacity: 52,000. **Colours:** Black and white hooped shirts, white shorts.
Coach: John McCormack.
League Appearances: Agostini D 5(4); Alexander D 24(2); Brown J 13(1); Carmichael D 12(1); Caven R 27; Chalmers J 17; Connaghan D 26(4); Cooke B 6; Edgar S 29(7); Elder G 11(2); Ferguson P 11(3); Ferry D 31(4); Finlayson K 26(9); Finlayson R (1); Graham D 19(1); Hamilton W (3); Inglis N 11; Little T 13(9); Martin A 4(5); Martin P 28; McColl B 2(9); McGhee D 3; McGill D 4; McGuffie R 5(6); Monaghan M 2; Orr G 4(2); Parks G 7(13); Reid A 7(3); Rossiter B 26(1); Tyrrell P 15(4); Whelan J 8.
Goals – League (41): Edgar 7, Carmichael 6, Finlayson K 6, Martin P 6, Brown 3, Graham 2, Caven 1, Elder 1, Ferry 1, Little 1, McGill 1 (pen), McGuffie 1, Orr 1, Parks 1, Whelan 1, own goals 2.
Scottish Cup (6): Edgar 2, Brown 1, Finlayson K 1, Graham 1, Parks 1.
League Cup (1): Graham 1.

RAITH ROVERS   DIV. 1

Ground: Stark's Park, Pratt Street, Kirkcaldy KY1 1SA (01592) 263514
Ground capacity: 10,271 (all seated). **Colours:** Navy blue shirts, white shorts.
Manager: John McVeigh.
League Appearances: Andrews M 19(5); Bowman D 23; Britton G 5; Browne P 31(1); Brownlie P 2(7); Byers K 10(5); Cameron I 26(2); Clark A (1); Cormack P 1; Dair J 27; Dair L (2); Dargo C 21(1); Ellis L 4(5); Fotheringham G 1(4); Fotheringham K 26; Grant C (1); Hartley P 18; Holmes D 13(1); Kirkwood D 5(1); Lennon D 21(4); Maughan R 1; McCulloch G 23(8); McEwan C 23(3); McGeown M 3; McInally D 1; McLeish K 1(1); McPherson D 3(1); McQuade J 3(3); Nicol K 1(1); Robertson G 3(3); Shields P 6(8); Smart C 3(2); Stein J 6(14); Tosh S 23(2); Van De Kamp G 33; Venables R 2; Wright K 8(4).
Goals – League (37): Dargo 8 (1 pen), Holmes 6, Cameron 4, Hartley 4 (2 pens), Tosh 4, Dair J 3, Wright 2, Andrews 1, Britton 1, Fotheringham K 1, McQuade 1, Stein 1, own goal 1.
Scottish Cup (0).
League Cup (4): Dair J 1, Hartley 1, Shields 1, Wright 1.

RANGERS   PREMIER LEAGUE

Ground: Ibrox Stadium, Glasgow G51 2XD (0141) 427 8500
Ground capacity: 50,403. **Colours:** Royal blue shirts, red and blue panels, white shorts.
Manager: Dick Advocaat.
League Appearances: Albertz J 33(1); Amato G 13(7); Amoruso L 33; Charbonnier L 11; Durie G 1(4); Feeney L (1); Ferguson B 23; Ferguson I 4(9); Gattuso G 3(2); Graham D (3); Guivarc'h S 11(3); Hendry C 16(3); Johansson J 13(12); Kanchelskis A 29(1); Klos S 18; McCann N 15(4); McInnes D (7); Miller C 2(14); Moore C 8; Nicholson B 3(3); Niemi A 7; Numan A 8(2); Porrini S 35; Reyna C 6; Riccio L (1); Rozental S (3); Stensaas S 1; Thern J 1; Van Bronckhorst G 35; Vidmar A 26(2); Wallace R 34; Wilson S 7(5).
Goals – League (78): Wallace 18, Albertz 11 (7 pens), Johansson 8, Kanchelskis 8, Van Bronckhorst 7, Amato 6 (1 pen), Guivarc'h 5, McCann 5, Miller 3, Porrini 2, Amoruso 1, Ferguson B 1, Moore 1, Vidmar 1, Wilson 1.
Scottish Cup (15): Johansson 3, McCann 3, Wallace 3, Albertz 1 (pen), Amoruso 1, Guivarc'h 1, Kanchelskis 1, Van Bronckhorst 1, Vidmar 1.
League Cup (13): Albertz 3, Wallace 2, Amato 1, Amoruso 1, Durie 1, Ferguson B 1, Ferguson I 1, Guivarc'h 1, Johansson 1, Miller 1.

ROSS COUNTY   DIV. 2

Ground: Victoria Park, Dingwall IV15 9QW (01349) 862253
Ground capacity: 5400. **Colours:** Dark blue shirts, white shorts.
Manager: Neale Cooper.
League Appearances: Adams D 4; Campbell C 1(7); Den Bieman I 2; Escalon F 17(1); Ewing G 1(2); Ferguson S 26; Ferries K 15(7); Furphy W 6(4); Gilbert K 25; Golabek S 18(5); Haro M 26; Hart R 1; Herd W 5(2); Higgins G 1(2); Hunter M 3(3); Kinnaird P 10; Mackay D 16(4); Mackay S (2); Matheson D 7; Maxwell I 36; McBain R 33; McGlashan J 16(1); McKee C (1); McLeod B 1(2); Meldrum C 2; Munro G 1; Ross D 19(9); Stewart G 1; Tarrant N 27(6); Taylor A 24(8); Tully C 8; Walker J 31; Williamson R 1(2); Wood G 12(15).
Goals – League (87): Ferguson 17 (1 pen), Tarrant 17 (4 pens), Wood 12, Ross 7, McGlashan 6, McBain 5, Ferries 4, Taylor 4, Adams 3, Maxwell 3, Golabek 2, Escalon 1, Haro 1, Kinnaird 1, own goals 4.
Scottish Cup (6): Tarrant 5 (1 pen), McBain 1.
League Cup (8): Adams 5, Tarrant 2, McBain 1.

ST JOHNSTONE   PREMIER LEAGUE

Ground: McDiarmid Park, Crieff Road, Perth PH1 2SJ (01738) 459090
Ground capacity: 10,673. **Colours:** Royal blue shirts with white trim, white shorts.
Manager: Sandy Clark.
League Appearances: Bollan G 32(1); Connolly P 6(3); Dasovic N 31; Dods D 34; Ferguson A 2(1); Grant R 14(11); Griffin D 14(5); Kane P 33(1); Kernaghan A 26; Lowndes N 12(17); Main A 34; McAnespie K 8(10); McBride J 2(1); McCluskey S 5(2); McMahon G 13(6); McQuillan J 27(1); O'Boyle G 12(1); O'Halloran K 10(6);

O'Neil J 33; Parker K (2); Preston A 8(7); Scott P 14(2); Simao M 20(6); Weir D 6(1); Whiteford A (1).
Goals – League (39): Bollan 4 (2 pens), Grant 4 (1 pen), Simao 4, Kane 3, Kernaghan 3, Dods 2, Lowndes 2, McAnespie 2, O'Boyle 2, O'Neil 2, Scott 2, Connolly 1, Dasovic 1, Griffin 1, McMahon 1, McQuillan 1, O'Halloran 1, Preston 1, Weir 1, own goal 1.
Scottish Cup (6): Grant 2, Dods 1, O'Neil 1, Scott 1, Simao 1.
League Cup (12): Dasovic 2, Lowndes 2, O'Boyle 2, Connolly 1, Kane 1, McMahon 1, O'Halloran 1, O'Neil 1, Preston 1.

ST MIRREN   DIV. 1

Ground: St Mirren Park, Paisley PA3 2EJ (0141) 889 2558, 840 1337
Ground capacity: 14,950. **Colours:** Black and white striped shirts, black shorts.
Manager: Tom Hendrie.
League Appearances: Brown T 23(3); Cameron D 3(8); Creaney G 11(1); Drew C 15(1); Innes C 9; Kerr C 24(4); McGarry S 27(7); McLaughlan B 23; McNamee D 30(1); McQuilter R 29; McWhirter N 24(1); Mendes J 13(9); Milne D 7(2); Murray H 27(2); Nicolson I 24(6); O'Brien B 17(5); Prentice A 1(5); Robinson R (1); Rodden P 18(8); Roy L 17; Scrimgour D 19; Turner T 13(1); Walker P (1); Yardley M 22(13)
Goals – League (42): Yardley 11 (1 pen), McGarry 8, Brown 4 (2 pens), Mendes 4, Nicolson 4, Creaney 3 (2 pens), Cameron 2, Kerr 2, McLaughlin 1, O'Brien 1, own goals 2.
Scottish Cup (1): Mendes 1.
League Cup (1): Brown 1.

STENHOUSEMUIR   DIV. 2

Ground: Ochilview Park, Stenhousemuir FK5 5QL (01324) 562992
Ground capacity: 3520. **Colours:** Maroon shirts with silver trim, white shorts.
Manager: Graeme Armstrong.
League Appearances: Armstrong G 35; Banks A 20(7); Baptie C 25(2); Brown S (1); Budinaukas K 2; Christie M 3; Craig A 32; Davidson G 23(1); Fisher J 29; Gibson J 17(5); Graham T 22(2); Hall M 15(3); Hamilton L 34; Hamilton R 34(1); Huggon R (2); Hunter P (2); Hutchison G 2; Kane K 3(3); Lansdowne A 10(7); Lawrence A 33; McKinnon C 6(1); Middlemist R (1); Miller K 11; Sprott A 17(13); Watters W 18(11); Wood D 5(3).
Goals – League (62): Hamilton R 11, Watters 9, Lawrence 8, Miller 8, Craig 7, Graham 4, Gibson 3, Sprott 3, Armstrong 2 (2 pens), McKinnon 2, Banks 1, Baptie 1, Christie 1, Huggon 1, Wood 1.
Scottish Cup (6): Craig 2, Miller 2, Hall 1, Watters 1.
League Cup (1): Watters 1.

STIRLING ALBION   DIV. 2

Ground: Forthbank Stadium, Springkerse Industrial Estate, Stirling FK7 7UJ (01786) 450399
Ground capacity: 3808. **Colours:** Red and white halves.
Manager: John Philliben.

League Appearances: Aitken A (1); Bell D 1(16); Bone A 27(1); Bradley M 4(3); Clark P 30(3); Cormack B 6; Donald G 18(4); Forrest E 24(3); Gow G 27; Graham A 23; Grant B 7; Hendry J 6(1); Jackson C 21(1); Jaffa G 1(2); Martin B 33; McCallion K (2); McCallum D 28(2); McGeown M 9; McKee C 1(1); Mortimer P 15(8); Nicholas S 27; Paterson A 36; Philliben J 20(2); Price G 14(5); Provan A 8(10); Wood C 10(14).
Goals – League (50): Bone 20 (4 pens), Graham 5, Nicholas 5, Donald 4, Paterson 3, Price 3, Hendry 2, Wood 2, Grant 1, Jackson 1, McCallum 1, Martin 1, Provan 1, own goal 1.
Scottish Cup (5): Graham 2, Jackson 1, McCallum 1, Nicholas 1.
League Cup (3): Bone 2, Price 1.

STRANRAER DIV. 2

Ground: Stair Park, Stranraer DG9 8BS (01776) 703271
Ground capacity: 6100. **Colours:** Blue shirts, white shorts.
Manager: Billy McLaren.
League Appearances: Abbott S 2(2); Adams M (2); Archdeacon P 4; Bell R 12(8); Black T 26; Blaikie A 4(1); Brownlie P 2; Bruce G 11; Campbell M 26; Friels G 9(10); Galloway G 4(4); George D 17(1); Hamilton B 1; Harty I 13(8); Jenkins A 9(10); Johnstone D 21(3); Kinnaird P 21; Knox K 25(1); Matthews G 18; McIntyre P 22(1); McMartin G 13; Meldrum C 7; O'Neill M 1; Ronald P 25(4); Skilling M 25(3); Smith J 4; Walker P 8(1); Watson P 36; Wright F (2); Young G 17(10); Young J 13(2).
Goals – League (29): Ronald 5, Young G 5, Campbell 3, Black 2 (1 pen), George 2, Harty 2, Knox 2 (pens), Young J 2, Bell 1, Friels 1, Jenkins 1, Kinnaird 1 (pen), Skilling 1, Walker 1.
Scottish Cup (2): Friels 1, Knox 1.
League Cup (1): Ronald 1.

SCOTTISH LEAGUE HONOURS

*On goal average (ratio)/difference. †Held jointly after indecisive play-off.
‡Won on deciding match. ††Held jointly. ¶Two points deducted for
fielding ineligible player. Competition suspended 1940–45 during war;
Regional Leagues operating.
‡‡Two points deducted for registration irregularities.

PREMIER LEAGUE
Maximum points: 108

	First	Pts	Second	Pts	Third	Pts
1998–99	Rangers	77	Celtic	71	St Johnstone	57

PREMIER DIVISION
Maximum points: 72

	First	Pts	Second	Pts	Third	Pts
1975–76	Rangers	54	Celtic	48	Hibernian	43
1976–77	Celtic	55	Rangers	46	Aberdeen	43
1977–78	Rangers	55	Aberdeen	53	Dundee U	40
1978–79	Celtic	48	Rangers	45	Dundee U	44
1979–80	Aberdeen	48	Celtic	47	St Mirren	42
1980–81	Celtic	56	Aberdeen	49	Rangers*	44
1981–82	Celtic	55	Aberdeen	53	Rangers	43
1982–83	Dundee U	56	Celtic*	55	Aberdeen	55
1983–84	Aberdeen	57	Celtic	50	Dundee U	47
1984–85	Aberdeen	59	Celtic	52	Dundee U	47
1985–86	Celtic*	50	Hearts	50	Dundee U	47

Maximum points: 88

	First	Pts	Second	Pts	Third	Pts
1986–87	Rangers	69	Celtic	63	Dundee U	60
1987–88	Celtic	72	Hearts	62	Rangers	60

Maximum points: 72

	First	Pts	Second	Pts	Third	Pts
1988–89	Rangers	56	Aberdeen	50	Celtic	46
1989–90	Rangers	51	Aberdeen*	44	Hearts	44
1990–91	Rangers	55	Aberdeen	53	Celtic*	41

Maximum points: 88

	First	Pts	Second	Pts	Third	Pts
1991–92	Rangers	72	Hearts	63	Celtic	62
1992–93	Rangers	73	Aberdeen	64	Celtic	60
1993–94	Rangers	58	Aberdeen	55	Motherwell	54

Maximum points: 108

	First	Pts	Second	Pts	Third	Pts
1994–95	Rangers	69	Motherwell	54	Hibernian	53
1995–96	Rangers	87	Celtic	83	Aberdeen*	55
1996–97	Rangers	80	Celtic	75	Dundee U	60
1997–98	Celtic	74	Rangers	72	Hearts	67

DIVISION 1
Maximum points: 52

	First	Pts	Second	Pts	Third	Pts
1975–76	Partick T	41	Kilmarnock	35	Montrose	30

Maximum points: 78

	First	Pts	Second	Pts	Third	Pts
1976–77	St Mirren	62	Clydebank	58	Dundee	51
1977–78	Morton*	58	Hearts	58	Dundee	57
1978–79	Dundee	55	Kilmarnock*	54	Clydebank	54
1979–80	Hearts	53	Airdrieonians	51	Ayr U*	44
1980–81	Hibernian	57	Dundee	52	St Johnstone	51
1981–82	Motherwell	61	Kilmarnock	51	Hearts	50
1982–83	St Johnstone	55	Hearts	54	Clydebank	50
1983–84	Morton	54	Dumbarton	51	Partick T	46
1984–85	Motherwell	50	Clydebank	48	Falkirk	45
1985–86	Hamilton A	56	Falkirk	45	Kilmarnock	44

Maximum points: 88

| 1986–87 | Morton | 57 | Dunfermline Ath | 56 | Dumbarton | 53 |
| 1987–88 | Hamilton A | 56 | Meadowbank T | 52 | Clydebank | 49 |

Maximum points: 78

1988–89	Dunfermline Ath	54	Falkirk	52	Clydebank	48
1989–90	St Johnstone	58	Airdrieonians	54	Clydebank	44
1990–91	Falkirk	54	Airdrieonians	53	Dundee	52

Maximum points: 88

1991–92	Dundee	58	Partick T*	57	Hamilton A	57
1992–93	Raith R	65	Kilmarnock	54	Dunfermline Ath	52
1993–94	Falkirk	66	Dunfermline Ath	65	Airdrieonians	54

Maximum points: 108

1994–95	Raith R	69	Dunfermline Ath*	68	Dundee	68
1995–96	Dunfermline Ath	71	Dundee U*	67	Morton	67
1996–97	St Johnstone	80	Airdrieonians	60	Dundee*	58
1997–98	Dundee	70	Falkirk	65	Raith R*	60
1998–99	Hibernian	89	Falkirk	66	Ayr U	62

DIVISION 2

Maximum points: 52

| 1975–76 | Clydebank* | 40 | Raith R | 40 | Alloa | 35 |

Maximum points: 78

1976–77	Stirling A	55	Alloa	51	Dunfermline Ath	50
1977–78	Clyde*	53	Raith R	53	Dunfermline Ath	48
1978–79	Berwick R	54	Dunfermline Ath	52	Falkirk	50
1979–80	Falkirk	50	East Stirling	49	Forfar Ath	46
1980–81	Queen's Park	50	Queen of the S	46	Cowdenbeath	45
1981–82	Clyde	59	Alloa*	50	Arbroath	50
1982–83	Brechin C	55	Meadowbank T	54	Arbroath	49
1983–84	Forfar Ath	63	East Fife	47	Berwick R	43
1984–85	Montrose	53	Alloa	50	Dunfermline Ath	49
1985–86	Dunfermline Ath	57	Queen of the S	55	Meadowbank T	49
1986–87	Meadowbank T	55	Raith R*	52	Stirling A*	52
1987–88	Ayr U	61	St Johnstone	59	Queen's Park	51
1988–89	Albion R	50	Alloa	45	Brechin C	43
1989–90	Brechin C	49	Kilmarnock	48	Stirling A	47
1990–91	Stirling A	54	Montrose	46	Cowdenbeath	45
1991–92	Dumbarton	52	Cowdenbeath	51	Alloa	50
1992–93	Clyde	54	Brechin C*	53	Stranraer	53
1993–94	Stranraer	56	Berwick R	48	Stenhousemuir*	47

Maximum points: 108

1994–95	Morton	64	Dumbarton	60	Stirling A	58
1995–96	Stirling A	81	East Fife	67	Berwick R	60
1996–97	Ayr U	77	Hamilton A	74	Livingston	64
1997–98	Stranraer	61	Clydebank	60	Livingston	59
1998–99	Livingston	77	Inverness CT	72	Clyde	53

DIVISION 3

Maximum points: 108

1994–95	Forfar Ath	80	Montrose	67	Ross Co	60
1995–96	Livingston	72	Brechin C	63	Caledonian T	57
1996–97	Inverness CT	76	Forfar Ath*	67	Ross Co	67
1997–98	Alloa	76	Arbroath	68	Ross Co*	67
1998–99	Ross Co	77	Stenhousemuir	64	Brechin C	59

185

DIVISION 1 to 1974–75

Maximum points: a 36; b 44; c 40; d 52; e 60; f 68; g 76; h 84.

	First	Pts	Second	Pts	Third	Pts
1890–91a	Dumbarton††	29	Rangers††	29	Celtic	21
1891–92b	Dumbarton	37	Celtic	35	Hearts	34
1892–93a	Celtic	29	Rangers	28	St Mirren	20
1893–94a	Celtic	29	Hearts	26	St Bernard's	23
1894–95a	Hearts	31	Celtic	26	Rangers	22
1895–96a	Celtic	30	Rangers	26	Hibernian	24
1896–97a	Hearts	28	Hibernian	26	Rangers	25
1897–98a	Celtic	33	Rangers	29	Hibernian	22
1898–99a	Rangers `	36	Hearts	26	Celtic	24
1899–						
1900a	Rangers	32	Celtic	25	Hibernian	24
1900–01c	Rangers	35	Celtic	29	Hibernian	25
1901–02a	Rangers	28	Celtic	26	Hearts	22
1902–03b	Hibernian	37	Dundee	31	Rangers	29
1903–04d	Third Lanark	43	Hearts	39	Celtic*	38
1904–05d	Celtic‡	41	Rangers	41	Third Lanark	35
1905–06e	Celtic	49	Hearts	43	Airdrieonians	38
1906–07f	Celtic	55	Dundee	48	Rangers	45
1907–08f	Celtic	55	Falkirk	51	Rangers	50
1908–09f	Celtic	51	Dundee	50	Clyde	48
1909–10f	Celtic	54	Falkirk	52	Rangers	46
1910–11f	Rangers	52	Aberdeen	48	Falkirk	44
1911–12f	Rangers	51	Celtic	45	Clyde	42
1912–13f	Rangers	53	Celtic	49	Hearts*	41
1913–14g	Celtic	65	Rangers	59	Hearts*	54
1914–15g	Celtic	65	Hearts	61	Rangers	50
1915–16g	Celtic	67	Rangers	56	Morton	51
1916–17g	Celtic	64	Morton	54	Rangers	53
1917–18f	Rangers	56	Celtic	55	Kilmarnock*	43
1918–19f	Celtic	58	Rangers	57	Morton	47
1919–20h	Rangers	71	Celtic	68	Motherwell	57
1920–21h	Rangers	76	Celtic	66	Hearts	50
1921–22h	Celtic	67	Rangers	66	Raith R	51
1922–23g	Rangers	55	Airdrieonians	50	Celtic	46
1923–24g	Rangers	59	Airdrieonians	50	Celtic	46
1924–25g	Rangers	60	Airdrieonians	57	Hibernian	52
1925–26g	Celtic	58	Airdrieonians*	50	Hearts	50
1926–27g	Rangers	56	Motherwell	51	Celtic	49
1927–28g	Rangers	60	Celtic*	55	Motherwell	55
1928–29g	Rangers	67	Celtic	51	Motherwell	50
1929–30g	Rangers	60	Motherwell	55	Aberdeen	53
1930–31g	Rangers	60	Celtic	58	Motherwell	56
1931–32g	Motherwell	66	Rangers	61	Celtic	48
1932–33g	Rangers	62	Motherwell	59	Hearts	50
1933–34g	Rangers	66	Motherwell	62	Celtic	47
1934–35g	Rangers	55	Celtic	52	Hearts	50
1935–36g	Celtic	66	Rangers*	61	Aberdeen	61
1936–37g	Rangers	61	Aberdeen	54	Celtic	52
1937–38g	Celtic	61	Hearts	58	Rangers	49
1938–39g	Rangers	59	Celtic	48	Aberdeen	46
1946–47e	Rangers	46	Hibernian	44	Aberdeen	39
1947–48e	Hibernian	48	Rangers	46	Partick T	36

186

1948–49*e*	Rangers	46	Dundee	45	Hibernian	39
1949–50*e*	Rangers	50	Hibernian	49	Hearts	43
1950–51*e*	Hibernian	48	Rangers*	38	Dundee	38
1951–52*e*	Hibernian	45	Rangers	41	East Fife	37
1952–53*e*	Rangers*	43	Hibernian	43	East Fife	39
1953–54*e*	Celtic	43	Hearts	38	Partick T	35
1954–55*e*	Aberdeen	49	Celtic	46	Rangers	41
1955–56*f*	Rangers	52	Aberdeen	46	Hearts*	45
1956–57*f*	Rangers	55	Hearts	53	Kilmarnock	42
1957–58*f*	Hearts	62	Rangers	49	Celtic	46
1958–59*f*	Rangers	50	Hearts	48	Motherwell	44
1959–60*f*	Hearts	54	Kilmarnock	50	Rangers*	42
1960–61*f*	Rangers	51	Kilmarnock	50	Third Lanark	42
1961–62*f*	Dundee	54	Rangers	51	Celtic	46
1962–63*f*	Rangers	57	Kilmarnock	48	Partick T	46
1963–64*f*	Rangers	55	Kilmarnock	49	Celtic*	47
1964–65*f*	Kilmarnock*	50	Hearts	50	Dunfermline Ath	49
1965–66*f*	Celtic	57	Rangers	55	Kilmarnock	45
1966–67*f*	Celtic	58	Rangers	55	Clyde	46
1967–68*f*	Celtic	63	Rangers	61	Hibernian	45
1968–69*f*	Celtic	54	Rangers	49	DunfermlineAth	45
1969–70*f*	Celtic	57	Rangers	45	Hibernian	44
1970–71*f*	Celtic	56	Aberdeen	54	St Johnstone	44
1971–72*f*	Celtic	60	Aberdeen	50	Rangers	44
1972–73*f*	Celtic	57	Rangers	56	Hibernian	45
1973–74*f*	Celtic	53	Hibernian	49	Rangers	48
1974–75*f*	Rangers	56	Hibernian	49	Celtic	45

DIVISION 2 to 1974–75

Maximum points: a 76; b 72; c 68; d 52; e 60; f 36; g 44.

1893–94*f*	Hibernian	29	Cowlairs	27	Clyde	24
1894–95*f*	Hibernian	30	Motherwell	22	Port Glasgow	20
1895–96*f*	Abercorn	27	Leith Ath	23	Renton	21
1896–97*f*	Partick T	31	Leith Ath	27	Kilmarnock*	21
1897–98*f*	Kilmarnock	29	Port Glasgow	25	Morton	22
1898–99*f*	Kilmarnock	32	Leith Ath	27	Port Glasgow	25
1899–						
1900*f*	Partick T	29	Morton	28	Port Glasgow	20
1900–01*f*	St Bernard's	25	Airdrieonians	23	Abercorn	21
1901–02*g*	Port Glasgow	32	Partick T	31	Motherwell	26
1902–03*g*	Airdrieonians	35	Motherwell	28	Ayr U*	27
1903–04*g*	Hamilton A	37	Clyde	29	Ayr U	28
1904–05*g*	Clyde	32	Falkirk	28	Hamilton A	27
1905–06*g*	Leith Ath	34	Clyde	31	Albion R	27
1906–07*g*	St Bernard's	32	Vale of Leven*	27	Arthurlie	27
1907–08*g*	Raith R	30	Dumbarton ‡‡	27	Ayr U	27
1908–09*g*	Abercorn	31	Raith R*	28	Vale of Leven	28
1909–10*g*	Leith Ath‡	33	Raith R	33	St Bernard's	27
1910–11*g*	Dumbarton	31	Ayr U	27	Albion R	25
1911–12*g*	Ayr U	35	Abercorn	30	Dumbarton	27
1912–13*d*	Ayr U	34	Dunfermline Ath	33	East Stirling	32
1913–14*g*	Cowdenbeath	31	Albion R	27	Dunfermline Ath*	26
1914–15*d*	Cowdenbeath*	37	St Bernard's*	37	Leith Ath	37

1921–22a	Alloa	60	Cowdenbeath	47	Armadale	45
1922–23a	Queen's Park	57	Clydebank ¶	50	St Johnstone ¶	45
1923–24a	St Johnstone	56	Cowdenbeath	55	Bathgate	44
1924–25a	Dundee U	50	Clydebank	48	Clyde	47
1925–26a	Dunfermline Ath	59	Clyde	53	Ayr U	52
1926–27a	Bo'ness	56	Raith R	49	Clydebank	45
1927–28a	Ayr U	54	Third Lanark	45	King's Park	44
1928–29b	Dundee U	51	Morton	50	Arbroath	47
1929–30a	Leith Ath*	57	East Fife	57	Albion R	54
1930–31a	Third Lanark	61	Dundee U	50	Dunfermline Ath	47
1931–32a	East Stirling*	55	St Johnstone	55	Raith R*	46
1932–33c	Hibernian	54	Queen of the S	49	Dunfermline Ath	47
1933–34c	Albion R	45	Dunfermline Ath*	44	Arbroath	44
1934–35c	Third Lanark	52	Arbroath	50	St Bernard's	47
1935–36c	Falkirk	59	St Mirren	52	Morton	48
1936–37c	Ayr U	54	Morton	51	St Bernard's	48
1937–38c	Raith R	59	Albion R	48	Airdrieonians	47
1938–39c	Cowdenbeath	60	Alloa*	48	East Fife	48
1946–47d	Dundee	45	Airdrieonians	42	East Fife	31
1947–48e	East Fife	53	Albion R	42	Hamilton A	40
1948–49e	Raith R*	42	Stirling A	42	Airdrieonians*	41
1949–50e	Morton	47	Airdrieonians	44	Dunfermline Ath*	36
1950–51e	Queen of the S*	45	Stirling A	45	Ayr U*	36
1951–52e	Clyde	44	Falkirk	43	Ayr U	39
1952–53e	Stirling A	44	Hamilton A	43	Queen's Park	37
1953–54e	Motherwell	45	Kilmarnock	42	Third Lanark*	36
1954–55e	Airdrieonians	46	Dunfermline Ath	42	Hamilton A	39
1955–56b	Queen's Park	54	Ayr U	51	St Johnstone	49
1956–57b	Clyde	64	Third Lanark	51	Cowdenbeath	45
1957–58b	Stirling A	55	Dunfermline Ath	53	Arbroath	47
1958–59b	Ayr U	60	Arbroath	51	Stenhousemuir	46
1959–60b	St Johnstone	53	Dundee U	50	Queen of the S	49
1960–61b	Stirling A	55	Falkirk	54	Stenhousemuir	50
1961–62b	Clyde	54	Queen of the S	53	Morton	44
1962–63b	St Johnstone	55	East Stirling	49	Morton	48
1963–64b	Morton	67	Clyde	53	Arbroath	46
1964–65b	Stirling A	59	Hamilton A	50	Queen of the S	45
1965–66b	Ayr U	53	Airdrieonians	50	Queen of the S	47
1966–67a	Morton	69	Raith R	58	Arbroath	57
1967–68b	St Mirren	62	Arbroath	53	East Fife	49
1968–69b	Motherwell	64	Ayr U	53	East Fife*	48
1969–70b	Falkirk	56	Cowdenbeath	55	Queen of the S	50
1970–71b	Partick T	56	East Fife	51	Arbroath	46
1971–72b	Dumbarton*	52	Arbroath	52	Stirling A	50
1972–73b	Clyde	56	Dumfermline Ath	52	Raith R*	47
1973–74b	Airdrieonians	60	Kilmarnock	58	Hamilton A	55
1974–75a	Falkirk	54	Queen of the S*	53	Montrose	53

Elected to Division 1: 1894 Clyde; 1895 Hibernian; 1896 Abercorn; 1897 Partick T; 1899 Kilmarnock; 1900 Morton and Partick T; 1902 Port Glasgow and Partick T; 1903 Airdrieonians and Motherwell; 1905 Falkirk and Aberdeen; 1906 Clyde and Hamilton A; 1910 Raith R; 1913 Ayr U and Dumbarton.

RELEGATED CLUBS

From Premier League

1998–99 Dunfermline Ath

From Premier Division

1974–75 *No relegation due to League reorganisation*
1975–76 Dundee, St Johnstone
1976–77 Hearts, Kilmarnock
1977–78 Ayr U, Clydebank
1978–79 Hearts, Motherwell
1979–80 Dundee, Hibernian
1980–81 Kilmarnock, Hearts
1981–82 Partick T, Airdrieonians
1982–83 Morton, Kilmarnock
1983–84 St Johnstone, Motherwell
1984–85 Dumbarton, Morton
1985–86 *No relegation due to League reorganization*
1986–87 Clydebank, Hamilton A
1987–88 Falkirk, Dunfermline Ath, Morton
1988–89 Hamilton A
1989–90 Dundee
1990–91 None
1991–92 St Mirren, Dunfermline Ath
1992–93 Falkirk, Airdrieonians
1993–94 *See footnote*
1994–95 Dundee U
1995–96 Partick T, Falkirk
1996–97 Raith R
1997–98 Hibernian

From Division 1

1974–75 *No relegation due to League reorganisation*
1975–76 Dunfermline Ath, Clyde
1976–77 Raith R, Falkirk
1977–78 Alloa Ath, East Fife
1978–79 Montrose, Queen of the S
1979–80 Arbroath, Clyde
1980–81 Stirling A, Berwick R
1981–82 East Stirling, Queen of the S
1982–83 Dunfermline Ath, Queen's Park
1983–84 Raith R, Alloa
1984–85 Meadowbank T, St Johnstone
1985–86 Ayr U, Alloa
1986–87 Brechin C, Montrose
1987–88 East Fife, Dumbarton
1988–89 Kilmarnock, Queen of the S
1989–90 Albion R, Alloa
1990–91 Clyde, Brechin C
1991–92 Montrose, Forfar Ath
1992–93 Meadowbank T, Cowdenbeath
1993–94 *See footnote*
1994–95 Ayr U, Stranraer
1995–96 Hamilton A, Dumbarton
1996–97 Clydebank, East Fife
1997–98 Partick T, Stirling A
1998–99 Hamilton A, Stranraer

Relegated from Division 2

1994–95 Meadowbank T, Brechin C
1995–96 Forfar Ath, Montrose
1996–97 Dumbarton, Berwick R
1997–98 Stenhousemuir, Brechin C
1998–99 East Fife, Forfar Ath

Relegated from Division 1 1973–74

1921–22 *Queen's Park, Dumbarton, Clydebank
1922–23 Albion R, Alloa Ath
1923–24 Clyde, Clydebank
1924–25 Third Lanark, Ayr U
1925–26 Raith R, Clydebank
1926–27 Morton, Dundee U
1927–28 Dunfermline Ath, Bo'ness
1928–29 Third Lanark, Raith R
1929–30 St Johnstone, Dundee U
1930–31 Hibernian, East Fife
1931–32 Dundee U, Leith Ath
1932–33 Morton, East Stirling
1933–34 Third Lanark, Cowdenbeath

1934–35 St Mirren, Falkirk
1935–36 Airdrieonians, Ayr U
1936–37 Dunfermline Ath, Albion R
1937–38 Dundee, Morton
1938–39 Queen's Park, Raith R
1946–47 Kilmarnock, Hamilton A
1947–48 Airdrieonians, Queen's Park
1948–49 Morton, Albion R
1949–50 Queen of the S, Stirling A
1950–51 Clyde, Falkirk
1951–52 Morton, Stirling A
1952–53 Motherwell, Third Lanark
1953–54 Airdrieonians, Hamilton A
1954–55 *No clubs relegated*
1955–56 Stirling A, Clyde
1956–57 Dunfermline Ath, Ayr U
1957–58 East Fife, Queen's Park
1958–59 Queen of the S, Falkirk

1959–60 Arbroath, Stirling A
1960–61 Ayr U, Clyde
1961–62 St Johnstone, Stirling A
1962–63 Clyde, Raith R
1963–64 Queen of the S, East Stirling
1964–65 Airdrieonians, Third Lanark
1965–66 Morton, Hamilton A
1966–67 St Mirren, Ayr U
1967–68 Motherwell, Stirling A
1968–69 Falkirk, Arbroath
1969–70 Raith R, Partick T
1970–71 St Mirren, Cowdenbeath
1971–72 Clyde, Dunfermline Ath
1972–73 Kilmarnock, Airdrieonians
1973–74 East Fife, Falkirk

*Season 1921–22 – only 1 club promoted. 3 clubs relegated.

Scottish League championship wins: Rangers 47, Celtic 36, Aberdeen 4, Hearts 4, Hibernian 4, Dumbarton 2, Dundee 1, Dundee U 1, Kilmarnock 1, Motherwell 1, Third Lanark 1.

The Scottish Football League was reconstructed into three divisions at the end of the 1974–75 season, so the usual relegation statistics do not apply. Further reorganization took place at the end of the 1985–86 season. From 1986–87, the Premier and First Division had 12 teams each. The Second Division remained at 14. From 1988–89, the Premier Division reverted to 10 teams, and the First Division to 14 teams but in 1991–92 the Premier and First Division reverted to 12. At the end of the 1997–98 season, the top nine clubs in Premier Division broke away from the Scottish League to form a new competition, the Scottish Premier League, with the club promoted from Division One.

PAST SCOTTISH LEAGUE CUP FINALS

1946–47	Rangers	4	Aberdeen	0
1947–48	East Fife	0 4	Falkirk	0* 1
1948–49	Rangers	2	Raith Rovers	0
1949–50	East Fife	3	Dunfermline	0
1950–51	Motherwell	3	Hibernian	0
1951–52	Dundee	3	Rangers	2
1952–53	Dundee	2	Kilmarnock	0
1953–54	East Fife	3	Partick Thistle	2
1954–55	Hearts	4	Motherwell	2
1955–56	Aberdeen	2	St Mirren	1
1956–57	Celtic	0 3	Partick Thistle	0 0
1957–58	Celtic	7	Rangers	1
1958–59	Hearts	5	Partick Thistle	1
1959–60	Hearts	2	Third Lanark	1
1960–61	Rangers	2	Kilmarnock	0
1961–62	Rangers	1 3	Hearts	1 1
1962–63	Hearts	1	Kilmarnock	0
1963–64	Rangers	5	Morton	0
1964–65	Rangers	2	Celtic	1
1965–66	Celtic	2	Rangers	1
1966–67	Celtic	1	Rangers	0
1967–68	Celtic	5	Dundee	3
1968–69	Celtic	6	Hibernian	2
1969–70	Celtic	1	St Johnstone	0
1970–71	Rangers	1	Celtic	0
1971–72	Partick Thistle	4	Celtic	1
1972–73	Hibernian	2	Celtic	1
1973–74	Dundee	1	Celtic	0
1974–75	Celtic	6	Hibernian	3
1975–76	Rangers	1	Celtic	0
1976–77	Aberdeen	2	Celtic	1
1977–78	Rangers	2	Celtic	1*
1978–79	Rangers	2	Aberdeen	1
1979–80	Aberdeen	0 0	Dundee U	0* 3
1980–81	Dundee	0	Dundee U	3
1981–82	Rangers	2	Dundee U	1
1982–83	Celtic	2	Rangers	1
1983–84	Rangers	3	Celtic	2
1984–85	Rangers	1	Dundee U	0
1985–86	Aberdeen	3	Hibernian	0
1986–87	Rangers	2	Celtic	1
1987–88	Rangers†	3	Aberdeen	3*
1988–89	Aberdeen	2	Rangers	3*
1989–90	Aberdeen	2	Rangers	1
1990–91	Rangers	2	Celtic	1
1991–92	Hibernian	2	Dunfermline Ath	0
1992–93	Rangers	2	Aberdeen	1*
1993–94	Rangers	2	Hibernian	1
1994–95	Raith R†	2	Celtic	2*
1995–96	Aberdeen	2	Dundee	0
1996–97	Rangers	4	Hearts	3
1997–98	Celtic	3	Dundee U	0

*†Won on penalties *After extra time*

SCOTTISH COCA-COLA CUP 1998–99

FIRST ROUND

Arbroath	(0) 0	Clydebank	(0) 1
Brechin C	(0) 2	Hamilton A	(1) 2

(aet; Hamilton A won 3-2 on penalties)

Clyde	(0) 1	Berwick R	(0) 1

(aet; Berwick R won 4-3 on penalties)

Cowdenbeath	(0) 0	Livingston	(1) 2
Dumbarton	(0) 0	Alloa Athletic	(2) 4
East Fife	*(1) 3	Partick T	(2) 2
Forfar Ath	(0) 0	Stirling Albion	(0) 1
Queen of the S	(0) 1	Inverness CT	(2) 4
Queen's Park	(1) 1	Ayr U	(1) 3
Ross Co	(1) 4	Montrose	(0) 1
Stenhousemuir	(0) 1	East Stirling	(0) 0
Stranraer	(0) 1	Albion R	(0) 1

(aet; Stranraer won 4-3 on penalties)

SECOND ROUND

Berwick R	(0) 1	Falkirk	(3) 5
Dundee	(0) 0	Alloa Ath	(1) 1
Dundee U	(2) 2	Stirling Albion	(1) 2

(aet; Dundee U won 3-0 on penalties)

East Fife	(0) 0	Motherwell	*(0) 1
Greenock Morton	(0) 0	Ross Co	(0) 1
Hamilton A	(0) 1	Hibernian	(1) 2
Inverness CT	(0) 0	Aberdeen	(1) 3
Livingston	*(0) 1	Dunfermline Ath	(0) 0
Raith R	(0) 2	Clydebank	(0) 0
St Johnstone	(0) 3	Stranraer	(0) 0
St Mirren	(0) 1	Ayr U	(2) 3
Stenhousemuir	(0) 0	Airdrieonians	(1) 2

THIRD ROUND

Falkirk	(0) 0	St Johnstone	(0) 1
Kilmarnock	*(1) 3	Livingston	(1) 1
Motherwell	(0) 0	Ayr U	(1) 2
Rangers	(2) 4	Alloa Ath	(0) 0
Airdrieonians	(1) 1	Celtic	(0) 0
Hearts	*(2) 4	Raith R	(1) 2
Hibernian	(0) 1	Aberdeen	(0) 0
Ross Co	*(0) 2	Dundee U	(0) 0

QUARTER-FINALS

Ayr U	(0) 0	Rangers	(1) 2
Kilmarnock	(0) 0	Airdrieonians	*(0) 1
St Johnstone	(3) 4	Hibernian	(0) 0
Hearts	(0) 1	Ross Co	(1) 1

(aet; Hearts won 3-0 on penalties)

SEMI-FINALS

Rangers	(2) 5	Airdrieonians	(0) 0
St Johnstone	(2) 3	Hearts	(0) 0

FINAL

Rangers	(2) 2	St Johnstone	(1) 1

*aet

TENNENT'S SCOTTISH CUP 1998–99

FIRST ROUND

Arbroath	(1) 1	Partick T	(2) 2
Dumbarton	(0) 1	Livingston	(0) 1
Queen's Park	(0) 2	Berwick R	(0) 0
Stenhousemuir	(1) 1	Alloa Ath	(1) 1

FIRST ROUND REPLAYS

Livingston	(1) 3	Dumbarton	(0) 0
Alloa Ath	(0) 0	Stenhousemuir	(0) 2

SECOND ROUND

Civil Service Stroll	(0) 0	Albion R	(2) 3
Dalbeattie Star	(1) 1	East Stirling	(1) 2
Forfar Ath	(0) 2	East Fife	(2) 2
Huntly	(3) 3	Peterhead	(0) 0
Inverness CT	(1) 1	Livingston	(1) 2
Keith	(0) 0	Brechin C	(0) 0
Montrose	(0) 0	Stirling Albion	(0) 0
Partick T	(2) 5	Cowdenbeath	(1) 2
Spartans	(1) 1	Clyde	(1) 1
Whitehill Welfare	(1) 1	Stenhousemuir	(0) 1
Queen of the S	(0) 1	Ross Co	(3) 3
Queen's Park	(0) 1	Clachnacuddin	(0) 1

SECOND ROUND REPLAYS

Clyde	(2) 5	Spartans	(0) 0
Brechin C	(1) 3	Keith	(0) 1
East Fife	(0) 0	Forfar Ath	(1) 1
Stenhousemuir	(0) 2	Whitehill Welfare	(0) 0
Stirling Albion	(1) 2	Montrose	(0) 1
Clachnacuddin	(0) 2	Queen's Park	(1) 3

THIRD ROUND

Aberdeen	(0) 0	Livingston	(0) 1
Ayr U	(1) 3	Kilmarnock	(0) 0
Brechin C	(0) 1	Albion R	(0) 1
Celtic	(1) 3	Airdrieonians	(1) 1
Falkirk	(0) 3	Huntly	(0) 0
Greenock Morton	(2) 2	Dundee	(1) 1
Hibernian	(0) 1	Stirling Albion	(1) 1
Partick T	(1) 1	Dunfermline Ath	(2) 2
Raith R	(0) 0	Clyde	(2) 4
Rangers	(2) 2	Stenhousemuir	(0) 0
St Johnstone	(0) 1	Forfar Ath	(0) 0
St Mirren	(1) 1	Hamilton A	(0) 1
Stranraer	(1) 1	East Stirling	(0) 0
Motherwell	(1) 3	Hearts	(0) 1
Queen's Park	(0) 0	Dundee U	(0) 0
Clydebank	(0) 1	Ross Co	(0) 1

THIRD ROUND REPLAYS

Albion R	(1) 3	Brechin C	(1) 1
Hamilton A	(0) 1	St Mirren	(0) 0

Stirling Albion	(1) 2	Hibernian	(1) 1
Dundee U	(1) 1	Queen's Park	(0) 0
Ross Co	(1) 2	Clydebank	(0) 3

(aet)

FOURTH ROUND

Ayr U	(0) 1	Albion R	(0) 0
Celtic	(4) 4	Dunfermline Ath	(0) 0
Livingston	(0) 1	St Johnstone	(2) 3
Motherwell	(0) 2	Stirling Albion	(0) 0
Stranraer	(0) 1	Falkirk	(1) 2
Greenock Morton	(3) 6	Clyde	(0) 1
Hamilton A	(0) 0	Rangers	(2) 6
Clydebank	(1) 2	Dundee U	(0) 2

FOURTH ROUND REPLAY

| Dundee U | (1) 3 | Clydebank | (0) 0 |

QUARTER-FINALS

Motherwell	(0) 0	St Johnstone	(0) 2
Rangers	(0) 2	Falkirk	(0) 1
Greenock Morton	(0) 0	Celtic	(1) 3
Ayr U	(0) 0	Dundee U	(0) 0

QUARTER-FINAL REPLAY

| Dundee U | (1) 2 | Ayr U | (0) 1 |

SEMI-FINALS

| Celtic | (2) 2 | Dundee U | (0) 0 |
| St Johnstone | (0) 0 | Rangers | (2) 4 |

FINAL

| Rangers | (0) 1 | Celtic | (0) 0 |

PAST SCOTTISH CUP FINALS

Year				
1874	Queen's Park	2	Clydesdale	0
1875	Queen's Park	3	Renton	0
1876	Queen's Park	1 2	Third Lanark	1 0
1877	Vale of Leven	0 1 3	Rangers	0 1 2
1878	Vale of Leven	1	Third Lanark	0
1879	Vale of Leven	1	Rangers	1
	Vale of Leven awarded cup, Rangers did not appear for replay			
1880	Queen's Park	3	Thornlibank	0
1881	Queen's Park	2 3	Dumbarton	1 1
	Replayed because of protest			
1882	Queen's Park	2 4	Dumbarton	2 1
1883	Dumbarton	2 2	Vale of Leven	2 1
1884	*Queen's Park awarded cup when Vale of Leven did not appear for the final*			
1885	Renton	0 3	Vale of Leven	0 1
1886	Queen's Park	3	Renton	1
1887	Hibernian	2	Dumbarton	1
1888	Renton	6	Cambuslang	1
1889	Third Lanark	3 2	Celtic	0 1
	Replayed because of protest			
1890	Queen's Park	1 2	Vale of Leven	1 1
1891	Hearts	1	Dumbarton	0
1892	Celtic	1 5	Queen's Park	0 1
	Replayed because of protest			
1893	Queen's Park	2	Celtic	1
1894	Rangers	3	Celtic	1
1895	St Bernards	3	Renton	1
1896	Hearts	3	Hibernian	1
1897	Rangers	5	Dumbarton	1
1898	Rangers	2	Kilmarnock	0
1899	Celtic	2	Rangers	0
1900	Celtic	4	Queen's Park	3
1901	Hearts	4	Celtic	3
1902	Hibernian	1	Celtic	0
1903	Rangers	1 0 2	Hearts	1 0 0
1904	Celtic	3	Rangers	2
1905	Third Lanark	0 3	Rangers	0 1
1906	Hearts	1	Third Lanark	0
1907	Celtic	3	Hearts	0
1908	Celtic	5	St Mirren	1
1909	*After two drawn games between Celtic and Rangers, 2.2, 1.1, there was a riot and the cup was withheld*			
1910	Dundee	2 0 2	Clyde	2 0 1
1911	Celtic	0 2	Hamilton Acad	0 0
1912	Celtic	2	Clyde	0
1913	Falkirk	2	Raith R	0
1914	Celtic	0 4	Hibernian	0 1
1920	Kilmarnock	3	Albion R	2
1921	Partick Th	1	Rangers	0
1922	Morton	1	Rangers	0
1923	Celtic	1	Hibernian	0
1924	Airdrieonians	2	Hibernian	0
1925	Celtic	2	Dundee	1
1926	St Mirren	2	Celtic	0
1927	Celtic	3	East Fife	1
1928	Rangers	4	Celtic	0
1929	Kilmarnock	2	Rangers	0
1930	Rangers	0 2	Partick Th	0 1
1931	Celtic	2 4	Motherwell	2 2

1932	Rangers	1 3	Kilmarnock	1 0
1933	Celtic	1	Motherwell	0
1934	Rangers	5	St Mirren	0
1935	Rangers	2	Hamilton Acad	1
1936	Rangers	1	Third Lanark	0
1937	Celtic	2	Aberdeen	1
1938	East Fife	1 4	Kilmarnock	1 2
1939	Clyde	4	Motherwell	0
1947	Aberdeen	2	Hibernian	1
1948	Rangers	1 1	Morton	1 0
1949	Rangers	4	Clyde	1
1950	Rangers	3	East Fife	0
1951	Celtic	1	Motherwell	0
1952	Motherwell	4	Dundee	0
1953	Rangers	1 1	Aberdeen	1 0
1954	Celtic	2	Aberdeen	1
1955	Clyde	1 1	Celtic	1 0
1956	Hearts	3	Celtic	1
1957	Falkirk	1 2	Kilmarnock	1 1
1958	Clyde	1	Hibernian	0
1959	St Mirren	3	Aberdeen	1
1960	Rangers	2	Kilmarnock	0
1961	Dunfermline Ath	0 2	Celtic	0 0
1962	Rangers	2	St Mirren	0
1963	Rangers	1 3	Celtic	1 0
1964	Rangers	3	Dundee	1
1965	Celtic	3	Dunfermline Ath	2
1966	Rangers	0 1	Celtic	0 0
1967	Celtic	2	Aberdeen	0
1968	Dunfermline Ath	3	Hearts	1
1969	Celtic	4	Rangers	0
1970	Aberdeen	3	Celtic	1
1971	Celtic	1 2	Rangers	1 1
1972	Celtic	6	Hibernian	1
1973	Rangers	3	Celtic	2
1974	Celtic	3	Dundee U	0
1975	Celtic	3	Airdrieonians	1
1976	Rangers	3	Hearts	1
1977	Celtic	1	Rangers	0
1978	Rangers	2	Aberdeen	1
1979	Rangers	0 0 3	Hibernian	0 0 2
1980	Celtic	1	Rangers	0
1981	Rangers	0 4	Dundee U	0 1
1982	Aberdeen	4	Rangers	1 (aet)
1983	Aberdeen	1	Rangers	0 (aet)
1984	Aberdeen	2	Celtic	1 (aet)
1985	Celtic	2	Dundee U	1
1986	Aberdeen	3	Hearts	0
1987	St Mirren	1	Dundee U	0 (aet)
1988	Celtic	2	Dundee U	1
1989	Celtic	1	Rangers	0
1990	Aberdeen†	0	Celtic	0
1991	Motherwell	4	Dundee U	3 (aet)
1992	Rangers	2	Airdrieonians	1
1993	Rangers	2	Aberdeen	1
1994	Dundee U	1	Rangers	0
1995	Celtic	1	Airdrieonians	0
1996	Rangers	5	Hearts	1
1997	Kilmarnock	1	Falkirk	0
1998	Hearts	2	Rangers	1

†*won on penalties*

WELSH FOOTBALL 1998–99

LEAGUE OF WALES

	P	Home W	D	L	Goals F	A	Away W	D	L	Goals F	A	GD	Pts
Barry Town	32	13	2	1	46	13	10	5	1	36	10	+59	76
Inter Cable-Tel	32	9	2	5	35	14	10	4	2	26	12	+35	63
Cwmbran Town	32	9	1	6	38	26	8	5	3	35	18	+29	57
Aberystwyth Town	32	9	4	3	28	20	7	5	4	31	28	+11	57
Caernarfon Town	32	9	5	2	29	19	4	6	6	16	27	−1	50
Newtown	32	8	7	1	25	9	5	3	8	20	26	+10	49
Conwy United	32	7	4	5	26	24	7	3	6	29	25	+6	49
Total Network Solutions	32	7	5	4	28	19	5	6	5	27	23	+13	47
Carmarthen Town	32	7	4	5	25	19	6	4	6	21	27	0	47
Caersws	32	7	3	6	29	29	5	5	6	20	26	−6	44
Bangor City	32	6	2	8	26	23	5	4	7	18	26	−5	39
Connah's Quay Nomads	32	6	5	5	28	23	4	3	9	16	24	−3	38
Haverfordwest County	32	6	4	6	25	24	3	3	10	18	36	−17	34
Afan Lido	32	3	4	9	14	27	4	6	6	14	19	−18	31
Rhayader Town	32	3	7	6	14	23	2	4	10	15	31	−25	26
Rhyl	32	4	2	10	21	33	3	0	13	20	48	−40	23
Holywell Town	32	2	7	7	22	33	1	2	13	16	53	−48	18

NORTHERN IRISH FOOTBALL 1998–99

IFL SMIRNOFF

Premiership

	P	W	D	L	F	A	GD	Pts
Glentoran	36	24	6	6	74	35	+39	78
Linfield	36	20	10	6	68	39	+29	70
Crusaders	36	18	8	10	48	39	+9	62
Newry Town	36	17	9	10	52	46	+6	60
Glenavon	36	13	12	11	49	35	+14	51
Ballymena United	36	11	8	17	40	42	−2	41
Coleraine	36	10	9	17	34	53	−19	39
Portadown	36	9	10	17	41	47	−6	37
Cliftonville	36	7	14	15	31	47	−16	35
Omagh Town	36	5	6	25	25	79	−54	21

LEAGUE OF WALES—RESULTS 1998–99

	Aberystwyth Town	Afan Lido	Bangor City	Barry Town	Caernarfon Town	Caersws	Carmarthen Town	Connah's Quay Nomads	Conwy United	Cwmbran Town	Haverfordwest County	Holywell Town	Inter Cable-Tel	Newtown	Rhayader Town	Rhyl	Total Network Solutions
Aberystwyth Town	—	2-1	3-0	1-1	1-1	0-5	3-2	2-1	3-1	1-3	2-1	0-0	1-1	5-0	2-1	2-1	0-1
Afan Lido	2-2	—	0-2	0-0	1-3	0-1	1-1	1-3	0-1	0-4	0-2	2-0	0-2	0-2	2-0	2-1	3-3
Bangor City	1-2	0-1	—	0-3	1-1	0-1	4-0	0-2	1-3	2-2	3-0	5-2	1-0	2-3	0-1	4-1	2-1
Barry Town	5-1	0-2	4-2	—	3-0	5-2	6-2	1-0	1-1	2-1	2-0	4-0	1-1	1-0	7-1	2-0	2-0
Caernarfon Town	2-0	2-0	1-0	0-4	—	2-2	3-2	1-1	1-1	2-4	2-0	2-2	1-1	3-1	2-0	3-0	2-1
Caersws	2-3	2-1	2-0	2-4	3-2	—	1-2	2-0	0-3	1-3	4-4	3-2	0-2	1-1	0-0	3-1	3-1
Carmarthen Town	2-5	1-1	1-2	2-1	0-0	0-1	—	6-2	2-1	1-1	3-1	3-0	0-1	1-0	1-1	1-2	1-0
Connah's Quay Nomads	0-0	0-0	1-1	0-3	2-2	0-0	0-2	—	1-2	1-0	3-1	4-2	1-2	3-0	4-1	6-2	2-3
Conwy United	1-1	2-0	3-1	1-3	1-1	2-1	1-2	1-3	—	2-4	4-2	2-1	3-0	1-0	1-1	2-1	3-3
Cwmbran Town	0-1	0-4	2-4	0-4	6-0	2-1	2-0	2-1	3-0	—	4-0	4-0	0-0	3-0	3-6	6-1	0-4
Haverfordwest County	2-6	1-1	0-0	0-0	0-2	1-1	1-2	1-0	1-3	2-1	—	7-2	0-1	2-0	1-0	5-2	1-4
Holywell Town	3-6	0-0	1-1	2-3	1-2	0-0	1-1	0-0	4-3	0-4	4-0	—	1-2	0-3	2-2	0-3	3-3
Inter Cable-Tel	6-1	0-1	3-0	1-2	3-0	6-0	1-2	1-1	3-0	0-1	1-0	5-1	—	0-2	1-0	3-2	1-1
Newtown	1-1	4-0	3-1	0-0	1-1	4-0	0-0	1-0	2-1	0-0	1-1	4-0	1-3	—	3-0	2-1	0-0
Rhayader Town	0-2	1-1	0-0	0-0	2-0	1-3	1-0	2-0	2-2	1-1	2-2	1-3	0-5	0-2	—	1-2	0-0
Rhyl	1-0	2-0	1-2	0-6	0-1	1-1	1-2	1-2	0-3	1-4	1-2	5-1	1-2	3-3	3-1	—	0-3
Total Network Solutions	0-0	1-1	1-2	1-2	2-0	2-1	1-1	2-0	1-4	2-2	0-2	2-0	1-3	1-1	1-0	6-0	—

EUROPEAN REVIEW 1998–99

There have been many more exciting and skilfully exhilarating European Cup finals than the one staged at the Nou Camp in Barcelona on 26 May, but none of them had such a dramatic ending as when Manchester United scored twice in the last minute of injury time to overturn Bayern Munich's single goal lead which they had held since the sixth minute.

For once it was the Germans who completely underestimated the English team, who had careered cavalier fashion through a run of 32 unbeaten matches. Bayern only had themselves to blame for the defeat. In the closing stages of a game in which they had had the edge, they twice hit the woodwork with United ripped apart. The Germans made the crucial mistake of taking off their two most effective players, Lothar Matthaus and the scorer Mario Basler, though one of the substitutes Mehmet Scholl did well in an offensive role and was responsible for striking the goal frame shortly after coming on with some 20 minutes remaining.

The tiring Matthaus came off with ten minutes to go and it was then that United began to make headway for the first time in the match. Teddy Sheringham was already making inroads down the left flank and when Ole Gunnar Solskjaer took over from Andy Cole once Alex Ferguson had noted the departure of Matthaus, the tide was beginning to turn in United's favour.

But it was only after Basler's replacement on the stroke of full time that advantage turned to fulfilment. Where he had patrolled the right side of Bayern's midfield area, gaps appeared at last. Yet it was a mis-hit from Ryan Giggs right foot which found its way towards Sheringham who did not get a real touch of any force but still swung a boot in the same straight direction and it was enough to level matters in the first minute of time added on.

One could sense the disbelief on the part of the Germans and there seemed only one likely winner in extra time. But it was not needed and two minutes later, David Beckham's corner was headed on by Sheringham and nudged into the roof of the net by Solskjaer's instinctive reaction.

The very last Cup-Winners' Cup final staged at Villa Park a week earlier between Mallorca and Lazio had proved a fitting occasion with both teams scoring early before Pavel Nedved put Lazio into a winning lead in the 81st minute with a half-volley. Christian Vieri, a snip of a signing at £17 million, had opened the scoring in the seventh minute with a well judged header. Four minutes later Dani levelled matters.

Thus Italy's crop of crowns was handsomely added to, because only seven days before Parma had comprehensively beaten Marseille 3-0 in Moscow. It was their third European success in the 1990s.

Alas for the French team, weakened by suspensions, it was a disastrous night. None suffered more than their captain Laurent Blanc, who was at fault with all three goals.

His attempted back header only found Hernan Crespo who lobbed Parma in front in the 26th minute. Ten minutes later Blanc's interception was only diverted to Diego Fuser whose deep cross was headed in by Paolo Ventoll.

Within ten minutes of the restart, the game virtually ended as a contest when Blanc hesitated and Enrico Chiesa drove home the third goal.

At international level, the European Championship produced mixed fortunes for the home countries striving to reach the finals to be played in Holland and Belgium in the summer of 2000. The Republic of Ireland were at the top of Group Eight. Wales' poor set of results in Group One led to manager Bobby Gould resigning and Northern Ireland's prospects in Group Three fell into a similar category. Even England with a change at the helm from Glenn Hoddle to Kevin Keegan disappointed, knowing they had to win in Poland to be sure of even a play-off place.

In Group Nine, Scotland edged out twice by the Czech Republic, the first team to qualify for the finals, were still hoping to secure runners-up position.

EUROPEAN CUP 1998–99

FIRST QUALIFYING ROUND, FIRST LEG

Beitar Jerusalem	(3) 4	B36 Torshavn	(0) 1
Celtic	(0) 0	St Patrick's Athletic	(0) 0
Cliftonville	(1) 1	Kosice	(3) 5
Dynamo Kiev	(4) 8	Barry Town	(0) 0
Dynamo Tbilisi	(0) 1	Vllaznia	(0) 0

UEFA declared the match to be 3-0

Grasshoppers	(3) 6	Jeunesse Esch	(0) 0
HJK Helsinki	(0) 2	Erevan	(0) 0
Kareda	(0) 0	Branik Maribor	(1) 3
Litets	(1) 2	Halmstad	(0) 0
LKS Lodz	(1) 4	Kapaz	(0) 1
Obilic	(1) 2	IBV	(0) 0
Sileks	(0) 0	FC Brugge	(0) 0
Skonto Riga	(0) 0	Dynamo Minsk	(0) 0
Steaua	(2) 4	Flora Tallinn	(1) 1
Valletta	(0) 0	Anorthosis	(0) 2
Zimbru Chisinau	(1) 1	Ujpest	(0) 0

FIRST QUALIFYING ROUND, SECOND LEG

Anorthosis	(3) 6	Valletta	(0) 0
B36 Torshavn	(0) 0	Beitar Jerusalem	(0) 1
Barry Town	(1) 1	Dynamo Kiev	(1) 2
Branik Maribor	(0) 1	Kareda	(0) 0
Dynamo Minsk	(1) 1	Skonto Riga	(1) 2
Erevan	(0) 0	HJK Helsinki	(2) 3
FC Brugge	(2) 2	Sileks	(0) 1
Flora Tallinn	(1) 3	Steaua	(0) 1
Halmstad	(2) 2	Litets	(0) 1
IBV	(1) 1	Obilic	(0) 2
Jeunesse Esch	(0) 0	Grasshoppers	(2) 2
Kapaz	(0) 1	LKS Lodz	(1) 3
Kosice	(3) 8	Cliftonville	(0) 0
St Patrick's Athletic	(0) 0	Celtic	(1) 2
Ujpest	(1) 3	Zimbru Chisinau	(1) 1
Vllaznia	(1) 3	Dynamo Tbilisi	(0) 1

SECOND QUALIFYING ROUND, FIRST LEG

Bayern Munich	(0) 4	Obilic	(0) 0
Benfica	(2) 6	Beitar Jerusalem	(0) 0
Branik Maribor	(1) 2	PSV Eindhoven	(0) 1
Celtic	(0) 1	Croatia Zagreb	(0) 0
Dynamo Kiev	(0) 0	Sparta Prague	(1) 1
Dynamo Tbilisi	(2) 2	Athletic Bilbao	(0) 1
Galatasaray	(0) 2	Grasshoppers	(0) 1
HJK Helsinki	(0) 1	Metz	(0) 0
Internazionale	(3) 4	Skonto Riga	(0) 0
Kosice	(0) 0	Brondby	(0) 2
Litets	(0) 0	Spartak Moscow	(0) 5
Manchester United	(1) 2	LKS Lodz	(0) 0
Olympiakos	(2) 2	Anorthosis	(0) 1
Rosenborg	(0) 2	FC Brugge	(0) 0
Steaua	(1) 2	Panathinaikos	(1) 2
Sturm Graz	(1) 4	Ujpest	(0) 0

SECOND QUALIFYING ROUND, SECOND LEG

Anorthosis	(1) 2	Olympiakos	(0) 4
Athletic Bilbao	(0) 1	Dynamo Tbilisi	(0) 0
Beitar Jerusalem	(2) 4	Benfica	(1) 2
Brondby	(0) 0	Kosice	(1) 1
Croatia Zagreb	(2) 3	Celtic	(0) 0
FC Brugge	(1) 4	Rosenborg	(1) 2
Grasshoppers	(1) 2	Galatasaray	(2) 3
LKS Lodz	(0) 0	Manchester United	(0) 0
Metz	(0) 1	HJK Helsinki	(0) 1
Obilic	(0) 1	Bayern Munich	(0) 1
Panathinaikos	(3) 6	Steaua	(2) 3
PSV Eindhoven	(1) 4	Branik Maribor	(1) 1
Skonto Riga	(1) 1	Internazionale	(1) 3
Sparta Prague	(0) 0	Dynamo Kiev	(1) 1

aet; Dynamo Kiev won 3-1 on penalties.

Spartak Moscow	(3) 6	Litets	(1) 2
Ujpest	(1) 2	Sturm Graz	(1) 3

CHAMPIONS LEAGUE

GROUP A

Croatia Zagreb	(0) 0	Ajax	(0) 0
Porto	(0) 2	Olympiakos	(0) 2
Ajax	(0) 2	Porto	(0) 1
Olympiakos	(1) 2	Croatia Zagreb	(0) 0
Olympiakos	(1) 1	Ajax	(0) 0
Porto	(2) 3	Croatia Zagreb	(0) 0
Ajax	(1) 2	Olympiakos	(0) 0
Croatia Zagreb	(2) 3	Porto	(1) 1
Ajax	(0) 0	Croatia Zagreb	(0) 1
Olympiakos	(1) 2	Porto	(0) 1
Croatia Zagreb	(1) 1	Olympiakos	(0) 1
Porto	(0) 3	Ajax	(0) 0

Final table	P	W	D	L	F	A	Pts
Olympiakos	6	3	2	1	8	6	11
Croatia Zagreb	6	2	2	2	5	7	8
Porto	6	2	1	3	11	9	7
Ajax	6	2	1	3	4	6	7

GROUP B

Athletic Bilbao	(1) 1	Rosenborg	(0) 1
Juventus	(1) 2	Galatasaray	(1) 2
Galatasaray	(1) 2	Athletic Bilbao	(1) 1
Rosenborg	(0) 1	Juventus	(1) 1
Athletic Bilbao	(0) 0	Juventus	(0) 0
Rosenborg	(0) 3	Galatasaray	(0) 0
Galatasaray	(0) 3	Rosenborg	(0) 0
Juventus	(0) 1	Athletic Bilbao	(1) 1
Galatasaray	(0) 1	Juventus	(0) 1
Rosenborg	(1) 2	Athletic Bilbao	(0) 1
Athletic Bilbao	(1) 1	Galatasaray	(0) 0
Juventus	(2) 2	Rosenborg	(0) 0

Final table	P	W	D	L	F	A	Pts
Juventus	6	1	5	0	7	5	8
Galatasaray	6	2	2	2	8	8	8
Rosenborg	6	2	2	2	7	8	8
Athletic Bilbao	6	1	3	2	5	6	6

GROUP C

Real Madrid	(0) 2	Internazionale	(0) 0
Sturm Graz	(0) 0	Spartak Moscow	(0) 2
Internazionale	(0) 1	Sturm Graz	(0) 0
Spartak Moscow	(0) 2	Real Madrid	(0) 1
Internazionale	(1) 2	Spartak Moscow	(0) 1
Real Madrid	(2) 6	Sturm Graz	(1) 1
Spartak Moscow	(0) 1	Internazionale	(0) 1
Sturm Graz	(1) 1	Real Madrid	(2) 5
Internazionale	(0) 3	Real Madrid	(0) 1
Spartak Moscow	(0) 0	Sturm Graz	(0) 0
Real Madrid	(1) 2	Spartak Moscow	(0) 1
Sturm Graz	(0) 0	Internazionale	(0) 2

Final table	P	W	D	L	F	A	Pts
Internazionale	6	4	1	1	9	5	13
Real Madrid	6	4	0	2	17	8	12
Spartak Moscow	6	2	2	2	7	6	8
Sturm Graz	6	0	1	5	2	16	1

GROUP D

Brondby	(0) 2	Bayern Munich	(0) 1
Manchester United	(2) 3	Barcelona	(0) 3
Barcelona	(1) 2	Brondby	(0) 0
Bayern Munich	(1) 2	Manchester United	(1) 2
Bayern Munich	(1) 1	Barcelona	(0) 0
Brondby	(1) 2	Manchester United	(3) 6
Barcelona	(1) 1	Bayern Munich	(0) 2
Manchester United	(4) 5	Brondby	(0) 0
Barcelona	(1) 3	Manchester United	(1) 3
Bayern Munich	(0) 2	Brondby	(0) 0
Brondby	(0) 0	Barcelona	(2) 2
Manchester U	(1) 1	Bayern Munich	(0) 1

Final table	P	W	D	L	F	A	Pts
Bayern Munich	6	3	2	1	9	6	11
Manchester United	6	2	4	0	20	11	10
Barcelona	6	2	2	2	11	9	8
Brondby	6	1	0	5	4	18	3

GROUP E

Lens	(0) 1	Arsenal	(0) 1
Panathinaikos	(0) 2	Dynamo Kiev	(1) 1
Arsenal	(0) 2	Panathinaikos	(0) 1
Dynamo Kiev	(0) 1	Lens	(0) 1
Arsenal	(0) 1	Dynamo Kiev	(0) 1
Lens	(0) 1	Panathinaikos	(0) 0
Dynamo Kiev	(1) 3	Arsenal	(0) 1
Panathinaikos	(0) 1	Lens	(0) 0
Arsenal	(0) 0	Lens	(0) 1
Dynamo Kiev	(0) 2	Panathinaikos	(1) 1
Lens	(0) 1	Dynamo Kiev	(0) 3
Panathinaikos	(0) 1	Arsenal	(0) 3

Final table	P	W	D	L	F	A	Pts
Dynamo Kiev	6	3	2	1	11	7	11
Lens	6	2	2	2	5	6	8
Arsenal	6	2	2	2	8	8	8
Panathinaikos	6	2	0	4	6	9	6

GROUP F

PSV Eindhoven	(0) 2	HJK Helsinki	(1) 1
Kaiserslautern	(1) 1	Benfica	(0) 0
Benfica	(0) 2	PSV Eindhoven	(0) 1
HJK Helsinki	(0) 0	Kaiserslautern	(0) 0
HJK Helsinki	(1) 2	Benfica	(0) 0
PSV Eindhoven	(0) 1	Kaiserslautern	(0) 2
Benfica	(0) 2	HJK Helsinki	(1) 2
Kaiserslautern	(0) 3	PSV Eindhoven	(1) 1
Benfica	(1) 2	Kaiserslautern	(0) 1
HJK Helsinki	(0) 1	PSV Eindhoven	(1) 3
Kaiserslautern	(1) 5	HJK Helsinki	(1) 2
PSV Eindhoven	(1) 2	Benfica	(0) 2

Final table	P	W	D	L	F	A	Pts
Kaiserslautern	6	4	1	1	12	6	13
Benfica	6	2	2	2	8	9	8
PSV Eindhoven	6	2	1	3	10	11	8
HJK Helsinki	6	1	2	3	8	12	5

QUARTER-FINALS, FIRST LEG

Bayern Munich	(2) 2	Kaiserslautern	(0) 0
Juventus	(1) 2	Olympiakos	(0) 1
Manchester United	(2) 2	Internazionale	(0) 0
Real Madrid	(0) 1	Dynamo Kiev	(0) 1

QUARTER-FINALS, SECOND LEG

Dynamo Kiev	(0) 2	Real Madrid	(0) 0
Internazionale	(0) 1	Manchester United	(0) 1
Kaiserslautern	(0) 0	Bayern Munich	(3) 4
Olympiakos	(1) 1	Juventus	(0) 1

SEMI-FINALS, FIRST LEG

Dynamo Kiev	(2) 3	Bayern Munich	(1) 3
Manchester United	(0) 1	Juventus	(1) 1

SEMI-FINALS, SECOND LEG

Bayern Munich	(1) 1	Dynamo Kiev	(0) 0
Juventus	(2) 2	Manchester United	(2) 3

FINAL

Manchester U (0) 2, Bayern Munich (1) 1

(in Barcelona, 26 May 1999, 90,000)

Manchester U: Schmeichel; Neville G, Irwin, Johnsen, Butt, Stam, Beckham, Blomqvist (Sheringham 66), Cole (Solskjaer 80), Yorke, Giggs.
Scorers: Sheringham 89, Solskjaer 90.
Bayern Munich: Kahn; Babbel, Tarnat, Linke, Matthaus (Fink 80), Kuffour, Basler (Salihamidzic 89), Effenberg, Jancker, Zickler (Scholl 70), Jeremies.
Scorer: Basler 6.
Referee: Collina (Italy).

EUROPEAN CUP-WINNERS' CUP 1998–99

QUALIFYING ROUND, FIRST LEG

Amica	(1) 4	Hibernians	(0) 0
Apolonia	(1) 1	Genk	(3) 5
Bangor City	(0) 0	Haka	(1) 2
FC Copenhagen	(4) 4	Karabakh	(2) 2
Cork City	(2) 2	CSKA Kiev	(0) 1
Ekranas	(1) 1	Apollon	(1) 2
Glentoran	(0) 0	Maccabi Haifa	(1) 1
GI Gotu	(1) 1	MTK Budapest	(2) 3
Grevenmacher	(1) 2	Rapid Bucharest	(1) 6
Lantana	(0) 0	Hearts	(1) 1
Lausanne	(1) 5	Tsement	(1) 1
Levski	(5) 8	Lokomotiv 96	(0) 1
Metalurgs	(0) 4	IBK Keflavik	(0) 2
Partizan Belgrade	(2) 2	Dynamo Batumi	(0) 0
Rudar	(1) 2	Constructorul	(0) 0
Vaduz	(0) 0	Helsingborg	(1) 2
Vardar	(0) 0	Spartak Trnava	(1) 1

QUALIFYING ROUND, SECOND LEG

Apollon	(0) 3	Ekranas	(2) 3
Constructorul	(0) 0	Rudar	(0) 0
CSKA Kiev	(1) 2	Cork City	(0) 0
Dynamo Batumi	(1) 1	Partizan Belgrade	(0) 0
Genk	(1) 4	Apolonia	(0) 0
Haka	(1) 1	Bangor City	(0) 0
Hearts	(3) 5	Lantana	(0) 0
Helsingborg	(1) 3	Vaduz	(0) 0
Hibernians	(0) 0	Amica	(0) 1
IBK Keflavik	(1) 1	Metalurgs	(0) 0
Karabakh	(0) 0	FC Copenhagen	(0) 4
Lokomotiv 96	(0) 1	Levski	(0) 1
Maccabi Haifa	(1) 2	Glentoran	(1) 1
MTK Budapest	(3) 7	GI Gotu	(0) 0
Rapid Bucharest	(0) 2	Grevenmacher	(0) 0
Spartak Trnava	(0) 2	Vardar	(0) 0
Tsement	(1) 1	Lausanne	(0) 2

FIRST ROUND, FIRST LEG

Apollon	(1) 2	Jablonec	(1) 1
Besiktas	(2) 3	Spartak Trnava	(0) 0
Chelsea	(1) 1	Helsingborg	(0) 0
CSKA Kiev	(0) 0	Lokomotiv Moscow	(1) 2
Duisburg	(0) 1	Genk	(0) 1
Hearts	(0) 0	Mallorca	(1) 1
Heerenveen	(2) 3	Amica	(0) 1
Lazio	(1) 1	Lausanne	(0) 1
Levski	(0) 0	FC Copenhagen	(1) 2
Metalurgs	(0) 0	Braga	(0) 0
Newcastle U	(1) 2	Partizan Belgrade	(0) 1
Panionios	(1) 2	Haka	(0) 0
Paris St Germain	(0) 1	Maccabi Haifa	(0) 1
Rapid Bucharest	(0) 2	Valerengen	(0) 2
Ried	(1) 2	MTK Budapest	(0) 0
Rudar	(0) 0	Varteks	(0) 1

FIRST ROUND, SECOND LEG

Amica	(0) 0	Heerenveen	(1) 1
Braga	(2) 4	Metalurgs	(0) 0
FC Copenhagen	(1) 4	Levski	(0) 1
Genk	(2) 5	Duisburg	(0) 0
Haka	(0) 1	Panionios	(2) 3
Helsingborg	(0) 0	Chelsea	(0) 0

| Jablonec | (2) 2 | Apollon | (0) 1 |

aet; Appollon won 4-3 on penalties.

Lausanne	(1) 2	Lazio	(2) 2
Lokomotiv Moscow	(1) 3	CSKA Kiev	(1) 1
Maccabi Haifa	(0) 3	Paris St Germain	(0) 2
Mallorca	(0) 1	Hearts	(0) 1
MTK Budapest	(0) 0	Ried	(1) 1
Partizan Belgrade	(0) 1	Newcastle U	(0) 0
Spartak Trnava	(0) 2	Besiktas	(1) 1
Valerengen	(0) 0	Rapid Bucharest	(0) 0
Varteks	(1) 1	Rudar	(0) 0

SECOND ROUND, FIRST LEG

Chelsea	(0) 1	FC Copenhagen	(0) 1
Genk	(0) 1	Mallorca	(0) 1
Heerenveen	(0) 2	Varteks	(0) 1
Lazio	(0) 0	Partizan Belgrade	(0) 0
Lokomotiv Moscow	(2) 3	Braga	(0) 1
Panionios	(2) 3	Apollon	(2) 2
Ried	(1) 2	Maccabi Haifa	(1) 1
Valerengen	(0) 1	Besiktas	(0) 0

SECOND ROUND, SECOND LEG

Apollon	(0) 0	Panionios	(1) 1
Besiktas	(3) 3	Valerengen	(0) 3
Braga	(1) 1	Lokomotiv Moscow	(0) 0
FC Copenhagen	(0) 0	Chelsea	(1) 1
Maccabi Haifa	(1) 4	Ried	(0) 1
Mallorca	(0) 0	Genk	(0) 0
Partizan Belgrade	(1) 2	Lazio	(1) 3
Varteks	(0) 4	Heerenveen	(1) 2

QUARTER-FINALS, FIRST LEG

Chelsea	(2) 3	Valerengen	(0) 0
Lokomotiv Moscow	(0) 3	Maccabi Haifa	(0) 0
Panionios	(0) 0	Lazio	(2) 4
Varteks	(0) 0	Mallorca	(0) 0

QUARTER-FINALS, SECOND LEG

Lazio	(0) 3	Panionios	(0) 0
Maccabi Haifa	(0) 0	Lokomotiv Moscow	(0) 1
Mallorca	(0) 3	Varteks	(0) 1
Valerengen	(2) 2	Chelsea	(3) 3

SEMI-FINALS, FIRST LEG

| Chelsea | (0) 1 | Mallorca | (1) 1 |
| Lokomotiv Moscow | (0) 1 | Lazio | (0) 1 |

SEMI-FINALS, SECOND LEG

| Lazio | (0) 0 | Lokomotiv Moscow | (0) 0 |
| Mallorca | (1) 1 | Chelsea | (0) 0 |

FINAL

Mallorca (1) 1, Lazio (1) 2

(at Villa Park, 19 May 1999, 33,021)

Mallorca: Roa; Olaizola, Soler M, Lauren, Marcelino, Siviero, Engonga, Ibagaza, Biagini (Paunovic 73), Dani, Stankovic.
Scorer: Dani 11.
Lazio: Marchegiani; Pancaro, Favalli, Almeyda, Mihajlovic, Nesta, Stankovic (Conceicao 56), Mancini (Fernando Couto 89), Vieri, Salas, Nedved (Lombardo 84).
Scorers: Vieri 7, Nedved 81.
Referee: Benko (Austria).

UEFA CUP 1998–99

FIRST QUALIFYING ROUND, FIRST LEG

Arges	(2) 5	Dynamo Baku	(1) 1
Belshina	(0) 0	CSKA Sofia	(0) 0
Donetsk	(0) 2	Birkirkara	(0) 1
Ekeren	(3) 4	Sarajevo	(0) 1
Ferencvaros	(2) 6	Principat	(0) 0
Hapoel Tel Aviv	(1) 3	FinnPa	(1) 1
HB Torshavn	(1) 2	VPS Vaasa	(0) 0
IA Akranes	(1) 3	Zalgiris	(1) 2
Inter Bratislava	(1) 2	SK Tirana	(0) 0
Kolkheti	(0) 0	Red Star Belgrade	(1) 4
Mura	(5) 6	Daugava	(0) 1
Newtown	(0) 0	Wisla	(0) 0
Omonia	(2) 5	Linfield	(0) 1
Otelul	(2) 3	Sloga	(0) 0
Sadam	(0) 0	Polonia	(1) 2
Shelbourne	(2) 3	Rangers	(0) 5
Shirak	(0) 0	Malmo	(0) 2
Tiligul	(0) 0	Anderlecht	(0) 1
Union Luxembourg	(0) 0	IFK Gothenburg	(0) 3
Zeljeznicar	(0) 1	Kilmarnock	(0) 1

FIRST QUALIFYING ROUND, SECOND LEG

Anderlecht	(2) 5	Tiligul	(0) 0
Birkirkara	(0) 0	Donetsk	(1) 4
CSKA Sofia	(2) 3	Belshina	(0) 1
Daugava	(0) 1	Mura	(0) 2
Dynamo Baku	(0) 0	Arges	(0) 2
FinnPa	(0) 1	Hapoel Tel Aviv	(2) 3
IFK Gothenburg	(1) 4	Union Luxembourg	(0) 0
Kilmarnock	(0) 1	Zeljeznicar	(0) 0
Linfield	(3) 5	Omonia	(3) 3
Malmo	(3) 5	Shirak	(0) 0
Polonia	(3) 3	Sadam	(1) 1
Principat	(1) 1	Ferencvaros	(2) 8
Rangers	(1) 2	Shelbourne	(0) 0
Red Star Belgrade	(2) 7	Kolkheti	(0) 0
Sarajevo	(0) 0	Ekeren	(0) 0
SK Tirana	(0) 0	Inter Bratislava	(0) 2
Sloga	(1) 1	Otelul	(0) 1
VPS Vaasa	(2) 4	HB Torshavn	(0) 0
Wisla	(2) 7	Newtown	(0) 0
Zalgiris	(1) 1	IA Akranes	(0) 0

SECOND QUALIFYING ROUND, FIRST LEG

Arges	(2) 2	Istanbul	(0) 0
Brann	(0) 1	Zalgiris	(0) 0
Ekeren	(0) 1	Servette	(2) 4
Ferencvaros	(2) 4	AEK Athens	(0) 2
Hajduk Split	(1) 1	Malmo	(0) 1
Hapoel Tel Aviv	(0) 1	Stromsgodset	(0) 0
IFK Gothenburg	(1) 2	Fenerbahce	(0) 1
Molde	(0) 0	CSKA Sofia	(0) 0
Mura	(0) 0	Silkeborg	(0) 0
Olomouc	(1) 2	Kilmarnock	(0) 0
Omonia	(1) 3	Rapid Vienna	(1) 1
Osijek	(1) 3	Anderlecht	(0) 1
Polonia	(0) 0	Dynamo Moscow	(0) 1
Rangers	(0) 2	PAOK Salonika	(0) 0

Red Star Belgrade	(0) 2	Volgograd	(0) 1
Slavia Prague	(1) 4	Inter Bratislava	(0) 0
Vejle	(2) 3	Otelul	(0) 0
VPS Vaasa	(0) 0	Graz	(0) 0
Wisla	(2) 5	Trabzonspor	(0) 1
Zurich	(1) 4	Donetsk	(0) 0

SECOND QUALIFYING ROUND, SECOND LEG

AEK Athens	(3) 4	Ferencvaros	(0) 0
Anderlecht	(1) 2	Osijek	(0) 0
CSKA Sofia	(1) 2	Molde	(0) 0
Donetsk	(1) 3	Zurich	(2) 2
Dynamo Moscow	(0) 1	Polonia	(0) 0
Fenerbahce	(0) 1	IFK Gothenburg	(0) 0
Graz	(0) 3	VPS Vaasa	(0) 0
Inter Bratislava	(1) 2	Slavia Prague	(0) 0
Istanbul	(2) 4	Arges	(0) 2
Kilmarnock	(0) 0	Olomouc	(2) 2
Malmo	(0) 1	Hajduk Split	(1) 2
Otelul	(0) 0	Vejle	(2) 3
PAOK Salonika	(0) 0	Rangers	(0) 0
Rapid Vienna	(1) 2	Omonia	(0) 0
Servette	(0) 1	Ekeren	(2) 2
Silkeborg	(0) 2	Mura	(0) 0
Stromsgodset	(1) 1	Hapoel Tel Aviv	(0) 0

aet; Stromsgodset won 4-2 on penalties.

Trabzonspor	(0) 1	Wisla	(0) 2
Volgograd	(0) 1	Red Star Belgrade	(0) 2
Zalgiris	(0) 0	Brann	(0) 0

FIRST ROUND, FIRST LEG

Anderlecht	(0) 0	Grasshoppers	(0) 2
Arges	(0) 0	Celta Vigo	(1) 1
Aston Villa	(0) 3	Stromsgodset	(2) 2
Atletico Madrid	(1) 2	Obilic	(0) 0
Beitar Jerusalem	(1) 1	Rangers	(0) 1
Blackburn Rovers	(0) 0	Lyon	(0) 1
Bordeaux	(1) 1	Rapid Vienna	(0) 1
Branik Maribor	(0) 0	Wisla	(2) 2
Brann	(1) 2	Werder Bremen	(0) 0
Dynamo Moscow	(1) 2	Skonto Riga	(1) 2
Fenerbahce	(1) 1	Parma	(0) 0
Fiorentina	(0) 2	Hajduk Split	(1) 1
Guimaraes	(0) 1	Celtic	(1) 2
Kosice	(0) 0	Liverpool	(2) 3
Leeds United	(0) 1	Maritimo	(0) 0
Litets	(0) 1	Graz	(0) 1
LKS Lodz	(1) 1	Monaco	(0) 3
Olomouc	(2) 2	Marseille	(1) 2
Red Star Belgrade	(2) 2	Metz	(0) 1
Schalke	(1) 1	Slavia Prague	(0) 0
Servette	(0) 2	CSKA Sofia	(1) 1
Silkeborg	(0) 0	Roma	(0) 2
Sparta Prague	(2) 2	Real Sociedad	(1) 4
Sporting Lisbon	(0) 0	Bologna	(1) 2
Steaua	(1) 3	Valencia	(2) 4
Stuttgart	(1) 1	Feyenoord	(3) 3
Udinese	(0) 1	Leverkusen	(1) 1
Ujpest	(0) 0	FC Brugge	(3) 5
Vejle	(0) 1	Betis	(0) 0
Vitesse	(0) 3	AEK Athens	(0) 0
Willem II	(0) 3	Dynamo Tbilisi	(0) 0
Zurich	(1) 4	Anorthosis	(0) 0

FIRST ROUND, SECOND LEG

AEK Athens	(1) 3	Vitesse	(2) 3
Anorthosis	(1) 2	Zurich	(2) 3
Betis	(2) 5	Vejle	(0) 0
Bologna	(0) 2	Sporting Lisbon	(0) 1
Celta Vigo	(4) 7	Arges	(0) 0
Celtic	(1) 2	Guimaraes	(0) 1
CSKA Sofia	(1) 1	Servette	(0) 0
Dynamo Tbilisi	(0) 0	Willem II	(1) 3
FC Brugge	(1) 2	Ujpest	(0) 2
Feyenoord	(0) 0	Stuttgart	(1) 3
Grasshoppers	(0) 0	Anderlecht	(0) 0
Graz	(1) 2	Litets	(0) 0
Hajduk Split	(0) 0	Fiorentina	(0) 0
Leverkusen	(0) 1	Udinese	(0) 0
Liverpool	(1) 5	Kosice	(0) 0
Lyon	(2) 2	Blackburn Rovers	(1) 2
Maritimo	(1) 1	Leeds United	(0) 0

aet; Leeds United won 4-1 on penalties.

Marseille	(2) 4	Olomouc	(0) 0
Metz	(1) 2	Red Star Belgrade	(1) 1

aet; Red Star Belgrade won 4-3 on penalties.

Monaco	(0) 0	LKS Lodz	(0) 0
Obilic	(0) 0	Atletico Madrid	(0) 1
Parma	(2) 3	Fenerbahce	(0) 1
Rangers	(2) 4	Beitar Jerusalem	(1) 2
Rapid Vienna	(1) 1	Bordeaux	(1) 2
Real Sociedad	(0) 1	Sparta Prague	(0) 0
Roma	(0) 1	Silkeborg	(0) 0
Skonto Riga	(0) 2	Dynamo Moscow	(1) 3
Slavia Prague	(1) 1	Schalke	(0) 0

aet; Slavia Prague won 5-4 on penalties.

Stromsgodset	(0) 0	Aston Villa	(2) 3
Valencia	(0) 3	Steaua	(0) 0
Werder Bremen	(1) 4	Brann	(0) 0
Wisla	(0) 3	Branik Maribor	(0) 0

SECOND ROUND, FIRST LEG

Bologna	(0) 2	Slavia Prague	(0) 1
Celta Vigo	(0) 0	Aston Villa	(1) 1
Celtic	(1) 1	Zurich	(0) 1
CSKA Sofia	(0) 2	Atletico Madrid	(2) 4
Dynamo Moscow	(0) 2	Real Sociedad	(3) 3
Grasshoppers	(0) 0	Fiorentina	(1) 2
Graz	(1) 3	Monaco	(1) 3
Leverkusen	(0) 1	Rangers	(1) 2
Liverpool	(0) 0	Valencia	(0) 0
Red Star Belgrade	(0) 1	Lyon	(0) 2
Roma	(1) 1	Leeds United	(0) 0
Stuttgart	(1) 1	FC Brugge	(0) 1
Vitesse	(0) 0	Bordeaux	(1) 1
Werder Bremen	(0) 1	Marseille	(0) 1
Willem II	(0) 1	Betis	(0) 1
Wisla	(0) 1	Parma	(1) 1

SECOND ROUND, SECOND LEG

Aston Villa	(1) 1	Celta Vigo	(2) 3
Atletico Madrid	(1) 1	CSKA Sofia	(0) 0
Betis	(1) 3	Willem II	(0) 0
Bordeaux	(1) 2	Vitesse	(1) 1
FC Brugge	(0) 3	Stuttgart	(0) 2

| Fiorentina | 2 | Grasshoppers | 1 |

(Match abandoned at half time; tie awarded to Grasshoppers)

Leeds United	(0) 0	Roma	(0) 0
Lyon	(3) 3	Red Star Belgrade	(1) 2
Marseille	(1) 3	Werder Bremen	(0) 2
Monaco	(2) 4	Graz	(0) 0
Parma	(1) 2	Wisla	(0) 1
Rangers	(0) 1	Leverkusen	(0) 1
Real Sociedad	(0) 3	Dynamo Moscow	(0) 0
Slavia Prague	(0) 0	Bologna	(0) 2
Valencia	(1) 2	Liverpool	(0) 2
Zurich	(0) 4	Celtic	(0) 2

THIRD ROUND, FIRST LEG

Bologna	(1) 4	Betis	(0) 1
Celta Vigo	(0) 3	Liverpool	(1) 1
Grasshoppers	(2) 3	Bordeaux	(2) 3
Lyon	(1) 1	FC Brugge	(0) 0
Monaco	(1) 2	Marseille	(2) 2
Rangers	(0) 1	Parma	(0) 1
Real Sociedad	(1) 2	Atletico Madrid	(1) 1
Roma	(0) 1	Zurich	(0) 0

THIRD ROUND, SECOND LEG

Atletico Madrid	(2) 4	Real Sociedad	(0) 1
Betis	(1) 1	Bologna	(0) 0
Bordeaux	(0) 0	Grasshoppers	(0) 0
FC Brugge	(0) 3	Lyon	(1) 4
Liverpool	(0) 0	Celta Vigo	(0) 1
Marseille	(0) 1	Monaco	(0) 0
Parma	(0) 3	Rangers	(1) 1
Zurich	(0) 2	Roma	(1) 2

QUARTER-FINALS, FIRST LEG

Atletico Madrid	(1) 2	Roma	(0) 1
Bologna	(1) 3	Lyon	(0) 0
Bordeaux	(2) 2	Parma	(0) 1
Marseille	(1) 2	Celta Vigo	(0) 1

QUARTER-FINALS, SECOND LEG

Celta Vigo	(0) 0	Marseille	(0) 0
Lyon	(2) 2	Bologna	(0) 0
Parma	(2) 6	Bordeaux	(0) 0
Roma	(1) 1	Atletico Madrid	(0) 2

SEMI-FINALS, FIRST LEG

| Atletico Madrid | (1) 1 | Parma | (2) 3 |
| Marseille | (0) 0 | Bologna | (0) 0 |

SEMI-FINALS, SECOND LEG

| Bologna | (1) 1 | Marseille | (0) 1 |
| Parma | (1) 2 | Atletico Madrid | (0) 1 |

FINAL

Parma (2) 3, Marseille (0) 0

(in Moscow, 12 May 1999, 61,000)

Parma: Buffon; Fuser, Vanoli, Thuram, Sensini, Cannavaro, Dino Baggio, Boghossian, Crespo (Asprilla 82), Chiesa (Balbo 72), Veron (Fiore 78).
Scorers: Crespo 26, Vanoli 36, Chiesa 55.
Marseille: Porato; Blondeau, Edson (Camara 46), Issa, Blanc, Domoraud, Pires, Brando, Maurice, Gourvennec, Bravo.
Referee: Dallas (Scotland).

PAST EUROPEAN CUP FINALS

Year	Winner		Runner-up	
1956	Real Madrid	4	Stade de Rheims	3
1957	Real Madrid	2	Fiorentina	0
1958	Real Madrid	3	AC Milan	2*
1959	Real Madrid	2	Stade de Rheims	0
1960	Real Madrid	7	Eintracht Frankfurt	3
1961	Benfica	3	Barcelona	2
1962	Benfica	5	Real Madrid	3
1963	AC Milan	2	Benfica	1
1964	Internazionale	3	Real Madrid	1
1965	Internazionale	1	SL Benfica	0
1966	Real Madrid	2	Partizan Belgrade	1
1967	Celtic	2	Internazionale	1
1968	Manchester U	4	Benfica	1*
1969	AC Milan	4	Ajax	1
1970	Feyenoord	2	Celtic	1*
1971	Ajax	2	Panathinaikos	0
1972	Ajax	2	Internazionale	0
1973	Ajax	1	Juventus	0
1974	Bayern Munich	1 4	Atletico Madrid	1 0
1975	Bayern Munich	2	Leeds U	0
1976	Bayern Munich	1	St Etienne	0
1977	Liverpool	3	Borussia Moenchengladbach	1
1978	Liverpool	1	FC Brugge	0
1979	Nottingham F	1	Malmö	0
1980	Nottingham F	1	Hamburg	0
1981	Liverpool	1	Real Madrid	0
1982	Aston Villa	1	Bayern Munich	0
1983	Hamburg	1	Juventus	0
1984	Liverpool†	1	Roma	1
1985	Juventus	1	Liverpool	0
1986	Steaua Bucharest†	0	Barcelona	0
1987	Porto	2	Bayern Munich	1
1988	PSV Eindhoven†	0	Benfica	0
1989	AC Milan	4	Steaua Bucharest	0
1990	AC Milan	1	Benfica	0
1991	Red Star Belgrade†	0	Marseille	0
1992	Barcelona	1	Sampdoria	0
1993	Marseille	1	AC Milan	0

(Marseille subsequently stripped of title)

Year	Winner		Runner-up	
1994	AC Milan	4	Barcelona	0
1995	Ajax	1	AC Milan	0
1996	Juventus†	1	Ajax	1
1997	Borussia Dortmund	3	Juventus	1
1998	Real Madrid	1	Juventus	0

PAST EUROPEAN CUP-WINNERS FINALS

Year	Winner		Runner-up	
1961	Fiorentina	4	Rangers	1‡
1962	Atletico Madrid	1 3	Fiorentina	1 0
1963	Tottenham H	5	Atletico Madrid	1
1964	Sporting Lisbon	3 1	MTK Budapest	3* 0
1965	West Ham U	2	Munich 1860	0
1966	Borussia Dortmund	2	Liverpool	1*
1967	Bayern Munich	1	Rangers	0*
1968	AC Milan	2	Hamburg	0

1969	Slovan Bratislava	3	Barcelona	2
1970	Manchester C	2	Gornik Zabrze	1
1971	Chelsea	1 2	Real Madrid	1* 1*
1972	Rangers	3	Dynamo Moscow	2
1973	AC Milan	1	Leeds U	0
1974	Magdeburg	2	AC Milan	0
1975	Dynamo Kiev	3	Ferencvaros	0
1976	Anderlecht	4	West Ham U	2
1977	Hamburg	2	Anderlecht	0
1978	Anderlecht	4	Austria Vienna	0
1979	Barcelona	4	Fortuna Dusseldorf	3*
1980	Valencia†	0	Arsenal	0
1981	Dynamo Tbilisi	2	Carl Zeiss Jena	1
1982	Barcelona	2	Standard Liege	1
1983	Aberdeen	2	Real Madrid	1*
1984	Juventus	2	Porto	1
1985	Everton	3	Rapid Vienna	1
1986	Dynamo Kiev	3	Atletico Madrid	0
1987	Ajax	1	Lokomotiv Leipzig	0
1988	Mechelen	1	Ajax	0
1989	Barcelona	2	Sampdoria	0
1990	Sampdoria	2	Anderlecht	0
1991	Manchester U	2	Barcelona	1
1992	Werder Bremen	2	Monaco	0
1993	Parma	3	Antwerp	1
1994	Arsenal	1	Parma	0
1995	Real Zaragoza	2	Arsenal	1*
1996	Paris St Germain	1	Rapid Vienna	0
1997	Barcelona	1	Paris St Germain	0
1998	Chelsea	1	Stuttgart	0

PAST FAIRS CUP FINALS

1958	Barcelona	8	London	2‡
1960	Barcelona	4	Birmingham C	1‡
1961	Roma	4	Birmingham C	2‡
1962	Valencia	7	Barcelona	3‡
1963	Valencia	4	Dynamo Zagreb	1‡
1964	Real Zaragoza	2	Valencia	1
1965	Ferencvaros	1	Juventus	0
1966	Barcelona	4	Real Zaragoza	3‡
1967	Dynamo Zagreb	2	Leeds U	0‡
1968	Leeds U	1	Ferencvaros	0‡
1969	Newcastle U	6	Ujpest Dozsa	2‡
1970	Arsenal	4	Anderlecht	3‡
1971	Leeds U	3**	Juventus	3‡

PAST UEFA CUP FINALS

1972	Tottenham H	2 1	Wolverhampton W	1 1
1973	Liverpool	3 0	Borussia Moenchengladbach	0 2
1974	Feyenoord	2 2	Tottenham H	2 0
1975	Borussia Moenchengladbach	0 5	Twente Enschede	0 1
1976	Liverpool	3 1	FC Brugge	2 1
1977	Juventus**	1 1	Athletic Bilbao	0 2
1978	PSV Eindhoven	0 3	SEC Bastia	0 0
1979	Borussia Moenchengladbach	1 1	Red Star Belgrade	1 0

1980	Borussia Moenchengladbach ...3	0	Eintracht Frankfurt**	2	1
1981	Ipswich T	3 2	AZ 67 Alkmaar	0	4
1982	IFK Gothenburg	1 3	SV Hamburg	0	0
1983	Anderlecht	1 1	Benfica	0	1
1984	Tottenham H†	1 1	RSC Anderlecht	1	1
1985	Real Madrid	3 0	Videoton	0	1
1986	Real Madrid	5 0	Cologne	1	2
1987	IFK Gothenburg	1 1	Dundee U	0	1
1988	Bayer Leverkusen†	0 3	Espanol	0	3
1989	Napoli	2 3	Stuttgart	1	3
1990	Juventus	3 0	Fiorentina	1	0
1991	Internazionale	2 0	AS Roma	0	1
1992	Ajax**	0 2	Torino	0	2
1993	Juventus	3 3	Borussia Dortmund	1	0
1994	Internazionale	1 1	Salzburg	0	0
1995	Parma	1 1	Juventus	0	1
1996	Bayern Munich	2 3	Bordeaux	0	1
1997	Schalke*†	1 0	Internazionale	0	1
1998	Internazionale	3	Lazio	0	

After extra time ** *Won on away goals* † *Won on penalties* ‡ *Aggregate score*

EUROPEAN CUP DRAWS 1999–2000

EUROPEAN CUP

FIRST QUALIFYING ROUND
Barry Town v Valletta
Litets v Glentoran
St Patrick's Ath v Zimbru

SECOND QUALIFYING ROUND
Rapid Vienna v Barry Town or Valletta
Litets or Glentoran v Widzew Lodz
Haka or HB Torshavn v Rangers
Dynamo Tbilisi v St Patrick's Ath or Zimbru

Draw British and Irish Clubs only

UEFA CUP

QUALIFYING ROUND

GROUP 1
Gorica v Inter Cardiff

GROUP 3
Vaasa v St Johnstone
Portadown v CSKA Sofia

GROUP 4
Grasshoppers v Bray Wanderers

GROUP 5
IFK Gothenburg v Cork City
KR Reykjavik v Kilmarnock
Lokomotiv Tbilisi v Linfield

GROUP 6
Cwmbran Town v Celtic

Matches played August 12 and August 26.

EURO 2000

GROUP 1

Minsk, 5 September 1998, 35,000

Belarus (0) 0

Denmark (0) 0

Belarus: Satsunkevich; Yakhimovic, Ostrovski, Shtanyuk, Romashchenko M (Geraschenko 40), Gurenko, Khatskevich, Baranov, Lavrik, Belkevich, Makovski V (Romashchenko M A 89).

Denmark: Schmeichel; Tobiasen, Rieper, Hogh, Heintze, Helveg, Nielsen A, Thomsen, Tomasson (Frederiksen 81), Jorgensen (Andersen 67), Moller (Gravesen 67).

Referee: Dardenne (Germany).

Anfield, 5 September 1998, 23,160

Wales (0) 0

Italy (1) 2 *(Fuser 19, Vieri 76)*

Wales: Jones P; Robinson, Barnard, Symons, Williams, Coleman, Speed, Johnson, Blake (Saunders 66), Hughes M (Savage 80), Giggs.

Italy: Peruzzi; Panucci, Pessotto, Albertini (Di Biagio 68), Cannavaro, Iuliano, Fuser, Dino Baggio, Vieri, Del Piero (Roberto Baggio 74), Di Francesco (Serena 82).

Referee: Hauge (Norway).

Copenhagen, 10 October 1998, 36,009

Denmark (0) 1 *(Frederiksen 57)*

Wales (0) 2 *(Williams 58, Bellamy 86)*

Denmark: Krogh; Tobiasen, Rieper, Hogh, Heintze, Helveg, Frandsen (Gravesen 76), Steen-Nielsen, Jorgensen, Frederiksen, Beck (Sand 65).

Wales: Jones P; Savage, Barnard, Williams, Symons, Coleman, Saunders (Robinson 81), Blake (Bellamy 69), Hughes M, Johnson (Pembridge 62), Speed.

Referee: Piller (Hungary).

Udine, 10 October 1998, 35,247

Italy (1) 2 *(Del Piero 19, 61)*

Switzerland (0) 0

Italy: Buffon; Panucci, Cannavaro, Maldini, Torricelli, Fuser, Dino Baggio, Albertini, Di Francesco (Bachini 63), Inzaghi, Del Piero (Totti 70).

Switzerland: Hilfiker; Wolf (Chassot 68), Vega, Henchoz, Vogel, Wicky (Celestini 86), Sforza, Rothenbuhler, Sesa, Chapuisat, Muller.

Referee: Sars (France).

Zurich, 14 October 1998, 12,500

Switzerland (0) 1 *(Chapuisat 58)*

Denmark (0) 1 *(Tobiasen 90)*

Switzerland: Hilfiker; Jeanneret (Rothenbuhler 76), Sforza, Henchoz, Vogel, Wicky, Sesa (Haas 89), Fournier, Celestini, Chapuisat, Muller (Di Jorio 78).

Denmark: Krogh; Tobiasen, Rieper, Hogh, Heintze, Helveg, Frandsen (Colding 39), Steen-Nielsen, Tomasson (Beck 78), Fredriksen (Sand 61), Jorgensen.

Referee: Radoman (Yugoslavia).

Cardiff, 14 October 1998, 11,975

Wales (1) 3 *(Robinson 15, Coleman 54, Symons 85)*

Belarus (1) 2 *(Gurenko 21, Belkevich 48)*

Wales: Jones P; Robinson, Barnard, Savage, Symons, Coleman, Saunders, Johnson, Blake, Hughes M, Pembridge.

Belarus: Satsunkevich; Yakhimovic, Ostrovski, Lavrik, Shtanyuk, Baranov (Gerasimets 70), Khatskevich, Geraschenko (Romashchenko M 88), Gurenko, Belkevich, Makovski V (Katchuro 73).

Referee: Sammut (Malta).

Minsk, 27 March 1999, 44,000

Belarus (0) 0

Switzerland (0) 1 *(Fournier 72)*

Belarus: Tumilovich; Lavrik, Lukhvich, Yakhimovic, Gurenko, Khatskevich, Belkevich, Geraschenko (Skripchenko 86), Baranov (Chaika 56), Romashchenko, Makovski (Ostrovski 87).
Switzerland: Brunner; Hodel, Henchoz, Vogel, Fournier, Jeanneret, Wicky (Muller 66), Sforza, Sesa (De Napoli 74), Chapuisat, Comisetti.
Referee: Sarvan (Turkey).

Copenhagen, 27 March 1999, 41,429

Denmark (0) 1 *(Sand 56)*

Italy (1) 2 *(Inzaghi 1, Conte 68)*

Denmark: Schmeichel; Helveg, Henriksen, Hogh, Heintze, Goldbaek (Colding 82), Thomsen, Nielsen A (Tofting 77), Gronkjaer (Molnar 53), Jorgensen, Sand.
Italy: Buffon; Panucci, Nesta, Cannavaro, Maldini, Fuser (Conte 46), Dino Baggio, Di Biagio, Di Francesco, Inzaghi, Chiesa (Totti 63).
Referee: Lopez (Spain).

Ancona, 31 March 1999, 20,735

Italy (1) 1 *(Inzaghi 31 (pen))*

Belarus (1) 1 *(Belkevich 24)*

Italy: Buffon; Panucci, Nesta, Cannavaro, Maldini, Conte, Dino Baggio, Di Biagio (Giannichedda 46), Totti (Di Francesco 46), Inzaghi, Chiesa (Roberto Baggio 64).
Belarus: Tumilovich; Lavrik, Lukhvich, Yakhimovic, Gurenko, Orlovski, Belkevich, Ostrovski, Baranov, Romashchenko, Makovski V.
Referee: Piraux (Belgium).

Zurich, 31 March 1999, 13,500

Switzerland (1) 2 *(Chapuisat 4, 70)*

Wales (0) 0

Switzerland: Brunner; Jeanneret, Henchoz, Wolf, Muller, Vogel, Sforza, Fournier, Wicky, Chapuisat, Comisetti (Buhlmann 67).
Wales: Jones P (Crossley 26); Robinson, Pembridge, Symons, Coleman, Johnson, Saunders, Savage, Blake (Hartson 63), Hughes M (Bellamy 73), Speed.
Referee: Liba (Czech Republic).

Copenhagen, 5 June 1999, 24,876

Denmark (1) 1 *(Heintze 22)*

Belarus (0) 0

Denmark: Schmeichel; Colding, Henriksen, Hogh, Heintze, Goldbaek, Nielsen A, Tofting (Steen-Nielsen 87), Gronkjaer, Jorgensen, Sand (Molnar 78).
Belarus: Tumilovich; Lavrik, Lukhvich, Yakhimovic, Gurenko, Orlovski, Belkevic, Yaskovich (Kulchi 70), Ostrovski (Romashchenko 46), Baranov, Makovski V (Ryndyuk 85).
Referee: Baptista (Portugal).

Bologna, 5 June 1999, 12,392

Italy (3) 4 *(Vieri 6, Inzaghi 36, Maldini 39, Chiesa 89)*

Wales (0) 0

Italy: Buffon; Panucci, Maldini, Fuser (Di Livio 68), Negro, Cannavaro, Conte, Albertini, Vieri (Montella 46), Inzaghi (Chiesa 80), Di Francesco.
Wales: Jones P; Robinson (Jenkins 77), Barnard, Page, Melville, Williams, Giggs, Bellamy (Pembridge 79), Saunders (Hartson 46), Hughes M, Speed.
Referee: Steinborn (Germany).

Lausanne, 9 June 1999, 15,800

Switzerland (0) 0

Italy (0) 0

Switzerland: Huber; Wicky (Haas 70), Muller, Hodel, Geanneret (Di Jorio 78), Vogel, Sforza, Rothenbuhler, Sesa, Chapuisat, Comisetti (Celestini 57).
Italy: Buffon; Panucci (Pancaro 72), Negro, Cannavaro, Maldini, Fuser (Di Livio 61), Albertini, Conte, Vieri (Chiesa 61), Inzaghi, Di Francesco.
Referee: Poll (England).

Liverpool, 9 June 1999, 10,000
Wales (0) 0
Denmark (0) 2 *(Tomasson 84, Tofting 90 (pen))*
Wales: Jones P; Jenkins, Barnard (Legg 90), Robinson (Pembridge 87), Melville, Coleman, Speed, Saunders, Hartson (Bellamy 89), Hughes M, Giggs.
Denmark: Schmeichel; Colding, Heintze, Gronkjaer, Hogh, Henriksen, Goldbaek, Nielsen A (Tofting 85), Jorgensen (Frandsen 90), Sand, Molnar (Tomasson 72).
Referee: Ancion (Belgium).

Group 1	P	W	D	L	F	A	Pts
Italy	6	4	2	0	11	2	14
Denmark	6	2	2	2	6	5	8
Switzerland	5	2	2	1	4	3	8
Wales	6	2	0	4	5	13	6
Belarus	5	0	2	3	3	6	2

GROUP 2

Tbilisi, 5 September 1998, 35,000
Georgia (0) 1 *(Arveladze A 65)*
Albania (0) 0
Georgia: Gvaramadze; Kaladze, Tskitishvili, Silagadze (Kiknadze 42), Tsereteli, Kobiashvili, Nemsadze, Jamarauli, Ketsbaia (Janashia 56), Kinkladze, Iashvili (Arveladze A 60).
Albania: Strakosha; Lala, Shulku, Xhumba, Vata, Pinari, Haxhi, Bushi (Galo 74), Kola, Rrakli, Tare (Peco 67) (Maxhuni 87).
Referee: Tetrucci (Switzerland).

Athens, 6 September 1998, 29,000
Greece (0) 2 *(Mahlas 56 (pen), Frantzeskos 58)*
Slovenia (1) 2 *(Zahovic 19, 73)*
Greece: Atmatsidis; Kalitzakis, Ouzounidis, Dabizas, Borbokis (Liberopoulos 83), Markos, Zagorakis, Tsartas (Frantzeskos 46), Kassapis (Georgatos 78), Mahlas, Nikolaidis.
Slovenia: Simeunovic; Milanic, Galic, Knavs, Novak, Ceh, Zahovic, Pavlin, Rudonja, Udovic (Englaro 46), Osterc (Siljak 68) (Acimovic 72).
Referee: Trentalange (Italy).

Oslo, 6 September 1998, 11,030
Norway (1) 1 *(Solbakken 17)*
Latvia (1) 3 *(Pakhar 11, Shtolcers 53, Zemlinsky 65 (pen))*
Norway: Baardsen; Heggem (Berg 61), Bjornebye, Johnsen, Hoftun, Rekdal, Rudi (Flo H 79), Solbakken, Strandli, Flo T, Solskjaer (Flo J 62).
Latvia: Karavayev; Laizans (Lukashevich 51), Lobanyov, Zemlinsky, Ivanov, Bleidelis, Zakreshevsky, Babichev, Sharando (Boulders 73), Pakhar (Isakov 81), Shtolcers.
Referee: Shmolik (Belarus).

Riga, 10 October 1998, 1900
Latvia (1) 1 *(Shtolcers 2)*
Georgia (0) 0
Latvia: Karavayev; Lukashevich, Zemlinsky, Lobanyov, Sharando, Ivanov, Astafyev (Isakov 75), Bleidelis (Laizans 51), Babichev, Pakhar (Boulders 89), Shtolcers.
Georgia: Gvaramadze; Kaladze, Shekiladze, Kavelashvili, Gakhokidze (Demetradze 60), Kobiashvili, Nemsadze, Jamarauli, Ketsbaia, Kinkladze, Arveladze S.
Referee: Zotta (Romania).

Ljubljana, 10 October 1998, 7000
Slovenia (1) 1 *(Zahovic 24)*
Norway (1) 2 *(Flo T 43, Rekdal 80)*
Slovenia: Simeunovic; Galic, Milanic, Knavs, Rudonja, Novak, Ceh, Zahovic, Pavlin, Osterc (Englaro 46), Udovic (Acimovic 65).
Norway: Grodas; Haaland, Berg, Hoftun, Bjornebye, Heggem (Riseth 86), Strand (Hestad 77), Rekdal, Solbakken, Flo J, Flo T (Rushfeldt 89).
Referee: Schluchter (Switzerland).

Maroussi, 14 October 1998, 15,000

Greece (3) 3 *(Mahlas 13, Liberopoulos 15, Ouzounidis 36)*

Georgia (0) 0

Greece: Atmatsidis; Kalitzakis, Ouzounidis, Dabizas, Zagorakis, Markos, Poursanidis, Frantzeskos (Tsartas 74), Georgatos, Liberopoulos (Yannakopoulos 67), Mahlas (Mavroyenidis 85).

Georgia: Togonidze; Kobiashvili, Kaladze, Shelia, Nemsadze, Shekiladze, Ketsbaia, Jamarauli, Kinkladze, Kavelashvili (Gakhokidze 59), Arveladze S.

Referee: Ouzounov (Bulgaria).

Oslo, 14 October 1998, 17,770

Norway (0) 2 *(Rekdal 80 (pen), Berg 87)*

Albania (1) 2 *(Bushi 38, Tare 53)*

Norway: Grodas; Haaland (Iversen 12), Berg, Hoftun, Bjornebye, Heggem, Strand, Rekdal, Solbakken (Rushfeldt 90), Flo J (Solskjaer 57), Flo T.

Albania: Strakosha; Shulku, Lala, Xhumba, Haxhi, Bushi (Halili 84), Vata, Kola (Dalipi 90), Fakaj, Tare, Rrakli.

Referee: Grabher (Austria).

Maribor, 14 October 1998, 4700

Slovenia (0) 1 *(Udovic 86)*

Latvia (0) 0

Slovenia: Simeunovic; Galic, Milanic, Knavs (Gliha 46), Novak, Istenic (Acimovic 65), Pavlin, Englaro, Zahovic, Udovic (Milinovic 88), Rudonja.

Latvia: Karavayev; Lukashevich, Zemlinsky, Ivanov (Rimkus 87), Lobanyov, Sharando, Bleidelis (Mikholap 51), Astafyev (Boulders 79), Isakov, Pakhar, Shtolcers.

Referee: Nalbandyan (Armenia).

Tirana, 18 November 1998, 14,000

Albania (0) 0

Greece (0) 0

Albania: Strakosha; Dalipi (Halili 52), Haxhi, Vata, Xhumba, Shulku, Fakaj, Kola, Bushi, Rrakli, Tare.

Greece: Atmatsidis; Dabizas (Vokolos 90), Ouzounidis, Kalitzakis, Zagorakis, Poursanidis, Frantzeskos (Liberopoulos 46), Georgatos, Mahlas, Nikolaidis (Konstantinidis 68), Markos.

Referee: Torres (Spain).

Tbilisi, 27 March 1999, 20,000

Georgia (1) 1 *(Janashia 42)*

Slovenia (0) 1 *(Zahovic 52)*

Georgia: Grishikashvili; Kaladze, Bashvili, Chkhaidze, Tsereteli, Aleksidze (Kinkladze 46), Nemsadze, Jamarauli (Daraselia 82), Kobiashvili, Janashia, Demetradze (Kavelashvili 74).

Slovenia: Simeunovic; Galic, Milanic, Knavs, Rudonja (Mitrakovic 89), Bulajic, Milinovic, Ceh, Pavlin (Istenic 78), Udovic (Acimovic 60), Zahovic.

Referee: Hamer (Luxembourg).

Athens, 27 March 1999, 42,571

Greece (0) 0

Norway (1) 2 *(Solskjaer 38, 87)*

Greece: Atmatsidis; Dabizas, Ouzounidis, Anatolikis, Zagorakis (Mavrogenidis 46), Yannakopoulos, Poursanidis, Markos (Mahlas 55), Georgatos, Liberopoulos (Frantzeskos 75), Nikolaidis.

Norway: Myhre; Heggem, Berg, Johnsen, Bergdolmo (Halle 65), Iversen, Strand (Bohinen 60), Solbakken, Mykland, Rudi, Solskjaer (Carew 88).

Referee: Irvine (Republic of Ireland).

Riga, 31 March 1999, 3200

Latvia (0) 0

Greece (0) 0

Latvia: Karavayev; Lukashevich, Astafyev, Zemlinsky, Lobanyov, Ivanov (Isakov 27), Sharando (Stepanov 62), Mikholap (Boulders 46), Blagonadezhdin, Pakhar, Shtolcers.

Greece: Atmatsidis; Kassapis, Ouzounidis, Dabizas, Poursanidis, Mavrogenidis, Zagorakis (Yannakopoulos 75), Liberopoulos, Georgatos (Frantzeskos 75), Mahlas (Anastasiou 81), Nikolaidis.
Referee: Fisker (Denmark).

Tbilisi, 28 April 1999, 20,000
Georgia (0) 1 *(Janashia 58)*
Norway (4) 4 *(Shekiladze 16 (og), Flo T 26, 38, Solskjaer 35)*

Georgia: Togonidze; Shekiladze (Popkhadze 46), Didava, Tsereteli, Kaladze, Nemsadze, Revazishvili (Kiknadze 81), Jamarauli, Kobiashvili, Janashia, Ketsbaia (Demetradze 46).
Norway: Myhre; Haaland, Pedersen, Hoftun, Bergdolmo, Solskjaer (Strand 46), Iversen, Solbakken, Mykland, Rudi (Riseth 82), Flo T (Carew 88).
Referee: Puhl (Hungary).

Riga, 28 April 1999, 2700
Latvia (0) 0
Albania (0) 0

Latvia: Karavayev; Stepanov (Sharando 84), Isakov, Lukashevich, Lobanyov, Blagonadezhdin, Ivanov, Boulders, Rubins, Mikholap (Dobretsov 70), Shtolcers (Laizans 60).
Albania: Strakosha; Lala, Shulku, Xhumba, Vata (Jupi 77), Fakaj, Haxhi, Bushi (Halili 87), Kola, Rrakli (Dalipi 82), Tare.
Referee: Romain (Belgium).

Oslo, 30 May 1999, 18,236
Norway (1) 1 *(Iversen 4)*
Georgia (0) 0

Norway: Olsen; Heggem, Pedersen, Hoftun, Bergdolmo, Iversen (Dahlum 85), Leonhardsen (Rudi 46), Solbakken, Mykland, Riseth (Rekdal 70), Flo T.
Georgia: Gvaramadze; Guchua (Tskitishvili 62), Kaladze, Didava (Popkhadze 46), Tsereteli, Tskitishvili, Nemsadze, Ketsbaia, Jamarauli, Kavelashvili, Demetradze (Ashvetia 77).
Referee: Huyghe (Belgium).

Tirana, 5 June 1999, 5000
Albania (1) 1 *(Tare 16)*
Norway (1) 2 *(Iversen 4, Flo T 83)*

Albania: Strakosha; Lala, Shulku, Xhumba, Vata, Haxhi, Bushi, Kola (Duro 69), Fakaj (Bellaj 62), Tare, Rrakli (Bogdani 80).
Norway: Olsen; Haaland, Pedersen (Bragstad 62), Hoftun, Bergdolmo, Iversen, Solbakken (Riseth 89), Rekdal, Mykland, Rudi (Dahlum 78), Flo T.
Referee: Stoica (Romania).

Tbilisi, 5 June 1999, 15,000
Georgia (0) 1 *(Ketsbaia 55)*
Greece (0) 2 *(Mavrogenidis 88, Mahlas 90)*

Georgia: Gvaramadze; Chichveishvili (Didava 10), Khizaneishvili O, Akhvlediani (Khizaneishvili Z 67), Tsereteli, Tskitishvili (Alexidze 56), Nemsadze, Ketsbaia, Jamarauli, Ashvetia, Kobiashvili.
Greece: Atmatsidis; Mavrogenidis, Ouzounidis, Anatolakis, Kassapis, Konstantinidis (Froussas 46), Poursanidis, Zagorakis (Frantzeskos 81), Niniadis, Georgatos (Anastasiou 61), Mahlas.
Referee: Young (Scotland).

Riga, 5 June 1999, 2500
Latvia (1) 1 *(Pakhar 18)*
Slovenia (2) 2 *(Zahovic 25, 38 (pen))*

Latvia: Kolinko; Lukashevich, Astafyev (Rubins 41), Zemlinsky, Lobanyov (Korablov 43), Sharando (Bleidelis 69), Laizans, Shtolcers, Pakhar, Babichev, Mikholap.
Slovenia: Simeunovic; Rudonja (Osterc 88), Milinovic, Karic, Galic (Acimovic 66), Knavs, Novak, Ceh, Udovic, Zahovic, Pavlin (Istenic 79).
Referee: Arceo (Spain).

Tirana, 9 June 1999, 8000

Albania (0) 0

Slovenia (1) 1 *(Zahovic 26 (pen))*

Albania: Strakosha; Lala, Shulku, Xhumba, Vata, Duro, Bushi, Bellaj, Bogdani (Dalipi 75), Rrakli (Halili 46), Tare.
Slovenia: Simeunovic; Galic, Knavs, Osterc (Tsentic 80), Milinovic, Karic, Novak, Ceh, Udovic (Acimovic 66), Rudonja, Zahovic.
Referee: Stoica (Romania).

Athens, 9 June 1999, 15,000

Greece (1) 1 *(Niniadis 38 (pen))*

Latvia (1) 2 *(Verpakovskis 24, Zemlinsky 90 (pen))*

Greece: Atmatsidis; Mavrogenidis, Ouzounidis, Anatolakis, Kassapis, Zikos, Zagorakis, Frantzeskos (Anastasiou 60), Niniadis (Froussos 79), Georgatos (Markos 73), Mahlas.
Latvia: Kolinko; Lukashevich, Astafyev (Bleidelis 54), Zemlinsky, Rubins (Sismannovs 64), Pakhar, Babichev, Laizans, Verpakovskis (Mikholap 46), Korablovs, Lobanyov.
Referee: Pucek (Czech Republic).

Group 2	P	W	D	L	F	A	Pts
Norway	7	5	1	1	14	8	16
Slovenia	6	3	2	1	8	6	11
Latvia	7	3	2	2	7	5	11
Greece	7	2	3	2	8	7	9
Georgia	7	1	1	5	4	12	4
Albania	6	0	3	3	3	6	3

GROUP 3

Helsinki, 5 September 1998, 18,716

Finland (2) 3 *(Kolkka 8, Johansson 44, Paatelainen 62)*

Moldova (2) 2 *(Oprea 10, 11)*

Finland: Niemi; Ylonen, Tuomela, Hyypia, Turpeinen (Reini 46), Wiss, Kautonen, Litmanen, Johansson (Sumiala 80), Paatelainen, Kolkka (Mahlio 73).
Moldova: Coselev; Fistican (Tabanov 76), Rebeja (Pusca 46), Testimitanu, Guzun, Stroenco, Oprea, Gaidamasciuc, Epureanu (Suharev 76), Curtianu, Clescenco.
Referee: Barber (England).

Istanbul, 5 September 1998, 26,500

Turkey (1) 3 *(Oktay 18, 58, Tayfur 49 (pen))*

Northern Ireland (0) 0

Turkey: Rustu; Saffet, Mert, Alpay, Okan (Arif 87), Sergen, Tayfur, Tugay (Oguz 75), Abdullah, Oktay (Hami 79), Hakan Sukur.
Northern Ireland: Fettis; Hughes A, Horlock, Mulryne, Hill, Morrow, Gillespie (Jim Whitley 78), Lennon, Dowie, Rowland (Quinn 46), Hughes M.
Referee: Wojcik (Poland).

Belfast, 10 October 1998, 10,002

Northern Ireland (1) 1 *(Rowland 31)*

Finland (0) 0

Northern Ireland: Fettis; Hughes A, Horlock, Mulryne, Morrow, Patterson, Gillespie (McCarthy 71), Lennon, Dowie (O'Boyle 80), Rowland (Quinn 89), Hughes M.
Finland: Niemi; Ylonen, Ilola, Hyypia, Kautonen, Reini, Riihilahti (Litmanen 75), Valakari, Kolkka, Paatelainen, Johansson.
Referee: Arsic (Yugoslavia).

Bursa, 10 October 1998, 20,000

Turkey (0) 1 *(Hakan Sukur 70)*

Germany (0) 0

Turkey: Rustu; Fatih, Ogun (Unsal 89), Alpay, Tayfun, Tayfur, Tugay (Oktay 61), Abdullah, Mert, Sergen (Saffet 81), Hakan Sukur.
Germany: Kahn; Babbel, Nowotny, Rehmer, Ricken (Bode 81), Ramelow, Beinlich, Jeremies, Heinrich (Neuville 76), Bierhoff, Kirsten.
Referee: Dallas (Scotland).

Chisinau, 14 October 1998, 5000

Moldova (1) 1 *(Guzun 6)*

Germany (3) 3 *(Kirsten 20, 36, Bierhoff 38)*

Moldova: Coselev; Fistican, Stroenco, Testimitanu, Gaidamasciuc, Rebeja, Guzun, Oprea, Curtianu (Suharev 53), Clescenco, Epureanu.

Germany: Kahn; Babbel, Nowotny, Rehmer, Ricken (Neuville 53), Ramelow, Beinlich (Wosz 83), Nerlinger, Tarnat, Kirsten (Jancker 74), Bierhoff.

Referee: Marin (Spain).

Istanbul, 14 October 1998, 25,000

Turkey (0) 1 *(Ogun 73)*

Finland (1) 3 *(Paatelainen 5, Johansson 51, Litmanen 90)*

Turkey: Rustu; Alpay, Ogun, Fatih, Okan (Hami 46), Tugay (Mert 46), Sergen (Hasan Sas 83), Tayfur, Abdullah, Hakan Sukur, Oktay.

Finland: Niemi; Reini, Ylonen (Kolkka 61), Hyypia, Kautonen, Tuomela, Riihilahti (Valakari 76), Litmanen, Ilola, Johansson (Saastamoinen 90), Paatelainen.

Referee: Krondl (Czech Republic).

Belfast, 18 November 1998, 11,137

Northern Ireland (0) 2 *(Dowie 49, Lennon 63)*

Moldova (1) 2 *(Gaidamasciuc 22, Testimitanu 57)*

Northern Ireland: Fettis; Griffin, Kennedy, Lomas, Patterson, Morrow, Gillespie (McCarthy 88), Lennon, Dowie, Rowland (Gray 77), Hughes.

Moldova: Dinov; Fistican, Guzun, Stroenco, Rebeja, Curtian, Stratulat (Suharev 62), Testimitanu (Maeivic 86), Epureanu, Gaidamasciuc, Clescenco.

Referee: Hrinak (Slovakia).

Belfast, 27 March 1999, 14,270

Northern Ireland (0) 0

Germany (2) 3 *(Bode 11, 42, Hamann 62)*

Northern Ireland: Taylor; Patterson, Horlock, Lomas, Williams, Morrow, Gillespie (McCarthy 84), Lennon (Sonner 68), Dowie, Rowland (Kennedy 69), Hughes M.

Germany: Kahn; Babbel, Worns, Jeremies, Matthaus (Nowotny 46), Strunz, Heinrich, Hamann, Bierhoff, Neuville (Jancker 69), Bode (Preetz 79).

Referee: Cesari (Italy).

Istanbul, 27 March 1999, 30,000

Turkey (1) 2 *(Hakan Sukur 34, Sergen 90)*

Moldova (0) 0

Turkey: Rustu; Fatih, Ogun, Alpay, Okan, Tugay (Ayhan 85), Sergen, Tayfur, Abdullah, Hakan Sukur, Oktay (Hami 9) (Arif 74).

Moldova: Dinov; Fistican, Rebeja, Tabanov, Guzun, Stroenco, Sischin, Stratulat, Gaidamasciuc, Epureanu, Clescenco (Suharev 81).

Referee: Plautz (Austria).

Nuremberg, 31 March 1999, 40,758

Germany (2) 2 *(Jeremies 31, Neuville 37)*

Finland (0) 0

Germany: Kahn; Babbel, Matthaus, Worns, Strunz, Hamann (Nowotny 72), Jeremies, Heinrich, Neuville (Kirsten 65), Bierhoff, Bode (Jancker 76).

Finland: Niemi; Reini (Lehkosuo 89), Hyypia, Ylonen, Kautonen (Kolkka 72), Kinnunen, Riihilahti, Litmanen, Ilola, Johansson, Paatelainen (Saastamoinen 46).

Referee: Koussainov (Russia).

Chisinau, 31 March 1999, 9237

Moldova (0) 0

Northern Ireland (0) 0

Moldova: Dinov; Fistican, Stroenco, Sosnovsky, Oprea (Stratulat 90), Gaidamasciuc, Epureanu, Rebeja, Guzun, Clescenco, Suharev.

Northern Ireland: Taylor; Patterson (Hughes A 62), Horlock, Lomas, Williams M, Morrow, Gillespie, Lennon, Dowie, Robinson, Hughes M.

Referee: Trivkovic (Croatia).

Leverkusen, 4 June 1999, 21,000

Germany (3) 6 *(Bierhoff 2, 56, 82, Kirsten 27, Bode 38, Scholl 71)*

Moldova (0) 1 *(Stratulat 76)*

Germany: Kahn; Nowotny, Matthaus (Babbel 75), Strunz, Hamann, Jeremies (Scholl 46), Heinrich, Neuville, Bierhoff, Kirsten (Ramelow 54), Bode.

Moldova: Dinov; Fistican, Malevici (Stratulat 55), Storenco, Rebeja, Gaidamasciuc (Belous 74), Epureanu, Guzun, Curtianu, Oprea, Clescenco (Sischin 81).

Referee: Coroado (Portugal).

Helsinki, 5 June 1999, 36,042

Finland (2) 2 *(Tihinen 10, Paatelainen 14)*

Turkey (2) 4 *(Tayfur 25, 84, Hakan Sukur 34, 87)*

Finland: Niemi; Ylonen, Hyppia, Kuivasto, Tihinen, Riihilahti, Valakari, Litmanen, Kolkka, Paatelainen, Johansson.

Turkey: Rustu; Fatih, Ali Eren, Alpay, Saffet, Sergen (Daval 89), Tayfur, Abdullah (Hakan Unsal 90), Tayfun, Hakan Sukur, Ayhan (Tugay 74).

Referee: Jol (Holland).

Chisinau, 9 June 1999, 8000

Moldova (0) 0

Finland (0) 0

Moldova: Dinov; Fistican, Stratulat, Stroenco, Rebeja, Siskin (Belous 75), Guzun, Epureanu, Curtianu, Oprea (Gaidamascius 79), Suharev (Chirilov 89).

Finland: Niemi; Ylonen, Reini (Lehkosuo 85), Hyypia, Tininen (Kautonen 46), Riihilahti, Valakari, Paatelainen, Kolkka, Ilola, Johansson (Forssell 60).

Referee: Treossi (Italy).

Group 3	P	W	D	L	F	A	Pts
Germany	5	4	0	1	14	3	12
Turkey	5	4	0	1	11	5	12
Finland	6	2	1	3	8	10	7
N. Ireland	5	1	2	2	3	8	5
Moldova	7	0	3	4	6	16	3

GROUP 4

Erevan, 5 September 1998, 2300

Armenia (1) 3 *(Avalyan 40, Yessayan 71, 90)*

Andorra (0) 1 *(Lucendo 86 (pen))*

Armenia: Berezovski; Soukiassian, Krbachian, Hovsepian, Oganessian (Khodgoyan 83), Vardanian, Sarkissian, Arm Adamian (Gsepyan 86), Art Adamian, Shahgeldian, Avalyan (Yessayan 68).

Andorra: Koldo; Ramirez, Chema, Martin, Lima, Escurza, Garcia, Oscar, Sanchez, Lucendo, Justo.

Referee: O'Hanlon (Republic of Ireland).

Reykjavik, 5 September 1998, 10,500

Iceland (1) 1 *(Dadason 33)*

France (1) 1 *(Dugarry 36)*

Iceland: Kristinsson B; Helgason, Sigurdsson L, Sverrisson E, Marteinsson, Hreidarsson, Kolvidsson, Gudjonsson T, Kristinsson R, Dadason, Gunnlaugsson A (Thordarson 69).

France: Barthez; Karembeu, Thuram, Leboeuf, Lizarazu, Dugarry (Henry 66), Deschamps, Djorkaeff, Zidane, Pires, Laslandes.

Referee: Blareau (Belgium).

Kiev, 5 September 1998, 18,000

Ukraine (2) 3 *(Popov 14, Skachenko 24, Rebrov 74 (pen))*

Russia (0) 2 *(Varlamov 67, Onopko 87)*

Ukraine: Shovkovskyi; Gusin, Mikitin, Golovko, Vashchuk, Dmitrulin, Skachenko (Kalitvintsev 46), Popov, Kovalov (Kriventsov 87), Shevchenko, Rebrov.

Russia: Kharine; Minko, Chugainov, Kovtun, Yanovski, Semak (Cheryshev 72), Onopko, Alenichev (Mostovoi 64), Kanchelskis (Karpin 71), Kolyvanov, Varlamov.

Referee: Merk (Germany).

Andorra, 10 October 1998, 850

Andorra (0) 0

Ukraine (2) 2 *(Kossovski V 30, Rebrov 43)*

Andorra: Koldo; Ramirez, Chema, Martin, Lima A, Lima I, Pol, Oscar, Emiliano, Sanchez (Jimenez 87), Ruiz.
Ukraine: Shovkovskyi; Luzhny, Golovko, Vashchuk, Mikitin (Kovalov 46), Popov, Maximov (Kriventsov 51), Gusin, Kossovski V, Shevchenko (Mikhailenko 69), Rebrov.
Referee: Guetzov (Bulgaria).

Erevan, 10 October 1998, 6,000

Armenia (0) 0

Iceland (0) 0

Armenia: Berezovski; Soukiassian, Vardanian, Khachatrian, Hovsepian, Sarkissian, Art Petrossian (Oganessian 40), Arm Adamian, Shahgeldian, Mikaelian, Assadourian (Yessayan 25).
Iceland: Kristinsson B; Jonsson O, Hreidarsson, Adolfsson, Helgason, Kristinsson R, Kolvidsson, Gunnlaugsson A, Dadason, Gudjonsson T, Sigurdsson H.
Referee: Norman (Sweden).

Moscow, 10 October 1998, 32,500

Russia (1) 2 *(Yanovski 45, Mostovoi 55)*

France (2) 3 *(Anelka 12, Pires 28, Boghossian 81)*

Russia: Ovchinnikov; Kovtun, Onopko, Varlamov, Khlestov, Karpin, Yanovski, Alenichev (Semak 69), Mostovoi, Tikhonov, Bestchastnykh (Gerasimenko 62).
France: Lama; Thuram, Blanc, Desailly, Lizarazu, Deschamps, Petit (Boghossian 46), Pires, Zidane, Djorkaeff (Vieira 54), Anelka (Vairelles 88).
Referee: Ceccarini (Italy).

Saint-Denis, 14 October 1998, 75,000

France (0) 2 *(Candela 53, Djorkaeff 61)*

Andorra (0) 0

France: Lama; Candela, Leboeuf, Blanc, Lizarazu, Deschamps, Zidane, Djorkaeff (Boghossian 82), Dugarry (Pires 71), Trezeguet (Anelka 71), Vairelles.
Andorra: Koldo; Ramirez (Sanchez 80), Chema, Martin, Lima A, Lima I, Pol, Oscar, Lucendo (Jimenez 88), Ruiz, Emiliano.
Referee: Koren (Israel).

Reykjavik, 14 October 1998, 3500

Iceland (0) 1 *(Kovtun 88 (og))*

Russia (0) 0

Iceland: Kristinsson B; Jonsson S, Hreidarsson, Adolfsson, Helgason, Kristinsson R, Kolvidsson (Thordarson 85), Gunnlaugsson A, Dadason, Sigurdsson L, Gudjonsson T (Sigurdsson H 6).
Russia: Cherchesov; Kovtun, Onopko, Smertin, Yanovski, Shalimov, Varlamov (Solomatin 59), Mostovoi, Tikhonov (Igonin 12), Karpin (Khokhlov 59), Titov.
Referee: Temmink (Holland).

Kiev, 14 October 1998, 25,000

Ukraine (1) 2 *(Skachenko 31, Gusin 83)*

Armenia (0) 0

Ukraine: Shovkovskyi; Luzhny, Dmitrulin, Golovko, Vashchuk, Popov (Maximov 75), Skachenko (Kovalov 61), Gusin, Kossovski V, Shevchenko (Kriventsov 80), Rebrov.
Armenia: Berezovski; Soukiassian, Vardanian, Khachatrian, Hovsepian, Kropochian (Oganessian 85), Art Petrossian, Arm Adamian, Shahgeldian, Mikaelian (Avalyan 65), Assadourian (Yessayan 73).
Referee: Lica (Romania).

La Vella, 27 March 1999, 1400

Andorra (0) 0

Iceland (0) 2 *(Sverrisson E 58, Adolfsson 67.)*

Andorra: Alvarez; Ramirez (Gonzalez 77), Garcia, Martin, Lima T, Lima I, Pol, Sonejee, Jimenez (Sanchez 73), Lucendo, Ruiz (Imbernon 83).

Iceland: Kristinsson B; Jonsson, Gunnarsson B (Hreidarsson 70), Adolfsson, Helgason, Kristinsson R, Thordarsson, Gunnlaugsson A (Gudmundsson T 81), Sverrisson E (Gretarsson 70), Sigurdsson H, Gudjonsson T.
Referee: Agius (Malta).

Erevan, 27 March 1999, 20,000
Armenia (0) 0
Russia (1) 3 *(Karpin 7, 63 (pen), Bestchastnykh 89)*
Armenia: Berezovski; Mkrtichian, Hovsepian, Oganessian, Karbanian (Arotonian 65), Vardanian, Art Petrossian, Voskanian (Kakosian 78), Sarkissian, Shahgeldian, Mikalian (Yessayan 81).
Russia: Filimonov; Khlestov, Onopko, Drozdov, Tsymbalar, Karpin, Alenichev (Tikhonov 65), Yanovski, Titov, Yuran (Khokhlov 85), Panov (Bestchastnykh 46).
Referee: Hauge (Norway).

Saint-Denis, 27 March 1999, 78,500
France (0) 0
Ukraine (0) 0
France: Barthez; Thuram, Lizarazu, Deschamps, Blanc, Desailly, Pires (Dhorasoo 85), Djorkaeff, Petit (Boghossian 78), Anelka, Dugarry (Wiltord 69).
Ukraine: Shovkovskyi; Luzhny, Vashchuk, Golovko, Mikitin, Gusin (Skrypnyk 85), Popov, Kovalov (Kossovski 55), Rebrov, Skachenko (Maximov 69), Shevchenko.
Referee: Benko (Austria).

Saint-Denis, 31 March 1999, 78,852
France (2) 2 *(Wiltord 3, Dugarry 45)*
Armenia (0) 0
France: Barthez; Thuram (Karembeu 79), Blanc, Desailly, Deschamps, Vieira, Djorkaeff (Pires 69), Boghossian, Anelka, Wiltord, Dugarry (Trezeguet 46).
Armenia: Berezovski; Soukiassian (Khachatrian 40), Mkritician, Vardanian, Hovsepian, Oganessian, Art Petrossian, Voskanian (Hyropetian 77), Sarkissian, Shahgeldian (Yessayan 53), Mikaelian.
Referee: Bikas (Greece).

Moscow, 31 March 1999, 20,000
Russia (3) 6 *(Titov 8, Bestchastnykh 11, 62, Onopko 42, Tsymbalar 50, Alenichev 90)*
Andorra (0) 1 *(Sanchez 73)*
Russia: Filimonov; Khlestov, Smertin, Tsymbalar, Yevseyev (Tikhonov 46), Alenichev, Onopko, Karpin, Titov, Chirko, Bestchastnykh.
Andorra: Alvarez; Alonso (Gonzalez 57), Garcia, Martin, Lima T, Lima I, Pol, Sonejee, Jimenez, Lucendo (Sanchez 65), Ruiz.
Referee: Vuorela (Finland).

Kiev, 31 March 1999, 50,000
Ukraine (0) 1 *(Vashchuk 59)*
Iceland (0) 1 *(Sigurdsson L 66)*
Ukraine: Shovkovskyi; Luzhny, Vashchuk, Golovko, Mikitin, Gusin, Popov (Kalitvintsev 75), Kossovski V, Rebrov, Skachenko (Maximov 46), Shevchenko.
Iceland: Kristinsson B; Jonsson, Gunnarsson B, Adolfsson, Helgason, Kristinsson R (Kolvidsson 80), Sigurdsson L, Gunnlaugsson A, Sverrisson E, Sigurdsson H (Sverrisson S 86), Gudjonsson T.
Referee: Dani (Israel).

Saint-Denis, 5 June 1999, 78,000
France (0) 2 *(Petit 48, Wiltord 54)*
Russia (1) 3 *(Panov 40, 75, Karpin 85)*
France: Barthez; Thuram, Blanc, Desailly, Candela (Pires 88), Deschamps, Petit, Djorkaeff (Boghossian 90), Dugarry (Vieira 59), Anelka, Wiltord.
Russia: Filimonov; Khlestov, Onopko, Smertin, Varlamov, Karpin, Semak (Bestchastnykh 60), Mostovoi (Khokhlov 26), Titov, Tikhonov (Tsymbalar 71), Panov.
Referee: Durkin (England).

Reykjavik, 5 June 1999, 5565

Iceland (1) 2 *(Dadason 30, Gunnarsson B 46)*

Armenia (0) 0

Iceland: Kristinsson B; Helgason (Kolvidsson 72), Hreidarsson, Jonsson S, Marteinsson, Gunnarsson B, Kristinsson R, Sverrisson, Sigurdsson (Danielsson 81), Gudjonsson T, Dadason (Helguson 69).

Armenia: Berezovski; Soukiassian (Nkrchian 65), Khachatrian, Hovsepian, Voskanian (Gregorian 84), Vardanian, Art Petrossian (Hayrapepian 75), Harutyunian, Sarkissian, Shahgeldian, Mikaelian.

Referee: Peltola (Finland).

Kiev, 5 June 1999, 45,000

Ukraine (2) 4 *(Popov 38, Rebrov 41, Dmitrulin 56, Husin 89)*

Andorra (0) 0

Ukraine: Vorobyev; Luzhny, Mikitin (Mizin 72), Golovko, Vashchuk, Dmitrulin (Maximov 78), Tsykhmeistruk, Popov, Gusin, Shevchenko (Skachenko 67), Rebrov.

Andorra: Alvarez; Pol, Martin (Lucendo 53), Garcia, Lima T, Lima I, Gonzalez, Sonajee, Ramirez, Sanchez, Ruiz.

Referee: Georgiou (Cyprus).

Barcelona, 9 June 1999, 4000

Andorra (0) 0

France (0) 1 *(Leboeuf 85 (pen))*

Andorra: Alvarez; Pol, Ramirez, Lima T, Lima I, Chema (Jonas 70), Gonzalez, Sonejee, Ruiz, Jimenez (Genis 89), Lucendo (Martin 77).

France: Rame; Karembeu, Candela, Boghossian, Leboeuf, Desailly, Wiltord, Dugarry, Anelka, Petit (Vieira 56), Dhorasoo (Pires 60).

Referee: Ross (Northern Ireland).

Erevan, 9 June 1999, 10,000

Armenia (0) 0

Ukraine (0) 0

Armenia: Berezovski; Petrossian T (Gregorian 63), Khachatrian, Hovsepian, Oganessian (Harutiunian 46), Vardanian, Art Petrossian, Voskanian, Sarkissian, Shahgeldian, Mikaelian (Mkritichian 46).

Ukraine: Vorobyev; Luzhny, Mikitin, Golovko, Vashchuk, Dmitrulin, Tsykhmeistruk, Popov (Konovalov 34), Gusin, Shevchenko (Cardash 80), Rebrov (Skachenko 70).

Referee: Boggi (Italy).

Moscow, 9 June 1999, 36,000

Russia (1) 1 *(Karpin 44)*

Iceland (0) 0

Russia: Filimonov; Khlestov, Varlamov (Yanovski 56), Onopko, Semak (Bulatov 46), Smertin, Karpin, Khokhlov, Tikhonov, Bestchastnykh (Tsymbalar 71), Panov.

Iceland: Kristinsson B; Helgason, Hreidarsson (Adolfsson 60), Jonsson S (Kolvidsson 46), Marteinsson, Kristinsson R, Gunnarsson B (Helguson 82), Sverrisson, Sigurdsson L, Gudjonsson T, Dadason.

Referee: Tokat (Turkey).

Group 4	P	W	D	L	F	A	Pts
Ukraine	7	4	3	0	12	3	15
France	7	4	2	1	11	6	14
Russia	7	4	0	3	17	10	12
Iceland	7	3	3	1	7	3	12
Armenia	7	1	2	4	3	10	5
Andorra	7	0	0	7	2	20	0

Stockholm, 5 September 1998, 35,394

Sweden (2) 2 *(Andersson A 30, Mjallby 32)*

England (1) 1 *(Shearer 2)*

Sweden: Hedman; Nilsson, Andersson P, Bjorklund, Kamark (Lucic 82), Schwarz, Andersson A (Andersson D 90), Mjallby, Ljungberg, Larsson, Pettersson.
England: Seaman; Anderton (Lee 42), Le Saux, Southgate, Adams, Campbell (Merson 74), Redknapp, Ince, Shearer, Owen, Scholes (Sheringham 85).
Referee: Collina (Italy).

Bourgas, 6 September 1998, 20,000

Bulgaria (0) 0

Poland (2) 3 *(Czereszewski 19, 45, Iwan 47)*

Bulgaria: Zdravkov; Ginchev, Zagorcic (Petkov I 50), Yordanov, Petkov M (Trendafilov 46), Sirakov, Kishishev, Bachev, Borimirov (Gruiev 46), Stoichkov, Donev.
Poland: Sidorczuk; Bak, Zielinski, Lapinski, Siadaczka, Hajto (Klos 68), Brzeczek, Czereszewski, Swierczewski (Michalski 76), Iwan, Trzeciak (Juskowiak 83).
Referee: Batta (France).

Wembley, 10 October 1998, 72,974

England (0) 0

Bulgaria (0) 0

England: Seaman; Anderton (Batty 67), Hinchcliffe (Le Saux 34), Neville G, Southgate, Campbell, Lee, Scholes (Sheringham 77), Shearer, Owen, Redknapp.
Bulgaria: Zdravkov; Yordanov, Zagorcic, Kirilov, Kishishev, Iliev (Gruiev 63), Yankov, Petkov M, Naidenov, Stoichkov (Bachev 60), Hristov (Ivanov G 90).
Referee: Vagner (Hungary).

Warsaw, 10 October 1998, 8000

Poland (2) 3 *(Brzeczek 18, Juskowiak 35, Trzeciak 65)*

Luxembourg (0) 0

Poland: Matysek; Zielinski, Lapinski, Ratajczyk (Siadaczka 69), Hajto (Majak 62), Czereszewski, Iwan, Brzeczek (Bak 75), Swierczewski, Juskowiak, Trzeciak.
Luxembourg: Koch; Ferron, Birsens, Funck, Strasser, Holtz (Afrika 69), Theis (Deville F 46), Saibene, Cardoni, Deville L, Christophe (Thill 63).
Referee: Pregia (Albania).

Bourgas, 14 October 1998, 12,000

Bulgaria (0) 0

Sweden (0) 1 *(Larsson 62)*

Bulgaria: Zdravkov; Zagorcic, Yordanov, Kirilov (Parushev 17), Naidenov (Ivanov G 69), Iliev (Bachev 61), Yankov, Petkov M, Petkov I, Stoichkov, Hristov.
Sweden: Hedman; Nilsson, Andersson P, Bjorklund, Lucic (Sundgren 76), Ljungberg, Mild, Mjallby, Schwarz, Larsson (Erlingmark 88), Aslund (Blomqvist 71).
Referee: Heynemann (Germany).

Luxembourg, 14 October 1998, 8000

Luxembourg (0) 0

England (2) 3 *(Owen 19, Shearer 40 (pen), Southgate 90)*

Luxembourg: Koch; Ferron, Deville L, Funck, Deville F, Theis (Holtz 62), Saibene, Strasser, Posing, Cardoni, Christophe.
England: Seaman; Anderton (Lee 64), Neville P, Southgate, Ferdinand, Campbell, Beckham, Batty, Shearer, Owen, Scholes (Wright 76).
Referee: Vorgias (Greece).

Wembley, 27 March 1999, 73,836

England (2) 3 *(Scholes 11, 21, 70)*

Poland (1) 1 *(Brzeczek 29)*

England: Seaman; Neville G, Le Saux, Sherwood, Keown, Campbell, Beckham (Neville P 77), Scholes (Redknapp 83), Shearer, Cole, McManaman (Parlour 69).

Poland: Matysek; Hajto, Zielinski, Lapinski, Ratajczyk, Swierczewski (Klos 46), Bak, Brzeczek, Siadaczka (Kowalczyk 87), Iwan, Trzeciak (Juskowiak 83).
Referee: Pereira (Portugal).

Gothenburg, 27 March 1999, 37,728
Sweden (1) 2 *(Mjallby 34, Larsson 87)*
Luxembourg (0) 0

Sweden: Hedman; Kamark (Lucic 68), Andersson P, Bjorklund, Sundgren, Schwarz, Alexandersson, Mjallby, Ljungberg (Andersson D 79), Larsson, Andersson K.
Luxembourg: Felgen; Ferron, Funck, Birsens, Strasser, Theis (Holtz 70), Vanek, Saibene (Deville F 89), Cardoni, Deville L, Christophe (Zaritski 81).
Referee: Melnitjuk (Ukraine).

Luxembourg, 31 March 1999, 3004
Luxembourg (0) 0
Bulgaria (2) 2 *(Stoichkov 18, Yordanov 38)*

Luxembourg: Felgen; Ferron (Holtz 75), Vanek, Strasser, Deville L, Saibene, Birsens, Theis (Deville F 88), Posing (Zaritski 46), Cardoni, Christophe.
Bulgaria: Zdravkov; Kishishev, Yankov, Stoianov (Petkov I 48), Petkov M, Markov, Yordanov, Petrov, Iliev, Jovov (Ivanov 79), Stoichkov (Todorov 71).
Referee: Mitrovic (Slovakia).

Chorzow, 31 March 1999, 32,000
Poland (0) 0
Sweden (1) 1 *(Ljungberg 36)*

Poland: Sidorczuk; Waldoch, Lapinski, Zielinski, Siadaczka (Adamczuk 82), Iwan, Michalski (Bak 87), Brzeczek, Majak (Kowalczyk 70), Juskowiak, Trzeciak.
Sweden: Hedman; Kamark, Andersson P, Bjorklund, Lucic, Mild (Andersson D 72), Schwarz, Mjallby, Ljungberg, Larsson (Pettersson 89), Andersson K.
Referee: Merk (Germany).

Warsaw, 4 June 1999, 8000
Poland (1) 2 *(Hajto 16, Iwan 62)*
Bulgaria (0) 0

Poland: Matysek; Waldoch, Lapinski, Zielinski, Hajto (Majak 80), Nowak (Brzeczek 73), Michalski, Iwan, Siadaczka, Wichniarek (Frankowski 64), Trzeciak.
Bulgaria: Ivankov; Kirilov, Zagorcic, Markov, Kishishev, Petrov, Stoilov, Petkov M, Petkov I (Iliev 80), Stoichkov (Ivanov 63), Jovov (Bachev 46).
Referee: Braschi (Italy).

Wembley, 5 June 1999, 75,824
England (0) 0
Sweden (0) 0

England: Seaman; Neville P, Le Saux (Gray 46), Batty, Keown (Ferdinand R 35), Campbell, Beckham (Parlour 76), Sherwood, Shearer, Cole, Scholes.
Sweden: Hedman; Nilsson R, Kamark, Schwarz, Andersson P, Bjorklund, Mild (Alexandersson 7), Mjallby (Andersson D 82), Andersson K, Larsson (Svensson 70), Ljungberg.
Referee: Aranda (Spain).

Sofia, 9 June 1999, 22,000
Bulgaria (1) 1 *(Markov 18)*
England (1) 1 *(Shearer 15)*

Bulgaria: Ivankov; Kirilov, Stoilov, Kishishev, Zagorcic, Markov, Petrov S, Iliev (Borimirov 61), Petkov M, Stoichkov (Bachev 75), Yovov (Petrov M 46).
England: Seaman; Neville P, Gray, Southgate, Woodgate (Parlour 65), Campbell, Redknapp, Batty, Shearer, Fowler (Heskey 81), Sheringham.
Referee: Van der Ende (Holland).

Luxembourg, 9 June 1999, 2806

Luxembourg (0) 2 *(Birsens 76, Vanek 82)*

Poland (2) 3 *(Siadaczka 22, Wichniarek 45, Iwan 68)*

Luxembourg: Felgen; Vanek, Funck, Birsens, Strasser, Saibene (Alverdi 80), Theis (Schneider 46), Deville F, Cardoni, Christophe, Zaritski (Posing 65).
Poland: Matysek; Waldoch, Lapinski, Klos, Hajto (Brzeczek 65), Novak, Michalski, Iwan, Siadaczka, Wichniarek (Majak 87), Trzeciak.
Referee: Ivanov (Russia).

Group 5	P	W	D	L	F	A	Pts
Sweden	5	4	1	0	6	1	13
Poland	6	4	0	2	12	6	12
England	6	2	3	1	8	4	9
Bulgaria	6	1	2	3	3	7	5
Luxembourg	5	0	0	5	2	13	0

GROUP 6

Vienna, 5 September 1998, 20,000

Austria (1) 1 *(Reinmayr 7)*

Israel (0) 1 *(Nimni 68 (pen))*

Austria: Wohlfahrt; Schottel (Hiden 73), Feiersinger, Pfeffer, Cerny (Stoger 74), Kuhbauer, Mahlich, Reinmayr, Amerhauser, Vastic, Haas (Mayrleb 73).
Israel: Cohen; Harazi A, Shelach (Nimni 46), Ben Shimon, Amsalem, Abuksis (Mizrahi 46), Berkovic, Revivo, Benado, Harazi R (Graiev 61), Badir.
Referee: Frisk (Sweden).

Larnaca, 5 September 1998, 3500

Cyprus (1) 3 *(Engomitis 44, Gogic 48, Spoljaric 77)*

Spain (0) 2 *(Raul 72, Morientes 85)*

Cyprus: Panayiotou; Costa, Ioannou D (Ioakim 84), Charalambous, Pittas, Melanarkitis, Spoljaric, Christodolou M, Engomitis, Gogic (Agathocleous 61), Malekos (Pounnas 55).
Spain: Canizares; Michel, Nadal (Amor 65), Alkorta, Sergi, Etxeberria J (Ezquerro 59), Hierro, Raul, Luis Enrique, Alfonso (Kiko 39), Morientes.
Referee: Guseinov (Russia).

Larnaca, 10 October 1998, 10,000

Cyprus (0) 0

Austria (0) 3 *(Cerny 53, 61, Reinmayr 74)*

Cyprus: Panayiotou; Engomitis, Ioannou D, Costa, Charalambous, Pittas (Georgiou 67), Spolianis, Melanarkitis (Okkas 67), Christodolou M, Agathocleous (Pounnas 46), Gogic.
Austria: Wohlfahrt; Hiden, Schottel, Pfeffer, Cerny, Kuhbauer, Mahlich, Reinmayr (Stoger 78), Wetl, Vastic (Glieder 82), Haas (Mayrleb 78).
Referee: Meese (Belgium).

Serravalle, 10 October 1998, 872

San Marino (0) 0

Israel (3) 5 *(Revivo 16, Nimni 19, Mizrahi 31, 64, Graiev 83)*

San Marino: Gasperoni F; Gennari, Guerra, Valentini M, Bacciocchi (Valentini V 55), Marani, Montagna (Gualtieri 78), Muccioli, Della Valle (Francini 67), Matteoni, Selva.
Israel: Cohen; Harazi A, Ben Shimon, Telasnikov, Badir, Benado (Shelach 68), Nimni (Banin 59), Graiev, Revivo, Berkovic (Shitrit 74), Mizrahi.
Referee: Khudiev (Azerbaijan).

Tel Aviv, 14 October 1998, 42,000

Israel (0) 1 *(Hazan 63)*

Spain (0) 2 *(Hierro 65, Etxeberria J 77)*

Israel: Cohen; Harazi A, Ben Shimon, Benado, Hazan (Banin 75), Badir, Telasnikov (Mizrahi 59), Graiev, Nimni, Revivo, Berkovic.
Spain: Canizares; Michel, Hierro, Alkorta, Aranzabal, Luis Enrique, Engonga, Alkiza, De Pedro (Etxeberria J 72), Kiko (Urzaiz 88), Raul (Marcos Vales 90).
Referee: Elleray (England).

Serravalle, 14 October 1998, 1000
San Marino (0) 1 *(Selva 80 (pen))*
Austria (0) 4 *(Vastic 58, Mayrleb 63, Hiden 68, Glieder 76)*
San Marino: Gasperoni F; Gennari, Guerra, Valentini M (Della Valle 80), Bacciocchi, Marani, Muccioli, Francini (Valentini S 69), Ugolini (Montagna 62), Matteoni, Selva.
Austria: Wohlfahrt; Hiden, Schottel, Pfeffer, Cerny, Kuhbauer, Heraf, Reinmayr (Mayrleb 46), Wetl, Vastic (Stoger 70), Haas (Glieder 66).
Referee: Onufer (Ukraine).

Serravalle, 18 November 1998, 600
San Marino (0) 0
Cyprus (1) 1 *(Spoljaric 41)*
San Marino: Gasperoni F; Gennari, Valentini M, Guerra, Valentini V, Marani, Gasperoni B, Muccioli (Mularoni 83), Matteoni (Francini 75), Montagna (Bacchiocchi 67), Ugolini.
Cyprus: Panayiotou N; Pittas, Panayiotou P, Charalambous, Sophocleous, Engomitis, Melanarkitis, Spoljaric, Agathocleous (Constandinou 73), Malekos (Ioannou D 73), Gogic (Okkas 86).
Referee: McDermott (Republic of Ireland).

Nicosia, 10 February 1999, 3000
Cyprus (3) 4 *(Melanarkitis 18, Constantinou 32, 45, Christodoulou 88)*
San Marino (0) 0
Cyprus: Panayiotou; Theodotou, Christodoulou, Ioachim, Charalambous, Pittas, Melanarkitis, Spoljaric, Gogic (Ioannou 80), Constantinou (Okkas 80), Malekos (Aristocleous 89).
San Marino: Gasperoni F; Gennari, Marani (Vanucci 84), Gobbi, Vittorio, Guerra, Zonzini, Della Valle (Manzaroli 70), Ugolini (Bacciocchi 46), Mularoni L, Selva.

Valencia, 27 March 1999, 40,000
Spain (5) 9 *(Raul 5, 17, 47, 74, Urzaiz 30, 44, Hierro 35 (pen), Wetl 76 (og), Fran 84)*
Austria (0) 0
Spain: Canizares; Michel, Hierro, Marcelino, Sergi, Etxeberria J (Dani 84), Guardiola, Valeron (Mendieta 71), Fran, Raul, Urzaiz (Munitis 61).
Austria: Wohlfahrt; Schottel, Feiersinger (Kogler 54), Pfeffer, Cerny, Mahlich, Neukirchner, Prosenik (Reinmayr 58), Wetl, Herzog, Haas (Mayrleb 69).
Referee: Veissiere (France).

Tel Aviv, 28 March 1999, 30,000
Israel (1) 3 *(Banin 11, Mizrahi 47, 53)*
Cyprus (0) 0
Israel: Davidovich; Harazi A, Graiev, Shelach, Badir (Talkar 46), Banin, Benado, Berkovic, Revivo (Tikva 85), Harazi R (Mizrahi 46), Nimni.
Cyprus: Panayiotou; Theodotou, Pittas, Ioannou, Charalambous, Constandinou (Okkas 65), Melanarkitis, Spoljaric (Agathocleous 79), Malekos (Nicolaou 46), Sophocleous, Christodolou.
Referee: Lica (Romania).

Serravalle, 31 March 1999, 1000
San Marino (0) 0
Spain (2) 6 *(Fran 20, Raul 45, 59, 66, Urzaiz 49, Etxeberria J 72)*
San Marino: Gasperoni F; Gennari, Marani, Valentini V, Zonzoni, Valentini M, Manzaroli, Gasperoni B (Muccioli 75), Gobbi (Della Valle 51), Selva, Montagna (Gualtieri 60).
Spain: Canizares; Michel, Marcelino, Paco, Sergi, Etxeberria J, Guardiola (Engonga 68), Valeron (Helguera 78), Fran, Raul, Urzaiz (Dani 61).
Referee: Maric (Croatia).

Graz, 28 April 1999, 15,000
Austria (3) 7 *(Mayrleb 24, 53, Vastic 42, 44, 84, Amerhauser 71, Herzog 82 (pen))*
San Marino (0) 0
Austria: Wohlfahrt; Winklhofer (Rohseano 80), Feiersinger, Neukirchner, Cerny (Kitzbichler 71), Schopp (Glieder 71), Herzog, Prosenik, Amerhauser, Mayrleb, Vastic.
San Marino: Gasperoni F; Gennari (Bacciocchi S 46), Della Valle, Guerra, Gobbi, Vanucci, Gasperoni B (Manzaroli 15), Zonzini, Muccioli, Selva, Montagna (Bacciocchi N 78).
Referee: Vassaros (Greece).

Villarreal, 5 June 1999, 16,000

Spain (4) 9 *(Hierro 8 (pen), Luis Enrique 22, 67, 71, Etxeberria J 25, 45, Raul 56, Gennari 85 (og), Mendieta 90)*

San Marino (0) 0

Spain: Canizares; Michel (Munitis 60), Marcelino, Hierro, Aranzabal, Etxeberria J, Guardiola, Guerrero (Mendieta 74), Luis Enrique, Raul (Urzaiz 60), Morientes.

San Marino: Gasperoni F; Gennari (Vanucci 90), Marani, Della Balda, Gobbi, Guerra, Bacciocchi, Della Valle, Zonzini, Manzaroli (Valentini V 75), Montagna (Ugolini 58).

Referee: Perry (Republic of Ireland).

Tel Aviv, 6 June 1999, 43,000

Israel (2) 5 *(Berkovic 26, 47, Revivo 45, Mizrahi 54, Graiev 75)*

Austria (0) 0

Israel: Davidovich; Shelach, Benado, Harazi A, Graiev, Banin, Abuksis (Tal 82), Hazan, Mizrahi (Silivia 77), Berkovic (Tikva 79), Revivo.

Austria: Wohlfahrt; Winklhofer, Barisic, Kogler, Cerny, Mahlich, Herzog, Neukirchner, Amerhauser (Prosenik 46), Mayrleb (Haas 67), Vastic (Glieder 57).

Referee: Michel (Slovakia).

Group 6	P	W	D	L	F	A	Pts
Spain	5	4	0	1	28	4	12
Israel	5	3	1	1	15	3	10
Austria	6	3	1	2	15	16	10
Cyprus	5	3	0	2	8	8	9
San Marino	7	0	0	7	1	36	0

GROUP 7

Bucharest, 2 September 1998, 6000

Romania (4) 7 *(Gheorge Popescu 18, Munteanu C 30, Ilie A 32, 45, 51, Moldovan 56, Haas 60 (og))*

Liechtenstein (0) 0

Romania: Stelea (Lobont 80); Petrescu, Batranu, Gheorge Popescu, Contra, Petre, Galca, Munteanu C (Sabau 72), Munteanu D, Moldovan, Ilie A (Mihalcea 69).

Liechtenstein: Oehry M; Hefti, Hanselmann, Michael Stocklasa, Telser M (Ender 89), Ritter, Zech, Lingg (Buchel 62), Beck, Oehri R, Haas (Martin Stocklasa 63).

Referee: Prolic (Bosnia).

Kosice, 5 September 1998, 3243

Slovakia (3) 3 *(Fabus 17, Dubovsky 26 (pen), Moravcik 40)*

Azerbaijan (0) 0

Slovakia: Vencel; Varga, Tomaschek, Tittel, Spilar, Kinder, Sovic, Moravcik, Fabus (Jancula 62), Majoros (Ujlaky 46), Dubovsky (Zvara 62).

Azerbaijan: Kramarenko; Gaisumov, Abusev, Jabarov, Agayev, Lichkin (Rzayev 66), Kasumov (Guseynov 79), Asadov, Sirkhaev, Suleimanov (Kuliyev 46), Kurbanov K.

Referee: Snoddy (Northern Ireland).

Budapest, 6 September 1998, 50,000

Hungary (1) 1 *(Horvath 32)*

Portugal (0) 3 *(Sa Pinto 56, 76, Rui Costa 84)*

Hungary: Kiraly; Feher C (Korsos 78), Lakos, Hrutka, Matyus, Lisztes (Dardai 46), Halmai, Illes, Dombi (Kovacs Z 78), Horvath, Hamar.

Portugal: Vitor Baia; Secretario, Jorge Costa, Paulo Madeira, Dimas, Figo, Paulo Bento, Rui Costa, Paulinho Santos, Joao Pinto, Sa Pinto.

Referee: Meier (Switzerland).

Baku, 10 October 1998, 10,000

Azerbaijan (0) 0

Hungary (0) 4 *(Dardai 58, Illes 85 (pen), Pisont 87, Feher M 90)*

Azerbaijan: Kramarenko (Jidkov 59); Guseynov, Agayev, Abusev, Kerimov, Asadov, Lichkin, Sirkhaev, Rzayev, Kambarov (Kasumov 46), Kurbanov K.

Hungary: Kiraly; Sebok, Feher C, Hrutka, Matyus, Dardai, Pisont, Illes, Lisztes (Dombi 75), Horvath, Hamar (Feher M 46).

Referee: Bre (France).

Vaduz, 10 October 1998, 1900
Liechtenstein (0) 0
Slovakia (3) 4 *(Sovic 3, Dubovsky 13, Tomaschek 36, 61)*
Liechtenstein: Oehry M; Ritter, Hanselmann, Zech, Hefti (Lingg 76), Haas (Martin Stocklasa 33), Oehri R (Ospelt 46), Hasler, Michael Stocklasa, Frick M, Telser M.
Slovakia: Vencel; Varga (Timko 65), Tittel, Spilar, Sovic, Tomaschek, Moravcik, Dubovsky, Kinder (Kozak 30), Majoros, Fabus (Jancula 61).
Referee: Antonov (Moldova).

Porto, 10 October 1998, 40,000
Portugal (0) 0
Romania (0) 1 *(Munteanu D 90)*
Portugal: Vitor Baia; Abel Xavier (Dani 85), Jorge Costa, Fernando Couto, Dimas, Figo, Paulo Bento (Conceicao 70), Rui Costa, Paulinho Santos, Joao Pinto (Nuno Gomes 79), Sa Pinto.
Romania: Stelea; Petrescu (Contra 83), Filipescu, Gheorge Popescu, Ciobotariu, Petre, Munteanu C (Lupescu 61), Galca, Munteanu D, Rosu, Moldovan (Mihalcea 89).
Referee: Krug (Germany).

Budapest, 14 October 1998, 40,000
Hungary (0) 1 *(Hrutka 82)*
Romania (0) 1 *(Moldovan 51)*
Hungary: Kiraly; Feher C, Sebok, Hrutka, Matyus, Pisont, Dardai, Illes, Egressy (Lisztes 78), Feher M (Hamori 75), Hamar (Toth 70).
Romania: Stelea; Petrescu, Filipescu, Georghe Popescu, Ciobotariu, Petre (Serban 70), Galca, Lupescu, Munteanu D, Moldovan (Mihalcea 85), Craioveanu (Munteanu C 75).
Referee: Nielsen (Denmark).

Vaduz, 14 October 1998, 1900
Liechtenstein (0) 2 *(Frick M 47 (pen), Telser M 49)*
Azerbaijan (0) 1 *(Kurbanov K 59)*
Liechtenstein: Jehle; Ritter, Zech, Hasler, Martin Stocklasa, Bicker (Ospelt 67), Lingg, Michael Stocklasa, Beck (Buchel 74), Frick M, Telser M.
Azerbaijan: Jidkov; Jadulayev, Gaisumov, Agayev, Kerimov, Abusev (Kuliyev 76), Kurbanov M (Suleimanov 25), Rzayev, Kambarov, Kurbanov K (Mamedov 61), Sirkhaev.
Referee: Barr (N Ireland).

Bratislava, 14 October 1998, 22,059
Slovakia (0) 0
Portugal (2) 3 *(Joao Pinto 16, 31, Abel Xavier 72)*
Slovakia: Vencel; Spilar, Kinder, Tittel, Varga, Sovic (Pinte 82), Tomaschek, Fabus (Nemeth 57), Moravcik, Majoros, Dubovsky.
Portugal: Vitor Baia; Abel Xavier, Jorge Costa, Fernando Couto, Dimas, Figo (Capucho 89), Paulo Bento, Rui Costa (Costinha 67), Paulinho Santos, Joao Pinto (Conceicao 46), Sa Pinto.
Referee: Sarvan (Turkey).

Guimaraes, 26 March 1999, 20,000
Portugal (2) 7 *(Sa Pinto 28, Joao Pinto 36, 77, Paulo Madeira 67, Conceicao 75, Pauleta 82, 83)*
Azerbaijan (0) 0
Portugal: Vitor Baia (Espinha 83); Secretario, Paulo Madeira, Fernando Couto, Dimas, Paulo Sousa, Rui Costa (Pedro Barbosa 83), Conceicao, Figo (Pauleta 74), Sa Pinto, Joao Pinto.
Azerbaijan: Kramarenko; Agayev, Asadov, Akhmedov, Stukas, Abusev, Gambarov (Vasiliev 72), Musaev (Rzayev 69), Sirkhaev, Lichkin, Kurbanov G.
Referee: Granat (Poland).

Budapest, 27 March 1999, 9534
Hungary (3) 5 *(Sebok J 17, Sebok V 33, 41, 86, Illes 74)*
Liechtenstein (0) 0
Hungary: Kiraly; Hrutka (Simogyi 79), Sebok V, Korsos, Matyus, Halmai, Sebok J (Dombi 71), Pisont, Illes, Feher, Toth (Hamar 76).

Liechtenstein: Jehle; Hanselmann (Hefti 46), Martin Stocklasa, Lingg, Ritter, Michael Stocklasa, Wohlwend, Frick M, Hasler, Telser M, Beck (Ospelt J 78).
Referee: Kapitanis (Cyprus).

Bucharest, 27 March 1999, 15,000

Romania (0) 0

Slovakia (0) 0

Romania: Stelea; Petrescu, Batranu, Gheorge Popescu, Rosu, Petre, Galca, Munteanu C (Lupescu 66), Munteanu D, Moldovan (Craioveanu 64), Illie A.
Slovakia: Konig; Varga, Zeman, Karhan, Kratochvil, Zatek (Dzurik 75), Tomaschek, Balic, Labant, Dubovsky (Suchanok 78), Majoros (Slicho 62).
Referee: Barber (England).

Baku, 31 March 1999, 25,000

Azerbaijan (0) 0

Romania (0) 1 *(Petre 49)*

Azerbaijan: Magomedov; Gerimov, Pusuchatev, Asadov, Agayev (Kuliyev 75), Paki-Zadeh (Gambarov 69), Kurbanov M (Asaev 67), Akhmedov, Lichkin, Sirkhaev, Kurbanov K.
Romania: Lobont; Contra, Filipescu, Ciobotariu, Munteanu D, Petre, Galca, Lupescu, Rosu (Florea 75), Moldovan, Craioveanu (Mihalcea 89).
Referee: Luinge (Holland).

Vaduz, 31 March 1999, 3000

Liechtenstein (0) 0

Portugal (1) 5 *(Rui Costa 16 (pen), 79, Figo 49, Paulo Madeira 54, 60)*

Liechtenstein: Jehle; Lingg, Hasler, Zech, Hefti, Ritter (Ospelt 85), Telser, Frick C, Michael Stocklasa (Beck 66), Wohlwend (Burgmeier 83), Frick M.
Portugal: Vitor Baia; Secretario, Paulo Madeira, Fernando Couto, Dimas, Conceicao (Capucho 88), Paulo Sousa, Rui Costa, Figo, Sa Pinto (Pauleta 61), Joao Pinto (Nuno Gomes 75).
Referee: Orrason (Iceland).

Bratislava, 31 March 1999, 19,400

Slovakia (0) 0

Hungary (0) 0

Slovakia: Konig; Kratochvil, Zeman (Dzuric 13), Varga, Karhan, Balis, Tomaschek, Dubovsky, Zatek (Hrncar 79), Majoros, Pinte (Slicho 83).
Hungary: Kiraly; Korsos, Sebok V, Hrutka, Matyus, Pisont, Halmai, Illes, Sebok J (Dombi 56), Feher M (Hamar 64), Toth.
Referee: Colombo (France).

Baku, 5 June 1999, 8500

Azerbaijan (2) 4 *(Kurbanov G 16, Lichkin 42, Tagizade 60, Isajev 73)*

Liechtenstein (0) 0

Azerbaijan: Kramarenko; Agayev, Jadoelajev, Akhmedov, Kerimov, Kurbanov M, Tagizade (Isajev 68), Vasiljev (Khankishijev 61), Sirkhaev, Lichkin, Kurbanov G.
Liechtenstein: Jehle; Lingg, Hasler, Zech, Martin Stocklasa, Ritter, Telser, Michael Stocklasa (Wohlwend 74), Frick C, Bicker (Beck M 59), Benz (Beck T 46).
Referee: Stadskaar (Denmark).

Lisbon, 5 June 1999, 25,000

Portugal (0) 1 *(Capucho 62)*

Slovakia (0) 0

Portugal: Vitor Baia; Xavier (Conceicao 31), Fernando Couto, Paulo Madeira, Teixeira, Paulo Sousa, Paulo Bento, Rui Costa, Figo (Barbosa 89), Joao Pinto (Capucho 61), Sa Pinto.
Slovakia: Konig; Varga, Timko, Karhan, Kratochvil, Zvara (Valachovic 30), Tomaschek, Pinte (Slicho 64), Labant, Dubovsky, Majoros (Kosuch 83).
Referee: Larsen (Denmark).

Bucharest, 5 June 1999, 23,000

Romania (2) 2 *(Ilie 2, Munteanu D 15)*

Hungary (0) 0

Romania: Lobont; Petrescu, Filipescu, Gheorge Popescu, Nanu, Petre, Hagi (Lupescu 46), Galca, Munteanu D, Moldovan (Ganea 64), Ilie A (Craioveanu 86).
Hungary: Kiraly; Sebok V, Hrutka, Matyus, Korsos, Dardai, Halami, Illes (Preisinger 81), Egressy, Sebok J, Feher M (Pisont 46).
Referee: Pedersen (Norway).

Gyor, 9 June 1999, 16,500

Hungary (0) 0

Slovakia (0) 1 *(Fabus 53)*

Hungary: Kiraly; Sebok V, Hrutka, Matyus, Korsos G, Dardai, Halmai (Pisont 73), Illes, Egressy (Dombi 60), Sebok J, Somogyi (Preisinger 78).
Slovakia: Konig; Varga, Timko, Karhan, Kratochvil, Zvara (Dzurik 81), Valachovic, Pinte, Labant, Nemeth, Fabus.
Referee: Vega (Spain).

Coimbra, 9 June 1999, 25,000

Portugal (3) 8 *(Sa Pinto 28, 44, Joao Pinto 40, 59, 67, Ritter 52 (og), Rui Costa 80, 90 (pen))*

Liechtenstein (0) 0

Portugal: Vitor Baia; Secretario (Capucho 14), Fernando Couto, Paulo Madeira, Teixeira, Paulo Sousa (Barbosa 63), Conceicao, Rui Costa, Figo, Joao Pinto, Sa Pinto.
Liechtenstein: Jehle; Zech, Hasler, Ospelt, Ritter, Telser D (Lingg 53), Michael Stocklasa (Burgmeier 67), Wohlwend, Telser M (Buchel 73), Bicker, Beck T.
Referee: Drabek (Austria).

Bucharest, 9 June 1999, 8000

Romania (2) 4 *(Ganea 35, Munteanu D 44 (pen), Vladiou 50, Rosu 90)*

Azerbaijan (0) 0

Romania: Lobont; Petrescu, Filipescu, Gheorge Popescu, Nanu, Petre (Moldovan 68), Galca, Lupescu, Munteanu D, Ganea (Craioveanu 59), Vladiou (Rosu 79).
Azerbaijan: Kramarenko; Agayev (Getman 71), Jadulayev, Akhmedov, Isayev (Vasilyev 82), Kerimov, Kurbanov M (Musayev 59), Tagizade, Kurbanov G, Poshehontzev, Sirkhaev.
Referee: Siric (Croatia).

Group 7	P	W	D	L	F	A	Pts
Portugal	7	6	0	1	27	2	18
Romania	7	5	2	0	16	1	17
Slovakia	7	3	2	2	8	4	11
Hungary	7	2	2	3	11	7	8
Azerbaijan	7	1	0	6	5	21	3
Liechtenstein	7	1	0	6	2	34	3

GROUP 8

Dublin, 5 September 1998, 34,000

Republic of Ireland (2) 2 *(Irwin 4 (pen), Roy Keane 15)*

Croatia (0) 0

Republic of Ireland: Given; Irwin, Staunton, McAteer, Cunningham, Babb, Kinsella, Roy Keane, O'Neill (Cascarino 9), Robbie Keane (Carsley 62), Duff (Kenna 46).
Croatia: Ladic; Soldo (Tokic 77), Stimac, Simic, Tudor (Krpan 62), Jurcic, Boban, Asanovic, Jarni, Stanic, Maric (Panic 46).
Referee: Pereira (Portugal).

Skopje, 6 September 1998, 5000

Macedonia (1) 4 *(Bozinov 20, 48, Sakiri 75, 80)*

Malta (0) 0

Macedonia: Milosevski; Lazarevski, Stojkovski (Gosev 80), Nikolovski (Sainovski 78), Sedloski, Micevski, Stojanoski (Sakiri 70), Trenevski, Zaharievski, Stavrevski, Bozinov.
Malta: Muscat; Said, Overend, Debono, Chetcuti, Turner, Agius (Suda 70), Brincat, Zahra (Carabott 78), Busuttil, Camilleri.
Referee: Wegereef (Holland).

Ta'Qali, 10 October 1998, 8000
Malta (1) 1 *(Suda 28 (pen))*
Croatia (0) 4 *(Simic 54, Vugrinec 68, 74, Suker 85)*
Malta: Muscat; Buhagiar (Sixsmith 77), Overend, Debono, Chetcuti, Suda, Agius (Zammit 11), Brincat, Zahra (Turner 58), Busuttil, Camilleri.
Croatia: Ladic; Simic (Tokic 81), Soldo, Tudor, Saric, Maric, Boban, Asanovic, Jarni (Cvitanovic 87), Suker, Vucko (Vugrinec 60).
Referee: Benedik (Slovakia).

Zagreb, 14 October 1998, 20,000
Croatia (2) 3 *(Suker 16, Boban 45, 70)*
Macedonia (1) 2 *(Ciric 2, Sainovski 55)*
Croatia: Ladic; Tudor, Stimac, Simic, Stanic (Jurcic 81), Soldo, Boban, Asanovic (Saric 61), Jarni, Maric, Suker.
Macedonia: Milosevski; Sedloski, Stavrevski, Nikolovski (Stojanoski 77), Sainovski, Zaharievski, Micevski (Gosev 46), Lazarevski (Bozinov 60), Trenevski, Sakiri, Ciric.
Referee: Levnikov (Russia).

Dublin, 14 October 1998, 34,500
Republic of Ireland (2) 5 *(Robbie Keane 16, 18, Roy Keane 54, Quinn 63, Breen 82)*
Malta (0) 0
Republic of Ireland: Given; Kenna, Staunton, McAteer (Carsley 85), Cunningham, Breen, Kinsella, Roy Keane, Quinn (Cascarino 66), Robbie Keane (Kennedy 81), Duff.
Malta: Cini; Debono, Buttigieg, Spiteri, Carabott, Brincat, Zahra (Zammit 70), Sixsmith (Camilleri 66), Chetcuti, Turner, Suda (Agius 65).
Referee: Olsen (Norway).

Valletta, 18 November 1998, 4000
Malta (0) 1 *(Sixsmith 69)*
Macedonia (0) 2 *(Nikolovski 49, Zaharievski 62)*
Malta: Muscat; Sixsmith, Camilleri, Buttigieg, Spiteri, Debono, Busuttil, Saliba (Turner 67), Brincat, Nwoko (Carabott 54), Cutajar (Agius 59).
Macedonia: Milosevski; Lazarevski, Nikolovski, Sedloski, Babunski, Stavrevski, Zaharievski, Micevski, Sainovski, Bozinov (Trenevski 65), Sakiri.
Referee: Smolik (Belarus).

Belgrade, 18 November 1998, 44,000
Yugoslavia (0) 1 *(Mijatovic 65)*
Republic of Ireland (0) 0
Yugoslavia: Kralj; Djukic, Djorovic, Mihajlovic, Jokanovic, Jugovic (Grodzic 77), Stojkovic (Kovacevic 46), Stankovic J, Stankovic D, Mijatovic, Milosevic (Drulovic 77).
Republic of Ireland: Given; Cunningham, Irwin, McLoughlin (Connolly 72), Breen, Staunton, Kinsella, Roy Keane, Quinn (Cascarino 72), McAteer (O'Neill 83), Duff.
Referee: Nilsson (Sweden).

Valletta, 10 February 1999, 7000
Malta (0) 0
Yugoslavia (1) 3 *(Nadj 22, 55, Milosevic 90)*
Malta: Barry; Said, Turner, Spiteri, Camilleri (Sixsmith 73), Buttigieg, Busuttil, Saliba, Carabott, Nwoko (Cutajar 82), Agius (Bencini 59).
Yugoslavia: Kralj; Mirkovic, Djorovic, Jokanovic, Djukic, Mihajlovic, Stankovic (Tomic 75), Nadj, Stankovic (Grodzic 87), Mijatovic, Kovacevic (Milosevic 70).
Referee: Garibian (France).

Skopje, 5 June 1999, 14,000
Macedonia (0) 1 *(Hristov 80)*
Croatia (1) 1 *(Suker 19)*
Macedonia: Milosevski; Nikolovski, Stojanovski, Stavrevski, Babunski (Zaharievski 60), Sainovski, Micevski, Trenevski (Bozinov 46), Trajcov (Hristov 80), Sakiri, Ciric.
Croatia: Ladic; Juric, Simic, Soldo, Saric, Boban, Asanovic, Vugrinec (Vlaovic 19), Jarni, Suker, Boksic (Rapajic 19).
Referee: Dallas (Scotland).

Salonika, 8 June 1999, 2000
Yugoslavia (1) 4 *(Mijatovic 36, Milosevic 49, 90, Kovacevic 75)*
Malta (1) 1 *(Saliba 7)*
Yugoslavia: Kralj; Mirkovic, Djukic, Djorovic, Saveljic, Stojkovic (Drulovic 77), Nadj (Milosevic 46), Jokanovic, Stankovic D (Grozdic 63), Mijatovic, Kovacevic.
Malta: Barry; Buhagiar (Cutajar 80), Said, Debono, Chetcuti, Ruttieg, Saliba, Camilleri D (Brincat 64), Carabott, Busuttil, Nwoko (Sultana 83).
Referee: Stahl (Sweden).

Dublin, 9 June 1999, 28,108
Republic of Ireland (0) 1 *(Quinn 67)*
Macedonia (0) 0
Republic of Ireland: Kelly; Carr, Irwin, Duff (Kilbane 63), Cunningham, Breen, Kennedy, Kinsella, Quinn (Connolly 83), Robbie Keane (Cascarino 67), Carsley.
Macedonia: Milosevski; Stavrevski, Babunski, Stojanoski, Trajcev (Medmendi 46), Micevski, Trenevski (Hristov 75), Sainovski (Sedloski 70), Nikolovski, Ciric, Sakiri.
Referee: Meier (Switzerland).

Group 8	P	W	D	L	F	A	Pts
Yugoslavia	3	3	0	0	8	1	9
Republic of Ireland	4	3	0	1	8	1	9
Croatia	4	2	1	1	8	6	7
Macedonia	5	2	1	2	9	6	7
Malta	6	0	0	6	3	22	0

GROUP 9

Tallinn, 4 June 1998, 3500
Estonia (2) 5 *(Viikmae 13, Reim 43 (pen), Terehhov 76, Oper 87, Kirs 90)*
Faeroes (0) 0
Estonia: Poom; Lemsalu, Kirs, Hohlov-Simson, Meet, Viikmae (O'Konnel-Bronin 80), Terehhov, Oper, Kristal, Reim, Zelinski.
Faeroes: Knudsen; Dam, Hansen J, Thorsteinsson, Hansen O (Jarnskor H 83), Morkore A, Joensen, Johnsson, Petersen, Muller (Mikkelsen 41), Jonsson (Arge 83).

Sarajevo, 19 August 1998, 20,000
Bosnia (0) 1 *(Baljic 65)*
Faeroes (0) 0
Bosnia: Dedic; Kapetanovic, Barbarez (Mujdza 75), Konjic, Varesanovic, Hibic, Bolic (Mujcin 65), Halilovic, Kodro, Salihamidzic (Sabic 81), Baljic.
Faeroes: Mikkelsen; Hansen H, Hansen J, Thorsteinsson, Johannesen O, Jarnskor H, Joensen, Johnsson, Morkore A, Arge (Borg 77), Petersen.

Sarajevo, 5 September 1998, 21,000
Bosnia (0) 1 *(Barbarez 75 (pen))*
Estonia (1) 1 *(Hibic 28 (og))*
Bosnia: Dedic; Varesanovic, Konjic, Hibic, Kapetanovic, Salihamidzic, Katana (Mujcin 55), Halilovic (Bolic 77), Mujdza (Sabic 65), Barbarez, Baljic.
Estonia: Poom; Rooba U (Meet 81), Kirs, Hohlov-Simson, Reim, Smirnov, Terehov, Kristal, Alonen, Zelinski (Viikmae 81), Oper.
Referee: Agius (Malta).

Vilnius, 5 September 1998, 5112
Lithuania (0) 0
Scotland (0) 0
Lithuania: Stauce; Shugzda (Buitkus 61), Semberas, Zutautas R, Zvirgzdauskas, Mikulenas (Slekys 90), Skerla, Baltusnikas, Preitsaitis, Jankauskas, Skarbalius.
Scotland: Leighton; Dailly, Boyd, Elliott, Hendry, Calderwood (Davidson 70), Lambert, Gallacher, McCoist (McCann 82), Jackson (Ferguson B 56), Collins.
Referee: Zotta (Romania).

Toftir, 6 September 1998, 2000

Faeroes (0) 0

Czech Republic (0) 1 *(Smicer 84)*

Faeroes: Mikkelsen; Johannesen O, Hansen JK, Thorsteinsson, Hansen H, Jarnskor H, Leiftur (Jarnskor M 78), Johnsson, Morkore, Jonsson T, Petersen.
Czech Republic: Postulka; Rada, Bejbl (Latal 81), Suchoparek, Votava, Cizek (Berger 55), Nemec, Nedved, Lokvenc, Poborsky (Sloncik 81), Smicer.
Referee: Hirviniemi (Finland).

Sarajevo, 10 October 1998, 30,000

Bosnia (0) 1 *(Topic 88)*

Czech Republic (1) 3 *(Baranek 13, Smicer 59, Kuka 90)*

Bosnia: Dedic; Varesanovic, Konjic, Hibic, Kapetanovic, Salihamidzic (Demirovic 66), Katana, Halilovic, Mujcin (Topic 63), Barbarez, Baljic (Besirevic 71).
Czech Republic: Postulka; Baranek (Rada 71), Repka, Suchoparek, Latal, Votava, Nemec, Bejbl, Lokvenc (Kuka 80), Smicer (Sloncik 85), Berger.
Referee: Messina (Italy).

Vilnius, 10 October 1998, 1500

Lithuania (0) 0

Faeroes (0) 0

Lithuania: Stauce; Skerla, Mikalajunas (Zvingilas 74), Zutautas R, Baltusnikas, Zvirgzdauskas, Mikulenas (Buitkus 46), Ivanauskas, Skarbalius, Preitsaitis, Jankauskas.
Faeroes: Mikkelsen; Johannesen O, Hansen J, Thorsteinsson, Hansen H, Joensen, Jarnskor H, Johnsson, Arge (Borg 88), Jonsson T, Petersen.
Referee: Schaack (Luxembourg).

Edinburgh, 10 October 1998, 16,930

Scotland (0) 3 *(Dodds 70, 85, Hohlov-Simson 78 (og))*

Estonia (1) 2 *(Hohlov-Simson 35, Smirnov 76)*

Scotland: Leighton; Weir, Davidson, Calderwood (Donnelly 56), Hendry, Boyd, McKinlay W, Durrant, McCoist (Dodds 68), Gallacher (Jackson 17), Johnston.
Estonia: Poom; Kirs, Hohlov-Simson, Reim, Rooba U, Kristal, Smirnov, Alonen, Terehov, Zelinski (Viikmae 86), Oper.
Referee: Marques (Portugal).

Teplice, 14 October 1998, 13,123

Czech Republic (4) 4 *(Nedved 8, Berger 21, 41, Meet 44 (og))*

Estonia (0) 1 *(Arbeiter 90)*

Czech Republic: Postulka; Latal, Suchoparek, Repka, Votava (Rada 53), Nedved, Nemec, Bejbl (Cizek 80), Berger, Lokvenc (Kuka 61), Smicer.
Estonia: Poom; Smirnov (Nommik 46), Meet, Hohlov-Simson, Rooba U, Alonen, Terehov (O'Konnel-Bronin 63), Oper, Viikmae (Arbeiter 46), Reim, Zelinski.
Referee: Olafsson (Iceland).

Vilnius, 14 October 1998, 2000

Lithuania (0) 4 *(Ivanauskas 10, 67, 75, Baltusnikas 90)*

Bosnia (0) 2 *(Konjic 4, Baljic 68)*

Lithuania: Stauce; Skerla, Mikalajunas (Baltusnikas 87), Zutautas R, Gleveckas, Zvirgzdauskas, Semberas, Ivanauskas, Skarbalius (Zvingilas 62), Preitsatis, Jankauskas (Danilicevas 79).
Bosnia: Dedic; Varesanovic, Konjic, Ramcic, Kapetanovic (Mujdza 80), Salihamidzic, Katana (Topic 75), Halilovic, Mujcin, Barbarez, Baljic.
Referee: Schuttengruber (Austria).

Aberdeen, 14 October 1998, 18,517

Scotland (2) 2 *(Burley 22, Dodds 45)*

Faeroes (0) 1 *(Petersen 86 (pen))*

Scotland: Sullivan; Weir, Davidson, Elliott, Hendry, Boyd, McKinlay W (Durrant 46), Donnelly, Dodds, Burley, Johnston (Glass 79).
Faeroes: Mikkelsen; Hansen H, Johannesen O, Hansen JC, Thorsteinsson, Petersen, Joensen, Johnsson, Jarnskor H (Hansen J 80), Arge (Borg 69), Jonsson T.
Referee: Kapitanis (Cyprus).

Teplice, 27 March 1999, 14,658
Czech Republic (1) 2 *(Hornak 10, Berger 74 (pen))*
Lithuania (0) 0

Czech Republic: Srnicek; Repka, Suchoparek, Hornak, Poborsky (Kuka 63), Hasek, Nemec, Berger, Nedved, Lokvenc (Koller 71), Smicer (Baranek 80).
Lithuania: Stauce; Skerla, Zvirgzdauskas, Zutautas, Semberas, Vainoras, Preitsaitis, Skarbalius, Mikalajunas, Ivanauskas (Buitkas 83), Jankauskas (Zvingilas 67).
Referee: Juhos (Hungary).

Vilnius, 31 March 1999, 3000
Lithuania (0) 1 *(Fomenka 83)*
Estonia (0) 2 *(Terehov 49, 77)*

Lithuania: Stauce; Skerla, Zutautas, Zvirgzdauskas, Semberas, Vainoras, Preitsaitis, Maciulevicius, Mikalajunas, Skarbalius (Gleveckus 35) (Buitkus 52), Mikulenas (Fomenka 46).
Estonia: Poom; Lemsalu, Kirs, Hohlov-Simson, Saviauk, Svets (Kristal 69), Terehov, Oper (Zelinski 67), Viikmae, Smirnov (Alonen 90), Reim.
Referee: Trentalange (Italy).

Glasgow, 31 March 1999, 44,513
Scotland (0) 1 *(Jess 68)*
Czech Republic (2) 2 *(Elliott 27 (og), Smicer 35)*

Scotland: Sullivan; Hopkin, Davidson (Johnston 51), Elliott, Boyd, Weir, Burley, Lambert, McCann, McAllister (Hutchison 62), Jess.
Czech Republic: Srnicek; Hornak, Votava, Suchoparek, Poborsky (Rada 74), Hasek, Nedved, Berger, Nemec, Smicer (Baranek 82), Lokvenc (Kuka 69).
Referee: Nielsen (Denmark).

Sarajevo, 5 June 1999, 5000
Bosnia (1) 2 *(Kodro 26 (pen), Bolic 90)*
Lithuania (0) 0

Bosnia: Dedic; Smajic, Kapetanovic, Varesanovic, Hibic, Repuh (Bolic 87), Besirevic, Sabic, Topic (Turkovic 90), Kodro (Mujcin 79), Salihamidzic.
Lithuania: Leus; Skerla, Marius, Darius, Kancelskis, Mikalajunas, Zvirgzdauskas, Semberas (Grozveydos 71), Maciulevicius, Ivanauskas, Preitsatis.
Referee: Ibanez (Spain).

Tallin, 5 June 1999, 3000
Estonia (0) 0
Czech Republic (1) 2 *(Berger 45, Koller 83)*

Estonia: Poom; Lemsalu, Kirs, Hohlov-Simson, Saviauk, Alonen (Smirnov 65) (O'Konnel-Bronin 74), Terehov (Svets 80), Kristal, Oper, Reim, Viikmae.
Czech Republic: Srnicek; Suchoparek, Repka, Hornak, Poborsky, Hasek, Nedved (Galasek 85), Berger, Nemec, Smicer (Kuka 65), Lokvenc (Koller 70).
Referee: Roca (Spain).

Toftir, 5 June 1999, 4500
Faeroes (0) 1 *(Hansen H 90)*
Scotland (1) 1 *(Johnston 38)*

Faeroes: Mikkelsen; Johannesen O, Hansen H, Thorsteinsson, Hansen O (Hansen J 87), Johnsson J, Joensen J (Borg 73), Joensen S, Jonsson T, Morkore A, Petersen (Arge 82).
Scotland: Sullivan; Weir, Davidson, Elliott, Calderwood, Boyd, Durrant (Cameron 46), Gallacher (Jess 88), Dodds, Lambert, Johnston (Gemmill 85).
Referee: Kalt (France).

Prague, 9 June 1999, 22,000
Czech Republic (0) 3 *(Repka 65, Kuka 75, Koller 87)*
Scotland (1) 2 *(Ritchie 30, Johnston 62)*

Czech Republic: Srnicek; Poborsky (Kuka 68), Berger, Hornak, Suchoparek, Repka, Nedved, Hasek (Baranek 60), Nemec, Lokvenc (Koller 68), Smicer.
Scotland: Sullivan; Johnston, Davidson, Weir, Boyd, Ritchie, Lambert, Calderwood, Gallacher, Dodds, Durrant (Jess 70).
Referee: Krug (Germany).

Tallinn, 9 June 1999, 2500
Estonia (1) 1 *(Oper 10)*
Lithuania (0) 2 *(Bahelis 52, Maciulevicius 56)*
Estonia: Poom; Lemsalu, Kirs, Kaal, Viikmae, Alonen, Terehov (O'Konnel-Bronin 73), Kristal (Svets 80), Oper, Reim, Zelinski.
Lithuania: Leus; Skerla, Skinderis, Zutautas D (Maciulevicius 46), Zutautas R, Mikalajunas, Zvirgzdauskas, Bahelis, Bazanauskas, Skarbalius, Ivanauskas (Preitsaitis 87).
Referee: Albrecht (Germany).

Toftir, 9 June 1999, 4600
Faeroes (1) 2 *(Arge 38, 48)*
Bosnia (1) 2 *(Bolic 13, 50)*
Faeroes: Mikkelsen; Johannesen O, Joensen S, Thorsteinsson, Hansen O (Jarnskor H 65), Johnsson J, Hansen H, Arge (Joensen J 85), Morkore A, Jonsson T, Petersen.
Bosnia: Dedic; Smajic, Besirevic, Varesanovic, Hibic, Repuh (Osmanhodzic 78), Sabic, Topic, Turkovic (Joulic 63), Bolic, Mujcin (Muratovic 85).
Referee: Jones (England).

Group 9	P	W	D	L	F	A	Pts
Czech Republic	7	7	0	0	17	5	21
Scotland	6	2	2	2	9	9	8
Bosnia	6	2	2	2	9	10	8
Lithuania	7	2	2	3	7	9	8
Estonia	7	2	1	4	12	13	7
Faeroes	7	0	3	4	4	12	3

EURO 2000 – Remaining Fixtures

GROUP 1
Italy, Denmark, Switzerland, Wales, Belarus
04.09.99	Denmark v Switzerland
04.09.99	Belarus v Wales
08.09.99	Italy v Denmark
08.09.99	Switzerland v Belarus
09.10.99	Wales v Switzerland
09.10.99	Belarus v Italy

GROUP 2
Norway, Greece, Georgia, Latvia, Slovenia, Albania
04.09.99	Norway v Greece
04.09.99	Latvia v Albania
04.09.99	Slovenia v Georgia
08.09.99	Greece v Albania
08.09.99	Norway v Slovenia
08.09.99	Georgia v Latvia
09.10.99	Albania v Georgia
09.10.99	Slovenia v Greece
09.10.99	Latvia v Norway

GROUP 3
Germany, Turkey, Finland, Northern Ireland, Moldova
04.09.99	Finland v Germany
04.09.99	Northern Ireland v Turkey
08.09.99	Germany v Northern Ireland
08.09.99	Moldova v Turkey
09.10.99	Germany v Turkey
09.10.99	Finland v Northern Ireland

GROUP 4
Russia, France, Ukraine, Iceland, Armenia, Andorra
04.09.99	Ukraine v France
04.09.99	Iceland v Andorra
04.09.99	Russia v Armenia
08.09.99	Andorra v Russia
08.09.99	Iceland v Ukraine
08.09.99	Armenia v France
09.10.99	France v Iceland
09.10.99	Russia v Ukraine
09.10.99	Andorra v Armenia

GROUP 5
England, Bulgaria, Sweden, Poland, Luxembourg
04.09.99	England v Luxembourg
05.09.99	Sweden v Bulgaria
08.09.99	Poland v England
08.09.99	Luxembourg v Sweden
09.10.99	Sweden v Poland
10.10.99	Bulgaria v Luxembourg

GROUP 6
Spain, Austria, Israel, Cyprus, San Marino
04.09.99	Austria v Spain
05.09.99	Cyprus v Israel
08.09.99	Israel v San Marino
08.09.99	Spain v Cyprus
09.10.99	Spain v Israel
10.10.99	Austria v Cyprus

GROUP 7
Romania, Portugal, Slovakia, Hungary, Liechtenstein, Azerbaijan
03.09.99	Azerbaijan v Portugal
04.09.99	Liechtenstein v Hungary
04.09.99	Slovakia v Romania
08.09.99	Hungary v Azerbaijan
08.09.99	Romania v Portugal
08.09.99	Slovakia v Liechtenstein
09.10.99	Liechtenstein v Romania
09.10.99	Azerbaijan v Slovakia
10.10.99	Portugal v Hungary

GROUP 8
Yugoslavia, Croatia, Rep. of Ireland, Macedonia, Malta
04.09.99	Croatia v Rep. of Ireland
08.09.99	Malta v Rep. of Ireland
08.09.99	Macedonia v Yugoslavia
10.10.99	Croatia v Yugoslavia
10.10.99	Rep. of Ireland v Macedonia

GROUP 9
Scotland, Czech Republic, Lithuania, Bosnia, Faeroes, Estonia
04.09.99	Bosnia v Scotland
04.09.99	Faeroes v Estonia
04.09.99	Lithuania v Czech Republic
08.09.99	Czech Republic v Bosnia
08.09.99	Faeroes v Lithuania
08.09.99	Estonia v Scotland
09.10.99	Estonia v Bosnia
09.10.99	Czech Republic v Faeroes
09.10.99	Scotland v Lithuania

PAST EUROPEAN CHAMPIONSHIP FINALS

Paris, 10 July 1960
USSR 2, YUGOSLAVIA 1*
USSR: Yachin; Tchekeli, Kroutikov, Voinov, Maslenkin, Netto, Metreveli, Ivanov, Ponedelnik, Bubukin, Meshki. **Scorers:** Metreveli, Ponedelnik.
Yugoslavia: Vidinic; Durkovic, Jusufi, Zanetic, Miladinovic, Perusic, Sekularac, Jerkovic, Galic, Matus, Kostic. **Scorer:** Netto (og).

Madrid, 21 June 1964
SPAIN 2, USSR 1
Spain: Iribar; Rivilla, Calleja, Fuste, Olivella, Zoco, Amancio, Pereda, Marcellino, Suarez, Lapetra. **Scorers:** Pereda, Marcellino.
USSR: Yachin; Chustikov, Mudrik, Voronin, Shesternjev, Anitchkin, Chislenko, Ivanov, Ponedelnik, Kornaev, Khusainov. **Scorer:** Khusainov.

Rome, 8 June 1968
ITALY 1, YUGOSLAVIA 1
Italy: Zoff; Burgnich, Facchetti, Ferrini, Guarneri, Castano, Domenghini, Juliano, Anastasi, Lodetti, Prati. **Scorer:** Domenghini.
Yugoslavia: Pandelic; Fazlagic, Damjanovic, Pavlovic, Paunovic, Holcer, Petkovic, Acimovic, Musemic, Trivic, Dzajic, **Scorer:** Dzajic.

Replay: Rome, 10 June 1968
ITALY 2, YUGLOSLAVIA 0
Italy: Zoff; Burgnich, Facchetti, Rosato, Guarneri, Salvadore, Domenghini, Mazzola, Anastasi, De Sista, Riva. **Scorers:** Riva, Anastasi.
Yugoslavia: Pantelic; Fazlagic, Damjanovic, Pavlovic, Paunovic, Holcer, Hosic, Acimovic, Musemic, Trivic, Dzajic.

Brussels, 18 June 1972
WEST GERMANY 3, USSR 0
West Germany: Maier; Hottges, Schwarzenbeck, Beckenbauer, Breitner, Hoeness, Wimmer, Netzer, Heynckes, Müller, Kremers. **Scorers:** Müller 2, Wimmer.
USSR: Rudakov; Dzodzuashvili, Khurtsilava, Kaplichny, Istomin, Troshkin, Kolotov, Baidachni, Konkov (Dolmatov), Banishevski (Konzinkievits), Onishenko.

Belgrade, 20 June 1976
CZECHOSLOVAKIA 2, WEST GERMANY 2*
Czechoslovakia: Viktor; Dobias (Vesely F), Pivarnik, Ondrus, Capkovic, Gogh, Moder, Panenka, Svehlik (Jurkemik), Masny, Nehoda. **Scorers:** Svehlik, Dobias.
West Germany: Maier; Vogts, Beckenbauer, Schwarzenbeck, Dietz, Bonhof, Wimmer (Flohe), Müller D, Beer (Bongartz), Hoeness, Holzenbein. **Scorers:** Müller, Holzenbein.
Czechoslovakia won 5-3 on penalties.

Rome, 22 June 1980
WEST GERMANY 2, BELGIUM 1
West Germany: Schumacher; Briegel, Forster K, Dietz, Schuster, Rummenigge, Hrubesch, Müller, Allofs, Stielike, Kalz. **Scorers:** Hrubesch 2.
Belgium: Pfaff; Gerets, Millecamps, Meeuws, Renquin, Cools, Van der Eycken, Van Moer, Mommens, Van der Elst, Ceulemans. **Scorer:** Van der Eycken.

Paris, 27 June 1984
FRANCE 2, SPAIN 0
France: Bats; Battiston (Amoros), Le Roux, Bossis, Domergue, Giresse, Platini, Tigana, Fernandez, Lacombe (Genghini), Bellone. **Scorers:** Platini, Bellone.
Spain: Arconada; Urquiaga, Salva (Roberto), Gallego, Camacho, Francisco, Julio Alberto (Sarabia), Senor, Victor, Carrasco, Santilana.

Munich, 25 June 1988
HOLLAND 2, USSR 0
Holland: Van Breukelen; Van Aerle, Van Tiggelen, Wouters, Koeman R, Rijkaard, Vanenburg, Gullit, Van Basten, Muhren, Koeman E. **Scorers:** Gullit, Van Basten.
USSR: Dassayev; Khidiatulin, Aleinikov, Mikhailichenko, Litovchenko, Demianenko, Belanov, Gotsmanov (Baltacha), Protasov (Pasulko), Zavarov, Rats.

Gothenburg, 26 June 1992
DENMARK 2, GERMANY 0
Denmark: Schmeichel; Sivebaek (Christiansen), Nielsen K, Olsen L, Christofte, Jensen, Povlsen, Laudrup, Piechnik, Larsen, Vilfort. **Scorers:** Jensen, Vilfort.
Germany: Illgner; Reuter, Brehme, Kohler, Buchwald, Hässler, Riedle, Helmer, Sammer (Doll), Effenberg (Thon), Klinsmann.

Wembley, 30 June 1996
GERMANY 2, CZECH REPUBLIC 1†
Germany: Kopke; Helmer, Sammer, Scholl (Bierhoff), Hassler, Kuntz, Babbel, Ziege, Klinsmann, Strunz, Eilts (Bode). **Scorer:** Bierhoff 2.
Czech Republic: Kouba; Suchoparek, Nedved, Kadlec, Nemec, Poborsky (Smicer), Kuka, Bejbl, Berger, Hornak, Rada. **Scorer:** Berger (pen).
* *After extra time*
† *Won on sudden death*

OLYMPIC FOOTBALL
Previous winners

1896	Athens*	1.	Denmark	1960	Rome	1.	Yugoslavia
		2.	Greece			2.	Denmark
1900	Paris*	1.	England			3.	Hungary
		2.	France	1964	Tokyo	1.	Hungary
1904	St Louis**	1.	Canada			2.	Czechoslovakia
		2.	USA			3.	East Germany
1908	London	1.	England	1968	Mexico City	1.	Hungary
		2.	Denmark			2.	Bulgaria
		3.	Holland			3.	Japan
1912	Stockholm	1.	England	1972	Munich	1.	Poland
		2.	Denmark			2.	Hungary
		3.	Holland			3.	East Germany/
1920	Antwerp	1.	Belgium				USSR joint bronze
		2.	Spain	1976	Montreal	1.	East Germany
		3.	Holland			2.	Poland
1924	Paris	1.	Uruguay			3.	USSR
		2.	Switzerland	1980	Moscow	1.	Czechoslovakia
		3.	Sweden			2.	East Germany
1928	Amsterdam	1.	Uruguay			3.	USSR
		2.	Argentina	1984	Los Angeles	1.	France
		3.	Italy			2.	Brazil
1932	Los Angeles		no competition			3.	Yugoslavia
1936	Berlin	1.	Italy	1988	Seoul	1.	USSR
		2.	Austria			2.	Brazil
		3.	Norway			3.	West Germany
1948	London	1.	Sweden	1992	Barcelona	1.	Spain
		2.	Yugoslavia			2.	Poland
		3.	Denmark			3.	Ghana
1952	Helsinki	1.	Hungary	1996	Atlanta	1.	Nigeria
		2.	Yugoslavia			2.	Argentina
		3.	Sweden			3.	Brazil
1956	Melbourne	1.	USSR				
		2.	Yugoslavia				
		3.	Bulgaria				

*No official tournament
**No official tournament but gold medal later awarded by IOC

PAST WORLD CUP FINALS

Uruguay 1930
URUGUAY 4, ARGENTINA 2 (1-2) *Montevideo*
Uruguay: Ballesteros; Nasazzi (capt), Mascheroni, Andrade, Fernandez, Gestido, Dorado, Scarone, Castro, Cea, Iriarte. **Scorers:** Dorado, Cea, Iriarte, Castro.
Argentina: Botasso; Della, Torre, Paternoster, Evaristo, J., Monti, Suarez, Peucelle, Varallo, Stabile, Ferreira (capt), Evaristo, M. **Scorers:** Peucelle, Stabile.
Leading scorer: Stabile (Argentina) 8.

Italy 1934
ITALY 2, CZECHOSLOVAKIA 1 (0-0) (1-1)* *Rome*
Italy: Combi (capt); Monseglio, Allemandi, Ferraris IV, Monti, Bertolini, Guaita, Meazza, Schiavio, Ferrari, Orsi. **Scorers:** Orsi, Schiavio.
Czechoslovakia: Planicka (capt); Zenisek, Ctyroky, Kostalek, Cambal, Krcil, Junek, Svoboda, Sobotka, Nejedly, Puc. **Scorer:** Puc.
Leading scorers: Schiavio (Italy), Nejedly (Czechoslovakia), Conen (Germany) each 4.

France 1938
ITALY 4, HUNGARY 2 (3-1) *Paris*
Italy: Olivieri; Foni, Rava, Serantoni, Andreolo, Locatelli, Biaveti, Meazza (capt), Piola, Ferrari, Colaussi. **Scorer:** Colaussi 2, Piola 2.
Hungary: Szabo; Polgar, Biro, Szalay, Szucs, Lazar, Vincze, Sarosi (capt), Szengeller, Titkos. **Scorers:** Titkos, Sarosi.
Leading scorer: Leonidas (Brazil) 8.

Brazil 1950
Final pool (replaced knock-out system)

Uruguay 2, Spain 2	Brazil 6, Spain 1
Brazil 7, Sweden 1	Sweden 3, Spain 1
Uruguay 3, Sweden 2	Uruguay 2, Brazil 1

Final positions	P	W	D	L	F	A	Pts
Uruguay	3	2	1	0	7	5	5
Brazil	3	2	0	1	14	4	4
Sweden	3	1	0	2	6	11	2
Spain	3	0	1	2	4	11	1

Leading scorers: Ademir (Brazil) 7, Schiaffino (Uruguay), Basora (Spain) 5.

Switzerland 1954
WEST GERMANY 3, HUNGARY 2 (2-2) *Berne*
West Germany: Turek; Posipal, Kohlmeyer, Eckel, Liebrich, Rahn, Morlock, Walter, O., Walter, F. (capt), Schaefer. **Scorers:** Morlock, Rahn 2.
Hungary: Grosics; Buzansky, Lantos, Bozsik, Lorant, Zakarias, Czibor, Kocsis, Hidegkuti, Puskas (capt), Toth, J. **Scorers:** Puskas, Czibor.
Leading scorer: Kocsis (Hungary) 11.

Sweden 1958
BRAZIL 5, SWEDEN 2 (2-1) *Stockholm*
Brazil: Gilmar; Santos, D., Santos, N., Zito, Bellini, Orlando, Garrincha, Didi, Vavà, Pelé, Zagalo. **Scorers:** Vavà 2, Pelé 2, Zagalo.
Sweden: Svensson; Bergmark, Axbom, Boerjesson, Gustavsson, Parling, Hamrin, Gren, Simonsson, Liedholm, Skoglund. **Scorers:** Liedholm, Simonsson.
Leading scorer: Fontaine (France) 13 (present record total).

Chile 1962
BRAZIL 3, CZECHOSLOVAKIA 1 (1-1) *Santiago*
Brazil: Gilmar; Santos, D., Mauro, Zozimo, Santos, N., Zito, Didi, Garrincha, Vavà, Amarildo, Zagalo. **Scorers:** Amarildo, Zito, Vavà.
Czechoslovakia: Schroiff; Tichy, Novak, Pluskal, Popluhar, Masopust, Pospichal, Scherer, Kvasniak, Kadraba, Jelinek. **Scorer:** Masopust.
Leading scorer: Jerkovic (Yugoslavia) 5.

England 1966
ENGLAND 4, WEST GERMANY 2 (1-1) (2-2)* *Wembley*
England: Banks; Cohen, Wilson, Stiles, Charlton, J., Moore, Ball, Hurst, Hunt, Charlton, R., Peters. **Scorers:** Hurst 3, Peters.
West Germany: Tilkowski; Hottges, Schulz, Weber, Schnellinger, Haller, Beckenbauer, Overath, Seeler, Held, Emmerich. **Scorers:** Haller, Weber.
Leading scorer: Eusebio (Portugal) 9.

Mexico 1970
BRAZIL 4, ITALY 1 (1-1) *Mexico City*
Brazil: Felix; Carlos Alberto, Piazza, Everaldo, Gerson, Clodoaldo, Jairzinho, Pelé, Tostäo, Rivelino. **Scorers:** Pelé, Gerson, Jairzinho, Carlos Alberto.
Italy: Albertosi; Burgnich, Cera, Rosato, Fachetti, Bertini (Juliano), Riva, Domenghini, Mazzola, De Sista, Boninsegna (Rivera). **Scorer:** Boninsegna.
Leading scorer: Müller (West Germany) 10.

West Germany 1974
WEST GERMANY 2, HOLLAND 1 (2-1) *Munich*
West Germany: Maier; Vogts, Schwarzenbeck, Beckenbauer, Breitner, Bonhof, Hoeness, Overath, Grabowski, Müller, Holzenbein. **Scorers:** Breitner (pen), Müller.
Holland: Jongbloed; Suurbier, Rijsbergen (De Jong), Haan, Krol, Jansen, Van Hanegem, Neeskens, Rep (Nanninga), Cruyff, Rensenbrink (Van der Kerkhof, R.)
Scorer: Neeskens (pen).
Leading scorer: Lato (Poland) 7.

Argentina 1978
ARGENTINA 3, HOLLAND 1 (1-1)* *Buenos Aires*
Argentina: Fillol; Olguin, Passarella, Galvan, Tarantini, Ardiles (Larrosa), Gallego, Ortiz (Houseman), Bertoni, Luque, Kempes. **Scorers:** Kempes 2, Bertoni.
Holland: Jongbloed; Poortvliet, Brandts, Krol, Jansen (Suurbier), Neeskens, Van der Kerkhof, W., Van der Kerkhof, R., Haan, Rep (Nanninga), Rensenbrink.
Scorer: Nanninga.
Leading scorer: Kempes (Argentina) 6.

Spain 1982
ITALY 3, WEST GERMANY 1 (0-0) *Madrid*
Italy: Zoff; Bergomi, Cabrini, Collovati, Scirea, Gentile, Oriali, Tardelli, Conti, Graziani (Altobelli), Rossi (Causio). **Scorers:** Rossi, Tardelli, Altobelli.
West Germany: Schumacher; Kaltz, Forster, K-H., Stielike, Forster, B., Breitner, Dremmler (Hrubesch), Littbarski, Briegel, Fischer, Rummenigge (Müller). **Scorer:** Breitner.
Leading scorer: Rossi (Italy) 6.

Mexico 1986
ARGENTINA 3, WEST GERMANY 2 (1-0) *Mexico City*
Argentina: Pumpido; Cuciuffo, Olarticoechea, Ruggeri, Brown, Giusti, Burruchaga (Trobbiani), Batista, Valdano, Maradona, Enrique. **Scorers:** Brown, Valdano, Burruchaga.
West Germany: Schumacher; Berthold, Briegel, Jacobs, Forster, Eder, Brehme, Matthäus, Allofs (Völler), Magath (Hoeness), Rummenigge. **Scorers:** Rummenigge, Völler.
Leading scorer: Lineker (England) 6.

Italy 1990
WEST GERMANY 1, ARGENTINA 0 (0-0) *Rome*
West Germany: Ilgner; Berthold (Reuter), Kohler, Augenthaler, Buchwald, Brehme, Littbaski, Hässler, Matthäus, Völler, Klinsmann. **Scorer:** Brehme (pen).
Argentina: Goycochea; Lorenzo, Serrizeula, Sensini, Ruggeri (Monzon), Simon, Basualdo, Burruchago (Calderon), Maradona, Troglio, Dezotti.
Referee: Codesal (Mexico). Monzon and Dezotti sent off.
Leading scorer: Schillaci (Italy) 6.

USA 1994
BRAZIL 0, ITALY 0* (0-0) *Los Angeles*
Brazil: Taffarel; Jorginho (Cafu 21), Marcio Santos, Aldair, Branco, Mazinho, Mauro Silva, Dunga, Zinho (Viola 109), Bebeto, Romario.
Italy: Pagliuca; Mussi (Apolloni 34), Maldini, Baresi, Benarrivo, Donadoni, Albertini, Dino Baggio (Evani 101), Berti, Roberto Baggio, Massaro.
Brazil won 3-2 on penalties
Referee: Puhl (Hungary).
Penalty sequence: Baresi (shot over); Marcio Santos (saved); Albertini (scored); Romario (scored off upright); Evani (scored); Branco (scored); Massaro (saved); Dunga (scored); Roberto Baggio (shot over).
Leading scorers: Salenko (Russia) 6, Stoichkov (Bulgaria) 6.

France 1998
FRANCE 3, BRAZIL 0 (2-0) *Saint-Denis*
France: Barthez, Thuram, Leboeuf, Desailly, Lizarazu, Karembeu (Boghossian 56), Deschamps, Petit, Zidane, Djorkaeff (Vieira 75), Guivarc'h (Dugarry 66).
Scorers: Zidane 2, Petit.
Brazil: Taffarel, Cafu, Junior Baiano, Aldair, Roberto Carlos, Dunga, Leonardo (Denilson 46), Cesar Sampaio (Edmundo 74), Rivaldo, Bebeto, Ronaldo.
Referee: Belqola (Morocco).
Leading scorer: Suker (Croatia) 6.

** After extra time*

WORLD CLUB CHAMPIONSHIP

Played annually up to 1974 and intermittently since then between the winners of the European Cup and the winners of the South American Champions Cup — known as the Copa Libertadores. In 1980 the winners were decided by one match arranged in Tokyo in February 1981 and the venue has been the same since. AC Milan replaced Marseille who had been stripped of their European Cup title in 1993.

1960   Real Madrid beat Penarol 0-0, 5-1
1961   Penarol beat Benfica 0-1, 5-0, 2-1
1962   Santos beat Benfica 3-2, 5-2
1963   Santos beat AC Milan 2-4, 4-2, 1-0
1964   Inter-Milan beat Independiente 0-1, 2-0, 1-0
1965   Inter-Milan beat Independiente 3-0, 0-0
1966   Penarol beat Real Madrid 2-0, 2-0
1967   Racing Club beat Celtic 0-1, 2-1, 1-0
1968   Estudiantes beat Manchester United 1-0, 1-1
1969   AC Milan beat Estudiantes 3-0, 1-2
1970   Feyenoord beat Estudiantes 2-2, 1-0
1971   Nacional beat Panathinaikos* 1-1, 2-1
1972   Ajax beat Independiente 1-1, 3-0
1973   Independiente beat Juventus* 1-0
1974   Atlético Madrid* beat Independiente 0-1, 2-0
1975   Independiente and Bayern Munich could not agree dates; no matches.
1976   Bayern Munich beat Cruzeiro 2-0, 0-0
1977   Boca Juniors beat Borussia Moenchengladbach* 2-2, 3-0
1978   Not contested
1979   Olimpia beat Malmö* 1-0, 2-1
1980   Nacional beat Nottingham Forest 1-0
1981   Flamengo beat Liverpool 3-0
1982   Penarol beat Aston Villa 2-0
1983   Gremio Porto Alegre beat SV Hamburg 2-1
1984   Independiente beat Liverpool 1-0
1985   Juventus beat Argentinos Juniors 4-2 on penalties after a 2-2 draw
1986   River Plate beat Steaua Bucharest 1-0
1987   FC Porto beat Penarol 2-1 after extra time
1988   Nacional (Uru) beat PSV Eindhoven 7-6 on penalties after 1-1 draw
1989   AC Milan beat Atletico Nacional (Col) 1-0 after extra time
1990   AC Milan beat Olimpia 3-0
1991   Red Star Belgrade beat Colo Colo 3-0
1992   Sao Paulo beat Barcelona 2-1
1993   Sao Paulo beat AC Milan 3-2
1994   Velez Sarsfield beat AC Milan 2-0
1995   Ajax beat Gremio Porto Alegre 4-3 on penalties after 0-0 draw
1996   Juventus beat River Plate 1-0
1997   Borussia Dortmund beat Cruzeiro 2-0
*European Cup runners-up; winners declined to take part.

1998
1 December in Tokyo

Real Madrid (1) 2

Vasco da Gama (0) 1   51,514
Real Madrid: Illgner; Panucci, Sanchis, Sanz, Hierro, Roberto Carlos, Raul, Redondo, Seedorf, Savio (Suker 90), Mijatovic (Jarni 81).
Scorers: Naza 26 (og), Raul 83.
Vasco da Gama: Germano; Mauro Galvao, Odvan, Felipe, Luizinho (Guilherme 85), Naza, Ramon (Valver 88), Vagner (Vitor 81), Juninho, Donizete, Luizao.
Scorer: Juninho 57.
Referee: Yanten (Chile).

EUROPEAN SUPER CUP

Played annually between the winners of the European Champions' Cup and the European Cup-Winners' Cup. AC Milan replaced Marseille in 1993–94.

Previous Matches
1972   Ajax beat Rangers 3-1, 3-2
1973   Ajax beat AC Milan 0-1, 6-0
1974   Not contested
1975   Dynamo Kiev beat Bayern Munich 1-0, 2-0
1976   Anderlecht beat Bayern Munich 4-1, 1-2
1977   Liverpool beat Hamburg 1-1, 6-0
1978   Anderlecht beat Liverpool 3-1, 1-2
1979   Nottingham F beat Barcelona 1-0, 1-1
1980   Valencia beat Nottingham F 1-0, 1-2
1981   Not contested
1982   Aston Villa beat Barcelona 0-1, 3-0
1983   Aberdeen beat Hamburg 0-0, 2-0
1984   Juventus beat Liverpool 2-0
1985   Juventus v Everton not contested due to UEFA ban on English clubs
1986   Steaua Bucharest beat Dynamo Kiev 1-0
1987   FC Porto beat Ajax 1-0, 1-0
1988   KV Mechelen beat PSV Eindhoven 3-0, 0-1
1989   AC Milan beat Barcelona 1-1, 1-0
1990   AC Milan beat Sampdoria 1-1, 2-0
1991   Manchester U beat Red Star Belgrade 1-0
1992   Barcelona beat Werder Bremen 1-1, 2-1
1993   Parma beat AC Milan 0-1, 2-0
1994   AC Milan beat Arsenal 0-0, 2-0
1995   Ajax beat Zaragoza 1-1, 4-0
1996   Juventus beat Paris St Germaine 6-1, 3-1
1997   Barcelona beat Borussia Dortmund 2-0, 1-1

1998

28 August 1998, Monaco

Real Madrid (0) 0

Chelsea (0) 1 *(Poyet 83)*   9762

Real Madrid: Illgner; Panucci, Sanchis, Hierro, Roberto Carlos, Karembeu (Morientes 58), Seedorf, Redondo, Savio, Mijatovic (Jarni 74), Raul.
Chelsea: De Goey; Ferrer, Le Saux, Duberry, Leboeuf, Desailly, Babayaro, Di Matteo (Poyet 63), Casiraghi (Flo 90), Zola (Laudrup 83), Wise.
Referee: Batta (France).

SOUTH AMERICAN CHAMPIONSHIP

(Copa America)

1916	Uruguay	1937	Argentina	1959	Uruguay
1917	Uruguay	1939	Peru	1963	Bolivia
1919	Brazil	1941	Argentina	1967	Uruguay
1920	Uruguay	1942	Uruguay	1975	Peru
1921	Argentina	1945	Argentina	1979	Paraguay
1922	Brazil	1946	Argentina	1983	Uruguay
1923	Uruguay	1947	Argentina	1987	Uruguay
1924	Uruguay	1949	Brazil	1989	Brazil
1925	Argentina	1953	Paraguay	1991	Argentina
1926	Uruguay	1955	Argentina	1993	Argentina
1927	Argentina	1956	Uruguay	1995	Uruguay
1929	Argentina	1957	Argentina	1997	Brazil
1935	Uruguay	1959	Argentina		

SOUTH AMERICAN CUP

(Copa Libertadores)

1960	Penarol (Uruguay)	1980	Nacional
1961	Penarol	1981	Flamengo (Brazil)
1962	Santos (Brazil)	1982	Penarol
1963	Santos	1983	Gremio Porto Alegre (Brazil)
1964	Independiente (Argentina)	1984	Independiente
1965	Independiente	1985	Argentinos Juniors (Argentina)
1966	Penarol	1986	River Plate (Argentina)
1967	Racing Club (Argentina)	1987	Penarol
1968	Estudiantes (Argentina)	1988	Nacional (Uruguay)
1969	Estudiantes	1989	Nacional (Colombia)
1970	Estudiantes	1990	Olimpia
1971	Nacional (Uruguay)	1991	Colo Colo (Chile)
1972	Independiente	1992	São Paulo (Brazil)
1973	Independiente	1993	São Paulo
1974	Independiente	1994	Velez Sarsfield (Argentina)
1975	Independiente	1995	Gremio Porto Alegre
1976	Cruzeiro (Brazil)	1996	River Plate
1977	Boca Juniors (Argentina)	1997	Cruzeiro
1978	Boca Juniors	1998	Vasco da Gama
1979	Olimpia (Paraguay)	1999	Palmeiras

OTHER BRITISH AND IRISH INTERNATIONAL MATCHES 1998–99

FRIENDLIES

Wembley, 18 November 1998, 38,535

England (2) 2 *(Anderton 22, Merson 39)*
Czech Republic (0) 0

England: Martyn; Anderton, Le Saux, Keown, Ferdinand R, Campbell, Beckham, Butt, Dublin, Wright (Fowler 71), Merson (Hendrie 77).
Czech Republic: Kouba; Novotny (Baranek 46), Votava, Repka, Poborsky, Bejbl, Nemec (Kotulek 46), Berger, Latal (Vonasek 46), Smicer (Lokvenc 46), Kuka.
Referee: Meier (Switzerland).

Wembley, 10 February 1999, 74,111

England (0) 0
France (0) 2 *(Anelka 69, 76)*

England: Seaman (Martyn 46); Dixon (Ferdinand R 71), Le Saux, Keown (Wilcox 86), Adams, Redknapp (Scholes 85), Beckham, Ince, Shearer, Owen (Cole 65), Anderton.
France: Barthez; Thuram, Blanc (Leboeuf 46), Desailly, Lizarazu, Pires (Dugarry 46), Zidane, Deschamps (Candela 90), Petit, Djorkaeff (Wiltord 83), Anelka (Vieira 83).
Referee: Krug (Germany).

Dublin, 10 February 1999, 27,600

Republic of Ireland (1) 2 *(Irwin 37 (pen), Connolly 74)*
Paraguay (0) 0

Republic of Ireland: Given (Kelly A 66); Irwin, Harte (Babb 71), McAteer (McLoughlin 81), Cunningham, Breen, Kinsella (Carsley 66), Roy Keane, Quinn (Cascarino 69), Robbie Keane (Connolly 66), Duff.
Paraguay: Tavarelli; Rolon, Caniza, Ortiz, Valdez, Aguilera, Paredes, Acosta, Franco (Esquivel 79), Caballero (Britez 71), Roman (Peralta 63).
Referee: Orrason (Iceland).

Belfast, 27 April 1999, 7663

Northern Ireland (0) 1 *(Parker 90 (og))*
Canada (0) 1 *(Bircham 67)*

Northern Ireland: Taylor (Wright 46); Hughes A, Horlock, Williams M, Hunter, Lomas, McCarthy (Hamill 60), Mulryne (Sonner 81), Dowie (Ferguson 74), Coote (McVeigh 74), Rowland.
Canada: Forrest; Clark, Brennan, Watson, Parker, Devos, Xausa (Bircham 59), Dasovic, Staltari (Kusch 65), Peschisolido, Bent.
Referee: McCurry (Scotland).

Bremen, 28 April 1999, 27,000

Germany (0) 0
Scotland (0) 1 *(Hutchison 66)*

Germany: Lehmann; Nowotny, Matthaus, Worns, Strunz (Jancker 88), Jeremies (Ramelow 46), Hamann (Ballack 59), Heinrich, Neuville, Bierhoff (Kirsten 59), Heldt.
Scotland: Sullivan; Weir, Davidson (Whyte 79), Boyd, Hendry (Ritchie 66), Lambert (Cameron 84), Gemmill (Jess 59), Durrant (Winters 72), Dodds, Hutchison, Johnston (O'Neil 88).
Referee: Meier (Switzerland).

Budapest, 28 April 1999, 20,000

Hungary (0) 1 *(Hrutka 76)*
England (1) 1 *(Shearer 21 (pen))*

Hungary: Kiraly; Korsos (Toth 65), Hrutka, Sebok, Matyus, Halmai, Pisont (Somogyi 46), Dardal, Dombi, Illes, Korsos.
England: Seaman; Brown (Gray 73), Neville P, Keown, Ferdinand R (Carragher 62), Batty, McManaman (Redknapp 85), Sherwood, Shearer, Phillips (Heskey 83), Butt.
Referee: Frohlick (Germany).

Dublin, 28 April 1999, 29,300

Republic of Ireland (0) 2 *(Kavanagh 75, Kennedy 77)*
Sweden (0) 0

Republic of Ireland: Given; Carr, Staunton, McAteer (Kilbane 46), Cunningham, Breen (Babb 46), Kinsella (Kavanagh 46), McLoughlin, Quinn (Robbie Keane 79), Connolly (Cascarino 71), Kennedy (Duff 79).
Sweden: Kihlstedt; Kamark, Lucic, Andersson P, Bjorklund (Jakobsson 46), Mild (Alexandersson 46), Andersson D, Schwarz, Pettersson (Jonsson M 81), Larsson, Blomqvist.
Referee: Garibian (France).

Dublin, 29 May 1999, 12,100

Republic of Ireland (0) 0
Northern Ireland (0) 1 *(Griffin 85)*

Republic of Ireland: Given; Carr, Maybury, Carsley (McLoughlin 46), Cunningham, Babb, Kinsella (Kavanagh 82), Robbie Keane (Connolly 56), Quinn (Cascarino 72), Duff (O'Neill 56), Kennedy.
Northern Ireland: Taylor (Carroll 46); Patterson, Hughes A, Williams M, Hunter, Lennon (Griffin 79), McCarthy, Robinson, Dowie (Coote 46), Quinn, Rowland (Johnson 73).
Referee: Richards (Wales).

ENGLAND UNDER-21 TEAMS 1998–99

ENGLAND UNDER-21 INTERNATIONALS

4 Sept

Sweden (0) 0
England (1) 2 *(Carragher 8, Lampard 86 (pen))*   5266
England: Wright; Dyer K (Curtis 78), Ball, Mills, Brown, Upson, Lampard, Carragher, Heskey, Jansen (Euell 81), Hendrie (Clemence 88).

9 Oct

England (0) 1 *(Lampard 61 (pen))*
Bulgaria (0) 0   11,577
England: Wright; Dyer K (Mills 63), Ball, Curtis, Brown, Upson, Lampard, Carragher, Heskey (Euell 90), Jansen (Morris 74), Hendrie.

13 Oct

Luxembourg (0) 0
England (2) 5 *(Hendrie 27, Upson 34, Lampard 52, Cort 68. 98)*   3500
England: Wright; Curtis, Ball, Mills, Brown, Upson, Lampard (Johnson 75), Carragher, Heskey, Jansen (Cort 59), Hendrie (Morris 49).

17 Nov

England (0) 0
Czech Republic (0) 1 *(Dosek 41)*   13,768
England: Simonsen; Dyer K, Ball (Beattie 79), Curtis, Brown (Johnson 79), Barry, Lampard, Carragher, Davies, Cort (Cadamarteri 70), Morris (Dunn 46).

9 Feb

England (0) 2 *(Bowyer 54, Upson 62)*
France (1) 1 *(Christanual 21)*   32,865
England: Simonsen; Curtis, Upson (Marshall L 88), O'Brien, Barry, Williams, Lampard (Jansen 46), Carragher, Bridges (Beattie 46), Bowyer (Cresswell 68), Hendrie.

26 Mar

England (1) 5 *(Bowyer 41, 80, Lampard 54 (pen), 59, Hendrie 71)*
Poland (0) 0   15,202
England: Wright; Mills, Ball, Johnson, Brown, Carragher, Lampard (Mullins 79), Beattie, Jansen (Euell 61), Bowyer, Hendrie (Curtis 73).

27 Apr

Hungary (2) 2 *(Rosa 3, 25)*
England (0) 2 *(Mills 53, Beattie 56 (pen))*   5000
England: Wright; Curtis, Griffin (Bridge 28), Mills, Young, Barry (Vassell 60), Greening, Mullins, Beattie (Cort 67), Euell (Cresswell 46), Woodhouse.

4 June

England (2) 3 *(Cort 30, 80, Cresswell 45)*
Sweden (0) 0   13,045
England: Wright; Dyer K, Johnson, Mills, Brown, Robinson, Lampard, Carragher, Cresswell (Greening 71), Cort, Woodhouse (Curtis 57).

8 June

Bulgaria (0) 0
England (0) 1 *(Cort 87)*   2000
England: Simonsen; Curtis, Johnson, Mullins, Brown, Robinson, Greening, Carragher, Cresswell, Cort, Woodhouse.

B INTERNATIONALS

9 Feb

Wales (0) 1 *(Williams 72)*
Northern Ireland (0) 0   1270
Wales: Ward (Coyne 48); Trollope, Lloyd, Page, Edwards, Mardon (Hughes 48), Oster (Davies 58), Robinson, Nogan (Williams 71), Lloyd-Williams (Roberts N 86), Coates.
Northern Ireland: Taylor; Griffin (Jeff Whitley 46), McGlinchey, Sonner, McGibbon (Hunter 46), Williams M, Hamill, Jim Whitley, Ferguson (Coote 78), Black (Healy 66), O'Neill.

9 Feb
Republic of Ireland (3) 4 *(Fenn 1, 3, Clare 13, 51)*   1125
National League Selection (1) 3 *(Coughlan 40, Gormley 56 (pen) Cousins 62)*
Republic of Ireland: Kiely (Colgan 46); Worrell, Quinn, Butler, Hardy, Finnan, Holland (Savage 46), Whalley (Kavanagh 46), Moore, Clare, Fenn (Scully 72).

POST-WAR INTERNATIONAL APPEARANCES
As at July 1999

ENGLAND
A'Court, A. (5) (Liverpool) 1957/8, 1958/9.
Adams, T.A. (57) (Arsenal) 1986/7, 1987/8, 1988/9, 1990/91, 1992/93, 1993/94, 1994/95, 1995/96, 1996/97, 1997/98, 1998/99.
Allen, A. (3) (Stoke City) 1959/60.
Allen, C. (5) (QPR) 1983/4, 1986/7 (Tottenham Hotspur) 1987/8.
Allen, R. (5) (West Bromwich Albion) 1951/2, 1953/4, 1954/5.
Anderson, S. (2) (Sunderland) 1961/2.
Anderson, V. (30) (Nottingham Forest) 1978/9, 1979/80, 1980/1, 1981/2, 1983/84, (Arsenal) 1984/5, 1985/6, 1986/7, (Manchester United) 1987–8.
Anderton, D.R. (27) (Tottenham Hotspur) 1993/94, 1994/95, 1995/96, 1997/98, 1998/99.
Angus, J. (1) (Burnley) 1960/1.
Armfield, J. (43) (Blackpool) 1958/9, 1959/60, 1960/1, 1961/2, 1962/3, 1963/4, 1965/6.
Armstrong, D. (3) (Middlesbrough) 1979/80, (Southampton) 1982/3, 1983/4.
Armstrong, K. (1) (Chelsea) 1954/5.
Astall, G. (2) (Birmingham) 1955/6.
Astle, J. (5) (West Bromwich Albion) 1968/9, 1969/70.
Aston, J. (17) (Manchester United) 1948/9, 1949/50, 1950/1.
Atyeo, J. (6) (Bristol City) 1955/6, 1956/7.

Bailey, G.R. (2) Manchester United) 1984/5.
Bailey, M. (2) (Charlton) 1963/4, 1964/5.
Baily, E. (9) (Tottenham Hotspur) 1949/50, 1950/1, 1951/2, 1952/3.
Baker, J. (8) (Hibernian) 1959/60, 1965/6, (Arsenal).
Ball, A. (72) (Blackpool) 1964/5, 1965/6, 1966/7, (Everton) 1967/8, 1968/9, 1969/70, 1970/1, 1971/2 (Arsenal) 1972/3, 1973/4, 1974/5.
Banks, G. (73) (Leicester City) 1962/3, 1963/4, 1964/5, 1965/6, 1966/7, 1967/8, (Stoke City) 1968/9, 1969/70, 1970/1, 1971/2.
Banks, T. (6) (Bolton Wanderers) 1957/8, 1958/9.
Bardsley, D. (2) (QPR) 1992/93.
Barham, M. (2) (Norwich City) 1982/3.
Barlow, R. (1) (West Bromwich Albion) 1954/5.
Barmby, N.J. (10) (Tottenham Hotspur) 1994/95, (Middlesbrough) 1995/96, 1996/97 (Everton).
Barnes, J. (79) (Watford) 1982/3, 1983/4, 1984/5, 1985/6, 1986/7, (Liverpool) 1987/8, 1988/9, 1989/90, 1990/91, 1991/2, 1992/93, 1994/95, 1995/96.
Barnes, P. (22) (Manchester City) 1977/8, 1978/9, 1979/80 (West Bromwich Albion) 1980/1, 1981/2 (Leeds United).
Barrass, M. (3) (Bolton Wanderers) 1951/2, 1952/3.
Barrett, E.D. (3) (Oldham Athletic) 1990/91 (Aston Villa) 1992/93.
Barton, W.D. (3) (Wimbledon) (Blackburn Rovers) 1994/95.
Batty, D. (40) (Leeds United) 1990/91, 1991/2, 1992/93, (Blackburn Rovers) 1993/94, 1994/95, (Newcastle United) 1996/97, 1997/98 (Leeds United) 1998/99.
Baynham, R. (3) (Luton Town) 1955/6.
Beardsley, P.A. (59) (Newcastle United) 1985/6, 1986/7 (Liverpool) 1987/8, 1988/9, 1989/90, 1990/1, (Newcastle United) 1993/94, 1994/95, 1995/96.
Beasant, D.J. (2) (Chelsea), 1989/90.
Beattie, T.K. (9) (Ipswich Town) 1974/5, 1975/6, 1976/7, 1977/8.
Beckham, D.R.J. (23) (Manchester United) 1996/97, 1997/98, 1998/99.

Bell, C. (48) (Manchester City) 1967/8, 1968/9, 1969/70, 1971/2, 1972/3, 1973/4, 1974/5, 1975/6.
Bentley, R. (12) (Chelsea) 1948/9, 1949/50, 1952/3, 1954/5.
Berry, J. (4) (Manchester United) 1952/3, 1955/6.
Birtles, G. (3) (Nottingham Forest) 1979/80, 1980/1.
Blissett, L. (14) (Watford) 1982/3, 1983/4 (AC Milan).
Blockley, J. (1) (Arsenal) 1972/3.
Blunstone, F. (5) (Chelsea) 1954/5, 1956/7.
Bonetti, P. (7) (Chelsea) 1965/6, 1966/7, 1967/8, 1969/70.
Bould, S.A. (2) (Arsenal) 1993/94.
Bowles, S. (5) (QPR) 1973/4, 1976/7.
Boyer, P. (1) (Norwich City) 1975/6.
Brabrook, P. (3) (Chelsea) 1957/8, 1959/60.
Bracewell, P.W. (3) (Everton) 1984/5, 1985/6.
Bradford, G. (1) (Bristol Rovers) 1955/6.
Bradley, W. (3) (Manchester United) 1958/9.
Bridges, B. (4) (Chelsea) 1964/5, 1965/6.
Broadbent, P. (7) (Wolverhampton Wanderers) 1957/8, 1958/9, 1959/60.
Broadis, I. (14) (Manchester City) 1951/2, 1952/3 (Newcastle United) 1953/4.
Brooking, T. (47) (West Ham United) 1973/4, 1974/5, 1975/6, 1976/7, 1977/8, 1978/9, 1979/80, 1980/1, 1981/2.
Brooks, J. (3) (Tottenham Hotspur) 1956/7.
Brown, A. (1) (West Bromwich Albion) 1970/1.
Brown, K. (1) (West Ham United) 1959/60.
Brown, W.M. (1) (Manchester United) 1998/99.
Bull, S.G. (13) (Wolverhampton Wanderers) 1988/9, 1989/90, 1990/1.
Butcher, T. (77) (Ipswich Town) 1979/80, 1980/1, 1981/2, 1982/3, 1983/4, 1984/5, 1985/6, 1986/7 (Rangers) 1987/8, 1988/9, 1989/90.
Butt, N. (8) (Manchester United) 1996/97, 1997/98, 1998/99.
Byrne, G. (2) (Liverpool) 1962/3, 1965/6.
Byrne, J. (11) (Crystal Palace) 1961/2, 1962/3, (West Ham United) 1963/4, 1964/5.
Byrne, R. (33) (Manchester United) 1953/4, 1954/5, 1955/6, 1956/7, 1957/8.

Callaghan, I. (4) (Liverpool) 1965/6, 1977/8.
Campbell, S. (27) (Tottenham Hotspur) 1995/96, 1996/97, 1997/98, 1998/99.
Carragher, J.L. (1) (Liverpool) 1998/99.
Carter, H. (7) (Derby County) 1946/7.
Chamberlain, M. (8) (Stoke City) 1982/3, 1983/4, 1984/5.
Channon, M. (46) (Southampton) 1972/3, 1973/4, 1974/5, 1975/6, 1976/7, (Manchester City) 1977/8.
Charles, G.A. (2) (Nottingham Forest) 1990/1.
Charlton, J. (35) (Leeds United) 1964/5, 1965/6, 1966/7, 1967/8, 1968/9, 1969/70.
Charlton, R. (106) (Manchester United) 1957/8, 1958/9, 1959/60, 1960/1, 1961/2, 1962/3, 1963/4, 1964/5, 1965/6, 1966/7, 1967/8, 1968/9, 1969/70.
Charnley, R. (1) (Blackpool) 1961/2.
Cherry, T. (27) (Leeds United) 1975/6, 1976/7, 1977/8, 1978/9, 1979/80.
Chilton, A. (2) (Manchester United) 1950/1, 1951/2.
Chivers, M. (24) (Tottenham Hotspur) 1970/1, 1971/2, 1972/3, 1973/4.
Clamp, E. (4) (Wolverhampton Wanderers) 1957/8.
Clapton, D. (1) (Arsenal) 1958/9.
Clarke, A. (19) (Leeds United) 1969/70, 1970/1, 1972/3, 1973/4, 1974/5, 1975/6.
Clarke, H. (1) (Tottenham Hotspur) 1953/4.
Clayton, R. (35) (Blackburn Rovers) 1955/6, 1956/7, 1957/8, 1958/9, 1959/60.
Clemence, R (61) (Liverpool) 1972/3, 1973/4, 1974/5, 1975/6, 1976/7, 1977/8, 1978/9, 1979/80, 1980/1, 1981/2, (Tottenham Hotspur) 1982/3, 1983/4.
Clement, D. (5) (QPR) 1975/6, 1976/7.

Clough, B. (2) (Middlesbrough) 1959/60.
Clough, N.H. (14) (Nottingham Forest) 1988/9, 1990/91, 1991/2, 1992/93.
Coates, R. (4) (Burnley) 1969/70, 1970/1, (Tottenham Hotspur).
Cockburn, H. (13) (Manchester United) 1946/7, 1947/8, 1948/9, 1950/1, 1951/2.
Cohen, G. (37) (Fulham) 1963/4, 1964/5, 1965/6, 1966/7, 1967/8.
Cole, A. (5) (Manchester United) 1994/95, 1996/97, 1998/99.
Collymore, S. V. (3) (Nottingham Forest) 1994/95, 1997/98.
Compton, L. (2) (Arsenal) 1950/1.
Connelly J. (20) (Burnley) 1959/60, 1961/2, 1962/3, 1964/5 (Manchester United) 1965/6.
Cooper, C. T. (2) (Nottingham Forest) 1994/95.
Cooper, T. (20) (Leeds United) 1968/9, 1969/70, 1970/1, 1971/2, 1974/5.
Coppell, S. (42) (Manchester United) 1977/8, 1978/9, 1979/80, 1980/1, 1981/2, 1982/3.
Corrigan J. (9) (Manchester City) 1975/6, 1977/8, 1978/9, 1979/80, 1980/1, 1981/2.
Cottee, A. R. (7) (West Ham United) 1986/7, 1987/8, (Everton) 1988/9.
Cowans, G. (10) (Aston Villa) 1982/3, 1985/6 (Bari) 1990/1 (Aston Villa).
Crawford, R. (2) (Ipswich Town) 1961/2.
Crowe, C. (1) (Wolverhampton Wanderers) 1962/3.
Cunningham, L. (6) (West Bromwich Albion) 1978/9 (Real Madrid) 1979/80, 1980/1.
Curle, K. (3) (Manchester City) 1991/2.
Currie, A. (17) (Sheffield United) 1971/2, 1972/3, 1973/4, 1975/6 (Leeds United) 1977/8, 1978/9.

Daley, A. M. (7) (Aston Villa) 1991/2.
Davenport, P. (1) (Nottingham Forest) 1984/5.
Deane, B. C. (3) (Sheffield United) 1990/91, 1992/93.
Deeley, N. (2) (Wolverhampton Wanderers) 1958/9.
Devonshire, A. (8) (West Ham United) 1979/80, 1981/2, 1982/3, 1983/4
Dickinson, J. (48) (Portsmouth) 1948/9, 1949/50, 1950/1, 1951/2, 1952/3, 1953/4, 1954/5, 1955/6, 1956/7.
Ditchburn, E. (6) (Tottenham Hotspur) 1948/9, 1952/3, 1956/7.
Dixon, K. M. (8) (Chelsea) 1984/5, 1985/6, 1986/7.
Dixon, L. M. (22) (Arsenal) 1989/90, 1990/1, 1991/2, 1992/93, 1993/94, 1998/99.
Dobson, M. (5) (Burnley) 1973/4, 1974/5 (Everton).
Dorigo, A. R. (15) (Chelsea) 1989/90, 1990/1, (Leeds United) 1991/2, 1992/93, 1993/94.
Douglas, B. (36) (Blackburn Rovers) 1957/8, 1958/9, 1959/60, 1960/1, 1961/2, 1962/3.
Doyle, M. (5) (Manchester City) 1975/6, 1976/7.
Dublin, D. (4) (Coventry City) 1997/98, (Aston Villa) 1998/99.
Duxbury, M. (10) (Manchester United) 1983/4, 1984/5.

Eastham, G. (19) (Arsenal) 1962/3, 1963/4, 1964/5, 1965/6.
Eckersley, W. (17) (Blackburn Rovers) 1949/50, 1950/1, 1951/2, 1952/3, 1953/4.
Edwards, D. (18) (Manchester United) 1954/5, 1955/6, 1956/7, 1957/8.
Ehiogu, U. (1) (Aston Villa) 1995/96.
Ellerington, W. (2) (Southampton) 1948/9.
Elliott, W. H. (5) (Burnley) 1951/2, 1952/3.

Fantham, J. (1) (Sheffield Wednesday) 1961/2.
Fashanu, J. (2) (Wimbledon) 1988/9.
Fenwick, T. (20) (QPR) 1983/4, 1984/5, 1985/6 (Tottenham Hotspur) 1987/8.
Ferdinand, L. (17) (QPR) 1992/93, 1993/94, 1994/95 (Newcastle United) 1995/96, 1996/97 (Tottenham Hotspur) 1997/98.

Ferdinand, R. G. (8) (West Ham United) 1997/98, 1998/99.
Finney, T. (76) (Preston North End) 1946/7, 1947/8, 1948/9, 1949/50, 1950/1, 1951/2, 1952/3, 1953/4, 1954/5, 1955/6, 1956/7, 1957/8, 1958/9.
Flowers, R. (49) (Wolverhampton Wanderers) 1954/5, 1958/9, 1959/60, 1960/1, 1961/2, 1962/3, 1963/4, 1964/5, 1965/6.
Flowers, T. (11) (Southampton) 1992/93, (Blackburn Rovers) 1993/94, 1994/95, 1995/96, 1996/97, 1997/98.
Foster, S. (3) (Brighton) 1981/2.
Foulkes, W. (1) (Manchester United) 1954/5.
Fowler, R. B. (9) (Liverpool) 1995/96, 1996/97, 1997/98, 1998/99.
Francis, G. (12) (QPR) 1974/5, 1975/6.
Francis, T. (52) (Birmingham City) 1976/7, 1977/8 (Nottingham Forest) 1978/9, 1979/80, 1980/1, 1981/2 (Manchester City) 1982/3, (Sampdoria) 1983/4, 1984/5, 1985/6.
Franklin, N. (27) (Stoke City) 1946/7, 1947/8, 1948/9, 1949/50.
Froggatt, J. (13) (Portsmouth) 1949/50, 1950/1, 1951/2, 1952/3.
Froggatt, R. (4) (Sheffield Wednesday) 1952/3.

Garrett, T. (3) (Blackpool) 1951/2, 1953/4.
Gascoigne, P. J. (57) (Tottenham Hotspur) 1988/9, 1989/90, 1990/1 (Lazio) 1992/93, 1993/94, 1994/95 (Rangers) 1995/96, 1996/97 (Middlesbrough) 1997/98.
Gates, E. (2) (Ipswich Town) 1980/1.
George, F. C. (1) (Derby County) 1976/7.
Gidman, J. (1) (Aston Villa) 1976/7.
Gillard, I. (3) (QPR) 1974/5, 1975/6.
Goddard, P. (1) (West Ham United) 1981/2.
Grainger, C. (7) (Sheffield United) 1955/6, 1956/7 (Sunderland).
Gray, A. A. (1) (Crystal Palace) 1991/2.
Gray, M. (3) (Sunderland) 1998/99.
Greaves, J. (57) (Chelsea) 1958/9, 1959/60, 1960/1, 1961/2 (Tottenham Hotspur) 1962/3, 1963/4, 1964/5, 1965/6, 1966/7.
Greenhoff, B. (18) (Manchester United) 1975/6, 1976/7, 1977/8, 1979/80.
Gregory, J. (6) (QPR) 1982/3, 1983/4.

Hagan, J. (1) (Sheffield United) 1948/9.
Haines, J. (1) (West Bromwich Albion) 1948/9.
Hall, J. (17) (Birmingham City) 1955/6, 1956/7.
Hancocks, J. (3) (Wolverhampton Wanderers) 1948/9, 1949/50, 1950/1.
Hardwick, G. (13) (Middlesbrough) 1946/7, 1947/8.
Harford, M. G. (2) (Luton Town) 1987/8, 1988/9.
Harris, G. (1) (Burnley) 1965/6.
Harris, P. (2) (Portsmouth) 1949/50, 1953/4.
Harvey, C. (1) (Everton) 1970/1.
Hassall, H. (5) (Huddersfield Town) 1950/1, 1951/2 (Bolton Wanderers) 1953/4.
Hateley, M. (32) (Portsmouth) 1983/4, 1984/5, (AC Milan) 1985/6, 1986/7, (Monaco) 1987/8, (Rangers) 1991/2.
Haynes, J. (56) (Fulham) 1954/5, 1955/6, 1956/7, 1957/8, 1958/9, 1959/60, 1960/1, 1961/2.
Hector, K. (2) (Derby County) 1973/4.
Hellawell, M. (2) (Birmingham City) 1962/3.
Hendrie, L.A. (1) (Aston Villa) 1998/99.
Henry, R. (1) (Tottenham Hotspur) 1962/3.
Heskey, E.W. (2) (Leicester City) 1998/99.
Hill, F. (2) (Bolton Wanderers) 1962/3.
Hill, G. (6) (Manchester United) 1975/6, 1976/7, 1977/8.
Hill, R. (3) (Luton Town) 1982/3, 1985/6.

Hinchcliffe, A. G. (7) (Everton) 1996/97 (Sheffield W) 1997/98, 1998/99.
Hinton A. (3) (Wolverhampton Wanderers) 1962/3, 1964/5 (Nottingham Forest).
Hirst, D. E. (3) (Sheffield Wednesday) 1990/91, 1991/2.
Hitchens, G. (7) (Aston Villa) 1960/1, (Internazionale) 1961/2.
Hoddle, G. (53) (Tottenham Hotspur) 1979/80, 1980/1, 1981/2, 1982/3, 1983/4, 1984/5, 1985/6, 1986/7 (Monaco) 1987/8.
Hodge, S. B. (24) (Aston Villa) 1985/6, 1986/7, (Tottenham Hotspur), (Nottingham Forest) 1988/9, 1989/90, 1990/1.
Hodgkinson, A. (5) (Sheffield United) 1956/7, 1960/1.
Holden, D. (5) (Bolton Wanderers) 1958/9.
Holliday, E. (3) (Middlesbrough) 1959/60.
Hollins, J. (1) (Chelsea) 1966/7.
Hopkinson, E. (14) (Bolton Wanderers) 1957/8, 1958/9, 1959/60.
Howe, D. (23) (West Bromwich Albion) 1957/8, 1958/9, 1959/60.
Howe, J. (3) (Derby County) 1947/8, 1948/9.
Howey, S. N. (4) (Newcastle United) 1994/95, 1995/96.
Hudson, A. (2) (Stoke City) 1974/5.
Hughes, E. (62) (Liverpool) 1969/70, 1970/1, 1971/2, 1972/3, 1973/4, 1974/5, 1976/7, 1977/8, 1978/9 (Wolverhampton Wanderers) 1979/80.
Hughes, L. (3) (Liverpool) 1949/50.
Hunt, R. (34) (Liverpool) 1961/2, 1962/3, 1963/4, 1964/5, 1965/6, 1966/7, 1967/8, 1968/9.
Hunt, S. (2) (West Bromwich Albion) 1983/4.
Hunter, N. (28) (Leeds United) 1965/6, 1966/7, 1967/8, 1968/9, 1969/70, 1970/1, 1971/2, 1972/3, 1973/4, 1974/5.
Hurst, G. (49) (West Ham United) 1965/6, 1966/7, 1967/8, 1968/9, 1969/70, 1970/1, 1971/2.

Ince, P. (45) (Manchester United) 1992/93, 1993/94, 1994/95, (Internazionale) 1995/96, 1996/97 (Liverpool) 1997/98, 1998/99.

James, D. B. (1) (Liverpool) 1996/97.
Jezzard, B. (2) (Fulham) 1953/4, 1955/6.
Johnson, D. (8) (Ipswich Town) 1974/5, 1975/6, (Liverpool) 1979/80.
Johnston, H. (10) (Blackpool) 1946/7, 1950/1, 1952/3, 1953/4.
Jones, M. (3) (Sheffield United) 1964/5 (Leeds United) 1969/70.
Jones, R. (8) (Liverpool) 1991/2, 1993/94, 1994/95.
Jones, W. H. (2) (Liverpool) 1949/50.

Kay, A. (1) (Everton) 1962/3.
Keegan, K. (63) (Liverpool) 1972/3, 1973/4, 1974/5, 1975/6, 1976/7 (SV Hamburg) 1977/8, 1978/9, 1979/80 (Southampton) 1980/1, 1981/2.
Kennedy, A. (2) (Liverpool) 1983/4.
Kennedy, R. (17) (Liverpool) 1975/6, 1977/8, 1979/80.
Keown, M. R. (23) (Everton) 1991/2 (Arsenal) 1992/93, 1996/97, 1997/98, 1998/99.
Kevan, D. (14) (West Bromwich Albion) 1956/7, 1957/8, 1958/9, 1960/1.
Kidd, B. (2) (Manchester United) 1969/70.
Knowles, C. (4) (Tottenham Hotspur) 1967/8.

Labone, B. (26) (Everton) 1962/3, 1966/7, 1967/8, 1968/9, 1969/70.
Lampard, F. (2) (West Ham United) 1972/3, 1979/80.
Langley, J. (3) (Fulham) 1957/8.
Langton, R. (11) (Blackburn Rovers) 1946/7, 1947/8, 1948/9, (Preston North End) 1949/50, (Bolton Wanderers) 1950/1.
Latchford, R. (12) (Everton) 1977/8, 1978/9.
Lawler, C. (4) (Liverpool) 1970/1, 1971/2.

Lawton, T. (15) (Chelsea) 1946/7, 1947/8, (Notts County) 1948/9.
Lee, F. (27) (Manchester City) 1968/9, 1969/70, 1970/1, 1971/2.
Lee, J. (1) (Derby County) 1950/1.
Lee, R. M. (21) (Newcastle United) 1994/95, 1995/96, 1996/97, 1997/98, 1998/99.
Lee, S. (14) (Liverpool) 1982/3, 1983/4.
Le Saux, G. P. (35) (Blackburn Rovers) 1993/94, 1994/95, 1995/96, 1996/97, (Chelsea) 1997/98, 1998/99.
Le Tissier, M. P. (8) (Southampton) 1993/94, 1994/95, 1996/97.
Lindsay, A. (4) (Liverpool) 1973/4.
Lineker, G. (80) (Leicester City) 1983/4, 1984/5 (Everton) 1985/6, 1986/7, (Barcelona) 1987/8, 1988/9 (Tottenham H) 1989/90, 1990/1, 1991/2.
Little, B. (1) (Aston Villa) 1974/5.
Lloyd, L. (4) (Liverpool) 1970/1, 1971/2, (Nottingham Forest) 1979/80.
Lofthouse, N. (33) (Bolton Wanderers) 1950/1, 1951/2, 1952/3, 1953/4, 1954/5, 1955/6, 1958/9.
Lowe, E. (3) (Aston Villa) 1946/7.

Mabbutt, G. (16) (Tottenham Hotspur) 1982/3, 1983/4, 1986/7, 1987/8, 1991/2.
Macdonald, M. (14) (Newcastle United) 1971/2, 1972/3, 1973/4, 1974/5, 1975/6.
Madeley, P. (24) (Leeds United) 1970/1, 1971/2, 1972/3, 1973/4, 1974/5, 1975/6, 1976/7.
Mannion, W. (26) (Middlesbrough) 1946/7, 1947/8, 1948/9, 1949/50, 1950/1, 1951/2.
Mariner, P. (35) (Ipswich Town) 1976/7, 1977/8, 1979/80, 1980/1, 1981/2, 1982/3, 1983/4, 1984/5 (Arsenal).
Marsh, R. (9) (QPR) 1971/2 (Manchester City) 1972/3.
Martin, A. (17) (West Ham United) 1980/1, 1981/2, 1982/3, 1983/4, 1984/5, 1985/6, 1986/7.
Martyn, A.N. (9) (Crystal Palace) 1991/2, 1992/93 (Leeds United) 1996/97, 1997/98, 1998/99.
Marwood, B. (1) (Arsenal) 1988/9.
Matthews, R. (5) (Coventry City) 1955/6, 1956/7.
Matthews, S. (37) (Stoke City) 1946/7, (Blackpool) 1947/8, 1948/9, 1949/50, 1950/1, 1953/4, 1954/5, 1955/6, 1956/7.
McDermott, T. (25) (Liverpool) 1977/8, 1978/9, 1979/80, 1980/1, 1981/2.
McDonald, C. (8) (Burnley) 1957/8, 1958/9.
McFarland, R. (28) (Derby County) 1970/1, 1971/2, 1972/3, 1973/4, 1975/6, 1976/7.
McGarry, W. (4) (Huddersfield Town) 1953/4, 1955/6.
McGuinness, W. (2) (Manchester United) 1958/9.
McMahon, S. (17) (Liverpool) 1987/8, 1988/9, 1989/90, 1990/1.
McManaman, S. (24) (Liverpool) 1994/95, 1995/96, 1996/97, 1997/98, 1998/99.
McNab, R. (4) (Arsenal) 1968/9.
McNeil, M. (9) (Middlesbrough) 1960/1, 1961/2.
Meadows, J. (1) (Manchester City) 1954/5.
Medley, L. (Tottenham Hotspur) 1950/1, 1951/2.
Melia, J. (2) (Liverpool) 1962/3.
Merrick, G. (23) (Birmingham City) 1951/2, 1952/3, 1953/4.
Merson, P. C. (21) (Arsenal) 1991/2, 1992/93, 1993/94, 1996/97 (Middlesbrough) 1997/98, (Aston Villa) 1998/99.
Metcalfe, V. (2) (Huddersfield Town) 1950/1.
Milburn, J. (13) (Newcastle United) 1948/9, 1949/50, 1950/1, 1951/2, 1955/6.
Miller, B. (1) (Burnley) 1960/1.
Mills, M. (42) (Ipswich Town) 1972/3, 1975/6, 1976/7, 1977/8, 1978/9, 1979/80, 1980/1, 1981/2.
Milne, G. (14) (Liverpool) 1962/3, 1963/4, 1964/5.
Milton, C. A. (1) (Arsenal) 1951/2.

Moore, R. (108) (West Ham United) 1961/2, 1962/3, 1963/4, 1964/5, 1965/6, 1966/7, 1967/8, 1968/9, 1969/70, 1970/1, 1971/2, 1972/3, 1973/4.
Morley, A. (6) (Aston Villa) 1981/2, 1982/3.
Morris, J. (3) (Derby County) 1948/9, 1949/50.
Mortensen, S. (25) (Blackpool) 1946/7, 1947/8, 1948/9, 1949/50, 1950/1, 1953/4.
Mozley, B. (3) (Derby County) 1949/50.
Mullen, J. (12) (Wolverhampton Wanderers) 1946/7, 1948/9, 1949/50, 1953/4.
Mullery, A. (35) (Tottenham Hotspur) 1964/5, 1966/7, 1967/8, 1968/9, 1969/70, 1970/1, 1971/2.

Neal, P. (50) (Liverpool) 1975/6, 1976/7, 1977/8, 1978/9, 1979/80, 1980/1, 1981/2, 1982/3, 1983/4.
Neville, G. A. (32) (Manchester United) 1994/95, 1995/96, 1996/97, 1997/98, 1998/99.
Neville, P. J. (17) (Manchester United) 1995/96, 1996/97, 1997/98, 1998/99.
Newton, K. (27) (Blackburn Rovers) 1965/6, 1966/7, 1967/8, 1968/9, (Everton) 1969/70.
Nicholls, J. (2) (West Bromwich Albion) 1953/4.
Nicholson, W. (1) (Tottenham Hotspur) 1950/1.
Nish, D. (5) (Derby County) 1972/3, 1973/4.
Norman, M. (23) (Tottenham Hotspur) 1961/2, 1962/3, 1963/4, 1964/5.

O'Grady, M. (2) (Huddersfield Town) 1962/3, 1968/9 (Leeds United).
Osgood, P. (4) (Chelsea) 1969/70, 1973/4.
Osman, R. (11) (Ipswich Town) 1979/80, 1980/1, 1981/2, 1982/3, 1983/4.
Owen, M. J. (13) (Liverpool) 1997/98, 1998/99.
Owen, S. (3) (Luton Town) 1953/4.

Paine, T. (19) (Southampton) 1962/3, 1963/4, 1964/5, 1965/6.
Pallister, G. (22) (Middlesbrough) 1987/8, 1990/91 (Manchester United), 1991/2, 1992/93, 1993/94, 1994/95, 1995/96, 1996/97.
Palmer, C. L. (18) (Sheffield Wednesday) 1991/2, 1992/93, 1993/94.
Parker, P. A. (19) (QPR) 1988/9, 1989/90, 1990/1, (Manchester United) 1991/2, 1993/94.
Parkes, P. (1) (QPR) 1973/4.
Parlour, R. (3) (Arsenal) 1998/99.
Parry, R. (2) (Bolton Wanderers) 1959/60.
Peacock, A. (6) (Middlesbrough) 1961/2, 1962/3, 1965/6 (Leeds United).
Pearce, S. (76) (Nottingham Forest) 1986/7, 1987/8, 1988/9, 1989/90, 1990/1, 1991/2, 1992/93, 1993/94, 1994/95, 1995/96, 1996/97.
Pearson, Stan (8) (Manchester United) 1947/8, 1948/9, 1949/50, 1950/1, 1951/2.
Pearson, Stuart (15) (Manchester United) 1975/6, 1976/7, 1977/8.
Pegg, D. (1) (Manchester United) 1956/7.
Pejic, M. (4) (Stoke City) 1973/4.
Perry, W. (3) (Blackpool) 1955/6.
Perryman, S. (1) (Tottenham Hotspur) 1981/2.
Peters, M. (67) (West Ham United) 1965/6, 1966/7, 1967/8, 1968/9, 1969/70, (Tottenham Hotspur) 1970/1, 1971/2, 1972/3, 1973/4.
Phelan, M. C. (1) (Manchester United) 1989/90.
Phillips, K. (1) (Sunderland) 1998/99.
Phillips, L. (3) (Portsmouth) 1951/2, 1954/5.
Pickering, F. (3) (Everton) 1963/4, 1964/5.
Pickering, N. (1) (Sunderland) 1982/3.
Pilkington, B. (1) (Burnley) 1954/5.
Platt, D. (62) (Aston Villa) 1989/90, 1990/1, (Bari) 1991/2 (Juventus), 1992/93 (Sampdoria) 1993/94, 1994/95, (Arsenal) 1995/96.

Pointer, R. (3) (Burnley) 1961/2.
Pye, J. (1) (Wolverhampton Wanderers) 1949/50.

Quixall, A. (5) (Sheffield Wednesday) 1953/4, 1954/5.

Radford, J. (2) (Arsenal) 1968/9, 1971/2.
Ramsey, A. (32) (Southampton) 1948/9, 1949/50, (Tottenham Hotspur) 1950/1, 1951/2, 1952/3, 1953/4.
Reaney, P. (3) (Leeds United) 1968/9, 1969/70, 1970/1.
Redknapp, J. F. (14) (Liverpool) 1995/96, 1996/97, 1998/99.
Reeves, K. (2) (Norwich City) 1979/80.
Regis, C. (5) (West Bromwich Albion) 1981/2, 1982/3, (Coventry City) 1987–88.
Reid, P. (13) (Everton) 1984/5, 1985/6, 1986/7.
Revie, D. (6) (Manchester City) 1954/5, 1955/6, 1956/7.
Richards, J. (1) (Wolverhampton Wanderers) 1972/3.
Richardson, K. (1) (Aston Villa) 1993/94.
Rickaby, S. (1) (West Bromwich Albion) 1953/4.
Rimmer, J. (1) (Arsenal) 1975/6.
Ripley, S. E. (2) (Blackburn Rovers) 1993/94, 1997/98.
Rix, G. (17) (Arsenal) 1980/1, 1981/2, 1982/3, 1983/4.
Robb, G. (1) (Tottenham Hotspur) 1953/4.
Roberts, G. (6) (Tottenham Hotspur) 1982/3, 1983/4.
Robson, B. (90) (West Bromwich Albion) 1979/80, 1980/1, 1981/2, (Manchester United) 1982/3, 1983/4, 1984/5, 1985/6, 1986/7, 1987/8, 1988/9, 1989/90, 1990/1, 1991/2.
Robson, R. (20) (West Bromwich Albion) 1957/8, 1959/60, 1960/1, 1961/2.
Rocastle, D. (14) (Arsenal) 1988/9, 1989/90, 1991/2.
Rowley, J. (6) (Manchester United) 1948/9, 1949/50, 1951/2.
Royle, J. (6) (Everton) 1970/1, 1972/3, (Manchester City) 1975/6, 1976/7.
Ruddock, N. (1) (Liverpool) 1994/95.

Sadler, D. (4) (Manchester United) 1967/8, 1969/70, 1970/1.
Salako, J. A. (5) (Crystal Palace) 1990/91, 1991/2.
Sansom, K. (86) (Crystal Palace) 1978/9, 1979/80, 1980/1, (Arsenal) 1981/2, 1982/3, 1983/4, 1984/5, 1985/6, 1986/7, 1987/8.
Scales, J. R. (3) (Liverpool) 1994/95.
Scholes, P. (17) (Manchester United) 1996/97, 1997/98, 1998/99.
Scott, L. (17) (Arsenal) 1946/7, 1947/8. 1948/9.
Seaman, D. A. (52) (QPR) 1988/9, 1989/90, 1990/1 (Arsenal) 1991/2, 1993/94, 1994/95, 1995/96, 1996/97, 1997/98, 1998/99.
Sewell, J. (6) (Sheffield Wednesday) 1951/2, 1952/3, 1953/4.
Shackleton, L. (5) (Sunderland) 1948/9, 1949/50, 1954/5.
Sharpe, L. S. (8) (Manchester United) 1990/1, 1992/93, 1993/94.
Shaw, G. (5) (Sheffield United) 1958/9, 1962/3.
Shearer, A. (51) (Southampton) 1991/2 (Blackburn Rovers), 1992/93, 1993/94, 1994/95, 1995/96 (Newcastle United) 1996/97, 1997/98, 1998/99.
Shellito, K. (1) (Chelsea) 1962/3.
Sheringham, E. (38) (Tottenham Hotspur) 1992/93, 1994/95, 1995/96, 1996/97 (Manchester United) 1997/98, 1998/99.
Sherwood, T. A. (3) (Tottenham Hotspur) 1998/99.
Shilton, P. (125) (Leicester City) 1970/1, 1971/2, 1972/3, 1973/4, 1974/5, (Stoke City) 1976/7, (Nottingham Forest) 1977/8, 1978/9, 1979/80, 1980/1, 1981/2, (Southampton) 1982/3, 1983/4, 1984/5, 1985/6, 1986/7, (Derby County) 1987/8, 1988/9, 1989/90.
Shimwell, E. (1) (Blackpool) 1948/9.
Sillett, P. (3) (Chelsea) 1954/5.

Sinton, A. (12) (QPR) 1991/2, 1992/93 (Sheffield Wednesday) 1993/94.
Slater, W. (12) (Wolverhampton Wanderers) 1954/5, 1957/8, 1958/9, 1959/60.
Smith, A. M. (13) (Arsenal) 1988/9, 1990/1, 1991/2.
Smith, L. (6) (Arsenal) 1950/1, 1951/2, 1952/3.
Smith, R. (15) (Tottenham Hotspur) 1960/1, 1961/2, 1962/3, 1963/4.
Smith, Tom (1) (Liverpool) 1970/1.
Smith, Trevor (2) (Birmingham City) 1959/60.
Southgate, G. (31) (Aston Villa) 1995/96, 1996/97, 1997/98, 1998/99.
Spink, N. (1) (Aston Villa) 1982/3.
Springett, R. (33) (Sheffield Wednesday) 1959/60, 1960/1, 1961/2, 1962/3, 1965/6.
Staniforth, R. (8) (Huddersfield Town) 1953/4, 1954/5.
Statham, D. (3) (West Bromwich Albion) 1982/3.
Stein, B. (1) (Luton Town) 1983/4.
Stepney, A. (1) (Manchester United) 1967/8.
Sterland, M. (1) (Sheffield Wednesday) 1988/9.
Steven, T. M. (36) (Everton) 1984/5, 1985/6, 1986/7, 1987/8, 1988/9 (Rangers)
 1989/90, 1990/1, (Marseille) 1991/2.
Stevens, G. A. (7) (Tottenham Hotspur) 1984/5, 1985/6.
Stevens, M. G. (46) (Everton) 1984/5, 1985/6, 1986/7, 1987/8 (Rangers) 1988/9,
 1989/90, 1990/1, 1991/2.
Stewart, P. A. (3) (Tottenham Hotspur) 1991/2.
Stiles, N. (28) (Manchester United) 1964/5, 1965/6, 1966/7, 1967/8, 1968/9, 1969/70.
Stone, S. B. (9) (Nottingham Forest) 1995/96.
Storey-Moore, I. (1) (Nottingham Forest) 1969/70.
Storey, P. (19) (Arsenal) 1970/1, 1971/2, 1972/3.
Streten, B. (1) (Luton Town) 1949/50.
Summerbee, M. (8) (Manchester City) 1967/8, 1971/2, 1972/3.
Sunderland, A. (1) (Arsenal) 1979/80.
Sutton, C. R. (1) (Blackburn Rovers) 1997/98.
Swan, P. (19) (Sheffield Wednesday) 1959/60, 1960/1, 1961/2.
Swift, F. (19) (Manchester City) 1946/7, 1947/8, 1948/9.

Talbot, B. (6) (Ipswich Town) 1976/7, 1979/80.
Tambling, R. (3) (Chelsea) 1962/3, 1965/6.
Taylor, E. (1) (Blackpool) 1953/4.
Taylor, J. (2) (Fulham) 1950/1.
Taylor, P. H. (3) (Liverpool) 1947/8.
Taylor, P. J. (4) (Crystal Palace) 1975/6.
Taylor, T. (19) (Manchester United) 1952/3, 1953/4, 1955/6, 1956/7, 1958/9.
Temple, D. (1) (Everton) 1964/5.
Thomas, Danny (2) (Coventry City) 1982/3.
Thomas, Dave (8) (QPR) 1974/5, 1975/6.
Thomas, G. R. (9) (Crystal Palace) 1990/1, 1991/2.
Thomas, M. L. (2) (Arsenal) 1988/9, 1989/90.
Thompson, P. (16) (Liverpool) 1963/4, 1964/5, 1965/6, 1967/8, 1969/70.
Thompson, P. B. (42) (Liverpool) 1975/6, 1976/7, 1978/9, 1979/80, 1980/1, 1981/2,
 1982/3.
Thompson, T. (2) (Aston Villa) 1951/2, (Preston North End) 1956/7.
Thomson, R. (8) (Wolverhampton Wanderers) 1963/4, 1964/5.
Todd, C. (27) (Derby County) 1971/2, 1973/4, 1974/5, 1975/6, 1976/7.
Towers, T. (3) (Sunderland) 1975/6.
Tueart, D. (6) (Manchester City) 1974/5, 1976/7.

Ufton, D. (1) (Charlton Athletic) 1953/4.
Unsworth, D. G. (1) (Everton) 1994/95.

Venables, T. (2) (Chelsea) 1964/5.
Venison, B. (2) (Newcastle United) 1994/95.
Viljoen, C. (2) (Ipswich Town) 1974/5.
Viollet, D. (2) (Manchester United) 1959/60, 1961/2.

Waddle, C. R. (62) (Newcastle United) 1984/5, (Tottenham Hotspur) 1985/6, 1986/7, 1987/8, 1988/9, (Marseille) 1989/90, 1990/1, 1991/2.
Waiters, A. (5) (Blackpool) 1963/4, 1964/5.
Walker, D. S. (59) (Nottingham Forest) 1988/9, 1989/90, 1990/1, 1991/2 (Sampdoria) 1992/93, (Sheffield Wednesday) 1993/94.
Walker, I. M. (3) (Tottenham Hotspur) 1995/96, 1996/97.
Wallace, D. L. (1) (Southampton) 1985/6.
Walsh, P. (5) (Luton Town) 1982/3, 1983/4.
Walters, K. M. (1) (Rangers) 1990/91.
Ward, P. (1) (Brighton) 1979/80.
Ward, T. (2) (Derby County) 1947/8, 1948/9.
Watson, D. (12) (Norwich City) 1983/4, 1984/5, 1985/6, 1986/7 (Everton) 1987/8.
Watson D.V. (65) (Sunderland) 1973/4, 1974/5, 1975/6 (Manchester City) 1976/7, 1977/8, (Southampton) 1978/9 (Werder Bremen), 1979/80, (Southampton) 1980/1, 1981/2, (Stoke City).
Watson, W. (4) (Sunderland) 1949/50, 1950/1.
Webb, N. (26) (Nottingham Forest) 1987/8, 1988/9 (Manchester United) 1989/90, 1991/2.
Weller, K. (4) (Leicester City) 1973/4.
West, G. (3) (Everton) 1968/9.
Wheeler, J. (1) (Bolton Wanderers) 1954/5.
White, D. (1) (Manchester City) 1992/93.
Whitworth, S. (7) (Leicester City) 1974/5, 1975/6.
Whymark, T. (1) (Ipswich Town) 1977/8.
Wignall, F. (2) (Nottingham Forest) 1964/5.
Wilcox, J. M. (2) (Blackburn Rovers) 1995/96, 1998/99.
Wilkins, R. (84) (Chelsea) 1975/6, 1976/7, 1977/8, 1978/9, (Manchester United) 1979/80, 1980/1, 1981/2, 1982/3, 1983/4, 1984/5, (AC Milan) 1985/6, 1986/7.
Williams, B. (24) (Wolverhampton Wanderers) 1948/9, 1949/50, 1950/1, 1951/2, 1954/5, 1955/6.
Williams, S. (6) (Southampton) 1982/3, 1983/4, 1984/5.
Willis, A. (1) (Tottenham Hotspur) 1951/2.
Wilshaw, D. (12) (Wolverhampton Wanderers) 1953/4, 1954/5, 1955/6, 1956/7.
Wilson, R. (63) (Huddersfield Town) 1959/60, 1961/2, 1962/3, 1963/4, 1964/5, (Everton) 1965/6, 1966/7, 1967/8.
Winterburn, N. (2) (Arsenal) 1989/90, 1992/93.
Wise, D. F. (12) (Chelsea) 1990/91, 1993/94, 1994/95, 1995/96.
Withe, P. (11) (Aston Villa) 1980/1, 1981/2, 1982/3, 1983/4, 1984/5.
Wood, R. (3) (Manchester United) 1954/5, 1955/6.
Woodcock, A. (42) (Nottingham Forest) 1977/8, 1978/9, 1979/80 (FC Cologne) 1980/1, 1981/2, (Arsenal) 1982/3, 1983/4, 1984/5, 1985/6.
Woodgate, J.S. (1) (Leeds United) 1998/99.
Woods, C.C.E. (43) (Norwich City) 1984/5, 1985/6, 1986/7, (Rangers) 1987/8, 1988/9, 1989/90, 1990/1, (Sheffield Wednesday) 1991/2. 1992/93.
Worthington, F. (8) (Leicester City) 1973/4, 1974/5.
Wright, I. E. (33) (Crystal Palace) 1990/1, 1991/2 (Arsenal) 1992/93, 1993/94, 1994/95, 1996/97, 1997/98, (West Ham United) 1998/99.
Wright M. (45) (Southampton) 1983/4, 1984/5, 1985/6, 1986/7, (Derby County) 1987/8, 1988/9, 1989/90, 1990/1, (Liverpool) 1991/2, 1992/93, 1995/96.
Wright, T. (11) (Everton) 1967/8, 1968/9, 1969/70.

Wright, W. (105) (Wolverhampton Wanderers) 1946/7, 1947/8, 1948/9, 1949/50, 1950/1, 1951/2, 1952/3, 1953/4, 1954/5, 1955/6, 1956/7, 1957/8, 1958/9.

Young, G. (1) (Sheffield Wednesday) 1964/5.

NORTHERN IRELAND

Aherne, T. (4) (Belfast Celtic) 1946/7, 1947/8, 1948/9, 1949/50 (Luton Town).
Anderson, T. (22) (Manchester United) 1972/3, 1973/4, 1974/5, (Swindon Town) 1975/6, 1976/7, 1977/8, (Peterborough United) 1978/9.
Armstrong, G. (63) (Tottenham Hotspur) 1976/7, 1977/8, 1978/9, 1979/80, 1980/1, (Watford) 1981/2, 1982/3, (Real Mallorca) 1983/4, 1984/5, (West Bromwich Albion) 1985/6 (Chesterfield).

Barr, H. (3) (Linfield) 1961/2, 1962/3, (Coventry City).
Best, G. (37) (Manchester United) 1963/4, 1964/5, 1965/6, 1966/7, 1967/8, 1968/9, 1969/70, 1970/1 , 1971/2, 1972/3, 1973/4 (Fulham) 1976/7, 1977/8.
Bingham, W. (56) (Sunderland) 1950/1, 1951/2, 1952/3, 1953/4, 1954/5, 1955/6, 1956/7, 1957/8, 1958/9 (Luton Town) 1959/60, 1960/1 (Everton) 1961/2, 1962/3, 1963/4 (Port Vale).
Black, K. (30) (Luton Town) 1987/8, 1988/9, 1989/90, 1990/1, (Nottingham Forest) 1991/2, 1992/93, 1993/94.
Blair, R. (5) (Oldham Athletic) 1974/5, 1975/6.
Blanchflower, D. (54) (Barnsley) 1949/50, 1950/1 (Aston Villa) 1951/2, 1952/3, 1953/4, 1954/5, (Tottenham Hotspur) 1955/6, 1956/7, 1957/8, 1958/9, 1959/60, 1960/1, 1961/2, 1962/3.
Blanchflower, J. (12) (Manchester United) 1953/4, 1954/5, 1955/6, 1956/7, 1957/8.
Bowler, G. (3) (Hull City) 1949/50.
Braithwaite, R. (10) (Linfield) 1961/2, 1962/3 (Middlesbrough) 1963/4, 1964/5.
Brennan, R. (5) (Luton Town) 1948/9, 1949/50 (Birmingham City) (Fulham), 1950/1.
Briggs, R. (2) (Manchester United) 1961/2, 1964/5 (Swansea).
Brotherston, N. (27) (Blackburn Rovers) 1979/80, 1980/1, 1981/2, 1982/3, 1983/4, 1984/5.
Bruce, W. (2) (Glentoran) 1960/1, 1966/7.

Campbell, A. (2) (Crusaders) 1962/3, 1964/5.
Campbell, D. A. (10) (Nottingham Forest) 1985/6, 1986/7, 1987/8 (Charlton Athletic).
Campbell, J. (2) (Fulham) 1950/1.
Campbell, R. M. (2) (Bradford City) 1981/2.
Campbell, W. (6) (Dundee) 1967/8, 1968/9, 1969/70.
Carey, J. (7) (Manchester United) 1946/7, 1947/8, 1948/9.
Carroll, R. E. (2) (Wigan Ath) 1996/97, 1998/99.
Casey, T. (12) (Newcastle United) 1954/5, 1955/6, 1956/7, 1957/8, 1958/9, (Portsmouth).
Caskey, A. (7) (Derby County) 1978/9, 1979/80, 1981/2 (Tulsa Roughnecks).
Cassidy, T. (24) (Newcastle United) 1970/1, 1971/2, 1973/4, 1974/5, 1975/6, 1976/7, 1979/80 (Burnley) 1980/1, 1981/2.
Caughey, M. (2) (Linfield) 1985/6.
Clarke, C. J. (38) (Bournemouth) 1985/6, 1986/7 (Southampton) 1987/8, 1988/9, 1989/90, 1990/1 (Portsmouth), 1991/2, 1992/93.
Cleary, J. (5) (Glentoran) 1981/2, 1982/3, 1983/4, 1984/5.
Clements, D. (48) (Coventry City) 1964/5, 1965/6, 1966/7, 1967/8, 1968/9, 1969/70, 1970/1, 1971/2 (Sheffield Wednesday) 1972/3 (Everton) 1973/4, 1974/5, 1975/6 (New York Cosmos).
Cochrane, D. (10) (Leeds United) 1946/7, 1947/8, 1948/9, 1949/50.

Cochrane, T. (26) (Coleraine) 1975/6, (Burnley) 1977/8, 1978/9, (Middlesbrough) 1979/80, 1980/1, 1981/2, (Gillingham) 1983/4.
Coote, A. (2) (Norwich City) 1998/99.
Cowan, J. (1) (Newcastle United) 1969/70.
Coyle, F. (4) (Coleraine) 1955/6, 1956/7, 1957/8 (Nottingham Forest).
Coyle, L. (1) (Derry C) 1988/9.
Coyle, R. (5) (Sheffield Wednesday) 1972/3, 1973/4.
Craig, D. (25) (Newcastle United) 1966/7, 1967/8, 1968/9, 1969/70, 1970/1, 1971/2, 1972/3, 1973/4, 1974/5.
Crossan, E. (3) (Blackburn Rovers) 1949/50, 1950/1, 1954/5.
Crossan, J. (23) (Rotterdam Sparta) 1959/60, 1962/3 (Sunderland), 1963/4, 1964/5, (Manchester City) 1965/6, 1966/7, 1967/8 (Middlesbrough).
Cunningham, W. (30) (St Mirren) 1950/1, 1952/3, 1953/4, 1954/5, 1955/6, 1956/7, (Leicester City) 1957/8, 1958/9, 1959/60, 1960/1 (Dunfermline Athletic) 1961/2.
Cush, W. (26) (Glentoran) 1950/1, 1953/4, 1956/7, 1957/8 (Leeds United) 1958/9, 1959/60, 1960/1 (Portadown) 1961/2.

D'Arcy, S. (5) (Chelsea) 1951/2, 1952/3 (Brentford).
Davison, A. J. (3) (Bolton Wanderers) 1995/96 (Bradford City) 1996/97 (Grimsby Town) 1997/98.
Dennison, R. (18) (Wolverhampton Wanderers) 1987/8, 1988/9, 1989/90, 1990/1, 1991/2, 1992/93, 1993/94, 1996/97.
Devine, J. (1) (Glentoran) 1989/90.
Dickson, D. (4) (Coleraine) 1969/70, 1972/3.
Dickson, T. (1) (Linfield) 1956/7.
Dickson, W. (12) (Chelsea) 1950/1, 1951/2, 1952/3 (Arsenal) 1953/4, 1954/5.
Doherty, L. (2) (Linfield) 1984/5, 1987/8.
Doherty, P. (6) (Derby County) 1946/7, (Huddersfield Town) 1947/8, 1948/9, (Doncaster Rovers) 1950/1.
Donaghy, M. (91) (Luton Town) 1979/80, 1980/1, 1981/2, 1982/3, 1983/4, 1984/5, 1985/6, 1986/7, 1987/8, (Manchester United) 1988/9, 1989/90, 1990/1, 1991/2 (Chelsea) 1992/93, 1993/94.
Dougan, D. (43) (Portsmouth) 1957/8, 1959/60, (Blackburn Rovers), 1960/1, 1962/3 (Aston Villa) 1965/6 (Leicester City), 1966/7 (Wolverhampton Wanderers) 1967/8, 1968/9, 1969/70, 1970/1, 1971/2, 1972/3.
Douglas, J. P. (1) (Belfast Celtic) 1946/7.
Dowd, H. (3) (Glentoran) 1972/3, 1974/5 (Sheffield Wednesday).
Dowie, I. (56) (Luton Town) 1989/90, 1990/1 (West Ham United) (Southampton) 1991/2, 1992/93, 1993/94, 1994/95 (Crystal Palace) 1995/96 (West Ham United) 1996/97 (Queens Park Rangers) 1997/98, 1998/99.
Dunlop, G. (4) (Linfield) 1984/5, 1986/7.

Eglington, T. (6) (Everton) 1946/7, 1947/8, 1948/9.
Elder, A. (40) (Burnley) 1959/60, 1960/1, 1961/2, 1962/3, 1963/4, 1964/5, 1965/6, 1966/7, (Stoke City) 1967/8, 1968/9, 1969/70.

Farrell, P. (7) (Everton) 1946/7, 1947/8, 1948/9.
Feeney, J. (2) (Linfield) 1946/7 (Swansea City) 1949/50.
Feeney, W. (1) (Glentoran) 1975/6.
Ferguson, G. (1) (Linfield) 1998/99.
Ferguson, W. (2) (Linfield) 1965/6, 1966/7.
Ferris, R. (3) (Birmingham City) 1949/50, 1950/1, 1951/2.
Fettis, A. (25) (Hull City) 1991/2, 1992/93, 1993/94, 1994/95, (Nottingham Forest) 1995/96, 1996/97 (Blackburn Rovers) 1997/98, 1998/99.
Finney, T. (14) (Sunderland) 1974/5, 1975/6 (Cambridge United), 1979/80.

Fleming, J. G. (31) (Nottingham Forest) 1986/7, 1987/8, 1988/9 (Manchester City) 1989/90, 1990/1 (Barnsley), 1991/2, 1992/93, 1993/94, 1994/95.
Forde, T. (4) (Ards) 1958/9, 1960/1.

Gallogly, C. (2) (Huddersfield Town) 1950/1.
Garton, R. (1) (Oxford United) 1968/9.
Gillespie, K. R. (26) (Manchester United) 1994/95 (Newcastle United) 1995/96, 1996/97, 1997/98, (Blackburn R) 1998/99.
Gorman, W. (4) (Brentford) 1946/7, 1947/8.
Graham, W. (14) (Doncaster Rovers) 1950/1, 1951/2, 1952/3, 1953/4, 1954/5, 1955/6, 1958/9.
Gray, P. (21) (Luton Town) 1992/93, (Sunderland) 1993/94, 1994/95, 1995/96 (Nancy) 1996/97, (Luton Town) 1998/99.
Gregg, H. (25) (Doncaster Rovers) 1953/4, 1956/7, 1957/8, (Manchester United) 1958/9, 1959/60, 1960/1, 1961/2, 1963/4.
Griffin, D. J. (9) (St Johnstone) 1995/96, 1996/97, 1997/98, 1998/99.

Hamill, R. (1) (Glentoran) 1998/99.
Hamilton, B. (50) (Linfield) 1968/9, 1970/1, 1971/2 (Ipswich Town), 1972/3, 1973/4, 1974/5, 1975/6 (Everton) 1976/7, 1977/8, (Millwall), 1978/9, (Swindon Town) 1979–80.
Hamilton, W. (41) (QPR) 1977/8, 1979/80 (Burnley) 1980/1, 1981/2, 1982/3, 1983/4, 1984/5, (Oxford United) 1985/6.
Harkin, T. (5) (Southport) 1967/8, 1968/9 (Shrewsbury Town), 1969/70, 1970/1.
Harvey, M. (34) (Sunderland) 1960/1, 1961/2, 1962/3, 1963/4, 1964/5, 1965/6, 1966/7, 1967/8, 1968/9, 1969/70, 1970/1.
Hatton, S. (2) (Linfield) 1962/3.
Healy, F. (4) (Coleraine) 1981/2 (Glentoran) 1982/3.
Hegan, D. (7) (West Bromwich Albion) 1969/70, 1971/2 (Wolverhampton Wanderers) 1972/3.
Hill, C. F. (27) (Sheffield United), 1989/90, 1990/1, 1991/2, 1994/95 (Leicester City) 1995/96, 1996/97 (Trelleborg) (Northampton Town) 1997/98, 1998/99.
Hill, J. (7) (Norwich City) 1958/9, 1959/60, 1960/1, (Everton) 1961/2, 1963/4.
Hinton, E. (7) (Fulham) 1946/7, 1947/8 (Millwall) 1950/1.
Horlock, K. (17) (Swindon Town), 1994/95 (Manchester City) 1996/97, 1997/98, 1998/99.
Hughes, A. W. (8) (Newcastle United) 1997/98, 1998/99.
Hughes, M. E. (47) (Manchester City) 1991/2 (Strasbourg) 1992/93, 1993/94, 1994/95, 1995/96 (West Ham United) 1996/97 (Wimbledon) 1997/98, 1998/99.
Hughes, P. (3) (Bury) 1986/7.
Hughes, W. (1) (Bolton Wanderers) 1950/1.
Humphries, W. (14) (Ards) 1961/2 (Coventry City) 1962/3, 1963/4, 1964/5 (Swansea Town).
Hunter, A. (53) (Blackburn Rovers) 1969/70, 1970/1, 1971/2 (Ipswich Town) 1972/3, 1973/4, 1974/5, 1975/6, 1976/7, 1977/8, 1978/9, 1979/80.
Hunter, B. V. (13) (Wrexham) 1994/95, 1995/96 (Reading) 1996/97, 1998/99.

Irvine, R. (8) (Linfield) 1961/2, 1962/3 (Stoke City) 1964/5.
Irvine, W. (23) (Burnley) 1962/3, 1964/5, 1965/6, 1966/7, 1967/8, 1968/9 (Preston North End) (Brighton & Hove Albion) 1971/2.

Jackson, T. (35) (Everton) 1968/9, 1969/70, 1970/1 (Nottingham Forest) 1971/2, 1972/3, 1973/4, 1974/5 (Manchester United) 1975/6, 1976/7.
Jamison, A. (1) (Glentoran) 1975/6.
Jenkins, I. (5) (Chester City) 1996/97 (Dundee United) 1997/98.

Jennings, P. (119) (Watford) 1963/4, 1964/5, (Tottenham Hotspur) 1965/6, 1966/7, 1967/8, 1968/9, 1969/70, 1970/1, 1971/2, 1972/3, 1973/4, 1974/5, 1975/6, 1976/7, (Arsenal) 1977/8, 1978/9, 1979/80, 1980/1, 1981/2, 1982/3, 1983/4, 1984/5, (Tottenham Hotspur) 1985/6 (Everton)(Tottenham Hotspur).
Johnson, D.M. (1) (Blackburn Rovers) 1998/99.
Johnston, W. (1) (Glentoran) 1961/2, (Oldham Athletic) 1965/6.
Jones, J. (3) (Glenavon) 1955/6, 1956/7.

Keane, T. (1) (Swansea Town) 1948/9.
Kee, P. V. (9) (Oxford United), 1989/90, 1990/91, (Ards) 1994/95.
Keith, R. (23) (Newcastle United) 1957/8, 1958/9, 1959/60, 1960/1, 1961/2.
Kelly, H. (4) (Fulham) 1949/50 (Southampton) 1950/1.
Kelly, P. (1) (Barnsley) 1949/50.
Kennedy, P.H. (2) (Watford) 1998/99.

Lawther, I. (4) (Sunderland) 1959/60, 1960/1, 1961/2 (Blackburn Rovers).
Lennon, N. F. (27) (Crewe Alexandra) 1993/94, 1994/95, (Leicester City) 1995/96, 1996/97, 1997/98, 1998/99.
Lockhart, N. (8) (Linfield) 1946/7, 1949/50, (Coventry City) 1950/1, 1951/2, 1953/4, (Aston Villa) 1954/5, 1955/6.
Lomas, S. M. (30) (Manchester City) 1993/94, 1994/95, 1995/96 (West Ham United) 1996/97, 1997/98, 1998/99.
Lutton, B. (6) (Wolverhampton Wanderers) 1969/70, 1972/3 (West Ham United) 1973/4.

Magill, E. (26) (Arsenal) 1961/2, 1962/3, 1963/4, 1964/5, 1965/6 (Brighton & Hove Albion).
Magilton, J. (39) (Oxford United) 1990/1, 1991/2, 1992/93, (Southampton) 1993/94, 1994/95, 1995/96, 1996/97 (Sheffield Wednesday) 1997/98.
Martin, C. (6) (Glentoran) 1946/7, 1947/8 (Leeds United) 1948/9 (Aston Villa) 1949/50.
McAdams, W. (15) (Manchester City) 1953/4, 1954/5, 1956/7, 1957/8, 1960/1 (Bolton Wanderers) 1961/2 (Leeds United).
McAlinden, J. (2) (Portsmouth) 1946/7, 1948/9, (Southend United).
McBride, S. (4) (Glenavon) 1990/1, 1991/2.
McCabe, J. (6) (Leeds United) 1948/9, 1949/50, 1950/1, 1952/3, 1953/4.
McCarthy, J. D. (12) (Port Vale) 1995/96, 1996/97 (Birmingham City) 1997/98, 1998/99.
McCavana, T. (3) (Coleraine) 1954/5, 1955/6.
McCleary, J. W. (1) (Cliftonville) 1954/5.
McClelland, J. (6) (Arsenal) 1960/1, 1965/6 (Fulham).
McClelland, J. (53) (Mansfield Town) 1979/80, 1980/1, 1981/2 (Rangers) 1982/3, 1983/4, 1984/5 (Watford) 1985/6, 1986/7, 1987/8, 1988/9 (Leeds U) 1989/90.
McCourt, F. (6) (Manchester City) 1951/2, 1952/3.
McCoy, R. (1) (Coleraine) 1986/7.
McCreery, D. (67) (Manchester United) 1975/6, 1976/7, 1977/8, 1978/9, 1979/80 (QPR) 1980/1 (Tulsa Roughnecks) 1981/2, 1982/3 (Newcastle United), 1983/4, 1984/5, 1985/6, 1986/7, 1987/8, 1988/9 (Hearts) 1989/90.
McCrory, S. (1) (Southend United) 1957/8.
McCullough, W. (10) (Arsenal) 1960/1, 1962/3, 1963/4, 1964/5, 1966/7, (Millwall).
McCurdy, C. (1) (Linfield) 1979/80.
McDonald, A. (52) (QPR) 1985/6, 1986/7, 1987/8, 1988/9, 1990/1, 1991/2, 1992/93, 1993/94, 1994/95, 1995/96.
McElhinney, G. (6) (Bolton Wanderers) 1983/4, 1984/5.
McFaul, I. (6) (Linfield) 1966/7, 1969/70 (Newcastle United) 1970/1, 1971/2, 1972/3, 1973/4.
McGarry, J. K. (3) (Cliftonville) 1950/1.

McGaughey, M. (1) (Linfield) 1984/5.
McGibbon, P.C.G. (6) (Manchester United) 1994/95, 1995/96, 1996/97 (Wigan Athletic) 1997/98.
McGrath, R. (21) (Tottenham Hotspur) 1973/4, 1974/5, 1975/6 (Manchester United) 1976/7, 1977/8, 1978/9.
McIlroy, J. (55) (Burnley) 1951/2, 1952/3, 1953/4, 1954/5, 1955/6, 1956/7, 1957/8, 1958/9, 1959/60, 1960/1, 1961/2, 1962/3, 1965/6 (Stoke City).
McIlroy, S. B. (88) (Manchester United) 1971/2, 1973/4, 1974/5, 1975/6, 1976/7, 1977/8, 1978/9, 1979/80, 1980/1, 1981/2, (Stoke City), 1982/3, 1983/4, 1984/5 (Manchester City) 1985/6, 1986/7.
McKeag, W. (2) (Glentoran) 1967/8.
McKenna, J. (7) (Huddersfield Town) 1949/50, 1950/1, 1951/2.
McKenzie, R. (1) (Airdrieonians) 1966/7.
McKinney, W. (1) (Falkirk) 1965/6.
McKnight, A. (10) (Celtic) 1987/8, (West Ham United) 1988/9.
McLaughlin, J. (12) (Shrewsbury Town) 1961/2, 1962/3 (Swansea Town), 1963/4, 1964/5, 1965/6.
McMahon, G. J. (17) (Tottenham Hotspur) 1994/95, 1995/96 (Stoke City) 1996/97, 1997/98.
McMichael, A. (39) (Newcastle United) 1949/50, 1950/1, 1951/2, 1952/3, 1953/4, 1954/5, 1955/6, 1956/7, 1957/8, 1958/9, 1959/60.
McMillan, S. (2) (Manchester United) 1962/3.
McMordie, E. (21) (Middlesbrough) 1968/9, 1969/70, 1970/1, 1971/2, 1972/3.
McMorran, E. (15) (Belfast Celtic) 1946/7 (Barnsley) 1950/1, 1951/2, 1952/3, (Doncaster Rovers) 1953/4, 1955/6, 1956/7.
McNally, B. A. (5) (Shrewsbury Town) 1985/6, 1986/7, 1987/8.
McParland, P. (34) (Aston Villa) 1953/4, 1954/5, 1955/6, 1956/7, 1957/8, 1958/9, 1959/60, 1960/1, 1961/2 (Wolverhampton Wanderers).
McVeigh, P. (1) (Tottenham Hotspur) 1998/99.
Montgomery, F. J. (1) (Coleraine) 1954/5.
Moore, C. (1) (Glentoran) 1948/9.
Moreland, V. (6) (Derby County) 1978/9, 1979/80.
Morgan, S. (18) (Port Vale) 1971/2, 1972/3, 1973/4 (Aston Villa), 1974/5, 1975/6 (Brighton & Hove Albion) (Sparta Rotterdam) 1978/9.
Morrow, S. J. (37) (Arsenal) 1989/90, 1990/1, 1991/2, 1992/93, 1993/94, 1994/95, 1995/96 (Queens Park Rangers) 1996/97, 1997/98, 1998/99.
Mullan, G. (4) (Glentoran) 1982/3.
Mulryne, P. P. (8) (Manchester United) 1996/97, 1997/98, (Norwich City) 1998/99.

Napier, R. (1) (Bolton Wanderers) 1965/6.
Neill, T. (59) (Arsenal) 1960/1, 1961/2, 1962/3, 1963/4, 1964/5, 1965/6, 1966/7, 1967/8, 1968/9, 1969/70 (Hull City) 1970/1, 1971/2, 1972/3.
Nelson, S. (51) (Arsenal) 1969/70, 1970/1, 1971/2, 1972/3, 1973/4, 1974/5, 1975/6, 1976/7, 1977/8, 1978/9, 1979/80, 1980/1, 1981/2 (Brighton & Hove Albion).
Nicholl, C. (51) (Aston Villa) 1974/5, 1975/6, 1976/7 (Southampton), 1977/8, 1978/9, 1979/80, 1980/1, 1981/2, 1982/3 (Grimsby Town) 1983/4.
Nicholl, J. M. (73) (Manchester United) 1975/6, 1976/7, 1977/8, 1978/9, 1979/80, 1980/1, 1981/2 (Toronto Blizzard) 1982/3 (Sunderland) (Toronto Blizzard) (Rangers) 1983/4 (Toronto Blizzard) 1984/5 (West Bromwich Albion) 1985/6.
Nicholson, J. (41) (Manchester United) 1960/1, 1961/2, 1962/3, 1964/5, (Huddersfield Town) 1965/6, 1966/7, 1967/8, 1968/9, 1969/70, 1970/1, 1971/2.
Nolan, I. R. (7) (Sheffield Wednesday) 1996/97, 1997/98.

O'Boyle, G. (13) (Dunfermline Athletic) 1993/94 (St Johnstone) 1994/95, 1995/96, 1996/97, 1997/98, 1998/99.

O'Doherty, A. (2) (Coleraine) 1969/70.
O'Driscoll, J. (3) (Swansea City) 1948/9.
O'Kane, L. (20) (Nottingham Forest) 1969/70, 1970/1, 1971/2, 1972/3, 1973/4, 1974/5.
O'Neill, C. (3) (Motherwell) 1988/9, 1989/90, 1990/91.
O'Neill, J. (1) (Sunderland) 1961/2.
O'Neill, J. P. (39) (Leicester City) 1979/80, 1980/1, 1981/2, 1982/3, 1983/4, 1984/5, 1985/6.
O'Neill, M. A. (31) (Newcastle United) 1987/8, 1988/9 (Dundee United) 1989/90, 1990/1, 1991/2, 1992/93, (Hibernian) 1993/94, 1994/95, 1995/96 (Coventry City) 1996/97.
O'Neill, M. H. M. (64) (Distillery) 1971/2 (Nottingham Forest) 1972/3, 1973/4, 1974/5, 1975/6, 1976/7, 1977/8, 1978/9, 1979/80, 1980/1 (Norwich City) 1981/2 (Manchester City) (Norwich City) 1982/3 (Notts County) 1983/4, 1984/5.

Parke, J. (13) (Linfield) 1963/4 (Hibernian), 1964/5 (Sunderland), 1965/6, 1966/7, 1967/8.
Patterson, D. J. (17) (Crystal Palace) 1993/94, 1994/95, (Luton Town) 1995/96, 1997/98, (Dundee United) 1998/99.
Peacock, R. (31) (Celtic) 1951/2, 1952/3, 1953/4, 1954/5, 1955/6, 1956/7, 1957/8, 1958/9, 1959/60, 1960/1 (Coleraine) 1961/2.
Penney, S. (17) (Brighton & Hove Albion) 1984/5, 1985/6, 1986/7, 1987/8, 1988/9.
Platt, J. A. (23) (Middlesbrough) 1975/6, 1977/8, 1979/80, 1980/1, 1981/2, 1982/3, (Ballymena United) 1983/4 (Coleraine) 1985/6.

Quinn, J. M. (46) (Blackburn Rovers) 1984/5, 1985/6, 1986/7 (Swindon Town) 1987/8 (Leicester City) 1988/9 (Bradford City) 1989/90 (West Ham United), 1990/1, (Bournemouth) 1991/2 (Reading) 1992/93, 1993/94, 1994/95, 1995/96.
Quinn, S. J. (15) (Blackpool) 1995/96, 1996/97 (West Bromwich Albion) 1997/98, 1998/99.

Rafferty, P. (1) (Linfield) 1979/80.
Ramsey, P. (14) (Leicester City) 1983/4, 1984/5, 1985/6, 1986/7, 1987/8, 1988/9.
Rice, P. (49) (Arsenal) 1968/9, 1969/70, 1970/1, 1971/2, 1972/3, 1973/4, 1974/5, 1975/6, 1976/7, 1977/8, 1978/9, 1979/80.
Robinson, S. (3) (Bournemouth) 1996/97, 1998/99.
Rogan, A. (18) (Celtic) 1987/8, 1988/9, 1989/90, 1990/1 (Sunderland) 1991/2 (Millwall) 1996/97.
Ross, E. (1) (Newcastle United) 1968/9.
Rowland, K. (19) (West Ham United) 1994/95, 1995/96, 1996/97, 1997/98, 1998/99.
Russell, A. (1) (Linfield) 1946/7.
Ryan, R. (1) (West Bromwich Albion) 1949/50.

Sanchez, L. P. (3) (Wimbledon) 1986/7, 1988/9.
Scott, J. (2) (Grimsby Town) 1957/8.
Scott, P. (10) (Everton) 1974/5, 1975/6, (York City) 1977/8, (Aldershot) 1978/9.
Sharkey, P. (1) (Ipswich Town) 1975/6.
Shields, J. (1) (Southampton) 1956/7.
Simpson, W. (12) (Rangers) 1950/1, 1953/4, 1954/5, 1956/7, 1957/8, 1958/9.
Sloan, D. (2) (Oxford) 1968/9, 1970/1.
Sloan, T. (3) (Manchester United) 1978/9.
Sloan, W. (1) (Arsenal) 1946/7.
Smyth, S. (9) (Wolverhampton Wanderers) 1947/8, 1948/9, 1949/50 (Stoke City) 1951/2.
Smyth, W. (4) (Distillery) 1948/9, 1953/4.
Sonner, D. J. (3) (Ipswich Town) 1997/98 (Sheffield Wednesday) 1998/99.

Spence, D. (29) (Bury) 1974/5, 1975/6, (Blackpool) 1976/7, 1978/9, 1979/80, (Southend United) 1980/1, 1981/2.
Stevenson, A. (3) (Everton) 1946/7, 1947/8.
Stewart, A. (7) (Glentoran) 1966/7, 1967/8 (Derby County) 1968/9.
Stewart, D. (1) (Hull City) 1977/8.
Stewart, I. (31) (QPR) 1981/2, 1982/3, 1983/4, 1984/5, (Newcastle United) 1985/6, 1986/7.
Stewart, T. (1) (Linfield) 1960/1.

Taggart, G. P. (45) (Barnsley) 1989/90, 1990/1, 1991/2, 1992/93, 1993/94, 1994/95 (Bolton Wanderers) 1996/97, 1997/98.
Taylor, M. S. (4) (Fulham) 1998/99.
Todd, S. (11) (Burnley) 1965/6, 1966/7, 1967/8, 1968/9, 1969/70 (Sheffield Wednesday) 1970/1.
Trainor, D. (1) (Crusaders) 1966/7.
Tully, C. (10) (Celtic) 1948/9, 1949/50, 1951/2, 1952/3, 1953/4, 1955/6, 1958/9.

Uprichard, N. (18) (Swindon Town) 1951/2, 1952/3 (Portsmouth) 1954/5, 1955/6, 1957/8, 1958/9.

Vernon, J. (17) (Belfast Celtic) 1946/7 (West Bromwich Albion) 1947/8, 1948/9, 1949/50, 1950/1 , 1951/2.

Walker, J. (1) (Doncaster Rovers) 1954/5.
Walsh, D. (9) (West Bromwich Albion) 1946/7, 1947/8, 1948/9, 1949/50.
Walsh, W. (5) (Manchester City) 1947/8, 1948/9.
Watson, P. (1) (Distillery) 1970/1.
Welsh, S. (4) (Carlisle United) 1965/6, 1966/7.
Whiteside, N. (38) (Manchester United) 1981/2, 1982/3, 1983/4, 1984/5, 1985/6, 1986/7, 1987/8, (Everton) 1989/90.
Whitley, Jeff (3) (Manchester City) 1996/97, 1997/98.
Whitley, Jim (2) (Manchester City) 1997/98, 1998/99.
Williams, M. S. (4) (Chesterfield) 1998/99.
Williams, P. (1) (WBA) 1990/1.
Wilson, D. J. (24) (Brighton & Hove Albion) 1986/7 (Luton Town) 1987/8, 1988/9, 1989/90, 1990/1, (Sheffield Wednesday) 1991/2.
Wilson, K. J. (42) (Ipswich Town) 1986/7 (Chelsea) 1987/8, 1988/9, 1989/90, 1990/1, 1991/2 (Notts County) 1992/93, 1993/94 (Walsall) 1994/95.
Wilson, S. (12) (Glenavon) 1961/2, 1963/4, (Falkirk) 1964/5 (Dundee), 1965/6, 1966/7, 1967/8.
Wood, T. J. (1) (Walsall) 1995/96.
Worthington, N. (66) (Sheffield Wednesday) 1983/4, 1984/5, 1985/6, 1986/7, 1987/8, 1988/9, 1989/90, 1990/1, 1991/2, 1992/93, 1993/94 (Leeds United) 1994/95, 1995/96 (Stoke City) 1996/97.
Wright, T. J. (30) (Newcastle United) 1988/9, 1989/90, 1991/2, 1992/93 (Nottingham Forest) 1993/94 (Manchester City) 1996/97, 1997/98, 1998/99.

SCOTLAND
Aird, J. (4) (Burnley) 1953/4.
Aitken, G. G. (8) (East Fife) 1948/9, 1949/50, 1952/3 (Sunderland) 1953/4.
Aitken, R. (57) (Celtic) 1979/80, 1982/3, 1983/4, 1984/5, 1985/6, 1986/7, 1987/8, (Newcastle United) 1989/90, (St Mirren) 1991/2.
Albiston, A. (14) (Manchester United) 1981/2, 1983/4, 1984/5, 1985/6.
Allan, T. (2) (Dundee) 1973/4.
Anderson, J. (1) (Leicester City) 1953/4.

Archibald, S. (27) (Aberdeen) 1979/80 (Tottenham Hotspur) 1980/1, 1981/2, 1982/3, 1983/4, 1984/5, (Barcelona) 1985/6.
Auld, B. (3) (Celtic) 1958/9, 1959/60.

Baird, H. (1) (Airdrieonians) 1955/6.
Baird, S. (7) (Rangers) 1956/7, 1957/8.
Bannon, E. (11) (Dundee United) 1979/80, 1982/3, 1983/4, 1985/6.
Bauld, W. (3) (Heart of Midlothian) 1949/50.
Baxter, J. (34) (Rangers) 1960/1, 1961/2, 1962/3, 1963/4, 1964/5 (Sunderland) 1965/6, 1966/7, 1967/8.
Bell, W. (2) (Leeds United) 1965/6.
Bernard, P. R.(2) (Oldham Athletic) 1994/95.
Bett, J. (25) (Rangers) 1981/2, 1982/3 (Lokeren) 1983/4, 1984/5 (Aberdeen) 1985/6, 1986/7, 1987/8, 1988/9, 1989/90.
Black, E. (2) (Metz) 1987/8.
Black, I. (1) (Southampton) 1947/8.
Blacklaw, A. (3) (Burnley) 1962/3, 1965/6.
Blackley, J. (7) (Hibernian) 1973/4, 1975/6, 1976/7.
Blair, J. (1) (Blackpool) 1946/7.
Blyth, J. (2) (Coventry City) 1977/8.
Bone, J. (2) (Norwich City) 1971/2, 1972/3.
Booth, S. (17) (Aberdeen) 1992/93, 1993/94, 1994/95, 1995/96 (Borussia Dortmund) 1997/98.
Bowman, D. (6) (Dundee United) 1991/2, 1992/93, 1993/94.
Boyd, T. (65) (Motherwell) 1990/1 (Chelsea) 1991/2 (Celtic) 1992/93, 1993/94, 1994/95, 1995/96, 1996/97, 1997/98, 1998/99.
Brand, R. (8) (Rangers) 1960/1, 1961/2.
Brazil, A. (13) (Ipswich Town) 1979/80, 1981/2, 1982/3 (Tottenham Hotspur).
Bremner, D. (1) (Hibernian) 1975/6.
Bremner, W. (54) (Leeds United) 1964/5, 1965/6, 1966/7, 1967/8, 1968/9, 1969/70, 1970/1, 1971/2, 1972/3, 1973/4, 1974/5, 1975/6.
Brennan, F. (7) (Newcastle United) 1946/7, 1952/3, 1963/4.
Brogan, J. (4) (Celtic) 1970/1.
Brown, A. (14) (East Fife) 1949/50 (Blackpool) 1951/2, 1952/3, 1953/4.
Brown, H. (3) (Partick Thistle) 1946/7.
Brown, J. (1) (Sheffield United) 1974/5.
Brown, R. (3) (Rangers) 1946/7, 1948/9, 1951/2.
Brown, W. (28) (Dundee) 1957/8, 1958/9, 1959/60 (Tottenham Hotspur) 1961/2, 1962/3, 1963/4, 1964/5, 1965/6.
Brownlie, J. (7) (Hibernian) 1970/1, 1971/2, 1972/3, 1975/6.
Buchan, M. (34) (Aberdeen) 1971/2 (Manchester United), 1972/3, 1973/4, 1974/5, 1975/6, 1976/7, 1977/8, 1978/9.
Buckley, P. (3) (Aberdeen) 1953/4, 1954/5.
Burley, C. W. (30) (Chelsea) 1994/95, 1995/96, 1996/97 (Celtic) 1997/98, 1998/99.
Burley, G. (11) (Ipswich Town) 1978/9, 1979/80, 1981/2.
Burns, F. (1) (Manchester United) 1969/70.
Burns, K. (20) (Birmingham City) 1973/4, 1974/5, 1976/7 (Nottingham Forest) 1977/8, 1978/9, 1979/80, 1980/1.
Burns, T. (8) (Celtic) 1980/1, 1981/2, 1982/3, 1987/8.

Calderwood, C. (34) (Tottenham Hotspur) 1994/95, 1995/96, 1996/97, 1997/98, (Aston Villa) 1998/99.
Caldow, E. (40) (Rangers) 1956/7, 1957/8, 1958/9, 1959/60, 1960/1, 1961/2, 1962/3.
Callaghan, W. (2) (Dunfermline) 1969/70.
Cameron, C. (2) (Heart of Midlothian) 1998/99.
Campbell, R. (5) (Falkirk) 1946/7 (Chelsea) 1949/50.

Campbell, W. (5) (Morton) 1946/7, 1947/8.
Carr, W. (6) (Coventry City) 1969/70, 1970/1, 1971/2, 1972/3.
Chalmers, S. (5) (Celtic) 1964/5, 1965/6, 1966/7.
Clark, J. (4) (Celtic) 1965/6, 1966/7.
Clark, R. (17) (Aberdeen) 1967/8, 1969/70, 1970/1, 1971/2, 1972/3.
Clarke, S. (6) (Chelsea) 1987/8, 1993/94.
Collins, J. (53) (Hibernian) 1987/8, 1989/90, 1990/1 (Celtic) 1991/2, 1992/93, 1993/94, 1994/95, 1995/96 (Monaco) 1996/97, 1997/98, (Everton) 1998/99.
Collins, R. (31) (Celtic) 1950/1, 1954/5, 1955/6, 1956/7, 1957/8, 1958/9, (Everton) 1964/5, (Leeds United).
Colquhoun, E. (9) (Sheffield United) 1971/2, 1972/3.
Colquhoun, J. (1) (Hearts) 1987/8.
Combe, R. (3) (Hibernian) 1947/8.
Conn, A. (1) (Heart of Midlothian) 1955/6.
Conn, A. (2) (Tottenham Hotspur) 1974/5.
Connachan, E. (2) (Dunfermline Athletic) 1961/2.
Connelly, G. (2) (Celtic) 1973/4.
Connolly, J. (1) (Everton) 1972/3.
Connor, R. (4) (Dundee) 1985/6 (Aberdeen) 1987/8, 1988/9, 1990/91.
Cooke, C. (16) (Dundee) 1965/6 (Chelsea) 1967/8, 1968/9, 1969/70, 1970/1, 1974/5.
Cooper, D. (22) (Rangers) 1979/80, 1983/4, 1984/5, 1985/6, 1986/7 (Motherwell) 1989/90.
Cormack, P. (9) (Hibernian) 1965/6, 1969/70 (Nottingham Forest) 1970/1, 1971/2.
Cowan, J. (25) (Morton) 1947/8, 1948/9, 1949/50, 1950/1, 1951/2 (Motherwell).
Cowie, D. (20) (Dundee) 1952/3, 1953/4, 1954/5, 1955/6, 1956/7, 1957/8.
Cox, C. (1) (Hearts) 1947/8.
Cox, S. (24) (Rangers) 1947/8, 1948/9, 1949/50, 1950/1, 1951/2, 1952/3, 1953/4.
Craig, J. (1) (Celtic) 1976/7.
Craig, J. P. (1) (Celtic) 1967/8.
Craig, T. (1) (Newcastle United) 1975/6.
Crawford, S. (1) (Raith Rovers) 1994/95.
Crerand, P. (16) (Celtic) 1960/1, 1961/2, 1962/3 (Manchester United) 1963/4, 1964/5, 1965/6.
Cropley, A. (2) (Hibernian) 1971/2.
Cruickshank, J. (6) (Heart of Midlothian) 1963/4, 1969/70, 1970/1, 1975/6.
Cullen, M. (1) (Luton Town) 1955/6.
Cumming, J. (9) (Heart of Midlothian) 1954/5, 1959/60.
Cunningham, W. (8) (Preston North End) 1953/4, 1954/5.
Curran, H. (5) (Wolverhampton Wanderers) 1969/70, 1970/1.

Dailly, C. (14) (Derby County) 1996/97, 1997/98, (Blackburn Rovers) 1998/99.
Dalglish, K. (102) (Celtic) 1971/2, 1972/3, 1973/4, 1974/5, 1975/6, 1976/7, (Liverpool) 1977/8, 1978/9, 1979/80, 1980/1, 1981/2, 1982/3, 1983/4, 1984/5, 1985/6, 1986/7.
Davidson, C.I. (7) (Blackburn Rovers) 1998/99.
Davidson, J. (8) (Partick Thistle) 1953/4, 1954/5.
Dawson, A. (5) (Rangers) 1979/80, 1982/3.
Deans, D. (2) (Celtic) 1974/5.
Delaney, J. (4) (Manchester United) 1946/7, 1947/8.
Dick, J. (1) (West Ham United) 1958/9.
Dickson, W. (5) (Kilmarnock) 1969/70, 1970/1.
Docherty, T. (25) (Preston North End) 1951/2, 1952/3, 1953/4, 1954/5, 1956/7, 1957/8, 1958/9 (Arsenal).
Dodds, D. (2) (Dundee United) 1983/4.
Dodds, W. (9) (Aberdeen) 1996/97, 1997/98, (Dundee United) 1998/99.

Donachie, W. (35) (Manchester City) 1971/2, 1972/3, 1973/4, 1975/6, 1976/7, 1977/8, 1978/9.
Donnelly, S. (10) (Celtic) 1996/97, 1997/98, 1998/99.
Dougall, C. (1) (Birmingham City) 1946/7.
Dougan, R. (1) (Heart of Midlothian) 1949/50.
Doyle, J. (1) (Ayr United) 1975/6.
Duncan, A. (6) (Hibernian) 1974/5, 1975/6.
Duncan, D. (3) (East Fife) 1947/8.
Duncanson, J. (1) (Rangers) 1946/7.
Durie, G. S. (43) (Chelsea) 1987/8, 1988/9, 1989/90, 1990/1, (Tottenham Hotspur) 1991/2, 1992/93, (Rangers) 1993/94, 1995/96, 1996/97, 1997/98.
Durrant, I. (16) (Rangers) 1987/8, 1988/9, 1992/93, 1993/94, (Kilmarnock) 1998/99.

Elliott, M. S. (7) (Leicester City) 1997/98, 1998/99.
Evans, A. (4) (Aston Villa) 1981/2.
Evans, R. (48) (Celtic) 1948/9, 1949/50, 1950/1, 1951/2, 1952/3, 1953/4, 1954/5, 1955/6, 1956/7, 1957/8, 1958/9, 1959/60 (Chelsea).
Ewing, T. (2) (Partick Thistle) 1957/8.

Farm, G. (10) (Blackpool) 1952/3, 1953/4, 1958/9.
Ferguson, B. (1) (Rangers) 1998/99.
Ferguson, D. (2) (Rangers) 1987/8.
Ferguson, D. (7) (Dundee United) 1991/2, 1992/93 (Everton) 1994/95, 1996/97.
Ferguson, I. (9) (Rangers) 1988/9, 1992/93, 1993/94, 1996/97.
Ferguson, R. (7) (Kilmarnock) 1965/6, 1966/7.
Fernie, W. (12) (Celtic) 1953/4, 1954/5, 1956/7, 1957/8.
Flavell, R. (2) (Airdrieonians) 1946/7.
Fleck, R. (4) (Norwich City) 1989/90, 1990/1.
Fleming, C. (1) (East Fife) 1953/4.
Forbes, A. (14) (Sheffield United) 1946/7, 1947/8 (Arsenal) 1949/50, 1950/1, 1951/2.
Ford, D. (3) (Heart of Midlothian) 1973/4.
Forrest, J. (1) (Motherwell) 1957/8.
Forrest, J. (5) (Rangers) 1965/6 (Aberdeen) 1970/1.
Forsyth, A. (10) (Partick Thistle) 1971/2, 1972/3 (Manchester United) 1974/5, 1975/6.
Forsyth, C. (4) (Kilmarnock) 1963/4, 1964/5.
Forsyth, T. (22) (Motherwell) 1970/1 (Rangers) 1973/4, 1975/6, 1976/7, 1977/8.
Fraser, D. (2) (West Bromwich Albion) 1967/8, 1968/9.
Fraser, W. (2) (Sunderland) 1954/5.

Gabriel, J. (2) (Everton) 1960/1, 1961/2.
Gallacher, K. W. (43) (Dundee United) 1987/8, 1988/9, 1990/91 (Coventry City), 1991/2 (Blackburn Rovers) 1992/93, 1993/94, 1995/96, 1996/97, 1997/98, 1998/99.
Galloway, M. (1) (Celtic) 1991/2.
Gardiner, W. (1) (Motherwell) 1957/8.
Gemmell, T. (2) (St Mirren) 1954/5.
Gemmell, T. (18) (Celtic) 1965/6, 1966/7, 1967/8, 1968/9, 1969/70, 1970/1.
Gemmill, A. (43) (Derby County) 1970/1, 1971/2, 1975/6, 1976/7, 1977/8 (Nottingham Forest) 1978/9 (Birmingham City) 1979/80, 1980/1.
Gemmill, S. (15) (Nottingham Forest) 1994/95, 1995/96, 1996/97, 1997/98, (Everton) 1998/99.
Gibson, D. (7) (Leicester City) 1962/3, 1963/4, 1964/5.
Gillespie, G. T. (13) (Liverpool) 1987/8, 1988/9, 1989/90, (Celtic) 1990/91.
Gilzean, A. (22) (Dundee) 1963/4, 1964/5 (Tottenham Hotspur) 1965/6, 1967/8, 1968/9, 1969/70, 1970/1.
Glass, S. (1) (Newcastle United) 1998/99.

Glavin, R. (1) (Celtic) 1976/7.
Glen, A. (2) (Aberdeen) 1955/6.
Goram, A. L. (43) (Oldham Athletic) 1985/6, 1986/7, (Hibernian) 1988/9, 1989/90, 1990/1, (Rangers) 1991/2, 1992/93, 1993/94, 1994/95, 1995/96, 1996/97, 1997/98.
Gough, C. R. (61) (Dundee United) 1982/3, 1983/4, 1984/5, 1985/6, 1986/7 (Tottenham Hotspur) 1987/8 (Rangers) 1988/9, 1989/90, 1990/1, 1991/2, 1992/93.
Govan, J. (6) (Hibernian) 1947/8, 1948/9.
Graham, A. (10) (Leeds United) 1977/8, 1978/9, 1979/80, 1980/1.
Graham, G. (12) (Arsenal) 1971/2, 1972/3 (Manchester United).
Grant, J. (2) (Hibernian) 1958/9.
Grant, P. (2) (Celtic) 1988/9.
Gray, A. (20) (Aston Villa) 1975/6, 1976/7, 1978/9 (Wolverhampton Wanderers) 1979/80, 1980/1, 1981/2, 1982/3, 1984/5 (Everton).
Gray, E. (12) (Leeds United) 1968/9, 1969/70, 1970/71, 1971/2, 1975/6, 1976/7.
Gray F. (32) (Leeds United) 1975/6, 1978/9, 1979/80 (Nottingham Forest) 1980/1, (Leeds United) 1981/2, 1982/3.
Green, A. (6) (Blackpool) 1970/1 (Newcastle United) 1971/2.
Greig, J. (44) (Rangers) 1963/4, 1964/5, 1965/6, 1966/7, 1967/8, 1968/9, 1969/70, 1970/1, 1975/6.
Gunn, B. (6) (Norwich C) 1989/90, 1992/93, 1993/94.

Haddock, H. (6) (Clyde) 1954/5, 1957/8.
Haffey, F. (2) (Celtic) 1959/60, 1960/1.
Hamilton, A. (24) (Dundee) 1961/2, 1962/3, 1963/4, 1964/5, 1965/6.
Hamilton, G. (5) (Aberdeen) 1946/7, 1950/1, 1953/4.
Hamilton, W. (1) (Hibernian) 1964/5.
Hansen, A. (26) (Liverpool) 1978/9, 1979/80, 1980/1, 1981/2, 1982/3, 1984/5, 1985/6, 1986/7.
Hansen J. (2) (Partick Thistle) 1971/2.
Harper, J. (4) (Aberdeen) 1972/3, 1975/6, 1978/9.
Hartford, A. (50) (West Bromwich Albion) 1971/2, 1975/6 (Manchester City) 1976/7, 1977/8, 1978/9, 1979/80 (Everton) 1980/1, 1981/2 (Manchester City).
Harvey, D. (16) (Leeds United) 1972/3, 1973/4, 1974/5, 1975/6, 1976/7.
Haughney, M. (1) (Celtic) 1953/4.
Hay, D. (27) (Celtic) 1969/70, 1970/1, 1971/2, 1972/3, 1973/4.
Hegarty, P. (8) (Dundee United) 1978/9, 1979/80, 1982/3.
Henderson, J. (7) (Portsmouth) 1952/3, 1953/4, 1955/6, 1958/9 (Arsenal).
Henderson, W. (29) (Rangers) 1962/3, 1963/4, 1964/5, 1965/6, 1966/7, 1967/8, 1968/9, 1969/70.
Hendry, E. C. J. (39) (Blackburn Rovers) 1992/93, 1993/94, 1994/95, 1995/96, 1996/97, 1997/98 (Rangers) 1998/99.
Herd, D. (5) (Arsenal) 1958/9, 1960/1.
Herd, G. (5) (Clyde) 1957/8, 1959/60, 1960/1.
Herriot, J. (8) (Birmingham City) 1968/9, 1969/70.
Hewie, J. (19) (Charlton Athletic) 1955/6, 1956/7, 1957/8, 1958/9, 1959/60.
Holt, D. (5) (Heart of Midlothian) 1962/3, 1963/4.
Holton, J. (15) (Manchester United) 1972/3, 1973/4, 1974/5.
Hope, R. (2) (West Bromwich Albion) 1967/8, 1968/9.
Hopkin, D. (5) (Crystal Palace) 1996/97 (Leeds United) 1997/98, 1998/99.
Houliston, W. (3) (Queen of the South) 1948/9.
Houston, S. (1) (Manchester United) 1975/6.
Howie, H. (1) (Hibernian) 1948/9.
Hughes, J. (8) (Celtic) 1964/5, 1965/6, 1967/8, 1968/9, 1969/70.
Hughes, W. (1) (Sunderland) 1974/5.
Humphries, W. (1) (Motherwell) 1951/2.
Hunter, A. (4) (Kilmarnock) 1971/2, 1972/3, (Celtic) 1973/4.

Hunter, W. (3) (Motherwell) 1959/60, 1960/1.
Husband, J. (1) (Partick Thistle) 1946/7.
Hutchison, D. (2) (Everton) 1998/99.
Hutchison, T. (17) (Coventry City) 1973/4, 1974/5, 1975/6.

Imlach, S. (4) (Nottingham Forest) 1957/8.
Irvine, B. (9) (Aberdeen) 1990/1, 1992/93, 1993/94.

Jackson, C. (8) (Rangers) 1974/5, 1975/6.
Jackson, D. (28) (Hibernian) 1994/95, 1995/96, 1996/97 (Celtic) 1997/98, 1998/99.
Jardine, A. (38) (Rangers) 1970/1, 1971/2, 1972/3, 1973/4, 1974/5, 1976/7, 1977/8, 1978/9, 1979/80.
Jarvie, A. (3) (Airdrieonians) 1970/1.
Jess, E. (18) (Aberdeen) 1992/93, 1993/94, 1994/95 (Coventry City) 1995/96 (Aberdeen) 1997/98, 1998/99.
Johnston, A. (6) (Sunderland) 1998/99.
Johnston, M. (38) (Watford) 1983/4, 1984/5 (Celtic) 1985/6, 1986/7, (Nantes) 1987/8, 1988/9 (Rangers) 1989/90, 1991/2.
Johnston, W. (22) (Rangers) 1965/6, 1967/8, 1968/9, 1969/70, 1970/1 (West Bromwich Albion) 1976/7, 1977/8.
Johnstone, D. (14) (Rangers) 1972/3, 1974/5, 1975/6, 1977/8, 1979/80.
Johnstone, J. (23) (Celtic) 1964/5, 1965/6, 1966/7, 1967/8, 1968/9, 1969/70, 1970/1, 1971/2, 1973/4, 1974/5.
Johnstone, L. (2) (Clyde) 1947/8.
Johnstone, R. (17) (Hibernian) 1950/1, 1951/2, 1952/3, 1953/4, 1954/5, (Manchester City) 1955/6.
Jordan, J. (52) (Leeds United) 1972/3, 1973/4, 1974/5, 1975/6, 1976/7, 1977/8, (Manchester United) 1978/9, 1979/80, 1980/1, 1981/2 (AC Milan).

Kelly, H. (1) (Blackpool) 1951/2.
Kelly, J. (2) (Barnsley) 1948/9.
Kennedy, J. (6) (Celtic) 1963/4, 1964/5.
Kennedy, S. (8) (Aberdeen) 1977/8, 1978/9, 1981/2.
Kennedy, S. (5) (Rangers) 1974/5.
Kerr, A. (2) (Partick Thistle) 1954/5.

Lambert, P. (20) (Motherwell) 1994/95 (Borussia Dortmund) 1996/97 (Celtic) 1997/98, 1998/99.
Law, D. (55) (Huddersfield Town) 1958/9, 1959/60 (Manchester City) 1960/1, 1961/2 (Torino) 1962/3 (Manchester United) 1963/4, 1964/5, 1965/6, 1966/7, 1967/8, 1968/9, 1971/2, 1973/4 (Manchester City).
Lawrence, T. (3) (Liverpool) 1962/3, 1968/9.
Leggat, G. (18) (Aberdeen) 1955/6, 1956/7, 1957/8, 1958/9 (Fulham) 1959/60.
Leighton, J. (91) (Aberdeen) 1982/3, 1983/4, 1984/5, 1985/6, 1986/7, 1987/8, (Manchester United) 1988/9, 1989/90 (Hibernian) 1993/94, 1994/95, 1995/96, 1996/97 (Aberdeen) 1997/98, 1998/99.
Lennox, R. (10) (Celtic) 1966/7, 1967/8, 1968/9.
Leslie, L. (5) (Airdrieonians) 1960/1.
Levein, C. (16) (Hearts) 1989/90, 1991/2, 1992/93, 1993/94, 1994/95.
Liddell, W. (28) (Liverpool) 1946/7, 1947/8, 1949/50, 1950/1, 195/2, 1952/3, 1953/4, 1954/5, 1955/6.
Linwood, A. (1) (Clyde) 1949/50.
Little, A. (1) (Rangers) 1952/3.
Logie, J. (1) (Arsenal) 1952/3.
Long, H. (1) (Clyde) 1946/7.

Lorimer, P. (21) (Leeds United) 1969/70, 1970/1, 1971/2, 1972/3, 1973/4, 1974/5, 1975/6.

Macari, L. (24) (Celtic) 1971/2, 1972/3 (Manchester United) 1974/5, 1976/7, 1977/8, 1978/9.
Macaulay, A. (7) (Brentford) 1946/7 (Arsenal) 1947/8.
MacDougall, E. (7) (Norwich City) 1974/5, 1975/6.
Mackay, D. (22) (Heart of Midlothian) 1956/7, 1957/8, 1958/9 (Tottenham Hotspur) 1959/60, 1960/1, 1962/3, 1963/4, 1965/6.
Mackay, G. (4) (Heart of Midlothian) 1987/8.
Malpas, M. (55) (Dundee United) 1983/4, 1984/5, 1985/6, 1986/7, 1987/8, 1988/9, 1989/90, 1990/1, 1991/2, 1992/93.
Marshall, G. (1) (Celtic) 1991/2.
Martin, B. (2) (Motherwell) 1994/95.
Martin, F. (6) (Aberdeen) 1953/4, 1954/5.
Martin, N. (3) (Hibernian) 1964/5, 1965/6 (Sunderland).
Martis, J. (1) (Motherwell) 1960/1.
Mason, J. (7) (Third Lanark) 1948/9, 1949/50, 1950/1.
Masson, D. (17) (QPR) 1975/6, 1976/7, 1977/8 (Derby County) 1978/9.
Mathers, D. (1) (Partick Thistle) 1953/4.
McAllister, B. (3) (Wimbledon) 1996/97.
McAllister, G. (57) (Leicester City) 1989/90, 1990/1 (Leeds United), 1991/2, 1992/93, 1993/94, 1994/95, 1995/96 (Coventry City) 1996/97, 1997/98, 1998/99.
McAvennie, F. (5) (West Ham United) 1985/6 (Celtic) 1987/8.
McBride, J. (2) (Celtic) 1966/7.
McCall, S. M. (40) (Everton) 1989/90, 1990/1, (Rangers) 1991/2, 1992/93, 1993/94, 1994/95, 1995/96, 1996/97, 1997/98.
McCalliog, J. (5) (Sheffield Wednesday) 1966/7, 1967/8, 1968/9, 1970/1 (Wolverhampton Wanderers).
McCann, N.D. (2) (Heart of Midlothian) 1998/99, (Rangers).
McCann, R. (5) (Motherwell) 1958/9, 1959/60, 1960/1.
McClair, B. (30) (Celtic) 1986/7 (Manchester United) 1987/8, 1988/9, 1989/90, 1990/1, 1991/2, 1992/93.
McCloy, P. (4) (Rangers) 1972/3.
McCoist, A. (61) (Rangers) 1985/6, 1986/7, 1987/8, 1988/9, 1989/90, 1990/1, 1991/2, 1992/93, 1995/96, 1996/97, 1997/98, (Kilmarnock) 1998/99.
McColl, I. (14) (Rangers) 1949/50, 1950/1, 1956/7, 1957/8.
McCreadie, E. (23) (Chelsea) 1964/5, 1965/6, 1966/7, 1967/8, 1968/9.
MacDonald, A. (1) (Rangers) 1975/6.
MacDonald, J. (2) (Sunderland) 1955/6.
McFarlane, W. (1) (Heart of Midlothian) 1946/7.
McGarr, E. (2) (Aberdeen) 1969/70.
McGarvey, F. (7) (Liverpool) 1978/9 (Celtic) 1983/4.
McGhee, M. (4) (Aberdeen) 1982/3, 1983/4.
McGinlay, J. (13) (Bolton Wanderers) 1993/94, 1994/95, 1995/96, 1996/97.
McGrain, D. (62) (Celtic) 1972/3, 1973/4, 1974/5, 1975/6, 1976/7, 1977/8, 1979/80, 1980/1, 1981/2.
McGrory, J. (3) (Kilmarnock) 1964/5, 1965/6.
McInally, A. (8) (Aston Villa) 1988/9 (Bayern Munich) 1989/90.
McInally, J. (10) (Dundee United) 1986/7, 1987/8, 1990/1, 1991/2, 1992/93.
McKay, D. (14) (Celtic) 1958/9, 1959/60, 1960/1, 1961/2.
McKean, R. (1) (Rangers) 1975/6.
McKenzie, J. (9) (Partick Thistle) 1953/4, 1954/5, 1955/6.
McKimmie, S. (40) (Aberdeen) 1988/9, 1989/90, 1990/1, 1991/2, 1992/93, 1993/94, 1994/95, 1995/96.
McKinlay, T. (22) (Celtic) 1995/96, 1996/97, 1997/98.

McKinlay, W. (29) (Dundee United) 1993/94, 1994/95, 1995/96 (Blackburn Rovers) 1996/97, 1997/98, 1998/99.

McKinnon, R. (28) (Rangers) 1965/6, 1966/7, 1967/8, 1968/9, 1969/70, 1970/1.

McKinnon, R. (3) (Motherwell) 1993/94, 1994/95.

McLaren, A. (4) (Preston North End) 1946/7, 1947/8.

McLaren, A. (24) (Heart of Midlothian) 1991/2, 1992/93, 1993/94, 1994/95 (Rangers), 1995/96.

McLean, G. (1) (Dundee) 1967/8.

McLean, T. (6) (Kilmarnock) 1968/9, 1969/70, 1970/1.

McLeish, A. (77) (Aberdeen) 1979/80, 1980/1, 1981/2, 1982/3, 1983/4, 1984/5, 1985/6, 1986/7, 1987/8, 1988/9, 1989/90, 1990/1, 1992/93.

McLeod, J. (4) (Hibernian) 1960/1.

MacLeod, M. (20) (Celtic) 1984/5, 1986/7 (Borussia Dortmund) 1987/8, 1988/9, 1989/90, 1990/1 (Hibernian).

McLintock, F. (9) (Leicester City) 1962/3, 1964/5 (Arsenal) 1966/7, 1969/70, 1970/1.

McMillan, I. (6) (Airdrieonians) 1951/2, 1954/5, 1955/6 (Rangers) 1960/1.

McNamara, J. (9) (Celtic) 1996/97, 1997/98.

McNaught, W. (5) (Raith Rovers) 1950/1, 1951/2, 1954/5.

McNeill, W. (29) (Celtic) 1960/1, 1961/2, 1962/3, 1963/4, 1964/5, 1965/6, 1966/7, 1967/8, 1968/9, 1969/70, 1971/2.

McPhail, J. (5) (Celtic) 1949/50, 1950/1, 1953/4.

McPherson, D. (27) (Hearts) 1988/9, 1989/90, 1990/1, 1991/2 (Rangers) 1992/93.

McQueen, G. (30) (Leeds United) 1973/4, 1974/5, 1975/6, 1976/7, 1977/8, (Manchester United) 1978/9, 1979/80, 1980/1.

McStay, P. (76) (Celtic) 1983/4, 1984/5, 1985/6, 1986/7, 1987/8, 1988/9, 1989/90, 1990/1, 1991/2, 1992/93, 1993/94, 1994/95, 1995/96, 1996/97.

Millar, J. (2) (Rangers) 1962/3.

Miller, W. (6) (Celtic) 1946/7, 1947/8.

Miller, W. (65) (Aberdeen) 1974/5, 1977/8, 1979/80, 1980/1, 1981/2, 1982/3, 1983/4, 1984/5, 1985/6, 1986/7, 1987/8, 1988/9, 1989/90.

Mitchell, R. (2) (Newcastle United) 1950/1.

Mochan, N. (3) (Celtic) 1953/4.

Moir, W. (1) (Bolton Wanderers) 1949/50.

Moncur, R. (16) (Newcastle United) 1967/8, 1969/70, 1970/1, 1971/2.

Morgan, W. (21) (Burnley) 1967/8 (Manchester United) 1971/2, 1972/3, 1973/4.

Morris, H. (1) (East Fife) 1949/50.

Mudie, J. (17) (Blackpool) 1956/7, 1957/8.

Mulhall, G. (3) (Aberdeen) 1959/60, 1962/3 (Sunderland) 1963/4.

Munro, F. (9) (Wolverhampton Wanderers) 1970/1, 1974/5.

Munro, I. (7) (St Mirren) 1978/9, 1979/80.

Murdoch, R. (12) (Celtic) 1965/6, 1966/7, 1967/8, 1968/9, 1969/70.

Murray, J. (5) (Heart of Midlothian) 1957/8.

Murray, S. (1) (Aberdeen) 1971/2.

Narey, D. (35) (Dundee United) 1976/7, 1978/9, 1979/80, 1980/1, 1981/2, 1982/3, 1985/6, 1986/7, 1988/9.

Nevin, P. K. F. (28) (Chelsea) 1985/6, 1986/7, 1987/8 (Everton) 1988/9, 1990/1, 1991/2 (Tranmere Rovers) 1992/93, 1993/94, 1994/95, 1995/96.

Nicholas, C. (20) (Celtic) 1982/3, (Arsenal) 1983/4, 1984/5, 1985/6, 1986/7, (Aberdeen) 1988/9.

Nicol, S. (27) (Liverpool) 1984/5, 1985/6, 1987/8, 1988/9, 1989/90, 1990/1, 1991/2.

O'Donnell, P. (1) (Motherwell) 1993/94.

O'Hare, J. (13) (Derby County) 1969/70, 1970/1, 1971/2.

O'Neil, B. (2) (Celtic) 1995/96, (Wolfsburg) 1998/99.

Ormond, W. (6) (Hibernian) 1953/4, 1958/9.

Orr, T. (2) (Morton) 1951/2.

Parker, A. (15) (Falkirk) 1954/5, 1955/6, 1956/7, 1957/8.
Parlane, D. (12) (Rangers) 1972/3, 1974/5, 1975/6, 1976/7.
Paton, A. (2) (Motherwell) 1951/2.
Pearson, T. (2) (Newcastle United) 1946/7.
Penman, A. (1) (Dundee) 1965/6.
Pettigrew, W. (5) (Motherwell) 1975/6, 1976/7.
Plenderleith, J. (1) (Manchester City) 1960/1.
Provan, D. (5) (Rangers) 1963/4, 1965/6.
Provan, D. (10) (Celtic) 1979/80, 1980/1, 1981/2.

Quinn, P. (4) (Motherwell) 1960/1, 1961/2.

Redpath, W. (9) (Motherwell) 1948/9, 1950/1, 1951/2.
Reilly, L. (38) (Hibernian) 1948/9, 1949/50, 1950/1, 1951/2, 1952/3, 1953/4, 1954/5, 1955/6, 1956/7.
Ring, T. (12) (Clydebank) 1952/3, 1954/5, 1956/7, 1957/8.
Rioch, B. (24) (Derby County) 1974/5, 1975/6, 1976/7, (Everton) 1977/8, (Derby County) 1978/9.
Ritchie, P.S. (2) (Heart of Midlothian) 1998/99.
Robb, D. (5) (Aberdeen) 1970/1.
Robertson, A. (5) (Clyde) 1954/5, 1957/8.
Robertson, D. (3) (Rangers) 1991/2, 1993/94.
Robertson, H. (1) (Dundee) 1961/2.
Robertson, J. (1) (Tottenham Hotspur) 1964/5.
Robertson, J. (16) (Heart of Midlothian) 1990/1, 1991/2, 1992/93, 1994/95, 1995/96.
Robertson, J. N. (28) (Nottingham Forest) 1977/8, 1978/9, 1979/80, 1980/1, 1981/2, 1982/3 (Derby County) 1983/4.
Robinson, B. (4) (Dundee) 1973/4, 1974/5.
Rough, A. (53) (Partick Thistle) 1975/6, 1976/7, 1977/8, 1978/9, 1979/80, 1980/1, 1981/2, (Hibernian) 1985/6.
Rougvie, D. (1) (Aberdeen) 1983/4.
Rutherford, E. (1) (Rangers) 1947/8.

St John, I. (21) (Motherwell) 1958/9, 1959/60, 1960/1, 1961/2 (Liverpool) 1962/3, 1963/4, 1964/5.
Schaedler, E. (1) (Hibernian) 1973/4.
Scott, A. (16) (Rangers) 1956/7, 1957/8, 1958/9, 1961/2 (Everton) 1963/4, 1964/5, 1965/6.
Scott, J. (1) (Hibernian) 1965/6.
Scott, J. (2) (Dundee) 1970/1.
Scoular, J. (9) (Portsmouth) 1950/1, 1951/2, 1952/3.
Sharp, G. M. (12) (Everton) 1984/5, 1985/6, 1986/7, 1987/8.
Shaw, D. (8) (Hibernian) 1946/7, 1947/8, 1948/9.
Shaw, J. (4) (Rangers) 1946/7, 1947/8.
Shearer, D. (7) (Aberdeen) 1993/94, 1994/95, 1995/96.
Shearer, R. (4) (Rangers) 1960/1.
Simpson, N. (4) (Aberdeen) 1982/3, 1983/4, 1986/7, 1987/8.
Simpson, R. (5) (Celtic) 1966/7, 1967/8, 1968/9.
Sinclair, J. (1) (Leicester City) 1965/6.
Smith, D. (2) (Aberdeen) 1965/6, 1967/8 (Rangers).
Smith, E. (2) (Celtic) 1958/9.
Smith, G. (18) (Hibernian) 1946/7, 1947/8, 1951/2, 1954/5, 1955/6, 1956/7.
Smith, H. G. (3) (Heart of Midlothian) 1987/8, 1991/2.
Smith, J. (4) (Aberdeen) 1967/8, 1973/4 (Newcastle United).

Souness, G. (54) (Middlesbrough) 1974/5 (Liverpool) 1977/8, 1978/9, 1979/80, 1980/1, 1981/2, 1982/3, 1983/4, (Sampdoria) 1984/5, 1985/6.
Speedie, D. R. (10) (Chelsea) 1984/5, 1985/6, (Coventry City) 1988/9.
Spencer, J. (14) (Chelsea) 1994/95, 1995/96 (Queens Park Rangers) 1996/97.
Stanton, P. (16) (Hibernian) 1965/6, 1968/9, 1969/70, 1970/1, 1971/2, 1972/3, 1973/4.
Steel, W. (30) (Morton) 1946/7, 1947/8 (Derby County) 1948/9, 1949/50, (Dundee) 1950/1, 1951/2, 1952/3.
Stein, C. (21) (Rangers) 1968/9, 1969/70, 1970/1, 1971/2 (Coventry City) 1972/3.
Stephen, J. (2) (Bradford City) 1946/7, 1947/8.
Stewart, D. (1) (Leeds United) 1977/8.
Stewart, J. (2) (Kilmarnock) 1976/7 (Middlesbrough) 1978/9.
Stewart, R. (10) (West Ham United) 1980/1, 1981/2, 1983/4, 1986/7.
Strachan, G. (50) (Aberdeen) 1979/80, 1980/1, 1981/2, 1982/3, 1983/4 (Manchester United) 1984/5, 1985/6, 1986/7, 1987/8, 1988/9 (Leeds United) 1989/90, 1990/1, 1991/2.
Sturrock, P. (20) (Dundee United) 1980/1, 1981/2, 1982/3, 1983/4, 1984/5, 1985/6, 1986/7.
Sullivan, N. (8) (Wimbledon) 1996/97, 1997/98, 1998/99.

Telfer, W. (1) (St Mirren) 1953/4.
Thomson, W. (7) (St Mirren) 1979/80, 1980/1, 1981/2, 1982/3, 1983/4.
Thornton, W. (7) (Rangers) 1946/7, 1947/8, 1948/9, 1951/2.
Toner, W. (2) (Kilmarnock) 1958/9.
Turnbull, E. (8) (Hibernian) 1947/8, 1950/1, 1957/8.

Ure, I. (11) (Dundee) 1961/2, 1962/3 (Arsenal) 1963/4, 1967/8.

Waddell, W. (17) (Rangers) 1946/7, 1948/9, 1949/50, 1950/1, 1951/2, 1953/4, 1954/5.
Walker, A. (3) (Celtic) 1987/8, 1994/95.
Walker, J. N. (2) (Heart of Midlothian) 1992/93 (Partick Thistle) 1995/96.
Wallace, L. A. (3) (Coventry City) 1977/8, 1978/9.
Wallace, W. S. B. (7) (Heart of Midlothian) 1964/5, 1965/6, 1966/7 (Celtic) 1967/8, 1968/9.
Wardhaugh, J. (2) (Heart of Midlothian) 1954/5, 1956/7.
Wark, J. (29) (Ipswich Town) 1978/9, 1979/80, 1980/1, 1981/2, 1982/3, 1983/4 (Liverpool) 1984/5.
Watson, J. (2) (Motherwell) 1947/8 (Huddersfield Town) 1953/4.
Watson, R. (1) (Motherwell) 1970/1.
Weir, A. (6) (Motherwell) 1958/9, 1959/60.
Weir, D. G. (13) (Heart of Midlothian) 1996/97, 1997/98, (Everton) 1998/99.
Weir, P. (6) (St Mirren) 1979/80, 1982/3, (Aberdeen) 1983/4.
White, J. (22) (Falkirk) 1958/9, 1959/60 (Tottenham Hotspur) 1960/1, 1961/2, 1962/3, 1963/4.
Whyte, D. (12) (Celtic) 1987/8, 1988/9, 1991/2 (Middlesbrough) 1992/93, 1994/95, 1995/96, 1996/97 (Aberdeen) 1997/98, 1998/99.
Wilson, A. (1) (Portsmouth) 1953/4.
Wilson, D. (22) (Rangers) 1960/1, 1961/2, 1962/3, 1963/4, 1964/5.
Wilson, I. A. (5) (Leicester City) 1986/7, (Everton) 1987/8.
Wilson, P. (1) (Celtic) 1974/5.
Wilson, R. (2) (Arsenal) 1971/2.
Winters, R. (1) (Aberdeen) 1998/99.
Wood, G. (4) (Everton) 1978/9, 1981/2 (Arsenal).
Woodburn, W. (24) (Rangers) 1946/7, 1947/8, 1948/9, 1949/50, 1950/1, 1951/2.
Wright, K. (1) (Hibernian) 1991/2.
Wright, S. (2) (Aberdeen) 1992/93.
Wright, T. (3) (Sunderland) 1952/3.

Yeats, R. (2) (Liverpool) 1964/5, 1965/6.
Yorston, H. (1) (Aberdeen) 1954/5.
Young, A. (9) (Heart of Midlothian) 1959/60. 1960/1 (Everton) 1965/6.
Young, G. (53) (Rangers) 1946/7, 1947/8, 1948/9, 1949/50, 1950/1, 1951/2, 1952/3, 1953/4, 1954/5, 1955/6, 1956/7.
Younger, T. (24) (Hibernian) 1954/5, 1955/6, 1956/7 (Liverpool) 1957/8.

WALES

Aizlewood, M. (39) (Charlton Athletic) 1985/6, 1986/7 (Leeds United) 1987/8, 1988/9 (Bradford City) 1989/90, 1990/1 (Bristol City), 1991/2, 1992/93, 1993/94 (Cardiff City) 1994/95.
Allchurch, I. (68) (Swansea Town) 1950/1, 1951/2, 1952/3, 1953/4, 1954/5, 1955/6, 1956/7, 1957/8, 1958/9 (Newcastle United) 1959/60, 1960/1, 1961/2, 1962/3 (Cardiff City) 1963/4, 1964/5, 1965/6 (Swansea Town).
Allchurch, L. (11) (Swansea Town) 1954/5, 1955/6, 1957/8, 1958/9, 1961/2, (Sheffield United) 1963/4.
Allen, B. (2) (Coventry City) 1950/1.
Allen, M. (14) (Watford) 1985/6, (Norwich City) 1988/9 (Millwall) 1989/90, 1990/1, 1991/2, 1992/93 (Newcastle United) 1993/94.

Baker, C. (7) (Cardiff City) 1957/8, 1959/60. 1960/1, 1961/2.
Baker, W. (1) (Cardiff City) 1947/8.
Barnard, D. S. (6) (Barnsley) 1997/98, 1998/99.
Barnes, W. (22) (Arsenal) 1947/8, 1948/9, 1949/50, 1950/1, 1951/2, 1953/4, 1954/5.
Bellamy, C. D. (7) (Norwich City) 1997/98, 1998/99.
Berry, G. (5) (Wolverhampton Wanderers) 1978/9, 1979/80, 1982/3 (Stoke City).
Blackmore, C. G. (39) (Manchester United) 1984/5, 1985/6, 1986/7, 1987/8, 1988/9, 1989/90, 1990/1, 1991/2, 1992/93, 1993/94 (Middlesbrough) 1996/97.
Blake, N. (11) (Sheffield United) 1993/94, 1994/95, 1995/96 (Bolton Wanderers) 1997/98, (Blackburn Rovers) 1998/99.
Bodin, P.J. (23) (Swindon Town) 1989/90, 1990/1 (Crystal Palace), 1991/2 (Swindon Town) 1992/93, 1993/94, 1994/95.
Bowen, D. (19) (Arsenal) 1954/5, 1956/7, 1957/8, 1958/9.
Bowen, J. P. (2) (Swansea City) 1993/94 (Birmingham City) 1996/97.
Bowen, M. R. (41) (Tottenham Hotspur) 1985/6 (Norwich City) 1987/8, 1988/9, 1989/90, 1991/2, 1992/93, 1993/94, 1994/95, 1995/96 (West Ham United) 1996/97.
Boyle, T. (2) (Crystal Palace) 1980/1.
Browning, M. T. (5) (Bristol Rovers) 1995/96 (Huddersfield Town) 1996/97.
Burgess, R. (32) (Tottenham Hotspur) 1946/7, 1947/8, 1948/9, 1949/50, 1950/1, 1951/2, 1952/3, 1953/4.
Burton, O. (9) (Norwich City) 1962/3 (Newcastle United) 1963/4, 1968/9, 1971/2.

Cartwright, L. (7) (Coventry City) 1973/4, 1975/6, 1976/7 (Wrexham) 1977/8, 1978/9.
Charles, J. M. (19) (Swansea Town) 1980/1, 1981/2, 1982/3, 1983/4 (QPR), (Oxford United) 1984/5, 1985/6, 1986/7.
Charles, M. (31) (Swansea Town) 1954/5, 1955/6, 1956/7, 1957/8, 1958/9 (Arsenal) 1960/1, 1961/2 (Cardiff City) 1962/3.
Charles, W. J. (38) (Leeds United) 1949/50, 1950/1, 1952/3, 1953/4, 1954/5, 1955/6, 1956/7 (Juventus) 1957/8, 1959/60, 1961/2, 1962/3, (Leeds United) (Cardiff City) 1963/4, 1964/5.
Clarke, R. (22) (Manchester City) 1948/9, 1949/50, 1950/1, 1951/2, 952/3, 1953/4, 1954/5, 1955/6.
Coleman, C. (24) (Crystal Palace) 1991/2, 1992/93, 1993/94, 1994/95, 1995/96 (Blackburn Rovers) 1996/97 (Fulham) 1997/98, 1998/99.

Cornforth, J. M. (2) (Swansea City) 1994/95.
Coyne, D. (1) (Tranmere Rovers) 1995/96.
Crossley, M. G. (2) (Nottingham Forest) 1996/97, 1998/99.
Crowe, V. (16) (Aston Villa) 1958/9, 1959/60, 1960/1, 1961/2, 1962/3.
Curtis, A. (35) (Swansea City) 1975/6, 1976/7, 1977/8, 1978/9, (Leeds United) 1979/80, 1981/2, 1982/3, 1983/4 (Southampton) 1984/5, 1985/6, 1986/7 (Cardiff City).

Daniel, R. (21) (Arsenal) 1950/1, 1951/2, 1952/3, 1953/4 (Sunderland) 1954/5, 1956/7.
Davies, A. (13) (Manchester United) 1982/3, 1983/4, 1984/5, (Newcastle United) 1985/6 (Swansea City) 1987/8, 1988/9 (Bradford City) 1989/90.
Davies, G. (16) (Fulham) 1979/80, 1981/2, 1982/3, 1983/4, 1984/5 (Chelsea), (Manchester City) 1985/6.
Davies, R. Wyn (34) (Bolton Wanderers) 1963/4, 1964/5, 1965/6, 1966/7 (Newcastle United) 1967/8, 1968/9, 1969/70, 1970/1, 1971/2 (Manchester City), 1972/3 (Manchester United) 1973/4 (Blackpool).
Davies, Reg (6) (Newcastle United) 1952/3, 1953/4, 1957/8.
Davies, Ron (29) (Norwich City) 1963/4, 1964/5, 1965/6, 1966/7, (Southampton) 1967/8, 1968/9, 1969/70, 1970/1, 1971/2, 1973/4 (Portsmouth).
Davies, S. I. (1) (Manchester United) 1995/96.
Davies, W. D. (52) (Everton) 1974/5, 1975/6, 1976/7, 1977/8, (Wrexham) 1978/9, 1979/80, 1980/1 (Swansea City) 1981/2, 1982/3.
Davis, C. (1) (Charlton Athletic) 1971/2.
Davis, G. (4) (Wrexham) 1977/8.
Deacy, N. (11) (PSV Eindhoven) 1976/7, 1977/8 (Beringen) 1978/9.
Derrett, S. (4) (Cardiff City) 1968/9, 1969/70, 1970/1.
Dibble, A. (3) (Luton Town) 1985/6, (Manchester City) 1988/9.
Durban, A. (27) (Derby County) 1965/6, 1966/7, 1967/8, 1968/9, 1969/70, 1970/1, 1971/2.
Dwyer, P. (10) (Cardiff City) 1977/8, 1978/9, 1979/80.

Edwards. C. N. H. (1) (Swansea City) 1995/96.
Edwards, G. (12) (Birmingham City) 1946/7, 1947/8 (Cardiff City) 1948/9, 1949/50.
Edwards, I. (4) (Chester) 1977/8, 1978/9, 1979/80.
Edwards, R. W. (4) (Bristol City) 1997/98.
Edwards, T. (2) (Charlton Athletic) 1956/7.
Emanuel, J. (2) (Bristol City) 1972/3.
England, M. (44) (Blackburn Rovers) 1961/2, 1962/3, 1963/4, 1964/5, 1965/6, 1966/7 (Tottenham Hotspur) 1967/8, 1968/9, 1969/70, 1970/1, 1971/2, 1972/3, 1973/4, 1974/5.
Evans, B. (7) (Swansea City) 1971/2, 1972/3 (Hereford United) 1973/4.
Evans, I. (13) (Crystal Palace) 1975/6, 1976/7, 1977/8.
Evans, R. (1) (Swansea Town) 1963/4.

Felgate, D. (1) (Lincoln City) 1983/4.
Flynn, B. (66) (Burnley) 1974/5, 1975/6, 1976/7, 1977/8 (Leeds United) 1978/9, 1979/80, 1980/1, 1981/2, 1982/3 (Burnley) 1983/4.
Ford, T. (38) (Swansea Town) 1946/7 (Aston Villa) 1947/8, 1948/9, 1949/50, 1950/1 (Sunderland) 1951/2, 1952/3 (Cardiff City) 1953/4, 1954/5, 1955/6, 1956/7.
Foulkes, W. (11) (Newcastle United) 1951/2, 1952/3, 1953/4.

Giggs, R. J. (24) (Manchester United) 1991/2, 1992/93, 1993/94, 1994/95, 1995/96, 1996/97, 1997/98, 1998/99.
Giles, D. (12) (Swansea City) 1979/80, 1980/1, 1981/2 (Crystal Palace) 1982/3.
Godfrey, B. (3) (Preston North End) 1963/4, 1964/5.

Goss, J. (9) (Norwich City) 1990/1, 1991/2, 1993/94, 1994/95, 1995/96.
Green, C. (15) (Birmingham City) 1964/5, 1965/6, 1966/7, 1967/8, 1968/9.
Green, R. M. (2) (Wolverhampton Wanderers) 1997/98.
Griffiths, A. (17) (Wrexham) 1970/1, 1974/5, 1975/6, 1976/7.
Griffiths, H. (1) (Swansea Town) 1952/3.
Griffiths, M. (11) (Leicester City) 1946/7, 1948/9, 1949/50, 1950/1, 1953/4.

Hall, G. D. (9) (Chelsea) 1987/8, 1988/9, 1990/91, 1991/2.
Harrington, A. (11) (Cardiff City) 1955/6, 1956/7, 1957/8, 1960/1, 1961/2.
Harris, C. (24) (Leeds United) 1975/6, 1977/8, 1978/9, 1979/80, 1980/1, 1981/2.
Harris, W. (6) (Middlesbrough) 1953/4, 1956/7, 1957/8.
Hartson, J. (17) (Arsenal) 1994/95, 1995/96 (West Ham United) 1996/97, 1997/98, (Wimbledon) 1998/99.
Haworth, S. O. (5) (Cardiff City) 1996/97 (Coventry City) 1997/98.
Hennessey, T. (39) (Birmingham City) 1961/2, 1962/3, 1963/4, 1964/5, 1965/6, (Nottingham Forest) 1966/7, 1967/8, 1968/9, 1969/70 (Derby County) 1971/2, 1972/3.
Hewitt, R. (5) (Cardiff City) 1957/8.
Hill, M. (2) (Ipswich Town) 1971/2.
Hockey, T. (9) (Sheffield United) 1971/2, 1972/3 (Norwich City) 1973/4, (Aston Villa).
Hodges, G. (18) (Wimbledon) 1983/4, 1986/7 (Newcastle United) 1987/8, (Watford) 1989/90, (Sheffield United) 1991/2, 1995/96.
Holden, A. (1) (Chester City) 1983/4.
Hole, B. (30) (Cardiff City) 1962/3, 1963/4, 1964/5, 1965/6, 1966/7, (Blackburn Rovers) 1967/8, 1968/9 (Aston Villa) 1969/70 (Swansea City) 1970/71.
Hollins, D. (11) (Newcastle United) 1961/2, 1962/3, 1963/4, 1964/5, 1965/6.
Hopkins, J. (16) (Fulham) 1982/3, 1983/4, 1984/5 (Crystal Palace) 1989/90.
Hopkins, M. (34) (Tottenham Hotspur) 1955/6, 1956/7, 1957/8, 1958/9, 1959/60, 1960/1, 1961/2, 1962/3.
Horne, B. (59) (Portsmouth) 1987/8, (Southampton) 1988/9, 1989/90, 1990/1, 1991/2 (Everton) 1992/93, 1993/94, 1994/95, 1995/96 (Birmingham City) 1996/97.
Howells, R. (2) (Cardiff City) 1953/4.
Hughes, C. M. (8) (Luton Town) 1991/2, 1993/94, 1995/96, 1996/97 (Wimbledon) 1997/98.
Hughes, I. (4) (Luton Town) 1950/1.
Hughes, L. M. (72) (Manchester United) 1983/4, 1984/5, 1985/6, 1986/7 (Barcelona) 1987/8, 1988/9 (Manchester United) 1989/90, 1990/1, 1991/2, 1992/93, 1993/94, 1994/95 (Chelsea) 1995/96, 1996/97, 1997/98 (Southampton) 1998/99.
Hughes, W. (3) (Birmingham City) 1946/7.
Hughes, W. A. (5) (Blackburn Rovers) 1948/9.
Humphreys, J. (1) (Everton) 1946/7.

Jackett, K. (31) (Watford) 1982/3, 1983/4, 1984/5, 1985/6, 1986/7, 1987/8.
James, G. (9) (Blackpool) 1965/6, 1966/7, 1967/8, 1970/1.
James, L. (54) (Burnley) 1971/2, 1972/3, 1973/4, 1974/5, 1975/6 (Derby County) 1976/7, 1977/8 (QPR) (Burnley) 1978/9, 1979/80 (Swansea City) 1980/1, 1981/2 (Sunderland) 1982/3.
James, R. M. (47) (Swansea City) 1978/9, 1979/80, 1981/2, 1982/3 (Stoke City) 1983/4, 1984/5 (QPR) 1985/6, 1986/7 (Leicester City) 1987/8 (Swansea City).
Jarvis, A. (3) (Hull City) 1966/7.
Jenkins, S. R. (12) (Swansea City) 1995/96 (Huddersfield Town) 1996/97, 1997/98, 1998/99.
Johnson, A.J. (4) (Nottingham Forest) 1998/99.
Johnson, M. (1) (Swansea City) 1963/4.
Jones, A. (6) (Port Vale) 1986/7, 1987/8 (Charlton Athletic) 1989/90.

Jones, Barrie (15) (Swansea Town) 1962/3, 1963/4, 1964/5 (Plymouth Argyle) 1968/9 (Cardiff City).
Jones, Bryn. (4) (Arsenal) 1946/7, 1947/8, 1948/9.
Jones, C. (59) (Swansea Town) 1953/4, 1955/6, 1956/7, 1957/8 (Tottenham Hotspur) 1958/9, 1959/60, 1960/1, 1961/2, 1962/3, 1963/4, 1964/5, 1966/7, 1967/8, 1968/9 (Fulham) 1969/70.
Jones, D. (8) (Norwich City) 1975/6, 1977/8, 1979/80.
Jones, E. (4) (Swansea Town) 1946/7 (Tottenham Hotspur) 1948/9.
Jones, J. (72) (Liverpool) 1975/6, 1976/7, 1977/8 (Wrexham) 1978/9, 1979/80, 1980/1, 1981/2, 1982/3 (Chelsea) 1983/4, 1984/5 (Huddersfield Town) 1985/6.
Jones, K. (1) (Aston Villa) 1949/50.
Jones, P. L. (2) (Liverpool) 1996/97 (Tranmere Rovers) 1997/98.
Jones, P. S. (11) (Stockport County) 1996/97 (Southampton) 1997/98, 1998/99.
Jones, R. (1) (Sheffield Wednesday) 1993/94.
Jones, T. G. (13) (Everton) 1946/7, 1947/8, 1948/9, 1949/50.
Jones, V.P. (9) (Wimbledon) 1994/95, 1995/96, 1996/97.
Jones, W. (1) (Bristol City) 1970/1.

Kelsey, J. (41) (Arsenal) 1953/4, 1954/5, 1955/6, 1956/7, 1957/8, 1958/9, 1959/60, 1960/1, 1961/2.
King, J. (1) (Swansea Town) 1954/5.
Kinsey, N. (7) (Norwich City) 1950/1, 1951/2, 1953/4 (Birmingham City) 1955/6.
Knill, A. R. (1) (Swansea City) 1988/9.
Krzywicki, R. (West Bromwich Albion) 1969/70 (Huddersfield Town) 1970/1, 1971/2.

Lambert, R. (5) (Liverpool) 1946/7, 1947/8, 1948/9.
Law, B. J. (1) (QPR), 1989/90.
Lea, C. (2) (Ipswich Town) 1964/5.
Leek, K. (13) (Leicester City) 1960/1, 1961/2 (Newcastle United) (Birmingham City) 1962/3, 1964/5.
Legg, A. (5) (Birmingham City) 1995/96, 1996/97 (Cardiff City) 1998/99.
Lever, A. (1) (Leicester City) 1952/3.
Lewis, D. (1) (Swansea City) 1982/3.
Llewellyn, C. M. (2) (Norwich City) 1997/98.
Lloyd, B. (3) (Wrexham) 1975/6.
Lovell, S. (6) (Crystal Palace) 1981/2 (Millwall) 1984/5, 1985/6.
Lowndes, S. (10) (Newport County) 1982/3 (Millwall) 1984/5, 1985/6, 1986/7, (Barnsley) 1987/8.
Lowrie, G. (4) (Coventry City) 1947/8, 1948/9 (Newcastle United).
Lucas, M. (4) (Leyton Orient) 1961/2, 1962/3.
Lucas, W. (7) (Swansea Town) 1948/9, 1949/50, 1950/1.

Maguire, G. T. (7) (Portsmouth) 1989/90, 1991/2.
Mahoney, J. (51) (Stoke City) 1967/8, 1968/9, 1970/1, 1972/3, 1973/4, 1974/5, 1975/6, 1976/7 (Middlesbrough) 1977/8, 1978/9 (Swansea City) 1979/80, 1981/2, 1982/3.
Mardon, P. J. (1) (West Bromwich Albion) 1995/96.
Marriott, A. (5) (Wrexham) 1995/96, 1996/97, 1997/98.
Marustik, C. (6) (Swansea City) 1981/2, 1982/3.
Medwin, T. (30) (Swansea Town) 1952/3, 1956/7 (Tottenham Hotspur) 1957/8, 1958/9, 1959/60, 1960/1, 1962/3.
Melville, A. K. (34) (Swansea C), 1989/90, 1990/1 (Oxford United), 1991/2, 1992/93 (Sunderland) 1993/94, 1994/95, 1995/96, 1996/97, 1997/98 (Fulham) 1998/99.
Mielczarek, R. (1) (Rotherham United) 1970/1.

Millington, A. (21) (West Bromwich Albion) 1962/3, 1964/5 (Crystal Palace) 1965/6 (Peterborough United) 1966/7, 1967/8, 1968/9, 1969/70 (Swansea Town) 1970/1, 1971/2.
Moore, G. (21) (Cardiff City) 1959/60, 1960/1, 1961/2 (Chelsea) 1962/3, (Manchester United) 1963/4 (Northampton Town) 1965/6, 1968/9 (Charlton Athletic) 1969/70, 1970/1.
Morris, W. (5) (Burnley) 1946/7, 1948/9, 1951/2.

Nardiello, D. (2) (Coventry City) 1977/8.
Neilson, A. B. (5) (Newcastle United) 1991/2, 1993/94, 1994/95 (Southampton) 1996/97.
Nicholas, P. (73) (Crystal Palace) 1978/9, 1979/80, 1980/1 (Arsenal) 1981/2, 1982/3, 1983/4 (Crystal Palace) 1984/5, (Luton Town) 1985/6, 1986/7, 1987/8 (Aberdeen), (Chelsea) 1988/9, 1989/90, 1990/1 (Watford), 1991/2.
Niedzwiecki, E. A. (2) (Chelsea) 1984/5, 1987/8.
Nogan, L. M. (2) (Watford) 1991/2 (Reading) 1995/96.
Nurse, E. A. (2) (Chelsea) 1984/5, 1987/8.
Norman, A. J. (5) (Hull City) 1985/6, 1987/8.
Nurse, M. (12) (Swansea Town) 1959/60, 1960/1, 1962/3 (Middlesbrough) 1963/4.

O'Sullivan, P. (3) (Brighton & Hove Albion) 1972/3, 1975/6, 1978/9.
Oster, J. M. (2) (Everton) 1997/98.

Page, M. (28) (Birmingham City) 1970/1, 1971/2, 1972/3, 1973/4, 1974/5, 1975/6, 1976/7, 1977/8, 1978/9.
Page, R. J. (7) (Watford) 1996/97, 1997/98, 1998/99.
Palmer, D. (3) (Swansea Town) 1956/7, 1957/8.
Parry, J. (1) (Swansea Town) 1950/1.
Pascoe, C. (10) (Swansea Town) 1983/4, (Sunderland) 1988/9, 1989/90 1990/91, 1991/2.
Paul, R. (33) (Swansea Town) 1948/9, 1949/50 (Manchester City) 1950/1, 1951/2, 1952/3, 1953/4, 1954/5, 1955/6.
Pembridge, M. A. (33) (Luton Town) 1991/2 (Derby County) 1992/93, 1993/94, 1994/95 (Sheffield Wednesday) 1995/96, 1996/97, 1997/98 (Benfica) 1998/99.
Perry, J. (1) (Cardiff City) 1993/94.
Phillips, D. (62) (Plymouth Argyle) 1983/4 (Manchester City) 1984/5, 1985/6, 1986/7 (Coventry City) 1987/8, 1988/9 (Norwich City) 1989/90, 1990/1, 1991/2, 1992/93 (Nottingham Forest) 1993/94, 1994/95, 1995/96.
Phillips, J. (4) (Chelsea) 1972/3, 1973/4, 1974/5, 1977/8.
Phillips, L. (58) (Cardff City) 1970/1, 1971/2, 1972/3, 1973/4, 1974/5, (Aston Villa) 1975/6, 1976/7, 1977/8, 1978/9 (Swansea City) 1979/80, 1980/1, 1981/2 (Charlton Athletic).
Pontin, K. (2) (Cardiff City) 1979/80.
Powell, A. (8) (Leeds United) 1946/7, 1947/8, 1948/9 (Everton) 1949/50, 1950/1 (Birmingham City).
Powell, D. (11) (Wrexham) 1967/8, 1968/9 (Sheffield United) 1969/70, 1970/1.
Powell, I. (8) (QPR) 1946/7, 1947/8, 1948/9 (Aston Villa) 1949/50, 1950/1.
Price, P. (25) (Luton Town) 1979/80, 1980/1, 1981/2 (Tottenham Hotspur) 1982/3, 1983/4.
Pring, K. (3) (Rotherham United) 1965/6, 1966/7.
Pritchard, H. K. (1) (Bristol City) 1984/5.

Rankmore, F. (1 (Peterborough United) 1965/6.
Ratcliffe, K. (59) (Everton) 1980/1, 1981/2, 1982/3, 1983/4, 1984/5, 1985/6, 1986/7, 1987/8, 1988/9, 1989/90, 1990/1, 1991/2 (Cardiff City) 1992/93.
Ready, K. (5) (Queens Park Rangers) 1996/97, 1997/98.

Reece, G. (29) (Sheffield United) 1965/6, 1966/7, 1969/70, 1970/1, 1971/2, (Cardiff City) 1972/3, 1973/4, 1974/5.
Reed, W. (2) (Ipswich Town) 1954/5.
Rees, A. (1) (Birmingham City) 1983/4.
Rees, J. M. (1) (Luton Town) 1991/2.
Rees, R. (39) (Coventry City) 1964/5, 1965/6, 1966/7, 1967/8 (West Bromwich Albion) 1968/9 (Nottingham Forest) 1969/70, 1970/1, 1971/2.
Rees, W. (4) (Cardiff City) 1948/9 (Tottenham Hotspur) 1949/50.
Richards, S. (1) (Cardiff City) 1946/7.
Roberts, A. M. (2) (Queens Park Rangers) 1992/93, 1996/97.
Roberts, D. (17) (Oxford United) 1972/3, 1973/4, 1974/5 (Hull City) 1975/6, 1976/7, 1977/8.
Roberts, I. W. (7) (Watford) 1989/90, (Huddersfield Town) 1991/2, (Leicester City) 1993/94, 1994/95.
Roberts, J. G. (22) (Arsenal) 1970/1, 1971/2, 1972/3, (Birmingham City) 1973/4, 1974/5, 1975/6..
Roberts, J. H. (1) (Bolton Wanderers) 1948/9.
Roberts, P. (4) (Portsmouth) 1973/4, 1974/5.
Robinson, J. R. C. (16) (Charlton Athletic) 1995/96, 1996/97, 1997/98, 1998/99.
Rodrigues, P. (40) (Cardiff City) 1964/5, 1965/6 (Leicester City) 1966/7, 1967/8, 1968/9, 1969/70 (Sheffield Wednesday) 1970/1, 1971/2, 1972/3, 1973/4.
Rouse, V. (1) (Crystal Palace) 1958/9.
Rowley, T. (1) (Tranmere Rovers) 1958/9.
Rush, I. (73) (Liverpool) 1979/80, 1980/1, 1981/2, 1982/3, 1983/4, 1984/5, 1985/6, 1986/7 (Juventus) 1987/8, (Liverpool) 1988/9, 1989/90, 1990/1, 1991/2, 1992/93, 1993/94, 1994/95, 1995/96.

Saunders, D. (69) (Brighton & Hove Albion) 1985/6, 1986/7 (Oxford United) 1987/8, (Derby County) 1988/9, 1989/90, 1990/91, (Liverpool) 1991/2 (Aston Villa) 1992/93, 1993/94, 1994/95 (Galatasaray) 1995/96 (Nottingham Forest) 1996/97 (Sheffield United) 1997/98 (Benfica) 1998/99.
Savage, R. W. (13) (Crewe Alexandra) 1995/96, 1996/97 (Leicester City) 1997/98, 1998/99.
Sayer, P. (7) (Cardiff City) 1976/7, 1977/8.
Scrine, F. (2) (Swansea Town) 1949/50.
Sear, C. (1) (Manchester City) 1962/3.
Sherwood, A. (41) (Cardiff City) 1946/7, 1947/8, 1948/9, 1949/50, 1950/1, 1951/2, 1952/3, 1953/4, 1954/5, 1955/6, 1956/7 (Newport County).
Shortt, W. (12) (Plymouth Argyle) 1946/7, 1949/50, 1951/2, 1952/3.
Showers, D. (2) (Cardiff City) 1974/5.
Sidlow, C. (7) (Liverpool) 1946/7, 1947/8, 1948/9, 1949/50.
Slatter, N. (22) (Bristol Rovers) 1982/3, 1983/4, 1984/5 (Oxford United) 1985/6, 1986/7, 1987/8, 1988/9.
Smallman, D. (7 (Wrexham) 1973/4 (Everton) 1974/5, 1975/6.
Southall, N. (92) (Everton) 1981/2, 1982/3, 1983/4, 1984/5, 1985/6, 1986/7, 1987/8, 1988/9, 1989/90, 1990/1, 1991/2, 1992/93, 1993/94, 1994/95, 1995/96, 1996/97, 1997/98.
Speed, G. A. (52) (Leeds United), 1989/90, 1990/91, 1991/2, 1992/93, 1993/94, 1994/95, 1995/96 (Everton) 1996/97 (Newcastle U) 1997/98, 1998/99.
Sprake, G. (37) (Leeds United) 1963/4, 1964/5, 1965/6, 1966/7, 1967/8, 1968/9, 1969/70, 1970/1, 1971/2, 1972/3, 1973/4 (Birmingham City) 1974/5.
Stansfield, F. (1) (Cardiff City) 1948/9.
Stevenson, B. (15) (Leeds United) 1977/8, 1978/9, 1979/80, 1981/2 (Birmingham City).
Stevenson, N. (4) (Swansea City) 1981/2, 1982/3.

Stitfall, R. (2) (Cardiff City) 1952/3, 1956/7.
Sullivan, D. (17) (Cardiff City) 1952/3, 1953/4, 1954/5, 1956/7, 1957/8, 1958/9, 1959/60.
Symons, C. J. (31) (Portsmouth) 1991/2, 1992/93, 1993/94, 1994/95 (Manchester City) 1995/96, 1996/97 (Fulham) 1998/99.

Tapscott, D. (14) (Arsenal) 1953/4, 1954/5, 1955/6, 1956/7, 1958/9 (Cardiff City).
Taylor, G. K. (8) (Crystal Palace) 1995/96 (Sheffield United) 1996/97, 1997/98.
Thomas, D. (2) (Swansea Town) 1956/7, 1957/8.
Thomas, M. (51) (Wrexham) 1976/7, 1977/8, 1978/9 (Manchester United) 1979/80, 1980/1, 1981/2 (Everton) (Brighton) 1982/3 (Stoke City) 1983/4, (Chelsea) 1984/5, 1985/6 (West Bromwich Albion).
Thomas, M. R. (1) (Newcastle United) 1986/7.
Thomas, R. (50) (Swindon Town) 1966/7, 1967/8, 1968/9, 1969/70, 1970/1, 1971/2, 1972/3, 1973/4 (Derby County) 1974/5, 1975/6, 1976/7, 1977/8 (Cardiff City).
Thomas, S. (4) (Fulham) 1947/8, 1948/9.
Toshack, J. (40) (Cardiff City) 1968/9, 1969/70 (Liverpool) 1970/1, 1971/2, 1972/3, 1974/5, 1975/6, 1976/7, 1977/8 (Swansea City) 1978/9, 1979/80.
Trollope, P. J. (5) (Derby County) 1996/97 (Fulham) 1997/98.

Van Den Hauwe, P. W. R. (13) (Everton) 1984/5, 1985/6, 1986/7, 1987/8, 1988/9.
Vaughan, N. (10) (Newport County) 1982/3, 1983/4 (Cardiff City) 1984/5.
Vearncombe, G. (2) (Cardiff City) 1957/8, 1960/1.
Vernon, R. (32) (Blackburn Rovers) 1956/7, 1957/8, 1958/9, 1959/60 (Everton) 1960/1, 1961/2, 1962/3, 1963/4, 1964/5 (Stoke City) 1965/6, 1966/7, 1967/8.
Villars, A. (3) (Cardiff City) 1973/4.

Walley, T. (1) (Watford) 1970/1.
Walsh, I. (18) (Crystal Palace) 1979/80, 1980/1, 1981/2 (Swansea City).
Ward, D. (2) (Bristol Rovers) 1958/9, 1961/2 (Cardiff City).
Webster, C. (4) (Manchester United) 1956/7, 1957/8.
Williams, A. (12) (Reading) 1993/94, 1994/95, 1995/96 (Wolverhampton Wanderers) 1997/98, 1998/99.
Williams, A. P. (2) (Southampton) 1997/98.
Williams, D. G. (13) 1987/8 (Derby County) 1988/9, 1989/90 (Ipswich Town) 1992/93, 1995/96.
Williams, D. M. (5) (Norwich City) 1985/6, 1986/7.
Williams, G. (1) (Cardiff City) 1950/1.
Williams, G. E. (26) (West Bromwich Albion) 1959/60, 1960/1, 1962/3, 1963/4, 1964/5, 1965/6, 1966/7, 1967/8, 1968/9.
Williams, G.G. (5) (Swansea Town) 1960/1, 1961/2.
Williams, H. (4) (Newport County) 1948/9 (Leeds United) 1949/50, 1950/1.
Williams, Herbert (3) (Swansea Town) 1964/5, 1971/2.
Williams, S. (43) (West Bromwich Albion) 1953/4, 1954/5, 1955/6, 1957/8, 1958/9, 1959/60, 1960/1, 1961/2, 1962/3 (Southampton) 1963/4, 1964/5, 1965/6.
Witcomb, D. (3) (West Bromwich Albion) 1946/7 (Sheffield Wednesday).
Woosnam, P. (17) (Leyton Orient) 1958/9 (West Ham United) 1959/60, 1960/1, 1961/2, 1962/3 (Aston Villa).

Yorath, T. (59) (Leeds United) 1969/70, 1970/1, 1971/2, 1972/3, 1973/4, 1974/5, 1975/6 (Coventry City) 1976/7, 1977/8, 1978/9 (Tottenham Hotspur) 1979/80, 1980/1 (Vancouver Whitecaps).
Young, E. (21) (Wimbledon) 1989/90, 1990/1 (Crystal Palace), 1991/2, 1992/93, 1993/94, (Wolverhampton Wanderers) 1995/96.

EIRE

Aherne, T. (16) (Belfast Celtic) 1945/6 (Luton Town) 1949/50, 1950/1, 1951/2, 1952/3, 1953/4.

Aldridge, J. W. (69) (Oxford United) 1985/6, 1986/7 (Liverpool) 1987/8, 1988/9 (Real Sociedad) 1989/90, 1990/1, (Tranmere Rovers) 1991/2, 1992/93, 1993/94, 1994/95, 1995/96, 1996/97.

Ambrose, P. (5) (Shamrock Rovers) 1954/5, 1963/4.

Anderson, J. (16) (Preston North End) 1979/80, 1981/2 (Newcastle United) 1983/4, 1985/6, 1986/7, 1987/8, 1988/9.

Babb, P. (29) (Coventry City) 1993/94 (Liverpool) 1994/95, 1995/96, 1996/97, 1997/98, 1998/99.

Bailham, E. (1) (Shamrock Rovers) 1963/4.

Barber, E. (2) (Shelbourne) 1965/6 (Birmingham City) 1965/6.

Beglin, J. (15) (Liverpool) 1983/4, 1984/5, 1985/6, 1986/7.

Bonner, P. (80) (Celtic) 1980/1, 1981/2, 1983/4, 1984/5, 1985/6, 1986/7, 1987/8, 1988/9, 1989/90, 1990/1, 1991/2, 1992/93, 1993/94, 1994/95, 1995/96.

Braddish, S. (1) (Dundalk) 1977/8.

Brady, T.R. (6) (QPR) 1963/4.

Brady, W. L. (72) (Arsenal) 1974/5, 1975/6, 1976/7, 1977/8, 1978/9, 1979/80 (Juventus) 1980/1, 1981/2 (Sampdoria) 1982/3, 1983/4 (Internazionale) 1984/5, 1985/6 (Ascoli) 1986/7 (West Ham United) 1987/8, 1988/9, 1989/90.

Branagan, K. G. (1) (Bolton Wanderers) 1996/97.

Breen, G. (20) (Birmingham City) 1995/96 (Coventry City) 1996/97, 1997/98, 1998/99.

Breen, T. (3) (Shamrock Rovers) 1946/7.

Brennan, F. (1) (Drumcondra) 1964/5.

Brennan, S. A. (19) (Manchester United) 1964/5, 1965/6, 1966/7, 1968/9, 1969/70 (Waterford) 1970/1.

Browne, W. (3) (Bohemians) 1963/4.

Buckley, L. (2) (Shamrock Rovers) 1983/4 (Waregem) 1984/5.

Burke, F. (1) (Cork Athletic) 1951/2.

Byrne, A. B. (14) (Southampton) 1969/70, 1970/1, 1972/3, 1973/4.

Byrne, J. (23) (QPR) 1984/5, 1986/7, 1987/8 (Le Havre) 1989/90, 1990/1 (Brighton & Hove Albion), 1991/2 (Sunderland) 1992/93 (Millwall).

Byrne, P. (8) (Shamrock Rovers) 1983/4, 1984/5, 1985/6.

Campbell, A. (3) (Santander) 1984/5.

Campbell, N. (11) (St Patrick's Athletic) 1970/1 (Fortuna Cologne) 1971/2, 1972/3, 1974/5, 1975/6.

Cantwell, N. (36) (West Ham United) 1953/4, 1955/6, 1956/7, 1957/8, 1958/9, 1959/60, 1960/1 (Manchester United) 1960/1, 1961/2, 1962/3, 1963/4, 1964/5, 1965/6, 1966/7.

Carey, B. P. (3) (Manchester United) 1991/2, 1992/93 (Leicester City) 1993/94.

Carey, J. J. (21) (Manchester United) 1945/6, 1946/7, 1947/8, 1948/9, 1949/50, 1950/1, 1952/3.

Carolan, J. (2) (Manchester United) 1959/60.

Carr, S. (3) (Tottenham Hotspur) 1998/99.

Carroll, B. (2) (Shelbourne) 1948/9, 1949/50.

Carroll, T. R. (17) (Ipswich Town) 1967/8, 1968/9, 1969/70, 1970/1 (Birmingham City) 1971/2, 1972/3.

Carsley, L. K. (11) (Derby County) 1997/98 (Blackburn Rovers) 1998/99.

Cascarino, A. G. (83) (Gillingham) 1985/6 (Millwall) 1987/8, 1988/9, 1989/90 (Aston Villa), 1990/91 (Celtic) 1991/2 (Chelsea) 1992/93, 1993/94 (Marseille) 1994/95, 1995/96 (Nancy) 1996/97, 1997/98, 1998/99.

Chandler, J. (2) (Leeds United) 1979/80.
Clarke, J. (1) (Drogheda United) 1977/8.
Clarke, K. (2) (Drumcondra) 1947/8.
Clarke, M. (1) (Shamrock Rovers) 1949/50.
Clinton, T. J. (3) (Everton) 1950/1, 1953/4.
Coad, P. (11) (Shamrock Rovers) 1946/7, 1947/8, 1948/9, 1950/1, 1951/2.
Coffey, T. (1) (Drumcondra) 1949/50.
Colfer, M. D. (2) (Shelbourne) 1949/50, 1950/1.
Conmy, O. M. (5) (Peterborough United) 1964/5, 1966/7, 1967/8, 1969/70.
Connolly, D. J. (18) (Watford) 1995/96, 1996/97 (Feyenoord) 1997/98 (Wolverhampton Wanderers) 1998/99.
Conroy, G. A. (27) (Stoke City) 1969/70, 1970/1, 1972/3, 1973/4, 1974/5, 1975/6, 1976/7.
Conway, J. P. (20) (Fulham) 1966/7, 1967/8, 1968/9, 1969/70, 1970/1, 1973/4, 1974/5, 1975/6 (Manchester City) 1976/7.
Corr, P. J. (4) (Everton) 1948/9.
Courtney, E. (1) (Cork United) 1945/6.
Coyle, O. (1) (Bolton Wanderers) 1993/94.
Coyne, T. (22) (Celtic) 1991/2, (Tranmere Rovers) 1992/93, (Motherwell) 1993/94, 1994/95, 1995/96, 1997/98.
Cummins, G. P. (19) (Luton Town) 1953/4, 1954/5, 1955/6, 1957/8, 1958/9, 1959/60, 1960/1.
Cuneen, T. (1) (Limerick) 1950/1.
Cunningham, K. (23) (Wimbledon) 1995/96, 1996/97, 1997/98, 1998/99.
Curtis, D. P. (17) (Shelbourne) 1956/7 (Bristol City) 1956/7, 1957/8, (Ipswich Town) 1958/9, 1959/60, 1960/1, 1961/2, 1962/3 (Exeter City) 1963/4.
Cusack, S. (1) (Limerick) 1952/3.

Daish, L. S. (5) (Cambridge United) 1991/2, (Coventry City) 1995/96.
Daly, G. A. (48) (Manchester United) 1972/3, 1973/4, 1974/5, 1976/7 (Derby County) 1977/8, 1978/9, 1979/80 (Coventry City) 1980/1, 1981/2, 1982/3, 1983/4 (Birmingham City) 1984/5, 1985/6 (Shrewsbury Town) 1986/7.
Daly, M. (2) (Wolverhampton Wanderers) 1977/8.
Daly, P. (1) (Shamrock Rovers) 1949/50.
Deacy, E. (4) (Aston Villa) 1981/2.
Delap, R. J. (3) (Derby County) 1997/98.
De Mange, K. J. P. P. (2) (Liverpool) 1986/7, (Hull City) 1988/9.
Dempsey, J. T. (19) (Fulham) 1966/7, 1967/8, 1968/9 (Chelsea) 1968/9, 1969/70, 1970/1, 1971/2.
Dennehy, J. (11) (Cork Hibernian) 1971/2 (Nottingham Forest) 1972/3, 1973/4, 1974/5 (Walsall) 1975/6, 1976/7.
Desmond, P. (4) (Middlesbrough) 1949/50.
Devine, J. (12) (Arsenal) 1979/80, 1980/1, 1981/2, 1982/3 (Norwich City) 1983/4, 1984/5.
Donovan, D. C. (5) (Everton) 1954/5, 1956/7.
Donovan, T. (1) (Aston Villa) 1979/80.
Doyle, C. (1) (Shelbourne) 1958/9.
Duff, D. A. (9) (Blackburn Rovers) 1997/98, 1998/99.
Duffy, B. (1) (Shamrock Rovers) 1949/50.
Dunne, A. P. (33) (Manchester United) 1961/2, 1962/3, 1963/4, 1964/5, 1965/6, 1966/7, 1968/9, 1969/70, 1970/1 (Bolton Wanderers) 1973/4, 1974/5, 1975/6.
Dunne, J. C. (1) (Fulham) 1970/1.
Dunne, P. A. J. (5) (Manchester United) 1964/5, 1965/6, 1966/7.
Dunne, S. (15) (Luton Town) 1952/3, 1953/4, 1955/6, 1956/7, 1957/8, 1958/9, 1959/60.
Dunne, T. (3) (St Patrick's Athletic) 1955/6, 1956/7.

Dunning, P. (2) (Shelbourne) 1970/1.
Dunphy, E. M. (23) (York City) 1965/6 (Millwall) 1965/6, 1966/7, 1967/8, 1968/9, 1969/70, 1970/1.
Dwyer, N. M. (14) (West Ham United) 1959/60 (Swansea Town) 1960/1, 1961/2, 1963/4, 1964/5.

Eccles, P. (1) (Shamrock Rovers) 1985/6.
Eglington, T. J. (24) (Shamrock Rovers) 1945/6 (Everton) 1946/7, 1947/8, 1948/9, 1950/1, 1951/2, 1952/3, 1953/4, 1954/5, 1955/6.
Evans, M. J. (1) (Southampton) 1997/98.

Fagan, E. (1) (Shamrock Rovers) 1972/3.
Fagan, F. (8) (Manchester City) 1954/5, 1959/60 (Derby County) 1960/1.
Fairclough, M. (2) (Dundalk) 1981/2.
Fallon, S. (8) (Celtic) 1950/1, 1951/2, 1952/3, 1954/5.
Farrell, P. D. (28) (Shamrock Rovers) 1945/6 (Everton) 1946/7, 1947/8, 1948/9, 1949/50, 1950/1, 1951/2, 1952/3, 1953/4, 1954/5, 1955/6, 1956/7.
Farrelly, G. (5) (Aston Villa) 1995/96 (Everton) 1997/98.
Finucane, A. (11) (Limerick) 1966/7, 1968/9, 1969/70, 1970/1, 1971/2.
Fitzgerald, F. J. (2) (Waterford) 1954/5, 1955/6.
Fitzgerald, P. J. (5) (Leeds United) 1960/1 (Chester) 1961/2.
Fitzpatrick, K. (1) (Limerick) 1969/70.
Fitzsimons, A. G. (26) (Middlesbrough) 1949/50, 1951/2, 1952/3, 1953/4, 1954/5, 1955/6, 1956/7, 1957/8, 1958/9 (Lincoln City).
Fleming, C. (10) (Middlesbrough) 1995/96, 1996/97, 1997/98.
Fogarty, A. (11) (Sunderland) 1959/60, 1960/1, 1961/2, 1962/3, 1963/4, (Hartlepool United).
Foley, T. C. (9) (Northampton Town) 1963/4, 1964/5, 1965/6, 1966/7.
Fullam, J. (Preston North End) 1960/1 (Shamrock Rovers) 1963/4, 1965/6, 1967/8, 1968/9, 1969/70.

Gallagher, C. (2) (Celtic) 1966/7.
Gallagher, M. (1) (Hibernian) 1953/4.
Galvin, A. (29) (Tottenham Hotspur) 1982/3, 1983/4, 1984/5, 1985/6, 1986/7 (Sheffield Wednesday) 1987/8, 1988/9, (Swindon Town) 1989/90.
Gannon, E. (14) (Notts County) 1948/9 (Sheffield Wednesday) 1949/50, 1950/1, 1951/2, 1953/4, 1954/5 (Shelbourne).
Gannon, M. (1) (Shelbourne) 1971/2.
Gavin, J.T. (7) (Norwich City) 1949/50, 1952/3, 1953/4 (Tottenham Hotspur) 1954/5 (Norwich City) 1956/7.
Gibbons, A. (4) (St Patrick's Athletic) 1951/2, 1953/4, 1955/6.
Gilbert, R. (1) (Shamrock Rovers) 1965/6.
Giles, C. (1) (Doncaster Rovers) 1950/1.
Giles, M. J. (59) (Manchester United) 1959/60, 1960/1, 1961/2, 1962/3 (Leeds United) 1963/4, 1964/5, 1965/6, 1966/7, 1968/9, 1969/70, 1970/1, 1972/3, 1973/4, 1974/5 (West Bromwich Albion) 1975/6, 1976/7 (Shamrock Rovers) 1977/8, 1978/9.
Given, S. J. J. (23) (Blackburn Rovers) 1995/96, 1996/97 (Newcastle United) 1997/98, 1998/99.
Givens, D. J. (56) (Manchester United) 1968/9, 1969/70 (Luton Town), 1970/1, 1971/2 (QPR) 1972/3, 1973/4, 1974/5, 1975/6, 1976/7, 1977/8 (Birmingham City) 1978/9, 1979/80, 1980/1 (Neuchatel Xamax) 1981/2.
Glynn, D. (2) (Drumcondra) 1951/2, 1954/5.
Godwin, T. F. (13) (Shamrock Rovers) 1948/9, 1949/50 (Leicester City), 1950/1 (Bournemouth) 1955/6, 1956/7, 1957/8.
Goodman, J. (4) (Wimbledon) 1996/97.

Gorman, W. C. (2) (Brentford) 1946/7.
Grealish, A. (44) (Orient) 1975/6, 1978/9 (Luton Town) 1979/80, 1980/1, (Brighton & Hove Albion) 1981/2, 1982/3, 1983/4 (West Bromwich Albion) 1984/5, 1985/6.
Gregg, E. (8) (Bohemians) 1977/8, 1978/9, 1979/80.
Grimes, A. A. (17) (Manchester United) 1977/8, 1979/80, 1980/1, 1981/2, 1982/3 (Coventry City) 1983/4 (Luton Town) 1987/8.

Hale, A. (14) (Aston Villa) 1961/2 (Doncaster Rovers) 1962/3, 1963/4, (Waterford) 1966/7, 1967/8, 1968/9, 1969/70, 1970/1, 1971/2.
Hamilton, T. (2) (Shamrock Rovers) 1958/9.
Hand, E. K. (20) (Portsmouth) 1968/9, 1969/70, 1970/1, 1972/3, 1973/4, 1974/5, 1975/6.
Harte, I. P. (19) (Leeds United) 1995/96, 1996/97, 1997/98, 1998/99.
Hartnett, J. B. (2) (Middlesbrough) 1948/9, 1953/4.
Haverty, J. (32) (Arsenal) 1955/6, 1956/7, 1957/8, 1958/9, 1959/60, 1960/1, (Blackburn Rovers) 1961/2 (Millwall) 1962/3, 1963/4 (Celtic) 1964/5, (Bristol Rovers) 1964/5 (Shelbourne) 1965/6, 1966/7.
Hayes, A.W.P. (1) (Southampton) 1978/9.
Hayes, W. E. (2) (Huddersfield Town) 1946/7.
Hayes, W. J. (1) (Limerick) 1948/9.
Healey, R. (2) (Cardiff City) 1976/7, 1979/80.
Heighway, S. D. (34) (Liverpool) 1970/1, 1972/3, 1974/5, 1975/6, 1976/7, 1977/8, 1978/9, 1979/80, 1980/1 (Minnesota Kicks) 1981/2.
Henderson, B. (2) (Drumcondra) 1947/8.
Hennessy, J. (5) (Shelbourne) 1955/6, 1965/6 (St Patrick's Athletic) 1968/9.
Herrick, J. (3) (Cork Hibernians) 1971/2 (Shamrock Rovers) 1972/3.
Higgins, J. (1) (Birmingham City) 1950/1.
Holmes, J. (Coventry City) 1970/1, 1972/3, 1973/4, 1974/5, 1975/6, 1976/7 (Tottenham Hotspur) 1977/8, 1978/9, 1980/1 (Vancouver Whitecaps) 1980/1.
Houghton, R. J. (73) (Oxford United) 1985/6, 1986/7, 1987/8 (Liverpool), 1988/9, 1989/90, 1990/1, 1991/2 (Aston Villa) 1992/93, 1993/94 (Crystal Palace) 1994/95, 1995/96, 1996/97 (Reading) 1997/98.
Howlett, G. (1) (Brighton & Hove Albion) 1983/4.
Hughton, C. (53) (Tottenham Hotspur) 1979/80, 1980/1, 1981/2, 1982/3, 1983/4, 1984/5, 1985/6, 1986/7, 1987/8, 1988/9, 1989/90, 1990/1 (West Ham United), 1991/2.
Hurley, C. J. (40) (Millwall) 1956/7, 1957/8 (Sunderland) 1958/9, 1959/60, 1960/1, 1961/2, 1962/3, 1963/4, 1964/5, 1965/6, 1966/7, 1967/8 (Bolton Wanderers) 1968/9.

Irwin, D. J. (52) (Manchester United) 1990/1, 1991/2, 1992/93, 1993/94, 1994/95, 1995/96, 1996/97, 1997/98, 1998/99.

Kavanagh, G. A. (3) (Stoke City) 1997/98, 1998/99.
Keane, R. D. (9) (Wolverhampton Wanderers) 1997/98, 1998/99.
Keane, R. M. (42) (Nottingham Forest) 1990/1, 1991/2, 1992/93, (Manchester United) 1993/94, 1994/95, 1995/96, 1996/97, 1997/98, 1998/99.
Keane, T. R. (4) (Swansea Town) 1948/9.
Kearin, M. (1) (Shamrock Rovers) 1971/2.
Kearns, F. T. (1) (West Ham United) 1953/4.
Kearns, M. (18) (Oxford United) 1969/70 (Walsall) 1973/4, 1975/6, 1976/7, 1977/8, 1978/9 (Wolverhampton Wanderers) 1979/80.
Kelly, A. T. (22) (Sheffield United) 1992/93, 1993/94, 1994/95, 1995/96, 1996/97, 1997/98, 1998/99.
Kelly, D. T. (26) (Walsall) 1987/8 (West Ham United) 1988/9 (Leicester City) 1989/90, 1990/1 (Newcastle United) 1991/2, 1992/93 (Wolverhampton Wanderers) 1993/94, 1994/95 (Sunderland) 1995/96, 1996/97 (Tranmere Rovers) 1997/98.

Kelly, G. (28) (Leeds United) 1993/94, 1994/95, 1995/96, 1996/97, 1997/98.
Kelly, J. A. (48) (Drumcondra) 1956/7 (Preston North End) 1961/2, 1962/3, 1963/4, 1964/5, 1965/6, 1966/7, 1967/8, 1969/70, 1970/1, 1971/2, 1972/3.
Kelly, J. P. V. (5) (Wolverhampton Wanderers) 1960/1, 1961/2.
Kelly, M. J. (4) (Portsmouth) 1987/8, 1988/9, 1990/1.
Kelly, N. (1) (Nottingham Forest) 1953/4.
Kenna, J. J. (26) (Blackburn Rovers) 1994/95, 1995/96, 1996/97, 1997/98, 1998/99.
Kennedy, M. (22) (Liverpool) 1995/96, 1996/97, 1997/98 (Wimbledon) 1998/99.
Kennedy, M. F. (2) (Portsmouth) 1985/6.
Keogh, J. (1) (Shamrock Rovers) 1965/6.
Keogh, S. (1) (Shamrock Rovers) 1958/9.
Kernaghan, A. N. (22) (Middlesbrough) 1992/93 (Manchester City) 1993/94, 1994/95, 1995/96.
Kiernan, F. W. (5) (Shamrock Rovers) 1950/1 (Southampton) 1951/2.
Kilbane, K. D. (5) (West Bromwich Albion) 1997/98, 1998/99.
Kinnear, J. P. (26) (Tottenham Hotspur) 1966/7, 1967/8, 1968/9, 1969/70, 1970/1, 1971/2, 1972/3, 1973/4, 1974/5 (Brighton & Hove Albion) 1975/6.
Kinsella, M. A. (9) (Charlton Athletic) 1997/98, 1998/99.

Langan, D. (25) (Derby County) 1977/8, 1979/80 (Birmingham City) 1980/1, 1981/2 (Oxford United) 1984/5, 1985/6, 1986/7, 1987/8.
Lawler, J. F. (8) (Fulham) 1952/3, 1953/4, 1954/5, 1955/6.
Lawlor, J. C. (3) (Drumcondra) 1948/9 (Doncaster Rovers) 1950/1.
Lawlor, M. (5) (Shamrock Rovers) 1970/1, 1972/3.
Lawrenson, M. (38) (Preston North End) 1976/7 (Brighton & Hove Albion) 1977/8, 1978/9, 1979/80, 1980/1 (Liverpool) 1981/2, 1982/3, 1983/4, 1984/5, 1985/6, 1986/7, 1987/8.
Leech, M. (8) (Shamrock Rovers) 1968/9, 1971/2, 1972/3.
Lowry, D. (1) (St Patrick's Athletic) 1961/2.

McAlinden, J. (2) (Portsmouth) 1945/6.
McAteer, J. W. (30) (Bolton Wanderers) 1993/94, 1994/95 (Liverpool) 1995/96, 1996/97, 1997/98 (Blackburn Rovers) 1998/99.
McCann, J. (1) (Shamrock Rovers) 1956/7.
McCarthy, M. (57) (Manchester City) 1983/4, 1984/5, 1985/6, 1986/7 (Celtic) 1987/8, 1988/9 (Lyon) 1989/90, 1990/1 (Millwall), 1991/2.
McConville, T. (6) (Dundalk) 1971/2 (Waterford) 1972/3.
McDonagh, J. (24) (Everton) 1980/1 (Bolton Wanderers) 1981/2, 1982/3, (Notts County) 1983/4, 1984/5, 1985/6.
McDonagh, Joe (3) (Shamrock Rovers) 1983/4, 1984/5.
McEvoy, M. A. (17) (Blackburn Rovers) 1960/1, 1962/3, 1963/4, 1964/5, 1965/6, 1966/7.
McGee, P. (15) (QPR) 1977/8, 1978/9, 1979/80 (Preston North End) 1980/1.
McGoldrick, E. J. (15) (Crystal Palace) 1991/2, 1992/93, (Arsenal) 1993/94, 1994/95.
McGowan, D. (3) (West Ham United) 1948/9.
McGowan, J. (1) (Cork United) 1946/7.
McGrath, M. (22) (Blackburn Rovers) 1957/8, 1958/9, 1959/60, 1960/1, 1961/2, 1962/3, 1963/4, 1964/5, 1965/6 (Bradford Park Avenue) 1966/7.
McGrath, P. (83) (Manchester United) 1984/5, 1985/6, 1986/7, 1987/8, 1988/9 (Aston Villa) 1989/90, 1990/1, 1991/2, 1992/93, 1993/94, 1994/95, 1995/96 (Derby County) 1996/97.
Macken, A. (1) (Derby County) 1976/7.
Mackey, G. (3) (Shamrock Rovers) 1956/7.
McLoughlin, A. F. (39) (Swindon T) 1989/90, 1990/1 (Southampton) 1991/2 (Portsmouth) 1992/93, 1993/94, 1994/95, 1995/96, 1996/97, 1997/98, 1998/99.

McMillan, W. (2) (Belfast Celtic) 1945/6.
McNally, J. B. (3) (Luton Town) 1958/9, 1960/1, 1962/3.
Malone, G. (1) (Shelbourne) 1948/9.
Mancini, T. J. (5) (QPR) 1973/4 (Arsenal) 1974/5.
Martin, C. J. (30) (Glentoran) 1945/6, 1946/7 (Leeds United) 1947/8, (Aston Villa) 1948/9, 1949/50 1950/1, 1951/2, 1953/4, 1954/5, 1955/6.
Martin, M. P. (51) (Bohemians) 1971/2, 1972/3 (Manchester United) 1972/3, 1973/4, 1974/5 (West Bromwich Albion) 1975/6, 1976/7 (Newcastle United) 1978/9, 1979/80, 1981/2, 1982/3.
Maybury, A. (2) (Leeds United) 1997/98, 1998/99.
Meagan, M. K. (17) (Everton) 1960/1, 1961/2, 1962/3, 1963/4 (Huddersfield Town) 1964/5, 1965/6, 1966/7, 1967/8 (Drogheda) 1969/70.
Milligan, M. J. (1) (Oldham Athletic) 1991/2.
Mooney, J. (2) (Shamrock Rovers) 1964/5.
Moore, A. (8) (Middlesbrough) 1995/96, 1996/97.
Moran, K. (70) (Manchester United) 1979/80, 1980/1, 1981/2, 1982/3, 1983/4, 1984/5, 1985/6, 1986/7, 1987/8 (Sporting Gijon) 1988/9 (Blackburn Rovers) 1989/90, 1990/1, 1991/2, 1992/93, 1993/94.
Moroney, T. (12) (West Ham United) 1947/8, 1948/9, 1949/50, 1950/1, 1951/2, 1953/4.
Morris, C. B. (35) (Celtic) 1987/8, 1988/9, 1989/90, 1990/1, 1991/2 (Middlesbrough) 1992/93.
Moulson, G. B. (3) (Lincoln City) 1947/8, 1948/9.
Mucklan, C. (1) (Drogheda) 1977/8.
Mulligan, P. M. (50) (Shamrock Rovers) 1968/9, 1969/70 (Chelsea) 1970/1, 1971/2 (Crystal Palace) 1972/3, 1973/4, 1974/5 (West Bromwich Albion) 1975/6, 1976/7, 1977/8, 1978/9 (Shamrock Rovers) 1979/80.
Munroe, L. (1) (Shamrock Rovers) 1953/4.
Murphy, A. (1) (Clyde) 1955/6.
Murphy, B. (1) (Bohemians) 1985/6.
Murphy, J. (1) (Crystal Palace) 1979/80.
Murray, T. (1) (Dundalk) 1949/50.

Newman, W. (1) (Shelbourne) 1968/9.
Nolan, R. (10) (Shamrock Rovers) 1956/7, 1957/8, 1959/60, 1961/2, 1962/3.

O'Brien, F. (4) (Philadelphia Fury) 1979/80.
O'Brien, L. (16) (Shamrock Rovers) 1985/6 (Manchester United) 1986/7, 1987/8 (Newcastle United) 1988/9, 1991/2, 1992/93 (Tranmere Rovers) 1993/94, 1995/96, 1996/97.
O'Brien, R. (4) (Notts County) 1975/6, 1976/7.
O'Byrne, L. B. (1) (Shamrock Rovers) 1948/9.
O'Callaghan, B. R. (6) (Stoke City) 1978/9, 1979/80, 1980/1, 1981/2.
O'Callaghan, K. (20) (Ipswich Town) 1980/1, 1981/2, 1982/3, 1983/4, 1984/5, (Portsmouth) 1985/6, 1986/7.
O'Connnell, A. (2) (Dundalk) 1966/7 (Bohemians) 1970/1.
O'Connor, T. (4) (Shamrock Rovers) 1949/50.
O'Connor, T. (7) (Fulham) 1967/8 (Dundalk) 1971/2 (Bohemians) 1972/3.
O'Driscoll, J. F. (3) (Swansea Town) 1948/9.
O'Driscoll, S. (3) (Fulham) 1981/2.
O'Farrell, F. (9) (West Ham United) 1951/2, 1952/3, 1953/4, 1954/5, 1955/6 (Preston North End) 1957/8, 1958/9.
O'Flanagan, K. P. (3) (Arsenal) 1946/7.
O'Flanagan, M. (1) (Bohemians) 1946/7.
O'Hanlon, K. G. (1) (Rotherham United) 1987/8.
O'Keefe, E. (5) (Everton) 1980/1 (Port Vale) 1983/4, 1984/5.

O'Leary, D. (67) Arsenal) 1976/7, 1977/8, 1978/9, 1979/80, 1980/1, 1981/2, 1982/3, 1983/4, 1984/5, 1985/6, 1988/9, 1989/90, 1990/1, 1991/2, 1992/93.
O'Leary, P. (7) (Shamrock Rovers) 1979/80, 1980/1.
O'Neill, F. S. (20) (Shamrock Rovers) 1961/2, 1964/5, 1965/6, 1966/7, 1968/9, 1971/2.
O'Neill, J. (17) (Everton) 1951/2, 1952/3, 1953/4, 1954/5, 1955/6, 1956/7, 1957/8, 1958/9.
O'Neill, J. (1) (Preston North End) 1960/1.
O'Neill, K. P. (12) (Norwich City) 1995/96, 1996/97 (Middlesbrough) 1998/99.
O'Regan, K. (4) (Brighton & Hove Albion) 1983/4, 1984/5.
O'Reilly, J. (2) (Cork United) 1945/6.

Peyton, G. (33) (Fulham) 1976/7, 1977/8, 1978/9, 1979/80, 1980/1, 1981/2, 1984/5, 1985/6 (Bournemouth) 1987/8, 1988/9, 1989/90, 1990/1 (Everton) 1991/2.
Peyton, N. (6) (Shamrock Rovers) 1956/7 (Leeds United) 1959/60, 1960/1, 1962/3.
Phelan, T. (38) (Wimbledon) 1991/2 (Manchester City) 1992/93, 1993/94, 1994/95, 1995/96 (Chelsea) (Everton) 1996/97, 1997/98.

Quinn, N. J. (69) (Arsenal) 1985/6, 1986/7, 1987/8, 1988/9 (Manchester City) 1989/90, 1990/1, 1991/2, 1992/93, 1993/94, 1994/95, 1995/96 (Sunderland) 1996/97, 1997/98, 1998/99.

Richardson, D. J. (3) (Shamrock Rovers) 1971/2 (Gillingham) 1972/3, 1979/80.
Ringstead, A. (20) (Sheffield United) 1950/1, 1951/2, 1952/3, 1953/4, 1954/5, 1955/6, 1956/7, 1957/8, 1958/9.
Robinson, M. (23) (Brighton & Hove Albion) 1980/1, 1981/2, 1982/3, (Liverpool) 1983/4, 1984/5 (QPR) 1985/6.
Roche, P. J. (8) (Shelbourne) 1971/2 (Manchester United) 1974/5, 1975/6.
Rogers, E. (19) (Blackburn Rovers) 1967/8, 1968/9, 1969/70, 1970/1, (Charlton Athletic) 1971/2, 1972/3.
Ryan, G. (16) (Derby County) 1977/8 (Brighton & Hove Albion) 1978/9, 1979/80, 1980/1, 1981/2, 1983/4, 1984/5.
Ryan, R. A. (16) (West Bromwich Albion) 1949/50, 1950/1, 1951/2, 1952/3, 1953/4, 1954/5 (Derby County) 1955/6.

Savage, D. P. T. (5) (Millwall) 1995/96.
Saward, P. (18) (Millwall) 1953/4 (Aston Villa) 1956/7, 1957/8, 1958/9, 1959/60, 1960/1 (Huddersfield Town) 1960/1, 1961/2, 1962/3.
Scannell, T. (1) (Southend United) 1953/4.
Scully, P. J. (1) (Arsenal) 1988/9.
Sheedy, K. (45) (Everton) 1983/4, 1984/5, 1985/6, 1986/7, 1987/8, 1988/9, 1989/90, 1990/1 (Newcastle United) 1991/2, 1992/93.
Sheridan, J. J. (34) (Leeds United) 1987/8, 1988/9 (Sheffield Wednesday) 1989/90, 1990/1, 1991/2, 1992/93, 1993/94, 1994/95, 1995/96.
Slaven, B. (7) (Middlesbrough) 1989/90, 1990/91, 1992/93.
Sloan, J. W. (2) (Arsenal) 1945/6.
Smyth, M. (1) (Shamrock Rovers) 1968/9.
Stapleton, F. (70) (Arsenal) 1976/7, 1977/8, 1978/9, 1979/80, 1980/1 (Manchester United) 1981/2, 1982/3, 1983/4, 1984/5, 1985/6, 1986/7 (Ajax) 1987/8 (Derby County) (Le Havre) 1988/9 (Blackburn Rovers) 1989/90.
Staunton, S. (78) (Liverpool) 1988/9, 1989/90, 1990/1 (Aston Villa) 1991/2, 1992/93, 1993/94, 1994/95, 1995/96, 1996/97, 1997/98, 1998/99.
Stevenson, A. E. (6) (Everton) 1946/7, 1947/8, 1948/9.
Strahan, F. (5) (Shelbourne) 1963/4, 1964/5, 1965/6.
Swan, M. M. G. (1) (Drumcondra) 1959/60.
Synnott, N. (3) (Shamrock Rovers) 1977/8, 1978/9.

Thomas, P. (2) (Waterford) 1973/4.
Townsend, A. D. (70) (Norwich City) 1988/9, 1989/90, 1990/1 (Chelsea) 1991/2, 1992/93 (Aston Villa) 1993/94, 1994/95, 1995/96, 1996/97 (Middlesbrough) 1997/98.
Traynor, T. J. (8) (Southampton) 1953/4, 1961/2, 1962/3, 1963/4.
Treacy, R. C. P. (42) (West Bromwich Albion) 1965/6, 1966/7, 1967/8 (Charlton Athletic) 1967/8, 1968/9, 1969/70, 1970/1 (Swindon Town) 1971/2, 1972/3, 1973/4 (Preston North End) 1973/4, 1974/5, 1975/6 (West Bromwich Albion) 1976/7, 1977/8 (Shamrock Rovers) 1979/80.
Tuohy, L. (8) (Shamrock Rovers) 1955/6, 1958/9 (Newcastle United) 1961/2, 1962/3 (Shamrock Rovers) 1963/4, 1964/5.
Turner, P. (2) (Celtic) 1962/3, 1963/4.

Vernon, J. (2) (Belfast Celtic) 1945/6.

Waddock, G. (20) (QPR) 1979/80, 1980/1, 1981/2, 1982/3, 1983/4, 1984/5, 1985/6 (Millwall) 1989/90.
Walsh, D. J. (20) (Linfield) (West Bromwich Albion) 1945/6, 1946/7, 1947/8, 1948/9, 1949/50, 1950/1 (Aston Villa) 1951/2, 1952/3, 1953/4.
Walsh, J. (1) (Limerick) 1981/2.
Walsh, M. (21) (Blackpool) 1975/6, 1976/7 (Everton) 1978/9 (QPR) (Porto) 1980/1, 1981/2, 1982/3, 1983/4, 1984/5.
Walsh, M. (4) (Everton) 1981/2, 1982/3.
Walsh, W. (9) (Manchester City) 1946/7, 1947/8, 1948/9, 1949/50.
Waters, J. (2) (Grimsby Town) 1976/7, 1979/80.
Whelan, R. (2) (St Patrick's Athletic) 1963/4.
Whelan, R. (53) (Liverpool) 1980/1, 1981/2, 1982/3, 1983/4, 1984/5, 1985/6, 1986/7, 1987/8, 1988/9, 1989/90, 1990/1, 1991/2, 1992/93, 1993/94 (Southend United) 1994/95.
Whelan, W. (4) (Manchester United) 1955/6, 1956/7.
Whittaker, R. (1) (Chelsea) 1958/9.

BRITISH ISLES INTERNATIONAL GOALSCORERS SINCE 1946

ENGLAND

A'Court, A. 1
Adams, T.A. 4
Allen, R. 2
Anderson, V. 2
Anderton, D.R. 7
Astall, G. 1
Atyeo, P.J.W. 5

Baily, E.F. 5
Baker, J.H. 3
Ball, A.J. 8
Barnes, J. 11
Barnes, P.S. 4
Barmby, N.J. 3
Beardsley, P.A. 9
Beattie, J.K. 1
Beckham, D.R.J. 1
Bell, C. 9
Bentley, R.T.F. 9
Blissett, L. 3
Bowles, S. 1
Bradford, G.R.W. 1
Bradley, W. 2
Bridges, B.J. 1
Broadbent, P.F. 2
Broadis, I.A. 8
Brooking, T.D. 5
Brooks, J. 2
Bull, S.G. 4
Butcher, T. 3
Byrne, J.J. 8

Carter, H.S. 7
(inc. 2 scored pre-war)
Chamberlain, M. 1
Channon, M.R. 21
Charlton, J. 6
Charlton, R. 49
Chivers, M. 13
Clarke, A.J. 10
Connelly, J.M. 7
Coppell, S.J. 7
Cowans, G. 2
Crawford, R. 1
Currie, A.W. 3

Dixon, L.M. 1
Dixon, K.M. 4
Douglas, B. 11

Eastham, G. 2
Edwards, D. 5
Elliott, W.H. 3

Ferdinand, L. 5
Finney, T. 30
Flowers, R. 10
Fowler, R.B. 2
Francis, G.C.J. 3
Francis, T. 12
Froggatt, J. 2
Froggatt, R. 2

Gascoigne, P.J. 10
Goddard, P. 1
Grainger, C. 3
Greaves, J. 44

Haines, J.T.W. 2
Hancocks, J. 2
Hassall, H.W. 4
Hateley, M. 9
Haynes, J.N. 18
Hirst, D.E. 1
Hitchens, G.A. 5
Hoddle, G. 8
Hughes, E.W. 1
Hunt, R. 18
Hunter, N. 2
Hurst, G.C. 24

Johnson, D.E. 6

Kay, A.H. 1
Keegan, J.K. 21
Kennedy, R. 3
Keown, M.R. 1
Kevan, D.T. 8
Kidd, B. 1

Langton, R. 1
Latchford, R.D. 5
Lawler, C. 1
Lawton, T. 22
(inc. 6 scored pre-war)
Lee, F. 10
Lee, J. 1
Lee, R.M. 2
Lee, S. 2

Le Saux, G.P. 1
Lineker, G. 48
Lofthouse, N. 30

Mabbutt, G. 1
McDermott, T. 3
Macdonald, M. 6
Mannion, W.J. 11
Mariner, P. 13
Marsh, R.W. 1
Matthews, S. 11
(inc. 8 scored pre-war)
Medley, L.D. 1
Melia, J. 1
Merson, P.C. 3
Milburn, J.E.T. 10
Moore, R.F. 2
Morris, J. 3
Mortensen, S.H. 23
Mullen, J. 6
Mullery, A.P. 1

Neal, P.G. 5
Nicholls, J. 1
Nicholson, W.E. 1

O'Grady, M. 3
Owen, M.J. 4
Own goals 23

Paine, T.L. 7
Palmer, C.L. 1
Parry, R.A. 1
Peacock, A. 3
Pearce, S. 5
Pearson, J.S. 5
Pearson, S.C. 5
Perry, W. 2
Peters, M. 20
Pickering, F. 5
Platt, D. 27
Pointer, R. 2

Ramsay, A.E. 3
Revie, D.G. 4
Robson, B. 26
Robson, R. 4
Rowley, J.F. 6
Royle, J. 2

Sansom, K.	1	Brazil, A.	1	Henderson, W.	5
Scholes, P.	7	Bremner, W.J.	3	Hendry, E.C.J.	1
Sewell, J.	3	Brown, A.D.	6	Herd, D.G.	3
Shackleton, L.F.	1	Buckley, P.	1	Herd, G.	1
Shearer, A.	24	Burley, C.W.	3	Hewie, J.D.	2
Sheringham, E.P.	9	Burns, K.	1	Holton, J.A.	2
Smith, A.M.	2			Hopkin, D.	2
Smith, R.	13	Calderwood, C.	1	Houliston, W.	2
Southgate, G.	1	Caldow, E.	4	Howie, H.	1
Steven, T.M.	4	Campbell, R.	1	Hughes, J.	1
Stiles, N.P.	1	Chalmers, S.	3	Hunter, W.	1
Stone, S.B.	2	Collins, J.	11	Hutchison, D.	1
Summerbee, M.G.	1	Collins, R.V.	10	Hutchison, T.	1
		Combe, J.R.	1		
Tambling, R.V.	1	Conn, A.	1	Jackson, C.	1
Taylor, P.J.	2	Cooper, D.	6	Jackson, D.	4
Taylor, T.	16	Craig, J.	1	Jardine, A.	1
Thompson, P.B.	1	Crawford, S.	1	Jess, E.	2
Tueart, D.	2	Curran, H.P.	1	Johnston, A.	2
				Johnston, L.H.	1
Viollet, D.S.	1	Dailly, C.	1	Johnston, M.	14
		Dalglish, K.	30	Johnstone, D.	2
Waddle, C.R.	6	Davidson, J.A.	1	Johnstone, J.	4
Wallace, D.L.	1	Docherty, T.H.	1	Johnstone, R.	9
Walsh, P.	1	Dodds, D.	1	Jordan, J.	11
Watson, D.V.	4	Dodds, W.	3		
Webb, N.	4	Duncan, D.M.	1	Law, D.	30
Weller, K.	1	Durie, G.S.	7	Leggat, G.	8
Wignall, F.	2			Lennox, R.	3
Wilkins, R.G.	3	Fernie, W.	1	Liddell, W.	6
Wilshaw, D.J.	10	Flavell, R.	2	Linwood, A.B.	1
Wise, D.F.	1	Fleming, C.	2	Lorimer, P.	4
Withe, P.	1				
Woodcock, T.	16	Gallacher, K.W.	8	Macari, L.	5
Worthington, F.S.	2	Gemmell, T.K		McAllister, G.	5
Wright, I.E.	9	*(St Mirren)*	1	MacDougall, E.J.	3
Wright, M.	1	Gemmell, T.K		MacKay, D.C.	4
Wright, W.A.	3	*(Celtic)*	1	Mackay, G.	1
		Gemmill, A.	8	MacKenzie, J.A.	1
		Gibson, D.W.	3	MacLeod, M.	1
SCOTLAND		Gilzean, A.J.	12	McAvennie, F.	1
Aitken, R.	1	Gough, C.R.	6	McCall, S.M.	1
Archibald, S.	4	Graham, A.	2	McCalliog, J.	1
		Graham, G.	3	McClair, B.	2
Baird, S.	2	Gray, A.	5	McCoist, A.	19
Bannon, E.	1	Gray, E.	3	McGhee, M.	2
Bauld, W.	2	Gray, F.	1	McGinlay, J.	3
Baxter, J.C.	3	Greig, J.	3	McInally, A.	3
Bett, J.	1			McKimmie, S.I.	1
Bone, J.	1	Hamilton, G.	4	McKinlay, W.	4
Booth, S.	5	Harper, J.M.	2	McKinnon, R.	1
Boyd, T.	1	Hartford, R.A.	4	McLaren, A.	4
Brand, R.	8	Henderson, J.G.	1	McLean, T.	1
				McLintock, F.	1

McMillan, I.L. 2
McNeill, W. 3
McPhail, J. 3
McQueen, G. 5
McStay, P. 9
Mason, J. 4
Masson, D.S. 5
Miller, W. 1
Mitchell, R.C. 1
Morgan, W. 1
Morris, H. 3
Mudie, J.K. 9
Mulhall, G. 1
Murdoch, R. 5
Murray, J. 1

Narey, D. 1
Nevin, P.K.F. 5
Nicholas, C. 5

O'Hare, J. 5
Ormond, W.E. 1
Orr, T. 1
Own goals 9

Parlane, D. 1
Pettigrew, W. 2
Provan, D. 1

Quinn, J. 7
Quinn, P. 1

Reilly, L. 22
Ring, T. 2
Rioch, B.D. 6
Ritchie, P.S. 1
Robertson, A. 2
Robertson, J. 2
Robertson, J.N. 9

St John, I. 9
Scott, A.S. 5
Sharp, G. 1
Shearer, D. 2
Smith, G. 4
Souness, G.J. 4
Steel, W. 12
Stein, C. 10
Stewart, R. 1
Strachan, G. 5
Sturrock, P. 3

Thornton, W. 1

Waddell, W. 6
Wallace, I.A. 1
Wark, J. 7
Weir, A. 1
White, J.A. 3
Wilson, D. 9

Young, A. 2

WALES

Allchurch, I.J. 23
Allen, M. 3

Barnes, W. 1
Bellamy, C.D. 2
Blackmore, C.G. 1
Blake, N.A. 2
Bodin, P.J. 3
Bowen, D.I. 3
Bowen, M. 2
Boyle, T. 1
Burgess, W.A.R. 1

Charles, J. 1
Charles, M. 6
Charles, W.J. 15
Clarke, R.J. 5
Coleman, C. 4
Curtis, A. 6

Davies, G. 2
Davies, R.T. 9
Davies, R.W. 6
Deacy, N. 4
Durban, A. 2
Dwyer, P. 2

Edwards, G. 2
Edwards, R.I. 4
England, H.M. 4
Evans, I. 1

Flynn, B. 7
Ford, T. 23
Foulkes, W.J. 1

Giggs, R.J. 5
Giles, D. 2
Godfrey, B.C. 2
Griffiths, A.T. 6
Griffiths, M.W. 2

Harris, C.S. 1
Hartson, J. 2

Hewitt, R. 1
Hockey, T. 1
Hodges, G. 2
Horne, B. 2
Hughes, L.M. 16

James, L. 10
James, R. 7
Jones, A. 1
Jones, B.S. 2
Jones, Cliff 16
Jones, D.E. 1
Jones, J.P. 1

Kryzwicki, R.I. 1

Leek, K. 5
Lovell, S. 1
Lowrie, G. 2

Mahoney, J.F. 1
Medwin, T.C. 6
Melville, A.K. 3
Moore, G. 1

Nicholas, P. 2

O'Sullivan, P.A. 1
Own goals 5

Palmer, D. 1
Paul, R. 1
Pembridge, M.A. 5
Phillips, D. 2
Powell, A. 1
Powell, D. 1
Price, P. 1

Reece, G.I. 2
Rees, R.R. 3
Roberts, P.S. 1
Robinson, J.R.C. 2
Rush, I. 28

Saunders, D. 21
Savage R.W. 1
Slatter, N. 2
Smallman, D.P. 1
Speed, G.A. 3
Symons, C.J. 2

Tapscott, D.R. 4
Thomas, M. 4
Toshack, J.B. 12

Vernon, T.R. 8

Walsh, I. 7
Williams, A. 1
Williams, G.E. 1
Williams, G.G. 1
Woosnam, A.P. 3

Yorath, T.C. 2
Young, E. 1

NORTHERN IRELAND

Anderson, T. 4
Armstrong, G. 12

Barr, H.H. 1
Best, G. 9
Bingham, W.L. 10
Black, K. 1
Blanchflower, D. 2
Blanchflower, J. 1
Brennan, R.A. 1
Brotherston, N. 3

Campbell, W.G. 1
Casey, T. 2
Caskey, W. 1
Cassidy, T. 1
Clarke, C.J. 13
Clements, D. 2
Cochrane, T. 1
Crossan, E. 1
Crossan, J.A. 10
Cush, W.W. 5

D'Arcy, S.D. 1
Doherty, I. 1
Doherty, P.D. 3
(inc. 1 scored pre-war)
Dougan, A.D. 8
Dowie, I. 12

Elder, A.R. 1

Ferguson, W. 1
Ferris, R.O. 1
Finney, T. 2

Gillespie, K.R. 1
Gray, P. 5

Griffin, D.J. 1

Hamilton, B. 4
Hamilton, W. 5
Harkin, J.T. 2
Harvey, M. 3
Hill, C.F. 1
Humphries, W. 1
Hughes, M.E. 3
Hunter, A. 1
Hunter, B.V. 1

Irvine, W.J. 8

Johnston, W.C. 1
Jones, J. 1

Lennon, N.F. 2
Lockhart, N. 3
Lomas, S.M. 2

Magilton, J. 5
McAdams, W.J. 7
McClelland, J. 1
McCrory, S. 1
McCurdy, C. 1
McDonald, A. 3
McGarry, J.K. 1
McGrath, R.C. 4
McIlroy, J. 10
McIlroy, S.B. 5
McLaughlin, J.C. 6
McMahon, G.J. 2
McMordie, A.S. 3
McMorran, E.J. 4
McParland, P.J. 10
Moreland, V. 1
Morgan, S. 3
Morrow, S.J. 1
Mulryne, P.P. 1

Neill, W.J.T. 2
Nelson, S. 1
Nicholl, C.J. 3
Nicholl, J.M. 1
Nicholson, J.J. 6

O'Boyle, G. 1
O'Kane, W.J. 1
O'Neill, J. 2
O'Neill, M.A. 4
O'Neill, M.H. 8
Own goals 5

Patterson, D.J. 1
Peacock, R. 2
Penney, S. 2

Quinn, J.M. 12
Quinn, S.J. 1

Rowland, K. 1

Simpson, W.J. 5
Smyth, S. 5
Spence, D.W. 3
Stewart, I. 2

Taggart, G.P. 7
Tully, C.P. 3

Walker, J. 1
Walsh, D.J. 5
Welsh, E. 1
Whiteside, N. 9
Wilson, D.J. 1
Wilson, K.J. 6
Wilson, S.J. 7

EIRE

Aldridge, J. 19
Ambrose, P. 1
Anderson, J. 1

Bermingham, P. 1
Bradshaw, P. 4
Brady, L. 9
Breen, G. 3
Brown, D. 1
Byrne, J. *(Bray)* 1
Byrne, J. *(QPR)* 4

Cantwell, J. 14
Carey, J. 3
Carroll, T. 1
Cascarino, A. 19
Coad, P. 3
Connolly, D.J. 7
Conroy, T. 2
Conway, J. 3
Coyne, T. 6
Cummings, G. 5
Curtis, D. 8

Daly, G. 13
Davis, T. 4

Dempsey, J.	1	Hughton, C.	1	O'Keefe, E.	1
Dennehy, M.	2	Hurley, C.	2	O'Leary, D.A.	1
Donnelly, J.	3			O'Neill, F.	1
Donnelly, T.	1	Irwin, D.	4	O'Neill, K.P.	4
Duffy, B.	1			O'Reilly, J.	2
Duggan, H.	1	Jordan, D.	1	O'Reilly, J.	1
Dunne, J.	12			Own goals	7
Dunne, L.	1	Kavanagh, G.A.	1		
		Keane, R.D.	2	Quinn, N.	17
Eglinton, T.	2	Keane, R.M.	5		
Ellis, P.	2	Kelly, D.	9		
		Kelly, G.	1	Ringstead, A.	7
Fagan, F.	5	Kelly, J.	2	Robinson, M.	4
Fallon, S.	2	Kennedy, M.	1	Rogers, E.	5
Fallon, W.	2	Kernaghan, A.	1	Ryan, G.	1
Farrell, P.	3			Ryan, R.	3
Fitzgerald, J.	1	Lacey, W.	1		
Fitzgerald, P.	2	Lawrenson, M.	5	Sheedy, K.	9
Fitzsimons, A.	7	Leech, M.	2	Sheridan, J.	5
Flood, J.J.	4			Slaven, B.	1
Fogarty, A.	3	McAteer, J.W.	1	Sloan, W.	1
Fullam, J.	1	McCann, J.	1	Squires, J.	1
Fullam, R.	1	McCarthy, M.	2	Stapleton, F.	20
		McEvoy, A.	6	Staunton, S.	5
Galvin, A.	1	McGee, P.	4	Strahan, F.	1
Gavin, J.	2	McGrath, P.	8	Sullivan, J.	1
Geoghegan, M.	2	McLoughlin, A.	2		
Giles, J.	5	Mancini, T.	1		
Givens, D.	19	Martin, C.	6	Townsend, A.D.	7
Glynn, D.	1	Martin, M.	4	Treacy, R.	5
Grealish, T.	8	Mooney, J.	1	Tuohy, L.	4
Grimes, A.A.	1	Moore, P.	7		
		Moran, K.	6	Waddock, G.	3
Hale, A.	2	Moroney, T.	1	Walsh, D.	5
Hand, E.	2	Mulligan, P.	1	Walsh, M.	3
Harte, I.P.	2			Waters, J.	1
Haverty, J.	3	O'Callaghan, K.	1	White, J.J.	2
Holmes, J.	1	O'Connor, T.	2	Whelan, R.	3
Horlacher, A.	2	O'Farrell, F.	2		
Houghton, R.	6	O'Flanagan, K.	3		

UEFA UNDER-21 CHAMPIONSHIP 1998–99

GROUP 1
Belarus 0, Denmark 2
Wales 1, Italy 2
Denmark 2, Wales 2
Italy 1, Switzerland 0
Switzerland 2, Denmark 0
Wales 0, Belarus 0
Denmark 1, Italy 2
Switzerland 1, Wales 0
Italy 4, Belarus 1
Denmark 2, Belarus 0
Italy 6, Wales 2
Wales 1, Denmark 2
Switzerland 0, Italy 0

GROUP 2
Latvia 1, Georgia 2
Georgia 0, Albania 1
Slovenia 1, Norway 3
Norway 4, Albania 1
Greece 3, Georgia 2
Slovenia 0, Latvia 1
Norway 2, Latvia 0
Greece 2, Slovenia 2
Albania 0, Greece 5
Greece 2, Norway 1
Georgia 0, Slovenia 0
Latvia 0, Greece 2
Georgia 0, Norway 3
Latvia 0, Albania 0
Norway 0, Georgia 0
Albania 1, Norway 2
Georgia 1, Greece 1
Latvia 1, Slovenia 1
Albania 1, Slovenia 4
Greece 6, Latvia 0

GROUP 3
Turkey 2, N Ireland 0
N Ireland 1, Finland 1
Turkey 2, Germany 0
Moldova 0, Germany 2
Turkey 1, Finland 1
Finland 1, Moldova 0
N Ireland 1, Moldova 1
N Ireland 1, Germany 0
Turkey 2, Moldova 0
Moldova 0, N Ireland 0
Germany 2, Finland 0
Germany 2, Moldova 0
Finland 0, Turkey 0
Moldova 1, Finland 1

GROUP 4
Ukraine 1, Russia 0

Armenia 3, Iceland 1
Russia 2, France 1
Ukraine 8, Armenia 0
Iceland 1, Russia 2
Iceland 0, France 2
France 4, Ukraine 0
Armenia 0, Russia 2
Ukraine 5, Iceland 1
France 3, Armenia 1
Iceland 2, Armenia 0
France 2, Russia 0
Armenia 1, Ukraine 1
Russia 3, Iceland 0

GROUP 5
Sweden 0, England 2
England 1, Bulgaria 0
Poland 5, Luxembourg 0
Bulgaria 2, Sweden 1
Luxembourg 0, England 5
Bulgaria 2, Poland 2
Sweden 3, Luxembourg 0
England 5, Poland 0
Poland 2, Sweden 0
Luxembourg 0,
   Bulgaria 3
England 3, Sweden 0
Poland 3, Bulgaria 3
Bulgaria 0, England 1
Luxembourg 0, Poland 4

GROUP 6
Austria 0, Israel 1
Cyprus 1, Spain 3
Cyprus 2, Austria 1
Holland 3, Israel 0
Israel 0, Spain 4
Holland 3, Austria 2
Cyprus 0, Holland 3
Spain 4, Austria 0
Israel 1, Cyprus 1
Holland 0, Spain 1
Austria 0, Holland 1
Spain 4, Holland 1
Israel 2, Austria 1
Holland 5, Cyprus 1

GROUP 7
Portugal 1, Romania 1
Azerbaijan 2, Hungary 1
Slovakia 1, Portugal 0
Hungary 1, Romania 2
Hungary 0, Portugal 3
Slovakia 2, Azerbaijan 1

Portugal 5, Azerbaijan 0
Romania 0, Slovakia 1
Azerbaijan 0, Romania 2
Slovakia 4, Hungary 1
Romania 2, Hungary 1
Portugal 1, Slovakia 1
Romania 1, Azerbaijan 1
Hungary 3, Slovakia 0

GROUP 8
Republic of Ireland 2,
   Croatia 2
Malta 0, Croatia 3
Republic of Ireland 2,
   Malta 1
Croatia 4, Macedonia 0
Macedonia 1, Malta 0
Yugoslavia 1,
   Republic of Ireland 1
Malta 5, Macedonia 1
Malta 1, Yugoslavia 5
Macedonia 0, Croatia 2
Republic of Ireland 0,
   Macedonia 0
Yugoslavia 7, Malta 0

GROUP 9
Lithuania 0, Scotland 0
Scotland 2, Estonia 0
Bosnia 0,
   Czech Republic 0
Lithuania 0, Belgium 1
Lithuania 4, Bosnia 0
Czech Republic 3,
   Estonia 0
Belgium 2, Scotland 0
Belgium 0, Czech
   Republic 2
Bosnia 3, Estonia 2
Scotland 2, Belgium 2
Czech Republic 1,
   Lithuania 0
Lithuania 4, Estonia 1
Scotland 0, Czech
   Republic 1
Belgium 4, Bosnia 0
Bosnia 1, Lithuania 2
Estonia 0,
   Czech Republic 3
Czech Republic 3,
   Scotland 2
Estonia 0, Lithuania 2

NATIONWIDE CONFERENCE 1998–99

	P	W	D	L	F	A	W	D	L	F	A	Pts
		Home			*Goals*		*Away*			*Goals*		
Cheltenham Town	42	11	9	1	35	14	11	5	5	36	22	80
Kettering Town	42	11	5	5	31	16	11	5	5	27	21	76
Hayes	42	12	3	6	34	25	10	5	6	29	25	74
Rushden & Diamonds	42	11	4	6	41	22	9	8	4	30	20	72
Yeovil Town	42	8	4	9	35	32	12	7	2	33	22	71
Stevenage Borough	42	9	9	3	37	23	8	8	5	25	22	68
Northwich Victoria	42	11	3	7	29	21	8	6	7	31	30	66
Kingstonian	42	9	7	5	25	19	8	6	7	25	30	64
Woking	42	9	5	7	27	20	9	4	8	24	25	63
Hednesford Town	42	9	8	4	30	24	6	8	7	19	20	61
Dover Athletic	42	7	9	5	27	21	8	4	9	27	27	58
Forest Green Rovers	42	9	5	7	28	22	6	8	7	27	28	58
Hereford United	42	9	5	7	25	17	6	5	10	24	29	55
Morecambe	42	9	5	7	31	29	6	3	12	29	47	53
Kidderminster Harriers	42	9	4	8	32	22	5	5	11	24	30	51
Doncaster Rovers	42	7	5	9	26	26	5	7	9	25	29	48
Telford United	42	7	8	6	24	24	3	8	10	20	36	46
Southport	42	6	9	6	29	28	4	6	11	18	31	45
Barrow	42	7	5	9	17	23	4	5	12	23	40	43
Welling United	42	4	7	10	18	30	5	7	9	26	35	41
Leek Town	42	5	5	11	34	42	3	3	15	14	34	32
Farnborough Town	42	6	5	10	29	48	1	6	14	12	41	32

Leading Goalscorers 1998–99

Conf.		FAC	ECT	UT
26	Carl Alford (Stevenage Borough) +	4	—	3
20	Warren Patmore (Yeovil Town) +	4	—	2
19	John Norman (Morecambe) +	2	2	—
18	Lee Charles (Hayes) +	—	1	2
	Neil Grayson (Cheltenham Town) +	—	—	5
	Hugh McAuley (Leek Town) +	—	1	—
17	Darren Collins (Rushden & Diamonds) +	2	—	—
15	Dennis Bailey (Cheltenham Town) +	1	6	1
	Adrian Foster (Rushden & Diamonds) +	—	1	—
	Paul Tait (Northwich Victoria) +	—	1	—
13	Darran Hay (Woking) +	5	—	5
	Mark Hynes (Dover Athletic) +	4	—	1
	Adie Mike (Hednesford Town) +	3	—	—
12	Ian Duerden (Doncaster Rovers) +	2	4	—
	Marc McGregor (Forest Green Rovers) +	—	—	3
	Brett McNamara (Kettering Town) +	—	—	2
	Steve West (Woking) +	—	—	1
11	Scott Huckerby (Telford United) +	3	—	2
	Leroy May (Kidderminster Harriers) +	—	1	—
10	Lee Hudson (Kettering Town) +	—	—	1
	Neil Illman (Northwich Victoria) +	—	1	1
	Richard Leadbeater (Stevenage Borough) +	—	—	—
	David Leworthy (Kingstonian) +	2	—	5
	Owen Pickard (Yeovil Town) +	—	—	2
	Martin Randall (Hayes) +	2	—	—

FAC: FA Cup; ECT: Endsleigh Challenge Trophy; UT Umbro Trophy.

NATIONWIDE CONFERENCE RESULTS 1998–99

	Barrow	Cheltenham Town	Doncaster Rovers	Dover Athletic	Farnborough Town	Forest Green Rovers	Hayes	Hednesford Town	Hereford United	Kettering Town	Kidderminster Harriers	Kingstonian	Leek Town	Morecambe	Northwich Victoria	Rushden & Diamonds	Southport	Stevenage Borough	Telford United	Welling United	Woking	Yeovil Town
Barrow	—	1-1	2-2	1-0	1-0	2-1	0-1	0-2	0-1	0-0	0-4	0-1	2-1	2-1	0-1	0-2	0-0	0-1	1-1	2-1	1-2	2-0
Cheltenham Town	4-1	—	2-1	1-1	0-0	1-1	3-3	0-0	2-2	3-0	1-0	1-0	0-0	4-1	0-1	1-0	3-0	3-0	2-0	0-0	1-1	3-2
Doncaster Rovers	2-1	2-2	—	5-4	1-2	0-1	0-1	0-1	3-1	1-1	1-0	0-1	0-1	2-1	2-2	1-1	0-1	0-0	2-1	4-1	0-1	0-2
Dover Athletic	1-1	0-0	1-0	—	2-1	1-1	0-0	0-0	3-1	0-1	0-1	5-1	2-1	2-3	0-0	1-1	2-1	1-1	1-1	1-2	3-2	1-2
Farnborough Town	2-2	2-4	1-0	1-2	—	2-2	1-5	0-1	0-4	1-3	2-4	4-2	2-1	1-6	1-6	1-2	1-1	1-0	3-1	1-1	2-1	0-0
Forest Green Rovers	1-1	1-2	0-0	0-1	0-0	—	1-2	1-0	2-1	1-0	5-0	1-0	3-1	2-2	3-1	0-2	1-0	1-2	1-1	3-2	0-2	1-2
Hayes	1-0	3-2	2-0	1-2	1-0	0-3	—	1-0	1-2	0-2	2-1	3-0	2-0	1-2	1-0	2-1	3-0	2-2	4-3	1-2	2-2	1-1
Hednesford Town	1-0	3-2	1-1	1-2	0-0	1-1	0-0	—	3-1	0-2	2-1	1-2	1-1	1-0	1-0	1-1	3-1	2-2	1-1	3-2	2-1	2-3
Hereford United	3-0	0-2	1-0	2-0	2-0	4-0	0-1	0-0	—	0-2	1-3	2-0	1-0	2-0	2-2	3-2	2-2	0-1	0-0	0-0	0-1	0-1
Kettering Town	2-0	0-2	0-1	0-2	4-1	2-1	1-0	1-0	1-1	—	1-1	2-0	2-1	6-0	0-0	0-0	1-0	1-2	2-1	1-1	3-0	1-2
Kidderminster Harriers	1-2	0-1	3-3	1-0	2-0	2-2	0-1	1-2	1-0	1-1	—	0-1	1-2	5-2	4-0	0-0	2-1	2-0	3-0	0-1	3-2	0-1
Kingstonian	5-1	1-2	2-1	1-0	1-1	0-1	1-1	1-1	2-0	1-2	1-0	—	3-0	0-0	1-1	1-5	0-2	1-0	1-0	2-1	0-0	0-0
Leek Town	3-1	0-2	1-1	2-0	4-0	0-2	1-4	1-3	3-2	1-2	1-4	2-2	—	7-0	0-3	2-3	0-0	1-1	1-1	2-4	0-3	2-4
Morecambe	3-2	0-2	1-2	0-4	1-0	3-1	2-3	3-1	1-0	3-1	2-1	0-0	2-2	—	3-1	2-3	1-1	1-1	0-1	2-1	0-1	1-1
Northwich Victoria	1-0	1-0	1-3	2-0	3-0	1-0	2-1	1-1	1-0	4-0	1-0	2-3	0-2	1-1	—	2-1	1-2	0-1	1-1	3-0	0-3	1-2
Rushden & Diamonds	4-0	1-2	1-3	2-2	1-0	4-0	5-0	1-0	1-1	1-2	1-1	0-0	2-0	3-1	1-2	—	3-1	2-1	2-3	3-1	2-0	1-2
Southport	0-4	0-2	3-2	3-0	2-2	1-1	1-2	1-1	0-0	0-1	1-1	1-1	3-1	1-0	2-2	0-1	—	1-1	2-1	5-2	0-0	2-3
Stevenage Borough	1-2	2-2	2-0	1-0	3-1	1-1	2-1	3-1	0-3	2-2	3-0	3-3	2-0	2-0	1-3	0-0	0-0	—	2-2	1-1	5-0	1-1
Telford United	1-1	0-3	0-2	1-1	3-1	2-1	2-0	1-1	0-1	0-2	0-0	1-1	2-0	2-3	3-0	2-2	1-0	0-3	—	0-0	1-0	2-2
Welling United	1-1	2-1	1-1	0-3	0-0	0-2	0-2	1-1	2-2	0-2	0-0	1-3	1-0	3-2	2-3	0-1	2-1	1-1	0-1	—	0-1	1-2
Woking	2-3	1-0	2-0	1-2	4-0	1-1	2-0	2-1	0-1	0-0	2-1	0-1	1-0	0-3	2-1	1-1	2-3	1-2	3-0	0-0	—	0-0
Yeovil Town	1-0	2-2	2-2	1-1	6-3	0-4	1-1	1-2	3-0	2-1	3-1	1-3	2-0	0-1	1-2	0-1	3-1	1-3	4-0	1-3	0-1	—

DR MARTENS LEAGUE 1998–99

Premier Division

	P	W	D	L	F	A	Pts	GD
Nuneaton Borough	42	27	9	6	91	33	90	58
Boston United	42	17	16	9	69	51	67	18
Ilkeston Town	42	18	13	11	72	59	67	13
Bath City	42	18	11	13	70	44	65	26
Hastings Town	42	18	11	13	57	49	65	8
Gloucester City	42	18	11	13	57	52	65	5
Worcester City	42	18	9	15	58	54	63	4
Halesowen Town	42	17	11	14	72	60	62	12
Tamworth United	42	19	5	18	60	67	62	–7
King's Lynn	42	17	10	15	53	46	61	7
Crawley Town	42	17	10	15	57	58	61	–1
Salisbury City	42	16	12	14	56	61	60	–5
Burton Albion	42	17	7	18	58	52	58	6
Weymouth	42	14	14	14	56	53	56	3
Merthyr Tydfil	42	15	8	19	52	62	53	–10
Atherstone United	42	12	14	16	47	52	50	–5
Grantham Town	42	14	8	20	51	58	50	–7
Dorchester Town	42	11	15	16	49	63	48	–14
Rothwell Town	42	13	9	20	47	67	48	–20
Cambridge City	42	11	12	19	47	68	45	–21
Gresley Rovers	42	12	8	22	49	73	44	–24
Bromsgrove Rov*	42	8	7	27	38	84	30	–46

* 1 point deducted

**Leading Goalscorers 1998–99
(League and Cup)**

Premier Division

S. Piearce (Halesowen Town)	27
D. Laws (Weymouth)	25
M. Paul (Bath City)	24
A. Kiwomya (Nuneaton Borough)	19
B. Abbey (Crawley Town)	18
S. Keeble (King's Lynn)	18
M. Owen (Worcester City)	17
D. O'Hagan (Dorchester Town)	16
C. Griffith (Merthyr Tydfil)	15

DR MARTENS PREMIER LEAGUE RESULTS 1998–99

	Atherstone United	Bath City	Boston United	Bromsgrove Rovers	Burton Albion	Cambridge City	Crawley Town	Dorchester Town	Gloucester City	Grantham Town	Gresley Rovers	Halesowen Town	Hastings Town	Ilkeston Town	King's Lynn	Merthyr Tydfil	Nuneaton Borough	Rothwell Town	Salisbury City	Tamworth	Weymouth	Worcester City
Atherstone United	—	2-1	0-0	5-1	2-2	0-1	2-1	3-1	1-2	1-1	2-1	0-2	1-1	3-3	1-2	2-1	0-2	2-2	2-0	0-1	0-0	1-1
Bath City	3-1	—	8-0	3-0	2-0	1-0	2-0	0-1	1-2	1-1	3-0	0-0	0-2	1-2	2-0	3-0	1-3	2-0	3-5	3-0	2-1	0-0
Boston United	0-0	3-2	—	2-2	4-0	2-2	3-1	5-1	1-0	3-0	4-1	2-0	1-1	0-1	0-1	0-3	2-3	0-0	3-1	2-0	2-1	3-1
Bromsgrove Rovers	0-0	1-3	1-1	—	0-0	2-1	1-0	1-2	0-1	4-2	0-0	2-5	2-1	0-2	1-0	0-1	0-4	3-0	0-2	2-1	2-2	0-2
Burton Albion	0-3	0-1	0-2	2-1	—	4-1	1-2	7-0	5-3	0-1	1-0	0-1	3-1	1-2	0-1	0-1	1-1	0-0	1-2	2-1	1-2	0-1
Cambridge City	3-1	1-1	1-4	3-1	0-0	—	0-0	0-0	1-1	1-0	1-2	2-0	0-1	0-1	2-1	1-2	1-1	2-2	1-3	0-1	1-0	3-0
Crawley Town	3-0	0-2	2-2	4-1	1-1	1-1	—	1-1	2-1	2-0	2-0	1-1	3-1	2-1	3-1	0-2	0-3	1-0	1-1	1-0	2-2	2-1
Dorchester Town	2-1	1-1	0-0	3-0	2-1	1-1	1-2	—	0-0	3-2	1-0	2-0	1-2	0-1	2-1	1-1	0-1	3-1	4-0	0-1	1-1	1-2
Gloucester City	0-0	2-1	2-2	4-3	0-1	3-1	2-0	4-1	—	0-1	0-0	2-0	2-3	1-1	2-1	2-1	1-0	2-1	1-2	0-1	0-0	0-2
Grantham Town	1-1	0-1	1-3	4-1	2-3	0-1	1-2	1-1	0-1	—	3-1	0-0	1-2	3-1	0-1	5-3	2-0	3-0	2-1	1-2	2-0	0-3
Gresley Rovers	2-1	1-2	1-0	1-3	0-2	3-0	1-1	2-0	2-3	0-1	—	2-0	0-0	1-3	2-1	0-0	0-3	1-3	4-1	2-3	1-2	1-1
Halesowen Town	3-1	2-2	1-1	1-0	1-3	2-1	3-2	3-1	0-1	5-1	3-4	—	3-3	4-1	0-1	2-0	2-0	4-0	3-3	3-0	2-2	0-0
Hastings Town	0-0	2-2	1-0	2-0	1-4	2-0	3-0	1-0	0-0	1-3	1-2	2-0	—	3-0	1-0	0-2	0-4	1-1	3-2	1-2	0-1	1-0
Ilkeston Town	1-2	0-0	1-3	2-1	1-2	0-0	3-1	5-2	4-3	1-1	4-1	2-2	3-3	—	0-0	2-0	0-1	3-0	3-0	3-5	1-1	3-0
King's Lynn	0-0	1-0	1-2	0-0	2-0	0-3	2-0	1-1	2-0	1-1	4-0	1-1	0-0	1-1	—	3-0	2-4	2-0	3-3	4-2	1-2	2-0
Merthyr Tydfil	2-0	0-0	2-2	2-0	0-2	3-3	3-1	1-1	0-1	1-0	1-2	1-0	1-0	1-2	0-1	—	2-1	4-1	0-1	6-0	1-1	0-1
Nuneaton Borough	1-0	1-1	1-1	6-0	4-1	4-0	2-1	0-0	2-0	2-0	3-1	4-3	1-0	1-3	4-0	6-1	—	2-0	0-1	2-0	4-2	2-0
Rothwell Town	2-0	3-2	1-1	2-0	1-4	3-1	1-1	1-1	0-1	0-1	2-0	2-1	1-3	3-1	0-2	4-0	1-1	—	1-0	2-1	1-0	1-2
Salisbury City	0-2	3-2	0-0	1-0	0-2	4-1	0-2	3-3	1-1	1-0	2-2	1-2	1-0	0-0	2-2	1-0	1-1	0-2	—	2-1	1-0	2-0
Tamworth	2-1	1-1	4-2	1-0	0-1	6-1	3-1	1-0	1-1	1-1	0-1	3-1	1-5	2-2	0-2	4-2	1-1	3-2	2-1	—	1-3	0-1
Weymouth	0-1	2-1	1-1	3-1	0-0	1-2	1-3	2-1	5-3	1-0	3-1	1-2	1-2	2-2	1-0	0-0	1-1	5-0	1-1	0-3	—	2-1
Worcester City	1-2	0-3	1-0	3-1	2-0	4-2	1-2	2-2	2-2	1-2	3-3	3-4	0-0	2-0	3-2	6-1	0-4	1-0	0-0	1-0	3-0	—

UNIBOND LEAGUE 1998–99

Premier Division

	P	W	D	L	F	A	W	D	L	F	A	Pts
		Home			*Goals*		*Away*			*Goals*		
Altrincham	42	12	8	1	32	13	11	3	7	35	20	80
Worksop Town	42	16	3	2	37	15	6	7	8	29	33	76
Guiseley	42	15	3	3	41	17	6	6	9	23	30	72
Bamber Bridge	42	9	8	4	39	30	9	7	5	24	18	69
Gateshead	42	10	4	7	37	28	8	7	6	32	30	65
Gainsborough Trinity	42	10	4	7	35	28	9	4	8	30	31	65
Whitby Town	42	10	4	7	38	26	7	9	5	39	33	64
Leigh	42	6	10	5	30	22	10	5	6	33	28	63
Hyde United	42	9	6	6	37	23	7	5	9	24	26	59
Stalybridge Celtic	42	13	5	3	43	23	3	6	12	28	40	59
Winsford United	42	6	8	7	26	27	8	7	6	30	25	57
Runcorn	42	6	8	7	21	25	6	11	4	25	24	55
Emley	42	6	9	6	23	24	6	8	7	24	25	53
Blyth Spartans	42	7	5	9	29	32	7	4	10	27	32	51
Colwyn Bay	42	6	6	9	27	32	6	7	8	33	39	49
Frickley Athletic	42	6	6	9	28	32	5	9	7	27	39	48
Marine	42	6	7	8	37	41	4	10	7	24	28	47
Spennymoor United	42	7	7	7	27	26	5	4	12	25	45	47
Lancaster City	42	7	7	7	28	25	4	6	11	22	37	46
Bishop Auckland	42	5	10	6	25	31	5	5	11	24	36	45
Chorley	42	3	8	10	26	37	5	7	9	19	31	39
Accrington Stanley	42	5	5	11	24	37	4	4	13	23	40	36

Leading Goalscorers

(In order of League Goals)

Premier Division

Lge	Cup	Tot	
26	10	36	Tony Carroll (Chorley – 24+10 for Radcliffe Borough)
24	5	34	Mark Carter (Runcorn – 19+5 for Ashton United)
22	10	32	Billy O'Callaghan (Accrington Stanley)
20	9	29	Deiniol Graham (Colwyn Bay)
19	7	26	John Morgan (Marine)
18	6	24	Simon Yeo (Hyde United)
18	4	22	Leroy Chambers (Altrincham)
17	7	24	Peter Thomson (Lancaster City)
17	5	22	Carl Chillingsworth (Whitby Town)
17	5	22	Paul Heavey (Accrington Stanley – 11+2 for Congleton Town)
16	3	19	Phil Stafford (Worksop Town)
16	1	17	Keith Fletcher (Blyth Spartans)

UNIBOND LEAGUE—PREMIER DIVISION RESULTS 1998–99

	Accrington Stanley	Altrincham	Bamber Bridge	Bishop Auckland	Blyth Spartans	Chorley	Colwyn Bay	Emley	Frickley Athletic	Gainsborough Trinity	Gateshead	Guiseley	Hyde United	Lancaster City	Leigh	Marine	Runcorn	Spennymoor United	Stalybridge Celtic	Whitby Town	Winsford United	Worksop Town
Accrington Stanley	—	1-4	0-5	0-1	1-3	0-0	1-2	2-0	1-1	2-1	1-3	2-0	1-1	1-1	1-2	3-2	1-2	2-3	2-0	1-1	0-2	1-3
Altrincham	2-1	—	1-1	0-0	0-0	4-0	1-1	1-0	1-1	1-1	1-0	1-0	2-1	1-2	1-0	4-1	3-0	2-1	2-1	1-1	1-1	2-0
Bamber Bridge	1-1	0-1	—	2-2	1-0	1-0	1-1	1-2	3-2	1-4	3-1	4-1	1-1	4-3	1-1	2-2	1-2	5-1	2-1	1-1	1-1	3-2
Bishop Auckland	2-1	2-1	1-1	—	2-2	0-4	0-1	1-1	2-2	2-1	2-2	1-0	0-1	1-1	0-0	0-2	2-3	1-1	3-3	1-1	0-2	2-1
Blyth Spartans	0-1	0-0	0-1	2-1	—	0-0	4-4	0-2	2-2	0-2	1-2	4-1	1-2	1-0	4-1	2-1	1-1	4-0	3-2	0-5	0-3	0-1
Chorley	4-0	0-2	0-1	1-3	0-2	—	1-2	1-1	1-1	0-2	2-2	0-2	1-3	2-0	3-3	0-2	1-1	2-2	2-1	2-2	2-2	1-3
Colwyn Bay	3-1	1-1	0-1	0-3	2-0	2-1	—	3-3	0-2	3-4	1-1	0-0	2-1	0-0	0-1	1-0	1-3	1-3	1-2	3-1	1-2	2-2
Emley	3-1	0-3	0-1	2-0	2-1	1-0	0-0	—	1-1	3-2	1-2	0-1	1-1	1-1	0-2	1-1	1-1	1-0	2-2	0-1	1-1	2-2
Frickley Athletic	0-0	0-3	0-2	0-0	2-0	2-2	2-1	0-1	—	1-2	0-2	1-2	3-0	3-2	0-2	1-1	1-1	1-2	3-2	3-3	3-1	2-3
Gainsborough Trinity	0-4	0-3	0-1	2-1	3-4	3-0	3-1	1-2	4-1	—	1-1	2-2	0-1	1-0	2-0	3-0	1-1	3-1	1-4	2-0	0-0	3-1
Gateshead	3-0	0-1	2-0	4-1	0-1	0-0	3-2	2-1	2-3	0-2	—	1-0	0-3	7-1	1-3	2-2	2-2	0-1	2-1	1-1	2-1	3-2
Guiseley	4-0	2-0	3-0	1-0	1-2	4-0	2-2	1-1	3-0	2-1	3-2	—	1-0	1-0	2-0	2-0	2-0	2-1	1-1	0-3	2-3	2-1
Hyde United	3-2	0-1	1-1	5-0	0-1	3-4	2-2	0-1	2-0	1-2	3-0	3-1	—	1-1	1-2	1-1	2-0	3-0	1-1	3-2	2-0	0-0
Lancaster City	1-0	0-0	3-2	2-4	2-2	0-1	4-1	1-1	5-0	0-1	2-2	1-3	1-0	—	1-2	0-0	1-1	0-3	1-1	0-1	1-0	2-0
Leigh	1-2	3-2	0-1	1-1	3-2	0-1	3-2	0-0	0-1	3-0	2-2	3-2	2-2	0-2	—	0-0	0-0	1-1	3-0	2-2	2-2	1-1
Marine	2-0	2-1	1-2	2-2	1-3	4-1	1-4	2-2	1-4	1-2	0-1	1-1	1-0	2-1	1-1	—	1-4	5-2	2-2	3-3	3-3	1-2
Runcorn	2-2	0-3	2-2	1-0	1-0	2-1	0-1	1-1	1-1	0-0	1-0	1-3	1-1	1-2	0-2	1-1	—	2-0	1-0	2-3	0-1	1-1
Spennymoor United	2-0	0-2	0-0	2-0	2-1	0-0	4-0	2-1	0-1	1-1	2-2	0-0	2-0	2-2	2-4	0-2	0-0	—	1-0	4-5	1-3	0-2
Stalybridge Celtic	1-3	3-1	1-1	3-1	4-0	1-1	1-0	2-0	2-2	2-0	0-3	2-2	2-1	3-1	4-4	2-1	1-2	3-0	—	2-0	1-0	3-0
Whitby Town	3-2	1-4	1-0	2-1	2-1	1-1	4-3	1-0	4-0	5-1	1-2	0-0	2-3	1-2	0-2	0-2	0-0	4-1	4-1	—	1-2	1-1
Winsford United	2-2	2-1	1-0	1-2	2-2	1-2	1-1	3-2	2-2	2-0	1-2	0-1	0-2	1-0	2-0	2-2	0-0	1-1	1-2	0-2	—	1-1
Worksop Town	1-0	3-1	1-1	3-1	1-0	2-0	1-2	0-2	2-0	1-1	2-0	3-1	2-0	3-0	2-1	1-1	2-1	2-1	2-1	2-1	1-0	—

RYMAN FOOTBALL LEAGUE 1998–99

Premier Division	P	Home			Away			Total			Goals			Pts
		W	D	L	W	D	L	W	D	L	F	A	GD	
Sutton United	42	14	3	4	13	4	4	27	7	8	89	39	+50	88
Aylesbury United	42	12	3	6	11	5	5	23	8	11	67	38	+29	77
Dagenham & Redbridge	42	10	8	3	10	5	6	20	13	9	71	44	+27	73
Purfleet	42	15	2	4	7	5	9	22	7	13	71	52	+19	73
Enfield	42	13	4	4	8	5	8	21	9	12	73	49	+24	72
St Albans City	42	10	8	3	7	9	5	17	17	8	71	52	+19	68
Aldershot Town	42	11	4	6	5	10	6	16	14	12	83	48	+35	62
Basingstoke Town	42	10	7	4	7	3	11	17	10	15	63	53	+10	61
Harrow Borough	42	10	5	6	7	4	10	17	9	16	72	66	+6	60
Gravesend & Northfleet	42	11	2	8	7	4	10	18	6	18	54	53	+1	60
Slough Town	42	8	6	7	8	5	8	16	11	15	60	53	+7	59
Billericay Town	42	9	5	7	6	8	7	15	13	14	54	56	−2	58
Hendon	42	9	6	6	7	3	11	16	9	17	70	71	−1	57
Boreham Wood	42	9	8	4	5	7	9	14	15	13	59	63	−4	57
Chesham United	42	8	5	8	7	4	10	15	9	18	58	79	−21	54
Dulwich Hamlet	42	11	4	6	3	4	14	14	8	20	53	63	−10	50
Heybridge Swifts	42	8	4	9	5	5	11	13	9	20	51	85	−34	48
Walton & Hersham	42	8	3	10	4	4	13	12	7	23	50	77	−27	43
Hampton	42	6	9	6	4	3	14	10	12	20	41	71	−30	42
Carshalton Athletic	42	7	5	9	3	5	13	10	10	22	47	82	−35	40
Bishops Stortford	42	5	4	12	4	6	11	9	10	23	49	90	−41	37
Bromley	42	5	7	9	3	4	14	8	11	23	50	72	−22	35

Leading Goalscorers

Premier Division

		Lge	RLC	PC
40	Gary Abbott (Aldershot Town)	33	7	
28	Steve Clark (St Albans City)	28		
28	George Georgiou (Purfleet)	22	4	2
27	Mark Watson (Sutton United)	24	3	
26	Ian Mancey (Basingstoke Town)	23		3

Division One

		Lge	RLC	PC
27	Neil Selby (Chertsey Town)	26	1	
24	Billy Read (Leyton Pennant)	20	4	
23	Steve Tilson (Canvey Island)	20	2	1
20	Neil Scammell (Bognor Regis Town)	19	1	
20	Brian Jones (Wealdstone)	18		2

Division Two

		Lge	RLC	VT
30	Julian Hazel (Wivenhoe Town)	25		5
28	Dennis Greene (Windsor & Eton)	25		3
27	Robert Gibson (Marlow)	21	1	5
25	Warren Burton (Banstead Athletic)	20	3	2
24	Wayne Cort (Harlow Town)	24		

Division Three

		Lge	RLC	PC
38	Jeff Wood (Ford United)	35	3	
30	Deal Callcut (Ware)	28	2	
29	Clayton Whittle (Egham Town)	26	1	2
28	Ben Strevens (Wingate & Finchley)	28		
26	Del Francois (Tilbury)	23	2	1

Lge: Ryman League; RLC: Ryman League Cup; PC: Puma Cup;
VT: Vandanel Trophy

RYMAN FOOTBALL LEAGUE—PREMIER DIVISION RESULTS 1998–99

	Aldershot Town	Aylesbury United	Basingstoke Town	Billericay Town	Bishop's Stortford	Boreham Wood	Bromley	Carshalton Athletic	Chesham United	Dagenham & Redbridge	Dulwich Hamlet	Enfield	Gravesend & Northfleet	Hampton	Harrow Borough	Hendon	Heybridge Swifts	Purfleet	St Albans City	Slough Town	Sutton United	Walton & Hersham
Aldershot Town	—	0-1	0-1	0-1	5-0	6-0	3-0	4-0	0-0	4-3	3-1	3-1	3-0	5-0	5-2	0-2	1-1	1-1	1-2	1-1	1-2	7-2
Aylesbury United	0-1	—	3-2	3-0	4-2	0-0	2-1	2-0	0-3	0-1	3-0	1-2	2-0	3-0	2-0	1-0	0-1	2-1	0-0	0-0	1-4	1-0
Basingstoke Town	2-1	2-1	—	0-1	3-1	1-1	1-1	2-1	4-0	1-1	2-1	1-0	2-2	1-0	2-1	1-1	2-2	3-2	1-2	0-2	1-2	0-0
Billericay Town	1-1	0-3	0-0	—	3-2	1-0	2-2	2-0	3-0	1-2	1-0	0-1	0-2	2-0	2-2	2-1	2-1	0-1	3-3	1-2	1-2	1-0
Bishop's Stortford	0-8	0-3	0-0	1-1	—	2-0	1-3	1-2	5-2	0-3	2-1	1-2	3-1	0-2	0-3	0-3	1-3	0-0	1-1	0-1	1-2	1-0
Boreham Wood	1-1	1-6	1-1	0-0	1-2	—	0-3	4-4	0-0	0-2	4-0	3-2	3-1	4-2	1-0	2-0	1-1	2-1	1-1	1-0	2-0	0-0
Bromley	1-1	0-1	1-3	2-2	2-4	2-2	—	2-3	0-1	0-0	0-3	2-1	0-1	0-0	3-0	1-4	6-1	2-1	0-1	2-1	1-1	1-1
Carshalton Athletic	0-2	3-3	1-0	3-1	1-0	1-1	1-1	—	0-1	0-0	2-0	2-1	1-2	2-4	1-2	1-3	1-2	2-1	1-1	0-3	1-0	1-3
Chesham United	0-0	1-0	0-2	3-3	0-1	2-5	3-1	3-0	—	2-5	0-0	2-0	3-2	2-2	1-4	0-2	1-0	3-3	2-1	1-0	0-3	1-2
Dagenham & Redbridge	0-1	1-0	2-0	1-2	1-1	1-1	3-3	5-0	0-0	—	1-0	3-3	0-0	4-0	1-0	6-0	3-0	0-1	2-2	3-0	0-0	3-1
Dulwich Hamlet	4-3	0-1	2-0	2-4	1-1	2-0	2-0	0-0	3-2	1-2	—	0-1	1-0	2-1	0-2	3-1	4-3	1-2	2-2	2-2	2-1	3-2
Enfield	4-0	2-3	3-2	1-0	2-1	1-3	3-0	1-0	2-2	4-0	2-1	—	0-2	0-0	5-0	2-1	4-1	1-2	0-0	2-1	1-1	3-2
Gravesend & Northfleet	2-1	1-2	1-0	0-0	4-1	3-2	1-2	3-1	0-2	2-0	0-1	0-3	—	3-0	2-0	0-1	3-2	1-1	0-1	1-2	2-1	2-0
Hampton	0-0	0-0	2-1	0-0	0-0	3-3	2-1	1-1	0-1	1-2	0-0	0-2	1-0	—	0-0	3-1	4-0	2-3	1-2	2-2	0-3	2-0
Harrow Borough	1-0	1-4	0-2	3-3	2-2	3-0	2-0	8-2	5-4	2-1	3-2	0-0	0-1	4-0	—	2-2	2-0	5-0	0-0	0-2	0-3	0-1
Hendon	1-1	3-3	2-1	2-0	5-3	0-1	2-1	1-1	2-1	2-2	1-1	2-0	0-0	1-2	1-2	—	6-1	1-2	4-3	5-2	0-3	0-3
Heybridge Swifts	1-1	1-1	3-9	1-0	1-2	2-0	2-1	0-2	0-4	1-2	0-2	2-2	3-2	3-0	2-4	1-0	—	0-0	0-3	2-1	2-4	1-0
Purfleet	1-1	0-0	2-1	0-2	3-1	2-1	1-0	4-2	3-0	3-0	2-1	0-1	2-1	4-0	4-0	4-0	2-0	—	1-0	0-4	1-3	6-1
St Albans City	1-1	2-1	4-2	1-0	5-1	1-2	4-1	1-0	2-3	2-2	1-1	2-1	0-2	3-1	1-1	4-2	1-1	2-0	—	3-3	2-2	1-1
Slough Town	2-2	1-0	0-1	1-1	2-2	0-3	2-1	1-1	3-1	0-1	1-0	2-2	4-0	3-0	0-3	1-1	0-1	2-3	1-0	—	1-2	3-0
Sutton United	5-0	1-2	1-2	4-1	2-0	2-1	2-0	3-0	2-0	3-1	2-0	1-1	1-1	3-2	2-1	4-1	1-1	2-1	2-3	0-1	—	5-0
Walton & Hersham	0-4	0-2	2-1	3-4	2-2	1-1	1-0	3-2	9-1	0-1	3-1	0-4	1-3	0-1	2-2	0-3	0-1	1-0	1-0	2-0	0-2	—

PONTIN'S CENTRAL LEAGUE

Premier Division	P	W	D	L	F	A	Pts
Sunderland	24	14	7	3	46	18	49
Liverpool	24	13	7	4	28	16	46
Manchester U	24	13	4	7	48	28	43
Nottingham F	24	11	6	7	35	26	39
Everton	24	11	5	8	34	28	38
Blackburn R	24	8	7	9	31	26	31
Leeds U	24	9	3	12	40	43	30
Leicester C	24	8	6	10	30	41	30
Aston Villa	24	8	5	11	36	37	29
Stoke C	24	7	7	10	24	32	28
Preston NE	24	7	5	12	20	42	26
Birmingham C	24	5	9	10	24	33	24
Derby Co	24	3	7	14	26	52	16

Division One	P	W	D	L	F	A	Pts
Coventry C	24	12	6	6	36	21	42
Oldham Ath	24	13	3	8	36	31	42
Middlesbrough	24	12	5	7	48	38	41
Port Vale	24	11	4	9	31	30	37
Manchester C	24	10	6	8	53	38	36
Sheffield W	24	9	8	7	26	23	35
WBA	24	8	9	7	35	32	33
Wolverhampton W	24	10	3	11	43	45	33
Tranmere R	24	10	2	12	41	32	32
Bolton W	24	8	4	12	25	35	28
Barnsley	24	6	9	9	27	35	27
Burnley	24	6	8	10	20	35	26
Grimsby T	24	5	5	14	20	46	20

Division Two	P	W	D	L	F	A	Pts
Newcastle U	24	14	6	4	46	17	48
Huddersfield T	24	13	5	6	41	25	44
Shrewsbury T	24	9	9	6	29	24	36
Wrexham	24	11	3	10	41	37	36
Bradford C	24	10	4	10	41	41	34
Sheffield U	24	9	7	8	27	29	34
Stockport Co	24	9	6	9	41	32	33
York C	24	8	9	7	35	28	33
Rotherham U	24	9	6	9	33	36	33
Scarborough T	24	9	4	11	30	39	31
Notts Co	24	7	6	11	31	48	27
Lincoln C	24	7	3	14	31	47	24
Blackpool	24	3	8	13	25	48	17

Division Three	P	W	D	L	F	A	Pts
Scunthorpe U	22	13	5	4	48	27	44
Walsall	22	12	6	4	49	26	42
Hartlepool U	22	11	6	5	44	32	39
Rochdale	22	10	6	6	33	27	36
Bury	22	10	5	7	42	33	35
Chesterfield	22	10	4	8	28	30	34
Wigan Ath	22	9	4	9	32	30	31
Darlington	22	9	3	10	36	37	30
Halifax T	22	5	5	12	29	43	20
Chester C	22	5	5	12	23	47	20
Hull C	22	4	7	11	21	38	19
Carlisle U	22	5	2	15	31	46	17

AVON INSURANCE COMBINATION

	P	W	D	L	F	A	GD	Pts
Charlton Ath	28	19	3	6	60	24	+36	60
Tottenham H	28	18	3	7	56	24	+32	57
Chelsea	28	18	3	7	39	22	+17	57
Ipswich T	28	17	4	7	62	32	+30	55
Watford	28	14	9	5	56	28	+27	51
Southampton	28	15	4	9	53	37	+18	49
Peterborough U	28	14	6	8	50	38	+15	48
Fulham	28	14	5	9	83	44	+19	47
Arsenal	28	13	6	9	47	32	+15	45
Colchester U	28	13	4	11	48	43	+3	43
West Ham U	28	11	8	9	56	40	+16	41
Norwich C	28	12	5	11	38	34	+4	41
Northampton T	28	12	5	11	35	41	−8	41
Luton T	28	11	7	10	45	43	+2	40
QPR	28	11	5	12	44	34	+10	38
Portsmouth	28	11	5	12	40	37	+3	38
Wimbledon	28	9	11	8	38	38	0	38
Brighton & HA	28	9	10	9	27	31	−4	37
Bournemouth	28	10	6	12	43	39	+4	36
Crystal Palace	28	9	6	13	43	50	−7	33
Oxford U	28	10	3	15	33	52	−19	33
Reading	28	9	4	15	31	41	−10	31
Swindon T	28	8	6	14	28	47	−21	30
Cambridge U	28	8	6	14	41	55	−24	30
Barnet	28	8	5	15	33	55	−32	28
Millwall	28	7	6	15	33	58	−25	27
Brentford	28	5	7	16	25	56	−31	22
Wycombe W	28	5	7	16	24	58	−34	22
Gillingham	28	4	5	19	21	57	−36	17

FA ACADEMY UNDER-19

GROUP A

	P	W	D	L	F	A	GD	Pts
Everton	22	12	4	6	39	25	+14	40
Manchester U	22	12	4	6	38	25	+13	40
Crewe Alex	22	11	6	5	30	19	+11	39
Blackburn R	22	11	3	8	46	29	+17	36
Liverpool	22	9	9	4	33	17	+16	36
Aston Villa	22	7	4	11	34	44	−10	25
Manchester C	22	4	3	15	20	50	−30	15
Bolton W	22	3	3	16	28	63	−35	12

GROUP C

	P	W	D	L	F	A	GD	Pts
Nottingham F	22	13	6	3	53	23	+30	45
Sheffield W	22	10	5	7	37	36	+1	35
Sunderland	22	8	9	5	34	26	+8	33
Leeds U	22	10	3	9	34	37	−3	33
Barnsley	22	8	6	8	36	28	+8	30
Derby Co	22	8	5	9	34	35	−1	29
Middlesbrough	22	8	5	9	27	42	−15	29
Newcastle U	22	7	4	11	32	43	−11	25
Leicester C	22	5	5	12	27	37	−10	20

GROUP B

	P	W	D	L	F	A	GD	Pts
Fulham	22	12	3	7	34	27	+7	39
Crystal Palace	22	12	2	8	46	35	+11	38
Chelsea	22	11	4	7	43	36	+7	37
Charlton Ath	22	10	7	5	37	30	+7	37
Wimbledon	22	7	9	6	32	33	−1	30
Bristol C	22	7	5	10	34	39	−5	26
QPR	22	6	6	10	32	39	−7	24
Southampton	22	5	4	13	29	50	−21	19

GROUP D

	P	W	D	L	F	A	GD	Pts
West Ham U	22	17	3	2	53	20	+33	54
Arsenal	22	12	2	8	36	27	+9	38
Watford	22	9	6	7	37	40	−3	33
Tottenham H	22	8	6	8	35	31	+4	30
Coventry C	22	9	2	11	43	38	+5	29
Peterborough U	22	7	7	8	33	34	−1	28
Millwall	22	7	3	12	29	38	−9	24
Ipswich T	22	4	5	13	31	44	−13	17
Norwich C	22	5	2	15	23	49	−26	17

UNDER-19 PLAY-OFFS

Preliminary Round
Ipswich T 2 Leicester C 4
Newcastle U 0 Norwich C 6

First Round
Everton 7 Leicester C 1
Charlton Ath 3 Barnsley 1

Sunderland 3 Bristol C 0
Arsenal 4 Manchester C 0
Manchester U 4 Millwall 1

Chelsea 3 Derby Co 2
Leeds U 0 Wimbledon 3
West Ham U 2 Bolton W 1
Nottingham F 3
  Southampton 0
Blackburn R 5 Coventry C 2
Watford 3 Aston V 1
Crystal Palace 1
  Middlesbrough 2
Sheffield W 2 QPR 0
Crewe Alex 3
  Peterborough U 0
Tottenham H 2 Liverpool 1
Fulham 5 Norwich C 0

Second Round
Everton 4 Charlton Ath 0
Arsenal 3 Sunderland 1
Manchester U 1 Chelsea 2
  (aet)
West Ham U 2 Wimbledon 1
Nottingham F 1 Blackburn R 0
Middlesbrough 2 Watford 1
Sheffield W 1 Crewe Alex 1
  (aet)
*(Sheffield W won 3-0 on
  penalties)*
Fulham 1 Tottenham H 2

Third Round
Everton 2 Arsenal 1
Nottingham F 3
  Middlesbrough 2
West Ham U 2 Chelsea 2 *(aet)*
*(West Ham U won 5-3 on
  penalties)*
Tottenham H 0
  Sheffield W 2

Semi-Finals
West Ham U 1 Everton 0
Nottingham F 2 Sheffield W 3
  (aet)

Final
West Ham U 1 Sheffield W 0
  (aet)

FA ACADEMY UNDER-17

GROUP A	P	W	D	L	F	A	GD	Pts
Manchester U	22	14	7	1	66	20	+46	49
Blackburn R	22	14	5	3	56	23	+33	47
Liverpool	22	9	10	3	47	36	+11	37
Everton	22	10	5	7	44	33	+11	35
Manchester C	22	9	6	7	49	42	+7	33
Crewe Alex	22	6	8	8	30	32	–2	26
Aston Villa	22	7	3	12	27	54	–27	24

GROUP B	P	W	D	L	F	A	GD	Pts
Wimbledon	22	8	6	8	29	33	–4	30
Bristol C	22	8	4	10	40	42	–2	28
QPR	22	7	7	8	48	51	–3	28
Crystal Palace	22	7	6	9	25	37	–12	27
Southampton	22	7	4	11	37	50	–13	25
Fulham	22	5	4	13	37	69	–32	19
Charlton Ath	22	3	6	13	29	51	–22	15

GROUP C	P	W	D	L	F	A	GD	Pts
Newcastle U	22	16	3	3	45	19	+26	51
Leeds U	22	11	4	7	55	33	+22	37
Sunderland	22	11	4	7	39	24	+15	37
Sheffield W	22	11	2	9	45	41	+4	35
Leicester C	22	9	4	9	33	35	–2	31
Nottingham F	22	8	5	9	30	34	–4	29
Barnsley	22	8	3	11	29	44	–15	27
Middlesbrough	22	7	4	11	31	37	–6	25
Derby Co	22	5	3	14	25	54	–29	18

GROUP D	P	W	D	L	F	A	GD	Pts
Arsenal	22	15	4	3	54	23	+31	49
West Ham U	22	12	5	5	42	23	+19	41
Coventry C	22	11	1	10	52	42	+10	34
Tottenham H	22	6	9	7	26	32	–6	27
Watford	22	7	3	12	45	53	–8	24
Millwall	22	6	2	14	15	31	–16	20
Peterborough U	22	3	3	16	29	61	–32	12

UNDER-17 PLAY-OFFS

First Round
Crystal Palace 3
  Leicester C 4 *(aet)*
Sunderland 2 Fulham 1
West Ham U 2
  Aston Villa 3
Blackburn R 4
  Peterborough U 0
QPR 1 Nottingham F 2
Sheffield W 3
  Southampton 1
Arsenal 2 Derby Co 0
Everton 1 Watford 2
Coventry C 1 Crewe Alex 3
Leeds U 4 Charlton Ath 1
Liverpool 2 Millwall 0
Tottenham H 0
  Manchester C 2
Wimbledon 4
  Middlesbrough 2

Second Round
Manchester U 5
  Leicester C 4 *(aet)*
Aston Villa 1 Sunderland 7
Blackburn R 4
  Nottingham F 0
Arsenal 5 Sheffield W 0
Newcastle U 4 Watford 1
Barnsley 0 Crewe Alex 4
Leeds 1 Liverpool 1 *(aet)*
*(Liverpool won 5-4 on
  penalties)*
Wimbledon 1
  Manchester C 3

Third Round
Manchester U 3
  Sunderland 0
Arsenal 2 Blackburn R 2
  (aet)
*(Blackburn R won 6-5 on
  penalties)*
Newcastle U 2
  Crewe Alex 0
Manchester C 4 Liverpool 1

Semi-Finals
Manchester U 1
  Blackburn R 5 *(aet)*
Newcastle U 1
  Manchester C 2

Final
Blackburn R 4
  Manchester C 3 *(aet)*

REPUBLIC OF IRELAND LEAGUE

	P	W	D	L	F	A	Pts
St Patrick's Ath	33	22	7	4	58	21	73
Cork City	33	21	7	5	62	25	70
Shelbourne	33	13	8	12	37	35	47
Finn Harps	33	12	10	11	38	39	46
Derry City	33	12	9	12	34	32	45
UCD	33	10	12	11	31	32	42
Waterford United	33	11	9	13	21	37	42
Shamrock Rovers	33	9	13	11	34	40	40
Sligo Rovers	33	9	11	13	37	50	38
Bohemians	33	10	7	16	28	37	37
Bray Wanderers*	33	8	8	17	30	45	32
Dundalk*	33	6	9	18	23	40	27

HIGHLAND LEAGUE

	P	W	D	L	F	A	Pts
Peterhead	30	24	4	2	89	19	76
Huntly	30	23	3	4	86	38	72
Keith	30	22	4	4	92	41	70
Elgin City	30	21	1	8	71	39	64
Fraserburgh	30	18	6	6	86	39	60
Clachnacuddin	30	16	8	6	80	45	56
Cove Rangers	30	16	5	9	88	48	53
Forres Mechanics	30	11	6	13	60	60	39
Brora Rangers	30	11	5	14	61	63	38
Deveronvale	30	11	4	15	57	72	37
Rothes	30	8	5	17	46	64	29
Buckie Thistle	30	8	4	18	36	60	28
Lossiemouth	30	8	4	18	40	67	28
Wick Academy	30	7	2	21	33	85	23
Nairn County	30	3	2	25	32	114	11
Fort William	30	1	1	28	24	127	4

FA UMBRO TROPHY 1998–99

FINAL (at Wembley)

15 MAY

Forest Green Rovers (0) 0

Kingstonian (0) 1 *(Mustafa 49)*   20,037

Forest Green Rovers: Shuttlewood; Hedges, Kilgour, Forbes, Bailey (Smart), Honor (Winter), Wigg (Cook), Drysdale, Sykes, McGregor, Mehew.
Kingstonian: Farrelly; Stewart, Crossley, Harris, Mustafa, Patterson, Luckett, Rattray, Pitcher, Akuamoah, Leworthy (Francis).
Referee: A. Wilkie (Chester-le-Street).

FA CARLSBERG VASE 1998–99

FINAL (at Wembley)

16 MAY

Bedlington Terriers (0) 0

Tiverton Town (0) 1 *(Rogers 88)*   13,878

Bedlington Terriers: O'Connor; Bowes, Melrose, Teasdale, Pike, Bond, Cross, Middleton (Renforth), Boon (Ludlow), Milner, Gibb.
Tiverton Town: Edwards; Tallon, Tatterton, Saunders, Fallon, Nancekivell (Rogers), Daly, Conning (Pears), Leonard, Varley, Everett.
Referee: W. Burns (Scarborough).

THE TIMES FA YOUTH CUP 1998–99

FINAL FIRST LEG

7 MAY

Coventry City (0) 0

West Ham United (0) 3 *(Newton 70, Angus 75, Brayley 78)*   11,500

Coventry City: Kirkland; Mooney, Lewis, Betts, Burrows M, Cudworth, Graham (Grant), Pead (Doyle), Eribenne, McSheffrey, McPhee.
West Ham United: Bywater; Newton, Taylor, Forbes, Iriekpen, Angus, Carrick (Omonua), Cole, Garcia, Brayley (Riddle), Ferrante.
Referee: R. Harris (Oxford).

FINAL SECOND LEG

14 MAY

West Ham United (3) 6 *(Brayley 3, 59, Newton 28, Garcia 34 (pen), 70, Carrick 64)*

Coventry City (0) 0   18,438

West Ham United: Bywater; Newton (Cooper), Taylor, Forbes, Iriekpen, Angus, Carrick, Cole, Garcia, Brayley, Ferrante.
Coventry City: Kirkland; Mooney, Lewis (Strachan C), Burrows M, Cudworth, Betts (Doyle), Graham (Grant), Pead, Davenport, McSheffrey, McPhee.
Referee: R. Harris (Oxford).

USEFUL ADDRESSES

The Football Association: The Secretary, 16 Lancaster Gate, London W2 3LW *0171-262 4542*

Scotland: The Secretary, 6 Park Gardens, Glasgow G3 7YE. *0141-332 6372*

Northern Ireland (Irish FA): D. I. Bowen, 20 Windsor Avenue, Belfast BT9 6EG. *01232-669458*

Wales: A. Evans, 3 Westgate Street, Cardiff, South Glamorgan CF1 1JF. *01222-372325*

Republic of Ireland (FA of Ireland): B. O'Byrne, 80 Merrion Square South, Dublin 2. *00353-16766864*

International Federation (FIFA): M. Zen-Ruffinen, P. O. Box 85 8030 Zurich, Switzerland. *00 411 384 9595. Fax: 00 411 384 9696*

Union of European Football Associations: G. Aigner, Chemin de la Redoute 54, Case Postale 303 CH-1260 Nyon, Switzerland. *0041 22 994 4444. Fax: 0041 22 994 4488*

The Premier League: The Secretary, 11 Connaught Place, London W2 2ET. *0171-2981600*

The Football League: J. D. Dent, F.C.I.S., The Football League, Unit 5, Edward VII Quay, Navigation Way, Preston, Lancashire PR2 2YF. *01772 325800. Fax 01772 325801*

Scottish Premier League: R. Mitchell, Hampden Park, Somerville Drive, Glasgow G42 9BA. *0141 646 6962*

The Scottish League: P. Donald, 188 West Regent Street, Glasgow G2 4RY. *0141-248 3844*

The Irish League: H. Wallace, 87 University Street, Belfast BT7 1HP. *01232-242888*

Football League of Ireland: E. Morris, 80 Merrion Square South, Dublin 2. *003531 765120*

The Nationwide Football Conference: J. A. Moules, Collingwood House, Schooner Court, Crossways, Dartford DA2 6QQ. *01322-303120*

Northern Premier: R. D. Bayley, 22 Woburn Drive, Hale, Altrincham, Cheshire, WA15 8LZ. *0161-980 7007*

Isthmian League: N. Robinson, 226 Rye Lane, Peckham, SE15 4NL. *020 8409 1978. Fax 020 7639 5726*

English Schools FA: M. R. Berry, 1/2 Eastgate Street, Stafford ST16 2NN. *01785-51142*

Southern League: D. J. Strudwick, PO Box 90, Worcester WR3 8RX. *01905-757509.*

National Federation of Football Supporters' Clubs: Chairman: Ian D. Todd MBE, 8 Wyke Close, Wyke Gardens, Isleworth, Middlesex TW7 5PE. *0181-847-2905 (and fax). Mobile: 0961-558908.* National Secretary: Mark Agate, "The Stadium", 14 Coombe Close, Lordswood, Chatham, Kent ME5 8NU. *01634 319461 (and fax)*

Professional Footballers' Association: G. Taylor, 2 Oxford Court, Bishopsgate, Off Lower Mosley Street, Manchester M2 3WQ *0161-236 0575*

Referees' Association: A. Smith, 1 Westhill Road, Coundon, Coventry CV6 2AD. *01203 601701*

Women's Football Alliance: Miss K. Simmons, 9 Wyllyotts Place, Potters Bar, Herts EN6 2JD. *01707 651840*

The Association of Football Statisticians: R. J. Spiller, PO Box 5828, Basildon, Essex SS15 5GQ. *01268 416020 (and fax 01268-543559)*

The Football Programme Directory: David Stacey, 'The Beeches', 66 Southend Road, Wickford, Essex SS11 8EN. *01268 732041 (and fax)*

England Football Supporters Association: Publicity Officer, David Stacey, 66 Southend Road, Wickford, Essex SS11 8EN. *01268 732041 (and fax)*

World Cup (1966) Association: as above.

The Football Trust: Second Floor, Walkden House, 10 Melton Street, London NW1 2EJ. *0171-388 4504*

FA CARLING PREMIERSHIP
FIXTURES 1999–2000

	Arsenal	Aston Villa	Bradford C	Chelsea	Coventry C	Derby Co	Everton	Leeds U
Arsenal	–	11.9	25.8	6.5	25.3	27.11	16.10	28.12
Aston Villa	4.3	–	18.9	22.1	11.3	25.3	11.8	8.4
Bradford C	5.2	26.2	–	8.1	6.11	22.4	28.12	11.3
Chelsea	23.10	21.8	28.11	–	8.4	14.5	11.3	19.12
Coventry C	26.12	22.11	18.3	3.1	–	21.8	24.4	11.9
Derby Co	10.8	26.12	25.9	30.10	22.1	–	28.8	4.12
Everton	29.4	27.11	15.4	20.11	2.10	12.2	–	23.10
Leeds U	15.4	3.1	20.11	1.4	4.3	7.8	6.5	–
Leicester C	4.12	25.9	6.5	14.8	11.8	18.12	8.4	25.3
Liverpool	28.8	24.4	1.11	16.10	18.12	6.11	27.9	5.2
Manchester U	22.1	30.10	26.12	24.4	5.2	11.3	4.12	14.8
Middlesbrough	11.3	12.2	7.8	25.9	29.12	15.1	30.10	26.2
Newcastle U	14.5	7.8	1.4	4.3	29.4	25.10	8.11	22.4
Sheffield W	3.1	1.4	15.1	15.4	23.10	25.8	11.9	29.4
Southampton	18.9	18.3	3.1	26.12	4.12	4.10	22.1	11.8
Sunderland	14.8	18.10	24.4	4.12	29.8	26.2	25.3	22.1
Tottenham H	6.11	15.4	4.3	5.2	19.9	29.4	14.8	28.8
Watford	22.4	24.8	21.8	18.9	14.5	8.4	18.12	3.10
West Ham U	2.10	15.1	12.2	18.3	22.4	28.12	26.2	14.5
Wimbledon	1.4	6.5	16.10	28.8	14.8	11.9	5.2	7.11

Leicester C	Liverpool	Manchester U	Middlesbrough	Newcastle U	Sheffield W	Southampton	Sunderland	Tottenham H	Watford	West Ham U	Wimbledon
7.8	12.2	22.8	20.11	30.10	8.4	26.2	15.1	18.3	25.9	25.4	18.12
22.4	2.10	14.5	28.8	4.12	18.12	6.11	29.4	29.12	5.2	16.8	23.10
23.10	14.5	25.3	4.12	18.12	14.8	8.4	2.10	12.9	22.1	28.8	29.4
15.1	29.4	3.10	22.4	11.9	29.12	25.3	7.8	12.1	26.2	6.11	12.2
27.11	1.4	25.8	15.4	16.10	6.5	7.8	12.2	26.2	31.10	25.9	15.1
1.4	18.3	20.11	14.8	6.5	5.2	24.4	18.9	16.10	3.1	15.4	4.3
3.1	22.4	8.8	14.5	18.3	4.3	21.8	26.12	15.1	1.4	18.9	25.8
26.12	23.8	15.1	19.9	25.9	16.10	27.11	21.8	12.2	25.4	30.10	18.3
–	18.9	18.3	5.2	28.12	30.10	16.10	4.3	25.4	30.8	22.1	20.11
26.2	–	11.9	22.1	25.3	5.12	6.5	11.3	9.4	14.8	11.8	28.12
6.11	4.3	–	3.1	30.8	11.8	25.9	15.4	6.5	16.10	1.4	18.9
24.8	21.8	8.4	–	24.4	25.3	11.9	6.11	18.12	6.5	17.10	27.11
15.4	26.12	12.2	3.10	–	19.9	15.1	25.8	27.11	11.3	3.1	21.8
14.5	7.8	27.11	26.12	26.2	–	12.2	22.4	21.8	6.11	11.3	2.10
29.4	23.10	22.4	4.3	15.8	28.8	–	1.4	20.11	15.4	5.2	14.5
11.9	20.11	28.12	18.3	5.2	25.9	18.12	–	30.10	10.8	6.5	8.4
3.10	3.1	23.10	1.4	9.8	22.1	11.3	14.5	–	26.12	6.12	22.4
12.2	15.1	29.4	24.10	20.11	18.3	28.12	27.11	25.3	–	4.3	7.8
21.8	27.11	18.12	29.4	8.4	21.11	25.8	23.10	7.8	11.9	–	25.3
11.3	15.4	26.2	10.8	22.1	24.4	30.10	3.1	26.9	4.12	26.12	–

NATIONWIDE FOOTBALL LEAGUE FIXTURES 1999–2000

DIVISION ONE

	Barnsley	Birmingham C	Blackburn R	Bolton W	Charlton Ath	Crewe Alex	Crystal Palace	Fulham	Grimsby T	Huddersfield T
Barnsley	–	20.11	22.1	26.2	4.12	7.5	14.8	21.3	25.3	25.9
Birmingham C	18.3	–	13.11	12.2	30.10	30.8	16.10	7.8	7.5	3.1
Blackburn R	21.8	22.3	–	30.8	24.4	11.3	20.10	20.11	16.10	15.1
Bolton W	18.9	5.9	5.2	–	4.3	19.10	6.11	11.3	20.11	16.10
Charlton Ath	7.8	2.10	9.10	11.9	–	15.1	26.12	29.1	21.3	15.4
Crewe Alex	23.10	5.2	23.11	29.4	2.11	–	4.12	26.10	27.8	26.12
Crystal Palace	15.1	22.4	29.4	7.3	25.3	7.8	–	18.12	18.9	29.1
Fulham	13.11	4.12	18.3	23.11	28.8	25.9	1.4	–	22.1	7.5
Grimsby T	26.12	23.10	22.4	18.3	13.11	29.1	26.2	21.8	–	1.4
Huddersfield T	26.10	8.4	13.8	22.4	28.12	25.3	28.8	23.10	18.12	–
Ipswich T	30.8	18.9	7.3	21.8	19.10	27.11	24.4	25.3	30.10	12.2
Manchester C	24.11	29.4	23.10	29.1	18.3	8.4	11.9	15.1	28.12	27.11
Norwich C	9.10	14.8	28.8	24.10	22.1	11.9	11.3	2.10	19.2	26.2
Nottingham F	1.10	28.12	25.3	27.10	8.4	18.12	19.2	10.10	14.8	14.11
Port Vale	15.4	22.1	4.12	26.12	19.2	5.11	20.11	11.9	3.9	24.4
Portsmouth	29.1	6.11	28.12	27.11	16.10	20.11	30.10	12.2	25.9	30.8
QPR	27.11	27.10	2.10	15.1	18.12	28.12	22.3	26.2	11.3	7.8
Sheffield U	7.3	25.3	19.12	13.11	18.9	24.4	4.9	28.12	8.4	30.10
Stockport Co	4.3	27.8	19.2	1.4	5.2	16.10	3.1	6.11	4.12	19.10
Swindon T	29.4	19.2	4.9	2.10	23.11	26.2	22.1	22.4	5.2	7.3
Tranmere R	12.2	11.3	4.3	7.8	25.9	30.10	7.5	9.4	19.10	21.8
Walsall	1.4	8.10	26.10	3.1	7.3	21.8	15.4	26.11	4.3	23.11
WBA	3.1	4.3	18.9	15.4	7.5	12.2	25.9	30.8	24.4	18.3
Wolverhampton W	22.4	17.12	8.4	9.10	4.9	21.3	5.2	29.4	6.11	11.9

Ipswich T	Manchester C	Norwich C	Nottingham F	Port Vale	Portsmouth	QPR	Sheffield U	Stockport Co	Swindon T	Tranmere R	Walsall	WBA	Wolverhampton W
5.2	11.3	24.4	30.10	28.12	28.8	19.2	6.11	10.9	19.10	3.9	18.12	8.4	16.10
26.2	19.10	15.1	15.4	21.8	7.3	25.9	26.12	29.1	27.11	23.11	24.4	11.9	1.4
6.11	7.5	29.1	26.12	7.8	15.4	30.10	1.4	27.11	12.2	11.9	25.9	26.2	3.1
22.1	28.8	7.5	25.9	25.3	19.2	14.8	21.3	18.12	30.10	4.12	8.4	28.12	24.4
29.4	20.11	21.8	3.1	27.11	22.4	1.4	26.2	31.8	11.3	26.10	6.11	23.10	12.2
19.2	3.1	4.3	1.4	7.3	18.3	15.4	9.10	22.4	18.9	3.10	22.1	4.9	13.11
9.10	4.3	23.11	27.11	18.3	2.10	13.11	12.2	8.4	21.8	23.10	28.12	26.10	31.8
26.12	14.8	30.10	24.4	4.3	4.9	18.9	15.4	7.3	16.10	3.1	19.2	5.2	19.10
2.10	15.4	28.11	15.1	12.2	26.10	23.11	3.1	7.8	30.8	29.4	11.9	9.10	7.3
4.9	19.2	18.9	21.3	9.10	5.2	4.12	2.10	29.4	6.11	22.1	11.3	20.11	4.3
–	26.9	18.3	7.8	8.4	4.3	16.10	29.1	28.12	15.1	13.11	7.5	17.12	24.11
27.10	–	12.2	30.8	2.10	9.10	8.3	21.8	13.11	18.12	22.4	26.2	25.3	8.8
21.11	4.9	–	6.11	22.4	3.1	26.12	29.4	26.10	21.3	1.4	5.2	4.12	15.4
5.12	5.2	8.3	–	29.4	24.11	28.8	22.4	23.10	4.3	18.3	4.9	22.1	19.9
3.1	30.10	16.10	19.10	–	1.4	5.2	11.3	26.2	25.9	28.8	21.3	14.8	7.5
11.9	24.4	8.4	11.3	18.12	–	7.5	7.8	21.8	25.3	26.2	19.10	21.3	15.1
22.4	6.11	25.3	29.1	31.8	23.10	–	11.9	12.2	8.4	9.10	20.11	29.4	21.8
28.8	22.1	19.10	16.10	23.11	4.12	4.3	–	18.3	7.5	5.2	14.8	19.2	25.9
15.4	21.3	25.9	7.5	18.9	22.1	4.9	20.11	–	24.4	14.8	30.10	11.3	26.12
15.8	1.4	13.11	11.9	26.10	26.12	3.1	23.10	9.10	–	15.4	4.12	28.8	18.3
21.3	16.10	18.12	20.11	29.1	18.9	24.4	30.8	15.1	28.12	–	25.3	6.11	27.11
23.10	18.9	30.8	12.2	13.11	29.4	18.3	15.1	2.10	7.8	26.12	–	22.4	29.1
1.4	26.12	7.8	20.8	15.1	13.11	19.10	27.11	23.11	29.1	7.3	16.10	–	31.10
11.3	3.12	28.12	26.2	23.10	14.8	22.1	26.10	25.3	20.11	19.2	28.8	3.10	–

NATIONWIDE FOOTBALL LEAGUE FIXTURES 1999–2000

DIVISION TWO

	Blackpool	AFC Bournemouth	Brentford	Bristol C	Bristol R	Burnley	Bury	Cambridge U	Cardiff C	Chesterfield
Blackpool	–	18.9	29.1	12.2	24.4	21.3	16.10	27.11	11.3	6.5
AFC Bournemouth	26.2	–	23.11	15.1	19.10	12.2	25.9	7.8	6.11	25.4
Brentford	28.8	18.3	–	26.12	4.12	24.4	22.1	4.3	4.9	11.12
Bristol C	4.9	14.8	25.3	–	17.10	25.9	28.8	6.11	8.1	5.2
Bristol R	2.10	29.4	7.8	22.4	–	30.8	2.11	3.1	9.10	18.3
Burnley	13.11	4.9	2.10	23.10	5.2	–	25.3	29.4	18.12	14.8
Bury	22.4	23.10	21.8	29.1	11.3	26.12	–	11.12	2.10	15.4
Cambridge U	19.2	4.12	11.9	7.3	8.4	19.10	8.1	–	28.12	22.1
Cardiff C	2.11	7.3	12.2	11.12	6.5	1.4	24.4	15.4	–	13.11
Chesterfield	9.10	2.10	8.1	30.8	23.11	15.1	28.12	21.8	21.3	–
Colchester U	8.4	22.1	9.10	29.4	8.1	26.2	5.2	22.4	24.11	3.12
Gillingham	22.1	12.11	29.4	2.11	14.8	11.12	4.12	23.10	19.2	1.4
Luton T	14.8	5.2	26.2	15.4	19.2	6.11	4.9	21.3	28.8	26.12
Millwall	18.3	19.2	28.12	4.3	25.3	16.10	8.4	18.9	4.12	28.8
Notts Co	11.9	11.12	30.8	27.11	25.9	3.1	6.5	29.1	26.2	19.10
Oldham Ath	29.4	3.1	15.1	18.3	26.2	21.8	11.9	1.4	22.4	7.3
Oxford U	5.2	1.4	22.4	2.10	22.1	15.4	13.11	26.12	14.8	19.2
Preston NE	18.12	2.11	23.10	9.10	28.12	11.9	19.2	2.10	8.4	4.9
Reading	8.1	4.3	11.3	7.8	22.3	24.11	20.10	15.1	25.3	18.9
Scunthorpe U	28.12	28.8	21.3	18.9	4.9	6.5	18.12	11.3	5.2	25.9
Stoke C	25.3	22.4	8.4	13.11	18.12	29.1	8.3	12.2	29.4	4.3
Wigan Ath	7.3	9.10	18.12	21.8	11.9	27.11	18.3	30.8	23.10	2.11
Wrexham	4.12	15.4	6.11	3.1	28.8	11.3	14.8	23.11	22.1	16.10
Wycombe W	23.10	26.12	27.11	1.4	6.11	7.8	26.2	9.10	11.9	3.1

Colchester U	Gillingham	Luton T	Millwall	Notts Co	Oldham Ath	Oxford U	Preston NE	Reading	Scunthorpe U	Stoke C	Wigan Ath	Wrexham	Wycombe W
3.1	21.8	15.1	23.11	4.3	19.10	30.8	1.4	11.12	15.4	26.12	6.11	7.8	25.9
21.8	21.3	31.8	27.11	8.1	8.4	18.12	11.3	11.9	29.1	16.10	6.5	28.12	25.3
6.5	19.10	18.9	15.4	5.2	14.8	16.10	25.9	2.11	13.11	3.1	1.4	7.3	19.2
19.10	11.3	28.12	11.9	19.2	23.11	24.4	6.5	4.12	26.2	21.3	22.1	8.4	17.12
11.12	15.1	27.11	26.12	23.10	18.9	21.8	15.4	13.11	12.2	1.4	4.3	29.1	7.3
18.9	8.1	7.3	22.4	8.4	22.1	28.12	4.3	18.3	10.10	28.8	19.2	2.11	4.12
30.8	7.8	12.2	4.1	9.10	4.3	21.3	27.11	29.4	1.4	6.11	23.11	15.1	18.9
15.10	25.9	13.11	26.2	28.8	18.12	25.3	24.4	14.8	2.11	4.9	5.2	18.3	6.5
17.3	27.11	29.1	7.8	18.9	16.10	15.1	3.1	26.12	30.8	19.10	25.9	20.8	3.3
7.8	18.12	25.3	29.1	29.4	6.11	27.11	12.2	26.2	23.10	11.9	11.3	22.4	8.4
–	25.3	17.12	23.10	14.8	21.3	11.3	6.11	28.8	11.9	19.2	4.9	1.10	29.12
26.12	–	22.4	2.10	7.3	4.9	4.3	18.9	3.1	18.3	5.2	15.4	9.10	28.8
1.4	16.10	–	11.3	4.12	6.5	25.9	23.11	22.1	3.1	11.12	24.4	11.9	19.10
25.9	24.4	2.11	–	18.12	5.2	6.5	19.10	4.9	7.3	22.1	14.8	13.11	8.1
15.1	6.11	7.8	1.4	–	24.4	23.11	21.3	15.4	21.8	11.3	26.12	12.2	16.10
13.11	12.2	9.10	30.8	2.10	–	29.1	7.8	23.10	26.12	15.4	11.12	27.11	2.11
2.11	11.9	23.10	9.10	18.3	28.8	–	11.12	7.3	29.4	4.12	3.1	26.2	4.9
7.3	26.2	18.3	29.4	13.11	4.12	8.1	–	5.2	22.4	14.8	28.8	25.3	22.1
29.1	8.4	21.8	12.2	28.12	25.9	7.11	1.9	–	27.11	6.5	16.10	18.12	24.4
4.3	23.11	8.4	6.11	22.1	25.3	19.10	16.10	19.2	–	24.4	4.12	8.1	14.8
27.11	30.8	8.1	22.8	3.11	28.12	7.8	15.1	9.10	2.10	–	18.9	23.10	18.3
12.2	28.12	2.10	15.1	25.3	8.1	8.4	29.1	22.4	7.8	26.2	–	29.4	13.11
24.4	6.5	4.3	21.3	4.9	19.2	18.9	26.12	1.4	11.12	25.9	19.10	–	5.2
15.4	29.1	29.4	11.12	21.4	11.3	12.2	21.8	2.10	15.1	23.11	21.3	31.8	–

NATIONWIDE FOOTBALL LEAGUE FIXTURES 1999–2000

DIVISION THREE

	Barnet	Brighton & HA	Carlisle U	Cheltenham T	Chester C	Darlington	Exeter C	Halifax T	Hartlepool U	Hull C
Barnet	–	25.3	23.11	5.2	4.12	6.11	14.8	28.12	11.3	2.10
Brighton & HA	26.12	–	6.5	25.9	18.9	29.1	3.1	4.3	6.11	1.9
Carlisle U	18.3	9.10	–	7.3	3.1	29.4	22.4	23.10	21.8	1.4
Cheltenham T	30.8	23.10	6.11	–	29.4	22.4	26.12	11.3	29.1	21.8
Chester C	7.8	26.2	8.4	19.10	–	8.1	11.9	18.12	21.3	12.2
Darlington	7.3	28.8	19.10	16.10	11.12	–	4.9	4.12	24.4	26.12
Exeter C	15.1	8.4	16.10	25.3	4.3	12.2	–	21.3	18.12	7.8
Halifax T	15.4	11.9	25.9	2.11	1.4	7.8	13.11	–	15.1	18.3
Hartlepool U	2.11	7.3	22.1	28.8	13.11	2.10	1.4	14.8	–	9.10
Hull C	24.4	5.2	18.12	22.1	4.9	25.3	4.12	23.11	6.5	–
Leyton O	19.10	14.8	4.12	19.2	15.4	11.3	11.12	28.8	25.9	3.1
Lincoln C	21.8	18.3	4.3	8.4	23.10	9.10	2.10	25.3	14.12	15.1
Macclesfield T	12.2	13.11	28.12	8.1	22.4	15.1	23.10	9.10	27.11	29.1
Mansfield T	1.4	4.12	28.8	14.8	26.12	26.2	4.2	19.2	16.10	15.4
Northampton T	26.2	19.2	4.9	13.11	22.1	28.12	18.3	8.4	11.9	21.4
Peterborough U	27.11	2.10	21.3	18.9	9.10	30.8	15.4	22.4	7.8	11.12
Plymouth Arg	13.11	4.9	5.2	18.3	7.3	23.10	2.11	22.1	26.2	29.4
Rochdale	6.5	8.1	25.3	4.12	5.2	11.9	28.8	3.9	8.4	2.11
Rotherham U	16.10	28.12	19.2	24.4	14.8	18.12	22.1	8.1	19.10	7.3
Shrewsbury T	3.1	29.4	18.9	4.3	2.11	21.8	9.10	2.10	31.8	27.11
Southend U	11.12	2.11	24.4	6.5	18.3	27.11	7.3	18.9	12.2	13.11
Swansea C	11.9	18.12	14.8	4.9	19.2	23.11	29.4	5.11	8.1	26.2
Torquay U	25.9	22.1	8.1	18.12	28.8	21.3	19.2	5.2	23.11	11.9
York C	29.1	22.4	11.3	28.12	2.10	8.4	26.2	29.4	25.3	23.10

Leyton O	Lincoln C	Macclesfield T	Mansfield T	Northampton T	Peterborough U	Plymouth Arg	Rochdale	Rotherham U	Shrewsbury T	Southend U	Swansea C	Torquay U	York C
29.4	22.1	5.9	18.12	18.9	19.2	21.3	9.10	22.4	8.4	8.1	4.3	23.10	28.8
15.1	23.11	21.3	7.8	27.11	26.4	12.2	10.12	15.4	19.10	11.3	1.4	21.8	16.10
7.8	11.9	15.4	29.1	12.2	13.11	30.8	26.12	29.11	26.2	2.10	15.1	11.12	2.11
27.11	3.1	11.12	15.1	21.3	26.2	23.11	7.8	2.10	12.9	9.10	13.2	1.4	15.4
28.12	25.9	16.10	25.3	21.8	6.5	6.11	30.8	15.1	11.3	23.11	27.11	29.1	24.4
2.11	6.5	14.8	18.9	15.4	5.2	25.9	4.3	1.4	22.1	19.2	18.3	13.11	3.1
8.1	24.4	25.9	30.8	23.11	28.12	11.3	29.1	21.8	6.5	6.11	19.10	27.11	18.9
29.1	26.12	6.5	27.11	3.1	16.10	21.8	12.2	11.12	24.4	26.2	7.3	31.8	19.10
23.10	15.4	19.2	22.4	4.3	4.12	18.9	3.1	29.4	5.2	4.9	11.12	18.3	26.12
8.4	14.8	28.8	28.12	16.10	8.1	19.10	11.3	6.11	19.2	21.3	18.9	4.3	25.9
–	16.10	1.4	4.3	6.11	22.1	24.4	23.11	21.3	4.9	5.2	26.12	18.9	6.5
22.4	–	18.9	7.3	29.1	2.11	8.1	27.11	7.8	18.12	29.4	30.8	12.2	13.11
18.12	26.2	–	2.11	7.8	18.3	8.4	29.4	30.8	25.3	11.9	21.8	2.10	7.3
11.9	6.11	11.3	–	19.10	3.9	6.5	21.3	23.11	24.9	22.1	24.4	3.1	11.12
7.3	28.8	4.12	29.4	–	14.8	17.12	2.10	23.10	8.1	25.3	2.11	9.10	5.2
21.8	11.3	23.11	12.2	15.1	–	29.1	1.4	26.12	6.11	23.10	3.1	29.4	4.3
2.10	11.12	3.1	9.10	1.4	28.8	–	22.4	11.9	14.8	4.12	15.4	26.12	19.2
18.3	19.2	19.10	13.11	24.4	18.12	16.10	–	26.2	28.12	14.8	25.9	7.3	22.1
13.11	4.12	5.2	18.3	25.9	25.3	4.3	18.9	–	28.8	8.4	6.5	2.11	4.9
12.2	1.4	26.12	23.10	11.12	7.3	15.1	15.4	29.1	–	22.4	13.11	7.8	18.3
30.8	19.10	3.3	21.8	26.12	25.9	7.8	15.1	3.1	16.10	–	29.1	15.4	1.4
25.3	4.2	22.1	2.10	11.3	8.4	28.12	22.10	8.10	21.3	28.8	–	22.4	4.12
26.2	4.9	24.4	8.4	6.5	19.10	25.3	6.11	11.3	4.12	28.12	16.10	–	14.8
9.10	21.3	6.11	8.1	30.8	11.9	27.11	21.8	12.2	23.11	17.12	7.8	15.1	–

OTHER FIXTURES – SEASON 1999–2000

July 1999

1 Thu England v France – Under 16 Mini-Tournament at Northwich Victoria FC (7.05pm)

3 Sat France v Argentina – Under 16 Mini-Tournament at Kingstonian FC (3.30pm)
UEFA Intertoto Cup 2nd Round (1)

4 Sun England v Argentina – Under 16 Mini-Tournament at Wembley Stadium (3.00pm)
England v Scotland – Under 16 Women's International at Wembley Stadium (1.00pm)

10 Sat UEFA Intertoto Cup 2nd Round (2)

13/14 Tue/Wed UEFA Champions League 1st Qualifying Stage (1)

17 Sat UEFA Intertoto Cup 3rd Round (1)

20/21 Tue/Wed UEFA Champions League 1st Qualifying Stage (2)

24 Sat UEFA Intertoto Cup 3rd Round (2)

27/28 Tue/Wed UEFA Champions League 2nd Qualifying Stage (1)

28 Wed UEFA Intertoto Cup Semi-Final (1)

31 Sat Official Start of Season

August

1 Sun One-2-One F.A. Charity Shield
Nordic Under 16 Tournament in England (ends 8 Aug)

3/4 Tue/Wed UEFA Champions League 2nd Qualifying Stage (2)

4 Wed UEFA Intertoto Cup Semi-Final (2)

7 Sat F.A. Carling Premier League and Nationwide Leagues starting date

10 Tue UEFA Intertoto Cup Final (1)

10/11 Tue/Wed UEFA Champions League 3rd Qualifying Stage (1)

11 Wed Worthington Cup 1 (1)

12 Thu UEFA Cup Qualifying Round (1)

14 Sat Nationwide Conference starting date

18 Wed International (Friendly)

21 Sat F.A. Cup Sponsored by AXA Preliminary Round

22 Sun Denmark v England (Women's Friendly International)

24 Tue UEFA Intertoto Cup Final (2)

24/25 Tue/Wed UEFA Champions League 3rd Qualifying Stage (2)

25 Wed Worthington Cup 1 (2)

26 Thu UEFA Cup Qualifying Round (2)

30 Mon Bank Holiday

September

4 Sat England v Luxembourg UEFA European Championship
F.A. Cup Sponsored by AXA 1Q
The Times F.A. Youth Cup 1Q*

8 Wed Poland v England UEFA European Championship

11 Sat F.A. Carlsberg Vase 1Q

12 Sun AXA F.A. Women's Cup EP

14/15 Tue/Wed UEFA Champions League 1st Group – Match 1

15 Wed Worthington Cup 2 (1)

16 Thu UEFA Cup 1 (1)
England v France (Women's Friendly International)

18 Sat F.A. Cup Sponsored by AXA 2Q

21/22 Tue/Wed UEFA Champions League 1st Group – Match 2

22 Wed Worthington Cup 2 (2)

25 Sat F.A. Carlsberg Vase 2Q
The Times F.A. Youth Cup 2Q*

26 Sun AXA F.A. Women's Cup P

28/29 Tue/Wed UEFA Champions League 1st Group – Match 3

30 Thu UEFA Cup 1 (2)

October

2 Sat F.A. Cup Sponsored by AXA 3Q

9 Sat F.A. Umbro Trophy 1
The Times F.A. Youth Cup 3Q*
F.A. County Youth Cup 1*

10 Sun AXA F.A. Women's Cup 1
England v Belgium – Friendly International at Sunderland FC (3.00pm)

13 Wed Worthington Cup 3

15 Fri England v Northern Ireland (Victory Shield – Under 15 Schoolboy team)

16 Sat F.A. Cup Sponsored by AXA 4Q
Switzerland v England (Women's UEFA International)

17 Sun F.A. Umbro Sunday Cup 1

19/20 Tue/Wed UEFA Champions League 1st Group – Match 4

21 Thu UEFA Cup 2 (1)

23 Sat F.A. Carlsberg Vase 1P

26/27 Tue/Wed UEFA Champions League 1st Group – Match 5

28 Thu England v Wales (Victory Shield – Under 15 Schoolboy team)

30 Sat F.A. Cup Sponsored by AXA 1P
The Times F.A. Youth Cup 1P*

November

2/3 Tue/Wed UEFA Champions League 1st Group – Match 6

4 Thu UEFA Cup 2 (2)

7 Sun AXA F.A. Women's Cup 2

10 Wed F.A. Cup Sponsored by AXA 1P Replay

11 Thu Scotland v England (Victory Shield – Under 15 Schoolboy team)

13 Sat Possible Play-Off for UEFA European Championship
F.A. Carlsberg Vase 2P
The Times F.A. Youth Cup 2P*
F.A. County Youth Cup 2*
Under 18 UEFA Three Team Mini-Tournament in England (ends 20 Nov)

14 Sun F.A. Umbro Sunday Cup 2

17 Wed Possible Play-Off for UEFA European Championship

20 Sat F.A. Cup Sponsored by AXA 2P

23/24 Tue/Wed UEFA Champions League 2nd Group – Match 1

25 Thu UEFA Cup 3 (1)

27 Sat F.A. Umbro Trophy 2

December

1 Wed Worthington Cup 4
F.A. Cup Sponsored by AXA 2P Replay

4 Sat F.A. Carlsberg Vase 3P

5 Sun F.A. Umbro Sunday Cup 3

6 Mon	F.A. XI v Northern Premier League		16 Thu	UEFA Cup Quarter-Final (1)

6 Mon F.A. XI v Northern Premier League
7 Tue FIFA World Cup – Draw for Preliminary
Competition
F.A. XI v Southern League
7/8 Tue/Wed UEFA Champions League 2nd
Group – Match 2
8 Wed F.A. XI v Isthmian League
9 Thu UEFA Cup 3 (2)
11 Sat F.A. Cup Sponsored by AXA 3P
The Times F.A. Youth Cup 3P*
12 Sun AXA F.A. Women's Cup 3
15 Wed Worthington Cup 5
18 Sat F.A. County Youth Cup 3*
22 Wed F.A. Cup Sponsored by AXA 3P Replay
26 Sun Boxing Day
27 Mon Bank Holiday
28 Tue Bank Holiday

January 2000
1 Sat New Year's Day
3 Mon Bank Holiday
8 Sat F.A. Cup Sponsored by AXA 4P
9 Sun AXA F.A. Women's Cup 4
10 Mon F.A. XI v Combined Services
12 Wed Worthington Cup Semi-Final (1)
15 Sat F.A. Umbro Trophy 3
19 Wed F.A. Cup Sponsored by AXA 4P Replay
22 Sat F.A. Carlsberg Vase 4P
The Times F.A. Youth Cup 4P*
23 Sun F.A. Umbro Sunday Cup 4
26 Wed Worthington Cup Semi-Final (2)
29 Sat F.A. Cup Sponsored by AXA 5P
F.A. County Youth Cup 4*

February
5 Sat F.A. Umbro Trophy 4
6 Sun AXA F.A. Women's Cup 5
9 Wed F.A. Cup Sponsored by AXA 5P Replay
12 Sat F.A. Carlsberg Vase 5P
The Times F.A. Youth Cup 5P*
19 Sat F.A. Cup Sponsored by AXA 6P
20 Sun England v Poland (Women's UEFA International)
F.A. Umbro Sunday Cup 5
23 Wed International (Friendly)
26 Sat F.A. Umbro Trophy 5
27 Sun AXA F.A. Women's Cup 6
Worthington Cup Final
29 Tue England Semi-Professional International
29/1 Tue/Wed UEFA Champions League 2nd
Group – Match 3

March
1 Wed F.A. Cup Sponsored by AXA 6P Replay
2 Thu UEFA Cup 4 (1)
4 Sat F.A. Carlsberg Vase 6P
The Times F.A. Youth Cup 6P*
7 Tue Under 16 UEFA Three Team Mini-Tournament in Luxembourg (ends 12 March)
7/8 Tue/Wed UEFA Champions League 2nd
Group – Match 4
9 Thu UEFA Cup 4 (2)
England v Norway (Women's UEFA International)
11 Sat F.A. Umbro Trophy 6
F.A. County Youth Cup Semi-Final*
14/15 Tue/Wed UEFA Champions League 2nd
Group – Match 5

16 Thu UEFA Cup Quarter-Final (1)
18 Sat F.A. Carlsberg Vase SF1
19 Sun F.A. Umbro Sunday Cup SF
21 Tue England Semi-Professional International
21/22 Tue/Wed UEFA Champions League 2nd
Group – Match 6
23 Thu UEFA Cup Quarter-Final (2)
24 Fri England v Holland (Under 15 Schoolboy
Friendly International)
25 Sat F.A. Carlsberg Vase SF2
The Times F.A. Youth Cup SF1*
26 Sun AXA F.A. Women's Cup SF
29 Wed International (Friendly)

April
1 Sat F.A. Umbro Trophy SF1
4/5 Tue/Wed UEFA Champions League Quarter-
Final (1)
6 Thu UEFA Cup Semi-Final (1)
7 Fri England v Italy (Under 15 Schoolboy
Friendly International)
9 Sun F.A. Cup Sponsored by AXA Semi-Final
15 Sat F.A. Umbro Trophy SF2
The Times F.A. Youth Cup SF2*
18/19 Tue/Wed UEFA Champions League Quarter-
Final (2)
20 Thu UEFA Cup Semi-Final (2)
21 Fri Good Friday
22 Sat Portugal v England (Women's UEFA International)
24 Mon Easter Monday
26 Wed International (Friendly)
29 Sat F.A. County Youth Cup Final (fixed date)

May
1 Mon AXA F.A. Women's Cup Final
3 Wed UEFA Champions League Semi-Final (1)
5 Fri The Times F.A. Youth Cup Final 1st Leg
(fixed date)
6 Sat F.A. Carlsberg Vase Final
Final Nationwide League fixtures Divs 2&3
Final Nationwide Conference fixtures
7 Sun Final Nationwide League fixtures Div 1
10 Wed UEFA Champions League Semi-Final (2)
12 Fri The Times F.A. Youth Cup Final 2nd Leg
(fixed date)
13 Sat F.A. Umbro Trophy Final
14 Sun Nationwide League Play-Off Semi-Final (1)
Final F.A. Carling Premier League fixtures
England v Switzerland (Women's UEFA
International)
17 Wed UEFA Cup Final
Nationwide League Play-Off Semi-Final (2)
20 Sat F.A. Cup Sponsored by AXA Final
24 Wed UEFA Champions League Final
27 Sat Nationwide League 3rd Division Play-Off
28 Sun Nationwide Leage 2nd Division Play-Off
29 Mon Nationwide League 1st Division Play-Off

June
3 Sat Possible International Friendly
4 Sun Possible International Friendly
Norway v England (Women's UEFA International)
10 Sat European Championship Commences (ends
2 July)
* = closing date
to be dated – F.A. Umbro Sunday Cup Final

*If you enjoyed this book here is a selection of
other bestselling sports titles from Headline*

ROTHMANS FOOTBALL YEARBOOK 1999-2000	Glenda Rollin	£18.99	☐
PLAYFAIR FOOTBALL WHO'S WHO 2000	Jack Rollin	£6.99	☐
ROTHMANS BOOK OF FOOTBALL RECORDS	Jack Rollin	£25.00	☐
KICKING WITH BOTH FEET	Frank Clark	£16.99	☐
RED VOICES	Stephen F. Kelly	£17.99	☐
CHERRIES IN THE RED	Trevor Watkins	£16.99	☐
LEFT FOOT FORWARD	Garry Nelson	£5.99	☐
FERGIE	Stephen F. Kelly	£6.99	☐
DERBY DAYS	Dougie and Eddy Brimson	£6.99	☐
MANCHESTER UNITED RUINED MY LIFE	Colin Shindler	£5.99	☐

Headline books are available at your local bookshop or newsagent. Alternatively, books can be ordered direct from the publisher. Just tick the titles you want and fill in the form below. Prices and availability subject to change without notice.

Buy four books from the selection above and get free postage and packaging and delivery within 48 hours. Just send a cheque or postal order made payable to *Bookpoint Ltd* to the value of the total cover price of the four books. Alternatively, if you wish to buy fewer than four books the following postage and packaging applies:

UK and BFPO £4.30 for one book; £6.30 for two books; £8.30 for three books.

Overseas and Eire: £4.80 for one book; £7.10 for two or three books (surface mail).

Please enclose a cheque or postal order made payable to *Bookpoint Limited*, and send to: Headline Book Publishing Ltd, 39 Milton Park, Abingdon, OXON OX14 4TD, UK.

E-mail address: orders@bookpoint.co.uk

If you prefer to pay by credit card, our call team would be delighted to take your order by telephone. Our direct line is 01235 400 414 (lines open 9.00 am–6.00 pm Monday to Saturday, 24 hour message answering service). Alternatively you can send a fax on 01235 400 454.

Name ....

Address ....

....

....

If you would prefer to pay by credit card, please complete:

Please debit my Visa/Access/Diner's Card/American Express (delete as applicable) card number:

Signature .... Expiry Date ....